Holiday Greece

Katharine Wood-de Winne was [born in Scotland and] was educated there, reading Co[mbined Honours in] English Language and Literature at Edinburgh University. Following a period as a freelance public relations consultant and journalist she entered the world of travel journalism. An eighteen-month spell touring Europe and North Africa resulted in the guidebook *Europe by Train* (published by Fontana) which is one of the UK's top-selling guidebooks. As well as working on this series of Holiday Guides, she is currently involved in several projects encompassing every aspect of the travel industry – from backpacking students to round-the-world first-class tours. She regularly contributes to radio and TV programmes, both in the UK and USA, and writes articles freelance for numerous publications. In the course of her work she travels extensively, often in Greece, and has so far clocked up forty-eight countries. She is married and lives in Scotland with her husband, who works with her on various guides, and young sons, Andrew and Euan.

George McDonald was born in Dumfries in 1955 and was educated at Fettes College and Edinburgh University. Following a spell on the family farm he toured Europe and North Africa to research the guidebook *Europe by Train*. He continues to travel for a living as a full-time travel writer and is rarely in one place for more than three weeks at a time. Home, when he's there, is Guernsey in the Channel Islands.

Also by the same authors:

The Round the World Air Guide
Europe by Train
Holiday Yugoslavia
Holiday Turkey
Holiday Spain
Holiday Portugal
Holiday Ireland
The Winter Sun Guide

By Katie Wood:

The Best of British Country House Hotels and Restaurants
Holiday Scotland
European City Breaks

Holiday
GREECE

Compiled and Edited by
Katie Wood

Researcher: George McDonald

FONTANA/Collins

To my Mother

First published in 1987 by Fontana Paperbacks
8 Grafton Street, London W1X 3LA

This revised edition published in 1990

Copyright © Katie Wood and George McDonald 1987, 1988, 1989, 1990

Set in Linotron Plantin

Printed and bound in Great Britain
by William Collins Sons & Co. Ltd, Glasgow

CONDITIONS OF SALE
This book is sold subject to the condition
that it shall not, by way of trade or otherwise,
be lent, re-sold, hired out or otherwise circulated
without the publisher's prior consent in any form of
binding or cover other than that in which it is
published and without a similar condition
including this condition being imposed
on the subsequent purchaser.

Contents

Acknowledgements 13
What This Guide is About 15

Part One – BEFORE YOU GO 19

What to Expect 22

When to Go 25

The Climate 26
Winter Holidays 28

Where to Go for What 28
The Sunworshipper 30   The Sightseer 32   The Socialite 34
Healthy Holidays 37   The Nature Lover 39   The Recluse 42
The Family Holiday 43

Practicalities 44
Red Tape 44   Embassy Addresses 44   Health Formalities 44
Customs 45   Money 45   Banking 47   Insurance 47   Health 48
Pre-planning and Free Information 49   Budgeting 50

Getting Yourself Organized 52
What to Take With You 52

Part Two – HOW TO GO 55

Package v. Independent 57

Tour Operators in Britain offering Package Holidays to Greece 58
Who Specializes in What 86   *Self-catering* 87
Cost-consciousness 88   *Camping* 90
Private Accommodation 91   *Two-centre Holidays* 92
Coach Tours 92   *Holiday Clubs* 93
Cruising 94   *Sailing Holidays* 96
Special Interest Holidays 97   Summing Up 100   Checklist 101

Independent Means 103
The Options 103   By Air 106   By Rail 108   By Bus 110
By Car/Camper 110   Hitch-hiking 112   By Sea 113

Generally Useful Information 114
Time Differences 114   Electricity 114   Water 114

Part Three – WHEN YOU'RE THERE 115

Tourist Information 117   *Sightseeing* 118   *Shopping* 119
Food and Drink 120   *Nightlife* 125   *Communications* 126
Post Offices 127   Moving Around the Country 127
Car Hire 128   Trains 129   Buses 130   Taxis 131
Problems and Emergencies 131   Embassies and Consulates 132
Work 132   Women Alone 132

A Potted History 133

Part Four – THE COUNTRY 139

ATHENS AND ATTICA 141
Athens 141
Communications 143   *Tourist Information* 145
Where to Go For What 146   *Accommodation* 147
Sights 148   *Restaurants/Nightlife* 152

SOUTH-EAST ATTICA 154
Piraeus 154   Paleo Faliro 155   Glyfada 155   Voula 155
Vouliagmeni 156   Sounion 157

SOUTH-WEST ATTICA 158
Elefsina 158   Loutraki 159

EAST COAST/INLAND ATTICA 159
Lavrio 160   Messogia 160   Rafina 160   Marathon 161

EVIA 162
Communications 164   *Climate* 164   *Culinary Specialities* 165
Where to Go For What 165   Halkida 166   Gregolimano 168
Pefki 170   Edispos 171

CENTRAL GREECE 174
Practical Details 174   Lamia 174   Delphi 175   Meteora 179
Volos 180   Olympia 181

WESTERN GREECE 182
Practical Details 183   *Communications* 183
Tourist Information 184   *Climate* 184   *Culinary Specialities* 185
Where to Go For What 185
Ioanina 186   Metsova/Konitsa 189   East (Anatolika) 190
Central (Kentriko) 190   West (Ditoko) 192   Arta 193
Preveza 193

WESTERN MACEDONIA 195
Pella and Florina 195   Glanitsa 195   Grevena 197   Kozani 197
Kato Vermio 198   Katerini 199   Lithoro 200

NORTHERN GREECE 201
Practical Details 202   *Communications* 202
Tourist Information 203   *Climate* 204   *Culinary Specialities* 204
Where to Go For What 205

HALKIDIKI 205
Poligiros 206   Kassandra 206   Kalithea 208

SITHONIA 210
Porto Koufo 212   Porto Carras 212

WEST COAST 213
Fourka 213

Mount Athos and Environs 214
Amouliani 215   Karyes 217

Eastern Macedonia and Thrace 218
Kavala 218   Philippi 219   Alexandroupolis 220   Thassos 221
Makriamos 222   Limenaria 222

Thessaloniki 223

DOWN THE COAST 227

PELOPONNESE 231
History 232   *Practical Details* 232   *Communications* 232
Climate 233   *Culinary Specialities* 233
Where to Go For What 233
Corinth 234   Loutraki 236   Mycanae 236   Argos 236
Nafplio 237   Tolon 238   Porto Heli 238

SOUTHERN PELOPONNESE 239
Sparta 239   Mystra 240   Mani Peninsula 241
Monemvassia 242   Kythera 242

WESTERN PELOPONNESE 242
Kalamata 242   Pilos 243   Olympus 243   Patras 244

NORTHERN PELOPONNESE 245

THE ISLANDS 247

NORTH-EAST AEGEAN ISLANDS 249
Practical Details 249
Samothraki 250
Limnos 251
Lesbos 252 – Mytilini 252   Molyvos 253   Skala Eressos 253
Kalloni 254
Chios 254 – Chios 255   Psara 256
Samos 256 – Karlovassi 257   Pythagorion 258
Ikaria 259

SPORADES ISLANDS 260
Practical Details 261 *Communications* 261
Tourist Information 262 *Climate* 262 *Culinary Specialities* 263
Skiathos 263 – Skiathos Town 264 Koukkounaries 266
Kastro 266
Skopelos 268 – Skopelos Town 268 Loutraki 270
Alonissos 272 – Alonissos Town 272 Patitri 273
Excursions 276
Skyros 277

CYCLADES 280
Amorgos 282 – Katapola 282
Andros 283 – Gavrion 284 Vatsi 285
Folegandros 286
Ios 287 – Gaios 289
Kea 291 – Korissia 292
Kythnos 292
Milos 292 – Adamas 293 Plaka 294
Mykonos 295 – Mykonos Town 297 Excursions 300
Delos 301
Naxos 303 – Naxos Town 305
Paros 307 – Parikia 308 Naoussa 309
Antiparos 312
Santorini 314 – Thira 316 Kamari 319 Perissa 320 Oia 320
Serifos 321 – Livadi 322
Sifnos 322 – Plati Gialos 323 Kamares 323
Syros 323 – Ermoupolis 325 Galissas 326
Tinos 326 – Tinos Town 327

DODECANESE ISLANDS 330
Communications 331 *Climate* 333 *Culinary Specialities* 333
Karpathos 334 – Karpathos 335 Amopi Beach 335 Diafani 336
Halki 337 – Niborio 338
Kassos 338 – Emborio 339 Fri 339
Kastellorizo 340 – Megisti 340
Symi 341 – Ghialos 342 Pedi 344
Tilos 346 – Livadia 347 Megalochorio 347
Nissiros 348 – Mandraki 349

Astipalea 350 – Astipalea Town 351
Kos 352 – Kos Town 354   Kefalos 357
Kalymnos 360 – Pothia 362
Leros 366 – Platanos 367   Aghia Marina 368   Lakki 368
Patmos 369 – Skala 369
Lipsi 372

RHODES 373
History 376   *Practical Details* 377   *Communications* 377
Climate 379   *Culinary Specialities* 379
Where to Go For What 380
Rhodes Town 382   Accommodation 385
Restaurants/Nightlife 386   Excursions 388   Lindos 389

EAST COAST 392
Kalithea 392   Faliraki 393   Afandou 394   Haraki 395
Genadio and South of the Island 396

WEST COAST 396
Kritika and Ixia 397   Ancient Ialyssos 399   Ancient Kamiros 400

CRETE 402
History 403   *Practical Details* 405   *Tourist Information* 406
Climate 406   *Culinary Specialities* 406
Where to Go For What 407   Heraklion 409   Knossos 412
Gortys, Phaistos and Agia Triada 414

NORTH-EAST COAST 415
Herssonissos 416   Malia 416   Elounda 418
Aghios Nikolaos 419   Sitia 421

NORTH-WEST COAST 423
Rethymnon 424   Chania 427   Kastelli 430

SOUTH COAST 431
Ierapetra 431   Matala 432   Aghia Galini 432
Samaria Gorge 434

SARONIC GULF ISLANDS 436
Aegina 437 – Aegina Town 439   Perdika and Aghia Marina 441

Angistri 441 – Skala 441
Methana 442
Spetse 442 – Spetse Town 444
Salamis 446 – Salamina 447
Hydra 447 – Mandraki 451
Palamida and Aghios Nikolaos Bay 451
Poros 452 – Plaka Beach and Lemonodassos 456
Aliki Beach 456

CORFU 458
History 459   *Practical Details* 463   *Climate* 465
Culinary Specialities 465   Where to Go For What 466
Corfu Town 468   Sights 471   Excursions 479

NORTH-EAST COAST 481
Gouvia 483   Kommeno 486   Dassia 487   Ipsos 489
Nisaki 490   Kassiopi 491

NORTH COAST 493
Acharavi 494   Roda 495   Sidari 495

WEST COAST 497
Aghios Stefanos 497   Arillas 498   Aghios Georgeous 498
Paleokastritsa 499   Ermones 502   Glyfada 502   Yaliscari 504
Aghios Gordis 504   Aghios Georgios 504

SOUTH-EAST COAST 505
Kanoni 505   Perama 507   Benitses 509   Moraitika 511
Messonghi 512   Kavos 512

THE IONIAN ISLANDS 514
Paxos 515 – Lakka, Antipaxi and Voutoumi Bay 517
Lefkas 518 – Nidri 519   Vliho 520   Vassiliki 520
Ithaca 521 – Vathi 521   Frikes 523
Kefalonia 523 – Argostoli 526   Skala 530   Poros 530
Assos and Fiskado 531
Zakinthos 532 – Zante Town 534   Excursions 537   Argassi 537
Lagnas 538   Tsilivi 539

Vocabulary 541

ACKNOWLEDGEMENTS

RESEARCHERS

Devin Scobie – Western Greece, Northern Greece and the Sporades.
Peter Carroll – Dodecanese; Athens & Attica; Saronic Gulf.
Michael Bravo – Rhodes.
Patrick Robertson – Peloponnese; Central Greece; Cyclades; Ionian Islands, and North-East Aegean Islands.

Thanks to my ever-patient husband for his editing skills, and to my mother for help on the domestic front; and to all the researchers who worked so quickly, enthusiastically and thoroughly.

WHAT THIS GUIDE IS ABOUT

For too long now there has been a gap in the guidebook market. On the one hand there are the 'heavies' – such as Fodor, Michelin and Benn's Blue Guides – books which, though good in their way, assume the holidaymaker wants a stone-by-stone description of all the ancient remains of the country of their choice, and what's more, assume that their readership is middle-aged, middle-class and predominantly American, with a lot of cash to splash about. At the other end of the scale there are the backpacking, student-orientated, 'rough it on $10 a day' guides, which assume the traveller wants to cover the maximum amount of ground possible and spend the absolute minimum doing so (even if this does mean surviving on one bowl of vegetable rice a day and no bath for two weeks).

In between lies the vast majority of tourists. Normal, fun-loving people who go on holiday to unwind from a year's toil, and though not able to throw cash about indiscriminately, are willing to spend enough to enjoy themselves. Predominantly these people fall into the 18–45 age group, those keen to see the country they visit and have a good time in their own way. This guide is written for this sort of person. It does not wade into pages of history – it just gives you the basics to enable you to make sense of the monuments and places you'll see whilst on holiday. It does not pretend to be a specialist guide specifically for one group of people (water-sports enthusiasts, nature lovers, archaeologists, etc.), but it does point you in the direction of where to pursue these types of hobbies once you are in the country. If any one 'hobby' is highlighted more than most it is that of 'sun-worshipping' and where best to do it, as time after time surf, sea and sand still come top of most people's priorities for a good holiday.

Greece, a popular holiday destination for northern Europeans for the last decade, has reached a new high with the British in the last couple of years. It has for a long time been a country where students and independent travellers could be found, rucksack on back, wandering round the islands, but the increase now is in the package market. Tour operators are increasingly introducing more imaginative packages, and it is possible to take the sort of holiday you want, whether it be bird-watching on mainland Greece; a walking holiday on Crete; sailing in the Dodecanese, or wandering round the islands safe in the knowledge that someone has pre-arranged a bed for you – all these can be booked as packages which means that once in Greece the hassles are taken out of your holiday and all you have to do is enjoy yourself. The old image of being herded into coaches, force-fed your hospitality drink, and told to enjoy yourselves is fast disappearing from packages as the public become more discriminating and sophisticated in their holidaying expectations.

We look at the options open to the would-be traveller: both the pros and cons of the different packages on offer in 1990. But we do not forget the independent traveller. Though we don't concentrate on the camping, survive-on-200-dr-a-day crowd (for there simply is no need to do this in Greece – it's sufficiently cheap not to put yourself through unnecessary hardship), we do make mention of independent travellers, particularly those island-hopping. All the information you will need before deciding whether to take a package or go independently is given in Part One of this guide – 'Before You Go'.

Our recommendations for restaurants, nightlife, hotels and so on start at the lower end of the market, as no one has to be told how to spend money on holiday. Saving it without sacrificing the holiday spirit is the art.

We hope this guide will help you to have a rewarding time in Greece. It is, in the literal sense, an amazing country with so much to offer all types of holidaymakers. This guide is weighted to the popularity of the holiday resorts. There is no need for us to follow the time-honoured guidebook format of giving each section of the country equal emphasis. Accordingly the islands have many more pages than the mainland, and Corfu, Crete and Rhodes, as the big three holiday destinations, have more than the other islands. This is a different type of guide: informal and chatty, not academic and definitive. We are not setting ourselves up as *the* authority on Greece: we know a lot and have travelled there extensively, but our knowledge is more on where the best places for different types of holiday are than as Greek historians. If any of our recommendations fail to come up to the mark, or if you find a super undiscovered beach which you are willing to share, or a new lively taverna, write and tell us about it. After all, we all want the same in the end – the memory of at least two glorious, fun-filled weeks to sustain us through the long dark British winter nights.

Part One
BEFORE YOU GO

ENTRY REQUIREMENTS – British visitors with a full passport are allowed a 90-day stay without a visa. Holders of a British Visitor's Card are also allowed a 3-month stay.

NB: Those with a Turkish Republic of Cyprus or Turkish State of Cyprus stamp on their passport will *not* be admitted to Greece. Tourists arriving on charter flights are not allowed to leave Greece for the duration of their stay, and cannot visit Turkey, even on a day trip.

POPULATION – 9,000,000

CAPITAL – Athens (pop. 2,750,000)

CURRENCY – Drachma (£1 = 260 dr)

POLITICAL SYSTEM – Republic

RELIGION – Greek Orthodox

LANGUAGE – Greek (English spoken in most holiday resorts)

PUBLIC HOLIDAYS
    1, 6 January
    Shrove Tuesday
    25 March
    Good Friday
    1 May
    11 June
    15 August
    28 October
    25, 26 December

What to Expect

Many tourists to Greece go there quite simply for two weeks of sun-drenched relaxation; some still go as part of a Grand Tour, to gaze in wonder at the classical sights and see first-hand the 'cradle of civilization' in all its glory; and some travel to Greece for very specific reasons, such as visiting some of the world's most important archaeological sites, or touring round the islands. For most visitors however it is a combination of all these delightful pastimes which lures them to Europe's warmest country. Greece is still a cheap holiday destination. It offers most of the things that people want on a holiday, and as it's been in the business of mass tourism for the last decade, it knows what we northern Europeans want from our precious two weeks' holiday. Tour operators of all kinds offer holidays in Greece which means that every type of holiday is available there, from luxury cruises or grand hotels to bed and breakfast in simple tavernas where you can live for a few pounds a day and 'go native' on the beaches. Whatever you're looking for from a holiday the chances are that you will find it in Greece. The secret is knowing where to look, and working out at an early stage exactly what you want.

The commercial tourist centres such as Corfu, Rhodes, Crete and the Halkidiki lay on everything for those wanting a tailor-made package, but it is still possible to find quiet corners, even in these places, for the peace-seeking, and for those definitely looking to get away from it all there are still countless islands and parts of the mainland where the 1980s seem not to have arrived. The contrast of this country is its great asset, and it is the purpose of this guide to pinpoint the places best suited to your ideal holiday.

What Greece does best, in package terms, is offer a basic beach-based holiday: an unpretentious, relaxing time, where you live alongside the Greeks, taking life at their pace (which can mean little annoyances like unbelievably slow service in restaurants and asking for days on end to have your faulty plumbing put right), enjoying the simple things in life and unwinding from a year's toil. With only a couple of exceptions Greece does not cater for the 'smart set'. They would be better going to the South of France or resorts further north in Europe. Those wanting to live life at a city pace will find themselves bored by their second week, and will have to choose very carefully where they go, if Greece is their choice for 1990.

What we therefore do is show you all the options, but at the end of the day it is up to you to decide what you are looking for out of your holiday. This fundamental and crucial decision is one which many people overlook. Crazy as it seems many still spend the equivalent of two months' salary on a holiday they have spent only a day or two investigating, and in the end they base their choice of resort – *the* most crucial decision – on factors as arbitrary as what a travel agent recommends; a friend's subjective opinion, or simply what they read in a brochure. Though the trend is changing slowly, brochures only scrape the surface when it comes to describing the character of a resort, and it is unwise to spend hundreds of pounds on the basis of what you can glean from a paragraph of optimistic text. The more time you spend reading Parts One, Two and Three of this guide the higher the chances are that you will, in the end, select the right resort for your needs, and that you will enjoy your holiday to its full. List your idea of a perfect holiday; select what you want to see and do on holiday, and read through the 'Where to Go for What' section very carefully. Money is rarely the main criterion. You can spend just as much on an unsuitable holiday as you will on your perfect one, so don't fall into the great tourist trap of not doing your homework and then blaming the country or tour operator. Your homework has been done for you – it is Parts One and Two of this guide. We hope that after reading it you will select the right part of this wonderful country in which to enjoy your holiday.

In the '70s Greece became the new Spain, and it was overrun with British and northern Europeans searching for remote islands where they could live for a pittance. Its own success unfortunately caused some of its later partial demise, as the concrete boxes of new hotels and villas appeared on the landscape, scarring the beautiful countryside forever. The Greeks have realized their mistakes, but these concrete boxes are still being erected annually and let out to tourists, so it is important to choose your destination carefully. The authentic Greek islands do still exist, and sumptuous villas are still available for hire at reasonable prices, if you know where to look, but if you want an uncommercialized resort and to escape mass tourism your search will have to be that bit more thorough. That's where we come in . . .

Greece can be divided into several distinct sections: Athens and Attica, the area bordering the capital; the North Aegean islands; the Sporades; the Dodecanese, the Cyclades, Crete, the Saronic isles, the Ionian islands; and on the mainland Central Greece, Evia, Western Greece, Northern Greece and the Peloponnese. Historians will find the Peloponnese a fascinating place, and for those seeking solely the physical beauty of Greece the islands of Santorini, Corfu, Zakinthos, Lesbos and Cephalonia are commonly regarded as the most scenic. (More is said of suitable destinations for different people under the 'Where to Go for What' section.)

The contrast of Greece is best highlighted by looking at the rugged mountains of Central Greece – wild, barren places where western films are shot, life is hard, and tourists are few – and the green, lush Ionian islands with their Venetian architecture, British influence and popular resorts such as Corfu, Kefalonia and Zakinthos. Athens – a city of contrasts if ever there was one, where hectic traffic, perpetual pollution and ugly concrete blocks vie for attention with the world's symbols of classical beauty – the 5th-century B.C. Acropolis, where stands the sacred Erechtheion, Temple of Athena Nike, and the very symbol of civilization and ancient Greece – the Parthenon.

It is these contrasts which make this country such a fascinating place to travel in; which frustrate and excite you all at once. It is not an easy country on the independent traveller: public transport is notoriously unreliable; the Athenian taxi driver will undoubtedly try his best to rip you off, and by the end of the first week you will be longing for a change from Greek salad, kebabs and retsina, but the magical memories of island sunsets; the incredible blue of the seas; the sheer beauty of the ancient sites, and the warmth of the people will leave you desperate for more. That's Greece.

When to Go

July and August are peak periods as far as tour operators are concerned, and are consequently the busiest as well as the hottest months to go. You'll pay most for your holiday at this time of year however you do it, but in return you'll find everything open and the nightlife and social scene at its peak.

Athens in peak season can be unbearably hot and crowded; the inter-island ferries packed, and the meltemi wind in the Cyclades and Crete can be a nuisance.

April to mid-June is a good time to go for those who want the sun, but not in such burning proportions, and to escape the crowds and inflated peak period prices. At the beginning of the season you will also find people have more time for you (by the end of October they do not want to see any more tourists – ever), and as a result service is often better.

Nature lovers should plump for springtime to visit Greece. The abundance of wild flowers and lushness of the countryside make this the country's most attractive period.

Mainland Greece (as can be seen under the section on 'The Climate') is a different proposition, and as it's so much quieter here than on the islands you're better advised to stick to the more reliable months from June to September.

If you travel right at the beginning of the season (particularly if it's before Easter), you may find certain restaurants, museums and tourist-related shops are not yet open. Easter time in Greece is becoming increasingly popular, so if you want to escape the crowds be sure to choose a quiet resort.

June is a happy compromise for all these considerations and is one of the most pleasant months to visit Greece: the nights still have long daylight; the weather is perfect and the disadvantages of mass tourism are still at a minimum.

September finds the tourist season still in full swing, but strangely this month is generally quieter than October, when Crete in particular is still very busy with northern Europeans catching the last hot days before the onset of winter. Off season rates come in in October and bargains are to be found. On islands popular with students, for example Ios and Santorini, the first week of October is often as busy as peak season as students who have been working all summer spend their last days before the new academic year sunning themselves and partying until the early hours – a point to remember if you're looking for a peaceful time. The later in the season the further south you have to go to catch the hot sun, hence Crete's late season popularity.

The Climate

This is no doubt one of your most important considerations – a fact being recognized by many tour operators who now include temperature charts in their brochures for the various resorts they offer. There are marked differences in climate between the islands and northern Greece, and climatic extremes are a marked feature in Greece. Winter freezes in the north contrast with temperatures well over 100°F in the summer down in Crete. The meltemi, a northerly wind, makes the Aegean islands and the coast of Attica bearable in the summer, and sea bathing is possible all over Greece from April to October. Don't worry about the meltemi though, most Britons are very glad of it. It doesn't seem to affect the tanning process, and 99 per cent of people who holiday in Greece still return with a disgustingly good tan!

Average air temperatures

ATHENS

	JAN	FEB	MAR	APR	MAY	JUNE
°C	9	10	14	15	20	25
°F	48	50	59	60	68	76

	JULY	AUG	SEPT	OCT	NOV	DEC
°C	27	27	24	19	15	11
°F	81	81	76	66	59	32

CORFU

	JAN	FEB	MAR	APR	MAY	JUNE
°C	10	10	12	15	20	24
°F	50	51	54	59	67	75

	JULY	AUG	SEPT	OCT	NOV	DEC
°C	27	27	23	19	15	12
°F	80	80	73	66	59	53

CRETE

	JAN	FEB	MAR	APR	MAY	JUNE
°C	12	12	14	17	20	24
°F	54	54	57	62	69	76

	JULY	AUG	SEPT	OCT	NOV	DEC
°C	26	26	23	20	17	14
°F	79	79	75	68	63	57

THESSALONIKI

	JAN	FEB	MAR	APR	MAY	JUNE
°C	5	6	9	14	20	24
°F	43	44	49	58	68	75

	JULY	AUG	SEPT	OCT	NOV	DEC
°C	27	26	22	16	11	7
°F	80	79	71	61	53	44

Winter Greece

SKIING

There is a limited amount of skiing in northern Greece, but it hardly rates as a serious skiing destination. The main ski centres are on Mount Parnassus, Mount Vermio, Mestovo and Mount Falakro.

WINTER SUN

Greece does not set itself up to be a winter holiday destination. It has little in the way of winter holidays, and, unlike some other destinations, it does not pretend to have sunny weather when it doesn't. Basically it gets so many tourists from Easter to October that it needs the respite the winter brings in which to recover. Inland the winters are cold and harsh, though by the sea it can be splendid, bracing walking weather, and it is a good time to go for some serious sightseeing in somewhere like Crete.

Where to Go for What

So often people spend weeks deliberating which country to choose for their holiday destination, then leave the choice of where they stay within the country to either a photograph and brief optimistic write-up in a travel brochure, or the discretion and persuasive talk of a travel agent (most of whom haven't actually visited the country in any depth anyway). This lottery results, not surprisingly, in many having a disappointing holiday simply because they got the facts wrong on this crucial decision. If anything, the decision of which part of the country you base yourself in is more important than the choice of country itself, for there is good and bad in every country. Britain, for example, offers the tourist a superb holiday destination, but if the visitor were to opt for two weeks in Sheffield, when he really wanted a

Before You Go 29

get-away-from-it-all type break, he would be sadly disappointed. Don't think that the Greek equivalents of Sheffield aren't on offer. They are, but you will not know if you're landed with it until you've paid your hundreds of pounds and arrived at the resort.

In order to match your needs to the most suitable resorts we have divided holidaymakers into certain stereotypes. Doubtless most of you fall into several of the categories, but the idea is to find which resorts crop up in the areas you are interested in, and match your needs accordingly.

The following symbols representing the various interests appear throughout the text of the guide as a means of easy reference to spot the places likely to be of interest to you:

The Sun-worshipper

The Naturist

The Sightseer

The Socialite

Healthy Holidays

The Nature Lover

The Recluse

The Family Holidays

 **The Sun-worshipper**

Greece is a haven for beach bums. The beaches here are among the best in Europe – vast stretches of clean sand, lapped by warm blue seas, ideal for swimming and water sports. With over one thousand islands to choose from it is still possible to find the idyllic deserted beach if this is what you're after; alternatively there are naturist beaches (nudist); family beaches; pebbly beaches; rocky coves; beaches where the young congregate at night for parties, and beaches where manwatching is the main pastime. There are beaches to suit every taste, if you know where to look.

The best beaches are often a good walk away from the towns and resorts, and if it's seclusion you're after you may have to walk a good way to find it if you're on Corfu, Crete or Rhodes in high season. Some islands, it must be said, have very poor beaches, so if this is an important part of your holiday read this section carefully.

As a rough guide the Cyclades islands have better beaches than the Ionian; the Saronic islands vary dramatically; the Dodecanese have excellent beaches interspersed with poor; the North Aegean and East Aegean have too little in the way of tourist facilities to make them comfortable bases for beach holidays; the Sporades have beautiful beaches, and the Halkidiki has excellent, flat sandy expanses, particularly on the eastern side of the Kassandra peninsula.

Islands boasting particularly good sandy beaches are: NAXOS; ANTIPAROS; SKIATHOS; CORFU; MYKONOS; RHODES; MILOS; KIMOLOS and ZAKINTHOS.

Pebbly beaches and coves are good on CORFU, CRETE and RHODES, making these three major holiday centres particularly good islands for those looking for a beach-based holiday (which accounts for their popularity).

Naturist beaches are to be found all over on an impromptu basis (i.e. one week they are; the next week, after the Germans, Swedes and Brits have left, they're not – it just depends on the innovative few setting the trend for their stay), but on the following three major islands there are always naturist beaches: CRETE, MYKONOS (of course!) and RHODES. Generally the larger the island and more popular the resort the more chance there is there will be a naturist beach. Do bear in mind though that nudism is prohibited in some places, and if you find yourself in this position it's best to walk to a quiet cove somewhere before stripping off. Please also bear in mind that while no one will mind if you quietly sunbathe nude on a secluded beach somewhere, they will take objection if you disrobe in the middle of a family beach where children of all ages are playing. The Greeks are very family-minded and rarely strip off themselves. They expect visitors to the country, quite rightly, to show respect for their way of life, and to comply with their customs.

Water sports are at their best on the commercialized islands. Accordingly CORFU, RHODES and CRETE are good.

The Young Set congregate on IOS, SPETSE, CORFU, CRETE, NAXOS and SANTORINI.

Beach beds and sun shades can be hired in the major resorts, but as yet, unlike the Italians and Spaniards, the Greeks are not really into this profitable line of business on the smaller beaches. Rush beach mats can be widely bought as can suntan preparations, though you're still better advised to bring yours from the UK.

Detail on specific beaches on the islands can be found in the full geographical write-up in Part Four of this guide.

This list of some of Greece's best beaches is subjective, but well researched!

CORFU – Ypsos, Glyfada, Messongi, Agios Georgios
LEFKADA – Lefkada, Vassiliki
KEFALONIA – Platys Gialos, Lixouri & Sami
GULF OF CORINTH – Antirio, Rio
PELOPONNESE – Methoni, Kylini, Tolo, Dyros, Laganas
EVIA – Marmari, Karystos
SKIATHOS – Koukounaries
SKOPELOS – Skopelos Beach
HALKIDIKI – Agia Triada, Sani, Gerakina, Porto Carras
THRACE – Nea Hili, Lagos
NAXOS – Apollonas
ANDROS – Batsi
TINOS – Panormos
MYKONOS – Megali Amos & Agios Stefanos
SAMOS – Pythagorio

PAROS – Naoussa
SIFNOS – Platys Gialos
IOS – Gialos
RHODES – Faliraki, Ixia, Lindos
CRETE – Vai, Sitia, Elounda, Rethymnon, Gournes, Maleme, Matala, Kato Zakros, Kissamos.

 The Sightseer: *Sights, historical monuments, archaeological remains.*

Fortunately the best sights within Greece, an excellent country for a 'professional' sightseer, are on the major tourist circuit: ATHENS, CRETE, RHODES, the PELOPONNESE and CENTRAL GREECE. In the north inland MACEDONIA and THRACE will be of great interest to the archaeologist, though independent travel to these areas is about the only serious option. Package tourists to the capital city and major islands however can enjoy the sights without the hassles of organizing their own tours, and if you're prepared to do everything 'en masse' there are several packages put together which tour round the country's major sights and monuments, with expert guides to give you a full commentary as you go.

Just about every island or village has something of interest if you know where to look. The old quarter, generally built high on a hill, is invariably the most interesting, and there are very few islands or places in Greece which do not have an archaeological site and local museum filled with its finds (though note that the best finds are kept in Athens, in the National Archaeological Museum). A monastery is another 'sight' found in nearly every part of Greece. As a rule these have set opening hours now, and it is commonplace for them to insist that ladies cover their arms and no shorts are allowed.

Excursions are run by all the major tour operators to the local sights of interest, though often it is better to make the discoveries on your own.

All the major sites charge admission (25–250 dr), with admission on Sundays (and sometimes Thursdays as well) free. Long lunch breaks are commonplace, and in summer the average hours of opening are 8 or 9 a.m. to 4 or 5 p.m., Sundays and holidays 10 a.m. to 2 or 4 p.m.

Archaeological sites open from 7.30 a.m. to sunset in summer. Mondays and Tuesdays are the most popular closing days.

As a rough guide, keen historians should head for the Peloponnese where the sights include: the **citadel** and **tombs of Mycenae**; **Olympia**; the **amphitheatre at Epidavros** and the ancient cities of SPARTA and CORINTH. It is also possible to hop over to DELPHI from here. Northern Greece is another serious contender as a historian's destination within Greece. **Mount Athos** and the monasteries of METEORA will leave you in no doubt that you have made the right choice, and to add to this orgy of monumental reminders of the past there is the site of **Philippi**, where the fate of the Roman Empire was decided; and the birthplace of the great Macedonian who went on to build the strongest empire the world had known, Alexander the Great, born in PELLA, northern Greece.

Specific destinations worth considering therefore are: ATHENS for the **Acropolis, Temple of Zeus, Museums, Theseion** and **Pynx**; and as day trips from the capital the ruins at DELPHI; the temple of **Sounion** and **Dodona**, birthplace of the Hellenes.

THE METEORA in central Greece whose 14th-century metropolis is considered one of the wonders of the Middle Ages is worth seeking out, and definitely the high spot of any sightseer's trip to Greece will be **Mount Athos**, the monastic state, below this sacred mountain. (**Note:** women not allowed, men must have permit. See write-up in text.)

In the Peloponnese: EPIDAVROS, with the best-preserved amphitheatre in all Greece, and OLYMPIA, birthplace of the Panhellenic Games. Byzantine MYSTRAS and THE MANI are two further places of interest to the historically-minded.

In the Cyclades: the sacred island of DELOS, the sanctuary of Apollo; the catacombs on MILOS, and the incredible remains of the Bronze Age town of Akrotiri on SANTORINI.

On CRETE the palace of the Minoan King at Knossos; the acropolis at Lindos on RHODES in the Dodecanese, and also in this group of islands the remains of the sanctuary and medical school – the **Asklipio** – on KOS. The medieval remains on Kos and the island of PATMOS will also be of interest.

The Socialite: *Manwatching, Nightlife, etc.*

There are several places in Greece which qualify as places to see and be seen, and those concerned with such things should find the following information vital. Undoubtedly the most socially acceptable way to be seen in Greece is lounging on a yacht on your own Odyssey tour of the islands. Spending time in a villa ranks next on the social ladder, and in package terms it is *de rigueur* to travel with a socially acceptable firm. The rule here is the smaller and more exclusive the company, the better. Names to look out for with an executive appeal are: **Club Med**, **Small World**, and **Mark Warner** (not to be confused with Club 18-30 who cater for the other end of the market). Also the various yachting and cruising specialists: **Y.C.A.**, **Falcon** and **Island Sailing**. Often the Specialist Interest holidays are classy affairs, such as those operated by **Serenissima Travel, Swan Hellenic Art Treasure Tours**, or **Cox & Kings Special Interest Holidays**.

Greek islands come in and go out of fashion with amazing speed. One year it is Santorini, the next year after the large tour operators and the back-packing set have moved in, it is more than one's life is worth to be seen there. There remains however a core of islands where there is sufficient nightlife, large villas and good restaurants to carry a socialite through a holiday intact. Mykonos was *the* island a decade ago. Since then its popularity has peaked and troughed on numerous occasions, in the same way as somewhere like St. Tropez, but it is still an island of great appeal where a good time can be had. Perhaps more than any other island it has the necessary machinery of organized socialite activities: exclusive boutiques stay open until late; there is a selection of *haute cuisine* restaurants (unusual in Greece outside of Athens, though you do pay for the privilege); and there are discos and large-scale villa parties every night of the week, once you've wangled your way into the 'right' company and got onto the invitation lists.

Other islands for the socialite set are: DELOS, SANTORINI, SKIATHOS – becoming increasingly popular and building up a good reputation for its restaurants; HYDRA, which is *the* place to spend Easter; PAROS, RHODES, CORFU (though in the latter two cases it is assumed you will choose the resort most carefully to be well away from the great unwashed on their £200-for-two-weeks package. See the full write-ups on these islands); CEPHALONIA, KARPATHOS and LESBOS. The last three are still new arrivals on the scene. ATHENS itself would be worth a few days, particularly from June to September during the Athens Festival. The district for nightlife is the **Plaka**, in the shadow of the Acropolis.

Getting to the manwatching potential for holidaymakers: the Greeks enjoy an evening promenade at dusk and this is the opportunity to get into some serious manwatching. Pavement café space gets crowded with professionals, so get your seat around 7 p.m. in mid-season to be in with a chance. The Greeks don't go in much for beach-based manwatching; they leave that to the tourists, but the northern Europeans certainly make up for it, and if you're trying to meet someone this is as good a venue as any. Greek girls, particularly on remote islands, are still protected very much before marriage, so be aware of the local customs if asking one out (i.e. don't be too surprised when big brother turns up on the date too as official chaperone!).

Discos, dances in hotels, and restaurants with dancers and musicians constitute the basis of Greek holiday nightlife with many of the larger tour operators running organized 'Greek Evenings'.

RECORDING YOUR HOLIDAY

The trend is set and each year an increasing number of people discover the delights of taking their holiday on film, to be played back on their television and watched from the comfort of their armchair in the dark winter months ahead. Though a video rig-out is still an expensive business it is the sort of equipment once you've had you feel you can never do without. Photos, slides and cine films just aren't the same after a full colour and sound film, and on holiday where the sky and sea are *so* blue, and the colours so much more vibrant, a video camera really comes into its own.

Those on the market now are well adapted to travelling: lightweight and easy to handle.

If you still feel £1200 is a bit too much to splash out, consider hiring. That way you can have the fun of taking a film of your holiday for not much more than the equivalent you'd spend on conventional films, processing and so on. Hiring is widely available in all areas of the U.K. and is becoming, like the video camera itself, very much a thing of the future.

CULTURE VULTURES

Greece has some major festivals of interest to those of an artistic bent. The Athens Festival is a particularly noteworthy occasion, well worth getting to. At weekends in Epidavros, and off and on all season in the **Athens Herod Atticus Amphitheatre**, on the slopes of the Acropolis, open-air performances of classical Greek dramas are staged. The setting and atmosphere makes for a memorable event – an absolute 'must' for a theatre buff.

The ancient theatres of **Philippi**, **Dodona** and **Thassos** play host to theatrical performances also, and at the other end of the entertainments world is the Athens Fringe Festival (Rock, Jazz, etc). Many of its events are held in the open-air theatre on Likavitos Hill. If you're going specifically for the festival get hold of the N.T.O.G. publication called 'Greek Festivals'. Once in Athens tickets can be bought from the offices at Stadiou 4 or Voukourestiou 1.

Other major festivals (mainly days of religious significance) likely to influence your holiday are:

Easter – In Greece Easter is the biggest festival of the year. It is a particularly beautiful time to visit the country and even in the most remote village you will be unable to ignore the fact that a major national celebration is underway. They have many ritualistic ceremonies: the burning of Christ's funeral bier in the streets on Good Friday; the midnight candle-lit Mass on Holy Saturday; and the joyous pealing of bells and singing on Easter Sunday. All in all it is a wonderful experience to witness and be part of, and it will show you more of the true spirit of Greece and the Greeks than anything else you're likely to see on your holiday.

HYDRA, an island of 360 churches and monasteries, is a particularly magical place to spend Easter, and other places to aim for are ARAHOVA, near to Delphi, and **LIVADIA**.

Other festivals to note are:

25 March – *Independence Day* which celebrates the successful revolt against Turkish rule in 1821.

23 April – St George's Day, which as the patron saint of all shepherds is a big rural celebration.
May Day – the usual May Day celebration when Athenians descend on the coast in their hordes (making it a good time to be in the capital).
24 June – St John the Baptist's Day when bonfires are lit.
20 July – Prophet Ilias Day – marked by feasting and celebrations in the mountainous areas (Elijah displaced the god Apollo on the Greek mountains).
15 August – Assumption Day (religious holiday; everything closes).
28 October – 'Ochi' Day – ('No' Day). Marks the date of the Italian invasion in 1940 and recalls the answer to Mussolini's utlimatum.

Healthy Holidays: *The Great Outdoors; The Sportsman*

Water-based activities dominate the sporting scene in Greece, not surprisingly given the amount of water which surrounds the country, and for the swimmer, water-skier, windsurfer, diver, fisherman and yachtsman Greece will be a paradise.

Land-based sportsmen will have less to look forward to, though. The Greeks are not a particularly sporting nation, and most of the golf, tennis and squash facilities that exist in the country are there for the tourists, not the locals. From the package holidaymaker's point of view most sports which you could want or expect will be available at your, or a neighbouring hotel. The **HALKIDIKI** in Northern Greece is a particularly good place for sporting types. Many of the hotels here concentrate on sporting facilities to compensate for the lack of nightlife, accordingly table tennis, tennis, mini-golf, pool tables and large swimming pools are frequently found, as well as a good range of beach-based sports. *Mountaineering* is best pursued on the mainland, though there are some mountainous islands such as Crete. Rugged peaks, exhausting climbs and superb views are what's involved. The Greek Skiing and Alpine Federation have a system of some forty refuge huts which make the going easier. If you're keen on skiing or climbing contact them at Karageorgi Servias 7, Athens 126 (Tel: 323 4555), or, if you're heading for Northern Greece, contact the Thessaloniki office at Karalou Deal 15, Thessaloniki. The Greek

Touring Club will also supply information on mountain climbs. They're at 12 Politechnia Street, Athens.

Skiing: The main ski centres in Greece are **MOUNT PARNASSUS** and the **PINDUS RANGE**, where the season is from December to May; **MOUNT VERMIO**, **METSOVO**, **MOUNT FALAKRO** and **MOUNT PILIO**.

Caving: This is a popular sport in Greece due to the abundance of karstic formations to be found. Crete has over 3000 and in the Cyclades and on Cephalonia are the most outstanding examples. Though many are unguarded it is still necessary to gain permission to explore them (see the local Tourist Police). Several caves are open to the public, notable ones are **DRONGORATI** near to Haliotata, and **MELISSANI** in Karavomilos, both on Cephalonia.

Hunting: From August to March, wild boar, hare, quail, partridge, waterfowl and woodcock can be shot. Hunting is permitted for a fee in Greece on any open ground. Apply to the local Forestry Office. Permits are cheap and there are five main hunting regions: the islands of **ANTIPAXI**, **ATLANTONISI**, **DIA** on Crete, **ELAFONISI** and **SAPIENTZA**.

Golf is not a popular sport in Greece. There are only five courses in the country, all notably in tourist areas: **ATHENS** (just outside), **RHODES**, **CORFU**, **HALKIDIKI**, and **SKIATHOS**.

Tennis again is not popular. Hotels, sports stadiums and N.T.O.G. beaches are the only main venues. Equipment is not provided on N.T.O.G. courts.

Sailing is a different matter. Greece is a perfect place to learn the skills of the helm and many schools and clubs exist to this end. The schools are located in **ATHENS**, **THESSALONIKI**, **CORFU**, **VOLOS**, **SIROS**, **KALAMATA**, and **ALEXANDROUPOLIS**.

Numerous tour operators run flotilla and yachting holidays (see section on 'Who Specializes in What'). For further information write to the Hellenic Sailing Federation at 15a Xenofondos Street, Athens. One thing to bear in mind when cruising is that the meltemi wind is strong in July and August, so it's not the best time to be out.

Scuba-diving: There are restrictions on where and when in Greece you can dive with compressed air apparatus. It's best to check you're in the clear with the Captain of the Port involved. Scuba-diving schools are in **ATHENS, PIRAEUS, THESSALONIKI, CORFU** and **RHODES**.

Snorkelling: Equipment can be bought cheaply in all coastal resorts, and provided you don't take fish over 5 oz you can use a speargun.

Riding: Riding is not a particularly good idea in Greece. The few equestrian clubs there are expensive and even to hire an old nag is pricey.

Windsurfing: In the summer this seems to be the nation's favourite pastime. Every resort of any standing has boards for hire and lessons on offer. If this is your main reason for going to Greece write for further information to the Hellenic Wind Surfing Association, 7 Filelinon Street, Athens.

Fishing: No permits are required for sea fishing and boats and tackle are widely available at reasonable costs. Further information from Amateur Anglers & Maritime Sports Club, Akti Moutsopoulou, Zea Harbour, Piraeus.

 The Nature Lover

The flora of Greece is richer and more varied than that of any other European country – words sweet enough to entice any nature lover to explore the National Parks of Greece. However, in true Greek style, there exists in this same country a situation of desperate conflict: vast areas of forest and flora-rich vegetation are being grazed to infertility by the very animals which provide the main source of national employment – agriculture and small-scale husbandry. The pressure on the land has resulted in a strong conservation movement, but in truth it's a toothless tiger, and so the future is uncertain.

About the beauties of this country, however, there are no doubts. There are eight National Parks: **OLYMPUS**, which extends over the eastern part of the Olympus mountains and includes in its territory the highest peaks of Greece. Climbing from June to October is possible and the town of Litohoron is the preferred starting point for climbers. (Ayiou Dhionisiou is the exact point, just west of the town.) Forestry roads give access into the Park for those not keen or able to scale the heights, and a rich collection of birds (27 recorded species of geese, 3 recorded birds of prey), and endemic species of flowers and plants live there.

PARNASSUS is the highest mountain in central Greece and this peak and surrounding countryside is another of Greece's National Parks. Only experienced rock climbers should attempt a climb in this desolate but undeniably beautiful area of the country. The changing colours of the limestone cliffs are reason enough to make the effort to get there. Access is from Delphi, Arachova or Amphicleia. This park is particularly rich in both fauna (notably eagles and vultures) and flora.

MOUNT AINOS In the south-eastern corner of Cephalonia in the Ionian islands lies one of Greece's last remaining primaeval forests, noted for its endemic species – silver fir (*abies cephalonia*). Birdlife is extremely rich, making it an ideal place for ornithologists. Access is from Argostoli or Sami. There is a road through some of the park leading to a TV relay station at Chionistra.

THE SAMARIA GORGE This beautiful long gorge in the west of Crete is perhaps the most famous of Greece's natural features. Mass tourism on Crete has put the gorge on the tourist circuit, but even in peak season you needn't worry about crowds – there are 19 sq miles of beautiful countryside in which to lose yourself. A footpath runs the length of the gorge, which in some places is only a few feet wide, yet has limestone walls several hundred feet high. This gorge is the last natural habitat of the 'agrimini' – a long-horned goat, as well as boasting an interesting collection of 'chasmophytes' – plants adapted to shady situations. Permission is required to stray from the footpath or to be in the gorge outside the hours between sunrise and sunset. Access is from Xyloscao on the road from Chania, or Ayia Roumeli, reached by boat from Chora Skefion.

PINDUS In north-western Greece, on the border of Epirus and Thessaly, is the Pindus National Park which encompasses the highlands of the Pindus mountain range. Living in this area are the 'aromani' – semi-nomadic shepherds who speak a curious mixture of Greek and Romanian, and spend all their time in this wild, dramatic land where extreme temperatures are the norm, and wild animals such as the brown bear, wild boar and wolf still roam free. Access is from Metsova, the nearest village to the park.

MOUNT SETI This massive triangle of land in central Greece has crags, peaks and ridges reminiscent of the Swiss Alps. Broad-leaved woods and grazing land make up part of this Park, along with dramatic gorges and mountains over 2100 metres high. Of interest to botanists are the endemic species of orchid, found in the more remote parts of the Park. Also native to this area is the 'oeti wild goat'. Access is from Lamia or Ypati.

VIKOS-AOOS In north-west Greece, not far from the Albanian border, is a National Park best known for its two spectacular deep gorges. Unlike the Samaria Gorge in Crete, however, there is no footpath worth mentioning, and experience in climbing is necessary to negotiate the full length of the gorge.

Forests of black pine and beech add a dramatic backdrop to the literally dozens of streams which flow down the Papingos and Karoutia mountains into the Aoos gorge.

Access is from Konitsa or Ioannina to Monodendrion.

MIKRI PRESPA This is the newest of Greece's National Parks. It lies virtually on the Greek-Albanian border, and Little Lake Prespa ('mikri' means 'little') is divided from Greater Lake Prespa by a narrow isthmus, and this is the ideal area in which to birdwatch (notably aquatic birds). Thirteen endangered species have been identified here, and there are two kinds of pelican of particular interest. Access is from Florina or Kastoria to Mikrolimni.

For further information on all Greece's National Parks write to the Ministry of Agriculture & Forestry, National Parks Section, 3–5 Ippocratous Street, Athens.

If going to holiday in a National Park is too much of an undertaking for you any of the following islands will be of interest to a nature lover: Kythera, Kithnos, Serifos, Santorini, Nissiros, Amouliani, Aghios Efstratios and Lesbos.

N.B.: Note the information on page 81 regarding botanical and bird-watching organized holidays.

The Recluse

Despite mass tourism there are still many places in Greece where you can go to escape the crowds. Remember that vast areas of the mainland of Greece are still largely undiscovered by the tour operators, and that there are over 1000 islands, only 40 or so of which see any significant number of tourists. Information like this will change your perspective of Greece as a tourist haunt, and with a little homework you can ensure you get the right type of holiday. Independent arrangements are the most obvious solution to being hemmed in with other tourists, and one good piece of advice is to choose an island (assuming you want an island, not the mainland) which only receives about one ferry a week. Also read through all the package brochures to Greece that you can find, noting down the places they run to, and then avoid all those resorts. Islands worth considering are AGHIOS EFSTRATIOS, INOUSSA, PATMOS, AMORGOS, AMOULIANI, ANAFI, ASTIPALEA, HALKI, MONI, ANTIKYTHERA, DONOUSSA, KASTELORIZO, LIPSI, PSARA, SCHINOUSSA, TELENDOS and YIALI.

MOUNT ATHOS, the self-governing monastic state, has got to be high on your list too.

In Northern Greece SAMOTHRACE is an option. The old village of Samothrace, a few miles up the hills, is an ideal recluse's paradise. Alternatively try the mountain villages in Western Macedonia (head west from Thessaloniki). The peninsula of Sithonia, close to Thessaloniki, has good uncrowded beaches, particularly on the western coast, and the eastern coast town of VOURVOUROU is worth checking out.

The coast of the western Peloponnese in the south of the country is a good place for a quiet beach holiday, combined with ancient site-combing. The beaches at **KASTRO**, **SKAFIDIA** and **KIPARISSIA** are particularly good.

Those wanting a quiet time, but still keen on the odd bit of nightlife, could consider a package to the **HALKIDIKI**, or the islands in the Ionian group other than Corfu (e.g. **ZAKINTHOS** and **KEPHALONIA**).

Another area worth considering is the 'Olympian Coast' as the jargon goes (Western Peloponnese to you and I). So far only Enterprise and Sovereign, the British Airways tour operators, go there, but this ensures this lovely area remain relatively unspoilt.

 ## The Family Holiday

Greece is an ideal destination for a family holiday. It combines all the necessary ingredients; safe, sandy beaches, laid-on facilities, a family-loving people and plenty of new and interesting things to see and do for children of all ages.

If your children are of an age when it takes more than just a safe beach to keep them happy choose your resort carefully. Obviously the more commercialized it is the more facilities it will have, and the happier the older child will be. **CORFU** and **RHODES** are good for keeping children entertained if you choose the right resort, but the part of Greece most designed with the family holiday in mind is the **HALKIDIKI**. The hotels here, especially in Sithonia and Kassandra, have children's pools, electronic games and sports facilities for children. The only disadvantage about going to a place which caters specially for families (this is usually indicated in the brochure write-up) is that you can end up with the place being full of boisterous youngsters – great fun for the kids, but less so for you!

If your children are at an age where laid-on entertainment need not be a feature, the quiet areas of Corfu, Zakinthos and Skiathos will provide you with good safe beaches. If you're heading off to anywhere very remote do take your own supply of things like disposable nappies, baby foods and so on.

If babysitting is a consideration bear in mind that some Club-type holidays, such as **Club Med** and **Mark Warner** offer a babysitting service which means you can have a night out, safe in the knowledge that someone responsible is in charge.

Practicalities

Red Tape

British visitors holding a full passport are allowed to stay for up to 90 days without a visa. (American, Australian and Canadian visitors likewise.) Thereafter you must apply to the Athens Alien Bureau, 9 Halkokondili Street, 1st floor, Athens (Tel: 3628 301), or to the Aliens Centre, 37 Vass, Constantinou, Piraeus (Tel: 417 4023). Application to the Aliens Bureau must be in person and should be at least twenty days before the end of the first three months in Greece.

A British Tourist Passport (Visitors Card) valid for three months also allows you a maximum of 90 days in Greece without a visa. With any specific queries contact the British Embassy, 1 Plouttarchou Street, Athens (Tel: 723 9511), or before leaving contact the Greek Embassy in your own country. In London it is at 1a Holland Park, London W11 (Tel: 01-727 8040).
N.B.: Visitors with Turkish Republic of Cyprus stamps in their passports will not be admitted to Greece, and tourists using charter flights cannot visit Turkey on a holiday based in Greece.

Health Formalities

No health certificate is required for entry to citizens of the British Isles, North America, Australia or Canada. If you're coming from elsewhere you may require certificates. Contact the Greek National Tourist Organisation if in doubt. A Typhoid/Polio immunisation is advisable, according to the DHSS.

Customs

There are no real problems with customs in Greece, particularly for package tourists. If you've a Turkish stamp in your passport they may give you a rougher time; if you've been to the Turkish Republic of Cyprus you simply won't get in. But generally there are absolutely no problems, especially now Greece too is in the E.E.C.

The duty-free allowances for adults from the E.E.C. countries are: 300 cigarettes or 75 cigars or 150 cigarillos or 400 grams of tobacco; 1·5 litres of spirit or 4 litres of wines and liqueurs, and 4 litres in all of non-sparkling wines; 75g of perfume and 3·8 litres of eau de cologne, and goods which are not of commercial value up to the value of £112. Foreign banknotes in excess of US $500 must be declared for re-export, but there is no limit on how much currency or gold you bring into the country. There is no restriction on traveller's cheques. Only 3000 drachmas may be imported or exported. Animals require a health and rabies certificate and are cleared at the port of entry (unlikely to affect the average holidaymaker as there is no way you could get your pet back into Britain again at the end of the holiday without the long procedure of quarantine).

There is no restriction on the amount of souvenirs and gifts you can take back from Greece, but if you buy archaeological items or antiques (the replica busts sold in the museums do not count), an export licence is needed.

Money

The monetary unit in Greece is the drachma (dr). One drachma = 100 lepta, and it comes in the following denominations:

Coins: 1, 2, 5, 10, 20 and 50 drachmas.
Notes: 5000, 1000, 500 and 100.

A maximum of 3000 dr may be imported or exported. There is no limit to the amount of foreign currency which may be imported, though amounts over US $500 must be declared for re-exporting.
N.B.: Do not bring back notes over the value of 500 dr or you will not be able to change them.

HOW TO TAKE YOUR MONEY

Banks change money at the official rate and all banks will exchange foreign currencies and traveller's cheques. If you're buying drachmas in the U.K. you can often get a better rate if you buy a large sum – check first.

Traveller's cheques are a good way to take money if you're heading for any risky areas, for example, if you've to spend a day hanging around Piraeus docks waiting on a ferry, or if you're freelancing a lot, but generally, on a two-week package, you're pretty safe, and assuming you take good care of your possessions there is no real need to take traveller's cheques, which, after all, do cost extra and require you to wait in long queues to exchange them. If you do play safe buy your cheques in small denominations. That way you can change a small sum into drachmas, and if you're left with unspent cheques at the end of your holiday you can easily get the sterling back. If, however, you buy them in £20 or £50 sums and you have to change that all into drachmas, you may well be left with unspent foreign currency which you will then have to pay again to exchange.

Always go for a well known bank or credit card company, for example, American Express, Thomas Cook or Bank of England, otherwise you could have problems in the more rural parts of the country.

Credit Cards This is one of the best ways of taking money on holiday, assuming you're going to a large resort where they will be widely accepted. Hotels, shops and some restaurants will take the major cards: American Express, Visa and Access. In remote areas you will get nowhere with plastic money.

Personal Cheques With a Eurocheque Encashment Card and Eurocheques (available from your bank) you may cash cheques anywhere abroad, just as you would at home. This is the ideal way to take your money on holiday.

The best compromise is to take some ready drachmas, some sterling, any credit cards you have, and the bulk of your holiday money in Eurocheques, along with the Eurocheque encashment card.

Banking

Opening hours are 8 a.m. to 2 p.m. Monday to Friday, closed Saturday and Sunday and public holidays. In resorts, however, many banks stay open in the afternoons and during the evenings for currency exchange.

When closing time beckons it's more than your life's worth to try and get your foot in the door after 1.30 p.m. If the bank is closed and you want to exchange money or cheques head for a large hotel, but watch the exchange rate.

Insurance

It really is foolhardy to cut back on holiday insurance, yet each year thousands of people make this false economy and live to regret it. Increasingly if you're taking a package holiday you'll have no say in the matter and insurance will be added on to your final bill, whether you like it or not. While this at least makes sure you get some sort of cover, it also ensures the travel agent lines his pocket with a healthy commission. Note then that you are under no obligation to accept the insurance policy offered by your travel agent. In some instances these policies are not as detailed as those bought from large reputable companies and all too often the package policies mean long delays in the settlement of claims as they're snowed under at the peak of the tourist season. On their plus side is the fact that the rep at the resort will have been trained how to handle claims under these policies and that will take some of the strain off you. If you are not happy with the inclusive package insurance, the best advice is to go to an insurance broker, tell him what you're taking (remembering photographic equipment, etc.), what you envisage doing (if you plan spending a lot of time doing water sports, or more specifically skiing), and how long you'll be away. He can then give you the ideal policy, tailor-made to your needs. This is particularly sensible if you are taking a lot of new expensive equipment with you (many package policies put a limit of around £200 per item on your valuables), or if your chances of ending up requiring medical treatment are higher than average. Also check out the liability clause for flight delays if it's imperative you get back home by the date stipulated.

Lloyds of London are particularly good for travel insurance and will even provide cover for people who normally find it difficult, for example, just-pregnant women skiers or disabled people.

For most people a basic £15 insurance package deal will suffice, but the onus is on you to tell your insurance broker or travel agent if you are not just an average holidaymaker for one reason or another.

Independent travellers to Greece are particularly advised to procure a good insurance policy before going as they have no one (such as ABTA or a travel agent) to haggle for them.

If a theft occurs make sure you get a written statement from the police, no matter how unwilling they are to write it, as without this your insurance company will not want to know.

As regards medical assistance, British and all EEC citizens are entitled to the same health cover as Greek nationals – free medical care, but this only allows you to be admitted to the lowest grade of state hospital where nursing standards leave much to be desired. Form E111 is required to get any treatment free, so don't leave home without it. Apply at your local DHSS office. North American travellers and those from further afield are strongly advised to procure a good travel insurance cover before leaving home.

Health

Greece does not present any major health hazards to the average holidaymaker. Do not drink the water if you have a delicate disposition, and if travelling in remote areas take a good First Aid kit with you, but apart from these guidelines you will find Greece a safe place for you and your family. If a serious illness strikes ring either the Tourist Police (Tel: 104) or the British Consulate, where you will be put in touch with an English-speaking doctor. 'Farmakias' – chemists – are as good a bet as any for diagnosing and prescribing for minor complaints, and, as previously stated, the Form E111 will get you free medical care anywhere in Greece.

If you want to get yourself well insured for medical crises one of the best policies is arranged through Europ Assistance Ltd, 252

High Street, Croydon, Surrey CR0 11NF. For a relatively small premium they provide a 24-hour advice telephone link with the U.K. and a guarantee of on-the-spot cash for emergency services. This insurance also covers the expenses that can arise from a car accident (hiring another car, flying out spare parts etc).

No specific vaccinations or health certificates are required by Britons entering Greece, but if you're travelling into the more remote areas, or heading on to Turkey, it is a good idea to have a typhoid/cholera booster.

Pre-planning and Free Information

The more you know about a country before going, the more you'll get out of your holiday once you're there. Not only can you isolate where the things that interest you are located, but you'll be able to plan ahead to make sure you get to see them and ensure you don't waste any precious time waiting in tourist information queues. It's amazing how many people still leave on holiday with the picture of their hotel as their only image of the country they're going to.

The National Tourist Offices of virtually every country imaginable have an office in London, and Greece is no exception. Write to them ahead of your holiday (well ahead as they can take literally weeks to reply) asking for general tourist literature and, if you have any specific hobby or pursuit you're keen to indulge in on holiday, ask them their advice on where best to pursue it, and to send you any literature they might have on it (e.g. golfing or skiing). Request a map if you're considering touring, and accommodation listings if you're travelling independently. The National Tourist Organisation of Greece produce really sumptuous tourist bumpf – full colour glossies, way ahead of most country's literature, and it is well worth asking for the leaflet on the area you are travelling to (e.g. the pamphlet on Crete, Corfu, the Dodecanese if you're going to these places). The address to write to is the National Tourist Organisation of Greece, 195–197 Regent Street, London W1R 8DL (Tel: 01-734 5997).

Another source of free information on Greece is your local library. It needn't all be heavy reading. Apart from guidebooks and the

Lawrence Durrells, there are many interesting books on Greek history (modern as well as ancient) and if you have a particular interest, such as the fauna and flora of the country, this is probably the best place to do your pre-holiday research. Libraries are sadly neglected by many, and if your local one is of any reasonable size you will probably be amazed at the riches you can find there.

An extremely useful source of information (free and impartial) comes from the travel agent Hogg Robinson. They produce resort reports which go into detail on what to expect at the resorts, and give an unbiased report on all the hotels used by the tour operators. These files can be consulted free of charge in any of their agencies.

Thomas Cook produce resort reports too, and these can be taken away by the public. Much smaller and with no detail on specific hotels, these do however contain condensed information on the main resorts, sightseeing, best buys and so on, and they give a good idea how expensive drinks and meals will be once you're there.

As for bought sources: guidebooks on Greece are plentiful, though be sure you leaf well through the pages before buying one. If you want to learn a lot about the country's historic monuments a good investment is *Baedeker's Greece*, or the Collins Companion Guide. Fodor's guide is very much aimed at the middle-aged, middle-class American, but it is comprehensive if you're touring the country. The Berlitz series covers Rhodes, Crete and Corfu, but after a few pages the clichés get a bit hard to take, and the all-American extra-lightweight style does grate a bit; better to stick to the one you're reading, which is at least in touch with the British market! Backpackers will find the *Rough Guide to Greece* useful, and also the *Let's Go: Greece & the Turkish Coast*, though these books are really aimed at the 200 drachmas-a-day set who are aiming to cover every inch of Greece in the long student holidays. Whatever you read before making the trip will bring its rewards though, and remember the more you know before going, the more you will appreciate the country when you're there.

Budgeting

Despite inflation of around 20 per cent, Greece is still a reasonably cheap country to holiday in. Prices for food, hotels and souvenirs are very much on a par with prices at home, and meals out are still cheaper. Unless you're planning on continual splurges it's unlikely that you'll have to watch every drachma, and overall most holidaymakers find Greece a good place for a low-cost holiday. It is a country where if you're prepared to rough it a bit you can live unbelievably cheaply; sleeping on roofs and eating the set tourist menus can allow you to live for a couple of pounds a day, and even if you want to rent a reasonable but simple room in a pension and eat at a good taverna every night it is still possible to make it through a couple of weeks for around £200. If you're on a half-board package you can easily get by on spending money of around £100 for two weeks.

For those on a really tight budget here are some ways of saving money: consider doing your own thing. With so many charter flight companies running to Greece it is often possible to pick up a cheap flight to Athens or one of the major islands, find your own accommodation, and have a lower bill at the end of it than if you'd taken a package. This is a good idea off-season when rooms are plentiful, but as the season wears on finding a reasonably priced room can become a problem as it's very much a seller's market, and the Greeks can drive a hard bargain. (Be prepared to haggle, and always ask if they've nothing cheaper. Generally you'll find they have some little attic room tucked away which they'll let to you for a few drachmas a night.)

Taking a 'Budget' special with a tour operator is another way to cut costs. Many tour operators now offer this money-saving deal whereby you pay an appreciable amount less and take pot luck at the other end as to which resort and hotel you end up in. If all you're worried about is dossing on a beach somewhere, this could be the thing for you. Obviously as you're more likely to end up in a resort and hotel which no one else chose it has disadvantages, but occasionally you hear stories of people ending up in a 5-star hotel for a fraction of the cost that the other guests have had to pay because it was underbooked due to its being too expensive!

Picnicking is not really a good way to save money for as often as not you end up paying over the odds for your supplies of bread, cheese and fruit, and you find you could have had a set tourist menu for a similar if not lower cost.

Average prices for the type of things you're likely to need are as follows: room for two on half-board, moderate standard hotel – 7500 dr; meal with wine – 1000 dr; sports and drinks for a day – 800 dr; and disco or festival performance – 700 dr.

These are the top prices you should expect to pay in the big resorts. In smaller, rural areas you will live for a fraction of this cost. Wine and drinks can be very cheap indeed (75p a bottle), but if you sit on a waterfront taverna you can expect to pay three times that. It's the same the world over, and your commonsense will dictate which establishments are likely to be pricey.

Things to bring from home to make big savings are photographic films, toiletries, and a small jar of instant coffee – especially important if you do not like the strong Turkish coffee commonly served in Greece.

Moving around the country is likely to be your major expense if you insist on car hire. The average week's hire of a small car is in the region of £200. To compensate, buses, trains and ferries are all cheap, as are internal flights.

Students with an ISIC card qualify for up to 50 per cent off internal flights and ferries (that's why some islands seem to be extensions of university campuses), and reductions of up to 80 per cent are granted on museum entrances. For further information contact the Student Travel Service, 1 Fillellinon Street, Athens, or your local Student Travel Office.

Finally, when calculating the amount of spending money to take with you remember that it's easier to take too much (assuming it's in the safe form of a credit card or as eurocheques) than to have to have money sent on or transferred to your account. An extra £100 or so will not go amiss in the case of emergency.

Getting Yourself Organized

What to Take With You

Holidays in Greece are relaxing and simple affairs so only take the minimum of light, casual clothes with you, plus a showerproof rain jacket, just in case. Dress, even in 5-star hotels, is not formal (though you should take some evening clothes to dress for dinner if you really are going to a de luxe establishment), and do remember just how hot it is in Greece in mid summer. If you're going to a self-catering or informal taverna there really is no reason why you shouldn't be able to pack all your things into a piece of light hand luggage and travel without any of the hassles of baggage check-in and reclaim.

If you're travelling independently and camping or hostelling you'll obviously have to take slightly different things with you. For roughing it there is no substitute for a well-fitting backpack and a light tent (no need for a flysheet model in mid summer Greece, but *do* remember the mosquito repellent!).

For any independent traveller a plastic water bottle (jerry can idea) is an invaluable aid in the heat of the summer, as is a travelling alarm (see the 'Holiday Industry' section); a Swiss Army pen knife, and a money belt. A good First Aid kit is another 'must' (Boots sell a Trip Kit at £6.75 and a Holiday Kit for £3.55), and you'd be well advised to bring your camping gear from home as the Greeks don't go in much for the 'Great Outdoors', so their range of equipment is not too impressive.

The vast majority of holidaymakers, however, need not equip themselves for an overland expedition, and should take as little as possible. If you've a tiny space left in the corner of your suitcase a Greek phrase book (Berlitz do a good one) will win you many friends. The Greeks are one people who really appreciate foreigners having a go at their language, and even just a few phrases or words will endear you to them.

Below is a list of items definitely worth packing for a holiday in Greece, whether it be package or independent:

(1) Take all photographic equipment you're likely to need from home. The Greek equivalent is more expensive and not as good.

(2) Any English language books or magazines you're likely to want for beach reading. Some of the larger resorts do carry a stock of British and American books, but they're overpriced and generally of poor quality.

(3) If you're not keen on strong, sweet Turkish-style coffee, take a small jar of instant from home. If you're a coffee-junkie consider taking a mini kettle or immersion heater to make your own when you need a fix (see the 'Holiday Industry' section). This will save you a fortune as three or four coffees a day for a fortnight can mount up to about twenty-five pounds!

(4) If you're a smoker and have a preference for a particular British brand, buy your cigarettes in duty free. Greek cigarettes are much stronger (they resemble Turkish) and American or British cigarettes are more expensive. (Don't be fooled by the 20p a packet Marlboros you'll be offered by innocent-faced vendors, they're very good imitation cabbage-leaves!)

(5) Toiletries and medicines should be brought from home. This includes suntan preparations. The Greek equivalents are not as good and often more expensive. (Packs of tissues as emergency loo paper supplies come in handy in the more remote places.)

(6) If you're planning on visiting any of the beautiful Greek Orthodox churches or monasteries, ladies should take a scarf or shawl to cover their heads. It is still frowned upon in many cases to enter a place of worship with the female head uncovered, and in no circumstances should shorts be worn by either sex on such a visit.

Part Two
HOW TO GO

Package v. Independent

Holidaymakers to Greece are spoilt for choice when it comes to organized packages, yet there is also the very real option of going it alone and making up your own tour to Greece. This is one country where you can benefit from the high level of organized tourism and by taking advantage of the cheap charter flights on offer you can put together your own package for a low cost, ensuring you end up in the place you want, doing the things you want. It should be pointed out here, however, that only if you're after a very basic sun, sea and sand holiday can you hope to rival the prices of the major tour operators, who in this high volume market make only small profits on their holidays. If you're after something a bit more complicated (e.g. a two or three centre holiday, an activity holiday, or an up-market villa holiday) you are, nine times out of ten, better to buy a package where the arrangements are made for you, as once in Greece it is all too easy to get bogged down in bureaucracy and an unbelievable amount of red tape, and end up spending half your holiday filling in forms and waiting in queues. As you will see in the section on 'Tour Operators' not all the companies who run to Greece offer beer swilling, moussaka and chips type experiences, and it is perfectly possible to select a company who can provide you with exactly what you are looking for, at a good price, once you know where to look.

The main headaches for those travelling independently will be the comparatively poor communications within Greece; the ever-present risk of being 'ripped off', and the fact that in high season it really is essential to book ahead and writing/phoning Greece is not a terribly efficient or cost-effective way of getting your holiday organized. It *is* still possible, just so long as you're not planning anything too adventurous. The advantages are obvious: you really are your own boss; you can get well away from other Brits and have the experience of being a traveller in a foreign country, not a package tourist with everything done for you, and you stand a much better chance of seeing the real Greece – often a cliché, but in this case true!

The package holidaymaker has a choice of over 140 tour operators – the most impressive choice in the travel industry! These holidays range from two weeks in a busy resort such as Aghios Nikolaos, offered by over 60 operators, to something as obscure as a tour of the religious monuments of Greece, offered by one. The choice really is staggering and the following few pages should be given far greater attention than any biased selection of brochures from a travel agent (remember that many of the smaller – often better – tour operators never get their brochures in a travel agent as they cannot afford the 10 per cent commission the travel agent charges for selling his holidays. You must write off for the brochure. See the section following on 'Tour Operators' for details). This section aims to help you concentrate your thoughts on what you want from your holiday, and to put in front of you the options open to you.

Tour Operators List

(1) AEGINA CLUB
25a Hills Road, Cambridge CB2 1NW
Tel: (0223) 63256, Telex: 81684, ATOL

(2) AIRLINK HOLIDAYS LTD
9 Wilton Road, London SW1V 1LL
Tel: 01-828 7682, Telex: 8814454, ABTA - ATOL

(3) AIRTOURS PLC
Wavell House, Holcombe Road, Helmshore, Rossendale, Lancs BB4 4NB
Tel: (0706) 240033, Telex: 63126, ABTA - ATOL

(4) ALBANY TRAVEL (MANCHESTER) LTD
190 Deansgate, Manchester M3 3WD
Tel: 061-833 0202, Telex: 667174, ABTA - ATOL

(5) **ALECOS TOURS**
3a Camden Road, London NW1 9LG
Tel: 01-267 2092, Telex: 885110, ABTA - ATOL

(6) **ALL HOLIDAYS TRAVEL LTD**
293 Grays Inn Road, London WC1X 8QF
Tel: 01-837 3047, Telex: 914579, ABTA - ATOL

(7) **ALLEGRO HOLIDAYS**
15a Church Street, Reigate, Surrey RH2 8AP
Tel: (0737) 221323, Telex: 919114, ABTA - ATOL

(8) **ALLSUN HOLIDAYS**
Trafalgar House, 2 Chalkhill Road, London W6 8SB
Tel: 01-629 8870, Telex: 936055, ATOL

(9) **AMATHUS HOLIDAYS**
51 Tottenham Court Road, London W1P 0HS
Tel: 01-636 9873, Telex: 27900, ABTA - ATOL

(10) **ARISTA HOLIDAYS**
97a Beckenham Lane, Bromley, Kent BR2 0DN
Tel: 01-290 0542, Telex: 929599, ABTA - ATOL

(11) **ASPRO HOLIDAYS**
3 Bute Place, Cardiff CF1 6AL
Tel: (0222) 484151, Telex: 497168, ABTA - ATOL

(12) **BATH TRAVEL PALMAIR**
2 Albert Road, Bournemouth, Dorset BH1 1BY
Tel: (0202) 299299, Telex: 41168, ABTA - ATOL

(13) **BATTLEFIELD TOURS**
The Golden Key, 15 Market Street, Sandwich, Kent CT13 9DA
Tel: (0304) 612248

(14) BEACH VILLAS (HOLIDAYS) LTD
8 Market Passage, Cambridge CB2 3QR
Tel: (0223) 311113, Telex: 817428, ABTA - ATOL

(15) CHANDRIS HOLIDAYS LTD
5 St Helens Place, Bishopsgate, London EC3A 6BJ
Tel: 01-588 6991, Telex: 888024, ATOL

(16) CHART TRAVEL
9b Argyle Road, Southborough, Tunbridge Wells, Kent TN4 0SU
Tel: (0892) 22020

(17) CLUB MEDITERRANEE
106–108 Brompton Road, London SW3 1JJ
Tel: 01-225 1066, Telex: 299221, ABTA - ATOL

(18) CLUB 18-30 HOLIDAYS
Academic House, 24–28 Oval Road, London NW1 7DE
Tel: 01-267 7044, Telex: 295440, ABTA - ATOL

(19) CLUB CANTABRICA HOLIDAYS
146–148 London Road, St Albans, Herts AL1 1PQ
Tel: (0727) 66177, Telex: 8814162, ABTA - ATOL

(20) CORFU A LA CARTE
8 Deanwood House, Stockcross, Newbury, Berks RG16 8JP
Tel: (0635) 30621, Telex: 846811, ABTA - ATOL

(21) COSMOS AIR PLC
Tourama House, 17 Holmesdale Road, Bromley, Kent BR2 9LX
Tel: 01-464 3444, Telex: 896458, ABTA - ATOL

(22) COUNTRYWIDE HOLIDAY ASSOC.
Birch Heys, Cromwell Range, Manchester M14 6HU
Tel: 061-225 1000, Telex: 667047, ABTA - ATOL

(23) **COX & KINGS TRAVEL**
St James Court Hotel, Buckingham Gate, London SW1E 6AF
Tel: 01-931 9106, Telex: 23378, ABTA

(24) **CREATIVE HOLIDAYS & CRUISES**
8–10 Stamford Hill, London N16 6XS
Tel: 01-806 2123, Telex: 8955867

(25) **CRESTA HOLIDAYS**
Cresta House, 32 Victoria Street, Altrincham, Cheshire WA14 1ET
Tel: 061-927 7000, Telex: 667171, ABTA - ATOL

(26) **CV TRAVEL**
43 Cadogan Street, London SW3 2PR
Tel: 01-581 0851, Telex: 919773, ABTA - ATOL

(27) **EXODUS EXPEDITIONS**
All Saints Passage, 100 Wandsworth High Street, London SW18 4LE
Tel: 01-870 0151, Telex: 8951700, ATOL

(28) **EXPLORE WORLDWIDE**
7 High Street, Aldershot, Hants GU11 1BH
Tel: (0252) 319449, Telex: 858954

(29) **FALCON HOLIDAYS**
(Inc. Arrowsmith, Sunstart & Twenty's Holidays)
33 Notting Hill Gate, London W11 3JQ
Tel: 01-221 6298, Telex: 883256, ABTA - ATOL

(30) **FREEDOM HOLIDAYS**
224 King Street, London W6 0RA
Tel: 01-741 4471, Telex: 892928, ABTA - ATOL

(31) 3D GOLF PROMOTION LTD
62 Carcluie Crescent, Ayr KA7 4SZ
Tel: (0292) 42206, Telex: 776483, ABTA - ATOL

(32) GLOBAL AIR
26 Elmfield Road, Bromley, Kent BR1 1LR
Tel: 01-464 7515, Telex: 8953010, ABTA - ATOL

(33) GOLDEN SUN HOLIDAYS
15 Kentish Town Road, London NW1 8NH
Tel: 01-485 9555, Telex: 262563, ABTA - ATOL

(34) GRECIAN HOLIDAYS
31 Topsfield Parade, London N8 8PT
Tel: 01-444 3333, Telex: 25302, ABTA - ATOL

(35) GREEK CONNECTION
Bryslan House, Upper Street, Fleet, Hants GU13 9PE
Tel: (0252) 624660, Telex: 858039, ATOL

(36) GREEK ISLANDS CLUB
(Greek Islands Sailing Club)
66 High Street, Walton-on-Thames, Surrey KT12 1BU
Tel: (0932) 220477, Telex: 928561, ABTA - ATOL

(37) GREEK SUN HOLIDAYS
1 Bank Street, Sevenoaks, Kent TN13 1UW
Tel: (0732) 740317, Telex: 957138, ABTA - ATOL

(38) GREEK TOURIST AGENCY
Morley House, 320 Regent Street, London W1R 5AF
Tel: 01-580 3152, Telex: 267083, ATOL

(39) HAMILTON TRAVEL LTD
3 Heddon Street, London W1R 7LE
Tel: 01-734 9515, Telex: 299176, ABTA - ATOL

(40) HORIZON HOLIDAYS
Edgbaston Five Ways, Birmingham B15 1BB
Tel: 021-643 2727, Telex: 335641, ABTA - ATOL

(41) ILIOS ISLAND HOLIDAYS
18 Market Square, Horsham, W. Sussex RH12 1EU
Tel: (0403) 59788, Telex: 878168, ABTA - ATOL

(42) INFLIGHTS TRAVEL
145 White Hart Lane, Barnes, London SW13 0JP
Tel: 01-392 1111, Telex: 266765, ATOL

(43) INSIGHT INTERNATIONAL TOURS LTD
26 Cockspur Street, London SW1Y 5BY
Tel: 01-839 7060, Telex: 8814767, ABTA - ATOL

(44) INTASUN HOLIDAYS
Intasun House, Cromwell Avenue, Bromley, Kent BR2 9AQ
Tel: 01-290 0511, Telex: 896089, ABTA - ATOL

(45) INTER-CHURCH TRAVEL
The Saga Building, Middleburg Square, Folkestone, Kent CT20 1AZ
Tel: (0303) 47901, Telex: 966331, ABTA - ATOL

(46) INTER-ISLAND HOLIDAYS
152 Shirland Road, London W9 2BT
Tel: 01-286 9185, Telex: 261019, ABTA - ATOL

(47) JENNY MAY HOLIDAYS
2–10 St Johns Hill, London SW11 1TT
Tel: 01-228 0321, Telex: 915320, ATOL

(48) **KERKYRA (CORFU) TRAVEL**
16 Crwys Road, Cardiff CF2 4NJ
Tel: (0222) 493497, ATOL

(49) **KOSMAR VILLA HOLIDAYS**
87 Tottenham Court Road, London W1P 9HD
Tel: 01-323 2818, Telex: 267083, ABTA - ATOL

(50) **LANCASTER HOLIDAYS**
26 Elmfield Road, Bromley, Kent BR1 1LR
Tel: 01-697 8181, Telex: 8953010, ABTA - ATOL

(51) **LASKARINA HOLIDAYS**
St Mary's Gate, Wirksworth, Derbyshire DE4 4DQ
Tel: (062 982) 2203, Telex: 337197, ABTA - ATOL

(52) **LEISURE VILLAS LTD**
21 Palmerston Road, London SW19 1PG
Tel: 01-540 5720, Telex: 265451, ABTA - ATOL

(53) **LOGGOS TOURS LTD**
51 High Street, Newport, Gwent NP9 1GA
Tel: (0633) 842225, ABTA - ATOL

(54) **MANDEER HOLIDAYS LTD**
3 Replingham Road, London SW18 5LT
Tel: 01-871 4122, Telex: 9413430, ABTA - ATOL

(55) **MANOS (UK) LTD**
38–44 Gillingham Street, London SW1V 1HU
Tel: 01-630 0311, Telex: 297230, ABTA - ATOL

(56) **MARK WARNER**
20 Kensington Church Street, London W8 4EP
Tel: 01-938 1851, Telex: 24304, ABTA - ATOL

(57) MARTYN HOLIDAYS
Westleigh House, 390 London Road, Isleworth,
Middlesex TW7 5AD
Tel: 01-847 5955, Telex: 2469, ABTA - ATOL

(58) MEDINA HOLIDAYS
32 Cranbourn Street, London WC2H 7AD
Tel: 01-836 4995, Telex: 24931, ABTA - ATOL

(59) MEON TRAVEL LTD
Meon House, Petersfield, Hants GU32 3JN
Tel: (0730) 66561, Telex: 86181, ABTA - ATOL

(60) MERIDIAN TOURS LTD
12–16 Dering Street, London W1R 9AE
Tel: 01-493 2777, Telex: 22633, ABTA - ATOL

(61) NEXT ISLAND HOLIDAYS
113 Lower Richmond Road, London SW15 1EX
Tel: 01-780 2200, Telex: 927610, ABTA - ATOL

(62) OLYMPIC HOLIDAYS
30–32 Cross Street, London N1 2BG
Tel: 01-359 3500, Telex: 935628, ABTA - ATOL

(63) ORIENTOURS (LONDON) LTD
Kent House, 87 Regent Street, London W1R 8LS
Tel: 01-434 1551, Telex: 21337, ABTA - ATOL

(64) PAGE & MOY TRAVEL LTD
136–140 London Road, Leicester LE2 1EN
Tel: (0533) 542000, Telex: 34583, ABTA - ATOL

(65) **PEREGRINE HOLIDAYS LTD**
41 South Parade, Summertown, Oxford OX2 7JP
Tel: (0865) 511642, Telex: 837321

(66) **PETER PAN TRAVEL LTD**
18 James Street, London W1M 5HN
Tel: 01-491 2749, Telex: 264238, ATOL

(67) **PORTLAND HOLIDAYS**
218 Great Portland Street, London W1N 5HG
Tel: 01-388 5111, Telex: 299126, ATOL

(68) **RAMBLERS HOLIDAYS LTD**
Box 43, Welwyn Garden City, Herts AL8 6PQ
Tel: (0707) 331133, Telex: 24642, ABTA - ATOL

(69) **REDWING HOLIDAYS LTD**
(Inc. Enterprise, Flair, Martin Rooks, Sovereign & Sunmed Holidays)
Groundstar House, London Road, Crawley, Sussex RH10 2TB
Tel: (0293) 560777, Telex: 878791, ABTA - ATOL

(70) **SAGA HOLIDAYS PLC**
Middleburg Square, Folkestone, Kent CT20 1AZ
Tel: (0303) 47000, Telex: 966331, ABTA - ATOL

(71) **SELECT HOLIDAYS**
Centurion House, Hertford, Hertfordshire SG14 1BH
Tel: (0992) 554144, Telex: 817848, ABTA - ATOL

(72) **SERENISSIMA TRAVEL**
21 Dorset Square, London NW1 6QG
Tel: 01-730 9841, Telex: 28441, ABTA - ATOL

(73) SHERPA EXPEDITIONS
131a Heston Road, Hounslow, Middlesex TW3 0RD
Tel: 01-577 2717, Telex: 892512, ATOL

(74) SIMPLY CRETE LTD
480 Chiswick High Road, London W4 5TT
Tel: 01-994 4462, Telex: 8955503, ATOL

(75) SIMPLY SIMON HOLIDAYS
1–45 Nevern Square, London SW5 9PF
Tel: 01-373 1933

(76) SKIATHOS TRAVEL LTD
4 Holmesdale Road, Kew, Richmond, Surrey TW9 3JZ
Tel: 01-940 5157, Telex: 94015757, ATOL

(77) SMALL WORLD
2 Mount Sion, Tunbridge Wells, Kent TN1 1UE
Tel: (0892) 511733, Telex: 94070357

(78) SOL HOLIDAYS LTD
Churchfield House, 45–51 Woodhouse Road, London N12 9ET
Tel: 01-446 8500, Telex: 929692, ABTA - ATOL

(79) SOLAIR HOLIDAYS
101 Essex Road, London N1 2SJ
Tel: 01-354 3244, Telex: 927495, ATOL

(80) SOMETHING SPECIAL (TRAVEL) LTD
Bull Plain, Hertford, Hertfordshire SG14 1DT
Tel: (0992) 552231, Telex: 818168, ABTA - ATOL

(81) **SPORADES HOLIDAYS LTD**
The Coach House, Bull Lane, Winchcombe, Cheltenham,
Glos GL54 5HY
Tel: (0242) 603747, Telex: 43670

(82) **STALLARD HOLIDAYS**
29 Stoke Newington Road, London N16 8BL
Tel: 01-254 6444, Telex: 265010, ABTA

(83) **STARVILLAS LTD**
25 High Street, Chesterton, Cambs CB4 1ND
Tel: (0223) 311990, Telex: 817489, ATOL

(84) **SUNSCAPE HOLIDAYS LTD**
The Manor, Martin, Lincs LN4 3QS
Tel: (052) 67541, Telex: 21494, ABTA - ATOL

(85) **SUNSEEKER HOLIDAYS**
Revenue Chambers, St Peters Street, Huddersfield,
W. Yorks HD1 1DL
Tel: (0484) 511224, Telex: 51226, ABTA - ATOL

(86) **SUNVIL HOLIDAYS**
7–8 Upper Square, Old Isleworth, Middlesex TW7 7BJ
Tel: 01-568 4499, Telex: 8951529, ABTA - ATOL

(87) **SUNWHEEL TRAVEL LTD**
Radnor House, 93 Regent Street, London W1R 7TE
Tel: 01-434 4326, Telex: 261338, ATOL

(88) **SUPERTRAVEL LTD**
22 Hans Place, London SW1X 0EP
Tel: 01-589 5161, Telex: 263725, ABTA - ATOL

(89) SWAN HELLENIC ART TREASURE TOURS LTD
77 New Oxford Street, London WC1A 1PP
Tel: 01-831 1616, Telex: 885551, ABTA - ATOL

(90) THE BEST OF GREECE (TRAVEL) LTD
100 Week Street, Maidstone, Kent ME14 1RG
Tel: (0622) 692278, Telex: 965827, ABTA - ATOL

(91) TIMSWAY HOLIDAYS
Nightingales Corner, Little Chalfont, Bucks HP7 9QS
Tel: (02404) 5541, Telex: 837179, ABTA - ATOL

(92) THOMSON HOLIDAYS
(Inc. Skytours)
Greater London House, Hampstead Road, London NW1 7SD
Tel: 01-387 9321, Telex: 261123, ABTA - ATOL

(93) TJAEREBORG LTD
194 Campden Hill Road, London W8 7TH
Tel: 01-727 2680, Telex: 298910, ATOL

(94) THE TRAVEL CLUB OF UPMINSTER
Station Road, Upminster, Essex RM14 2TT
Tel: (04022) 25000, Telex: 897124, ABTA - ATOL

(95) TWELVE ISLANDS
Angel Way, Romford, Essex RM1 1AB
Tel: (0708) 752653, Telex: 8956938, ABTA - ATOL

(96) TOTAL HOLIDAYS LTD
10 Hill Street, Richmond, Surrey TW9 1TN
Tel: 01-948 6922, Telex: 94013570, ATOL

(97) **VELLA HOLIDAYS LTD**
43 Clayton Street, Newcastle upon Tyne NE1 5AG
Tel: 091-232 2652, Telex: 53642, ABTA - ATOL

(98) **VOYAGES JULES VERNE**
21 Dorset Square, London NW1 6QG
Tel: 01-724 6624, Telex: 27104, ABTA - ATOL

(99) **WAYMARK HOLIDAYS LTD**
295 Lillie Road, London SW6 7LL
Tel: 01-385 5015, ATOL

Irish Tour Operators

(Departures from Dublin Airport)

AER LINGUS HOLIDAYS LTD
Holiday House, 59 Dawson Street, Dublin 2, Eire
Tel: (0001) 795333, Telex: 93776

BUDGET TRAVEL
134–135 Lower Baggot Street, Dublin 2, Eire
Tel: (0001) 613122, Telex: 91084

JWT HOLIDAYS
8–11 Lower Baggot Street, Dublin 2, Eire
Tel: (0001) 789555, Telex: 93795

STUDENT & GROUP TRAVEL LTD
71 Dame Street, Dublin 2, Eire
Tel: (0001) 777834, Telex: 93527

Tour Destinations

(Note: Numbers in this section refer to tour operators listed above.)

ATHENS
2 4 6 8 9 10 13 15 23 25 28 34 37 39 42 43 45 61 63 68 69 70 75 79 81 82 86 90 92

APOLLO COAST
Anavyssos: 21 Faliro: 5 24 38 Glyfada: 5 18 21 24 33 34 38 44 50 60 61 62 66 79 87 92 Kalamaki: 5 38 Kavouri: 5 9 24 87 Lagonissi: 5 8 24 38 63 Sounion: 5 13 24 Varkiza: 5 10 24 34 Voula: 5 24 35 Vouliagmeni: 5 6 8 9 10 24 34 35 62 66 87 90

EAST COAST OF ATTICA
Ag Apostoli: 50 Marathon: 21 23 Nea Makri: 5 44 50 Porto Rafti: 35 Rafina: 1 5 44 Vraona: 44

SOUTH WEST COAST OF ATTICA
Ag Theodori: 35 Kinetta: 35 Loutraki: 9 24 35

CENTRAL GREECE
Ag Lavrentios: 68 Ag Theologos: 70 Amphissa: 68 Delphi: 1 8 13 23 24 28 38 63 65 68 86 98 Galaxidi: 75 Limni: 68 Kalambaka: 86 Kammena Vourla: 5 Karpenissi: 68 Larissa: 86 Meteora: 1 24 28 38 63 65 86 Mt Olympos: 100 Oropos: 35 50 Pelion: 35 37 65 68 Trizonia Island: 75 Volos: 5 35 65 68 86

WESTERN GREECE
Ioannina: 1 65 73 86 Metsovo: 86 98 Parga: 65 69 86 92 Pindos Mts: 27 73 Zagora: 68 73

NORTHERN GREECE
Kavala: 1 5 44 45 63 65 Thassos: 1 5 32 34 44 50 65 83 92 Thessaloniki: 1 5 6 8 9 24 45 63 65 86

HALKIDIKI
Afitos: 92 Ag Triada: 1 21 Gerakina: 21 40 55 67 Hanioti: 21 32 92 Kallithea: 9 21 32 40 44 67 92 93 Kriopigi: 40 44 93 Metamorfosis: 55 Neos Marmaras: 44 Ouranoupolis: 1 40 90 Pefkohori: 32 44 Polichrono: 93 Porto Carras: 9 40 67 Psakudia: 21 General: 6 8 24 34 42 62

PELOPONNESE
Ag Andreas: 79 Areopoli: 28 86 Corinth: 1 13 23 35 38 63 86 Eghion: 38 55 Galatas: 5 Gerolimni: 68 Gythion: 86 Itilion: 86 Kalamaki: 86 Kalamata: 5 73 79 86 Kitries: 79 Koroni: 1 Kosta: 79 Monemvassia: 1 28 Mycenae 28 Nafplion: 1 5 23 24 65 68 86 Olympia: 1 65 86 Patras: 86 Petalidi: 79 Porto Heli: 79 Pylos: 1 86 Rion: 24 Sparti: 1 23 24 28 65 68 86 Stoupa: 69 79 Tolon: 1 5 24 30 42 49 65 69 86 87 Valimitika: 55

KYTHIRA
5 36 84

EVIA
General: 35 Eretria: 44 Halkis: 5 17

NORTH EASTERN AEGEAN ISLANDS
Chios: 1 5 15 24 37 44 50 86 99 Lemnos: 1 9 24 37 62 66 84 86 88 90 Lesvos: 1 3 5 14 24 34 42 44 50 66 68 69 73 91 92 Samos: 1 5 10 24 34 37 38 42 44 50 66 68 92 99 Samothraki: 1

SPORADES ISLANDS
Alonissos: 5 30 34 51 55 76 77 81 86 91 Skiathos: 1 2 5 8 9 11 20 24 29 30 34 35 37 38 40 41 42 51 55 56 61 62 66 69 76 81 86 90 91 92 94 96 Skopelos: 1 5 24 28 30 34 37 40 41 51 55 76 77 81 86 91 92 Skyros: 1 5 24 38 81

DODECANESE ISLANDS
RHODES
Afandou: 11 32 44 50 62 85 87 Apollona: 95 Embona: 95 Faliraki: 9 11 18 32 38 40 44 50 55 62 66 67 69 78 87 92 Gennadi: 3 92 Haraki:

91 Ialyssos: 21 Ixia: 1 9 11 29 32 40 44 62 67 78 87 93 Kalithea: 87 92 Katavia: 95 Kolymbia: 11 Kremasti: 21 44 50 62 78 Lardos: 44 91 92 Lindos: 1 2 14 32 40 44 50 55 62 66 69 92 95 Pefkos: 2 14 44 50 55 62 69 91 95 Reni Koskinou: 44 Rhodes Town: 1 2 3 5 6 7 8 9 10 18 21 23 24 29 32 34 35 38 40 47 50 55 59 62 63 67 69 71 72 92 98 Tholos: 3 21 40 42 44 Trianta: 18 21 29 32 40 44 50 67 69 72 93 Zephyros: 21

OTHER DODECANESE ISLANDS
Astypalea: 1 35 47 51 95 Halki: 51 95 Kalymnos: 1 3 10 37 47 50 51 55 77 91 92 95 Karpathos: 1 5 37 47 51 59 91 95 Kassos: 1 37 Kastelorizo: 95 Kos: 1 2 3 5 8 9 10 17 24 29 32 34 38 40 42 44 47 50 55 58 59 62 66 69 71 72 78 87 91 92 95 Leros: 1 5 37 47 50 71 91 92 95 Lipsi: 1 95 Nissyros: 91 95 Patmos: 1 5 24 37 38 47 50 63 72 91 95 Pserimos: 91 95 Symi: 1 2 50 51 71 77 91 95 Telendos: 95 Tilos: 51 95

CYCLADES ISLANDS
Amorgos: 1 Andros: 1 5 24 29 30 33 34 38 49 55 86 87 91 92 Antiparos: 75 Ios: 1 5 24 28 30 34 38 61 62 68 75 79 86 Kea: 5 Milos: 1 5 30 37 75 86 101 Mykonos: 1 5 8 24 29 30 34 35 37 42 55 61 62 63 66 69 75 79 86 92 Naxos: 1 5 8 24 30 34 35 37 38 41 44 50 55 61 75 79 86 92 Paros: 1 5 8 24 28 29 30 34 35 37 38 42 44 47 50 55 61 62 75 79 86 92 Santorini: 1 5 8 24 28 30 34 35 38 42 47 61 62 63 66 68 69 75 86 90 Serifos: 1 5 30 37 84 Sifnos: 1 5 24 30 35 37 75 84 86 Syros: 1 5 28 38 50 79 Tinos: 1 5 24 38

CRETE
Ag Galini: 1 29 69 Ag Marina: 94 Ag Nikolaos: 1 2 3 5 8 9 11 14 18 24 29 32 34 38 40 42 44 47 49 50 55 57 60 61 62 66 67 68 69 87 88 89 90 92 93 Ag Pelaghia: 1 35 38 40 57 62 Almirida: 94 Almyros: 2 Ammoudara: 2 11 57 58 67 Amnisos: 21 Anoghia: 45 Axos: 45 Bali: 69 Chania: 1 5 8 9 16 22 24 28 34 35 38 42 45 47 57 59 62 66 68 69 73 74 83 84 86 92 93 94 Chryssi Akti: 57 Elounda: 1 2 3 5 8 9 11 24 32 34 38 40 44 49 50 55 57 61 62 66 69 78 87 90 93 Fodele: 45 Georgiopolis: 69 94 Gerani: 57 86 Gournia: 45 Gouves: 11 40 69 Heraklion: 1 5 8 9 13 21 23 24 28 34 38 41 45 47 66 84 86 89 Hersonissos: 5 8 9 10 11 21 24 32 34 35 38 40 41 43 44 50 55 57 58 60 62 66 69 74 78 84 87 92 93 Ierapetra: 5 8

24 38 40 86 87 Kalamaki: 57 Kalives: 69 86 94 Kalo Horio: 2 14 57 Kasteli: 86 Kokini Hani: 21 40 44 Kokinos Pyrgos: 89 Kolymvitirio: 21 Ligaria: 35 Linoperamata: 21 40 44 58 62 69 Loutro: 91 Makriyialos: 38 46 49 91 Maleme: 15 57 Malia: 11 18 21 32 38 44 50 57 62 69 92 Matala: 1 68 69 Paleohora: 16 86 91 Plaka: 3 Plakias: 1 49 62 69 86 Platanias: 86 Rethymnon: 1 5 6 8 9 10 24 28 34 38 40 45 47 56 57 62 67 68 86 89 92 93 Sissi: 3 57 91 Sitia: 1 38 46 86 Stalis: 3 11 32 44 50 62 67 93 Stalos: 57 86 Tavronitis: 94 Tersanas: 57

SARONIC ISLANDS
Aegina: 1 5 10 13 21 24 29 32 33 34 38 44 50 55 58 61 62 63 68 69 78 92 Angistri: 38 44 49 50 69 Hydra: 1 5 10 13 24 63 79 Poros: 1 2 5 10 13 21 24 28 32 33 34 38 44 49 50 55 58 60 61 62 63 66 69 78 79 87 92 Spetse: 1 2 5 13 18 24 29 32 34 37 38 44 50 51 55 60 61 62 66 69 78 79 92

CORFU
Acharavi: 3 14 34 50 55 92 Achilio: 21 Ag Georgios (North): 69 92 Ag Georgios (South): 11 18 29 34 44 50 58 69 Ag Gordis: 11 20 40 44 55 80 92 Ag Panteleimon: 52 Ag Stefanos (North East): 52 57 80 92 Ag Stefanos (North West): 14 35 41 66 80 86 92 Alepou: 48 Alykes: 3 40 48 86 Arillas: 86 91 92 Astrakeri: 29 Avliotes: 41 Barbati: 2 11 20 26 44 50 57 80 83 92 Benitses: 18 21 32 34 38 40 48 55 58 62 67 69 92 Corfu Town: 5 6 8 12 17 21 22 34 43 59 62 72 92 98 Dassia: 9 11 15 18 19 21 34 40 62 67 69 83 92 93 Doukades: 21 26 Ermones: 31 35 Glyfa: 50 57 Glyfada: 38 40 Gouvia: 3 11 12 18 29 40 61 62 67 83 92 Ipsos: 2 11 18 21 32 34 38 44 55 57 60 61 62 69 78 83 92 Kalami: 52 71 80 92 Kaminaki: 57 80 84 Kanoni: 9 21 44 92 Kassiopi: 11 14 18 26 29 32 34 44 55 69 92 Kavadades: 52 Kavos: 18 29 32 34 44 50 55 62 66 69 84 92 Kinopiastes: 26 Kokini: 52 Komeno: 9 11 67 83 92 Kontokali: 2 3 29 34 44 61 62 69 78 92 Liapades: 21 50 55 71 Linea: 50 Maltas: 86 Messonghi: 2 3 18 21 32 40 44 50 85 92 97 Moraitika: 2 3 9 11 21 29 32 34 44 48 58 78 85 97 Nissaki: 14 20 32 52 57 67 80 92 Paleokastritsa: 12 21 34 40 55 62 69 83 92 Perama: 21 34 44 50 67 92 93 Pirgi: 34 44 Platonas: 18 Potamos: 3 40 44 48 86 Roda: 29 32 34 50 55 92 Ropa Valley: 26 Sgombou: 86 Sidari: 34 35 38 55 57 62 67 69 86 92 Sinarades: 20 69 Tsavros: 11 Vigla: 52 Yaliskari: 40

OTHER IONIAN ISLANDS
Ithaca: 1 36 Kefalonia: 1 2 5 11 34 36 38 41 42 58 61 62 66 69 83 91 92
Lefkas: 5 29 30 41 42 69 83 91 92 Paxos: 14 20 26 34 36 38 47 52 53 59
62 69 Zakynthos: 1 2 5 10 11 29 32 34 35 36 38 40 41 42 44 50 55 58 62
66 67 69 78 83 91 92

Different types of holidays

Camping Holidays: 19 42 95
Fly-cruising Holidays: 1 6 9 10 15 18 21 24 34 36 38 43 50 61 62 63 70 72 77

Yacht Charterers/Brokers

CAMPER & NICHOLSONS
31 Berkely Street, London W1X 5FA
Tel: 01-491 2950, Telex: 918078

CAREFREE SAILING LTD
122 Pavilion Gardens, Laleham, Middlesex TW18 1HW
Tel: (0784) 62796

CREATIVE HOLIDAYS & CRUISES
8–10 Stamford Hill, London N16 6XS
Tel: 01-806 2123, Telex: 8955867

CRESTAR YACHT CHARTERS
Colette Court, 125–126 Sloane Street, London SW1X 9AU
Tel: 01-730 9962, Telex: 918951

HALSEY MARINE LTD
22 Boston Place, Dorset Square, London NW1 6HZ
Tel: 01-724 1303, Telex: 265131

LIZ FENNER-WORLDWIDE YACHTING HOLIDAYS
35 Fairfax Place, London NW6 4EJ
Tel: 01-328 1033, Telex: 262284

RIVIERA SAILING HOLIDAYS
45 Bath Road, Emsworth, Hants PO10 7ER
Tel: (0243) 374376

TEMPLECRAFT YACHT CHARTERS LTD
33 Grand Parade, Brighton BN2 2QA
Tel: (0273) 695094, Telex: 94013292

TENRAG YACHT CHARTERS
Bramling House, Bramling, Canterbury, Kent CT3 1NB
Tel: (0227) 721874, Telex: 965041

AIRSEALAND YACHTING HOLIDAYS
1 Station Approach, Kingston Road, Tolworth, Surrey KT5 9NX
Tel: 01-337 1383, Telex: 934999

Island-hopping Holidays: 1 10 24 28 29 30 35 38 42 50 51 54 61 71 75 79 81 86

Cruising Companies

CHANDRIS CRUISES LTD
5 St Helens Place, London EC3A 6BJ
Tel: 01-588 2598, Telex: 884111

COSTA LINE CRUISES LTD
Albany House, 324–326 Regent Street, London W1R 5AA
Tel: 01-436 9431, Telex: 296444

EPIROTIKI CRUISES (LONDON) LTD
Westmoreland House, 127–131 Regent Street, London W1R 7HA
Tel: 01-734 0805, Telex: 27751

EQUITY CRUISES LTD
(UK agents for Cycladic Cruises, Inter-Cruise and Sun Line Oceanic)
77–79 Great Eastern Street, London EC2A 3HU
Tel: 01-729 1929, Telex: 295576

SUN-TAL CRUISES LTD
2 Criterion Buildings, Portsmouth Road, Thames Ditton, Surrey KT7 0SS
Tel: 01-398 9861, Telex: 94014959

SWAN HELLENIC LTD
77 New Oxford Street, London WC1A 1PP
Tel: 01-831 1515, Telex: 885551

Fly-drive Holidays: 1 6 8 9 10 24 31 34 37 38 40 42 46 65 74 75 79 86 87 91

Fly-yachting Holidays: 10 24 36 42 47 52 74 75

For Flotilla Holidays you may contact:

FALCON SAILING
33 Notting Hill Gate, London W11 3JQ
Tel: 01-727 0232, Telex: 264242, ATOL

FLOTILLA SAILING HOLIDAYS LTD
2 St Johns Terrace, Harrow Road, London W10 4RB
Tel: 01-969 5423, Telex: 298915, ATOL

ISLAND SAILING AND YACHT CRUISING ASSOCIATION
The Port House, Port Solent, Portsmouth, Hants PO6 4TH
Tel: (0705) 219847, Telex: 86734 and 869110, ABTA - ATOL

ODYSSEUS YACHTING HOLIDAYS
33 Grand Parade, Brighton BN2 2QA
Tel: (0273) 695094, Telex: 94013292

Student Travel and Educational Trips

C.T.S. TRAVEL (UK) LTD
33 Windmill Street, London W1P 1HH
Tel: 01-637 5601, Telex: 261608, ATOL

SCHOOLPLAN TRAVEL LTD
Olivier House, 18 Marine Parade, Brighton BN2 1TL
Tel: (0273) 606688, Telex: 87374, ABTA - ATOL

SCHOOLS ABROAD
Grosvenor Hall, Bolnore Road, Haywards Heath,
West Sussex RH16 4BX
Tel: (0444) 441300, Telex: 877156

U.S.I.T. CHARTERS LTD
Terminal House, 52 Grosvenor Gardens, London SW1 0AG
Tel: 01-823 5151, Telex: 23472, ATOL

Greece by Coach

CONTIKI
Wells House, 15 Elmfield Road, Bromley, Kent BR1 1LS
Tel: 01-290 6777, Telex: 8952630

OLYMPIC BUS LTD
70 Brunswick Centre, London WC1 1AB
Tel: 01-837 9141, Telex: 298627

TOP DECK TRAVEL
131–133 Earls Court Road, London SW5 9RH
Tel: 01-244 8641, Telex: 8955339

Self-catering Holidays

ATTICA
Ag Apostoli: 50 Athens: 34 61 Glyfada: 34 44 50 60 61 88 Kavouri: 88 Nea Makri: 44 50 Rafina: 44 Varkiza: 34 Vouliagmeni: 34 88 Vraona: 44

CENTRAL GREECE
Oropos: 50 Pelion: 37

WESTERN GREECE
Parga: 65 69 86

NORTHERN GREECE
Halkidiki: 21 24 32 34 40 42 44 55 62 92 93 Kavala: 44 Thassos: 32 34 44 50 83 92

PELOPONNESE
Egion: 55 Kitries: 79 Stoupa: 69 Tolon: 24 30 38 42 49 65 69 86 88 Valimitika: 55

KYTHIRA
36

EVIA
44

NORTH EASTERN AEGEAN ISLANDS
Chios: 24 44 50 Lemnos: 1 24 37 62 86 Lesbos: 3 14 24 34 44 47 50 69 91 92 Samos: 1 24 29 34 37 44 50 92

SPORADES ISLANDS
Alonissos: 30 51 55 81 91 Skiathos: 11 20 24 29 30 37 40 41 42 51 55 61 62 66 69 76 81 86 91 92 94 96 Skopelos: 24 30 40 41 51 55 76 81 91 92 Skyros: 24 81

DODECANESE ISLANDS
Astypalea: 51 95 Halki: 51 95 Kalymnos: 3 10 50 51 55 91 92 95 Karpathos: 37 51 59 91 95 Kos: 3 10 24 29 32 34 40 42 44 50 55 58 59 62 69 71 78 88 91 92 95 Leros: 50 71 91 92 95 Patmos: 37 50 95 Pserimos: 91 Rhodes: 3 7 10 11 14 18 24 29 32 34 40 42 44 47 50 55 59 62 66 67 69 71 78 85 88 91 92 95 Symi: 47 50 51 71 91 95 Telendos: 95 Tilos: 51 95

CYCLADES ISLANDS
Andros: 29 30 34 38 49 55 86 88 91 92 Antiparos: 75 Ios: 30 34 61 62 Milos: 30 37 75 Mykonos: 24 29 30 34 42 55 61 62 69 75 79 92 Naxos: 30 34 44 50 55 61 79 92 Paros: 1 24 29 30 34 42 44 50 55 61 62 75 79 92 Santorini: 24 30 34 42 61 62 66 69 Serifos: 30 Sifnos: 30 Syros: 50

CRETE
3 10 11 14 16 18 21 24 29 32 34 35 38 40 41 42 44 46 49 50 55 57 58 59 60 61 62 65 66 67 69 74 78 83 86 88 91 92 93 94

SARONIC ISLANDS
Aegina: 10 21 24 29 32 34 38 44 50 55 61 62 69 78 92 Angistri: 38 44 49 50 69 Poros: 10 21 24 30 32 34 38 44 49 50 55 58 60 61 62 66 69 78 79 88 92 Spetse: 1 18 24 29 32 34 44 50 51 55 61 62 69 78 79 92

IONIAN ISLANDS
Corfu: 3 11 12 14 18 20 21 26 29 32 35 40 41 42 44 48 50 52 55 57 59 61 62 65 67 69 71 78 80 83 85 86 88 91 92 97 Ithaca: 35 Kefalonia: 11 34

36 41 61 62 69 83 91 92 Lefkas: 29 30 41 42 69 83 91 92 Paxos: 14 20 26 34 36 52 53 59 62 69 Zakynthos: 10 11 29 32 34 35 36 40 41 42 44 50 55 62 66 67 69 78 83 91 92

Special Interest Holidays

Most of the Tour Operators deal with special interest holiday requirements on application. Classical tours, for example, even if not featured, can be arranged by almost all tour operating companies.

Adventure: 28
Archaeological/historical: 1 9 10 13 24 38 65 72 89
Art History: 89
Battlefields: 13
Botany: 23 69 95 98
City Breaks: 3 25 39
Cultural: 23
Embroidery: 81
Flowers: 1 16 36 65 68 98
Golf: 31 35
Houseparty: 77
Natural History: 65
Ornithology: 65 69
Painting: 36 51 53 81 95 98
Photography: 10
Rambling: 28 68 69 81
Religion: 45 63
Robinson Crusoe: 95
Sailing: 36 56
Scuba-diving: 56
Steps of St Paul: 45 63
Tennis: 56
Water-skiing: 17 56 86
Walking: 22 27 36 69 73 101
Wind-surfing: 17 36 56 69 86 96

Working: 95
Yoga: 81
Young peoples: 18 29

Accommodation Only

2 5 6 9 10 11 14 16 17 22 23 24 25 26 31 32 35 36 37 38 42 46 47 48 50 52 53 55 56 58 61 63 65 69 72 73 74 75 76 77 78 79 80 81 82 85 86 89 90 95 96 97

Conference Arrangements

1 6 9 10 12 15 17 23 24 25 31 38 40 45 47 50 62 63 64 65 71 79 81 85 86 93 96

Arrangements for the disabled

3 10 11 12 14 15 18 21 24 26 31 32 34 36 38 40 41 45 48 52 56 58 62 63 69 71 78 79 82 83 85 92 95 97

Tailor-made Holidays

1 5 6 7 8 9 13 15 24 35 36 37 38 41 42 43 45 47 50 56 60 61 62 63 65 69 74 75 79 81 82 85 86 87 90 97

Taverna-Pension-Rooms Holidays

2 3 5 10 11 12 18 21 29 30 32 34 36 37 38 42 55 58 61 62 66 69 74 75 76 78 79 81 85 86 87 91 92 95 96 97

Two-/Multi-centre Holidays

1 2 6 9 13 15 18 20 24 26 30 34 36 37 38 41 44 47 49 50 51 52 55 59 61 62 63 65 68 69 70 71 74 75 79 80 81 86 90 91 92 95

Wanderer (Voucher) Holidays

10 29 79 87

IMPORTANT
Tourists who travel to and from Greece on board **Charter Flights** must have an Accommodation Voucher, issued by the tour operator or his agent, to cover accommodation.

Tour Operators, flights to Greece from the UK

TO AKTION/PREVEZA FROM:
Gatwick: 30 69 73 83 91 Manchester: 30 69 73

TO ATHENS FROM:
Birmingham: 18 29 32 34 42 44 50 54 66 69 81 92 Bristol: 54 58 East Midlands: 42 54 Gatwick: 2 5 6 9 10 13 15 18 21 25 28 29 30 32 33 34 37 38 42 44 47 49 50 51 54 55 58 60 61 62 65 66 68 69 70 73 75 77 78 79 81 86 87 88 91 92 Glasgow: 29 34 38 42 44 54 62 69 73 78 92 Heathrow: 1 6 8 9 10 13 15 17 18 23 24 25 33 36 37 38 42 43 44 54 62 63 65 66 75 79 81 82 86 88 90 98 99 Liverpool: 92 Luton: 18 32 42 44 47 49 50 54 66 79 92 Manchester: 2 4 5 6 9 18 21 25 29 30 32 33 34 38 42 44 47 49 50 55 58 60 62 66 69 78 79 81 87 92 Newcastle: 18 34 44 62 69 Stansted: 32 44 50

TO CORFU FROM:
Belfast: 11 18 32 34 44 50 69 Birmingham: 3 18 21 29 30 32 34 38 40 42 44 47 48 50 52 53 57 62 66 69 71 78 80 92 93 Bournemouth: 13 Bristol: 11 18 21 32 34 44 48 50 52 53 58 69 80 92 Cardiff: 10 18 32 44 48 50 52 92

East Midlands: 18 29 30 32 34 40 42 44 47 50 52 62 69 80 92
Edinburgh: 92 Gatwick: 2 5 6 9 10 14 15 17 18 19 20 21 22 26 27 29 30 31 32 34 35 36 38 40 41 42 44 47 48 50 52 53 55 57 58 59 60 61 62 65 66 67 69 71 78 80 83 85 86 87 91 92 93 Glasgow: 18 29 31 32 34 38 42 44 50 52 62 66 69 71 78 80 92 Heathrow: 5 6 8 10 24 38 48 65 66 80 98 Liverpool: 92 Luton: 14 18 21 29 30 32 34 40 42 44 47 48 50 52 55 66 67 69 80 83 92 Manchester: 2 3 9 14 18 19 20 21 22 29 30 31 32 34 35 36 40 42 44 47 50 52 53 55 57 58 60 62 66 67 69 71 78 80 83 85 87 92 93 Newcastle: 18 29 30 32 34 44 50 52 62 69 92 97 Stansted: 18 21 32 44 50 69 92

TO CRETE (HERAKLION) FROM:
Belfast: 11 32 34 44 50 61 Birmingham: 18 21 29 32 34 38 40 42 44 47 50 57 62 66 69 92 Bristol: 11 21 32 44 50 58 69 92 Cardiff: 11 18 92 East Midlands: 32 34 40 44 47 50 62 92 Gatwick: 1 2 5 6 9 10 13 14 15 18 21 22 29 30 32 34 35 38 40 41 42 44 46 47 49 50 55 56 57 58 59 60 61 62 65 66 67 69 73 74 78 83 86 87 88 90 91 92 93 94

Glasgow: 29 32 34 38 42 44 50 62 66 69 73 78 92 Liverpool: 92 Luton: 18 21 32 34 42 44 47 50 57 66 92 Manchester: 2 3 9 14 18 21 22 29 30 32 34 38 40 42 44 45 47 49 50 57 58 60 62 66 67 69 73 74 78 87 91 92 93 Newcastle: 18 29 32 34 44 50 62 69 92

TO CRETE (HANIA) FROM:
Gatwick: 57 69 Manchester: 57

TO KALAMATA FROM:
Gatwick: 69

TO KARPATHOS FROM:
Gatwick: 37 91 95

TO KAVALA FROM:
Gatwick: 32 44 50 83 Manchester: 32 44

TO KEFALONIA FROM:
Birmingham: 69 92 Bristol: 58 Cardiff: 11 Gatwick: 2 5 34 36 38 42 47 58 61 62 65 66 69 83 91 92 Liverpool: 92 Luton: 92 Manchester: 2 34 58 62 69 92

TO KOS FROM:
Birmingham: 18 32 34 42 44 50 71 92 Bristol: 58 East Midlands: 92 Gatwick: 1 2 5 9 10 17 18 29 32 34 37 38 40 42 44 47 50 51 55 58 59 62 69 71 77 78 87 91 92 95 Glasgow: 29 32 34 42 44 50 78 92 Liverpool: 92 Luton: 42 92 Manchester: 2 3 9 18 29 32 42 44 47 50 51 58 62 66 69 71 78 87 91 92 95 Newcastle: 18 92

TO LEMNOS FROM:
Gatwick: 9 37 86 90

TO LESVOS FROM:
Gatwick: 14 34 42 47 66 68 69 73 91 92 Manchester: 3 47 69

TO MYKONOS FROM:
Gatwick: 1 29 34 37 38 41 42 47 54 55 61 62 66 69 75 79 92 Luton: 92 Manchester: 29 34 55 79

TO RHODES FROM:
Belfast: 11 32 44 50 Birmingham: 18 21 29 32 34 40 42 44 47 50 62 69 71 92 93 Bristol: 11 21 32 40 44 50 69 92 Cardiff: 11 32 44 50 71 92 East Midlands: 32 34 40 42 44 47 50 92 Gatwick: 1 2 5 6 7 9 14 18 21 29 32 34 38 40 42 44 47 50 51 55 59 62 66 67 69 71 77 78 85 87 91 92 93 95 Glasgow: 18 29 32 34 38 42 44 47 50 62 69 71 92 Luton: 18 21 32 34 42 44 47 50 66 71 92 Manchester: 2 3 9 18 21 29 32 34 38 40 42 44 47 50 51 55 62 66 67 69 71 77 85 87 91 92 93 95 Newcastle: 18 32 34 44 47 50 62 69 71 92 Stansted: 18 32 44 50 69 71

TO SAMOS FROM:
Gatwick: 10 34

TO SANTORINI FROM:
Gatwick: 1 30 34 47 61 62 66 69 79 96 Manchester: 34 47 79

TO SKIATHOS FROM:
Cardiff: 11 Gatwick: 2 6 9 20 29 30 34 37 38 40 41 42 47 51 55 56 61 62 66 68 69 76 77 81 86 90 91 92 94 96 Luton: 66 81 Manchester: 2 29 30 34 38 40 42 47 51 55 62 69 77 81 91 92 96

TO THESSALONIKI FROM:
Birmingham: 40 92 Gatwick: 9 21 32 34 38 40 42 44 47 54 55 62 65 66 67 90 92 93 Heathrow: 1 8 9 24 54 62 63 65 66 90 98 Luton: 54 92 Manchester: 21 32 34 40 44 47 62 67 92 93 Newcastle: 34

TO ZAKYNTHOS (ZANTE) FROM:
Birmingham: 54 69 92 Bristol: 11 58 69 Cardiff: 11 54 East Midlands: 54 69 Gatwick: 2 5 10 29 32 34 35 36 38 40 41 42 44 47 50 54 55 58 62 66 67 69 83 91 92 Glasgow: 69 Luton: 66 92 Manchester: 2 29 32 34 44 47 50 54 55 58 62 69 83 91 92 Newcastle: 69

Who Specializes in What

GENERAL TOUR OPERATORS

With so many tour operators going to Greece, obviously not all of them specialize in certain areas of the market such as two-centre holidays, private accommodation and so on, and many are general operators, offering standard flight, transfer and hotel arrangements. Of the many on offer we have tested the vast majority and from our personal findings we highlight the following as having something exceptional to offer:

In the lower price bracket **Grecian** and **Tjaereborg** are well worth looking at. Their no frills approach keeps costs well down, but both are large enough companies to ensure a professional service is given and back-ups in terms of couriers and accommodation are available (an important point if you get to your destination only to find you are badly disappointed by the hotel and you find your courier less than helpful). In some small companies no alternative will be available.

While **Tjaereborg** only offer the main Greek islands, **Grecian** are specialists in the country, so offer many destinations on the mainland and on the islands.

In terms of good quality all-rounders **Thomson** and **Intasun** are worth checking out. The market share taken up by these companies is substantial, but it is clear why: they are all large companies of long standing, who cannot afford to let their standards drop as they have so many repeat customers, year after year. They are middle of the price range, with a wide family appeal (all offer good child discounts), and they give genuine value in terms of the standard of their accommodation, professionalism of rep, and flight efficiency.

SELF-CATERING

There is no real price advantage in package self-catering in Greece. One tends to pay just as much for a self-catering apartment as for a medium-grade hotel, once food has been bought, so it tends to be the people who very much want the freedom of their own place, or who have young noisy children who take up organized self-catering. Obviously if you're doing all your own arrangements and travelling independently self-catering can be a different story. You will find, however, that B & B in tavernas is still more commonly found, and cheaper, and that only in a few of the big resorts will you be able to hire out a self-contained apartment. Purpose-built, self-catering accommodation in Greece is of a relatively high standard internally (i.e. the kitchen facilities and general fittings) as they know what the northern European package market are expecting, but often the external appearance of the apartments is disappointing. Concrete boxes, brightened only by the continual sunshine and the odd plant, is the norm, and if you want a Greek villa you'll have to choose very carefully which tour operator to go with, and be prepared to pay well for it. The exception is in the Halkidiki where what there is in the way of self-catering accommodation is of a high standard, often with facilities such as a swimming pool, shop, taverna and gardens included in the complex. Increasingly the trend is for package self-catering to be in suites within hotels, as opposed to separate self-contained apartments. Bear this in mind if the main reason you're choosing to self-cater is to avoid crowds and be on your own. You will have no more privacy in one of these self-catering suites in a hotel than you would if you were staying as a boarding guest.

Many tour operators offer self-catering holidays: for a full list see the section on tour operators, specifically page 79. Among the best are **Grecian** for low-cost apartments. **Beach Villas** are also good value for the quality of villas on offer on the Greek islands. They sell direct to the public, so see the Tour Operator directory for their address.

If you're considering the Ionian islands, particularly Cephalonia or Zakinthos, get hold of the **Greek Islands Club** brochure. Their accommodation is of a very high standard and their prices only average. The 'Premier Class' packages they offer are aimed at the upper end of the market, offering little extras such as 'bucks fizz' on the flight, separate check-in desks etc. This is a small company, but with many original touches to their holidays. You won't find their brochure in many travel agents, but it's worth phoning for if you're looking for something that little bit more individual. Their Paxos villas account for much of their business and if you see the villas, you'll see why each year a third of their clients return.

COST-CONSCIOUSNESS

Because so many of the big tour operators run to Greece a holiday there can be a very low-cost operation. If you choose to go it alone you can benefit from the cheap charter flights offered by the tour operators, and though you will have to fly to one of the main resorts you can always head off to somewhere quieter from there. A cheap flight to Athens followed by a cruise from Piraeus to one of the smaller, less touristy islands can still set you back under £150 return. From a package viewpoint with over 100 tour operators in Britain running to Greece there is inevitably a lot of competition, and you're the one to benefit from this. If you're happy to take a popular destination and fairly basic accommodation, it is still perfectly possible to get a two-week package for under £250, which, considering the cost of flights alone, is a very good buy. Generally the bigger the tour operator the lower the cost can be. It's just a fact of life that the smaller operators generally cannot offer holidays in small quantities at small profits. Hence you find them specializing in certain types of holidays – sporting, up-market villas, cruising etc.

If you are really on a tight budget and want to get to Greece for as little as possible get hold of the following tour operators' brochures, and start your homework. (There is little point going to a travel agent, unless you have an exceptionally good one, as if you spell out that you're trying to do it as cheaply as possible, you'll generally be fobbed off with a 'there's nothing left at that price' line. Remember they're in it for the commission, and it's hardly worth their phone bill to chase round half a dozen tour operators for you.)

Grecian Holidays – one of the biggies who can offer low prices; **Intasun**; **Olympic**; **Lancaster**; **Simply Simon**; **Tjaereborg**; **Manos**; **Falcon Holidays** and **Club 18-30**. **Simply Simon** is a relatively new company offering well-priced tours to several popular islands and some little-known ones in package terms. A package with them is as close as you can get to not having the impression you're on a package. Their sensibly written brochure is worth seeking out if you're keen to avoid the one-of-a-herd feeling, and their prices are very competitive.

If you're willing to rough it there's always the option of going overland to Greece. See p.78 for the details of bus companies running to Greece, and apart from these there's the option of training it to Greece, though unless you're under 26 and can qualify for an Inter Rail or BIGE tickets, this is likely to work out more expensive than flying. If you've found a good charter flight, but don't like the thought of traipsing out to Greece only to discover that finding accommodation can be a nightmare, look at the details on p.82 of the companies who will deal in accommodation only. You will pay that bit extra for their tavernas, but you do gain peace of mind, and you'll still make a saving over a conventional package if your charter flight is cheap enough.

The budget option offered by many package companies is another alternative to cut costs. By taking pot luck at which resort and hotel you end up in, you can make savings of up to 30 per cent. If you're just wanting to rest in the sun, and you're not too fussed where you get it, this is an excellent way of trimming your costs. Many of the larger operators now run schemes like this.

Thomson's 'Simply Greece' packages are particularly good value. They offer basic accommodation on 15 islands, flying from ten airports, and for a holiday with no frills but lots of glimpses of authentic Greek life (especially if you choose the option to stay in village rooms), this is a good choice. These and their 'Freestyle' tours are particularly suited to young people.

Tjaereborg cut out the middle man by selling direct to the public. Their holidays tend to be well organised, no frills (major resorts only), but good value if you live close to the major airports and want to go to a leading resort.

CAMPING

Despite camping being the mainstay of many independent holidays, it is also possible to take a packaged camping holiday. Three tour operators run these types of tours – **Club Cantabrica, Inflights** and **Twelve Islands**. The main reason for a holiday under canvas is still the low cost involved, and if this is your main criterion for selecting a camping holiday, compare very carefully the costs of a budget (go-where-there's-space-left) type holiday (see 'Cost-consciousness' section) and a camping package. Often there is as little as £10 of difference involved. The more there are of you, the better value organized camping becomes. For a couple it's rarely worth your while. What you get laid on by the tour operator varies: it can be just the tent, sleeping bags, and basic equipment; it can be everything from loo paper to a torch. With so few operators in the organized camping game, it really is worth your while getting all the brochures and looking through them all before booking.

Independent camping is a different story, and if you're concerned with keeping costs to a minimum, this is a good option. If you're prepared to carry a light-weight tent, a couple of mattresses and sleeping bags, and a camping gas stove with you (which if you're flying doesn't amount to even one person's baggage allowance) you can live for pennies once in Greece. Organized campsites are far more abundant than they were a few years ago (part of the move to stop people sleeping free on the beaches, wrecking the environment, as was happening on most islands in the late '70s and early '80s), and facilities, although basic, are adequate. Many islands now have signs up forbidding freelance camping on the beaches, so unless you can find a very quiet spot, away from civilization (in which case you'll have to be prepared to have no fresh water for washing etc), your only choice is to use an official campsite. It is illegal to camp outside official sites, though in high season, when all tavernas and hotels are full the police do make allowances, providing you do not litter the area or harm the environment (try to use the toilets in local cafés where you buy your breakfast, not the beaches. Not surprisingly the locals take great exception to this unsavoury habit, practised by hordes of young northern Europeans each summer).

N.T.O.G. is the main authority running campsites in Greece. Write for a list of official campsites before going. N.T.O.G. sites generally have better facilities than privately run ones, which vary dramatically, and often they are located in sites of particular natural beauty. Expect to pay around 200 dr per person and 200 dr per tent. The Hellenic Touring Club also run sites; cheaper but with fewer facilities.

Islands particularly suited for freelance camping are CRETE, NAXOS, and on the mainland the HALKIDIKI and EVIA.

PRIVATE ACCOMMODATION

Going independently to Greece and staying as a paying guest in a private house makes for a cheap and interesting holiday. Not only do you get the authentic feeling of living with a Greek family and learning about the locals, but you leave all mass tourism behind, and save yourself a considerable sum into the bargain.

People with rooms to let generally make their presence felt in Greece, and rarely will you have to do the chasing to find rooms. They will meet you off the ferry boats, at the stations and in Tourist Information Office queues – don't be put off by their blatant approach; it's just the way things are done in Greece. Check that what they are charging is no more than a D-class hotel, and if in any doubt ask the local Tourist Police what the going rate should be. Around 600 dr per person is average. In Athens, where hordes of young students roam the likely places looking for people to fill their hostels/guest-houses, the practice of the really hard pressed is to sleep on a roof. It will cost next to nothing, and there is a shower and breakfast in the morning, but unless you're the type who can sleep on a log, forget it!

If you're not keen on taking risks, and the thought of travelling out to Greece without the knowledge that a bed is waiting at the other end does not appeal, consider the option of booking your accommodation from the U.K. Many tour operators offer accommodation only (see the list under the 'tour operators' section), and though you do pay for the booking, you are at least assured of accommodation in a taverna of a reasonable standard – and you have a come-back if there are problems. The operators vary from small specialists to large firms such as **Olympic**. Tailor-made holidays (see same section) are another option, whereby you can book the type of accommodation you want ahead of going, without losing the independent feel of your holiday. This represents good value in most cases, and allows you all the benefits of a package without any of the disadvantages.

TWO-CENTRE HOLIDAYS

These are becoming increasingly popular in the travel industry. The reason is simple – the variety worked into a holiday by going to two destinations makes for a particularly interesting time, and gives you the feeling of having had two holidays instead of one. More and more people are realizing that for the small extra cost involved it is well worth it, and consequently more are being put together each year. For those who get a bit bored with lying on a beach for 14 days, a two-centre is ideal as just as you're beginning to feel as though you know every stone of the resort you're in, you're off again to somewhere new. In the case where you combine a city or mountain resort with a beach-based resort the contrast is even more marked, and the change more pleasant.

With around forty tour operators to Greece offering two centres there is a good choice on offer. In the case of mainland Greece, Athens tends to be matched in with the nearby islands – Aegina, Poros etc, as it's impractical to tie in islands such as Crete and Rhodes with the capital because of the distance involved.

Neighbouring islands are also often paired up, but be sure that there is enough difference and variety between the two destinations to make the extra cost worthwhile. In many cases one beach resort looks much like another, so if it's variety you're after choose carefully.

COACH TOURS

There are two types of coach tours – those which originate in Britain and travel by coach to, among other places, Greece; and the tours which start once out in Greece, after a flight from the U.K. Generally the latter are more expensive, but far less tiring as a three- or four-day overland drive to Greece is not for the faint-hearted! (For details on bussing it to Greece as a way of saving money see the text on 'By Bus' in the Independent Section; page 110.)

Coach tour holidays tend to have an OAP image as the average age on coach holidays is usually over 50. But if you're keen to see a lot of the country a coach tour is as good a way as any of doing it. There is a short list of operators running coach tours from Britain in the tour operators' section.

If you're considering a tour following a flight, take a look at the following tours which are the pick of the bunch: **Thomson**'s Classical Greece Tour – flight to Athens followed by one-week tour of the major sights of Greece: well organized and about the best of its kind while **Olympic** do a four-night in Athens and three-day tour for those just wanting a taster and a longer stay in the capital.

HOLIDAY CLUBS

These are becoming more popular each season as tour operators recognize the demand for all-in holidays, aimed largely at families on a restricted budget. The basic idea of a holiday club is that all the facilities you are likely to need for your holiday – flights, accommodation, entertainment, sporting facilities, childminder services and so on, are all lumped in together in the packaged price, and once the initial payment is made the rest of your holiday is virtually free. Everyone in the club has the use of the facilities and for a value-for-money deal they are hard to beat. As most are in the confines of a large hotel complex it is possible that in all your time abroad you need not, if you don't want to, leave the confines of the club. If you're after a quiet time, away from the crowds, this is definitely not for you. If you have a couple of children who need constant entertainment, or are on your own and keen to meet people, this could be an ideal answer.

At one end of the club idea are the up-market operators such as **Club Med** and **Mark Warner**. Of the two Club Med offer more in the way of facilities and put more accent on style and entertainment. These clubs are *not* to be confused with the Club 18-30 type holidays which are aimed at the other end of the market. Club Med and the like have more the atmosphere of a large luxurious villa party – a concept which is in fact offered by the operator **Small World**. Club Med offer two international holiday villages (international implying that, unlike in their other clubs, French will not be the dominant language): both are on Corfu: IPSOS and HELIOS. Each offers over a dozen sports and the facilities in the villages are excellent. Ipsos is, if anything, more aimed at the young (accommodation is in straw huts, as opposed to the bungalows of Helios); and in Helios children over 8 years are welcomed, but no special facilities exist for them.

As in all Club Meds, the food and wine are limitless and excellent, and the complete holiday experience is rounded off at night by a live show performed by the hard-worked G.O.s who do everything from coaching the sports to organizing excursions and running the village for your enjoyment. At night they don the greasepaint and put on shows of international appeal to pass the time after dinner and before the nightclub gets going.

Club Med in Greece are particularly popular and good value when you take into account the cost of sports and good food in the resorts.

In the middle range are the Holiday Clubs and special deals for children such as those run by **Thomson**'s and many of the larger operators. Primarily these are aimed at families and the main advantages are those of supervised children's entertainment and good price reductions for children.

Club 18-30 is very much aimed at the young, 'out-for-a-laugh' set. Accommodation is basic and the only thing that is not skimped on is booze and entertainment.

At the other end of the age scale **Saga** offers holidays aimed at the retired market. While not real 'Club' holidays, they do go in for their clients sharing facilities and they offer all the advantages of specialized marketing to ensure the Club 18-30 set are not in the room next door.

CRUISING

Greece is a natural magnet for a cruising holiday. The blue seas, perfect sailing conditions, nautical experience of the Greeks, and guaranteed sunshine make it an ideal country to cruise around. Realizing this potential a dozen cruising companies have organized holidays through over two dozen different tour operators, meaning that many different types of cruises are available: lengthy, luxury affairs, specialist interest cruises, one-week moderately priced cruises, and cruises which take in Greece and other countries.

One of the best known and most prestigious companies in this line is **Swan Hellenic** (a division of P&O). Their cruises take in most of the major sights of the country, and on their staff are expert guides who will take you round the sights and leave you with a greater knowledge of the country from your 48-hour port of call stop, than most people gain in a two-week stay. The many cruises that Swan Hellenic offer to Greece are to be found in virtually any High Street for this company, perhaps more than any other in this field, have market penetration where it counts – in the travel agents. Their tours are not cheap, but then cruises rarely are. Really the best advice in the case of a cruising holiday is to go to a travel agent who is well used to dealing in cruises. Simply ask the person on the counter how much business they do in cruises, and if there is anything other than a very positive response, then find another agent. Cruising is a very specialized type of holiday. Not only does it cost twice as much as a conventional package, but there are many other considerations to take into account. Most of the brochures do not go into anything like enough detail on the accommodation and facilities side of things, and given that you spend so much of your time on the actual ship, this is the sort of information which your agent should have to hand. Another point to watch out for is how much time you actually want to spend on board, and how much ashore, sightseeing. At least half the fun of the holiday is the actual cruising, so if you're looking on the sailing side of things as merely a means to get you to your final destination, cruising is not for you.

For a full list of the companies who operate fly/cruise holidays to Greece see page 75.

Of the many companies available one worth noting is the small, but imaginative operators – **Small World**. This up-market company offer a cruising holiday on a small scale, in their own boat – **Small World II** – which takes in Greece and Turkey, and puts the emphasis on an informal time where like-minded people can enjoy the sort of luxury only afforded normally by those owning their own yachts. They also have the option of a one-week cruise combined with a week on land in a resort. Their Cyclades Cruise is a particularly exciting tour, as it takes in islands as remote as **AMORGOS**, **KOUFONISIA** and **PSERIMOS**. For a copy of their brochure write to them at the address shown on page 67.

Aegina Club, **Greek Islands Sailing Club**, **Amathus Holidays**, **Grecian**, **Thomson** and **Twelve Islands** are further companies which our researchers have singled out for special commendations.

SAILING HOLIDAYS

Flotilla has become one of the fastest growth areas in the travel world in the '80s. Desk-bound city types are realizing that this is an ideal opportunity to indulge in a healthy, outdoor holiday, without having to exert yourself too much, safe in the knowledge that you can learn as much as you want, and that someone with all the knowledge necessary is at the helm. Flotilla holidays are also great sociable occasions, and from a single person's point of view they offer a good opportunity to meet someone, without making it blatantly obvious that this is the sole purpose that you're there, à la Club 18-30.

Of the many operators in this market now, **Falcon**, **Island Sailing and Yacht Cruising Association** are among the best. They are all specialist companies who offer a good selection of flotilla holidays for all stages and most pockets. ISYCA offer a comprehensive range of sailing holidays: flotilla, 'villa flotilla' which combines a week in a villa with a week's sailing; bare boat sailing, and cruising in the Ionian and Sporades islands. In a market as specialized as this, though, it is best to collect all the relevant brochures and do your own homework as everyone's ideal flotilla holiday can be very different.

The list of Yacht Brokers in the directory of tour operators offers private yacht hire if you wish to put together your own itinerary and are prepared for the expense involved in doing it yourself. If there is a sufficiently large group of you, and you have the necessary crewing skills between you, this can actually work out as quite a realistic option, and if you find these companies too pricey there are always the ads in the Sunday newspapers.

The fly-yachting option is another to consider. See the list of operators in the directory.

SPECIAL INTEREST HOLIDAYS

As can be seen from the list on page 81 there are numerous operators in the market for special interest holidays to Greece. **Swan Hellenic** is one of the reputable names to look out for. They are well practised in the art of supplying a package that bit more specialized and cater to a minority interest market. The range of interests that can be pursued on holidays gets more diverse each year, but generally they can be grouped into five main areas: history/archaeology; fauna and flora; sport; general hobbies, such as painting and photography; and singles holidays. Other alternatives which allow a 'different' holiday to be arranged are to opt for a 'tailor-made holiday', designed specifically to suit your needs; to book 'accommodation only' and make your own travel arrangements; to take one of the 'Wanderer' type holidays which effectively give you the freedom to decide where you want to go once there, but take the hassle out of getting there and finding accommodation; or, for the disabled, to take a package designed specifically with them in mind. All the tour operator details for these sections are to be found in the section on 'Tour Operators'.

To take the five main categories of Special Interests though: the Historical/Archaeological tours are the most plentiful, hardly surprising given the rich historical legacy Greece can offer the visitor. On these tours the accent is on furthering your knowledge of Greek history, and what better way to bring it to life than to tour the country's ancient monuments and remains, and learn 'in situ' from an expert. If you're a serious antiquarian and you already possess a sound knowledge of your subject it is best to opt for a company which runs history tours and nothing else. These companies tend to have the most expert guides and take the educating side of the trip more seriously than general tour operators who run a history tour in their programme of 'normal' sea and sun packages. If all you're really looking for is to see the classical sights of Greece, you'd be better advised to opt for one of the many tours of 'Classical Greece' offered by the major tour operators (see the section on 'Coach Tours'). *All* the companies running History/Archaeology tours to Greece are reputable, reliable operators, but if you have any further specific area of interest within this general category you should collect in all the brochures to ensure you get the tour you want. You will also find that the prices vary dramatically, and it's not always the case that the bigger the company, the lower the prices, so check carefully.

The Fauna/Flora interest breaks down to hobbies such as ornithology, flower study, and botany. This is a small percentage of the Special Interest market in Greece, largely because the country does not have the strong, established bodies we do in Britain to promote and conserve the native natural resources of the land, but this does not mean that it is a barren land in ecological terms. There is much to wonder at in the expansive landmass of Greece, and the National Parks are Utopia for those of this interest. (See the section on 'The Nature Lover'; page 39.) **Cox & Kings** are established agents in this field, but with so few in the run, you'd be well advised to collect in all the brochures for comparison as the itineraries vary considerably. **Countrywide** offer a range of very well priced interesting activity holidays. Among their tours are two in Greece: one combines Kos and Rhodes at Easter; the other is a spring departure two-centre holiday on Crete and Santorini, taking in walks such as the Samaria Gorge. This offers five different locations on your stay on the islands, making it ideal for those who get bored lying on the same stretch of sand for 14 solid days. Get hold of a Countrywide brochure from the address in the tour operators' directory.

The 'general hobbies' category takes in what might be thought of as the slightly quirky, specific interests. Painting or Photography breaks in Santorini are not to be taken as seriously as, say, a Swan Hellenic tour of the sites of Minoan Crete, but they are good fun, and for beginners are a way of developing an interest and making new friends. If you want to pursue your interest very seriously, choose a small specialist company, and make rigorous enquiries into the standard of tuition etc.

Sports are the big growth sector of the Special Interest holidays market. Each summer thousands of desk-bound, city dwellers head off to sunny healthy climes and spend their time getting fit and indulging in an orgy of sport, exercise and sociable occasions. If you're tired of the promises of 'Sports Facilities' in your average package hotel turning out to be a couple of second-rate tennis courts which need booking days ahead, a crowded swimming pool, and a kid-infested mini-golf course, and you want some decent facilities with tuition on tap if needed, then a Sports Holiday is for you.

It needn't be all sweat and aching muscles, for sports as diverse as golfing, fishing, scuba diving, windsurfing, water skiing and sailing can be tackled in Greece. The annoying thing is that most really sporting people enjoy tackling a whole range of sports, not just flogging away at one for two weeks. This can be got round by taking one of the holidays listed under the general *Sports* heading on page 37, or by looking at the options **Club Med** and the like offer. In Greece Club Med have four Holiday Villages: GREGOLIMANO, AIGHION, and HELIOS and IPSOS on Corfu. The range of sporting facilities on offer at these resorts (and remember that they are all free) is most impressive. Between the four resorts all the following are on offer: all manner of water sports, tennis, mini-tennis, judo, basketball, rugby, football, gymnastics, aerobics, body-building, yoga, archery, volleyball, snorkelling, swimming, pétanque, table tennis and kayak racing. Club Med not only offer sports facilities, they also lay on other recreational pursuits such as batik, pottery, music seminars, bridge, backgammon, computer courses and things such as circus-schools for children. Basically, the Club Med philosophy is to lay on all the Special Interests, and let you drift from one to another as the mood takes you.

If you want to be more specific however, and concentrate on one activity, collect in the brochures of the relevant companies and start comparing facilities and costs. Under the heading of Water Sport holidays the operators work on the premise that if you've selected a holiday specifically aimed at water sport advancement, that is exactly what you will get. Given that water sports are generally available in all resorts now, if you choose a specific holiday on this you will find your interest being taken very seriously, which can mean a lot of hard work! Be warned if you're looking on it as a social activity. (For details of Sailing Holidays see the section on page 77.)

'Singles' holidays are offered by many large tour operators as part of their overall programme (e.g. special departure for singles on certain dates, with single room accommodation as standard), but if this isn't enough and you want to be surrounded solely by other single people, opt for one of the specialist singles holidays. **Saga** offer tours to several Greek isles as part of their programme for the elderly singles. At the other end of the timescale **Club 18-30** offers holidays where it's extremely unlikely you'll be in company with married couples or families. The special interest on these holidays needs no further expansion!

SUMMING UP

To sum up then on the package holiday scene to Greece: there is an impressive number of tour operators running to the country, giving the holiday-maker a wide choice and a good selection of different types of packages. In general they offer a good deal as they work on the premise that they make their money from the number of people they send out, so the profit from the individual is low. Increasingly specialist operators are entering the market, so it is no longer the case that you can only get a tour which involves beach-bumming and doing everything 'en masse'. The sort of villa and yachting holidays which only a few years ago were still very much the preserve of the wealthy, are now available as packages to the only 'moderately wealthy', and it is no longer accurate to think of every package being for the first time traveller and costing £300 per person per fortnight. Packages to Greece can range from £200 a fortnight to over £1000.

What Greece does best is the simple beach style holiday, and if this is all you're after it could still be worth your while working out the costs of doing it yourself. If you want to go to a quiet spot, it is still definitely best to make your own arrangements, but be aware of the potential hassles. **Grecian**, **Olympic**, **Thomson** and **Intasun** are the big names to look out for in terms of general packages. It is *always* worth comparing the brochures in the case of Greece.

Camping in Greece is really only for the hardy; sailing is wonderful; self-catering is O.K., but the lack of exciting food stores and the small price differential makes it hardly worth doing unless you have a particular reason to. The mainland, particularly the Halkidiki, looks set to be the next area of touristic development in Greece, so visit it now if you want to see the unspoiled version and are looking for a quiet time. Corfu, Rhodes and Crete are still the big three, but despite their submersion in mass tourism, they retain much of their charm and are deservedly popular holiday destinations. Skiathos, Kephalonia and Zante are changing every season as the influx of tourism takes over, so again, get in now if you want to sample their pleasures without the crowds.

In package terms Greece still represents good value for the British, but it is nothing like the cheap holiday paradise it was back in the early '70s.

If you don't need to cut corners, choose a good, reliable tour operator. An extra £50 or so spent with a company like Redwing or Thomson will make a disproportionate amount of difference to your holiday. This will show in everything from your airline to the size of your patio, and who you will have to share a swimming pool with!

The overall message is that there is a tremendous selection of packages to Greece, many of which completely escape the public's eye because they are offered by small companies who do not have their brochures in the High Street travel agents. It is very much in your interest to seek out as many brochures as you can get, and decide exactly what you want before booking anything. In a country which offers everything from perfecting the martial art of judo in Corfu to re-tracing the steps of St. Paul in Northern Greece; from the gay beaches of Mykonos to the ethereal solitude of Mount Athos, there just *has* to be a holiday to suit every taste!

Checklist

As a final reminder to anyone taking a package holiday anywhere, check the following points before booking:

1. Is your travel agent competent? Unfortunately many are not and all too often it's the large chains of High Street agents who give the worst advice and service. Try to avoid the obvious trainees when you go into the shop and have a list of questions prepared so you don't end up having to make several trips when one would do.

2. Is your travel agent a member of ABTA? If not, think seriously about finding one who is. There are plenty of them about, and it could make a big difference to you if things start to go wrong.

3. Having chosen your country of destination, do you really know all that is available on the market? Many of the small tour operators do not get their brochures into the High Street travel

agents, but that does not mean their holidays aren't reliable or worth checking out. Check against the Tour Operators' list and phone up for a brochure to any likely looking company. At least that way you'll know you've chosen the most suitable holiday for you.

4. If the travel agent can't book the holiday you finally selected, don't necessarily accept his/her substitute recommendations. Have your own second and third options sorted out beforehand, or if there really is no substitute, leave the whole idea and consider something completely different. Remember that travel agents are in the business of selling holidays for commissions – they often don't much care what they sell, but they do like to clinch a sale before you leave the shop.

5. As for the holiday itself . . . Check the following before paying your deposit:

(i) Does the holiday price include all airport or port taxes and security charges (for both the UK and abroad)?

(ii) Does it include meals on the journey?

(iii) Is it extra for a weekend flight or a daytime departure?

(iv) Is transfer between the point of arrival and your hotel included?

(v) Be clear you know on what basis you are booked in at the hotel: full/half-board/B&B

(vi) Are you clear about supplementary charges made for single rooms/balcony/sea view/bathroom etc?

(vii) Is the insurance sufficient for you? Does it cover pregnant women/disabled people/people going on sports holidays? Is the limit on personal baggage high enough to cover all you are taking? Does it include a clause on late departure for your return journey? What provisions does it make for cancellations? Finally, check you're clear about the procedure in the case of theft or loss – often these matters have to be reported within a specific time limit to the police and a police report procured.

6. And finally before handing your money over, ask:
   (i) What the position is on cancellations (from both parties' point of view).
   (ii) What happens if your holiday needs to be altered significantly – under the ABTA code you must be told and given the choice of accepting the new hotel/resort/flight, etc., or have the option of a full refund. (Alterations caused by bad weather or industrial disputes will only be covered by your insurance.)
   (iii) What's the score on over-booking? Is there a 'disturbance' compensation to be paid (there should be under the ABTA code); will the alternative accommodation be of an equally high standard (it must be under the ABTA code).

Once you have gone through all these points you should have a clear understanding of the contract you are signing, and your travel agent will undoubtedly be in such awe of your intimate knowledge of the travel industry that you will receive preferential treatment all the way!

If, despite all this good groundwork, you still have a case for complaint, ABTA's address is 55–57 Newman Street, London W1N 4AH. Write to them with full details of your complaint and enclose copies of all your correspondence with the travel agent or tour operator.

Independent Means

The Options

Travelling to Greece on an independent basis is perfectly possible, even for first-time travellers. There is a highly developed network of tourist-related services out there and plenty of choice in transport terms to get you there. Basically you can take advantage of the large package industry which exists from Britain to Greece and cash in on the cheap charter flights operated by the large tour operators. Once there you can either book yourself into hotels (though if you're going independent to save on the higher cost of a package you won't be able to afford the types of places packages use as they have bulk-buying power and receive large discounts), or explore the cheaper (and often better) alternative of taverna rooms, private accommodation, hostelling or camping. Really this is the only way that you can possibly make an independent trip more favourably priced than many packages, as such is the competition that in many cases you simply cannot better the deals offered by some tour operators.

The alternate ways of getting to Greece are discussed in the following pages, but here we will concentrate on the alternatives in accommodation for freelancing travellers:

Hotels are strictly categorized by the State: 'A'–'E' class, with 'L' at the top for 'Luxury', the only class which does not have to keep its prices within set limits. Local tax is added to the prices shown – by law they must be displayed on the back of hotel room doors – and you should watch out for the following tricks which some unscrupulous hoteliers will try to pull:

A 10 per cent extra charge can be made for a stay of less than three nights – they *can* legally do this, so be prepared; a 20 per cent extra charge is made for high season (July to September) – again, quite legal. Also they are likely to quote you prices for their best rooms which include breakfast, showers etc. If you're cutting costs always ask what the cheapest room they have costs, and if they've anything at all which costs less (they invariably have a little attic room tucked away somewhere at a quarter of the price, and if all you want to do is have a night's sleep this could well suit you). If you feel you are being taken for a ride, see the Tourist Police; generally just the mention of their name will resolve matters amicably. Showers and breakfasts are always extra in Greece.

Prices for 'C', 'D' and 'E' class hotels are as follows (if you want 'L', 'A' or 'B' class you'd be as well booking a package). In high season (July to September) expect:

	'C'	'D'	'E'
Single, no bath	800	700	550
Single, with bath	1000	800	700
Double, no bath	1300	1000	900
Double, with bath	1500	1200	1000

You can virtually double the 'D' prices to find out the 'A' prices.

Rooms to let (dhomatia) are perhaps the best bet in Greece. Again they are classified by the government into 'A', 'B' and 'C' categories. Often these are rooms in people's homes which are by far the best and offer a genuine insight into Greek life. Some are in purpose-built apartments, but even these tend to have more charm than hotel rooms. Pricewise they should be just about on a par with the 'D' class hotels: expect to pay around the 500 dr a single; 800 a double mark. As to how you find them – it's not something which can be booked from this end (unlike hotels), and generally they find you as much as you find them. People with rooms meet the ferries and approach you in the street if you look like you're looking for a place. If this doesn't happen ask the Tourist Information office or the Tourist Police, or even at a local taverna. In winter the rooms are no longer let in order to allow the hotels to make enough to keep going.

Hostels are for the hardy, whether they be youth hostels or the new breed of private Student Hostels (open to anyone, not just students) which abound in Greece, particularly in Athens. The latter have few rules, unlike traditional youth hostels, and are very cheap and very basic. They also tend to have complete no-hopers hanging about sleeping on the roofs and strumming guitars till the early hours, but if you're young and looking for company and a good time they are ideal meeting places!

The official Youth Hostels (for which you need to be a member of the IYHA) are actually excellent places for the hardy who want to live off a shoestring. For about 300 dr a night you get a clean bed and for around 100 dr a hearty breakfast and shower. Though stricter than Student Hostels they are nothing like as disciplined as their northern European counterparts, and rather than doors closing at 10 p.m., it tends to be midnight.

Camping is a cheap alternative if you're prepared to lug all the equipment from home. N.T.O.G. and the Hellenic Touring Club offer good sites for around 200 dr per person and 150 dr per tent. Freelance camping is very common on the islands, though it is illegal and you could be moved on. If you take to this completely free form of accommodation please tidy up behind you and do not soil or litter the site. It is getting to the stage where the authorities are likely to make the blanket ruling that all freelance camping will be immediately stamped out, which would spoilt it for everyone. In 1977 they went to the lengths of making it illegal, but in reality the police only move in when a large group gather or where the environment is under threat, so the rule here is to get as far away from other campers as you can and keep the place tidy.

Unfortunately the *Greek monasteries* had their hospitality abused to such an extent in the '70s that many of them no longer open their doors to travellers as they did in the past. You can still find a room in remote areas though, providing you dress respectfully and are not just looking on it as a cheap bed. To stay on Mount Athos you should apply in advance.

Finally, there is always the option of booking a villa or private apartment yourself through one of the Sunday papers. Check all the details carefully and insist on a recent photo of the place and a full inventory before making your final commitment.

If you have very definite ideas of what you want for your freelance holiday, but don't want the hassle, or don't know how to go about booking all the different components yourself, take a look at the operators who provide 'Tailor-made' holidays. (See the tour operators' directory section on page 58.) This is the expensive way of getting a holiday that bit different, but at least you have a come-back if things go wrong.

So much for the independent accommodation scene. Now let's turn our attention to the travelling to Greece alternatives.

By Air

A good travel agent is the key to finding a cheap air ticket to Greece. The Olympic and British Airways' scheduled flights are not the cheapest options, but they are reliable, convenient and on their full scheduled flights they offer luxuries such as stop-offs, which are impossible on charter flights. There are more scheduled flights going to Athens than other destinations, but there is a limited service to Thessaloniki and Corfu, and also flights to Crete, Salonika and Rhodes by Olympic. The Olympic Love-A-Fares are interesting for those travelling independently. This guarantees you a seat for a trip from 6 days to a month and they cover all the big holiday destinations. You must book at least 2 weeks in advance and by travelling mid-week you can make an average £20 saving. Overall Olympic are one of the better European airlines and it's always worth checking out their schemes if you're making an independent trip to Greece.

APEX and PEX fares offer an alternative for those cutting costs. Depending on the conditions which apply to your particular flight you can pay between £160 and £255 for a London–Athens return, which is sometimes cheaper than a charter flight and gives you a lot more security (schedules are delayed less frequently than charters).

With APEX you must buy your ticket at least 14 days in advance; PEX can be bought on the day of departure.

Charter flights are a convenient way of getting to Greece for a low price. They have become very popular in the last few years as more people have decided to try an independent holiday, and sales of charter flights in the last two years have trebled as a result. It is imperative therefore that you book early. Their popularity stems from several factors: they're cheap, not only do they cover more Greek destination airports, but they also fly out of more local airports in the U.K. The price difference can be as much as £100 of a saving on the APEX; over £300 on the schedule. Expect to pay around £175 return London–Athens, Crete, Rhodes, and slightly less to Corfu. To get a charter flight you must also take the basic accommodation offered with the ticket as part of the deal, even if you don't intend using it (in fact in most cases this is a bogus hotel and the accommodation does not even exist, or if it does it is so awful that no one would stay in it. Really this is a purely nominal thing which has to be seen to be done to get round the law on sale of Inclusive Air Holidays to Europe, which allows the company to claim they are actually selling you a package consisting of travel and accommodation.). The sort of companies who offer these cheap flights through travel agents are **Thomson**, **Intasun** and **Horizon**. This is a safer and altogether better way of flying to Greece on the cheap than going through a bucket shop. They cannot beat these prices anyway, and you have nothing like the same amount of come-back should things go wrong. **Tjaereborg** and **USIT** are two other firms worth checking out. USIT offer exceptionally low fares for students and people up to 26 years, from London-Athens with additional on internal flights from the capital to the major resort islands. Contact London Student Travel, 52 Grosvenor Gardens, London W1 (Tel: 01-734 5997).

British airports from which tour operators fly to Greece are: Aberdeen, Belfast, Birmingham, Bristol, Cardiff, East Midlands, Edinburgh, Exeter, Gatwick, Glasgow, Heathrow, Leeds, Liverpool, Luton, Manchester, Newcastle and Stansted. Gatwick, being the big charter flight airport, offers the most destinations (Heathrow generally only handles scheduled flights), and Manchester, Birmingham and Luton offer the next most destinations. Glasgow is under a lot of strain to cope with the 5 million Scots it serves, consequently you must book early for a Glasgow departure. Flying to Greece is really the only comfortable way of getting to the country, a fact to be borne in mind when considering the other options. It is just that bit too far to make training, bussing or driving a pleasure, and if tanning time is of the essence your only realistic option is to fly.

By Rail

As author of the guide book *Europe by Train* and as one who has spent many months travelling on the Greek rail network, I feel inclined to say that unless you have a masochistic streak in you, or are intent on saving every penny possible, don't consider travelling to Greece by train. There is no through service from Britain to Greece, and you have to get well into Germany before you can connect with a direct train to Greece. The upshot is that it will take you at least two-and-a-half days (longer if you're coming from up north) to get to Greece, and at the end of it you're likely to feel like a wet rag. In peak season the trains are crowded and to stand a chance of a couchette or sleeper you have to book months ahead. Even in first class the going can get rough, though undoubtedly there is a marked improvement in travelling in first as you can avoid the hordes of students and families which pack out second class in the summer months.

On the plus side, there is the advantage of taking your time to get to Greece. If you're not rushed you can make stop-offs and vary your route to make your trip to Greece a tour of Europe's greatest sights. Consider travelling via Germany, Austria and Yugoslavia one way, and returning by sailing to Italy and coming up through Italy and France. Generally the only people who have time to do this sort of Grand Tour are students, and they, or anyone under 26 years, should look into the possibilities of buying an Inter Rail card (go-as-you-please pass for unlimited travel on the railways of twenty-one countries, selling for around the £115 mark) or a B.I.J. rail discount ticket, available from Transalpino or Eurotrain. (If you are doing this type of holiday take a look at the guide *Europe by Train* which you should find helps you along the way!)

If, however, you just want to get to Greece as quickly as you can Munich, Dortmund or Venice are the best places to head for to catch a direct train to Athens. The Venice run is the fastest and most expensive. It is packed out with young 'eurorailers' in summer, so do reserve a seat/couchette ahead. From Dortmund to Athens is a 52 hour trip; Munich is approx 48 hours, and Venice 38 hours. From London to Dortmund is around 11 hrs; to Munich is approx 18 hours, and to Venice, 18 hours. The three International Express trains you will be told of if you ask in Britain about training it to Greece are the 'Hellas Express', the 'Acropolis Express', and the 'Venezia Express'. Don't be confused (many are) that these are super-fast different trains from those described above: they're not. The Hellas is Dortmund – Düsseldorf – Cologne – Stuttgart – Munich – Salzburg – Ljubljana – Zagreb – Beograd – Nis – Thessaloniki – Athens; the Acropolis Express is the same as above, but it originates in Munich; and the Venezia Express is Venice – Trieste – Ljubljana – Zagreb – Beograd – Nis – Thessaloniki – Athens. The ferry from Brindisi to Patras is worth every penny of the fare, not only for a chance of sailing to Greece (an experience in itself), but to save you the tortuous slow journey down through Yugoslavia and northern Greece. Bear in mind that delays are common (3-4 hours is thought of as a minor delay!); if you've only got two weeks it's fair to say that you can forget training it to Greece.

The London–Athens via Beograd fare is approx £260 2nd class; £375 1st.

By Bus

Only the truly masochistic will contemplate coaching or taking a bus to Greece. After all the scare publicity of drivers having not slept for two days and nights, and the vehicles being unfit to be on the road, it's surprising that people still consider this form of torture. However, having said that, a lot of what was put out a couple of summers ago on the subject was alarmist and exaggerated. It is still possible to find a safe, reliable coach trip to Greece from the U.K., and if you're desperately short of cash it is an alternative (or if you no longer qualify for the under 26 years cheap rail fares, and all the cheap flights are full).

The following London–Athens direct services are worth checking out: **Supabus** have two routes, either via Belgium, Germany, Austria and Yugoslavia, or by France, Italy (sail to Patras) and onto Athens. The latter is by far the most civilized. It takes about three and a half days and costs approx £125 return; the former a couple of hours more and costs around £150 return.

Magic Bus at 67 New Bond Street, London, are reasonably reliable and competitively priced, and **Miracle Bus** and **Magic Tours Budget Bus** also offer coach links between Europe's major cities. Budget Bus are at 53 Stamford Hill, London N16. Fares are around the £100 mark return, but it's a long slog!

It is not a good move to go with a Greek-owned coach company. They do not have the stringent laws on resting drivers and vehicle roadworthiness that British companies do, and they tend to get you to Greece with the very minimum of stops, even for nature's little emergencies!

The companies listed in the tour operators' directory under the heading Coach Tours are dealing with a different market. They offer the coach journey as part of an inclusive holiday. For those wanting a cheap way of getting to Athens this is no good, but if it's for the appeal of overland travel that you're considering a coach trip, get hold of these brochures, particularly **Top Deck Travel**. For the hardy they offer well organized, low-priced tours.

By Car/Camper

However you look on it, it's a long hard drive to Greece from the U.K.

and unless you have plenty of time and are looking on your holidays as a tour of the continent, driving to Greece is not a realistic option. If you do wish to drive the best routes are either: London – Ostend – Munich – Salzburg – Vienna – Budapest – Belgrade – Athens; or London – Paris – Basel – Innsbruck – Ljubljana – Belgrade – Athens. For a wonderful 'Grand Tour' go one way and return the other, with at least a month to complete your journey. If you're holidaying on the islands in Greece think carefully about leaving your car in Piraeus where car theft is not unheard of, but equally well check out car ferry prices before committing yourself. There are very few occasions when taking your own car to the islands is a sensible proposition.

The closest border crossing in to Greece is at Evzoni in Yugoslavia, and all Greek border stations are manned 24 hours. Ferrying your car across to one of Greece's major ports is another option to get your car over to Greece, and this way avoids all the tiring days of driving. Any good travel agent will be able to book this for you, choosing the port closest to your destination. Driving to Italy to the ferry ports of Bari, Ancona or Brindisi will get you to Corfu, Igoumentisa or Patras – a far less strenuous proposition than driving all the way through central Europe.

To enter Greece your car must be entered on your passport, or you must have a 'Carnet de passage en douanes', issued by the automobile or touring club of your country of origin. You also have to be able to prove third party insurance, and a Green Card, though not essential, is advised (the International Motor Insurance Certificate). Your vehicle registration documents are also useful in case of accident, but an International Drivers Licence is not essential – your British one will suffice.

As elsewhere in mainland Europe one drives on the right and overtakes on the left. Front seat-belts are compulsory, children must sit in the back, and drink-driving offences are harshly dealt with. The Greek roads are not comparable with roads in the U.K. There are few motorways and potholes on quite major roads are still commonplace. Road signs are International. A spare petrol can is a wise move as in rural areas service stations are few and far between, and when buying petrol (of a comparable price with at home), opt for 'Super' not 'Regular'.

Should you have a breakdown dial 104 if you are within 60 km of the major cities of Athens, Thessaloniki, Patras, Lamia and Larissa. Help will be on its way soon after. If you're outside these areas carry essential spares and your car's handbook (particularly if you own a car not likely to be common in Greece). The Tourist Police (Tel: 171) will get you organized with a mechanic, or you can always get help from the Automobile and Touring Club of Greece. They speak English and help foreign drivers free of charge (Tel: 104). In case of an accident pull into the roadside, put on your hazard warning lights and position a warning triangle 50 m from the car.

If you have an accident (which, given Greece has the second highest accident rate in Europe after Portugal, is not outside the bounds of possibility), note that it is an offence to drive away. You can end up in a Police Station for up to 24 hours trying to sort out the paperwork – ensure you have a lawyer who speaks English there if it is serious. Your Consul will help out.

The speed limit in town is 50 km (31 mph) and elsewhere it is 110 km (68 mph). So dense and chaotic is the traffic that it's unlikely you'd be able to exceed it.

Everyone has their own preferences when it comes to a driving holiday, but speaking as someone who has driven to the Continent in everything from a Daimler limousine to a battered old Mini, I feel it's worth putting in a word here about what to look for when choosing a car to drive abroad in. Obviously luggage capacity is an important consideration. Fuel economy, spare parts and comfort are the other major considerations. Don't try to squeeze too many people into a car, and remember, you'll return with more than you set out with. When we were researching this section of the guide we used our Honda Legend, which over any other car we'd tried gave us the best in terms of comfort, room and efficiency. It's worth bearing in mind if you intend doing a lot of holiday motoring, or if you're in a position to hire one out. A car with a bit extra power is well worth having on long journeys – and safer.

Hitch-hiking

Although hitching in Greece is a relaxed friendly affair, as in any country these days single women should not hitch-hike alone. Lifts are offered fairly regularly, but the only drawback is they tend to be short and the driving erratic. It can take an age to get from A to B, so only hitch if you have all summer to travel, or if you are getting from one major town to another (in which case get a piece of card and ask an English-speaking Greek to write on your destination and the word 'please' in Greek: this works wonders as the locals haven't yet thought of this system!).

Couples find hitching easiest, and truck drivers are likely to be your main takers: private cars tend to be full to bursting.

By Sea

Obviously the only direct way to get to Greece by sea is to take a cruise (see Cruising section on page 76), or to charter your own yacht. The alternative most people end up with however is to take a ferry from Italy. The Brindisi (on the south-eastern coast of Italy) to Corfu, Igoumenitsa or Patras sailings are the most commonly used. Count on about £20 per person for deck class for the Patras sailing which lasts 20 hours (Corfu is 10 hours; Igoumenitsa is 11-17 depending on company and route).

From mid-July to mid-August it is busy, more expensive and full of backpackers, so avoid these crossings if possible.

Book ahead if you must travel then, and whenever you travel be sure to check in at least three hours before sailing. You need this time to take the embarkation pass you will have received from the line you are travelling with, to the police on the second floor of the maritime station. Passports are presented on board the ship.

There are many ferry companies, but the most reliable tend to be **Adriatic-Hellenic Mediterranean Lines** and **Epirotiki Lines**. BARI is another option from where you can sail to Greece. Two hours up the coast, ferries are less hectic and often cheaper from here, but services less frequent. ANCONA has connections with Igoumenitsa and Patras, but fares are expensive (Ancona is north of Rome, making it a long journey). If money is no object take the plush car ferry from VENICE. Two days aboard this Adriatic Lines ferry, however, will cost you around £100.

LIMASSOL (Cyprus), ALEXANDRIA (Egypt), HAIFA (Israel), numerous **YUGOSLAVIAN** ports, **ODESSA** (USSR), **BULGARIA**, and **ISTANBUL** (Turkey) also have ferries to Greece, though none make logical sense if you're travelling from the UK.

Ferries to the islands leave Piraeus (Athens' port). Details can be found under the relevant islands later in the guide.

Generally Useful Information

TIME DIFFERENCES

Greece is on the same time as Eastern Europe which is 1 hour ahead of EEC countries and 2 hours ahead of G.M.T.

ELECTRICITY

The voltage in Greece is 220V AC, but on some of the more remote islands you can still find 110V DC. Take an International Adaptor with you from home.

WATER

In Athens do not drink the water unless you have the constitution of an ox; even elsewhere it is best to buy bottled mineral water, or boil the tap water for at least 10 minutes. The Authorities will tell you the water is fine to drink. It is, but you won't be anything like acclimatized to it until your holiday is over.

Part Three
WHEN YOU'RE THERE

Tourist Information

There are tourist offices (called E.O.T. in Greece; N.T.O.G. elsewhere), in all the major towns and resorts of Greece. The tourist literature they have in Greece is adequate but it is often not as good as that which can be sent to you from the London office of N.T.O.G. at 195–197 Regent Street, London W1R 8DL. If you have a specific interest (e.g. golfing, mountaineering, archaeological digs etc) let them know and they will send you out specialized leaflets. Their standards of efficiency and the quality of their promotional material is as high if not higher than most other tourist authorities, and they are particularly good for producing sumptuously illustrated brochures using very high-quality photography.

English is spoken by just about everyone working for the Tourist Board in Greece, and the only problems you're likely to encounter with them are long queues. Maps are not really their forte, so if you're doing a lot of touring it would be advisable to buy a good one in Britain before you go.

In smaller places where an E.O.T. office is not to be found contact the Tourist Police for help. This force has the same power as the ordinary police but are specially trained to help visitors to their country. They generally speak some English and can sort out accommodation problems (in the form of advice, not actually booking it for you) and can give general advice on local facilities. They are recognizable by their shoulder flash 'Tourist Police' on their uniforms.

E.O.T.'s head office is 2 Amerikis Street, Athens (Tel: 01 3223 111/9). This office does not generally deal with the public; it is more of the Admin Head Office. They have an information desk at the East Main Airport at Eliniko, and an office at 1 Karageorgi Servias Street, Athens. (This is actually in the building of the National Bank of Greece.)

These are the offices which will find you accommodation (as will most E.O.T. offices all over Greece). Opening hours of 8 a.m. to 8 p.m. are common in peak season in the larger resorts and Athens.

The E.O.T. office in Corfu is the Governor's House (Tel: 0661 30520/30360/39730).

On Rhodes it is 5 Archbishop Makarios and Papagou Streets (Tel: 0241 23655/23255).

On Crete it is in Chania, 6 Akti Tombazi (Tel: 0821 26426), and in Heraklion it is 1 Xanthoudidou Street (Tel: 081 222 487/8).

Details of all Tourist Offices are given under the relevant chapters.

In Athens the Tourist Police Headquarters are 7 Singrou Street (Tel: 9239 224). Open 8 a.m. to 9 p.m. There is also an office at the train station and at the airport. Dial 171 to reach the Tourist Police.

Sightseeing

Greece is a haven for sightseers and those historically minded. Details of the best places to sightsee are given under 'The Sightseer' on page 32. Here we discuss the practicalities of sightseeing in Greece. The sights are there in the thousands, concentrated in the Peloponnese, Athens, Crete and Rhodes. Being located thus, it is possible to hire a car and make your own tour of the 'big sights' of the country, and that's exactly what many of the coach touring companies do, packaging 'Classical Greece' into seven or ten days.

Museums, galleries and ancient archaeological sites generally charge a small admission fee. Standard opening hours are:

Spring (April 1st to May 15th): 9 a.m. to 1.30 p.m.; 4 to 6 p.m. weekdays. 10 a.m. to 4.30 p.m. Sundays and holidays.

Summer (May 16th to Aug 31st): 8.30 a.m. to 12.30 p.m.; 4 to 6 p.m. weekdays. 9 a.m. to 3 p.m. Sundays and holidays.

Autumn (Sep 1st to Oct 15th): 9 a.m. to 1 p.m.; 3 to 5 p.m. weekdays. 10 a.m. to 4 p.m. Sundays and holidays.

Winter (Oct 16th to Mar 31st): 9 a.m. to 3.30 p.m. weekdays. 10 a.m. to 4.30 p.m. Sundays and holidays.

Regional variations may occur and on the following days you can expect sites to be closed: Jan 1st, Mar 25th, Good Friday till 12.00, Easter Sunday, Christmas Day and *every Tuesday*, which is their day off. On Sundays admission is free.

One entertaining form of sightseeing is to attend some of the summer festivals held throughout Greece (see 'The Socialite' on page 34 for details).

Shopping

Standard shopping hours are Mon, Wed, Sat 8 a.m. to 2.30 p.m.; Tues, Thurs, Fri 8 a.m. to 1.30 p.m., and 4 to 8 p.m. These however vary widely and in tourist resorts it's quite normal to find 8 a.m. to 9 or 10 p.m. openings, with a 2 to 4 or 5 p.m. siesta.

Good buys in the souvenir stakes are handicrafts such as handwoven rugs, ceramics, earthenware and 'Komboli' – worry beads. One of the best places to get these sort of items is in the area surrounding Monastiraki Square and off Pandrosou Street in Athens.

If you're really stuck for something original and typically Greek, then there's always the ubiquitous Greek vases and coasters made in classical designs which sell for only a few pounds, or coppersmith's work, leather bags, chunky woollens or flokati rugs. All these are reasonably priced and authentically Greek. Or, on the edible front, pine honey, figs soaked in ouzo, olive oil, or a variety of fresh nuts. Replica statues of the Greek gods and goddesses are best bought in reliable souvenir shops or in the museums where the original statues are kept. (The National Archaeological Musuem in Athens has an excellent collection.)

And for the broad-minded relations at home there are replica symbols of fertility: generally gentlemen with extremely large assets, or, in poster form, scenes of orgies and generally debauched behaviour!

Look out for the National Organization of Greek Handicrafts. A sticker on a souvenir by this body assures it has been handmade to the authentic design, not turned out in its thousands in a factory somewhere. You can actually buy souvenirs in their shops which are located in Athens and the provincial capitals. Their showroom in Athens is at Mitropoleos 9.

Genuine antiques and archaeological remains cannot be exported without a licence which is obtained from the State Archaeological Service, Polygnotou 13, Athens.

Other souvenir ideas include fine silver work, particularly on the island of Ioannina, and Greek gold jewellery (very heavy and ornate) is renowned worldwide.

Sticking with luxury items, Greece is a very good place to pick up a bargain fur. The reason the coats and jackets are so reasonably priced is that cuttings and left-over bits of all different furs are sent from all over the world to the town of Kastoria in Macedonia, northern Greece. Here they are expertly sewn together and sold for a fraction of the price of the genuine 'one animal' item (or, in some cases, sold as the real thing at vast profit). Even the real thing is often cheaper in Greece where the furrier's skills are passed on generation after generation. Head for the back street factory shops and ask at Tourist Information for names. Don't wander into one of the exclusive fur shops if you want a bargain.

Handwoven cottons made up into blouses, dresses and skirts are still prevalent, especially in the Plaka flea market in Athens, as are the handmade 'Jesus' sandals, so popular in the early eighties.

Food and Drink

Greek cuisine and wine is not the main reason for travelling to the country, but having said that there are some deliciously tasty traditional dishes, and some very palatable wines, and though the food is unlikely to be the highlight of your holiday, it shouldn't be the undoing of it either. The Eastern Mediterranean (Turkish, Egyptian) influence of herbs, garlic and above all olive oil is what you will most remember about Greek dishes, but if your stomach cannot adjust to these richer ingredients, 'European' dishes (i.e. what you eat at home) are widely available in the larger resorts and international hotels. Restaurants are classified on the same scale system as hotels, so there are five categories. To be frank restaurants in Greece tend to be overpriced and overrated. (It's a well known fact that the best Greek restaurants are in New York, London and Sydney.) Far better to stick to a taverna, rotisserie or inn, where the national dishes are served with more enthusiasm and far less cost.

Places where the menu is written only in Greek and by hand should not be avoided. Indeed they should be positively sought out, for there the locals obviously eat, and if no one can translate the menu for you you can always honour the time-old tradition of going into the kitchen yourself and having a look at what's on offer. (Always do this if you're choosing fish – you will generally be invited to anyway – as fish and seafood in Greece is very expensive, so be sure you know what you're ordering and ask how much it will cost: the rate is worked out by weight.)

In most tourist-orientated centres menus will appear in Greek, English and German. (Great entertainment is trying to spot how many English errors you can find. Some are absolutely classic!) Apart from tavernas and restaurants the Greek coffee house (*kafenion*) has a very special role to play in Greek life. Here you will find the local worthies playing cards, discussing politics and catching up on news. These are wonderful places to sit with an ouzo (the national aniseed-flavoured firewater), accompanied by feta cheese and olive nibbles; or a coffee and the traditional glass of water. (A brief note here: the strong dark Turkish coffee, served in a small cup, does require water to wash it down, especially if you're feeling dehydrated already, but if your tummy is playing up, ask for a mineral water. What they bring otherwise is tap water which may exacerbate your problems.)

Coffee houses also serve the sweet pastries that Greece and most of the Eastern Mediterranean countries are famed for. Ask for *zakharoplastion*.

Getting back to the serious business of meal times and national dishes, breakfast is a light affair, generally just a cup of coffee or tea and a piece of bread with honey or jam. Lunch is also a smallish meal, generally served between 12.30 and 3 p.m. From 2.30 p.m. to 5 p.m. is the siesta. Lunch can be a mini-version of the dinner, and you can order any of the dishes served at night. Generally though, in the heat of the midday sun what you'll feel more like is a *choriatiki* – a Greek salad containing olives, tomatoes, onions, cucumber and feta cheese, accompanied by a basket of bread. If you need more, try the Greek salad as well as a *souvlaki pitta* – a delicious concoction of skewered spit-roasted lamb, onions, tomatoes and sauce wrapped in pitta bread (similar to the doner kebabs you get in this country in Turkish take-aways). It is also possible to have just the spit-roasted meat (lamb or beef) without the pitta bread. The *gyros pitta* is the de luxe version with the meat being carved from a huge leg of lamb. Souvlaki on wooden sticks are sold as snacks from stalls, known as *kalamaki*. Washed down by a beer, or retsina, and followed by some fresh fruit (fresh figs are particularly good in Greece) this should keep you going until evening! An alternative is the delicious freshly-made yoghurt available in Greece (*yiaourti*).

Dinner is the main meal of the day, and is a late and lengthy affair. In true Mediterranean style it is the social occasion of the day, and for the tourist this is the time to try a few of the national delicacies.

Fixed menus are common in tourist resorts, and if you're budgeting they can mean savings, but obviously you won't get the best of the national cuisine if you're eating what was left from lunch that day.

Most dinners start with a salad of greens and some dips, eaten with pitta bread. *Taramasalata* ('poor man's caviar') is a common sight in our supermarkets these days, but there is nothing to beat a good home-made authentic Greek tara, so make the most of it while you're here. *Melanzansalata* is a dip from aubergines, and *tzatziki* is a favourite: a yoghurt, cucumber and garlic-seasoned dip – delicious with hot pitta bread.

Assorted hors d'oeuvre (*orektika*) are served in the more upmarket restaurants. Nibbles of squid, olives, onions, cheese, seafood and *dolmadhes* – vine leaves stuffed with rice – are usual. (Take your mouthwash with you!) If these are put on your table as a matter of course be aware that they are not free and if eaten will have to be paid for.

Soups tend to be substantial affairs in Greece. They fall into two main categories: broths cooked with eggs, rice and lemon – *avgolemono*, or fish broths – *psarosoupa*. *Fasslada* is made with beans and is akin to a thick broth; *Piperi Supa* is a peppers, vegetables and meat concoction and *Kakavia* is a delicious rich garlicky fish soup.

Lamb (*arni*) is the favourite meat in Greece and it is served in many ways: grilled, roasted or spit-roasted. Suckling pig is a late summer delicacy when charcoal-roasted (*gourounopolo*), and pork (*chirino*) is good, though often more expensive. Beef outside expensive hotel restaurants is not found, and is of inferior quality and overpriced anyway.

Dishes to look for are *Giuvetsi* – a speciality in Athens consisting of roast lamb with pasta, served in a traditional earthenware pot; *Moussaka* – a pie made of aubergines and minced meat; *Styphado* is a tasty stew made of hare, tongue or veal and slowly cooked with wine and onions. Chicken (*kotopoulo*) outside the cities tends to be good as it is not battery-bred, and game is excellent when in season.

The many traditional dishes which use minced meat (meat balls – *keftedas*; *moussaka*, *dolmadhes*, and rice and meat balls served in a tomato or lemon sauce – *souzoukakia*) should only be ordered where you are sure that the establishment is good. It's all too easy to get away with mincing yesterday's leftover meat! Away from the back streets of Athens and the main resorts, however, you're unlikely to find too much of this type of sharp practice (which goes on in every country anyway). Places where the Greeks themselves eat are generally safe bets as if they found any restaurateur on the fiddle they would not be slow in bringing justice to bear!

Pollution and plundering of the seas have resulted in what was once the staple food of the islanders being reduced to a virtual luxury. Fish and seafood in Greece is fresh and well cooked but invariably more expensive than you would pay at home. Among the less pricey and tastier of the dishes available are: *xiphios* – swordfish – grilled pieces are served on skewers with onions, tomatoes and bay leaves; squid – *soupia* – casseroled in wine; prawn pilaff, and bream – *sinagrida*. Sole – *glossa* – can be excellent, but expensive.

Typical vegetables are aubergines (*melitsanes*); artichokes (*anginares*); courgettes (*kolokithakia*); peppers (*piperies*) and asparagus (*sparangia*).

On the sweet front there is not the trolley-full you will find at home. It tends to be fresh fruit (*fruta*), ice cream (*pagoton*) or a pastry (but only a tourist would end a meal with a pastry!). Greek ice cream can be wonderful – home-made, creamy and delicious enough to rival their Italian neighbours. Of the fruit on offer the melons (*mulkaiko*), peaches (*rodakino*), figs (*sika*) and grapes (*stafilia*) are the best choices to go for. Apples are often a disappointment, and oranges are not reliably good either.

Cheeses are not at their best in Greece. *Kaseri* is a hard cheese; *feta* is a soft one. *Manouri*, a goat's cheese from Crete, is worth trying, but far more tasty, and not to be missed (even if you don't like the sound of it!) is the sheep's milk yoghurt for which Greece is famous – *proveio*. Freshly made and eaten with honey, there is nothing better on a hot summer's afternoon.

DRINKS

Wine (*krasinos*) is most commonly drunk in Greece. White is *aspro krasi*; red is *mavro krasi*. Resin is used to preserve the wines, hence that uniquely Greek aftertaste to the wine which you either love or hate. (Give it time; you have to get used to the taste of *retsina*.) Retsina, which comes mainly from Attica, should be served chilled and can come from bottles or from barrels. It can be dirt cheap or moderately priced, but it is unusual to be charged more than £4 a bottle, even for the good stuff. *Kourtakis* is a good one to start with, or *kokkineli*, the rosé wine with less of the resinated taste.

Whilst in Greece try the following recommended wines: *Theotokis* from Corfu; *Verdea* from Zakinthos and *St Helena* from the Peloponnese in the whites; *Porto Carras* from the Halkidiki in white, rosé or red is excellent; *Mirabello* from Crete; *Hymettus* from Attica and *Aharnes* from Crete.

The best unresinated wines have 'VQPRD' on the labels. If you're giving up with the retsina variety, rather than stick to the *Demestica* (or as it's aptly known by many Brits 'Domestos'), try the *Petit Château*, white *Nihteri* from Thira, or the Macedonian red *Naoussa*.

These wines should change your mind if you've condemned all Greek wine as turpentine, and should cost you no more in a restaurant than the price of a supermarket bottle at home.

Beer in Greece means lager, and the national brand *Fix* is considerably cheaper than the German and Dutch imports, and there is little in the taste difference. It is still common to find a refrigerated bottle being pricier than an unrefrigerated one; unfortunately in the capitalistic mind of the Greek shopkeeper that's just business. Soft drinks including Coca-Cola and 7-Up are all over Greece, though again the prices for a chilled can can be extortionate. Better to stick to the mineral water (carbonated or still). *Loutraki* and *Sariza* are two good brands, though every region has its own and they are all acceptable. The Greek soft drinks tend to be very sweet and syrupy.

Local spirits tend to be a bit ropey. Ouzo is pretty rough stuff, but once bitten by the bug, you'll love it, and while in Rome . . . It is the traditional drink to be offered by a Greek and it is an insult to refuse. The only other spirit worth risking your health with is Metaxa, the local brandy.

Nescafé is widely available if the strong Turkish coffee is not to your taste, but do specify when asking. Tea is not widely drunk but in tourist areas it is available.

Nightlife

If you want an active nightlife on your holiday in Greece all you have to do is make sure you choose the right resort and come at the right time of year. There is a lively atmosphere in many Greek towns and tourist resorts in summer and if you're looking for a good dinner, followed by dancing, singing and a party atmosphere this shouldn't be hard to come by just about anywhere in Greece. The Greeks love a celebration, and if you've ever been in Greece at the time of any of their major festivals you'll be left in no doubt that the Greeks know how to enjoy themselves. There is obviously a dichotomy here: you will find nightlife laid on for the tourists by the professionals, and you will find the spontaneous 'natural' nightlife which bubbles through and requires no pre-planning. The latter is invariably the most enjoyable, but there's no planning for it. Organized nightlife involves Zorba the Greek style dancing, ouzo-drinking competitions and dancing on the terraces of the international hotels. For the younger set discos are laid on, and occasionally beach barbecues. All these stem from external influences and though the hoteliers think this is what people want, it often isn't. This same sort of nightlife could just as easily take place in Spain, Yugoslavia or Portugal; there is nothing particularly Greek about it, and to the locals it's all alien. The typical Greek idea of nightlife is more along the lines of starting the evening with a leisurely multi-course dinner with all the family and friends seated around a large table. Here the animated conversation will be on everything from what the next grandchild should be called to world politics. Leaving the old boys behind, the rest of the family then generally makes for the waterfront or the town square, where the ritual evening 'volta' is taken. This is the promenade at dusk; their opportunity to see and be seen, and after this the young members of the family are taken home and put to bed. A coffee and ouzo in a café finishes the night for the rest. It may sound a bit tame by European standards, but if you get in with a good crowd of Greeks this myth will be quickly dispelled. The dancing to the traditional folk music starts after dinner on a special occasion and then you can be up till dawn! Of course this is the sort of nightlife which tourists can hardly barge in on, but in my experience the very best evenings in Greece are being surrounded by Greeks (not fellow tourists), listening to the animated dialogues, watching the expressive gestures, and soaking up the foreignness of the situation. Dusk is also one of the most atmospheric times to see the ancient monuments of Greece. This may sound clichéd, but in fact very few people get themselves sufficiently organized to be at the temples and acropoli just at the right time.

If, by way of contrast, you want a knees-up there are plenty of restaurants offering entertainment as you eat in the large tourist resorts. There are also dances, bars and cafés a-plenty in the large resorts. The section on 'The Socialite' on page 34 lists the main islands and resorts to head for: Mykonos, Rhodes, Crete, Corfu, Skiathos, Hydra, Paros etc.

Note also the festivals which liven up the nightlife scene listed under this section. Try to coincide with a festival if you want a lively time among the Greeks.

If you want a consistently lively time in the way you would at home, and don't mind being surrounded by tourists, be sure that your resort is suitable. Read the brochure carefully; read what we say about the resort in the text, and ask your travel agent's opinion.

Communications

Keeping in touch with home from Greece is relatively simple. You can telephone direct to Britain (dial 010 44, then your number in the U.K.). Long-distance telephone calls can only be made from OTE offices, not local payphones. You pay for the call after making it so there's no chance of being cut off, and rates are cheaper between 9 p.m. and 5 a.m. It can take a while to get a line overseas if you're dialling from a remote island; a good dose of patience is required. For help on international calls dial 162.

To make a local call insert your coin before dialling. If you don't get through the coin will be returned.

The speed of the postal service is pretty awful (ten days for a postcard in peak season is doing very well), although it has improved in the last year or so.

Sending on money to Greece through a bank or American Express is still a lengthy and complicated procedure, so take an extra 'emergency supply' (or easier, take some credit cards with you) just in case you incur unforeseen expenditure.

POST OFFICES

The Post Office is identified by the letters 'ELTA'. Independent of this is the Telephone Network System 'OTE'.

Post offices open Mon to Fri 8 a.m. to 1 p.m., 3 to 7 p.m. If you just require stamps these can be bought from kiosks and shops selling postcards, thereby avoiding the long queues that are found in most major Greek post offices. Letter boxes are painted yellow. As the normal post takes so long the extra few drachmas for Air Mail is well worth it.

Telegrams can be sent from post offices or OTE centres.

Poste restante is a bit chaotic, but it is theoretically possible. The main post office in Athens is at Eolou Street 100. This and the Syntagma Square office are open Mon to Fri 7.30 a.m. to 8.30 p.m., Sat 7.30 a.m. to 3 p.m., and Sun 9 a.m. to 2 p.m. The Athens main OTE is at Stadiou 15. The 28 Patission Street no. 85 office is open 24 hours.

Moving Around the Country

Getting around Greece is not particularly easy if you're trying to stick to a tight budget. Car hire is expensive and for touring an area there is no comfortable alternative. If, however, you don't mind the squeeze or slow pace of travel, the train offers a chance to get to many corners of Greece. The inter-city buses are another option. Local buses are busy and not for the delicate.

It's actually much easier to get from one city to another within Greece than to tour an area. Internal flights are one of the best bargains in the country, though they do need pre-booking in the summer, and the inter-city buses already mentioned are also relatively efficient, cheap and fast. To get between the islands the ferries are the only option. These get crowded in high season and none can be described as luxurious, even if you're prepared to pay 1st class fares, but they are reasonably efficient at getting to the remote places, even if they do cancel sailings at ten minutes' notice and run hours late! To take each option in turn:

CAR HIRE

Car and moped hire is big business in Greece. The rental companies know that if you're stuck in a quiet beach resort, by the end of the first week you'll feel as though you were born there and will be looking to see what's over the other side of the mountain. Their prices are not cheap, and despite the high level of competition the cartel-type set-up ensures you can't win.

Given this you're as well going to an established firm. There are cowboys in Greece, so beware! Avis and Europcar offer a good deal and cover even the most remote areas. It's best to hire your car from them in the U.K. before you go. This way you get a guaranteed price in sterling which cannot be altered whatever happens to the exchange rates, and you also have an easier time if things go wrong as you can take it up with a British person rather than a Greek. You can make a booking through your travel agent or direct through their offices.

Avis operate in major towns and cities throughout Greece and have agencies in all major resorts. Hertz and Budget are the other two main rental agencies. Budget rent-a-car, the world's number three, are well worth considering for a vehicle. Operated under licences, they have a comprehensive service insurance and can be found in even the smallest locations. Today you can find Budget in every Western European country, including Yugoslavia, making them a serious contender for the package holiday market. The travel and leisure programmes they offer vary from year to year, but there will always be one aimed at the holiday market so enquire at any local Budget office.

Other points to note in Greece: check that your insurance is not just limited to third party, and that your holiday insurance is not invalid if you hire and ride a motor bike (some of the package covers specify this). You must have International Third Party Insurance (the Green Card), but given that the accident rate in Greece is the second highest in Europe, after Portugal, you'd be better with Comprehensive. (The little shrines you see on the roads every few miles are thanksgiving from those who survived accidents. Let these remind you how many accidents occur!)

Many companies specify that you must be over 23 years to hire a car and have an internationally valid (i.e. U.K.) driver's licence.

Roads have improved in recent years in Greece and major roads are quite acceptable. Smaller secondary roads are still badly surfaced though and on the islands you must drive with extreme care. Moped hire is increasingly popular due to the price difference, but do check the safety angles before setting off (brakes, crash helmet, number in case of breakdown etc.).

Expect to pay around £175 a week all-in from a reputable company (the dodgier ones are often cheaper, but it's a risk: the high price reflects the hefty tax put on car hire by the Greek Government. These cowboy outfits have to pay the same rate of tax so they cut their costs by offering cars that are less well maintained and often safety suffers). Moped hire should cost around £9 a day, though out of season haggle to reduce prices. Cycles come in around £2 a day, but usually the mountainous nature of Greece makes for heavy going, especially in the heat.

A couple of quick notes in case of problems:

It is an offence to drive away from an accident. Always report it.

AA and RAC members can get help from the Greek equivalent, ELPA, in case of a breakdown. In any of the major cities or towns dial 174.

In an emergency the Tourist Police will help. Dial 104.

For further information on driving in Greece see the 'By Car' section on page 110.

TRAINS

To get between major towns the rail network in Greece is adequate, but if you want to branch off to explore remote areas of the country you will quickly run into problems. The trains are also slow and erratic. However, if you are heading from one major centre to another the fares are cheap and it's a wonderful way of meeting both fellow travellers and the Greeks themselves.

The main line from Athens to Thessaloniki divides into two: one runs north to Yugoslavia, the other east to Turkey (and subsequently on to Bulgaria). Other lines in tourist areas include the line running west of Thessaloniki, which eventually gets up to Yugoslavia; the Athens–Corinth narrow gauge railway which splits between Patras, Olympia and Pylos on one line, and Nafplio and Tripoli on the other; both meeting up again at Kalamata.

The Greek Tourist Card is a rover ticket which allows you to use the railways as often as you like, where you like for 10, 20 or 30 days in 2nd class. It also entitles you to unlimited use of the buses owned by the railways, making it an excellent way of getting round the country in detail. It is very cheap (approx £2 a day for unlimited travel!) and is available from any travel agent or from the Greek Railway (OSE) Offices in Athens.

BUSES

Greece is still served by an impressive network of local buses, which are cheap and reasonably efficient (in comparison to the trains), but there ends the good news. They are also unbelievably crowded in summer, and if you suffer from claustrophobia, don't go anywhere near one. In the summer heat there are few things worse than being squashed into a corner in an over-loaded bus, travelling at 15 mph and stopping every mile or so. This is quite common. Having said this, if you reserve a seat, or can time it to avoid the worst of the crush, or you're in a remote area, it is a good way to get to grips with some of the country's hidden assets, and it is an independent person's answer to organized excursion phobia. Though you won't find bus routes planned to take in the sights of an area, you can often make up your own itinerary and see what interests you most for a fraction of the cost of an organized excursion, and avoid the worst of the mass tourism syndrome.

Timetables tend to be largely ignored, so enquire in the local Tourist Office, or a travel agency, or your hotel as to times and routes.

CHAT at Stadiou 4, Athens operate coach tours (half-day to a week) if you want a comfortable form of sightseeing which retains more of the dignity (the odd Greek can still be found on these tours, as well as largely independent travellers), and other buses are operated by the railway (OTE) and private companies. Overland bus routes operate between major centres on the mainland and the Ionian islands and Peloponnese. The bus stations in Athens for these services are at Liossion 260 and Kifissou 100.

TAXIS

The stories of Athenian taxi driver rip-offs are legion, and just about anyone who has travelled in Greece independently will tell you that taxi drivers are licensed criminals. Largely this is deserved, for undoubtedly unless you agree a fare beforehand or check the meter is on and accurate, you will be 'had'. Taxis are still relatively cheap when the price is accurate, though, and with the customary blaring bouzouki music, and photographs of all the family on the dashboard, they do make a rather dramatic and atmospheric mode of transport. There are no communal taxis in Greece as there are in Turkey, so only use taxis for short distances.

Problems and Emergencies

MEDICAL

In Athens dial 107 for a list of all late-night chemist's. Elsewhere a list is displayed in all chemist's (*farmakia's*) windows. If the problem is serious and a chemist can't help dial 166 for the Red Cross First Aid, or in Athens dial 166 to find out which First Aid Centre is admitting casualties. In other areas the emergency number is displayed near telephone kiosks. Usually if you are in or near a hotel the best thing is to contact reception and let them sort it all out for you in Greek.

Britons and other EEC nationals are entitled to free medical care, but this means being admitted to only the lowest grade of state hospitals. Unless it's anything serious this would suffice, but if you're likely to be in hospital for a while use your travel insurance to get into somewhere where the nursing standards are higher. And remember you'll need Form E111 from your local DHSS office with you, so get this before you go.

POLICE

Dial 100 for the Police in cities; 109 in the suburbs and rural areas. Remember if you have goods stolen to report it to the police and obtain a copy of their report for your insurance claim. (Also inform your travel rep if you're on a package.)

EMBASSIES AND CONSULATES

The British Embassy in Athens is at Ploutarhou 1, Kolonaki (Tel: 736 211). The consulate in Thessaloniki is at Vass. Konstantinou 15. Contact them in case of loss of passport and papers.

WORK

It is possible to find short-term work in Greece, though as it is rarely declared to the authorities it is usually under-paid and subject to a fair degree of exploitation. Bar work and work related to the tourist industry is easiest to find, especially for girls, and Corfu is noted for being a good place to start. Harvesting and agricultural work is a popular choice for many young men, and here Crete is the favoured destination for its many harvests and long summer.

Long-term work is often in the form of teaching English or au pairing. Be sure that you get all the paperwork fixed up and that your contract is to your liking before signing anything. It becomes very difficult once you are out in Greece to start legal proceedings against a Greek employer.

WOMEN ALONE

Women travelling alone in remote parts of Greece, particularly Crete, may still find the going tough. Women only got the vote here thirty years ago, and until literally a couple of years ago adulterous women were regularly taken to court where sentence was passed on them. In some rural parts women cannot own property, and it is still very much the case that the woman is her husband's chattel. Given this, it is not surprising that northern European women who sunbathe nude, have what would be regarded as 'loose morals' and lead independent lives, are regarded as easy prey for the local men. If you are in an area where the women you see are still living in the old traditional ways, for your own safety and enjoyment 'dress down' and act discreetly.

A Potted History

The Republic of Greece lies in the south-east of Europe, sharing a border with Turkey, Albania, Yugoslavia and Bulgaria, and surrounded by the Mediterranean, Aegean and Ionian seas. The mainland is divided into two parts, connected by a narrow isthmus, and the Pindus mountain range runs the length of the mainland. The mountainous area of Northern Greece contrasts with the flat Peloponnese, which lies south-west of the isthmus. Most of the country, however, is mountainous (four-fifths) with pine-covered upland areas and scrub-covered footlands.

Included in its land mass are many small islands (1,425 in total), scattered in groups throughout the Aegean and Eastern Mediterranean, the largest of which is Crete. These islands, where tourism is the main industry, represent one of the largest holiday areas in the world.

Power is in the hands today of a republican government, but only as recently as 1967–74 a military junta ruled, following the deposition of the King. In 1981 Greece became the tenth member of the EEC. Despite the fact that industry is becoming increasingly important to the country's economy and the standard of living has risen, it is essentially still a poor country in comparison to its EEC neighbours, with only 25 per cent of the land of any cultivatable use, and tourism still ranking as the country's main industry.

Recorded Greek history spans nearly thirty centuries. This country has as long and colourful a history as one could imagine, and what you see here makes no attempt to be a comprehensive or authoritative account. All this does is outline the basics so that you can begin to piece things together and make sense of the ancient monuments you will inevitably come across on your holiday in Greece.

Archaeological findings suggest that as long ago as 4000 BC the Hellenic peninsula was inhabited by migratory tribes. When the Indo-Europeans from the East introduced metalworking in the Bronze Age (2800 BC–1000 BC), great cities emerged, with powerful navies and armies to defend them. Three great civilizations emerged at this time: the Cycladic, the Minoan and the Mycenaean, with the latter two being based around a royal palace.

Thus it was that the oldest European civilizations stemmed from Greece, which became known as the 'cradle of civilization'.

The Minoans (2000–1580 BC) were powerful in the Peloponnese region and on Crete (see the Palace of Knossos on Crete). Their influence was greatly felt in the later Mycenaean civilization (1580–1100 BC) which dominated the Aegean region with its powerful navies for several centuries.

The Mycenaean decline was due to the Dorian Invasion, which occurred when four Hellenic tribes migrated en masse to the mainland in around 1100 BC. This pan-Hellenic movement marked the beginning of the Geometric Period (1100-700 BC), when recorded history began. Under the Dorians the first true cities appeared, a common alphabet was adopted, and religious worship organized.

Livestock breeding was introduced and a truly 'civilized' society resulted, at a time when the rest of Europe was still living in an unstructured and barbaric manner. Refugees from the mainland of Greece fled east in the 11th and 10th centuries BC and they formed the first Greek colonies on the coast of Asia Minor which later developed into independent cities.

The introduction of the Olympic Games in 776 BC was one of the highspots of this organized society.

Political differences divided the tribes and independent city states arose out of the disputes. This marked the beginning of the Archaic Period (700–500 BC). The two main city states of Sparta and Athens emerged. The Peloponnese cities clung to Sparta, which operated a harsh military code and expansionist policy. Athens on the other hand developed a more democratic society, with more emphasis on inter-state liaison and the development of the arts. Both rival states united, however, against Persia and from the Battle of Marathon in 490 BC to the Battle of Plataea in 479 BC the rivals fought as one in the Persian Wars.

The Classical Period (500-323 BC) saw the zenith of Greek achievement. Athens flourished as the world centre for the arts and science, and under Pericles the 'Golden Age' began. This was the time when many of the fine Classical buildings whose remains you see today were erected: the Agora and Parthenon in Athens were built with the wealth accrued from trading and shipping as Athens took its place as a leading world power. The intense rivalry between the Athenians and the Spartans turned to full-blooded war again, and the Peloponnesian War of 431-404 BC resulted. Sparta emerged victorious and Athens never again fully recovered her military strength, though there could be no quelling the tide of great philosophical achievement, spearheaded by men such as Plato, Aristotle and Socrates who lived in Athens in the 4th century BC.

Sparta's victory was short-lived for soon the rest of the Greek city states challenged its supremacy, and following the Battle of Chaeroneia in 338 BC, King Philip II of Macedonia became the leader of the Greeks in the next stage of their long campaign against the Persians. In the end the King's son, Alexander the Great, led the campaign in which Greece captured Egypt and the East as far as India.

The Hellenistic Period (323-146 BC) saw the dispersal of Alexander's conquests in Asia and Africa after his death in 323 BC. His generals and collaborators were put in command of the many outposts, but internal strife weakened Greece considerably, and Athens and Sparta took on a secondary role. The real centres of civilization moved outside Greece to Alexandria in Egypt and Pergamos in Asia Minor, etc. The Romans first appeared in Greece at this time, during the 3rd century BC. They were successful in defeating the Macedonian Kings three times, and one after the other the Greek states were subjugated to Roman domination. In 146 BC Greece became a Roman province.

In the Roman and Byzantine Period (146 BC-1453 AD) Corinth became the administrative capital of Greece and until the 3rd century AD the country had three centuries of peaceful domination. In AD 395 when the Roman Empire split into the Western Empire under Rome and Eastern under Constantinople, Greece went under the latter, and then began the Byzantine era. From the 4th century AD numerous tribes of barbarians invaded from the North. Athens slid into oblivion as Thessaloniki took its place and rose to the status of second city to

Constantinople. Christianity was adopted by the Roman Empire in AD 398 and with this the Greeks abandoned paganism. The Byzantine period saw the flowering of religious art (as can be seen by the many icons and ornate churches of this period) and during this era Greece was the administrative centre of the Byzantine Empire.

In 1204 troops of the 4th Crusade seized Constantinople and Greece fell into the hands of the Franks who established a number of feudal states throughout the land. This new influence and the emergence of new strong tribes from the East weakened Byzantium until in 1453 it fell to the Turks. This was Greece's darkest hour as the Ottomans subjugated Greece to a harsh, ruthless rule throughout the Middle Ages. Christians were persecuted and many either fled to monasteries or moved West.

The Greeks fought the Turks off and on throughout the Middle Ages, but in 1669 they lost Crete to them and this put all Greece under their control. It took until the early 19th century before the new state of Greece came into being. In 1821 an army of guerillas began the fight-back. Stalemate was reached, but at this point the three great Western powers of Britain, France and Russia intervened, and in the resultant Battle of Navarino, Turkey and Egypt were decisively beaten and Greece once more was able to return to self-government.

The twentieth century has been a turbulent time, and provides the explanation why the Greeks have such a predilection for discussing politics at any given opportunity. In 1909 the monarch was ousted in favour of a republican government, but in 1930 the army restored the monarchy, and democratic government again took a back seat. During World War II the Greeks fought with the Allies, with the communist-aided ELAS group putting up a valiant fight against the Germans and stemming their tide for several months. After the war the Communists attempted to take over the country, but the British and the monarchists put paid to this scheme, only in 1949 to find another Communist attempted take-over. American backing quelled this attempt, and from 1952–63 the republican government ruled. When the centre Union Party took over from this largely conservative government in 1963 there grew a fear that their weak control would open up the way again for a Communist take-over, so on 21 April a coup was staged by the military and a military dictatorship came into power. The junta, under General Papadopolous, held a harsh and repressive grip on the country and many Greeks (including the now famous Melina Mercouri) fled the country. This dictatorship fell in 1974 when General Ioannidis overthrew Papadopolous and also Archbishop Makarios in Cyprus – a move which very nearly resulted in war between Turkey and Greece when the Turks used this opportunity to invade the northern part of Cyprus. Fearing a full-scale war and a loss of public support, Constantine Karamanlis, the Prime Minister of the republican government in the period before the rule of the junta, was re-called to govern the country. He did so successfully, and during his office the monarchy was finally ousted from any power and a republican constitution was drawn up in 1975.

The balance today hangs with the Pan-Hellenic Socialist Party (PASOK), under Papandreou, though the situation now is generally stable and democratic. The situation with the Turks is still very delicately poised (which is why you cannot pass from Greece to Turkey and back again, and why if you have a Turkish stamp on your passport you will be given a hard time!), as the Turks still hold northern Cyprus and operate restrictive measures on any Greeks living in their country. Now that Greece is in the EEC an increasing amount of European standardization is taking place (for better or worse), and the other main issue which you can hardly fail to notice by the amount of graffiti it generates is the strong feeling concerning the American bases in Greece. The Communist parties (KKE and KNE) are opposed to their presence, hence the slogans 'Kato to PASOK' daubed on prominent buildings.

If you want to engage a Greek in conversation (and many of the younger people speak enough English to converse), raise the political issues of the day and you'll be there till dawn. They are one of the most politically aware nations in the world, but with a history like theirs, it's hardly surprising!

Part Four
THE COUNTRY

Athens and Attica

Athens

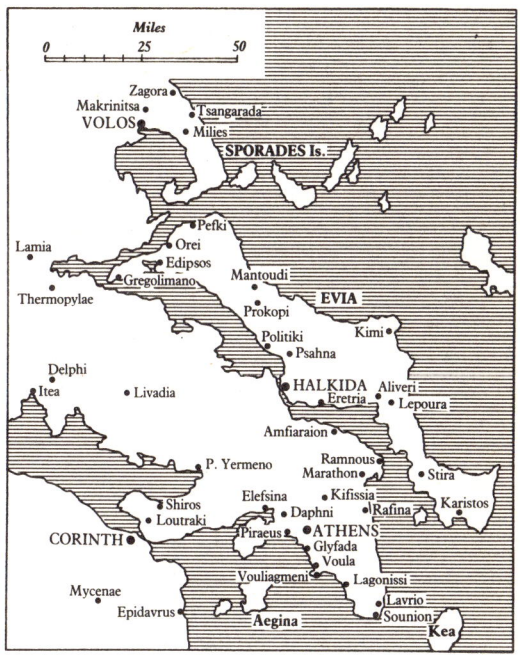

With its unrivalled classical monuments, Athens, capital of Greece and the birthplace of Western civilization, is too important to be missed by anybody with the remotest interest in history or culture. However, if you are expecting an elegant, dignified city, your illusions will be shattered. Modern Athens is a vast, ugly sprawl, ruined in recent years by the Colonels who allowed unscrupulous property developers to cram unattractive, squat buildings right next to ancient sites. The sites themselves have suffered from the ravages left by millions of visitors, and worst of all the terrible air pollution which still afflicts central Athens. The smog is referred to locally as 'the cloud' (*nephos*) and it combines with the heat and noise (Athens is the noisiest city in the world according to one recent survey) to guarantee headaches and a generally exhausting time for anyone imprudent enough to visit during the height of the summer.

The city's main problems can be put down to one simple cause: over-crowding. There is barely enough room for the 3½ million Greeks who live there, let alone the thousands of tourists who descend on Athens every year. There are dreadful traffic and pollution problems and you take your life in your hands every time you venture to cross a street. However, all is not lost and the present government is doing all it can to beautify the main tourist areas, and it has restricted the number of cars allowed in the city centre in an effort to cut down on air pollution and congestion.

According to Greek mythology Athens got its name when Poseidon and Athena had a bit of a set-to over who should rule the city. The gods of Olympus decided that whoever bestowed the most beneficial gift on the city would become its protector. Athena offered the first-ever olive tree, while all Poseidon could do was produce a torrent of salt water. Not surprisingly Athena won the contest and the city was named in her honour.

Archaeological finds on the south slope of the Acropolis have suggested that the site of Athens was already occupied by the Neolithic period around 2000 BC, and there is also evidence demonstrating that the city participated in the development of the Mycenaean world 1600 years later. However, Athens did not come into its own until the 6th century BC, when the city established itself as a great power and saw off the threat of the Persians in the historic Battle of Salamis in 480 BC. Under the great Pericles, both the arts and sciences flourished and Athens experienced its 'Golden Age': Iktinos designed the Parthenon – without the benefit of any technological gadgetry; Aeschylus set the standard for tragedy and was followed by the equally great Sophocles and Euripides; Aristophanes perfected the form of comedy; and Hippocrates developed the science of medicine virtually single handed. This explosion of talent is all the more remarkable when you think that these pioneers often had little or no tradition on which to draw.

Towards the end of the 5th century Athens became embroiled in the protracted Peloponnesian War with powerful Sparta, which it eventually lost through bad leadership. However, even during its decline it remained as the centre of learning and culture, and Plato and Aristotle developed their philosophical theories, while Demosthenes became the first great orator.

The city continued to flourish as an educational centre under the Roman Empire, but lost its importance during Byzantine rule. It was not until 1834 that the city was resurrected as capital of free Greece. The modern city, with its squares and wide boulevards, was largely designed by King Otto towards the end of the last century, though these efforts were negated under the rule of the Colonels in the late 1960s and early 1970s, when unrestricted redevelopment lost Athens its former elegance.

However, this unique city is still worth a few days of anybody's time. Its classical splendours are matchless and the modern city is friendly and welcoming, with nightlife of a standard you'd expect from a major European city.

Try to avoid the city in the heat of summer if you can at all help it. It is hot, crowded and exhausting. There is also a chronic shortage of rooms in peak season and you will have enough to keep you occupied without having to worry about finding accommodation.

Practical Details

COMMUNICATIONS

Make sure you know which terminal of Athens' Hellenikon International Airport you will be arriving at. There are two terminals: East Airport (*Anatoliko Aerodromio*) is used by foreign airlines while West Airport (*Dytiko Aerodromio*) is used by Olympic Airways, the Greek national airline. All flights to the islands and other Greek destinations are from this terminal. There is a shuttle service between the two terminals and a no. 018 bus or yellow express takes you from East Airport to Syntagma Square (the centre of Athens) while a blue no. 133 takes you from West Airport to the city centre. There is an official tourist office at East Airport which has lists of accommodation (hotels only), museums, buses and ferries (open 24 hrs). If you arrive in the small hours of the morning and haven't booked accommodation you're better off snatching a few hours of sleep at the airport than getting a taxi to the city centre (pay no more than 1000 dr).

There are two train stations – Larissa (Tel: 213882) is the main station (no.1 trolley-bus to Deligiani) and serves Northern Greece and Europe. The station serving the Peloponnese is over the bridge across the tracks and 100 yards to the left. Trains are normally chock-a-block in Greece and even if you've made a reservation you will generally have to hustle somebody to get your seat. Try to catch the earliest train possible as it will be less crowded, and travelling will be more comfortable. There is no air-conditioning in Greek trains. If you are leaving Greece by train book a seat well in advance. You simply will not get one if you do not book two months in advance during peak season. There are just two trains per day out of Greece: at eight in the morning and eight at night. The crowds of backpackers that gather to cram themselves into the carriages, corridors and even toilets of every train are a sight to behold. Generally, unless you're on an Inter-Rail ticket (unlimited travel for those under 26) you are better taking the bus to mainland destinations outside Athens.

However, before you take a bus, you've got to get to the main bus station, and Athens being what it is, there is do direct transport from the city centre (i.e. Syntagma) to the bus station, unless you take a taxi, which can set you back anything up to 1000 dr. The bus station for all destinations except Delphi, Evia, Larnia and Larissa is the Kiffisous Street Station (terminal A) at 100 Kiffisous Street on the northern fringes of town. You can get to the station from Syntagma via a no.1 trolley-bus to Omonia and a regular (blue) 051 bus from Agios Konstandinou Street. The other destinations listed are served by Liosson Street Station (terminal B) at 260 Liosson Street. This is connected with the city centre by the blue no. 24 bus. The N.T.O.G. offices have details of routes, fares and timetables within and outside of Athens.

Ferries depart from Piraeus harbour for all the islands and other Mediterranean destinations. To get to Piraeus take the green no. 040 bus which runs 24 hrs (free before 8 a.m.), from the first block off Fillelinon Street, just off Syntagma, or take the subway from either Omonia or Monastiraki. Schedules can be obtained from the N.T.O.G. tourist office just inside the National Bank in the north-west corner of Syntagma and tickets are purchased from the agencies which line the waterfront, or at the ferry dock itself. Hydrofoils depart from Zea Marina around half a mile east of the main harbour.

In Athens itself there is an efficient, if crowded, bus service. The blue buses bear three-digit numbers and cost 20 dr as do the yellow trolley buses, which bear one- or two-digit numbers. They get very crowded during the rush hour, but are cheap and convenient for short city hops. The services are free before 0800 and they terminate around midnight, although there are buses to the airport terminals throughout the night.

Taxis are cheap and a good bet if there are three or four of you. Drivers charge 20 dr per km plus 25 dr entrance fee, but if you look vulnerable they'll charge you more. Try to insist that the driver uses the meter.

There is a one-line subway system which begins at Kiffisia, just north of the city, and takes you through to Piraeus, via Omonia and Monastiraki in the centre of Athens.

You can hire cars and mopeds, but driving in Athens is not really recommended unless you're a fan of Mad Max!

TOURIST INFORMATION

The Greek National Tourist Organization (N.T.O.G., or E.O.T. in Greek) has an information desk in the National Bank of Greece in the north-west corner of Syntagma Square (Tel: 322 2545). It is open from 8 a.m. to 8 p.m., Mon to Sat, but crowded after 10 a.m. They will book you into accommodation, but only into hotels of 'D' class and above. There is also information on buses, ferries, museums and a free leaflet entitled *Athens and Attica*, which contains useful maps. There is another branch at East Airport which is manned 24 hours a day, as are the banks next door.

Tel. 171 for the tourist police, who always understand English. There are offices at the train station (Tel: 821 3574, open 7 a.m. to 11 p.m); the East Airport (Tel: 981 4093), open 24 hours and very helpful), and the main office is at 7 Singrou Street (Tel: 923 9224, open daily 8 a.m. to 9 p.m.).

The central post office is at 100 Eolou Street, Omonia Square, and there is another in Syntagma. Both are open Mon to Fri 7.30 a.m. to 8.30 p.m., Sat 7.30 a.m. to 2 p.m. and Sun 9 a.m. to 2 p.m.

There are OTEs at 28 Patission Street (open round the clock, no. 85 bus); Omonia Square, and 15 Stadiou Street (both open daily 7 a.m. to midnight); and at the train station (open Mon to Sat 7.30 a.m. to 10 p.m.). Call 171 for directory assistance and 162 for information on overseas calls.

The National Bank in Syntagma is open 9 a.m. to 8 p.m., but most banks close at 2 p.m. Some hotels will change money, but you won't get such a good rate.

If you don't buy a map you could end up in a fix. The *Hallway* city map (cost £2.50) is probably the clearest but the map in the *Athens and Attica* brochure, available free of charge from the tourist offices, is more than adequate. *This Week in Athens* has a map but its listings are far more useful. It costs 50 dr from kiosks and gives extensive details of nightlife, cinema and restaurants, etc. Other publications worth a look at are the English-language newspapers, the *Athens Star* (100 dr.) and the *Athens News* (60 dr.). These contain news as well as helpful listings and emergency telephone numbers. For cultural information, the *Athenian* (120 dr) is the most useful. It contains reviews and features and comes out every month.

WHERE TO GO FOR WHAT

There are well over three dozen British travel companies offering holidays to Greece's capital and all markets are catered for. You can stay in an economical pension or in a big, luxury hotel with classical tours included in the package; the choice is yours. We strongly recommend that you visit Athens out of peak season when sightseeing is more comfortable, though the city is no less interesting. The pounds in your pocket will probably be worth more during the low season as the Greek financial markets get a bit jittery when there are fewer tourists around and the drachma correspondingly falls in value.

A holiday in Athens will appeal to anyone who wants a lively time with plenty of ancient ruins and sights to see by day, and a good, varied nightlife to get stuck into after dark. Sun worshippers may like to consider staying in one of the resorts to the south-east of Athens so that a beach holiday may be combined with tours of the sights.

ACCOMMODATION

There is a shortage of rooms – especially in the summer – but you will find that prices are quite reasonable for a major European capital.

Hotels are situated in several areas, and many people will want to stay close to the Acropolis in a hotel which is convenient for sights and nightlife, with views of the Parthenon to boot. However, most of the hotels in the Acropolis/Agora area are pretty dull and many have terrible noise problems. A good middle of the range bet though is the **Herodion** (Tel: 923 6832), which is stylish and quiet, and has good views of the Acropolis.

Many people choose to stay just east of here in the famous Plaka region, which is now gradually being smartened up with the more seedy establishments being closed down. This is one of the most attractive areas of the city to stay in and all the archaeological sights are within easy reach on foot. The hotels in this area are generally small and basic, but several of them have more character than others in Athens. The **Acropolis House** (Tel: 322 2344) is recommended. It is a comfortable old building with plenty of character and the management are kind and helpful. The **Adonis** (Tel: 324 9737) is a simple pension with an attractive roof terrace which has views of the Acropolis, and **New Clare's House** (Tel: 922 2288) is clean and central. The English-speaking owner is a mine of useful information on how to get the best out of the city. Those on a pretty tight budget should consider the **Hotel Ideal** (Tel: 321 3195) and the **Hotel Tempi** (Tel: 321 3175) which are similar establishments near Monastiraki, with both representing good value for money.

To the east of the Plaka, around Syntagma Square, is where you'll find more up-market hotels. The **Grande Bretagne** (Tel: 323 0251) on Syntagma Square is one of Athens' most prestigious hotels, with lavishly decorated public rooms and superb service. Still in Syntagma the **King George** (Tel: 323 0651) is a more old-fashioned luxury hotel. Continuing east towards the fashionable district of Kolonaki and the **St. George Lykavittos** (Tel: 729 0711) is a well-equipped hotel pleasantly situated amongst pines, with fine views over the city. Further east is the district of Ilissia where there are several high-rise establishments, but this is not a particularly interesting or convenient area in which to stay.

There are several hotels in the vicinity of Omonia Square, a quarter of an hour's walk north of the Plaka. Some of them are quite seedy and the better ones are to be found on the smarter east side in Eolou Street. The **Athinea** (Tel: 524 3884) is quiet, cheap and a hotel of character while the **Athenée Palace** (Tel: 523 0791) has large, comfortable rooms.

South of the Acropolis, there are quite a few bargain hotels in Koukaki and Kinnosargous, though these areas are not well served by public transport.

Similarly the railway area has a few cheap hotels, but it is remote from the main sights. The hotels in Piraeus aren't up to much either, and you shouldn't bother staying here unless you arrive late at night, or have to leave early in the morning.

SIGHTS

There is no doubt that Athens' main attraction is its wealth of classical monuments. Chief of these is undoubtedly the Acropolis, which is crowned by the Parthenon: probably the most photographed building in the world, and the supreme achievement of classical Greek architecture.

The Acropolis – meaning 'high city' in Greek – is situated on a flat outcrop of rock around 600 ft in height, which can only be reached on foot. This virtually inaccessible location made it an easy site to defend and the Acropolis was a residential centre as long ago as the Neolithic Age. The four main monuments which remain today date from the 5th century BC and were built under the aegis of Pericles as replacements for the buildings which had been sacked by the Persians in 480 BC. **The Parthenon** is the most beautiful and well-known structure, and it certainly lives up to its reputation. It was begun in 447 BC and took 15 years to complete. Its main function was as a treasury, but it also housed a massive statue of the goddess Athena, and served as a memorial to the dead Marathonas. Iktinas, the architect, designed the building without using straight lines. Instead he expertly plotted and executed curves to create an optical illusion of straightness. The temple was originally decorated with a sculpted frieze by Phidias, the finest sculptor of antiquity. The Turks blew some of it up; some has simply corroded away; some sections of the frieze are in the Louvre in Paris; and, as the Greeks never tire of telling us, some sections are now in the British Museum, and are better known as the 'Elgin Marbles' after the Lord who commandeered them in the 19th century. If you fancy an argument that will probably rage as long as your holiday, try suggesting to a Greek that these sculptures remain in Britain – if you dare. The depth of feeling behind the Greeks' conviction that we have robbed them of a vital symbol of their past is quite phenomenal.

The Propylaea is the first building you see on the site. It was an ambitious undertaking, because the steepness of the ground on which it is built necessitated a split-level building. Over to the right is the tiny **Temple of Athena Nike**, dedicated to the memory of the Athenian victories over the Persians. The Turks destroyed the temple to make way for a gun battery, but they left the pieces scattered about and in 1936 it was finally rebuilt correctly. It is a delightful little temple and many people's favourite.

The Erectium originally housed three separate cults but was associated chiefly with the worship of Poseidon, as this was the site where the god allegedly caused salt water to spurt from the rock. Today it is best known for the **Caryatids**, which are sculptured columns in the shape of women. The originals have been badly damaged by the ravages of air pollution and have been replaced by plaster copies. The originals can now be seen at the **Acropolis Museum** on the same site, and entry to the museum is included in the price of your ticket. Apart from the Caryatids there are several other superb sculptures from the site including the few pieces of magnificent friezes of the Parthenon which were not removed by Lord Elgin. The Acropolis site is open Mon to Sat 7.30 a.m. to 7.15 p.m., Sun 8 a.m. to 5.30 p.m. Admission is 500 dr (students 125 dr) and you should hang onto your ticket so that you can visit the Acropolis Museum (open Mon and Wed to Sat 7.30 a.m. to 7.15 p.m., Tue midday to 5.30 p.m., Sun 8 a.m. to 5.30 p.m.). If you only go to one archaeological site in Athens, make sure this is it, but go as early as you can, for by 10 a.m. the place is literally swarming with coachloads of tourists.

Directly below the Acropolis are the reconstructed **Odeon of Herod Atticus**, which is still used for concerts and theatre performances, and, to the left of this, the ruins of the **Theatre of Dionysus**. Entry to the theatre costs 250 dr (students and children 100 dr), except for Sundays when admission is free, and also on the site and included in the admission price are the **Asclepion** and **Stoa of Eumenes** (open Mon to Sat 8 a.m. to 4 p.m., Sun 10 a.m. to 4 p.m.).

The second major site of Athens is the **Agora**. This is situated between Monastiraki Square and the bottom of the Acropolis rock and was the old market place and business centre of Athens. It is mainly rubble now, but the plan of the ancient site at the entrance at the far end of Ifestou Street demonstrates clearly what an impressive city centre it must have been. Two buildings of note remain. The first is the **Temple of Hephaestus**, which actually overlooks the Agora from a low hill nearby. This is the best preserved of all Greek temples and is on a similar scale to the Parthenon but somehow far less impressive. The colonnade building at the end of the Agora is the **Stoa of Attalus** which is a reconstruction of the original stoa, which was a sort of arcade for shops, though mercifully it is filled with museum exhibits rather than the tacky souvenirs which are all too common in nearby shops. The Agora and its museum are open in summer, Mon to Sat 7.30 a.m. to 7.30 p.m., Sun 8 a.m. to 6 p.m.; and in off-season, Mon to Sat 9 a.m. to 3 p.m., Sun 9.30 a.m. to 2.30 p.m. Admission is 300 dr for both.

Also worth a visit is the **Temple of Olympian Zeus** which is situated just below the National Gardens. This was the biggest temple ever built in Greece, though fifteen monumental columns are all that remain today. The site is open Mon to Sat 8.45 a.m. to 3 p.m., Sun 9.30 a.m. to 2.30 p.m. Admission 200 dr (students and children 100 dr). Nearby is **Hadrian's Arch,** which was built in the second century AD to mark the symbolic boundary between the ancient Greek city and its Roman extension.

No visit of Athens' classical antiquities would be complete without a visit to the truly superb **National Archaeological Museum** in Patisson Street. This is the finest collection of antiques in the world and you will no doubt be overwhelmed by the wealth of priceless pieces – including the 'Mask of Agamemnon' from Mycenae and other awesome sculptures and reliefs. However, if you do not arrive early at the museum, you will also be overwhelmed by the crowds of tourists. Admission is 200 dr (students 100 dr, flash-cameras 150 dr) and the museum is open Tue to Sun, 8 a.m. to 7 p.m.

It is worth remembering that Greek culture was also shaped by the Byzantine as well as the Classical period. There are numerous churches which perfectly illustrate the architecture of this period of Turkish occupation and the prime example is the **Church Kaprikaria** on the corner of Eolou and Ermou Streets. To get the full effect of religious Byzantine culture, attend one of the Sunday liturgies here, when you are likely to be hypnotized by the chants and incense into an intensely spiritual state. Some are enchanted by the experience, others incensed at it. There are two good museums containing Byzantine artefacts: the **Benaki**, on the corner of Koumbari and Vassilissis Sophias, houses a wonderfully diverse collection, while the **Byzantine Museum** just up Vassilissis Sophias has an excellent collection of Christian art from the fourth right up until the nineteenth centuries.

Other museums worth visiting are the **National Gallery** (paintings and sculptures); the **Theatre Museum** (costumes and photographs); the **Popular Art Museum**; and the **War Museum**. Full details are on the brochure available from the N.T.O.G. tourist offices at Syntagma and East Airport.

There is more to sightseeing in Athens than the classical monuments and the various museums, however. The changing of the guard on Sunday mornings at the Parliament Building to the east of Syntagma is popular, and the **National Gardens**, which surround the **Parliament** building on two sides, is a lovely spot for a relaxing, leafy stroll. There are also live entertainments here in the evenings. You should take the funicular railway up LYKAVITTOS HILL (60 dr) for a wonderful view of Athens – especially at night. The prices at the café on the summit are as steep as the hill itself.

Most people take a walk through the **Flea Market** which leads from Monastiraki up towards the Plaka. It's a great place to browse and you can get anything here from a flokati rug to a bouzouki. Whenever buying anything exercise your powers of haggling. If you're determined enough you may be surprised at the results. As you ascend the narrow winding streets the tourist shops give way to restaurants, which themselves give way to charming, period houses which have fine views of the Acropolis and the rest of the city. Most of the 'old town' of Athens has now been pedestrianized and its pleasant leafy squares are a good place to escape the noise and fumes of the city traffic.

Good buys in Athens include leather goods, traditional Greek clothes, rugs, handicrafts and gold and silver jewellery. Most people shop in the Plaka and around Monastiraki but there are smarter shops in the Kolonaki district at the foot of Lykavittos Hill.

There are several excursions on offer from Athens, many of which are extremely over-priced: 2000–3000 dr for a half-day's sightseeing tour of the city's sights is a bit steep and some of the excursions further afield are no better. Sightseers should try to see **CORINTH**, **MYCENAE** and **EPIDAVROS**, which can all be visited in a (tiring) day; but if you only make one trip out of the city then that trip should be to the Sanctuary at DELPHI, where the scenery is awe-inspiring and the atmosphere magical. Both excursions will cost around 3000 dr from Athenian travel agents, but you're better off taking the regular buses if you can face the hassle.

As the beaches along the Athenian riviera aren't really all that special it's worth taking a boat trip to one of the Saronic Islands. If you want to see as many islands as possible, by all means take the widely advertised trip to **HYDRA, AEGINA** and **POROS** at another whopping 3000 dr. However, bear in mind that you will spend most of the day on the boat with only about half an hour on each island. It is easy and convenient to arrange your own travel from Piraeus and you will get far more time on the island of your choice. We would recommend Hydra as the best island to see on a day trip and Agia Marina on Aegina as the nearest and best beach.

Finally, at **DAPHNI**, six miles west of Athens, there is a wonderful eleventh-century monastery which possesses what many consider to be the finest mosaics of any church in Greece. The mosaic depicting the *Pantocrator* (Christ Almighty) is considered by some art historians to be the finest in the world. There is also a wine festival which runs from June until September.

RESTAURANTS/NIGHTLIFE

In Athens you can eat reasonably well for less than most European capitals. The restaurants in the Plaka are an obvious tourist trap and beware of being hustled into an establishment which offers 'live music'. You will pay enormously inflated prices for an average meal and mediocre entertainment. As ever the best advice is to seek out where the locals eat and follow suit. In the Plaka, for example, many Athenians choose to frequent **To Fagadiko**, a taverna totally unspoilt by tourism, which offers basic Greek cooking at rock bottom prices. Also popular in the Plaka is the **Eden Vegetarian Restaurant**, situated in a beautiful rooftop garden atop an old Plaka mansion, and whose imaginative vegetarian specialities lure in many a carnivore. **Zafiris**, at Thespidos 4, is the best restaurant for game, and they should have had enough practice at preparing it for the restaurant has been in business since 1918. Another excellent Plaka taverna is the **Xynou** at Angelou Geronta 4. It's quite difficult to find but once you're there the cooking more than makes up for any problems you may have encountered locating the place. If you've only got time for a snack, grab a couple of souvlakis from **Kostas' Souvlaki Shop** in the Platia Lyssikratous. They're ridiculously cheap and totally delicious.

Kostoyannis at Zaimi 37, behind the Archaeological Museum, has an excellent reputation, while **Gerofinikas**, skilfully hidden at Pindarou 10, has a wide range of Greek and Turkish specialities and is widely considered to be one of the best restaurants in town.

If you want to eat fish, then make the short journey to Piraeus where Mikrolimano Harbour has a whole host of tavernas specializing in sea food. Of these, the **Black Goat** at the far end of the waterfront does reasonable crayfish and red mullet, while a better value alternative is the **Vassilena**, on Etolikou 72 which is facing the main harbour and to the right. You get several hors d'oeuvres before soup, chicken and fruit, all washed down with unlimited retsina, and all for an astonishingly low price.

The Kolonaki district has several smart cafés, with **Apotsos** near the university, being a typically trendy brasserie.

By our conservative standards the Athenians are noisy and gregarious, and seem to be perfectly content just to sit in an *ouzerie* all night long, animatedly discussing money, sex or politics, often all at the same time. However, there is also a wide range of night-time entertainment on offer with Athens being particularly well served by cinemas and theatres. The standard motto: 'When in doubt go to the Plaka' doesn't really apply to nightlife any longer, as most of the discos have moved out of the area as a consequence of the government's efforts to gentrify the Plaka. Clubs are now scattered all around the town and we would recommend the following for trendies: the **Ergostasion** at Vouliagmenis Ave 268; for jazz buffs: the **Half-Note** at Michalachopoulou 56; and for live rock: the **Kyttaro Club** at Ipinou and Acharnou Streets. Those looking for more traditional Athenian entertainment should visit one of the **Rebbetika** clubs which specialize in hard bouzouki music. Sotiria Bellou is famous for her deep, gravelly voice and she can be heard from October to May at the **Charama** in the Kaiserani district. **Quasimodo's**, at Tsakalou 13, is a modern club with a red-hot band, and the **Pigi to Rebetikou** at Agg. Glykerias 11 in the Glatsi district is popular with Athenians from all over the city.

The **National Garden** has free music and comedy shows in the summer, and those in search of more high-brow diversions can check out the **Athens Festival** which runs from June until September at the **Odeon of Herod Atticus**, below the Acropolis, and the **Lycabettus Theatre** at the top of Lycabettus Hill. The performances are generally of classical theatre, but occasionally there is classical music, and even, on occasions, rock.

Check the *Athens News, This Week in Athens,* or the *Athenian* for more up-to-date details of nightlife.

South-east and South-west Attica

PIRAEUS AND THE APOLLO COAST

Piraeus has been Athens' port since ancient times, and ferries and hydrofoils to the islands depart from here. To get to Piraeus from central Athens either take the subway from Omonia or Monastiraki (60 dr), or the no.040 bus from Filellinou Street just off Syntagma. Get off at the Public Theatre and head right for the port. The ferry embarkation points vary but there are numerous travel agents along the waterfront who will tell you where to go. Long-distance trains for the Peloponnese leave daily from the station on Akti Kallimassiati.

There is a well laid out Archaeological Museum at 31 Char.

Trikoupi Street (open Mon, Wed to Sat 9 a.m. to 3 p.m.; Sun 10 a.m. to 2 p.m. Admission 50 dr, students 30 dr, free on Sundays), and you can have a pleasant stroll around the harbours of Zea Marina, from where the hydrofoils depart, and Mikrolimano, which is crammed with pleasure vessels of all kinds. The sea-food restaurants lining Mikrolimano have an excellent reputation.

The 50 miles or so of coastline which stretch south-west from Piraeus to Cape Sounion are known as the Apollo coast or Athenian riviera. This is a particularly well developed stretch of coastline and its attractions include picturesque small coves, well appointed beaches, marinas, modern hotel complexes, and several first-class restaurants and nightclubs. The beaches get better (and less polluted) the further you go from Athens along the scenic coastal road, and the main two resorts are **GLYFADA** and **VOULIAGMENI** which offer unparalleled facilities for water sports and yachting.

The first resort south of Piraeus is **PALEO FALIRO**, which is pleasant enough, but bear in mind that the sea is far too polluted this close to Piraeus for swimming. However, this is a good base from which to explore Athens, which is only 5 miles distant.

There are developed beaches at KALAMAKI and ALIMOS, but the premier resort along this particular stretch of the Apollo coast is **GLYFADA** (11 miles from Athens) which, together with its near neighbour **VOULA**, has the largest concentration of hotels along the coast. It is a modern, well-equipped resort with shops, cafés, an 18-hole golf course, and a series of marinas and sandy beaches – though again the water isn't as clean as it could be. Athens is only half an hour on the bus and there is a connection every 20–30 minutes. The beaches here are in two parts: to the north is a series of coarse (i.e. little pebbles) strips divided by rocks, while to the south is the fine, long, privately owned ASTIR BEACH, which will cost you around 200 dr for a day's bask.

There are a number of good quality hotels in Glyfada, with the most prestigious probably being the luxury **Astir** bungalows (Tel: 8946 461) which are situated directly on the comprehensively equipped Astir Beach. The **Emmantina** (Tel: 8932 111) and the **Fenix** (Tel: 8944 863) are both smart and comfortable 'B'-class hotels while those wanting to be right next to the 'action' should opt for the **Riviera** (Tel: 8952 011) or the cheaper **Perla** (Tel: 8944 212) which are both situated adjacent to night clubs. Over at Voula the **Voula Beach** (Tel: 8953 851) is a smart, modern hotel with bathing from a wooden platform just across the road.

Glyfada has a number of excellent restaurants and nightclubs. Opposite the main marina, the **Antonopoulos** and **Psaropoulos** are renowned, if expensive, seafood restaurants, while **Antonis** offers shrimp ragout and wild boar. Far cheaper is the **Kanatakia** which serves pies and grills and wine from the barrel. You can dance at the **B.B.G. Disco** or **Esperides** and there are a host of nightclubs from which to choose, most of which are pretty expensive.

The main problem with Glyfada – apart from the polluted sea – is its close proximity to the extremely noisy Athens East Airport. Planes regularly zoom over your head at all hours and the noise problem isn't helped by Glyfada's situation astride the main coastal road. Hotels in the centre of the resort tend to be worse afflicted than those on the outskirts. Unless you are desperate to be close to the nightlife, it is worth grilling whichever of the twenty or so tour operators who run packages to Glyfada/Voula you have chosen, to ascertain the exact location of your hotel in relation to the airport's main runway. The **Emmantina**, for example, while it is an admirable hotel, also directly overlooks the end of the runway of the airport.

VOULIAGMENI, 15 miles from Athens, is the other big resort along the Apollo coast and if anything it is more exclusive than Glyfada. Together with **KAVOURI**, it forms a sprawl of hotels, restaurants and nightclubs, with there being no real centre to the resort. Buses run to Athens about once every half hour and the journey takes just under an hour.

Vouliagmeni has a natural lake set in beautiful surroundings, with warm, medicinal waters. It also boasts some of the best water-skiing in Greece, possessing its own water-skiing school, situated on the edge of the N.T.O.G.-run enclosed beach. This beach is excellent and less crowded than the one round the promontory at Kavouri, but again you have to pay to get in. Like Glyfada airport noise is once again a problem, though nothing like so bad.

The **Apollon Palace** (Tel: 8951 401) and the **Astir Palace** (Tel:

8960 211) are by far the best hotels in the area, with the former being a sumptuous ten-storey block near the Kavouri beach, well suited for children, while the latter lives up to its palatial name, being gloriously positioned in extensive tropical gardens on a small promontory with beaches at either side. The **Pine Hill** (Tel: 8960 871) is a smaller (and cheaper) hotel pleasantly situated in a quiet country location, with fine views over the bay. Generally, don't expect any bargain-priced accommodation, as Vouliagmeni is one of the most exclusive resorts in Greece.

If you've got the cash you can eat famously in the select restaurants overlooking the country's most elegant marina. Otherwise, you should head for the lake, on whose shores you will find several decent fish tavernas.

There are several more resorts – notably VARKIZA, LAGONISSI and ANAVISSOS – before you reach the main attraction of the Apollo coast, the majestic **Temple of Poseidon** at SOUNION.

SOUNION

Cape Sounion is two hours' drive from Athens and provides a suitably spectacular backdrop for the marvellous **Temple of Poseidon**, which is situated high on a promontory above the coast. This temple was built shortly after the Parthenon, and is as equally deserving of a visit as its more famous cousin in the capital. Countless photos have been taken of the temple at sunset, and this is the best time to view it – when the crowds have all left. The site is open daily 9 a.m. to sunset, and admission is 50 dr, or 30 dr for students (free on Sundays).

Several paths lead down to the sea, which is much cleaner than at the resorts nearer to Piraeus. There are some sandy beaches at the base of the hill on which the temple is situated, but it is more exciting to swim off the rocks directly below the temple.

Sounion – and indeed all the resorts along the Apollo coast – can be reached from Athens by taking the yellow bus from Filellinou Street, at Xerofondas Street, which leaves every hour at twenty-to. However, your chances of getting a seat are much better if you catch the bus at Mavromateon, in the square opposite Areos Park. The fare is 200 dr. It is worth hiring a car if you are going to be travelling along the

Athenian riviera, as public transport is sporadic rather than frequent, and you will have more freedom to visit the places of your choice.

South-west Attica

The coast directly to the west of Piraeus is industrial, unattractive and smelly, although **ELEFSINA**, the ancient sanctuary where the mysteries were enacted, is well worth a visit. The road follows the ancient route to a spot around eight miles west of Athens where the 'mysteries' – an initiation into the secrets of the underworld – were enacted once a year. Though thousands of ancients must have attended these ceremonies (they were held from roughly the eighth century BC until the fourth century AD, when the sanctuary was closed by the Roman Emperor Theodosius), nobody actually knows the secret of the mysteries today.

Though the ruins are quite impressive, there is little left standing above waist height, and you will need to investigate the model of the original layout of the sanctuary which is contained in the museum. The site is open Mon to Sat 9 a.m. to 3.30 p.m., Sun 10 a.m. to 3 p.m. and admission is 50 dr (students 30 dr). To get to Elefsina take the buses nos. 818, 853 and 862 from Platia Eleftherias. Get off at the second stop in Elefsina and continue across the square until you see a blue sign pointing the way.

After Elefsina the gulf is dominated by the dull north coast of Salamis and the giant oil tankers and other commercial vessels moored offshore. It is not until you pass **MEGARA**, over 30 miles from Athens, that there are any decent beaches. The first is at **KINETA**, which is situated on the scenic but dangerous old Corinth road, some 35 miles from Athens. The old road has since been superseded by a brash new dual-carriageway which is faster, but lacks the charisma of the old one. As you drive through Kineta people yell and wave from cafés whose tables virtually spill out into the road, and there are also several lively tavernas and restaurants in the village. Its main attraction for tourists, however, is its long shingle beach which is attractively fringed with pines and is a favourite spot for campers and picnickers. The water hereabouts is surprisingly clear and sparkling and always cool due to the amount of cross-currents off shore. Further along the old road there is a beach at the village-resort of **AGII THEODORI**, before you eventually arrive at the isthmus of Corinth, where Theseus is said to have slain Sinis the pine-bender, who had the nasty habit of bending back two pine trees until they met, whereupon he would tie the arms of some unfortunate traveller to each tree and then let them go, thus causing the victim to meet his death in a particularly gruesome and painful fashion.

Before you reach the bridge over the most famous canal in the world, the **Corinth Canal**, a road branches off towards the spa of **LOUTRAKI**, now a popular tourist resort – especially with the Greeks themselves. Loutraki has a fine shingle beach and is overlooked by the impressive Yerania mountains. Only half a dozen British firms offer packages here, but it makes a great base from which to explore ancient Corinth and the Argolid. The hotels lining the waterfront are all modern and fairly impersonal, but offer satisfactory facilities. The town itself is fairly sleepy but good nightlife is to be found in the outlying hotels and tavernas. A peaceful excursion from here is to the **BAY OF IREON** where there are the remains of the ancient **Sanctuary of Hera**. The ruins don't amount to much but the scenery is magnificent and the beach and the tavernas of the delightful lagoon-like inlet are pleasantly tranquil.

The resorts lining the Halcyonic Gulf to the north-east of Loutraki are well off the beaten tourist track, but they are getting more popular every year. The unpaved road from **SHIROS** to **ALEPOHORI** is a delight and it continues to **PORTO YERMENO**, which has a broad sandy beach and occupies the site of ancient **AIGOSTHENA**, whose fortifications are a superb example of Greek defensive architecture dating back to around 300 BC. These resorts are nicely undercrowded at present, but are sure to become more popular in the future.

East Coast and Inland Attica

The pine-fringed resorts and ports of east Attica are within easy day-tripping distance of Athens. They are smaller and less trendy than those on the Apollo (west) coast, but generally not so crowded. Inland there are pleasant villages where you can sample the 'real'

Attica; and there are enough archaeological sites – notably at Marathon – to keep historians well occupied. The area is quite mountainous and there is even a skiing resort on Mt Parnes, which is higher than Ben Nevis and only 25 miles north of the capital.

From Cape Sounion, where the west coast meets the east, the scenic coastal road sweeps down to **LAVRIO**, which was famed for its silver mines in antiquity, but is now a rather ugly port which serves as the main departure point for boats to the island of **KEA**. Nearby are the remains of ancient **Thorikos**, whose uniquely elliptical theatre is in an excellent state of preservation.

The district to the north of Lavrio and inland is known as **MESSOGIA** and its villages, particularly MARKOPOULU, are famed for their fine retsina wines. Though something of an acquired taste, an ice-cold bottle of retsina makes a superb accompaniment to the good, country cooking which is to be found in the many tavernas in this region. One of the villages, PEANIA, has the added attraction of the **Koutouki Cave**, whose artificial lighting is considered among the best in the world. The main section of the cave has several impressive stalactites and stalagmites and is only 14 miles east of Athens (open on weekdays 10 a.m. to 5.30 p.m.; holidays 9 a.m. to 5.30 p.m., tel: 664 2910).

On the coast to the east of Messogia, a coastal road begins at PORTO RAFTI, and extends up as far as the fine beach at SCHINIAS. Porto Rafti has an N.T.O.G.-run beach and several tavernas, while just round the coast at Vravona are the ancient ruins of BRAURON. On the site is a large, partly reconstructed **Temple of Artemis**, while the **Chapel of Agia Giorgiou** next to this contains some splendid, but fading frescoes dating from the fifteenth century (site open Mon, Wed to Sat 9 a.m. to 3 p.m.; Sun 9 a.m. to 2 p.m. Admission 50 dr, students 30 dr). On the road leading to the other side of the hill is the **Brauron Museum** which contains statues, pottery and unique wooden vases (open Mon, Wed to Sat 9 a.m. to 3.30 p.m.; Sun 10 a.m. to 3 p.m.).

Continuing north along the coastal road past LOUTSA (not a bad beach here), you come to the port of **RAFINA**. This is Attica's second most important ferry port and boats leave here for the Cyclades and Euboea. It is worth pointing out that fares to popular islands such as Mykonos and Andros are 100–300 dr cheaper than from Piraeus, and that journeys are in some cases only half as long. The number of the agent in Rafina is (0294) 286 02. There are several daily buses to Athens (Mavromateon Street), and the journey lasts 1½ hours.

From Rafina to the Bay of Marathon there are several beach resorts, of which the first is **MATI**. This is a huddle of modern houses, only 18 miles east of Athens, and an ideal spot to spend a few relaxing hours, or even days. The hotels **Costa Rica** (Tel: 71103) and **Mati** (Tel: 71511) are superior class 'A' establishments, and Athens is within easy reach for sights and nightlife.

Just north of Mati is the attractive village of **NEA MAKRI** which gives the impression of remoteness, even though it is only just over 20 miles from Athens and with buses every half hour. The village is handy for **MARATHON**, the area's most famous sight, and good hotels include the **Marathon Beach** (Tel: 91292) which is attractively laid out, and has picturesque views, with a fine beach nearby; and the **Nireus** (Tel: 91214), which is an older, cheaper hotel, 7 minutes from the village and again, opposite a good beach.

MARATHON

In 490 BC the Greeks won a famous victory when they ambushed the numerically superior Persian army at Marathon, and they promptly dispatched one Phidippedes to run the 26 miles back to Athens to convey the good news. Now 26 miles is a long way to run, particularly in hot sunshine, right after you've fought in a tough battle. However, Phidippedes made it – just – delivering his message with literally the last breath left in his body; for after he had related his glad tidings, he collapsed and expired. The 'Marathon' race, which was established to commemorate Phidippedes' worthy feat (feet?), is now more popular than ever, though running the original route in the blazing Attic sun is emphatically not recommended! However, you will have to be reasonably fit to visit all the sights at Marathon as they are scattered around the plain with little public transport connecting them.

Assuming you have taken one of the numerous buses from Athens (Mavromateon Street) you will be let off about two miles from the **Archaeological Museum**, which contains a large variety of artefacts from the Cave of Pan and nearby grounds, though these are poorly labelled and there is no guide (open Mon, Wed to Sat 9 a.m. to 3.30 p.m. Admission 50 dr, students 30 dr). A few hundred yards away is the **Tomb of the Plateans** which is the ancient burial mound built as a tribute to the Athenians' only allies at the Battle of Marathon. Two miles from the museum is the larger burial mound commemorating the 192 Athenians who fell during the battle (open Mon, Wed to Fri 9 a.m. to 6 p.m.; Sun and Tue 9 a.m. to 3 p.m. Admission 50 dr, students 30 dr).

More impressive than these mounds is the beautiful **Lake Marathon,** five miles to the west. With its massive marble dam, the lake was Athens' only supply of water until World War II. Also impressive are the several good beaches in this area, notably the long sandy one at SCHINIAS. There is a windsurfing centre at the **Galatzi Hotel,** but avoid the beach at weekends if all you want is a quiet dip.

After the beaches in the Marathon vicinity, the east coast becomes a lot quieter. There are interesting remains at RAMNOUS, just north of Schinias, and AMFIARAION, some twenty miles to the north-west, but other than this there is little of interest.

Further inland is **Mt Parnes,** at 5000 ft easily the highest mountain in Attica. At DEKELIA in the foothills is a lovely park containing the remains of Greece's royalty – including the parents of the Duke of Edinburgh. A tortuous, hairpinned road then slowly ascends the mountain before terminating at the military installations just beneath the summit. A more pleasant way of getting up the mountain is by the funicular railway which rises to an altitude of 3000 ft in four minutes. Where the railway ends there is a luxury hotel, the **Mont Parnes** (Tel: 246 9111/5), which has a casino, and spectacular views over Athens (when the smog lifts). At the fringe of the fir forest are several good, cheap tavernas.

To the south-west of the mountain lies Athens' summer hill-resort of KIFISSIA. The air here is cool and fresh, and every summer thousands of Athenians come here to escape the oppressive heat and noise of the capital. The resort is quite upmarket and there are several expensive restaurants and luxury hotels. Near here is MAROUSSI, which has some interesting pottery works and a large riding school which offers pony-trekking expeditions (Tel: 681 2506/682 6128).

EVIA (EUBOEA)

Separated from the mainland by an earthquake, Evia (also known by its ancient name, Euboea), is an island still undiscovered by the vacationing hordes. Mountains form the one hundred-mile backbone of the island and make for good hiking. These same peaks, dropping precipitously on the east coast, provide shelter for the green plains on the west side of the island. Picturesque mountains looking down on the plains, fertile valleys cradling the towns and secluded beaches hidden by the hills are the hallmarks of Evia.

You can still watch the Greeks whose way of life has changed little over the years. Fishermen rise in the early hours of the morning to put to sea and come back to unload their catch in the afternoon; tradesmen haggle over the price of their goods at country fairs; people from all over Greece visit the springs to heal their ills with the medicinal waters. A holiday in Evia offers you the chance to share the slow pace of life with the Greeks and to leave behind the urgencies of life.

Evia's strategic location on the Evripos Straits made it the prey of growing empires and, through the centuries, it has been conquered and reconquered by nearly everyone. There were seven city-states on the island in Ancient Greece, the two most powerful being Eretria and Chalkis, which for a time had overseas colonies of their own. These two cities, only twelve miles apart, were fierce rivals and continually fought to dominate the fertile Lelantine Plain, on which they are both situated. Only vestiges of these rich commercial centres remain. Evia has since been sacked by the Persians, the Attic League, the Turks, the Franks and the Venetians. Eretria paid the price of helping out in the Ionic revolt against Persia, who in retaliation razed the cities to the ground and enslaved the people in 490 BC.

Evidence of the warlike traditions can be seen in the castles from the Middle Ages, pinnacled on hilltops, dotting the countryside. The Venetians controlling the vital ports wrestled control of the interior from the Franks in the Middle Ages. They renamed the island Pontenegro, after the 'black bridge' joining Chalkis (now Halkida) to the mainland. The trade routes between Macedonia, Thessaly and Athens no longer hold such importance and Halkida is the island's main centre. Ancient Eretria lies mostly buried, and today the town's beaches play host to the tourists.

Practical Details

COMMUNICATIONS

Access to Evia is relatively easy. Buses leaving about every half hour and trains running ten times a day from Athens take 1½ hours to reach Halkida. Alternatively, the island is readily accessible by ferry from six ports. Karistos, Marmari and Agia Marina, all on the south of the island, are connected with Rafina on the mainland. Likewise, Edipsos from Arkitsa, Eretria from Oroposto, and Agiokambos from Glifa. The ferries operate on a regular schedule and all mainland ports are connected by bus with Athens, where most international flights arrive and depart.

Getting around Evia is straightforward but requires some patience because buses heading for the extremities of the island leave only once a day. They are cheap and the routes span the island, stopping at most towns along the way.

Travellers moving on to the Aegean islands of Skiathos and Skyros can pick up a ferry from Kimi on the east coast of Evia. Kimi can be reached by several buses from Eretria and Chalkis ten times a day. You would not, however, want to leave your connections to the last minute. The bus stops in the town of Kimi for a while, before descending the last two miles to the harbour. There are fewer buses on Sundays and the ferries to Skiathos run only four or five times a week.

The Tourist Police office in Halkida is at No. 32, Elefteriou Venizelou. The police office is open all the time, but the information office is only open Mon to Fri, 9 a.m. to 2 p.m. (Tel: 0221-24662). If you arrive at the train station, you can find the tourist police by crossing the bridge and taking your first left. Eleftheriou Venizelou is about five hundred yards up the street on your right. The office in Edipsos, summer months only, is at No.3, Okeanidon (Tel: 0226-22 456).

CLIMATE

The summers are sunny and hot (25–35°C), typical of the east coast of Greece. Bring a hat to cover the back of your neck and avoid

Athens and Attica

looking like a lobster by having a long-sleeved shirt for the days when the sun is a bit too much. Evenings can be cool, even in June and September, so bring along a sweater.

Winter daytime temperatures average around 10–15°C, and warm clothing for the nights is essential.

CULINARY SPECIALITIES

The Evians take great pride in their history as an island people and, accordingly, cook up enticing dishes of seafood. Try the prawns or *garides*, boiled and served in a sauce of oil and lemon juice. Watch the fishermen bringing in their catch and hanging the octopus and squid to dry. If you are still tempted, order the *oktopodi* and *soupia*, stewed in a Greek sauce. Enjoy your fish with a salad and a bottle of retsina.

WHERE TO GO FOR WHAT

Evia offers the traveller a window into the Greek way of life, unhurried and unchanging. The island's tourism centres around the coastal resorts, but there is much more that shouldn't be missed. At the same time, it is a good idea for novice travellers to plan out their excursions before leaving the main towns. What this also means is that you need not go far to find peace and tranquillity.

Travellers of any age may want to begin with a package holiday in ERETRIA or GREGOLIMANO. Eretria is a resort town on the west coast of the island. Hotels and bungalows are plentiful and there is organized tennis, bathing and sailing. The restaurants will keep you smiling with all varieties of seafood. The town itself has ancient archaeological sites with tales to tell to capture your imagination. Alternatively, Club Med offers package holidays in the small town of Gregolimano. Most water sports are available with instructors to help. Of special interest to families is the programme for children, which teaches them circus skills. At the end of each week, they can join in a small performance to show off their new-found abilities. The atmosphere is very relaxed and there is plenty to do, but nothing is forced upon you. Unfortunately the Club Med package is not being promoted for 1990.

Nature lovers will be at home on Evia. Much of the island is green and wooded, with wildlife roaming free. You can climb up to the castles perched high on the hilltops, many of which command exhilarating views of the Aegean reaches. You will not want to miss the enchanting scenery on the northern road, winding through the fertile valley between Psahna and Prokopi. Equally satisfying is a drive through the Dirfys Mountains to Kimi on the east coast, looking out from the 750-foot cliffs, over the glistening waters on which the Greeks have been sailing for thousands of years. Regardless of your location on the island, day trips hiking up into the hills with a daypack are both possible and enjoyable.

Climbing holidays are another popular way to explore the island. There are excellent trips, scaling peaks in the Dirfys Mountains. Further south, you can trek up to the ancient 'Dragon Houses' near Stira or Karistos. Even if you are hiking, it is worthwhile to get in touch with the Hellenic Alpine Club at No. 7 Karagiorgi in Athens (Tel: 3234 555), who can provide you with information about routes and climbing conditions.

HALKIDA – THE MAIN TOWN

Halkida, like all good Greek towns, has several English names including Chalkis, Halkis and Khalkis. Once a powerful city-state, it is now the capital of Evia and is linked to the mainland by a bridge. Any charm it had in days gone by has been lost to the heavy industry. It is still the largest town on the island and, like Rome, all roads will lead you to Halkida.

The Tourist Police office (9 a.m. to 2 p.m.) is at No. 32 Eleftheriou Venizelou (Tel: 0221-24662), where you can pick up a map of the island and Halkida and can plan your excursions. A few doors down is the OTE (6 a.m. to midnight). To find the bus station, coming out of the Tourist Police office, turn right, walk up the street, take your first right, and then your first left. It is only a few hundred yards. The buses connect with most parts of the island.

Sights that might be of interest are in the **KASTRO**, the old Turkish quarter with an aqueduct, fortress, a mosque and a Gothic cathedral. You can kill a few hours before the bus leaves, standing outside the **Archaeological Museum** across the street from the police office, which seems to be semi-permanently closed. The water channel in the Evripos Straits has such strange currents that the water whirls and can flow at seven knots in either direction. The illustrious Aristotle, frustrated and bewildered by this, threw himself into the river fully clothed.

Even should you decide not to swim in the Evripos, you might wish to try the seafood at the **O Zoes** or at any of the other restaurants along the waterfront. The medium-priced **Hilda** (Tel: 28-111/9). **John's** (Tel: 24-996) and the **Paliria** (Tel: 28-001/7) are all air-conditioned, reasonably clean and comfortable. For something a little less expensive, try the **Iris Hotel**, doubles 750 dr.

EXCURSIONS

Halkida is the most convenient place from which to organize excursions to any part of the island. They vary in the amount of effort required, from a scenic drive through the lush valleys near **PROKOPI** (it's a must!), to the blood, sweat and tears of a day's hike up **Mt Dirfys** (5725 ft), the highest mountain on the island. If you are content just to look up at the mountains, you might instead explore more of the beaches at **Nea Artaki**, **Politika**, or **Malakonda Beach**.

Take a bus or drive from Halkida along the north road winding to the top of the island. You will pass through **PSAHNA**, the gateway to the hills of the North. You may then detour to see the Byzantine church of the Theotokou in **POLITIKI**, but you won't want to miss the next leg of the ride. The road peaks at 2000 ft, providing a panoramic view of the countryside down to the Evripos. You then wind your way down to Prokopi, past ravines, wooded with pines and firs. Visit the **Church of Agios Ioannis Rossos** that attracts many Greek pilgrims. Explore the countryside or else surrender yourself to the health centre for a massage. Buses run in both directions, once a day.

THE BEACH RESORTS

Tour operators offer several holiday packages to Gregolimano and to Eretria.

Club Med plays host to the resort at **GREGOLIMANO** on the north coast. All activities are prepaid from the moment you step off the plane and you need not worry about a thing. Hostesses are there to meet you at the airport and to take you to the luxurious Gregolimano Village, reserved exclusively for Club Med guests. This is the best rest and relaxation package on the island, but is not available for 1990.

All meals are taken care of, leaving you to choose between the seafood, Greek food, or Western food as your palate desires. Sip on a long, cool drink and watch the waves roll in and the world go by.

You are quite free to join in on any of the sporting activities, ranging from golf and tennis to sailing and scuba-diving. Qualified instructors are always there to offer hints when you want them. The fun at night carries on from the day and the dancing is in a relaxed atmosphere.

This Club Med caters for families as well as for singles. Children over four years can safely learn circus skills like juggling and the swinging trapeze from trained professionals. At the end of the week, everyone has the chance to participate in a small show.

ERETRIA, once the dominant city-state of Evia, is now a resort town for Greek and foreign tourists. It lies on the edge of the Lelantine plain, guarding the Evripos Straits. Buses from Halkida take only thirty minutes and run all day. If you are coming from the mainland, you can take a ferry direct from Onoposto and miss out Halkida. Tours operate here throughout the summer and there are several good hotels to choose from. Eretria is an ideal place for resting weary bones. The beaches are a mixture of sand and shingles, the water is a deep blue, and if you are feeling energetic, there are tennis courts, but no ball boys, and sometimes no nets.

The **Chryssi Akti** is a large, clean medium-priced hotel. For something smaller, try the **Perigiali Eretrias**. Alternatively, you might want to consider taking a small bungalow further along at the

MALAKONTA BEACH resort or at the **Xenia** hotel on the island. For independent travellers on the cheap, there are rooms for rent in the town, starting at about 800 dr.

The nightlife here is not highly rated. There are at present only a few foreign tour operators in Evia and anyone seeking lively dancing will be limited to the discos in the hotels. On the other hand, the quiet evenings are much cooler than the day and it is a good time to explore the town and to watch the people. For an excellent Greek meal, seafood in particular, visit the **O Tsolias** fish tavern. It is not cheap, but it carries quite a reputation and it is worth it.

The archaeological sites of Eretria are worth a morning. Coming from the beach, you can cross the **Agora**, the marketplace of Ancient Eretria, and arrive at the **Temple of Daphnephoros Apollo**, an impressive monument. Turn left at the square and two blocks further on is the **Archaeological Museum**, noted for its bronze and pottery from the temple of Apollo. Past the museum is the impressive masonry of the **West Gate**, and up the hill are the remains of the ancient **Theatre**. A large square opening into the ground was originally used for the *Deus ex machina*. Just as the play appeared to be coming to an impossible, disastrous conclusion, a god, hence *deus*, would rise up the steps from the passage below and resolve all the conflicts. If you are still feeling energetic, a twenty-minute climb will take you up to the Acropolis on the top of the hill. You will see the Lelantine plain, the town and the shoreline, and on a clear day, you can see Attica on the mainland.

EXCURSIONS

When you feel sufficiently bronzed by the Eretrian sun, consider an excursion to KIMI on the windswept shores of the Aegean. En route, you will traverse the island and see a cross-section of everything it has to offer. A bus running every hour or two will drive south along the coast for twenty-five miles, passing through the quiet Greek village of ANO VATHIA with its Byzantine church and monastery, and skirting ALIVERI, where the water from the island's hydro-electric plant empties into the Notios Evoiros gulf. The road branches at LEPOURA and a turn to the left leaves the coast behind and leads into the green hill country. Climbing up to 1700 ft and winding through the hills, the Frankish towers stare down at you from either side. Peering out over the sea from a height of 750 ft, Kimi is the logical place to stop. The traditional architecture of white-stoned houses, the **amphitheatre** covered with olive vines and the serene surroundings contribute to the locals' simple way of life, and they like it that way. Spend a night at the **Hotel Krinon** or at the **Kimi Hotel** and enjoy the evening air with the townspeople, strolling around the cathedral in the plaza. Visit the **Folkloric Museum** of modern history, open (10 a.m. to 1 p.m., 6 p.m. to 9 p.m.) daily, or take a twenty-minute walk up to **HONEFTIKA** for the medicinal springs and the café. For the hardier sorts, a goatsherd track climbs up to the summit of Mt. Orari to **Cape Kalami** where the view is magnificent. Near Kimi is **ANO POTAMIA**, the remains of an ancient city and a fifteenth-century weather-beaten fortress.

The port of PARALIA KIMI, 4 km down the slope, is connected by bus and has daily ferries out to Skyros, as well as some connections with Skopolos, Ionnysos and Skiathos.

Northern Evia

PEFKI. Secluded spots for the independent traveller, where you can lie undisturbed, are in practice difficult to find. This is why we recommend the north coast of Evia. Not surprisingly, most open stretches of sand do not centre around major towns, which is why they are secluded. A good bet is to take the daily bus north from Halkida and get off at Pefki on the north shore, which is heavily touristed. Book a room at the medium-priced **Amaryllis, Galini** or **Myrtia** or at one of the small pensions. Take a daypack, including a couple of litres of water, and walk westward along the shore for a kilometre or two. The main road is diverted away from the coastline here, and your only company will be the cry of the gulls. There is no problem sleeping on the beach here if you want to avoid the town altogether.

If, in a few years' time, these empty beaches become full with readers of *Holiday Greece*, you could get off the bus in **OREI**, an ancient town separated into two halves by a Frankish fort. Walking east along the shore will give you the same peace of mind as the shores west of Pefki. The **Evia** hotel in Orei is quite reasonably priced.

Getting to Pefki and Orei can be a delight to your eyes. The daily bus from Halkida leaves around midday crossing mountain passes and the wooded ravines of the interior. If you are on the mainland, you can ferry across to AGIOKAMBOS from GLIFA and then it's only a short bus ride.

EXCURSIONS

When you have had your fill of sun worship and decide to move on, you might see the beautiful woods of GIALTA and LIHADA or stop at the Land's End village of AGIOS GEORGIOS. The damp cave near **Profitis Elias** is well worth the visit for its spectacular stalactites.

EDIPSOS is one of the best-known Greek holiday resorts, recommended by Aristotle, who no doubt preferred it to the Evripos Straits. Edipsos and nearby **LOUTRA EDIPSOU** attract masses of Greeks seeking a remedy for their rheumatism and arthritis at the ancient spas, once frequented by Sulla. If this appeals to you, there are at least eighty hotels to choose from in Edipsos.

From Edipsos, there are several alternatives. You can ride the steamer down to Halkida, ferry across to ARKITSA on the mainland, or take a bus down to the seaside town at LIMNI, where artists come seeking inspiration. The **Avra**, **Limni** and **Plaza** are all reputable hotels. Forty minutes up the road, the frescoes of the monastery at ROVIES are painted with consummate skill. The stretch of beach between Limni and ANGALI is empty and you can have it all to yourself.

Limni is accessible by bus from Halkida, which drives north to PROKOPI, turns west twelve miles after MANTOUDI, crosses a precipitous valley and passes through AGIA ANA and KEHRIES, two towns with a strong sense of tradition which fill for the country fairs.

Southern Evia

KARISTOS is a pleasant fishing town resort, lying on a broad bay where life moves at a snail's pace. You can travel to Karistos by daily ferry across the **KOLPOS PETALION** from Rafina or else take a bus from Halkida (2 hours). The banks do business Mon to Fri, 8 a.m. to 2 p.m., and the OTE is open seven days a week, 8 a.m. to 3 p.m. For comfortable accommodation, try the **Apollon Resort**, a medium-priced hotel with a view looking out over the bay. The **Karystion** and the **Plaza** are spartan, but quite adequate, and for budget travellers, the **Louloudi** is clean and the management are friendly. The **Melissa** restaurant on Theochari Kotsika is popular with the local fishermen, and who knows better? The **Peroulakis** restaurant down the road also offers good value for money.

Make up for the lack of nightlife with a walk along the sandy beach of Psili Amnos at sunrise. The air is tranquil and the light shimmers off the wet sand. The town is dead quiet. The fishermen have already begun their day and are out at sea. Follow the old track leading to the **Castel Rosso**. Take the path up to the Venetian fort, named after the red (rosso) stone in the towers. In the centre of town, you can visit the spacious galleries of the Agia Triado grotto.

EXCURSIONS

The paths and trails in the forests around Karistos are worth exploring. The ascent of **Mt. Orkh** near St Elias will appeal to climbers and ramblers. A goatsherd path winds up the mountain to the **Dragon Houses**, originally built as shelters for the quarrymen. You can spend the night there if you pick up the key from the city hall, although superstitious locals might advise you against it. Another good hiking area is around **STIRA**, a pleasant inland town. Visit the site of the ancient citadel. A half-hour walk past the ancient quarries brings you to more Dragon Houses and the Frankish castle of **Larmena** on the hill of Hagios Niklaos. The lookout here provides an excellent view of the surrounding countryside.

A daily bus to Stira comes from Karistos via MARMARI, an unexciting resort town. The nearby coastal town of NEA STIRA has a fine beach and reputable hotels including the **Aktion** and the **Evoikon**. If you prefer a place all to yourself, get a bungalow at the VENUS BEACH. Further north is one of the few Aegean resorts, situated at ALMIROPOTAMOS, with prehistoric fossils embedded in the rocks that overlook the beach.

Central Greece

This area has some very good scenery, of interest to the Naturalist, but its main attractions are the sights, the best of which is **DELPHI**, ideal for the sightseer. Few people actually base their holiday in the area and most simply visit it on a whistle stop coach tour. Nonetheless there are some small resorts and these are usually fairly empty of Brits, but sadly, for the recluse at least, they are jammed full of Greeks on holiday. The sights are remarkable at any time of year, but the dedicated sightseer would be well advised to come outside the peak season, when the weather will be cooler and the crowds smaller.

Practical Details

As mentioned above most people come to Central Greece on a large tourist coach, or in their own transport, for there are good roads all over the area. There are, however, flights from Athens to Ioannia, Kastoria and Kozani for those who like to travel quickly. The independent traveller is more likely to make use of the good bus network, or the rather more limited train service.

In what follows, the region is divided up into five main areas: Lamia, Delphi, Meteora, Volos and Olympia.

LAMIA
Lamia, on the south-east coast, is a lively, bustling town. Most people do not choose to come here but arrive as a consequence of the bus and train connections. There are good beaches nearby at RAHES and GLIFA. Just down the east coast is THERMOPYLAE. As you may dimly recall from your school days, when the Persians invaded Greece in 480 BC they were delayed here until a Greek traitor led them along a secret pass. This was controlled by Leonidas and 1000 Spartans, who all died in a heroic manner trying to stop the enemy getting through. Further down the coast is the pleasant spa town of KARENA VOURLA.

DELPHI

South of Lamia is Delphi. Even if you are the world's most indifferent sightseer drag yourself out of your stupor and come here. With good scenery, lots of ruins and an excellent museum this is the most wonderful archaeological sight in Greece.

Delphi was a sacred site from 1500 BC. Originally, probably because it was in an earthquake area, it was dedicated to Ge, mother earth, and Poseidon, the earth shaker. Ge's son, Python (yes, he was a snake) lived in a cave nearby and guarded the oracle. The god Apollo then arrived and killed him. To celebrate this, and to appease the locals, the Pythonian games, a kind of Olympics, were established. Also, since Apollo had travelled from Crete in the shape of a dolphin (*Delphoi* in Greek), the name of the oracle was changed from Pythos to Delphi. According to some myths Apollo had to purge himself in the River Pineas, in the valley of Tempe, and returned from there with a bay tree, the leaves of which were later used by the oracles to induce their trance. This is the traditional explanation for Delphi but it does not explain its popularity or what it did.

Even today, 3000 years after the oracle, the newspapers' horoscopes show people's interest in predictions of the future; to the ancient Greeks prophecies were even more important because they were regarded as the way in which the gods could communicate their knowledge. Whether the oracle was miraculous or not, people believed in it. Pilgrims would arrive, undergo a ritual spiritual and physical cleansing, sacrifice an animal, perhaps a goat, and then ask their question. The oracle herself was usually a simple village woman over 50, who would sit unseen in the temple, and inhaling drugs from an adyton, or tripod, cry out in strange words. Conveniently for them, only the priests could 'interpret' her strange chants. The 'success' of the oracle therefore depended on the knowledge of current events by the priests. They were well informed not only by the visitors who came to Delphi to consult the oracle but those who came because it was the centre of a kind of Greek United Nations, the Amphictyonic League. In addition they had their own paid informers in the various Greek cities. Prudently the predictions were usually vague and they were notoriously misleading. The most famous confusing prophecy was when King Croesus asked if he should go to war against Cyprus and the oracle replied that if he did, a great empire would be destroyed. Hearing only what he wanted to hear he assumed that this meant Cyprus; in fact the exact opposite was the result and he was defeated.

The other well known prediction was that Oedipus was told that he would murder his father and marry his mother. On his return from the oracle he killed a man who he later discovered was his father and then married a woman who, he later discovered, was his mother.

By the 8th century BC the oracle had become very popular and by the 6th century it was famous throughout the known world. So highly regarded was it that anyone who publicly questioned its veracity was liable to the death sentence. The richness of the ruins indicate the huge amounts of wealth which came to Delphi as the various states competed to give glory to the gods and themselves. Later the oracle's power diminished. Various battles for the control of this rich and enviable prize took place, known as the Sacred Wars. In the 5th century BC the oracle, more out of a sense of self-preservation than divine revelation, recommended to the Athenians that they should flee from the invading Persians rather than defend themselves. As a result of this decision the impartiality and reliability of the oracle became somewhat doubtful. It still remained very popular, however, but it was consulted over domestic matters rather than affairs of state. Pilgrims still came and perhaps the most famous was Nero. Annoyed by the oracle's correct accusation that he had killed his mother, he added to his list of crimes by stealing many of the very costly statues on the site. The oracle was finally ended by the Christian Emperors in the 4th century AD. Delphi was then left alone until 1892 when a French archaeological team arrived, moved a small number of people to what is now the site of modern Delphi, and began excavating. Go and look at the results!

Before exploring the site itself try to pick up the helpful Tourist Board leaflet on it, which has a very good map. The setting, with Mt. Parnassos on one side and a 2000 ft drop along the Pleastos Ravine on the other, is very dramatic, something like a large natural amphitheatre.

As you enter the site you come to the **Castalian Spring,** supposedly the site of Python's cave. Here a ritual purification, physical and mental, took place before the visitor passed in to Delphi. You then come to the Temple of Athens, more commonly called **Marmaria,** or marble quarry, because for years the locals took the stones from here to use in their own buildings. West from here is the Roman **gymnasium,** where you can still see two tracks and a plunge bath used after training. Nearer is the **Tholos,** a 4th century BC rotunda, which apart from having excellent views is also probably one of the most photographed ruins in Greece.

You then come to the **Sanctuary of Apollo** and the **Agora** where you can see the shops which would have sold religious offerings. Around this area you begin to notice the bases of the many statues which once filled the site. There is nothing new about one-upmanship, and each state would try to position its offerings to the gods in the most annoying places for their enemies. Thus the Arcadian monument, celebrating victory over the Spartans, is opposite the Spartan monument (with 37 statues) which recalls the defeat of the Athenians, whose monument, built to celebrate a previous victory over the Spartans, contains only 16 statues.

On the left is the **Siphnian Treasury,** which because there were large gold mines on Siphnos, was renowned for its heavy and ornate golden decorations. Next to this is the **Treasury of the Athenians.** The walls are covered with commemorative inscriptions recording famous Athenian visitors, Athenian representatives to the Pythonian Games and even a hymn to Apollo, complete with words and music. From these inscriptions the archaeologists were able to rebuild much of the temple, like a huge jigsaw, in 1905. There follows the **Bouleuterion,** the local town hall, and the **Threshing Floor,** where every seven years a play commemorating Apollo's killing of Python took place. Then there is the **Polygonal Wall,** inscribed with the name of freed slaves, Delphi being one of the few places in all Greece where slaves could be declared free men. The large rock with a crack about halfway along is traditionally where the Sibyl used to proclaim her prophecies.

You then reach the **Temple of Apollo.** On the terrace there once stood the monuments erected by Gelon, a tyrant of Syracuse, of four golden tripods each weighing over 1500 lb. Slightly less impressive are the pillars which the archaeologists erected to give some visual focus, even though they come from elsewhere on the site, and a large altar given by the island of Chios. Inside, the walls, once covered in marble and plaster, were inscribed with well known philosophical sayings which remain as true today as they were then, 'Know thyself'; 'nothing in excess'. The cave or the cleft of rock where the oracle inhaled the special fumes has disappeared, presumably as a result of earthquakes, though some have suggested that it never existed and was all a massive confidence trick by the priests.

Above the temple lies the **theatre**, built with 35 tiers of seats for about 5000 people. A fairly stiff walk then takes you to the best preserved **stadium** in Greece, well worth the energy it takes to reach. Also on the site is a very good **archaeological museum** which houses many of the findings of the site. The most famous exhibits are the **Frieze of the Sifnian temple** and the **charioteer** sculpture. It does not matter whether you visit the museum before or after you see the ruins, but make sure you visit it. The site is open 8.30 a.m. to 7 p.m., Sun 10 a.m. to 4.30 p.m. The museum is closed on Tuesday.

The modern town of Delphi is totally based around the tourist and is really of fairly limited interest to someone who is not a sightseer. Over 10 tour operators offer holidays here, however, and there are a number of suitable hotels such as the **Athina**, the **Flivos**, the **Aiolos** and the **Sybilla**. For those travelling on a budget there is a **Youth Hostel** at 39 Apollonos and there are two campsites on the Itea road, the **Apollon** and the **Delphi**.

The Tourist Police are very helpful in providing information and are situated on 45 Apollonos, open 8 a.m. to 10 p.m. (Tel: 82220). Below on Pavlou Street is the Post Office, open 7.30 a.m. to 2.30 p.m., the bank, open Mon to Fri 8 a.m. to 2 p.m., and the international telephone office, the OTE, where you can phone home between 7.30 a.m. to 9 p.m.

The large number of visitors has occasioned a surprisingly active nightlife. The two best Greek restaurants are the **Pan**, up a narrow alley near the Hotel Sybilla and the **Stamaks**, near the Hotel Zeus. Cheaper are the **Vakhos**, with excellent views, and the **Macedonia Grill**. There are even several discos, of which the most lively seem to be **Delphi by Night** and the **Zodiaque**.

The most popular excursions are to the beaches nearby at ITEA and KIRA. Further west is the lively resort of NEFPAKTOS, originally called Lepanto, and the site of a famous battle of that name where the Turkish fleet was defeated by the Christians. Also worth a day trip is

Ossios Loukas, a monastery with excellent frescoes and regarded as one of the best Byzantine-style buildings in Greece. Take a torch and explore the mosaics in the crypt as well as those in the main church. Incidentally the St Luke to whom the monastery is dedicated is not the Luke of the gospels, but a local saint, St Luke de Stiris who was a hermit with a great following. East of Delphi is LIVADIA. A pleasant town on a river famous for the **Oracle of Trophonios.** This worked on a slightly different principle from the Oracle at Delphi. The pilgrim drank first of the River of Forgetfulness to clear his mind, and then of the River of Remembrance so that he would remember what was to follow. He would then be placed in a dark hole. After some time, that day or even a few days later, he would reappear and the priest would explain the significance of whatever had happened to him. Near the well-positioned Xenia Café you can see the two caves which were once filled with votive offerings to the oracle. The town was taken by the Turks and, though there is now little left to suggest it, became the second city of Greece. The local Turkish governor used to come to the largest of these caves and sit inside smoking his pipe. Also worth visiting from Delphi is the scenically positioned village of ARACHORA. Quieter and less crammed with tourists, this makes a comfortable break away from the crowds and can indeed, with two good hotels, the **Apollon** and the **Parnassos,** make a good base. There are also a few pleasant restaurants such as the **Lycabethus** and the **Kastro.**

METEORA

Back in the centre of the mainland is Meteora. The name, in English, literally means 'rocks in the air' and refers to the monasteries perched upon the mountains for which the area is famous. Hermits lived in caves on the hills as early as the 9th century, but it was only in the 14th century that proper monasteries were established. This happened as a result of St Athanasios fleeing here from persecution on Mt Athos and, according to local tradition, being flown to the highest rock by an eagle. By the 16th century there were 24 monasteries and although now there are only six, you can visit four. This involves a fair amount of walking and you will soon start looking round for a friendly eagle. It is very important that you dress modestly, for these are still 'working' monasteries: anyone wearing shorts or short-sleeved shirts will not be admitted and girls must also wear skirts. Remember to wear sensible shoes, take some refreshments, and also a little money to give as donations. Roughly the monasteries are open 9 a.m. to 1 p.m., 3 p.m. to 6.30 p.m.

The most impressive monastery is the **Great Meteoron**, closed on Tuesdays. This was founded by the saint himself and as you approach by bridges and tunnels you wonder how anyone ever had the courage to use the original wooden windlasses. One visitor asked when the rope on the machinery was replaced and with monastic simplicity the abbot replied 'when it breaks'! Inside the church there are many good frescoes and outside is the large wooden gong or simantra, used to call the monks to prayer. There is also a small museum with a few interesting illustrated books. There is also an ossarium where the bones of dead monks were kept.

Perhaps the most beautiful of the monasteries is **Barlaam,** built in 1517 by two brothers: it is covered in frescoes, and reached by a memorable bridge across a gap in the rock. The first monastery you come to is **Ag Nikolaos,** quieter and smaller than the rest and worth the 15 minute climb up all the steps. Similar is the **Ag Triada,** easier to admire from a distance and not really worth all the effort of getting there. Film fans may recognize it from the Bond film 'For Your Eyes Only'. **Ag Stephanos** is the most accessible monastery from the road and for this reason tends to get rather crowded.

Nearby is the town of **KALAMBAKA,** reached by a road surrounded by strange shaped rocks. In addition to the beautiful **Church of the Assumption,** there are several good hotels, the **Divania** and the **Xenia,** and two good restaurants, the **Platanos** and **Tikos**.

VOLOS

On the east coast lies Volos, the main port for reaching the Sporades. Apart from this the town has little charm because it was destroyed by an earthquake in 1956 and rebuilt in a functional and rather unappealing style. There are, however, a number of popular hotels such as the **Xenia,** the **Alexandros** and the **Aigli**. Among the more simple establishments for the independent traveller are the **Avra** and the **Kypseli**.

There is an excellent Tourist Office on Riga Fereou Sq, a good place to stop before you travel on to the islands or head into the mainland. Open Mon to Fri 7.30 a.m. to 2.30 p.m. The Post Office is at 67 Pavlou Mela and nearby is the international telephone office, the OTE, at 24 Elef Venizelou.

There are no sights in the town apart from the **Archaeological Museum,** about a 20 minute walk from the centre, but this is very good. It is one of the few museums which actually manages to make a collection of pottery interesting and should be visited by anyone in the area. Open 9 a.m. to 1 p.m., 3 p.m. to 6 p.m., sun 10 a.m. to 2.30 p.m.

There is some nightlife in the town but during the tourist season everything tends to get fairly swamped. For simple Greek food, however, try one of two restaurants on Argonafton, the **Metaftis** at No. 23 and the **Socrates** at No. 33.

Volos is also the entrance to the **PELION**, a collection of 24 pretty villages which make a very interesting excursion. Perhaps the prettiest, and for this reason the most full of admiring tourists, is MAKRINITSA. Less packed but still very charming is PORTARIA nearby. There is also the added benefit of some very good beaches in the area. The best are at TSANGARADA and ZAGORA, but KISSOS, MILIES and KALANERA are all worth a look.

OLYMPIA

Finally we come to **Mt Olympus,** north of Volos. Traditionally this is the home of the gods and it was only climbed in 1913. The main village in the area is LITOCHORA, little more than a convenient base camp for those who want to climb the mountain. This is about a two-day trip and of the two routes the red is the most popular. English-speaking guides can be hired and there are special huts along the route where you can stay the night. For more information enquire at the **Federation of Mountaineering and Skiing** which has an office on Kentriki Sq. (Tel: 21 239). There is one reasonable hotel, the **Myrto,** but most people stay in the **Youth Hostel.**

Western Greece

Geographically, Western Greece is one of the two largest regions in Greece. From the bustling port of Igoumenitsa in the east, through the rolling mountains bordering distant Albania, to the grey industrial towns in the west, this is undoubtedly one of the least-explored areas on the tourist map of Europe.

From the 15th century onwards, Western Greece suffered more than its fair share of enemy invasions. The Turkish rule imposed on northern Greece for centuries forced many of the mountainous districts to nurture a degree of self-rule which enabled the region's economy – and culture – to flourish. Many of the region's picturesque modern-day towns retain evidence of their past importance as thriving artistic centres.

Countless tiny, traditional villages nestle virtually undisturbed amidst some of the most stunning natural scenery anywhere in

Greece. Away from the beaches along the eastern coast, so popular with the Greeks themselves in the summer, large-scale tourist developments are unknown. One of Western Greece's best-kept secrets is the existence of two fine ski resorts near both Florina and Veria in the west of the region.

This chapter covers the main resorts along the eastern coast of Western Greece, including Parga, as well as many lesser-known inland destinations. The regional capital Ioanina is an important feature we look at in addition to – briefly – some of the area's other large towns.

Unexplored natural beauty is here in abundance, but Western Greece also retains a traditional way of life which will not last forever. Much of this region really is a microcosm of the real Greece as it could be without the international influences so obvious in the better-known parts of the country. There is genuine potential in Western Greece for every type of tourist if you are prepared to look for it before it's too late.

Practical Details

COMMUNICATIONS

The region has three modest airports – at Ioanina, Kastoria, and Kozani – which handle predominantly domestic flights to and from Athens. A regular Ioanina–Thessaloniki service is also in operation but there is virtually no scheduled international traffic from any of the three airports.

There is hardly any rail network in Western Greece, other than a patchy service from Thessaloniki which is routed via Veria, Edessa and Florina as far as Kozani. Further south the line begins again near Trikala and heads eastwards towards Volos, meeting up with the main line south from Thessaloniki to Athens. The rest of the region is considered too mountainous and sparsely populated to justify a wider rail network.

The region does have an excellent bus service. As well as the main national bus company (operating, for example, at least seven daily departures to Thessaloniki from Ioanina) there are numerous smaller operators serving even the tiniest of villages. Buses are frequently crowded so do be prepared to stand, or sit on the floor, at peak periods. Most resorts seem to have a high number of taxis – all of which can negotiate the region's many steep hills and sharp curves with alarming speed!

Frequent ferry services from Igomenitsa, one of Greece's largest ports, are available to Corfu, Yugoslavia and Italy. A daily schedule from Parga over to Paxi island also operates.

TOURIST INFORMATION

The head office for Western Greece is situated in Ioanina at 2, Nap Zerva Street opposite the imposing fountain in the centre of town. The smart, oak-panelled, office has an almost library-like display of N.T.O.G. leaflets, in numerous languages, covering most of the country. There is surprisingly little information available on the region itself outside Ioanina unless you are prepared to sit patiently with one of the English-speaking members of staff and ask about specific places. The main tourist office is open every day until early evening and is situated conveniently close to the large Olympic Airways office in the town.

CLIMATE

Outside the sun-soaked coastal resorts of eastern Epirus, Western Greece tends to have a slightly cooler climate than the rest of the country. You can still expect year-round sunshine but bear in mind that much of this region is well above sea-level and can remain quite chilly right through the year. Snow remains on higher ground until the end of spring.

Nearby Corfu gives a fair indication of the average temperatures which can be expected in the region. Rising from a March/April average of around 12–16°C (54–60°F) the summer temperatures level off about 26°C (80°F) in July and August. Further inland the average temperatures fall by a few degrees. In Ioanina itself the Easter average is between 10–15°C (50–60°F) rising to between 22–28°C (70–82°F) June to August.

The northern part of this region is the coldest anywhere in Greece.

In January, around Florina, snow is normal and the temperatures scarcely rise above freezing level – thus making it a popular ski resort. Even by midsummer, the Florina average seldom breaches the mid 20°C (around 80°F) level.

CULINARY SPECIALITIES

Western Greece as a whole has surprisingly few regional delicacies peculiar to it. Along the shore of the islet of Nissi, in the lake of Ioanina, there are numerous small tavernas which specialize in fish dishes from the fresh-water lake's fish. In Ioanina itself various smart fish restaurants offer the same type of cuisine – including frog's legs and other specialities.

Sea-caught fish, including shell-fish, are the favourite delicacies along the region's main coastline. Wildfowl thrive further inland and are occasionally available cooked in the traditional Greek style.

WHERE TO GO FOR WHAT

Sightseers will enjoy the archaeological remains at Dodoni, Pela, Vergina and Dion whereas sun-worshippers ought to stick to Parga or coastal Macedonia. The Recluse will enjoy most of the smaller towns and villages of Epirus, particularly in the Zagohoria region and near the Albanian border where commercial tourism has yet to dawn. The Nature lover will appreciate most parts of this region where unspoilt natural splendour is plentiful. Visitors looking for Healthy Holidays should aim for spa resorts around Xyno Nero and Lontra Arideas, or coastal Macedonia if you prefer water sports.

Nightlife and organized festivals in Western Greece really don't happen. This is a predominantly rural area and, away from the few developing coastal resorts and larger towns like Ioanina and Florina, there is practically nothing in the way of organized entertainment. On certain dates each summer, village fairs are held all over the region to revive and observe old customs, folk dances and folk songs. The largest take place at Metsora on the 25th of July, Matsouki between the 15th and 18th of August, and at Vassikiko on the 24th of August.

Outside Parga, and the southern strip of coastal Macedonia, the beaches of Western Greece are pretty average. There are plenty of long, picturesque stretches of coastline between Igonmenitsa and Preveza – ideal for a day's picnic – but they really don't compare with the Halkidiki as mainland resorts. Beach facilities in Western Greece are an attractive complement to an all-round holiday, but as the overriding factor in your choosing a part of Greece to visit, they really rule out this peaceful part of the world.

Western Greece

The region known as Epirus occupies the north-west corner of Greece to the south of Albania, and is the most mountainous part of the country. The regional capital, and largest town in Western Greece, is Ioanina.

IOANINA *(JANENA)*
Built a third of a mile above sea level, this attractive regional centre has a population of scarcely 40,000 and remains largely undiscovered by British tourists. The geography of the town is basically long and narrow since it has developed along one wide shore of a massive natural lake.

Founded by the Roman Emperor Justinian, Ioanina retains many traces of its 1400-year history although little remains of that first Roman settlement – in its day a key defensive city known as Pamvotis. The modern town, however, has no shortage of points of interest to the visitor – more than enough to justify at least a brief stop if you visit Western Greece at all.

The main sight in the town itself, and the most impressive man-made feature in Ioanina, is the magnificent old municipal museum located in the former **Mosque of Aslan Pasha**. This dubious character built the original building in 1618 and had a string of wives and mistresses to look after him inside it. Most of his women ended up being murdered by him before he met a particularly gruesome death at the hands of several of his many enemies. Aslan Pasha was a former Governor of Epirus and is now remembered very much in the folklore legends of the region.

The modern-day museum still retains the glorious lake view Aslan Pasha valued so much and, inside, there is a wide range of predominantly folklore exhibits. There is a modest admission charge and the museum is open all week except Sunday. Close by the former mosque is a now sadly overgrown cemetery where the butchered, headless corpse of Pasha now lies buried.

Situated in the town's public park is the **archaeological museum** – the most significant in the region. This modern building contains an impressive collection of the best Roman finds from all over Epirus.

Other sights worth seeing within Ioanina itself are the few remaining old parts of the town. The fragments of the ancient city walls are easily located and worth seeking out as is Justinian's massive fortress. The structure was heavily strengthened in the eleventh century by later Norman invaders to the region who spread their influence almost as far as the Romans had a thousand years earlier.

Even an hour's stroll along some of the old town's many narrow backstreets will reveal a wealth of small shops and traditional Greek wooden crafts. Ioanina is a good shopping centre and has an efficient town bus service to help you get around.

The town has a considerable number of reasonable hotels but most are quite small; there are scarcely 2000 beds available for visitors. Advance booking, particularly for the independent travellers arriving on spec, is well-advised.

The town's highest grade hotels are two rated B-class; the **Hotel Palladion** at 26, October 28th Street and the **Xenia** on Dodonis Street. The latter is the smaller and least expensive, although it does have obligatory half-board. The Palladion has one of the finest dinner menus in Ioanina (open to non-residents) and a bar which serves draught beer – a very rare sight in Greece. Boiled fishheads are one of their specialities although, unfortunately, they cannot be favourably recommended!

The C-grade **Dioni** and **El Greco** hotels (both on Tsirigoti Street) are comfortable and good value for money, but the more central **Olympic** boasts the best restaurant in town. Their adjoining **La Fontanina** serves fillet steak to perfection and locally caught fish at their finest.

It has to be said that nightlife is not this region's strong point, away from the cosmopolitan coastal resorts. But what there is tends to centre around the few smart clubs and restaurants clustered in and around the town centre at Ioanina. Good eating places in particular are numerous and the **Ganymidis restaurant,** on Kapodistrion Street (just off the main Dodonis Street) is the only one in town which specializes exclusively in fish.

For a quick snack, look out for **Spitioko** on King George Street about 100 yards from the massive State House in the centre of town. Run by an exiled American, Spitioko's is probably the cleanest and best value fast-food place you'll find anywhere in this region. The jovial proprietor is also a gold-mine of useful tourist information!

EXCURSIONS

Hidden deep within the heart of one of the most naturally picturesque parts of Greece, Ioanina is also an ideal base for a host of varied excursions into the surrounding countryside. Organized excursions are scarce so hiring a car for a few days would be your best way of getting around.

PERAMA is a small village less than three miles out of Ioanina and site of the famous **Perama Cave.** Thousands visit this mile-long natural wonder each year, with its huge galleries and vaulted chambers. The cave is well-signposted from Ioanina. A few miles further along is the village of **Mouzakei.** This village has a museum containing wax effigies of the region's historical heroes through the ages and is renowned throughout Greece.

An interesting day-trip can be made in only ten minutes by boat from Ioanina to NISSI, situated on the islet in the lake of Ioanina. The village was originally constructed as late as the 17th century and contains several important Byzantine monuments. The Filantropinan monastery still houses frescoes which date back to the early 1500s.

The traditional villages of SIRAKO-KALANITES make an interesting drive from the town but undoubtedly one of Ioanina's more famous neighbours is nearby DODONI. Here you can wander round at leisure in Western Greece's most famous, and historically significant, archaeological sites.

Chosen as a place of settlement by religious tribes as long ago as 2000 BC, a truly magnificent **Roman amphitheatre** stands largely intact as a monument to some of the region's earliest settlers. Almost sixty tiers high, this massive spectacle will remain one of your abiding memories of Western Greece. Historically minded visitors will be able to find limited accommodation in nearby Dodoni village.

'Never before have I seen so splendid a sunset,' said Lord Byron 160 years ago when he visited nearby ZITSA. Although its wine and sunsets are famous (and rightly so) there is little more to recommend the village as a special attraction.

An excursion to PIGES LOUROS may prove more rewarding. A large trout farm lies close to the famed Louros springs. Although little to see in themselves, these health-giving springs have formed a little lake here high on the mountainside. From it, the source of the winding River Louros flows.

A picturesque traditional mansion has been restored in the little town of METSOVA and now serves as a folklore museum. Although the town is fast becoming a central base for winter sports, it retains a distinct tranquillity in the summer months. Rows of whitewashed houses, with smiling locals and the occasional bustling taverna, make the visitor feel genuinely welcome. Wander round the medieval church, still in daily use, or just sit back and absorb the atmosphere in one of the most typical Greek mountain villages you'll find in this region.

A more off-beat excursion, by regular bus service from Ioanina, will take you to KONITSA. The forty-mile journey takes you through some quite spectacular mountain scenery to this scattered little town where life progresses slowly. Built in tiers, the surrounding countryside is breathtaking and the atmosphere so peaceful with scarcely another tourist in sight. The wooded slopes of Mt Trapezitsa (nearly 7000 ft high) make a memorable backdrop.

On the horizon lie the distant, snow-covered, mountain peaks of southern Albania. An intriguing little excursion from Konitsa is to nearby MELISSOPETRA (about eight miles away). By twice-daily bus, or preferably by taxi, you can reach the tiny village from where you will find one of the clearest vantage points over into Albania. Greece's near neighbour has officially banned western visitors and casual tourism for decades, but from Melissopetra you can get a clear view of the mountains and the little Albanian town of Perat on the other side. You are less than a mile from the fortified border (which cannot be seen) so don't risk straying any closer!

The main road northwards, from Ioanina to Konitsa, is surrounded by dozens of small, traditional villages known collectively as the **ZAGOROHORIA**. The entire area forms part of the enormous Vikos-Aoos National Park – so designated in order to preserve the wild flowers and animals native to Western Greece.

East (Anatolika)

The national park area is divided into three unequal regions. Anatolika is the smallest, but also the most accessible. The area is strikingly untouristed – no large-scale resorts, sky-rise hotels or anything of that nature. And it is likely to stay that way since future commercial development has been expressly forbidden by the Greek Government.

On a single road north-east from Ioanina – which narrows and deteriorates as you climb higher – you will come across the region's three main villages, **TRISENTO**, **GREVENITI**, and **FLAMBOURARI**. Shopping and eating facilities are limited in all these small villages – and accommodation for visitors practically non-existent. Each of these villages is only a few miles apart from the next one in the region. Driving through, they tend to spring from the rich foliage with amazing frequency. Bring a picnic and simply absorb the peaceful, unspoiled atmosphere.

Central (Kentriko)

The heart of the undulating region of Epirus is a central area known as Kentriko. Here you will find the densest accumulation of any of the forty-six traditional villages which make up the whole area. Since there are so many similarities between the villages it would be worth your while concentrating a visit to just one or two, or alternatively take one of the numerous organized tours available from Ioanina. A useful mode of transport here is the

Western Greece

scheduled bus services from Ioanina which (miraculously) do reach all the villages. Bear in mind that services are seldom more than once daily except to the most popular villages such as **MONODENTRI** and **ASPRANGETI**. Out of the season, hiring transport is really the only way to see these lovely settlements without causing great inconvenience to yourself.

VITSA has two of the oldest churches in the region. **Agios Nikolaos** (St Nicholas) dates from 1610 and nearby **Taxiarchis** from around 1700. Kentriko is rich with impressive old churches but beyond those there is little to see once you tire of the natural beauty which surrounds you. In Vitsa you will find one or two refurbished guest-houses subtly hidden amongst the old homes. Nightlife is limited to the village's one or two small tavernas – informal and relaxed but unlikely to appeal to younger travellers looking for action.

The best-known, and most popular, of all the Zagorokoria villages is **MONODENTRI**. Particularly favoured by German tourists, little Monodentri is considered one of the most attractive villages by the natives of Western Greece. Buses run here daily and there are two particularly fine churches in the centre of the village worth seeing: **Agios Panteleyman,** built in 1630 and still retaining a collection of fine frescoes well-known in Greece, and the church **Agios Thanassis,** built two hundred years later, is a classical example of traditional church architecture from this later period.

High above the village there is an awkward little viewpoint, known as **Oxia,** from where you can enjoy one of the finest views over the whole gorge. It is a little off the beaten track but well worth the extra trek for a really spectacular picnic point. Ask a local for directions when you reach Monodentri.

As the road climbs higher, and veers further away from the main highway, you will come across the tiny villages of **ASPRANGETI**, **DILOFO**, **KIPI**, and **KONKONLI**. Depending on which approach road you've taken from Ioanina, the order in which these small villages run into each other will differ. In appearance and character they remain very similar. Most offer fine vantage points over the rest of the gorge but, really, very little distinguishes them from the previous one a mile or so earlier. Bear in mind that 'traditional' tends to imply normal tourist facilities are non-existent!

If you persevere along the narrow, isolated road as far as Tsepelovo you will be rewarded by the sight of the ancient **monastery of Rongovon**. This quite obscure old building was originally constructed by the Normans in the mid-11th century, about the time when Ioanina was being pulled apart and rebuilt. As the number of monks in Tsepelovo multiplied, the original building was pulled down and completely rebuilt on a much larger scale in 1749. It retains that 18th-century construction to the present day.

The only established resort in the Zagorohoria area is situated virtually next door to Tsepelovo. SKEMNELI offers limited, and quite modest, accommodation in spectacular surroundings. High-rise hotels are neither allowed, nor desired in Kentriko.

Skemneli itself is the most central of all the forty-six villages in the Zagorohoria area thereby making it an ideal base from which to explore any – or all – of the others. There is little more in the way of places of interest than in any of the other villages apart from two attractive old monasteries. Dating from the 17th century, **Agia Paraskevi** and **Agios Nikolaos** are reckoned to be amongst the most historically significant of any of the religious buildings in the area. Skemneli also has a further two churches which are open to visitors. The best bet for accommodation is at the B-class pension **Platanos** with thirty beds. In common with the other villages, many private houses offer basic accommodation – with the minimum of frills.

Still higher in this central region lie LAISTA and VRISSOHORI surrounded by snow-capped mountain peaks. Hidden within the lush green vegetation that makes the whole park special, these villages are the most secluded of any in the region. Other than the (very) occasional private room, there is no accommodation for visitors.

One of the most appealing places to visit in this area is in NEGADES. The village contains a quite unique church with striking murals of Orthodox saints, and the philosophers Plutarch and Aristotle.

West (Ditoko)

The west of Zagorohoria has a cluster of villages known collectively as **DITOKO**. Situated high above sea-level, the two finest are accessible only after a lengthy climb along narrow roads. Both MIKRO and MEGA PAPINGO are situated thirty-eight miles out of Ioanina – but the journey feels *much* longer!

Both villages represent traditional settlements set in an area of unsurpassed natural beauty. This area remains totally unspoiled by visitors from home or abroad. Ditoko offers little in the way of 'conventional' tourist attractions – night spots, good restaurants, places of interest to visit, good hotels and so on. But for a feeling of the real Greece, the natural uncommercialized Greece, this is the region to visit for tranquillity and natural splendour. Few afternoons will surpass a visit to West Zagori if only to sit and bask in the magnificent shadow of Mount Garmila – all 7500 feet of the region's highest peak.

Arta and Environs

After Ioanina, **ARTA** is the largest town on Epirus. It still maintains much of a small town atmosphere and is quite easily accessible by road from Ioanina or the other major towns further south.

A former capital of Epirus in ancient times, Arta retains considerable evidence of a prosperous market past. The most striking point of interest is an ancient stone bridge which spans the River Arahithos on the outskirts of the town. Numerous ancient ruins are accessible throughout the city, including a former Roman theatre and a temple to the god Apollo. Nightlife and accommodation are limited to what's on offer at the town's three or four B- and C-grade hotels as well as the usual tavernas.

Two typically Greek villages, MATSOUKI and MELISSOURGI, are situated nearby. A winding narrow road south-east of Arta itself will take you to the small villages of SKOULIKAVA and VELENTZIKO. Both retain quite charming, and well-kept old Orthodox monasteries. For peace and tranquillity, and very little else, Arta and her environs have it.

West Coast

An interesting drive (along good roads) would take you down the west coast of the region. The largest coastal town is **PREVEZA**, a bustling but largely uninteresting port resort. The only real sight is a Venetian clock tower in the centre of town. There are a sprinkling of moderate hotels, of which the large B-grade **Margarona Royal** is the smartest. But although coastal, the beaches around here are pretty average. NIKAPOLIS lies five miles further north and historians will remember its colourful past during the crusading centuries. Traces of Roman Emperor Octavius' original settlement can still be explored.

KASTOSIKIA is a fast-developing seaside resort next door to tiny KANALI. Both have good safe beaches but they are long stretches of busy coastline rather than the picture postcard-type inlets you'll find closer to Parga. Nightlife starts to pick up around about here – but don't expect Stringfellows just yet!

Nearby ZALONGO has an interesting, but tragic, past. Perched high on a hilltop cliff sits a sombre monument to the memory of sixty women who jumped to their deaths from here in 1803. Rather than risk capture by advancing Turkish armies, they first threw their children over before killing themselves.

The remaining traces of the once mighty city of **KATSOPI** lie sixteen miles north of Preveza. Occasional day-trips are organized from nearby resorts and the ruins of two large theatres – destroyed in the fourth century BC – are worth seeing. Take a picnic though since the ancient Greeks didn't build too many souvlaki stands near Katsopi!

You probably won't find MESSAPOTAMOS on any map, but the village still stands at the point where the rivers Acheron and Kokytos meet. Nothing to see here now, but in ancient times this was the point from where Charon supposedly rowed the souls of the dead across a vast underground lake to the Kingdom of Hades. The popular resort of PARGA, back again onto the coast, has considerably more life to offer modern-day visitors.

Parga is easily the most attractive resort along the west coast – and it is surrounded by the best beaches in Western Greece. The town itself rests at the foot of a sweeping arch of lushly wooded hills and the typically Greek white houses reach right down to the small harbour. Although Parga's own beach is small and usually quite crowded, there is no shortage of clean, safe, sandy beaches within a mile or two of the town.

The town's finest sight is another renowned Venetian fortress, plumped on top of the largest hill which you can see opposite the harbour. The steep climb to reach it is worthwhile on a clear day. Good fish restaurants and some decent hotels have sprung up over the past year – the **Parga Beach** (B-grade) is the town's best.

Further up the coast lies the small resort of PLATOPIA offering a genuine 'Away from it all' atmosphere, yet still within striking distance of the region's main towns. Beaches here are a close second to those around Parga but accommodation can be limited.

Western Greece's largest international port is at IGONMENITSA and from here it is possible to visit nearby Corfu in a day or else make a lengthy eight-hour crossing to Brindisi in Italy. Other than the comings and goings at the harbour, Igonmenitsa isn't worth a special trip. Island excursions are possible from here to the traditional old town of PARAMITIA or to FILIATES, once the base of a Turkish despot in mediaeval towns.

Western Macedonia (West of Thessaloniki)

North (Pella and Florina)

West of Thessaloniki lies a cluster of moderately sized towns and villages which see little in the way of foreign tour companies – rather like England's industrial northern counties. Only a few smaller tour operators venture to this region. The perception of Greece held by many of the larger companies stops beyond popular beach resorts!

GLANITSA is a dull, industrialized town and has little to offer other than as a good central base for this region. A crucial battle took place here in 1912, between the Greeks and the Turks, which led to the eventual liberation of Thessaloniki. An enjoyable excursion is possible to **PELA,** the ruined original capital of ancient Greece. A compact museum contains the best of countless archaeological finds around here, and it's not difficult to transport yourself two millenniums back in time as you wander round the surviving stone floor mosaics and early pillars.

SHIDRA is a modest and unimposing resort further west of **GLANITSA**, but much more worthy of a visit is **EDESSA** further north on the same main highway. This busy old town was once the centre of generations of pious crusades to the Holy Land. A massive archaeological site on the outskirts of town still testifies to Edessa's historic past – if you can recall anything of the history of the crusades from your schooldays. The town also has a natural waterfall and a flourishing carpet industry, much in evidence. Accommodation is limited to a few average hotels and private rooms. Evening entertainment in Edessa revolves around the streetside tavernas and good company!

The sheltered northern resort of **ARIDEA** is becoming more popular with people looking for a 'different' holiday away from sun-soaked beaches and other tourists. The small town is situated close to the Yugoslavian border but off a main road which continues across it thereby making foreign daytrips awkward. Its sound-alike neighbour **LONTRA ARIDEAS** is even closer and considered something special on account of its crystal-clear mountain spa waters.

One of Western Macedonia's busiest resorts is the prefecture of **FLORINA**, which borders both Albania and Yugoslavia. Amidst picturesque landscape, the town boasts a small zoo, an impressive little museum, and an art gallery displaying works by better known local artists. The town has numerous decent hotels and restaurants, including at least three at B-grade, and on a good night has a surprisingly lively night scene for a relatively out of the way place. The village of **NIMFEO**, south of Florina, is worth a brief detour to have a look at its mansions in traditional Macedonian style.

Nature enthusiasts ought to make the awkward trek to **MIKRA PREPSA**, a small national park for the last ten years. Although situated on a peninsula jutting out from Albania, this desolate nesting ground for pelicans is largely Greek so perfectly accessible for the casual visitor.

The town of **AMINDEON**, on the edge of its own small lake, has developed slowly into one of the most peaceful parts of the region for tourists. Typically Greek, Amindeon is a good base from which to visit **XYNO NERO** with its clean freshwater spa.

The capital of this northern region is **KASTORIA**. Boasting a small airport and precious little else, you would be well advised to avoid Kastoria if at all possible. To be fair, it has the usual facilities of a moderate-sized Greek town – main post office, banks, numerous hotels and restaurants, N.T.O.G. office and so on. But it has been gradually ruined by industrial pollution over a number of years and remains a sad, unattractive memory of the glossy N.T.O.G. photographs you will see in leaflets for the region.

South (Grevena, Kozani and Imathia)

Halfway between Thessaloniki and Ioanina lies the scattered region to the south of Western Macedonia. **GREVENA** is as far away from the coast as just about any town in Greece and, along with **KOZANI**, is one of two towns of any real size in this southern region. The town has little man-made for the casual visitor to see or do, but here again the natural surroundings are simply overwhelming. Fur trimming was formerly the region's main source of income, and evidence of a once prosperous industry can still be visited.

From here, a winding road leads south-east to **PERIVOLI**, an isolated mountain village offering a couple of peaceful tavernas and bags of natural charm. Halfway between Grevena and Kozani the town of **SIATISTA** belies the prosperous merchant centre which existed here a century previously. A fine old church, **Agia Pavashevi,** is still worth seeing on account of the magnificent hand-carved wooden altar inside.

KOZANI itself is the largest town in this immediate area offering the only proper large town facilities – telephone, office, doctors, N.T.O.G. office – for miles around. Once a centre of distinguished international learning, Kozani attracts many visitors each year to its famous library, founded over 400 years ago. Many traditional old mansions used by scholars and rich merchants alike still stand and there is also a folkloric museum in the centre of town which is open most days. Accommodation shouldn't be too great a problem since hotels – from grade B downwards – are quite numerous.

Close to Kozani lie **SENIA** and **PETRONA** allowing the opportunity for scenic day-trips from the main town. Of the two, Senia has the edge since the road along to it passes over the gloriously long, narrow banks of Lake Aliakman. The village itself has a clutter of Byzantine churches, and a few ancient ruins from the days when it was once at the heart of an important gold-mining area.

The modest winter resort of **PTOLEMAIDA** sits close to VERIA, the capital of the Imatia region with an impressive Roman pedigree. In its day, Veria was one of two capitals of Macedonia and, although the town still has traces of some of Greece's finest church architecture from a later period, the ancient ruins of **Vergina** (the old town) should be a must for a visit. Representing some of the most important archaeological discoveries anywhere in Greece, the famous tomb of Philip II was discovered here only a decade ago. The gold, silver and pottery found, as well as the bones of Philip II himself, are in the archaeological museum in Thessaloniki but the site itself still has much to be seen.

A small road north-east from Veria leads to Edessa passing, on the way, the excellent winter sports resort of **KATO VERMIO** – the largest and most popular in Greece. The only sizeable town on the road to Edessa is NAOSSA which retains a flourishing textile industry. Shattered by Turkish forces in 1822, the rebuilt town had to find a means of supporting itself and so the textile industry was born. The twenty-six-bed C-grade **Hellas Hotel,** in the centre of town, represents good value for money in this area. To the north-east of Naossa lies LEFKADIA where you can still see the excavated remains of an important royal tomb dating back to the 3rd century BC.

Coast

The best road in mainland Greece is a toll motorway which shoots southwards out of Thessaloniki towards Athens. The coastal region of Western Macedonia offers, in general, facilities broadly similar to those on the Halkidiki peninsula – only less of them and with noticeably fewer tourists. Only a few British tour operators venture to this stretch of coastline.

The tiny fishing settlement of **ORMOS METHANIS** lies a mile or so to the north of the beach resort of **METHONI**. Between the two you will find the best beaches along this part of the coast, and Methoni ought to be reckoned a reasonable base for this area as a whole. The village's own beach is sheltered and safe with a gently sloping gradient into the clear blue Aegean.

Good camping facilities lie just outside **MAKRIGIALOS** close to the beach. The village also has a couple of modest hotels and three A-grade pensions. It sits right next to the main road and rail connections north and south. **ALIKES**, a bit further down, is one of the area's smallest villages with virtually nowhere to stay. The beaches around here are terrible – dissolving into muddy marshland, so avoid it, if you can. A day excursion is recommended, however, to the Roman archaeological remains at **Pidna**. It was near here that Olympias, mother of Alexander the Great, was buried after Cassandros murdered her. Great place if you know your history!

KORINOS is tucked away behind a blanket of rolling green countryside as you venture further south. It doesn't merit a special visit, unless you want to look at its unremarkable church, and the beach is fully two miles away from the once decent (C-grade) hotel.

KATERINI is the coast's main town and is well-linked by rail and road to the rest of Greece. Although six miles from the nearest beach – a vast, but crowded, stretch of sand at Paralia – the town has a noticeable quaintness unequalled in any of the countless 'traditional' villages in the region. Katerini is a veritable gold mine of well-stocked little supermarkets and craft stores, and has enough to keep most visitors occupied for a few days. The municipal gardens in the centre of town are an ideal picnic location, and the old square church offers a peaceful haven from the bustle of the morning markets. The Tourist Police are located on M. Alexandron Street. There are numerous places to stay in the town – about twenty C-grade hotels alone! The B-grade **Alkyon,** by the seaside, has a good restaurant and in town either the **Pieria Pallas** or the **Modern,** both near the Central Place, will reward you with a good feast without charging the earth.

A definite must is a visit to nearby **DION**. By hourly coach from Katerini, you will find here the most significant collection of archaeological finds in Western Greece. In the 5th century BC a holy sanctuary to the god Zeus was expounded and developed and, believe me, the spirit of that sanctuary remains as strong as ever. The theatre, temples, and sanctuary to Isis are stunning – your picture postcard Greek ruins – and you'd be silly to miss the opportunity to see them.

LITOHORO lies five miles south cradled gently at the base of Greece's highest peak, Mount Olympus. This active little town has endless narrow, winding streets and still air tinged with the smell of wood-burning stoves. With an excellent restaurant (the **Enripieis** in the central square) and all the necessary facilities to make a short stay more enjoyable – including OTE and post office – Litohoro is the popular base from which to mount an assault on Olympus. Wise Greeks predicted this market early and there are numerous clean places to stay in town.

A string of magnificent beaches distinguish the next twenty miles of coast at **LEPTOKARIA, PARALIA SKOTINAS, LERTOKANA** and **PLATAMONAS**. The last one is particularly stunning and so far unexploited except for a single tower block hotel – the **Plataman Beach.** This part of the coastline has an excellent reputation for watersports and receives many visitors escaping southwards from Thessaloniki for a few days.

Northern Greece

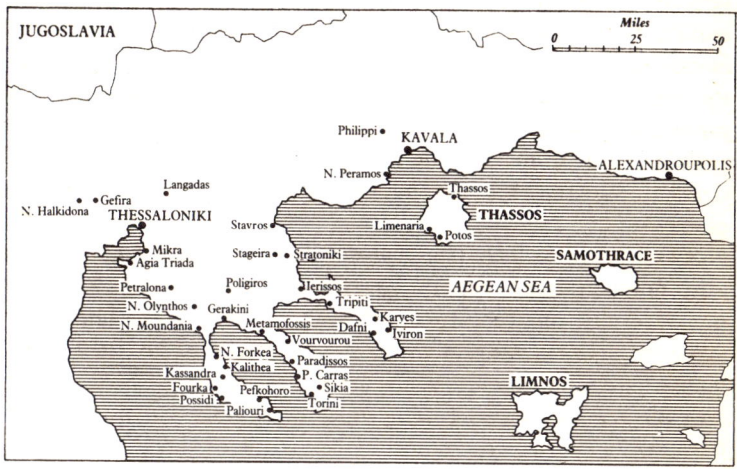

This large and diverse region stretches from Thessaloniki, the second city of Greece in the east, to Alexandroupolis by the Turkish border in the west. Encompassing the Greek regions known as Macedonia and Thrace, Northern Greece has a long history dating back to 2300 BC. It was in that period when the first Helladic tribes penetrated the broadest area of this large region from the north.

Generations of colourful settlers came and went – all leaving rich archaeological deposits, the best of which have found their way to Thessaloniki's massive archaeological museum. Tiny Pella, for instance, was once the capital of the thriving ancient state of Macedonia when King Philip II was on the throne. His son, Alexander the Great, helped spread the Greek civilization from Macedonia as far east as Central Asia.

For centuries after, Northern Greece was a key part of the Byzantine Empire. Thessaloniki fell to the Turks in 1430 and the region was lost to the Ottoman Empire in whose control it remained for five centuries. Northern Greece was one of the last parts of the country to be freed from Turkish rule – as recently as the Balkan Wars of 1912–13.

The sprawling, narrow region is rich in scenic beauty, as well as ological heritage. Stunning beaches cluster around the two Halkidiki prongs open to tourists, and all along the seaward edge of the region looking across the calm waters of the Aegean Sea. In addition to the finest mainland resorts anywhere in Greece, this varied region also includes the mysterious Mount Athos, banned to women for over a thousand years and also includes the only independent monastic state anywhere in the world.

Northern Greece is becoming increasingly popular with tour operators – particularly the glorious beach resorts of the Halkidiki. Nearly twenty package companies visit there and quite a few more offer holidays which take in Thassos island or the more interesting mainland cities of Thessaloniki, Kavala, and Alexandroupolis.

In this chapter we look in detail at Greece's second largest city, Thessaloniki, together with those popular Halkidiki beach resorts. The other major tourist centres of the region, including Kavala and Thassos, are covered and, in addition, a visit is made to the lesser-known third Halkidiki prong – Mount Athos.

Practical Details

COMMUNICATIONS

Outside the area around Athens itself, Northern Greece has the best communications. International borders link the region east, north and west with Yugoslavia, Bulgaria, and Turkey respectively. Road and rail links between all of them are numerous and well used. The main motorway link with the rest of Europe leads down through Yugoslavia, from Belgrade, towards Thessaloniki. Thereafter it follows the coast down towards Athens.

The region has three airports – at Thessaloniki, Kavala, and Alexandroupolis. The latter two handle predominantly domestic flights, and there are frequent daily connections with Athens throughout the year. Thessaloniki handles much more in the way of international traffic, and is Greece's second largest airport. Olympic Airways, the national airline, operate an impressive international service via Thessaloniki as well as domestic connections with Athens (up to eight times daily), Ioanina, and Skiathos during the summer timetable period from April to October.

Greece's hilly terrain does not lend itself to the construction of an impressive rail network. There are regular daily trains along the one line from Thessaloniki to Alexandroupolis, and onwards through Turkey to Istanbul. The trains are slow, but inexpensive, and wind their way gradually eastwards through the middle of the region. Other than a single branch line down to Limenas, onward connections to coastal resorts, including Kavala and the Halkidiki, must be made by road.

The bus network in this region is impressive and reasonably efficient. The main bus company in Greece has various departure points in Thessaloniki covering every major destination within the region beyond. Check with your hotel, or any tourist office, well in advance to find out precisely which depot you ought to go to.

Ferry services are available from various points along the coast. Numerous small companies operate from the harbour buildings in Thessaloniki, offering trips to Limnos, Kavala, Skiathos, Piraeus (for Athens) or occasionally smaller resorts further along the coast towards Turkey. Similar ferry services are available from Kavala and Alexandroupolis. From Kavala there are frequent hour-long crossings over to Thassos island, as well as trips further afield to Alexandroupolis, Limnos and even Skiathos on selected days of the week.

TOURIST INFORMATION

The head office for Northern Greece is at 8 Aristotelous Square in Thessaloniki (Tel: 031 222 935 or 271 888). It is open Monday to Friday 8.30 a.m. to 2.30 p.m. and 3.30 p.m. to 8.30 p.m., and Saturday 8 a.m. to 1 p.m. Situated quite close to the British Consulate, on the eighth floor at 8, Platia Eleftherias, there is another smaller branch at the airport. You'll also find tourist offices in one or two of the region's larger towns.

The public area of the main office is small and shop-like, with pleasant staff who mostly speak good English. As well as being willing to answer endless questions, information leaflets on most parts of Northern Greece are available free of charge. N.T.O.G. produce an excellent series of glossy, colour tourist leaflets, all in the same style. These include specific leaflets for Thessaloniki itself (with a good street map), Kavala and Thassos and the Halkidiki. Lists of A–C grade hotels are included and the tourist office can provide printed lists of D and E grade accommodation as well.

Train, ferry, bus and aeroplane timetables can be consulted and free (useful!) leaflets about regional cuisine, shopping in the city and general tourist attractions are also available. In addition, there are numerous glossy guidebooks to various parts of the region which can be purchased.

CLIMATE

The region generally enjoys a comfortable, temperate climate rather than year-round sunshine commonly associated with many of the popular island resorts. The inland areas of the region occasionally become quite chilly during the winter months with temperatures dipping under 5°C (40°F). January, February, and March are the coolest months when seasonal breezes seldom lift average temperatures over 10°C (50°F). Inland from the coastal resorts on the Halkidiki peninsula the temperature remains a few degrees noticeably cooler than by the seafront.

June, July, and August are the warmest months. The average temperature at Thessaloniki is around 26°C (80°F) for these three months and the daily average is consistently much higher. Average temperatures along the coast – Halkidiki, Kavala and Alexandroupolis – are virtually identical. You can reasonably expect ample sunshine as one of the outstanding features of the Greek climate as a whole. Northern Greece is no exception to this feature although it is always worth bearing in mind that inland resorts can be quite cool outside the main summer season.

CULINARY SPECIALITIES

The further east towards Turkey you travel, the greater the Turkish influence on the food and wine of the region becomes. In Thessaloniki you will be able to find every conceivable type of international cuisine. But many a rewarding, traditional snack (or full meal if you prefer) can be had in tiny cafés down just about any one of the city's countless side streets. The Thessaloniki souvlakis are considered by visitors and residents alike as being amongst the best in Greece!

Seafood is a particular speciality in the Halkidiki peninsula. Many tiny fishing villages cling to the coast and catch some of the finest large prawns and crabs anywhere in Greece. Locally produced retsina, and the white wines fermented by the monks of Mount Athos are amongst the better drink specialities to be sampled in this region.

WHERE TO GO FOR WHAT

The Sun worshipper should head for any of the stunning Halkidiki beach resorts. Likewise the Socialite should stick with the liveliest of these at Porto Carras. Gerakini and Thessaloniki are also worth considering. The Kassandra peninsula on the Halkidiki offers the best resorts for Family Holidays – just about any of the large hotels there offer ideal facilities for looking after and entertaining children of all ages. Sightseers will find plenty to visit in and around historic Thessaloniki, and at Kavala and Filipi. Healthy Holidays are possible at Kavala and, again, at the larger Halkidiki resorts like Kalithea, Haniotis and Porto Carras where watersports can be found in abundance. The ultimate holiday break for the Recluse (strictly males only allowed!) can be enjoyed on the mysterious monastic state of Mount Athos.

Halkidiki

Apart from Athens, the three-pronged Halkidiki peninsula is probably the best known part of mainland Greece and certainly an increasingly popular tourist destination because of its fine climate and extensive beaches. The clear Aegean Sea laps upon the shores of all three prongs; bustling Kassandra, picturesque Sithonia and mysterious Mount Athos which to this day remains the only independent monastic state.

Halkidiki's main land mass is the wide bulge between Thessaloniki and the three prongs, although it is sparsely populated, with little to see away from the coastline.

One notable exception is the town of **POLIGIROS** about 40 miles south-east of Thessaloniki. Poligiros is the capital of Halkidiki and has been built at the foot of Mount Holomon. To reach here from Thessaloniki take one of the dozen or so daily KTEL buses, but be prepared to hang on to your seat since the ninety-minute journey takes you almost 2000 ft above sea level along some of the most twisting and spectacular roads in the region.

The town has a good archaeological museum, just up from the bus station, and this contains many of the more notable finds from the surrounding area that haven't yet made their way to the main museum in Thessaloniki. Some traditional architecture has been preserved in the town's old quarter and, on a clear day, you have a glorious panoramic view of all three prongs of the Halkidiki if you climb to the top of the nearby Profitis Elias hill.

An excellent place to eat in Poligiros is the **Atha** taverna just 50 yards left of the bus station. The jovial English-speaking chef offers a wide choice of mouthwatering Greek dishes, including pork, lamb, moussaka, chicken, and – his speciality – veal. Try the local speciality, pronounced 'Kokorehtsee', if you can – kidneys, tripe and liver roasted together on an open spit. It sounds disgusting but tastes delicious!

There is no package tour accommodation in town, but the independent traveller should head for the C-grade hotel **Epicouros**, opened only in summer 1986, for a central place to rest. The hotel is only 100 yards down from the large post office and OTE.

KASSANDRA

The western coast road from Thessaloniki winds its way down through a host of picturesque villages towards Kassandra, one of the most developed tourist areas on mainland Greece. Just outside Thessaloniki lies PETRALONA, an appealing little sidetrip renowned for its huge cave by the same name. It was here that a primeval skull, dating back to 200,000 years BC, was found many years ago and the cave's spectacular vaults still attract a lot of visitors. Open daily from 9 a.m. to 6 p.m., it is an easy detour from the main road if you're travelling by car. A few operators based in the city offer daily excursions which normally include a brief stop in the village of Petralona as part of the tour.

PRIVATE. Keep Out

Travelling further south along the breezy western coast you will pass the traditional villages of DIONISIOU and ZOGRAFOU. Both are typical of the type of small, untouristed settlements found in this region a century ago with their low stone houses and sloped chimneys. They have little to offer the modern-day traveller other than nostalgia.

One of the first resorts is GERAKINI, situated on the bridge between the Kassandra and Sithonia peninsulas. Accommodation and things to see in the village are limited, but there is a modest little beach, offering good views east and west, which becomes quickly crowded in summer. There is a seedy disco near the beach which the locals largely ignore in favour of the more upmarket tourist nightspots further down the coast. The village of KALDIVE nearby has an almost identical, but larger, beach.

Two miles or so inland from here sits NEA OLYNTHOS. Like all the small Halkidiki villages in this region, there is no direct bus link from Thessaloniki. You must go via Poligiros and then change at Nea Moundania if approaching from the north. If you are staying in a Halkidiki resort already, then this same bus link northwards will be your main means of transport beyond Kassandra.

Olynthos itself isn't worth a special stop, and is unusually rundown-looking for this prosperous region. A sobering sight once you stray just a little from the most familiar tourist spots, Olynthos does, however, boast a few archaeological ruins which culture-seeking sightseers from the beach resorts further south might appreciate. Just a short walk outside the village, and across a small stream which (usually) dries up in summer, a few surviving remains sit atop a small hill representing all that is left of the capital of a once strong confederation of market towns destroyed finally in 348 BC by Philip II of Macedon.

At the tip of Kassandra lies NEA MOUDANIA, a bustling little coastal town with excellent transport connections throughout the region. Travelling by KTEL bus, you will almost certainly find yourself with an hour or two to spare here. Most of the obvious tavernas and cafés are clean and tidy, but do be wary of salads here. The Greek custom of drenching most foods in olive oil is particularly prevalent. For a relaxing walk, head for the seafront and the remains of the old harbour. For true romantics, the sunset at this point is stunning.

Heading south again, the undulating road crosses into the peninsula proper at **NEA POTIDEA**. The area around here is said to have once been occupied by ancient Mendi, a colony founded around the year 750 BC by the Eritreans. Nothing to stop for at Nea Potidea unless you fancy a quick bite at the self-service restaurant **Italos,** just past the bridge.

Green fields spread out for miles around and are interrupted again at **NEA FORKEA**. An impressive old Byzantine watch tower still stands guard at the far end of the village, looking seaward towards Sithonia. The clean, white beaches this region is famous for start around this point on the coast and begin to run into one another quite rapidly after here.

The east coast's main resort is at **KALITHEA,** just past the tiny village of **AFITOS** which actually lies on the slopes of the ancient citadel Kalithea. The modern-day resort has been well developed and has several enormous tourist hotel blocks situated near the beaches. The massive **Athos Palace** and **Pallini Beach** hotels (both A grades) are favoured by one or two major British operators and offer every conceivable facility from child-minding to thriving nightspots. It is an ideal resort for a good, all round, family holiday.

The beaches in and around Kalithea are superb – but popular. Long, white, spotless strips of sand with safe bathing are close by most of the larger hotels.

The village of Kalithea itself has a few remaining historic points of interest dating back to before the time of Christ. You can still see bits of an ancient temple to Zeus on the seafront, and a small museum in the village is open most days during the summer months. This is a great location for most sports, including watersports; and nightlife has a good reputation too because of the high turnover of money-spending foreign visitors! The resort's best nightspot is **Disco Annabel** about half a mile out of the village.

The peninsula's administrative centre is nearby **KASSANDRA,** an undeveloped island village with a couple of banks and the main bus stop for the east and west coast. The **Rainbow Pub** (fifty yards from the bus stop) does good midday snacks in a relaxed atmosphere.

Continuing down the east coast, three scattered fishing villages run into each other quickly: **KRIOPIGI, POLIHRONO** and **PEFKOHORO**. All sit more or less on the seafront and have numerous well-developed modern hotels between them. Neither Kriopigi nor Polihrono offer much beyond a few tavernas and the odd souvenir shop, except for the swinging nightspot **Athos** in Kriopigi.

Pefkohoro has a better reputation among more independent travellers since only modest pensions and private rooms are available. The beaches around the three villages narrow to fine pebble-covered strips of coast with clear waters for bathing. Even here, though, the beaches quickly fill up in summer.

The resort of **HANIOTIS** is sandwiched between Polihrono and Pefkohoro. A host of smaller hotels and apartments, including the hotel **Pella** and **Diomissos** apartments, make this thriving little town one of the liveliest resorts in the region. Watersports are a favourite attraction during the day and at night a myriad of bright tavernas and nightspots really come alive. The beaches are long and narrow, but the white sands and crystal-clear waters are as fine as anywhere you'll find on this stretch of coastline.

The village is cluttered round a central square that is lined with souvenir shops and small tavernas. Try and avoid the **Slippy** café with its English 'Egg and Bacon' type menu. Self-catering package holiday-makers will be well-rewarded if they spend an hour or so strolling around the well-stocked (for Greece) supermarkets in the village. Look out for the oddly named **Supermarket Australia** on your right as you enter.

At the southernmost tip of the peninsula is the village of **PALIOURI**. A modest resort, with only the B-grade **Xenia** hotel based just outside the village providing much in the way of tourist accommodation apart from private rooms.

Paliouri is an interesting excursion from anywhere in the region. The highlight of any visit would be a twenty-minute walk up the hill to the old Panafias church to take in the spectacular view. Numerous paths also exist down to the rocky beach at the very tip of the peninsula but it is not ideal for swimming because of its exposed position.

Buses leave Paliouri back to Nea Moudania every three hours from 6.15 a.m., detouring via most of the resorts on the way. Worth a stop whilst in the village is the spacious main **Café Giannikos** near where the buses park. Their sandwiches are excellent, but don't leave the village without trying the huge (six-inch!) prawns which are caught and cooked locally.

SITHONIA

The middle prong of the Halkidiki offers similar natural beauty to Kassandra yet has fewer small villages and fewer developed resorts. Driving down towards Sithonia you will pass ORMILIA, a compact village slightly off the beaten track. It is notable only for a large outdoor games arena, decorated with the five Olympic rings, which you'll spot on the left as you enter. A couple of traditional churches are worth a look if you've time to spare in the village, but neither merit a special visit.

Continuing south, the tiny village of VATOPEDI has managed to retain much of its traditional charm since few visitors seem to stop here. It has a fine golden beach with pine trees growing right down almost to the water's edge.

METAMOFOSSIS and NIKITI lie close to the main road, and are convenient stopover points if you need to visit a bank or maybe pick up a few groceries. The **Haus Dania** hotel in Metamofossis has a good restaurant, with an extensive Greek menu during the summer, if you fancy something to eat here. The road deteriorates sharply here as you enter the village.

Nikiti is a sprawling, traditional, small village that has grown up at the foot of several thousand acres of hilly farmland. The beach here is located a short distance down from the village and is both clean and safe. The sand is more golden than on Kassandra, and the view across the Halkidiki is magnificent on a clear day.

If you tire of the beach, a restored fifth-century early Christian church makes an interesting afternoon stroll about two miles further inland from the town. Also just outside Nikiti is the **Disco Alamo**, so named because it has been built (in dubious taste) to look like an enormous toy fort!

AGIOS NIKOLAOS makes an equally interesting alternative detour a mile or so north of the main road over into Sithonia. This is one of the cleanest of many similar such traditional villages that make a worthy trip in contrast to the bustling tourist resorts further down the coast. Sights and facilities are limited but the more relaxed atmosphere can be very welcome. The beach at Agios Nikolaos looks across the island of Amoliani at the top of the Mount Athos prong.

Nearby ORMOS PANOGIAS and VOURVOUROU next door are best reached by bus from Thessaloniki, unless you prefer to use a car, since there are no bus links here from Poligiros or the rest of the peninsula. Neither of the tiny coves have been disturbed by tourism yet and therefore offer a welcome backwards glance to a time when the entire Halkidiki area was no more than a handful of unknown fishing villages. All the tavernas thrive on the local catches, but accommodation is limited to private rooms and pensions. The beach at Vourvourou is awkward to find but when you do you will discover an idyllic, sheltered cove of yellow sand and calm waters. Ideal for safe family swimming, if you're prepared to make the trek.

The easternmost tip of the peninsula is SARTI, a sleepy seaside town that *feels* Greek as soon as you arrive. The pace of life is slow, and the town has one of the longest beaches on the Greek mainland; over a mile of gently curving coastline stretching down from the back gardens of half the town towards the Aegean. The uninterrupted view over to Mount Athos is spectacular. Try the **Restaurant Emanuel** on the seafront for local fish, or the small (twenty-one roomed) hotel **Akti Sarti**. A small tourist office is open near the beach in summer, and at least three KTEL buses run daily to Poligiros.

SIKIA is the only proper inland settlement on the peninsula, hiding at the foot of moors and hillside that bear an uncanny resemblance to the highlands of Scotland. This little resort is very peaceful and a well-connected central point for exploring the rest of the peninsula. The **Sithoria** restaurant in town is good and look out for the mouth-watering array of fresh oranges at the supermarket near the bus stop. Sikia has two discos; the **Amnesia** is best forgotten (sic), but the **White Lady** on the road to Kalomitsi really swings on a good night.

KALOMITSI itself is the southernmost village on Sithonia, sheltering another large campsite and a surprisingly secluded beach at Liniraki. You'll get a great view over to the snow-topped peak of Mount Athos from here.

The port of **PORTO KOUFO** shelters a semi-circular inlet beach – well hidden from the southern breezes but unfortunately not so well hidden from growing yacht traffic. A large campsite sits just behind the beach area too but there is no other obvious tourist accommodation available for several miles.

The village of TORINI is nearest, and still has one or two remains of ancient fortifications just on the outskirts of the village. These date from Roman and Byzantine times and sit a good 300 yards up a hill just a mile or two in from the coast from Porto Koufo.

Travelling up the west coast you'll find the luxurious resort of **PORTO CARRAS,** probably the most exclusive and well-developed resort on mainland Greece. Here you'll discover the brightest, trendiest and liveliest nightlife in Northern Greece, as well as every conceivable sporting facility (water and otherwise) centred around some of the finest beaches in Europe.

Porto Carras has some of Greece's most famous and luxurious hotels, including the exclusive Luxury grade **Meliton Beach** and the A-grade **Sithonia Beach** which between them have almost 1000 bedrooms. You'll also have access to an open-air theatre and a marina in Porto Carras, and might even rub shoulders with international stars like Mick Jagger or Jacqueline Kennedy Onassis who have been known to drop in here. International cuisine in this resort is at its finest, and tourist facilities are very well developed. Prices are accordingly higher too. This is a high quality luxury resort which is perfect for everything – except for uncovering a flavour of the real Greece.

The nearby village of NEA MARAMAS is the largest on the peninsula and a constantly bustling source of excellent grill houses and small supermarkets. The **Restaurant Georg** is superb for locally caught fish, and sample the ice cream in **Café Itmos**.

Despite its glamorous name, the village of PARADISSOS just before Nea Maramas sees few visitors and has little to offer other than basic amenities for campers based at the nearby campsite.

West Coast

Apart from **FOURKA,** the tiny settlements along the west coast of Kassandra have not yet been developed as tourist resorts. They are less easily accessible by public transport although KTEL buses do run from Poligiros down through the villages of SIRIRI, POSSIDI, and NEA SKIONI. The area is particularly popular with campers, and there is a large official campsite at SANI.

The southern village of NEA SKIONI is as far as you can normally get by scheduled bus. This unassuming little village has a few quiet beaches nearby, and is surprisingly popular with small groups of young Scandinavian tourists who don't seem to mind the spartan facilities here.

Continuing up the western coast you'll find numerous relatively unspoilt little villages tucked away off the main road. KALANDRA and POSSIDI are particularly appealing, although neither offer a great deal to see or do, nor receive many package tour visitors beyond the occasional casual arrival. There is another large campsite at Possidi with facilities for over five hundred visitors. All these small fishing villages are linked by varied strips of attractive coastline but, although quieter, the west coast beaches tend to be a little cooler than those down the east coast.

Nightlife simply doesn't happen in this part of Kassandra unless you are content with passing a few hours in a rustic little taverna. Seafood is the culinary speciality in all these villages; always cooked superbly, each taverna boasting its own recipes. Good local wine helps cultivate the general atmosphere of hospitality.

The coast's only developed resort is at **FOURKA**, another small fishing village situated between Kalandra and Siviri. Fourka itself has a fine beach which you'll find about three-quarters of a mile down a scruffy dirt track from Siviri. It's not exactly on your door-step, but it is extremely easy to find. If you're passing this way on one of the scheduled bus services the driver will let you off at the appropriate spot if you hail 'Stassis!' in good time.

Once there, you will be rewarded by a gloriously long, narrow stretch of fine white sand and crystal-clear water. The village of SIVIRI itself has little to offer other than one or two welcoming tavernas. The road continues through nearby KASSANDRIA which is said to boast the best-preserved windmill in the whole district. It appears now to be just about the only one remaining in the region. Kassandria ends with the fabulous beach AKITI SANI. Easily accessible, and surrounded by thick pine-woods, Sani's popularity has yet to reach its full potential so overcrowding shouldn't be too much of a problem during the summer season. Bear in mind though that only a few tour operators visit the area around Fourka (therefore coach excursions don't exist) and to take advantage of the fine beaches on the west coast, like Akiti Sani, you will have to hire a car or plan your day around local bus services.

MOUNT ATHOS AND ENVIRONS

The most easterly of the three fingers of the Halkidiki peninsula is the Holy Mountain of Athos, an independent monastic republic, dating back for over one thousand years, and strictly forbidden to women. Over the centuries, several attractive holiday settlements have, however, sprung up around the neck of the peninsula – and these are definitely accessible to men and women.

An interesting afternoon's drive, by car or coach, will take you to the villages of STAGEIRA and STRATONIKI towards the eastern coast of the main Halkidiki landmass. Both villages are similar in layout, though Stageira is the smarter of the two, having several inviting little tavernas and gift shops dotted along the narrow main street. A particular point of interest is the large marble statue of **Aristotle** in the village, which you can see from the road on the way into Stageira. The statue sits atop a small wooden knoll and was built in honour of a few nearby ruins which are said to be the remains of the philosopher's birth place.

Ten miles further down the coast lies the village of **IERISSOS**, partly hidden in a picturesque wooded landscape. The national bus company, KTEL, has services which run to Ierissos daily from Thessaloniki and from here you will be able to pick out the series of mountain ranges which constitute the Athos prong. The **Hotel Marcos** is the tidiest of one or two small hotels in the village. Excursions are possible from here to the nearby traditional settlements of **GOMATI** and **MEGALI PONAGIA**. The beaches around this area are not great so stick to Kassandra or Sithonia if it's purely sunshine you are after.

The bridge across into the peninsula proper occurs at **NEA RODA**, the narrowest point of the Athos neck and a bustling fishing port where seafood is a harbour speciality. Check out the **Restaurant Xeres** for good local produce.

From Nea Roda you get a glorious view over the island of **AMOULIANI**, a small inhabited island just off the north-west coast of the peninsula. The journey across takes about half an hour and caiques run once or twice a day from **TRIPITI** a nearby mainland village with a small harbour. Amouliani has only a few people living there now and, accordingly, facilities are limited. The fishing hamlet of Amouliani itself is, however, enchanting, and the opportunities for long rambles across the island are virtually limitless.

The last village before you reach the monastic republic is the resort of **OURANOPOLIS**. The village has an impressive Byzantine tower, built originally in AD 1292 by the Emperor Adronicus II. Weather and warfare have taken their toll over the centuries, and the tower can be viewed only from the outside. The reclusive English authoress Barbara Lock lived in the tower for many years before her death about ten years ago. Her furniture and many possessions have remained shut away inside since her death as legal investigations continue to clarify their rightful ownership. Her English secretary still lives in the village and this popular local character is quite a goldmine of local history if you happen to come across her!

Accommodation overnight is essential if you plan to catch the early morning (and only) boat to DAFNI in the monastic republic. The hotels **Kranopoli** and **Acrogiali** are good – C-grade – and the owner of the latter also owns the only boat to Dafni! You'll find the hotel Acrogiali just one hundred yards round the corner to the left from where the bus stops, with car parking space on the seafront.

For women, an afternoon's boat trip from Ouranopolis is as close to the Holy Republic as you can reach. Even then, the boat cannot come within 500 yards of the coastline lest the monks spot you and be led from the straight and narrow with the aid of a pair of powerful binoculars!

For men, however, a visit to Mount Athos promises to be one of the most memorable and truly unforgettable experiences of your life. Unless you are a Greek national, only ten foreigners daily are allowed in, and each of these *must* have an entry permit issued by either the Ministry of Foreign Affairs at No. 2 Zalokosta Street in Athens, or else at the Ministry of Northern Greece (Directorate of Civil Affairs) at Dioikitiriou Square in Thessaloniki. Before you can get the relevant permit you must first of all secure a letter of recommendation (for which there is a fee) from your Embassy or Consulate in Greece.

The last (ever) British Consul to Thessaloniki, Tony Bradfield, encouraged British visitors to visit Mount Athos, but he retired in the summer of 1986. A new consul was never appointed but Mr Bradfield's secretary, and an Honorary Consul, still operate from the old consular office. In theory, overnight stays on Mount Athos are forbidden except for men who have proven religious or scientific interests in the area. In practice, however, none will be refused a permit provided they understand the obvious need to respect the tranquillity and holy sanctity of Mount Athos.

Permits secured, the boat leaves early from Ouranopolis, skirts the Athos coastline for two hours, stopping at a few monasteries on the way to drop off the odd pilgrim or provision (anything from a tractor to a sack of potatoes). The boat eventually stops at Dafni and the place instantly looks and feels strange. The few run-down provisions shops are antiquated and poorly looked-after, and the absence of women and children is striking. A line of red-roofed, hut-like shops selling predominantly hand-made Athos souvenirs, sits opposite the quay. They include a 'café' that serves only bread and soup, and a customs shack where all passports will be checked and all bags searched when you leave. The Republic's only post office is in Dafni.

From Dafni you must make your way to **KARYES,** the Republic's 'capital' in the centre of the peninsula and reached only by a rickety old bus which runs from the harbour. This will cost you about one hundred drachmas. Quaint little signs, in English and in Greek, like 'PILGRIMS – BEWARE OF STARTING FOREST FIRE' adorn the untarred roads from here on.

Nothing can prepare you for Mount Athos, and you will be amazed at how time seems to have stood still, when you reach Karyes. All pilgrims must report to the administrative building, and surrender their entry permit. A large yellow certificate will be given in return assuring you of hospitality at any of the Republic's twenty surviving monasteries. Karyes is built around a beautiful tenth-century church – always open so have a look inside at the lovingly kept murals and icons. This is a taste of the feast of artistic Byzantine treasures about to unfold if you choose your monasteries with care.

The main street in town looks like an Elizabethan film set with its thick cobbles and tiny grocery stores selling the most basic of provisions at higher than average prices. No one in Karyes smiles and it is eerie in the extreme. Nor is there any noise, save for the occasional burst of pigeons ascending from a distant orchard. The silence here is truly deafening, and one of the things about this unusual place you'll never be able to forget.

From Karyes the choice is yours to go to any of the twenty inhabited monasteries. Be prepared (and clad accordingly) to walk everywhere. You may be lucky enough to hire a mule in Karyes, or even get a lift on *the* bus when it occasionally rumbles across country with provisions for a distant monastery. But don't count on it.

The busiest monasteries are those within a few miles of Karyes, **Pandeleimona Stavronokita** and **Iviron** but all have limited guest accommodation so get there as soon as possible after arrival. The roads are dry and dusty, and the sun unforgiving so take plenty to drink for your journey.

Guest accommodation is generally limited to a camp bed and simple food – but you *must* present yourself to the appropriate Guestmaster well before nightfall or else the monastery gate will be locked and not reopened under any circumstances. The Athos day runs from dawn to dusk (and their calendar is thirteen days behind the rest of the world's), but never forget when your return boat to Ouranopolis leaves Dafni. Of the monasteries near Karyes, head for any one but Iviron. This unclean, inhospitable place receives most visitors, but seems to welcome few, and the filthy bedlinen in cell-like dorms is unrepresentative of what you ought to expect.

Within the four-day limit allowed to visitors on Mount Athos, you are free to explore the landscape and visit as many monasteries as you wish. If you are lucky, you may be able to persuade a Guestmaster to show you some of the monastery's priceless art treasures. Sound and cine recording is forbidden, but photography is permitted. The Holy Mountain of Athos itself is a seven-hour climb each way, suitable only for groups and the super-fit but it truly is an experience that will take you to the roof of the world. Athos has to be seen to be believed. You will never forget the Holy Republic, so if you get the chance to visit it, take it while you can.

Eastern Macedonia and Thrace

KAVALA

One of Northern Greece's most attractive and accessible mainland resorts is Kavala. This bustling town is the principal port in Eastern Macedonia and lies on the slopes of Mount Symvolon. Kavala was founded in the 6th century BC by settlers from Paros. It became a Roman territory in 168 BC, later serving as a base for the fleet of Brutus and Cassius before their defeat at Philippi.

Modern-day Kavala is a busy passenger port (primarily to Thassos island) and a major centre for the comings and goings of the Greek cotton trade. The sightseer will be particularly rewarded by a visit to Kavala since traces of the town's rich history are very much in evidence.

Easiest to find is the harbour, always busy with the hourly Thassos ferries and morning fish markets. A host of good fish restaurants skirt the harbour front – the grillhouse in the large B-grade hotel **Galaxy** is outstanding. Above the harbour, occupying what was once the site of the ancient acropolis, is the magnificent **Byzantine Castle.** Standing defiantly on the top of the old Panagia district of the town, the ancient ramparts are only open to visitors in the summer months. The small admission charge is well worth it for the commanding views seaward, but beware not to get lost in the labyrinth of tiny passageways on your way up to the castle.

Nearby is the **House of Muhammad Ali** (not the boxer!). Narrow cobbled alleyways lead to this quaint old whitewashed timber house where the founder of a large dynasty of Egyptian kings was born in 1769. He was *not* born in the Byzantine Castle as some guidebooks say. The timber structure has been lovingly preserved, and an elderly (non-English-speaking) guide will gladly show you around the (totally empty) rooms for a modest tip. Other than what it says in this (or any other) guidebook, there is no indication whatsoever, beyond the old Greek guide, as to why the house is special!

Kavala's two other main points of interest are the massive late medieval **aqueduct,** and the **archaeological museum.** You cannot miss the aqueduct, towering over the town two huge tiers high. It was originally constructed by Suleiman the Magnificent to supply the expanding town, then under Turkish rule, with water from the nearby hills. You'll find the museum at the far end of the waterfront, away from the Panagia district and open most days. A good array of local finds, including much from **PHILIPPI** and **AUDIRA,** are on display.

Hotel accommodation, and eating out, in Kavala are excellent. In addition to the luxurious **Galaxy** on the seafront, the hotel **Egnatia,** with a well-kept roof garden, and the **Oceanis,** with a private swimming pool and discotheque, are good. Kavala's finest restaurants include two superb grills; in **Taverna Saloniki** (no. 2 bus to Songroulou), or the **Mikalas** in Platia Eleftherias for more traditional Greek fare.

A memorable excursion from Kavala is nearby **PHILIPPI,** one of the finest archaeological sites in Greece and one of unequalled religious significance outside the Holy Land. Settled from the fourth century BC, from when the mined theatre dates, the apostle Paul himself visited Philippi in the early years AD and established the first Christian community anywhere in Europe.

A host of magnificent ruins lie over a large site, including the old town walls, a large rectangular **forum** dating from the time of Marcus Aurelius (AD 161–180), several rock-cut **shrines** and two impressive **basilicas**. The larger of the two is easily recognizable from the massive masonry pillars, but it was the smaller one which was said to have been the prison in which the apostle Paul was confined and later executed.

The sense of history around Philippi is overwhelming. Regular trips are organized from different travel operators in Kavala and, during the summer months, classical drama performances are staged within the ruins of the Roman theatre. In such overpowering surroundings, the fact that you don't understand the Greek language is a mere detail.

Three popular sandy beaches lie within close reach of Kavala. Less than a mile away is **KALAMITSA**, very clean and surprisingly quiet too. The beach is privately owned by the B-grade hotel **Lucy**, which also has its own swimming pool and is one of the safest and cleanest hotels in this area.

A little up the coast are public beaches at **BATIS** and **TOSKA** which are equally appealing. Both comfortably manage to accommodate countless thousands each summer but in peak season Batis becomes over-crowded as hot, sweaty campers spill down from the adjoining N.T.O.G. campsite.

For more seclusion, and equally impressive sunbathing, head a little further down the coast to the tiny villages of **NEA IRAKLISTA** and **NEA PERAMOS**. Both these cosy fishing harbours have remained, so far, hidden from the bulk of sun-worshipping tourists. Wide beaches and great views over to Thassos island will be your reward.

A few hours east of Kavala lies **ALEXANDROUPOLIS,** the only other town of any size in this region. Barely twenty miles from the politically sensitive Greco-Turkish border, this dusty industrial town has very little to offer visitors other than a night's rest if you're planning to travel further east. There are no places of interest to speak of, and the town's long beach is filthy. Even in the summer, this place feels uncomfortably warmer and stickier than the rest of the region.

The Turkish influence is very strong. You occasionally see women wearing veils, the shops are poorly stocked, like those in Istanbul backstreets, and the telling Greek warmth towards strangers is noticeably absent from the locals. Hotel accommodation is limited to a few C-grade hostel-type places around Vass. Georgiou Street, or the B-grade **Alexander Beach** hotel a mile out of town.

If you've time to spare (and stacks of patience at the hopelessly under-staffed railway station), consider a quick jaunt across to **ISTANBUL**. There is no appreciable service to anywhere nearer than Istanbul, on the other side of the Turkish border, but if you have a couple of days' freedom to travel by train, bus or hire-car, the overnight trip is very worthwhile.

THASSOS (*Limenas*)

An hour's ferry journey (hourly from Kavala during the summer) will take you to the lush, attractive island of Thassos. Settlers first arrived on Thassos before the seventh century BC when the Parians, from the island of Paros, took a fancy to the then rich gold seams running through the island. A flourishing tourist trade is fast becoming the modern-day gold seam for the residents of Thassos.

The regular ferries from Kavala land at SKARA PRINOS, a small village with one or two reasonable cafés if you've time to kill before your ferry. From here you can catch one of two waiting KTEL buses to either **LIMENARIA,** in the south of the island, or **THASSOS TOWN** (*Limenas*) to the east.

 Thassos Town is the island's active little capital, with a population of two thousand, and is worth a visit. It has the island's best hotel, the B-grade **Timoleon,** together with at least seven C-grade places. Private rooms are available in abundance for the independent traveller, and the seafront Tourist Police will give you the (extensive) list on request.

The island's main point of interest is the remains of an ancient Roman theatre just outside Limenas. There's not a lot left at the site now but a small museum, close to the original port, contains most of the finds from the site. Thassos is a good shopping centre for a small town, and an absolute *must* for any visitor is **Gregory's Gift Shop.** This Aladdin's Cave is already an attraction in itself. Every possible souvenir – jewellery, leather, pottery, real sponges – are stocked high into all the possible spaces in this already groaning shop. Gregory himself speaks fluent English and is in his element when asked about the history of Thassos. He also produces the best map of the island, which includes a potted history, and this is well worth the hundred or so drachmas if you plan to stay more than a day or so. Modest nightlife on Thassos is limited to three reasonable nightspots in Limenas – discos **Zodiac**, **Arcouda** and **Lernos.**

Less than two miles down the coast lies **MAKRIAMOS**, one of the best known and most expensive parts of the island. So far, this is the only developed resort on Thassos. It is an idyllic location, even allowing for the hopelessly crowded beaches in July and August. A perfect sun-trap, Makriamos has one of those picture postcard yellow beaches merging gracefully with the clear blue Aegean. A stunning forest landscape blends into the background, stretching back from the edges of the sand. This is a safe, central, family location. Attractive A-grade bungalows are available for rent nearby and bus connections are good.

Further down the eastern coast is the village of KINIRA, a small place with a long, clean, but exposed beach. The village's beach lies within three-quarters of a mile of its island namesake – an energetic swim is perfectly feasible for experienced swimmers.

Still in the vicinity of Makriamos, and that stretch of coast, the finest beach is at AGIOS IONIS. A popular summer suntrap with a truly spectacular yellow core beach. A couple of tavernas open up around here to keep summer visitors fed and watered!

The island's second largest town, a sleepy village compared with Limenas, is **LIMENARIA.** The village has remarkably little to offer beyond a few basic shops and a handful of friendly tavernas. **Nikos Maramos** restaurant is particularly good for local fish. The small, and very public beach is the only poor one on the island. Luckily it is surrounded by many that are better.

Just a couple of miles away lie **POTOS** and **PEFKARIA**, two really quaint villages with superb sandy beaches. Surprisingly under-developed, these comfortable retreats are easily accessible to the rest of the island yet sufficiently off the beaten track not to be noticed by most casual tourists. Numerous private rooms are available in the villages, and the couple of really modest (D or E-grade) hotels there were due to be refurbished last season.

A small, Caribbean-like bay, known as **ARCHANGELOS** has been formed close to the monastery of Archangelon. The monastery (like most religious houses in Greece) does welcome sensibly dressed visitors, with legs and shoulders fully covered! The cove itself is immaculate and breathtaking, but swiftly crowded with the overflow from the equally popular twin coves of **ALIKI** a mile or two further east.

Overall, Thassos has a surprising amount to offer visitors and, to an extent, this is being recognized by the growing number of tour operators who include the island in their schedule. The best balance between being developed and undiscovered is always difficult to find but, for the time being, Thassos has achieved just that.

THESSALONIKI

Said to be first settled by the Phoenicians around the time of the Trojan War, Thessaloniki was properly founded by Kassandros in 315 BC and named after his wife Thessalonike, a sister of Alexander the Great. The city's reputation slumped during the Middle Ages before which time it had been the second city of the Byzantine Empire. Greeks began to return to the Turk-dominated city around the eighteenth century, and by 1912 Thessaloniki was finally liberated from Turkish forces.

Modern Thessaloniki is a vibrant sea-port and commercial city, renowned for its big international trade fair each September. It is the largest city in Greece after Athens, maintaining a fine university and many of the hallmarks of a long and colourful history spanning more than two millenniums.

Finding your way around Thessaloniki is relatively easy if you bear in mind that the city is built predominantly in blocks of streets. The city's main streets run parallel to one another but most of the points of interest are within walking distance of the city's main attraction: **Egnatia Street**. Here stands the impressive old **Arch of Galerius**, with carvings depicting the emperor's campaigns against the Persians in the late 3rd century AD. There isn't a great deal of the original Arch left now beyond a couple of central pillars and unfortunately these have been vandalized with spray-paint over the years.

In Roman times, a colonnaded street originally ran between the Arch and the huge **Rotunda** which you'll see about a hundred yards to the left of the Arch. Originally built as a mausoleum for Galerius, the huge round church was later converted into a Christian church dedicated to Saint George. The mosaics inside are quite magnificent if you get the chance to have a look at them, and the eighty-foot-wide golden dome is really quite stunning. Unfortunately the Rotunda has been closed to ordinary members of the public for almost a decade now as a result of some minor earthquake damage which seems to be taking an inordinate length of time to be put right. A reasonable alternative to visiting the Rotunda is to have a look inside the large **Greek Orthodox Church** which is situated just in front of the Arch. The murals of Jesus and the Virgin Mary are stunning, but do remember that this is a current place of worship so noisy tourists – especially with flash cameras – will not be welcome.

Continuing down Egnatia Street you will pass a few more ruins on your left. These have been transformed into part of a small – and very public – park with DO NOT TOUCH signs littering the well-tended flower beds! The ruins themselves are part of the original Roman settlement which turns up all over the city.

Egnatia Street ends at a huge road junction with the massive, normally empty, park-like site for the annual September trade fair on the left and the city's famous **archaeological museum** on the right. If you are lucky enough to visit Thessaloniki during the trade fair, you will find the city positively heaving with visitors and excited locals alike. Do *not* arrive in the city during the fair without arranging accommodation well in advance or else you will almost certainly be sleeping on a park bench.

The massive archaeological museum justly deserves its reputation as one of the country's finest outside Athens. Even if you are one of those people who loathe tramping round 'stuffy old museums' you cannot fail to be impressed with this place. Open every day (mornings only on Sunday) with discounts for students and children, this is Northern Greece's primary collection of treasures from Thessaloniki, Macedonia, and Thrace. Arranged roughly clockwise, the early years of the city's own history are revealed, with identification cards on all exhibits in Greek and English. The surviving glassware and pottery are very impressive and there are countless priceless finds from the **Tombs of Vergina,** including that of King Philip II himself. Philip's tomb was emptied in 1978 and, as well as numerous household items and pieces of jewellery, the King's complete skeleton was found and is on display in a glass case. He has survived in remarkably good shape considering he was assassinated in 338 BC!

Right on the seafront, at the far end of Vasileos Konstantinou, stands the city's renowned **White Tower.** The tower was built by the architect Sinaian in the first half of the 16th century on the site of the last remaining city walls constructed during the Byzantine era. The tower is now a small museum filled with artefacts found in archaeological digs nearby. It is normally possible to climb up inside almost to the top but, for safety reasons, it is not possible to reach the roof. Glass cabinets of well-documented exhibits fill each level inside and there is one particularly remarkable piece of eleventh-century silk to look out for. Beware of the low ceilings as you climb up the wide staircase – you'll need to duck if you're over 5'11"! Admission to the White Tower is free but it exists largely on donations so a modest contribution would be a good idea.

The city has one or two other points of interest which are less well known, including a **Folklore Museum** near the seafront, and a **Citadel,** with the remains of seven ancient towers. The imposing stronghold has walls still standing over thirty feet high and is flanked by lengthy sections of the original city walls on either side. A walk along these old walls will take you through some of the quainter old backstreets of Thessaloniki.

In addition to historical points of interest, Thessaloniki is a great shopping centre. The city is peppered with tiny backstreets that are just waiting to be discovered by bargain-hunting visitors and you'll find the busiest tend to be those which branch off the main (Egnatia) street such as Menexe and Chalkeon. Handcarved wooden goods, leather accessories, belts and so on, together with quality cotton goods are amongst the best bargains. Food shops seem to outnumber even the countless wooden huts which sell newspapers and lottery tickets – and without a doubt one of Thessaloniki's 'specials' are oranges. Most are grown locally and they are a real bargain to keep your vitamin C levels up.

Another bargain is a natural sponge. These were used for centuries before the invention of plastic substitutes and are considered quite a luxury in many parts of the world. For a couple of pounds any one of these backstreet shops will provide you with a truly Greek, original, and lasting souvenir of your visit. You'll also be pleasantly surprised if you ever see them on sale in Harrods or the like to remember how many pounds you saved!

One thing to avoid in Thessaloniki particularly are lottery tickets. These oblong football coupon-type tickets are on sale everywhere – shops, newspaper stands, even by beggars in the street desperate for a few extra drachmas. They are not expensive, but utterly useless if you don't understand the draw procedure. The winners are usually announced every couple of weeks for the really big prizes anyway, so even if you did understand the procedure you would be unlikely still to be in Greece at the time. The sellers can be a real nuisance in the streets, though, so you'd be best to politely refuse each time.

You will not be disappointed when you come to look for a place to dine out in Thessaloniki. Souvlaki places abound in the city. Virtually any sidestreet will reward you with a filling souvlaki for one hundred drachmas, usually with a wedge of bread and glass of water if you are prepared to sit in. For a more substantial meal, virtually any one of the major hotels in town will serve a respectable dinner to residents and non-residents. Because the competition is so great in the city, the choice and prices are good.

Try walking along the seafront, from the White Tower towards the harbour or vice versa, and any one of the small restaurants along there will do you proud. Probably the best is the **Restaurant Taverne** about half way along. Bear in mind that virtually all restaurants will have menus bearing two scales of price charges. You will always be expected to pay the greater of the two prices in order to take account of the various service taxes which are imposed at national and local government levels in Greece.

Accommodation in Thessaloniki shouldn't be too great a problem if you leave home without a definite booking. There is no shortage of hotels in the city, although undoubtedly the finest is the Luxury-grade **Makedonia Palace** on Leoforos Megalou Alexandrou – unashamed luxury at unashamed luxury prices! Perhaps surprisingly, there are only two A-grade hotels in the city. The 353-bed **Capitol** at 8, Monastirou and the **Electra Palace** just round from the tourist office.

The best of the hotels include the **Astor** (B), **Egnatia** (B), **Olympic** (B), **El Greco** (B with a good restaurant), **ABC** (C), **Continental** (C) and the **Grande Bretagne** (C). A few of the official N.T.O.G. hotel recommendations are over-generous but, on the whole, all are clean and tidy. Certainly those used by British operators are near the top end of the scale in view of the relative cost of staying in a Greek hotel as opposed to somewhere more expensive (for the time being anyway) like Spain or the Algarve.

Nightlife in Thessaloniki has the potential to be what you want to make it in a cosmopolitan city. In addition to cinemas and theatre – with a limited appeal for non-Greek speakers – there is an abundance of vibrant nightspots. Your own hotel will almost certainly be able to offer something but, failing that, most of the larger hotels are clueing up to the idea that foreign visitors like to be entertained. Wander along the seafront and you should be able to spot one or two of the tavernas offering traditional entertainment. One of the city's better nightspots is the **Blue Sky disco** just on the outskirts of town, heading towards the airport.

Down the Coast from Thessaloniki

A handful of smaller resorts are clustered along the western coast down from Thessaloniki towards the Halkidiki. Just past the outskirts of the city, close to where the airport is situated, is MIKRA. No more than a bright little village, each summer Mikra sees a high proportion of foreign visitors, keen to escape the city for a while. You will find a reasonable beach here but, like most of these coastal villages outside the city, they do get very crowded, very quickly, as the summer temperature in the city begins to start nudging 30°C (90°F). Mikra has a smart B-grade motel, the **Haris**, but its thirty beds fill quickly in summer.

Virtually alongside Mikra is NEI EPIRATES, a small village which tends to absorb the coastal overload. It has little to recommend it other than being an alternative choice of resort if the coastal ones prove full. It tends to get quite noisy in summer, and decent tourist accommodation is limited to a single C-grade hotel and a few private rooms.

Further down the coast, on a chunk of land that suddenly juts out from the rest of the coastline, lies AGIA TRIADA. The popularity of this appealing resort is growing annually, not least because the beach facilities here are the finest between the city and the Halkidiki. This place has fine golden sands with ample space for safe, family bathing although don't expect to have this paradise all to yourself at the height of summer!

Agia Triada is an ideal choice of resort if you want to combine a good beach holiday with some of the sights and advantages of the city on your doorstep. There are good bus connections into the city, and no shortage of reasonable hotels in the resort including the large 200-bed **Akti Ilou** (Sun Beach) hotel, B-grade. There's not much anywhere along this stretch of coast for the independent traveller (the packages use these large resort hotels) but the 148-bed (C-grade) **Galaxius** in Agia Triada sometimes has space available in summer.

Some of the overflow from Agia Triada end up at nearby ASVESTOHORI, not quite as well sited a resort but with one or two reasonable hotels and still conveniently close to the main bus routes north and south. An extensive **camping ground** is situated at AKTI THERMAIKOU, offering some of the best campsite facilities anywhere in this region.

Continuing down the coast you'll come to GEFIRA: by no means the best resort in this part of the region and, compared with those around it, mediocre. Accommodation and things to do in and around the village are very limited – it's less than hospitable to independently travelling foreigners, and in any case its eighteen beds quickly fill up in summer.

On the main road east from Thessaloniki, heading towards STAVROS, you'll come across the village of LANGADAS. The village is surprisingly secluded, even for an inland resort, and offers excellent views across **Peristeron,** the second and much larger of the two great lakes in Northern Greece which just about cut off the Halkidiki area entirely. Langadas has one particularly attractive, B-grade pension, the **Lido,** together with the usual basic facilities of a small village including a chemist and an OTE telephone office.

One of the most picturesque, and secluded, resorts in the area is **NEA APOLONIA**, scarcely more than an offshoot from the slightly larger town of Apolonia next door. Nea is not on the main bus route, but instead is a short (mile or so) walk up from the road. Nea Apolonia is becoming increasingly popular as a spa resort and already has at least one large hotel – the 116-bed **Aristotelis.**

This is an attractive little spot, but for a poignant reminder of all too recent events in Greece look out for the collapsed old stone footbridge on your right as you leave. This was one of the numerous victims of the major earthquake which hit this region in the late seventies and has, sadly, been replaced by an utterly unappealing modern-day concrete equivalent.

The two great lakes have produced a few fine-looking inland beaches but you ought to avoid these if you possibly can. Most of them have formed on private land and, in any case, they tend to conceal dangerous sands and unexpectedly steep gradients. Stick to the coasts for safe swimming.

One or two small villages inland are fast developing as tourist resorts. So far, **EYZONI**, **NEA HALKIDONA**, and **DREOKASTRO** are being noticed by tour operators. None of these smaller resorts have a great deal to offer someone looking for a conventional-type package holiday – beaches, nightlife, a good shopping centre and so on. For the time being though, accommodation is limited to small, home-like hotels and pensions and for a real get-away-from-it-all holiday, they are ideal. Unlike Western Greece, these resorts have the added advantage of being relatively central to Thessaloniki for the purpose of travelling there from Britain and for excursions when you're there.

As you head out, or return, to the city, look out for the small resort of **PANORAMA PEREA**. As the city continues to spread, Panorama is fast becoming the up-market commuter suburb. As the name implies, the views from Panorama are quite something. Thessaloniki nestles in a wide, shallow valley and from here you can see the lie of the land. The hotels are pricey – but good. Both the

A-grade **Nefeli** and **Panorama** do the view justice in the resort of Panorama Perea. If you can afford to stay here, it is an ideal base to explore this region including Thessaloniki.

Thessaloniki is fortunate in having so many satellite resorts around it. If you cannot stand the thought of a week or a fortnight in the city itself, particularly if you normally live in a city, yet cannot bear to miss out on the region's vibrant capital city, then head for one of the resorts touched on in this section. Unlike many of the Halkidiki resorts, those covered here are, by and large, in their early stages of development so may be of additional interest to visitors keen to avoid fellow tourists as much as possible.

Peloponnese

The Peloponnese, the most southerly part of the Greek mainland, is ideal for the first-time visitor to Greece. Its important (and for once really interesting!) historical sights, good resorts and deserted areas provide you with whatever type of holiday you wish. It most suits the Sightseer and the Recluse, however, as away from the sights it is a predominantly highland region, and there is a great variety of landscape from the hills of Arcadia in the centre, to the flat plains of the north-west and long, sandy beaches on the west coast.

Over 70 tour operators offer holidays in the area, most based around a few resorts. Prices can vary up to £100 for the same hotels so check the brochures carefully. Surprisingly it is the smaller operators who usually have a wider choice. Accommodation is also available for the independent traveller in all but the most remote areas, but at the resorts the earlier in the morning you can arrive to book a room, the better.

History

The island of Pelops is named after Pelops, in whose honour and at whose funeral the Olympic Games took place.

Between 2000 and 1000 BC the Peloponnese were dominated by Mycenae, and then for the next 1000 years by Sparta. In the Middle Ages the Slavs, the Frankish Crusaders and finally, from 1453 the Turks held it. It was against the Turks that the Peloponnese led the revolt which, aided by Britain, France and Russia, led to the founding of modern Greece.

Practical Details

COMMUNICATIONS

Access to the Peloponnese is very easy. Most people fly to Athens and are then taken by coach to their holiday resort, but there are also flights to Kalamata, Kythra and Sparta. Independent travellers can easily reach the area by train, bus or car. There are also ferries from Piraeus to most of the ports on the east coast, and a hydrofoil from the Zia marina nearby.

Getting around the Peloponnese itself is fairly straightforward if not always very quick. Trains run on a narrow gauge and tend to be picturesque rather than efficient. The buses, unlike the rail network, cover the whole of the area, but are even more crowded than the trains. In the very undeveloped parts like the south there is often only one bus a day, which can add an extra day to each stop you make unless you are prepared to take a taxi or hitch. The area is ideal for touring by car. The roads are quite good and clearly this is the most convenient way to travel, enabling you to stop where and when you wish, but hiring a car is, as always in Greece, very expensive. Bikes and mopeds can be hired for shorter distances, but beware of the huge tourist coaches! The good communications in the Peloponnese means that you can get around the many interesting sights without having to repeat any part of your journey.

CLIMATE

Although not humid, the summer is very hot, especially inland. The temperatures are between 26° and 32°C (about 85° to 90°F). The evenings are cool so bring a jumper. Homer's description of the Peloponnese as a 'thirsty' place is still true, for between April and September there is almost no rain. If you dislike the heat the spring and the autumn are cooler and there are fewer tourists.

CULINARY SPECIALITIES

There are no special foods within the Peloponnese, but the *anginares*, young artichokes, are particularly good and you should try the grapes from around Corinth and olives from Kalamatu. The region is one of the main wine-producing areas of Greece. The two best are Deneotika and St Helena, and though they may be the same price per gallon as petrol, they are particularly good. Other wines are Nemea, Castel and Daniels.

WHERE TO GO FOR WHAT

For the Sightseer this is one of the richest areas of Greece containing the ruins of Olympus, Mycenae, Epidavros, and moving forward to mediaeval times, Mystras and the Mani. The major sights are very crowded during the summer, but they should still not be missed. Try visiting them early or late in the day, or if you can withstand the heat and have a good hat, the siesta time. Food can be expensive here, so take a picnic and also try to pick up one of the local printed guides, for the ones at the site are frequently sold out. There is no need to stay near the sites since nearly all can be reached easily by a day trip from 'civilization'.

The main resorts in the area, with the best hotels for families and the most nightlife for socialites, tend to be on the best beaches. So for Families, Socialites and the Sun-worshipper, the same resorts are suitable: **TOLON, PORTO HELI, NAFPLIO** and **LOUTRAKI.**

The Recluse should steer clear of such areas. Their havens are found instead in the middle and the south of the region, especially the Mani. Here there are few Greeks and even fewer tourists. The only drawback is that transport can be very sporadic in the very remote areas, not that the true recluse would object to this. However, even the developed areas like the Argloid still contain quieter towns like Kranidi.

Sports enthusiasts will find that most facilities are available at the large resorts with everything from paragliding to scuba-diving. They will also be positively encouraged to drink the water at the spa towns of **LOUTRAKI**, near Corinth, **LOUTRA KYLLINIS** and **KAIFOS** in the west and **METHAN** in the Argloid.

Remember not to disregard an area simply because it does not have your symbol. For instance spa towns like Loutraki also have good beaches and hotels, equally the ancient ruins at Mycenae may be of historic importance to the sightseer, but to a child it may simply be a large playground, but to both the site is very enjoyable.

The Nature Lover will find many of the views from the ruins stunning, and can also enjoy many exhilarating, and exhausting, hikes. The dedicated hiker should head for the more mountainous areas in Arcadia and further south. For more information contact the Greek Alpine Club at 7 Karageorgis Servias, Athens (Tel: 323 4555).

To consider the Peloponnese in more detail it is divided into four areas: Corinth, the south, the west and the north.

Corinth

The outstanding ruins, good beaches, and the geological convenience of the main towns being near each other are the main appeal of this area.

After surviving three earthquakes (none recently) and a fire, the town of Corinth is now earthquake-proof but somewhat dull, though it does have a good park and a nice beach promenade. If you need somewhere to stay, among the best hotels are the **Bellevue** at 41 Damaskinou and the **Apollon** on Prinis Street. More simple are the **Ephira** and the **Kypsolos** on Ephira St. For the independent traveller there is also a campsite about 1½ miles out of the town on the road to Corinth.

To find the facilities in the town go straight to the park, where you will find everything you need. The Tourist Police are at no. 33 (Tel: 232 830) and the OTE, the international telephone office, at no. 47 Koliatsou. There is also a Post Office at 47 Adiamandau Street and a bank in Theotraki Street. The two best things in the town are perhaps the bus stations. The first is situated on the park and from here buses go to Ancient Corinth, about a 25-minute journey, every half-hour from 7 a.m. to 8 p.m. The second bus station is just above the first and from here, the buses go to Nafplio, Argos and Athens.

The visitor should go and see the **Corinth Canal,** ideally at a time when a ship is going through. This is a man-made shortcut across the isthmus, allowing ships to avoid going all the way round the Peloponnese, and is about 4 miles long, 30 yards wide and about 270 yards deep.

There are no outstanding restaurants but the **Anaxagoras** and **Kantina** are better than many others. The coffee shops along the lower Ethnikis Anistasis will be enjoyed by those with a sweet tooth. There are also two cinemas on Danaskinoa Street.

The most popular excursions from Corinth, and the main reason for coming here, is to visit the site of **ANCIENT CORINTH,** a must for everyone, not simply the Sightseer. Since it controls access to the Peloponnese, Corinth has been a fortified town since the Bronze Age. The town grew rich as the result of the tolls it levied on trade passing through it and soon became so notorious for its extravagant indulgence that St Paul came here to try to reform it. Of more interest to contemporaries perhaps is the **Temple of Aphrodite,** served by 1000 sacred prostitutes. So famous were they that in Roman times the term 'Corinthian woman' was synonymous with a whore.

The best view is from the north of the site and if it looks a rather disappointing heap of rubble to you, remember that 300,000 Romans and 450,000 slaves once lived here. The **Argora** shows our shopping arcades are nothing new. Note the 20 seat loo just on the left of the road. In the Argora you can see the raised platform, the **Bima,** where speakers addressed the crowd. St Paul spoke from here and was arrested for causing a riot! Take a torch and explore the **Fountain of Peirine** on the north-eastern edge of the Agora (the water has since been diverted to the village). Also worth visiting are the **Temple of**

Apollo on the hill, and a quite interesting **museum**. The site is open Mon to Sat 9 a.m. to 6.30 p.m., and 9 a.m. to 5.30 p.m. on Sundays.

Most people do not bother, but if you have the energy the 1½-hour walk up to **Acrocorinth** is well worth the visit. Apart from the castle there is also a stunning view. A Byzantine General committed suicide by riding his horse into the sea rather than surrender the castle.

There are other sights in the area apart from Ancient Corinth. Just north of the town is the spa town of **LOUTRAKI**. The beach is the largest in Greece, and almost uniquely it has large sand dunes. It makes a pleasant place to visit on a day trip or to use as a base. There are some good hotels such as the **Acropite**, the **Kontis**, the **Galaxy** and **Mon Repos**. The sporting type would probably enjoy the very well-equipped **Club Poseidon**. Just above Loutraki is PERACHORA, a small village with stunning views.

South of Corinth is the famous old city of **MYCENAE**. In 1874 the German archaeologist Heinrich Schliemann, a genius for discovery if not discernment, uncovered what he thought was the tomb of Agamemnon. In fact the tomb turned out to belong to someone else, but the site is still worth a visit. The supposed tomb of the hero is on the right as you walk up the road. The sheer size of the tomb (the lintel above the door is 28 ft long and weighs 220 tons) is perhaps less impressive than the expert masonry and excellent acoustics. You enter the main site through the famous **Lion Gates** which are shown in most of the brochures. Sadly these also show that vandalism is not a new problem, for the lions were damaged many years ago. Here you will also find the beehive tombs. Perhaps more memorable than the ruins themselves are the views.

If you do wish to stay here, follow in the footsteps not of Agamemnon but of Virginia Woolf and Debussy, who stayed at the now slightly expensive **Belle Helena**, or try the somewhat cheaper **La Petite Planete**. For independent travellers on the road to the site is **Mycenae Camping**.

Along from Corinth the next major town is **ARGOS**, the home of Jason and the Argonauts, which claims to be the oldest inhabited town in Europe. Whether this is true or not, today the town is rather drab and industrial, and you would be better advised to stay at Nafplio or Tolon. There are, however, some reasonable hotels such as the **Apollo**

Inn on 15 Korai Street and the **Hermes** on Konstantia. There are also some interesting sights. The **archaeological museum** contains some fine mosaics which look particularly good when wet (ask the guard to sponge them down). At the top of the town the castle has some excellent views. Further along are the ruins of the **Ancient Theatre**, on the street of that name, which although less impressive than those at Epidavros are well worth a visit. It has 81 tiers of seats and originally sat 20,000 people. Some time in the 4th century BC it was refitted and the orchestra pit was turned into a large pool for use in mock naval battles.

Near Argos is **Tiryns**, a fortified palace. The walls are so huge, between 20 and 60ft thick, that the ancients assumed that they could only have been built by the giant Cyclops. This excellent sight is surprisingly not very popular with tourists, but is worth making the effort to visit.

Three miles west of Argos is KEFALARI, where a church now stands on a site originally dedicated to the god Pan. Here there is a strange 4th century BC pyramid which the experts believe must be part of some kind of military fortification.

Just south of Argos is **NAFPLIO,** a large modern resort with an elegant atmosphere, which would make an ideal touring base. There are a number of good hotels such as the **Dioscouri** on Byrnos, the very pleasant **Kotto** at 3 Farakopdou, set amidst orange and lemon trees, and the very comfortable **Agamemnon** at 3 Miaoul. Rather more simple is the **campsite** just outside of town.

The Tourist Police, on Praxitelous Street, are very helpful in providing information (Tel: 27 776). The OTE office is in front of the bus station on Nikatara Sq and is open from 6 a.m. to midnight.

Apart from being a good place to sit, the main square contains some interesting sights, such as the **Archaeological Museum.** Although you frequently need to be an expert to fully enjoy such places, this one is well worth a visit. Note especially the frescoes and the Mycenaean armour from the 15th century BC – quite a thought! Above the town is the **Palamidi Castle,** the largest castle in Greece, of great importance in the war of independence. There are 899 steps up to the castle but fortunately it is also possible to visit it by bus or taxi. Open Mon to Fri 9 a.m. to 5 p.m., weekends 10 a.m. to 3 p.m.

There are also a number of good restaurants in the town. Try the

Naifara and the **Ellas** on Konstadinou Street. An elegant place to eat is the **Kondogiorgis** on the waterfront. Take a boat or walk along the causeway to the Bordzi and try the very civilized **Aktaion**. Also to be recommended is the **Alekos** at 71 Bouboulinis. In the square the **Zakoroplasteron** has a strange name but serves very good breakfasts. There is a beach in the town, but the sun-worshipper would be better heading for ASSINI or TOLON.

Easily reached from the resort is EPIDAVROS, a large 3rd-century BC Roman theatre which is still largely intact. It looks very impressive with 54 tiers of seats for 14,000 people. From every seat you can see and hear perfectly, and the place is full of tour guides dropping pins and whispering to prove this. Every year a festival of classical plays is held here, performed in Greek. The tickets, which sell very quickly, are available from the office here, or in Athens (4 Stadiou Street, Tel: 32 21 459). Epidavros was a kind of pagan version of Lourdes, dedicated to the god of healing, Asclepius, who apparently occasioned over 70 miracles. Apart from the baths you can also see the temple of sleep, where the god apparently cured patients whilst they slept. Most of the buildings were destroyed by Christians in the early 4th century. Most visitors stick to the main paths but the valley itself is very scenic and an ideal place for a picnic. On the coast nearby is PALZA EPIDAVROS, which once had a population of 70,000 but is now of interest because it has a good beach.

The final resort in the area is **TOLON**, just down the coast from Nafplio. Over 20 tour operators offer holidays here, mainly because of the excellent beaches and for this reason it should be suitable for families or sun-worshippers. The resort is also fairly developed and should thus interest the socialite, and with good water sports, the sporting types. Most of the hotels are very small but popular with the tour operators are the **Tolo**, the **Mino**, the **Epidavro**, and the **Aris**. There is also a **campsite** at Kastraki.

Apart from the beach and the water sports there are few sights to enjoy. There are a number of popular bars such as the **Bamboo** and the **Dionysos**. Also worth mentioning is the cinema, situated on the beach! Nearby are two less-crowded beaches at ASSINI, NEA KIOS and KASTRAKI.

Further down the Argloid is **PORTO HELI**, a good beach resort.

This is a fairly developed resort and among the more popular hotels are the **Alycon,** with a disco, and the **Galaxy** with a pleasant roof garden. Nearby is ERMIONI, a small fishing village set on a beautiful bay which is beginning to be developed. Of particular interest to the Healthy-holiday type will be the **Plepi Kappa Club,** with tennis, golf and similar facilities.

Southern Peloponnese

Apart from the area around Mycenae, this is a quiet part of Greece, ideal for the recluse.

Modern **SPARTA** is of less historical importance than the ancient town which bears its name, but some of the tour operators use it as a base. A mainly Victorian town with tree-lined streets, it has considerably more charm than many of the resorts. The best hotel is the very comfortable **Apollon** on Thomopylon. Less luxurious but clean and pleasant is the **Maniahs** on Paleyou. Among the more simple and less expensive establishments are the **Sparti** at 46 Aghissilaou, and two good but rather noisy hotels, the **Cecil** and the **Panelliaion.**

There is a helpful Tourist Police office at 8 Hilonos Street, Tel: 28701, open 7 a.m. to 1.30 p.m. A bank is situated on Lykorgou, open Mon to Fri 8 a.m. to 2 p.m. One street away is the OTE office, on Kleombrotou, open Mon to Fri 6 a.m. to midnight, and a Post Office open Mon to Fri 7.30 a.m. to 2 p.m.

The most obvious place for a meal is around the main square. Among the many restaurants here the pizzas at the **Hriso Klithi** are both appetizing and cheap. For more Greek food try the **Sparti,** at 69 Lykorgou, the **Richia** near the town hall, the **Leski,** and finally the **Kali Kardia** at 39 Agisilaos.

The main attraction of the town is ANCIENT SPARTA, never itself a town but a collection of villages. It rose to power in about 700 BC and for the next 400 years controlled most of the Peloponnese, a power explained mainly by their control of themselves. Lycurgus, a famous Spartan, laid down a series of laws to govern Spartan life from its very beginning. Husbands and wives were kept apart for a long time so that when they saw each other children would be conceived with much vigour. For this same reason young women married to older men were allowed, and indeed encouraged, to have affairs. Deformed or handicapped children were simply left to die. Those that did survive were underfed to encourage them to develop cunning by theft, and were punished not for stealing, but for being foolish enough to be caught. They were forced to look at the ground all the time to remind them of their humility; indeed a Roman joke of the time was that you were more likely to hear a statue speak than a Spartan child. However inhuman these codes may seem, they clearly had their desired effect of making the population strong, for Sparta was only defeated by a simultaneous combination of a declining population, natural disasters and attack from enemies.

It is ironical that despite the enormous fame of Sparta little remains to be seen today. The Spartans never erected many of the buildings you expect to see on ancient sites, for town walls were considered a sign of the weakness of the people they defended and temples were unnecessary ostentation. A contemporary once remarked that future visitors would find it hard to believe that Sparta was as powerful as her history records, and indeed some visitors are a little disappointed. What remains to be seen is a theatre, built by the Romans so that they could watch the public floggings which formed part of the initiation of a Spartan boy into manhood, parts of an acropolis, and a temple to Aphrodite. There is also a good **museum** in the town on Lykorgou Street near the central square.

About 3 miles west of Sparta is the ancient site of **MYSTRA**, historically much less important, but much more popular with most tourists since there is much more to see. It is a large mediaeval city, built mostly by the Byzantines around the 13th and 14th centuries, which once had a population of 42,000 but is now deserted . . . apart, that is, for what sometimes seems like 42,000 tourists. Mystra is thought by many to be one of the best archaeological sites in Greece and is certainly worth a visit. The town contains many monasteries and churches, so remember to go modestly dressed.

Entering by the main gate at the bottom of the town you are near most of the interesting buildings, the **Mitropolis**, once a church and now a museum, the **Vrontokhion Monastery** and the **Perivleptos Monastery** where all the walls are covered in frescoes. Finally there is the **Pantanassa Convent** with more impressive frescoes and an excellent view. At the top of the hill is the **Palace,** with its huge audience chamber, the beautiful church of **St Sofia,** and finally the castle itself, which although of no great interest offers more wonderful views.

Heading further south you come to the **MANI PENINSULA,** an ideal place for the Recluse with few Greeks and even fewer tourists. The area is famous for its towers, built by feuding families to protect themselves from their neighbours. It has always been an isolated part of the country: Christianity only reached here 500 years after the rest of the mainland for instance, and today it still remains a very rural and undeveloped part of Greece.

On the far south of the Peloponnese, of which the peninsula is a part, is GYTHION, a small port to which Paris and Helen fled after they had eloped from Sparta, the event which later occasioned the Trojan wars. Today the town has a nice harbour, hilly streets and good views and would make an excellent base for exploring the Mani. The best hotel is the **Milton** but there are several other hotels worth considering such as the **Pantheon** and the slightly cheaper **Andreas.** There is also a **campsite** about 2 miles south of the town.

The Police, situated near the harbour, speak little English but are helpful. On the square you will find the OTE office open Mon to Fri 7.30 a.m. to 10 p.m. Further down is the Post Office, open Mon to Fri 7.30 a.m. to 4 p.m. Whilst staying in the town visit the **ancient theatre,** off Ermou Street. There is a beach in the town but it would be a good idea to travel to the east a few miles, where you will find better beaches. There are also a few pleasant restaurants. Try the **Pizzeria** for cheap Italian food or the **Kali Karthia** for something a little more Greek.

On the West of the Mani Peninsula is AREOPOLIS, a small hill village, which most independent travellers will probably stop at because it is one of the major bus junctions in the area. The bank, the OTE, and the Post Office are all situated on Kapelan Matapa Street just off the main square.

At the tip of the Mani is GEROLIMENAS, a pleasant town for a short stay. Nearby are the **Pirgos Dirou Caves.** Greece is famous for its caves, and all the resorts that have any nearby advertise them as much as possible in order to attract the tourists. This is understandable, but it does mean that many are not really worth visiting. However, the

Pirgos Dirou are some of the best caves in Greece and if you are in the area are worth making a detour for. The caves are flooded by an underground river and thus you can have the enjoyable experience of touring round them by boat, rather than having to walk up flights of steep steps. The boat is pulled along by the boatman grabbing the stalactites hanging from the roof! Floating lamps illuminate the cave and provide something of a magical atmosphere. Less magical are the crowds outside the cave and the wait to get in, but there is a beach alongside so queueing up takes on a rather different form than it does at home.

On the south-eastern coast of the Peloponnese is **MONEM-VASSIA,** a fortified Byzantine city similar to Mystra, known as the 'Gibraltar of Greece'. The modern town itself is also very pretty and worth visiting. The best hotel is probably the excellent **Malvasia** in the castle, but there are some good hotels in the town itself such as the **Monemvassia,** the **Artaion** and the **Minoa,** with good views. There are also several good restaurants such as the quiet **Dionysus** and the **Castello** on the causeway, but best of all is the **Cyprus,** with a very good view.

Just off the coast from here is the island of **KYTHERA,** very quiet and with no facilities, but ideal for the recluse. There is a ferry from the port here and also from Piraeus and Porto Heli, as well as flights from Athens. The port, KAPASALI, is very pretty and above it a 25 minute walk takes you to the CHORA. There are rooms to rent in both places. There are reasonable beaches at AG PELAGIAS and PLATI AMOS in the North.

Western Peloponnese

The main resort in this area is **KALAMATA,** situated on a large bay surrounded by mountains, and as yet, not too developed. The main area is a large industrial city but there is a good beach and a number of pleasant hotels nearby such as the **America,** the **Vasilikon** and the **Haicis.** There are also a couple of fairly similar **campsites** towards the east end of the beach, **Camping Patistu** and the **Sun and Sea.**

There is a Tourist Office on the waterfront, open 8.30 a.m. to 1.30 p.m., 5.30 p.m. to 8 p.m. Here you can pick up helpful advice as well as some helpful literature. The Tourist Police, useful if disaster strikes or when the Tourist Office is closed, is at 46 Anstomenos, south of the main square. On this square you will find the OTE office, open round the clock, and the banks. The Post Office is off the bottom right of the square on Iatropolou.

The dedicated sightseer might wish to visit the ancient **MESSAE**, near Mavrommati, where large walls and a few buildings remain of an old town, or the monasteries of **Valonidia, Voulkanos** and **Almiros**. Round the bay are two very pleasant and quieter beach resorts, PETALIDON and KORONI. The road then crosses to the mediaeval town of METHONI. This was besieged by the Venetians and under their control became one of the main stop overs for pilgrims on the way to the Holy Land. Today it makes an excellent excursion for there are good views as well as an interesting castle to explore.

Further up the west coast is **PILOS**, an elegant town with a large harbour. The name is a shortened form of Paliokastro, old castle, which refers to the Venetian castle which is the main sight of the town. About 30 minutes' drive north-east from here lies **Nestors Palace**. This is much larger and much more interesting than Mycenae, and although of less historical significance makes a very interesting excursion. Among the interesting sights are the excellent frescoes, the throne room, the bathroom (complete with jug!) and a few beehive tombs. There is also a good museum, but more interesting than perhaps all of this are the wonderful views. The site is open from 8.30 a.m. to 12.30 p.m., 4 p.m. to 6 p.m., Sun 9 a.m. to 3 p.m.

Further north is KIPARISSIA, with a good beach and pleasant views, and KAIFOS, with an excellent, uncrowded beach and a mineral water spring. Nearby is ANDRITSEA, another quiet town with a good beach. Inland there is an excellent **temple** at BASSAE. This was dedicated to Apollo and designed by Iotinus, the same man who built the Parthenon in Athens. The roof has long since disappeared, but apart from this the temple is still largely intact and makes a very interesting excursion.

The modern town of **OLYMPUS** is a convenient but very crowded holiday base. The hotels used by the tour operators include the **Leonideon**, the **Hercules** and the **Phedias**. The best is the **Apollon**, a luxury hotel complete with rooftop pool.

Most people come here to see ANCIENT OLYMPIA nearby, the

original site of the Olympic games. The games sprang from a competition held in 776 BC between the gods and the mortals at the funeral of Pelops. By 576 BC entrance was confined to mortals only and the competition had become a regular event. Every year the games took place wars would be suspended and truces declared to enable all countries to enter. To begin with the only event was a running race, but soon the number of events grew. Rules were very strict and anyone who cheated was fined and the money was used to erect a statue to him shaming him, his father and his home town. Women were not allowed to compete or watch the games, mainly because the men were naked, but they had their own games, the Heraia, named after Zeus' wife. Under the Romans the games became increasingly secular and professional athletes chasing money replaced the amateurs pursuing honour. One of the most famous victors was Nero. He delayed the games two years to enable him to compete and then was very prudently declared by the judges to be the winner of the chariot race, even though he had fallen off twice and did not actually finish the course. The games finally ended in AD 393 when the Emperor Theodosus stopped them for being pagan rights. The modern Olympics were started in 1896 mainly by the enthusiasm of a Frenchman called Baron de Coubaton, who is now buried here.

Visitors to the site can walk through the tunnel on to the famous track, and indeed even dazzle the rest of the tourists with a quick burst of speed. The site is open 7.30 a.m. to 7 p.m., as is the interesting **Archaeological Museum.** Also worth a visit is the **Olympics' Museum** back in the town, open 8 a.m. to 3.30 p.m. Mon to Sat, 9 a.m. to 4.30 p.m. Sun. For those who have had enough of ancient ruins there is a good beach nearby at KATAKOLO.

North of Olympia, back on the coast, is LOUTAKI KYLLINI, a small spa resort with a good beach, and some good hotels such as the **Xenia** and the **Ionian.** You then come to **PATRAS,** the largest town in the Peloponnese and the third-largest town in Greece. Traditionally St Andrew preached and was buried here. After his death his relics were taken to many parts of the world, including of course the country of which he is the patron saint, Scotland. From a tourist point of view Patras is not a very pretty place, but it is one of the major ferry ports. There is a very good Tourist Office on Polytechnicou Street and a bank and a Post Office on Amalias Street. If you stay here the best hotel is perhaps the **Adonis**. Less expensive are the **Delphi** and the **Splendid**. There is also a **Youth Hostel** at 62 Polytechnicou, the same street as the tourist office, and about 2 miles out of town, **Avia Pata Camping**.

Northern Peloponnese

There are two small resorts in this area. EGIO is a pretty place with two inexpensive hotels, the **Galini** and the **Tels**. A most enjoyable excursion from here is to visit Kalavrita by the cog railway from Diakofto. The line runs up a 1 in 7 slope and offers excellent views. At the top is the now almost empty **Monastery of Mega Spileo.**

The other resort in this area is GALATI, also famous for its views.

THE ISLANDS

North East Aegean Islands

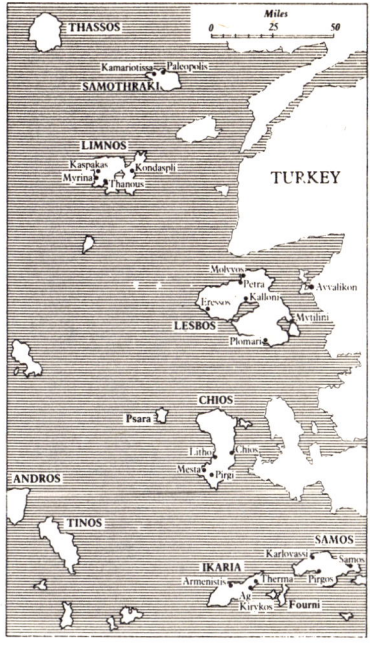

This collection of islands with good beaches and comparatively green scenery are beginning to be featured more and more in the holiday brochures. However, they are still relatively uncrowded and are a good place for quiet beach holidays. Samothraki, Chios and Ikaria are ideal for the Recluse and Sun-worshippers; Lesbos, Limnos and Samos are all more developed and suitable for Families and Sun-worshippers.

Practical Details

Most people fly out directly to the islands, but since not all have airports, some tour operators will fly you to Athens or one of the nearby islands first, and then take you by ferry to your destination. There are good ferry connections but the distances involved are fairly considerable. Most of the islands have a reasonable road network but the buses are all fairly limited and it is worth considering hiring a car or a moped if you intend to explore at all.

Samothraki

This quiet island is still uncrowded by tourists. Like Santorini it is a volcanic island with some excellent scenery, dominated by Mt Fengari, at 5500 ft the highest point in the Aegean. There are few facilities and even less accommodation and the island would suit the Recluse or keen hiker. For many years the only visitors the island attracted were archaeologists who came to visit the Sanctuary of the Great Gods. The dedicated sightseer, with a very strong interest in Greek history might find this of sufficient interest – at least to visit the island on a day trip.

The main reason for the island's lack of development is that it is not very easily accessible. It can only be reached by small ferries from Alexandroupolis, Kavala and Kymi. On the island both the roads and the buses leave a lot to be desired.

The main port is **KAMARIOTISSA**, where the best hotel is the **Niki Beach**. The main town is **CHORA** set below a Byzantine castle. Here you will find the **Xenia** hotel, the Post Office, the OTE office, and the bank.

There is a beach at the port but the sun-worshipper would be well advised to head for the sandy beach at AMMOS on the south-west coast.

The main excursion is to **PALEOPOLIS** on the north coast. First stop should be the excellent **museum** which explains the site you are about to see, open 9 a.m. to 3.30 p.m., 10 a.m. to 3 p.m., Sun, closed Tues. It contains a copy of the famous *Nike*, or the Winged Victory, now in the Louvre, which was originally found here. The site is the Sanctuary of the Great Gods. Although little but the foundations remains to be seen, with the help of the guide you can buy in the museum it makes an interesting excursion. Of particular interest is the **Arsinoe Rotunda,** the largest circular building in Ancient Greece. The site is open 9.30 a.m. to 3 p.m., Sun 10 a.m. to 3 p.m. Also of interest is THERMA on the north coast, a small spa resort. It is worth considering a day trip to the nearby islands of **THASSOS** and **LIMNOS.**

Limnos

Limnos, also known as Lemnos, is a large island which has too few facilities and is too isolated to attract large numbers of tourists. There are, however, good beaches and it would suit Sun-worshippers and Families. Inland the island is very quiet and would appeal to the Recluse. In its ancient past the island was dominated by women who on one occasion killed almost all their husbands (must have been interesting for the few men who were left!). During the First World War it was an Allied naval base in the Gallipoli campaign, and was visited by Churchill.

From the UK most people fly to Athens and then take domestic flights to the island. There are ferry connections to Kaiala, Thessaloniki, Lesbos, Chios, Samos, Ikaria, Patmos, Kos and Rhodes. On the island there is a very limited bus service and most people therefore travel by taxis, which are both numerous and cheap.

The main town is **MYRINA,** a pretty port full of old houses. The best hotel is the very luxurious **Akti Myrina,** known locally as 'Little Switzerland' because of the nationality of the owners. This is expensive but with a very comfortable number of rooms, a pool, tennis courts and no less than four restaurants, this is hardly surprising. The **Lemnos** and the **Castro Beach** are still comfortable but are less expensive. Finally there are the cheap and simple **Thraki** and **Aktaeon.**

The Post Office is on the harbour, and the bank and the OTE office are on the main square. There is a beach in the town but a 10 minute walk takes you to a much better beach at PLATIS. There is a less crowded beach further on at THANOUS and also at AVLONAS, KASPAKAS and KOTSIMAS.

With your own transport you can explore the island. Among the more interesting excursions are the isolated villages of ATSIKI, KOKINOS and KONDASPLI.

Lesbos

Lesbos is the third largest of the Greek islands and is mainly a resort for Greek holidaymakers. However, with good beaches, good scenery and plenty of interesting sights, as well as easy accessibility, it is almost certain that within a few years it will become a major British holiday destination. The major philosophers Aristotle, Plato and Epicurus all came to the island to study and to teach, and Sappho, the famous Greek poetess, was born here. Today the island offers good holidays to Families, Sun-worshippers and Nature lovers.

There are direct air connections from Gatwick but some tour operators will fly you to Athens first, and then on to Lesbos itself. There are ferry connections to Piraeus, Limnos, Chios, Samos, Patmos, Kos, Rhodes and Turkey. On the island, distances are very large and unless you are happy to stay on the beach all day you should consider hiring a car or a moped.

The island is famous for its drinks: Epom wine, no less than six varieties of ouzo and fine brandy.

For a lively time stay in MYKLINI or MOLYVOS, but for good beaches consider KALLONI, PLOMARI and SKALA ERESSOS.

The Island

The main town is **MYTILINI,** a large town built on low hills and surrounded by a castle. The best hotel is the **Blue Sea,** but also recommended are the **Sappho** and the **Lesvion**. The traveller will find it hard to find rooms in season.

Of some help to such people will be the Tourist Office next bus station. The Post Office is on Voumazon Street, open 7.30 a.m. 4 p.m., as is the OTE office, open 6 a.m. to midnight. The banks are on Koudourioutou Street, open 8 a.m. to 2 p.m.

The main sights in the town are the museums. The **Archaeological Museum** with some good sculptures, open Mon to Sat 9 a.m. to 7 p.m., Sun 10 a.m. to 2 p.m., closed Tues, is probably the most interesting. Also worth visiting is the small **Byzantine Museum** on the ground floor of the Philanthropic Society, open 9 a.m. to 1 p.m., and the **Folklore Museum**, open Mon to Fri 10 a.m. to 2 p.m., 3 p.m. to 7 p.m. Just outside the town there are two more museums at Varia. The **Teriade** houses some modern paintings and the **Theophilus** the works of a Greek folk artist of this name. If all these museums are too much for you, visit the **castle** above the town which has an excellent view. The district immediately below it is known as the KIOSKI and makes a pleasant place for an evening stroll. Day trips can be taken to the islands of **LIMNOS, CHIOS** and, on the mainland of Turkey, **AYVALIKON.**

The other main town is **MOLYVOS** or **METHIMNA,** very scenically located and also dominated by a large castle. The best hotel is the very comfortable and peaceful **Delfina.** Slightly less luxurious but still very good are the modern **Alkaios** and the **Molyvos.** On the steep 17th November Street is the Post Office, open Mon to Fri 7.30 a.m. to 2.30 p.m. and the OTE office, open 8 a.m. to 1 p.m., 6 p.m. to 10 p.m.

A good pebble beach can be reached through the **Hotel Delfina,** but it is worth travelling about 5 miles to the south to the beach at PETRA. If you get this far climb more than a hundred steps to the church, and once you have recovered, enjoy the wonderful view. About 30 minutes' walk to the north of the town is the small spa town of EFTALOU, with a good beach.

On the north coast of the islands is the popular resort of **SKALA ERESSOS,** popular mainly because of its huge beach. There is a reasonable choice of water sports and a few good bars such as the **Marianna** and the rather more lively **Silver Moon** and the **Seagull**. The beach at SIGRI, nearby, is not as good but it is considerably less crowded. Inland visit the petrified forest with tree stumps enshrined in lava. The largest trees, millions of years old, are about 20 ft high and with an 18ft circumference. On the road back towards Mytilene is the **Ipsilo Monastery,** with an excellent view and a small museum, open 9 a.m. to 1 p.m. Continuing along the road lies another pretty monastery, **Zeimonos.**

On the south-west coast is the resort of **KALLONI,** set on a very large and very beautiful bay. This is a highly popular resort with British tourists, with most of the accommodation in rooms rather than hotels. Among the many bars are the **Louis,** and **Maros** and the **Miltos.** An enjoyable way to spend a leisurely evening is the cinema in the resort.

Finally, on the south-east coast lies the resort of PLOMERI, with a pleasant beach and good water sports. Among the package hotels are the popular **Oceanis** and the **Isadoris.** In the village is the pretty little **Church of St Nicholas** which is worth a look. The most popular sight however is the ouzo factory about half a mile from the centre of town, the **Barbatabbi.** The island is a pleasant place to drift round and if you are setting out from here visit the quiet and rural village of AGIASSOS.

Chios

Chios, only 4 miles away from Turkey, is a large island with good beaches, pleasant scenery and few tourists. It would suit those who want a quiet holiday such as the Recluse or the Sun-worshipper.

Chios is one of the many islands which claims to be the birthplace of Homer. The most notorious fact in its history was the reprisal taken by the Turks when the locals joined in the war of independence in 1822: 35,000 islanders were killed and 40,000 sold into slavery. The Greeks took revenge on the Turkish admiral who ordered this but the island did not finally become part of Greece until 1912.

There are direct flights to the island from the UK, but many tour operators will fly you via Athens. For the independent traveller there are ferry connections to Lesbos, Piraeus, Limnos, Samos, Ikaria, Patmos, Kos and Rhodes. To explore the island the bus service is not really adequate and you should consider hiring your own transport.

The Island

The main town is **CHIOS** which, although full of tourists, is the most convenient base for exploring the island. The best hotel is the modern **Chandris**. Nearby is the older **Kyma,** slightly less comfortable but with rather more character. At the simpler end of the market consider the **Diana** or the **Filokenia.**

The Tourist Police are usually very helpful in providing information, either for excursions or for those seeking accommodation, and along with the banks are situated on the harbour. Up the first street on the right are the Post Office and the OTE office. In the evening there are a large number of good restaurants. Among the most popular are the **Tasos** and the well-positioned **Bella Vista.** There is a popular cinema in the town which usually shows American films.

The most convenient beach for the town is at KARFAS, about 32 miles to the south. Much the best beach on the island, however, is at EMBORIOS, on the far south of the island. The beach here is of black sand and above it are the remains of an ancient acropolis. Another good beach is KOMI nearby. There are several more good beaches on the island, NAGOS in the north, and LIMANI, LITHO, ST MARKELLA and VALLIS in the west.

There is, however, plenty to see on the island apart from all these beaches. About 15 miles south-east of the town is PIRGI, a charming medieval town with tiny streets, where all the houses are covered in grey and white geometric patterns, of which you can usually see photos in all the brochures. OLYMBAI and MESTA are two similar villages nearby which are equally pretty but are less visited by tourists. Pirgi itself is the only place in Greece where the mastic plant will grow. For some reason all attempts to grow the plant elsewhere, even in the north of the island, have not met with success.

About 6 miles to the west of the town is the very pretty 11th-century monastery of **Nea Moni** with some of the best mosaics in Greece. Apart from the mosaics note the clock, keeping Byzantine time according to which the sun rises and sets at 12. A few miles further inland is the ruined village of ANEVATOS. During the war of independence in the 1820s 400 families who lived here threw themselves off the cliff rather than surrender to the Turks. Even today the village has not really recovered and it is now very quiet.

It is worth considering the islands off the coast. **PSARA** is a small pretty place with some good beaches. In 1824 this was also caught up in the war of independence and after a Turkish attack only 3000 out of the population of 30,000 survived. Real Sun-worshippers should head for the small island of **INOUSSA** which has some excellent beaches and a pleasant harbour.

Samos

This is a large, pretty island with very good beaches and green scenery. It would suit Families, Sun-worshippers and Nature lovers. It is also the most popular of this chain of islands with British tourists, but away from the main resorts it remains a very Greek and very quiet island.

The island was once one of the richest of the Greek islands and a considerable intellectual centre. Pythagoras, of geometry fame, and Aesop, who wrote the fables, were both born here. Local tradition says that the god Bacchus taught the islanders the secret of making wine in gratitude for their help against the Amazons. Today the island is famous for its wines, supposedly the best in Greece. The best of these is *Samaina,* a dry white, and, if you can find it, *Fokianos,* a rosé. Also worth trying are *Dux, Anhemis* and *Nectar.*

There are direct flights to the island from the UK but many come via Athens. Ferries run from Piraeus, Ikaria, the other North Aegean islands, Syros and Mykonos. There is also a hydrofoil service to Patmos, Kos and Rhodes. On the island there is a good bus service but this stops early in the evening and many people find it easier to travel by car or taxi.

The main town is **SAMOS,** but there are also two popular beach resorts. **PYTHAGORION** is a very pretty and developed town which, although crowded, has a fair degree of charm; **KOKKARI** is rather more simple and very popular with the young.

The Island

Most of the ferries stop first at **KARLOVASSI** on the north-east coast. Apart from the dock there is little of interest. If you do stay here consider the **Merope Hotel,** or the rather more simple **Astir** and **Morpheus.** The OTE office and the Post Office are on the Ag Nicholas.

The ferries then pass on to **SAMOS** town, a lively and pretty place. The best hotels are the **Xenia** and the older but comfortable **Samos.** Among the modern package hotels are the **Edinis,** the **Galaxy,** the **Aelos** and the **Acropolis.** For the independent traveller there is a **youth hostel** on the harbour road.

The Tourist Police and the banks are also on this road. Behind the Hotel Xenia are the Post Office and the OTE office.

Of all the sights in the town perhaps the most enjoyable is VATHI, the old town below the castle. This is now a quiet residential area and is very pleasant to stroll around. Back in the town the **Archaeological Museum** contains some good sculptures, for which the island was once famous, and is open Mon to Sat 8 a.m. to 3 p.m., Sun 10 a.m. to 2 p.m., closed Tues. The **Byzantine Museum** in the palace of the Metropolis is a small ecclesiastical museum in which among other exhibits is the silver footprint of St George! Open 9 a.m. to 1 p.m., closed Tues. On a hot afternoon the town **gardens** make a quiet place to sit and also contain a small zoo.

The nightlife in the town is fairly active. One of the nicest restaurants is the **Samian** serving Greek food in a pretty garden. Rather more simple, but offering good food, are the **Gregori** and the **Kanarinya.** Of the many discos in the town try the **Samos Beach** in the north and the **Xenon** and the **Space** to the west. The nearest beach to the town is GAGOU, reached by a convenient bus. This gets very crowded and quieter beaches are TSAMADOU and LE MONAKIA to the north.

To the north-west of the town is the beach resort of **KOKKARI**. Several tour operators offer holidays here and although most people stay in rooms there are some popular package hotels such as the **Kokkari Beach** and the **Venus**. Further round the coast there are more good beaches at AVLAKIA, KONSTANTINOS and PIGE. Inland lie the quiet and pretty villages of PLATANOS and PIRGOS.

The main resort on the island is **PYTHAGORION** which, although developed, still retains something of a Greek atmosphere. Until recently it was known as Tigani but was renamed to celebrate the famous philosopher who was born here. Three good hotels are the **Doryssa**, the **Polixeni** and the **Acropole**. More simple establishments are the **Pythagoras** and the **Labito**.

The telephone office, the OTE, is on the harbour, open Mon to Fri 8 a.m. to 1 p.m., 4 p.m. to 9 p.m., the Post Office is on Likourogou Street, near the bus station, open Mon to Fri 7.30 a.m. to 2.30 p.m. and finally nearby is the bank, open 8.30 a.m. to 12.30 p.m.

Whilst in the resort visit the pretty **church of the Transfiguration**. Perhaps more interesting are some of the excellent restaurants on the harbour such as the **Troras**, the **Athena** and the **Samaina**. Among the many discos the most popular are the **Muppet** and the **Esmarelda**.

Near the town lie two of the ancient wonders of the world. The Eupalinos Tunnel is a 1030-yard-long tunnel built in the 6th century BC to carry water to the town and to offer an escape route in case of siege. Slaves took 11 years to build it and digging from opposite ends met only a few yards out in the middle. The tunnel may be closed for the installation of electric light, so check first at the travel agents. Further south, along what used to be the Sacred Way but is now the road to the airport, is the **Temple of Hera**. Little remains to be seen but this was once the second largest temple in Greece, 120 yards long, 60 yards wide and surrounded by 134 columns. Contemporaries were very impressed and the temple was widely copied. The site is open 9 a.m. to 3.15 p.m., Sun 9 a.m. to 2 p.m. Round the south coast there is a very good beach at VOTSALAKIA.

Ikaria

This is a small island famous for its thermal springs. Traditionally this is also where Icarus, the boy with the wings of wax and feathers made by his father to escape from Crete, fell after he flew too close to the sun. Today the island is ideal for those who want a quiet holiday in a very Greek atmosphere.

The main port is **AG KIRYKOS,** of little interest apart from the facilities on the harbour. Here you will find the banks, open Mon to Fri 8 a.m. to 2 p.m., and next door to the National Bank, the Post Office, open Mon to Fri 7.30 a.m. to 2 p.m., the OTE office, open 7.30 a.m. to 3 p.m.

Ten minutes around the coast is the spa resort of THERMA. The main beach resort is ARMENISTIS on the north-east coast which is very popular with young backpackers. The drive along the hairpin bends to the resort is very dramatic and also takes you to good beaches at YIALISEA, RAKIS and NAS.

Off the coast of Ikaria lies the island of **FOURNI,** a very Greek island bypassed by the tour operators and almost unnoticed by the backpackers.

The Sporades

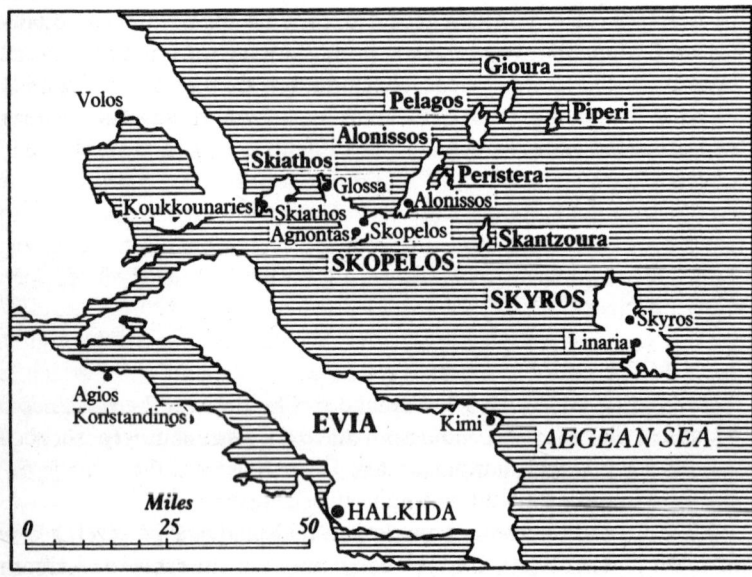

Like a scattered handful of bright emeralds, the Sporades lie across the clear blue Aegean just off the eastern mainland of Greece. Three inhabited northern islands – Skiathos, Skopelos and Alonissos – are surrounded by a host of smaller uninhabited ones. Skyros, the largest and most distant of the group, lies further south, close to the mainland port of Kimi.

Inhabited for many centuries, much of the region was a Cretan colony in ancient times. In later centuries the flourishing islands were repeatedly ravished by waves of Turkish invasions. There are poignant reminders of a tragic past all over the region. Earlier this century all the islands suffered heavily from natural disasters of earthquake and crop pestilence. Tiny Alonissos lost its picturesque old town and entire wine industry in less than a decade.

Attractive natural scenery – lush forests and green hills –

surrounded by clear blue seas are amongst the most appealing features of the region. All four main islands have their own distinct identities. All share a common geographical bond, yet remain very different in atmosphere, surroundings and facilities for visitors.

In this chapter we look at what each of the four main islands, in turn, has to offer. Working geographically through Skiathos, Skopelos and Alonissos we also look briefly at the various uninhabited islands in the group before concluding with the largest island – Skyros, to the south of all the others. As a group, these islands offer a warmth and diversity of regional life difficult to equal anywhere else in Greece.

Practical Details

COMMUNICATIONS

Travelling to and from the mainland to the three northern islands – Skiathos, Skopelos and Alonissos – or to the large southern island of Skyros is a relatively simple matter. Travelling from the three to the one is extremely difficult and quite time-consuming.

Skiathos and Skyros have modest airfields allowing at least three or four Olympic Airways' flights weekly (more in summer) to and from Athens. There is an additional summer service between Thessaloniki and Skiathos. Olympic have their office in Skiathos at 12 Papadiamanti Street. A few international charter flights fly direct to Skiathos and British Airways have an infrequent scheduled service from London. Small airstrips are being constructed on Skopelos and Alonissos at the moment but are not yet in commercial use.

The Sporades are served by regular ferry and hydrofoil services from three points – Velos, Kimi and Agios Konstandinos. The hydrofoil service is much quicker but ticket prices are approximately 50 per cent higher than the ferry equivalent. Small boats are available for charter from the harbours on all four islands if you wish to visit any of the smaller, uninhabited islands in the Sporades' group.

The islands have no rail network – and a very restricted bus service which reflects the very limited number of roads! Old, rickety, crowded buses rumble infrequently along the narrow island roads.

Skiathos, Skopelos and Skyros only have one main road each which becomes hopelessly crowded with motorcycles in the summer months. Alonissos has no proper roads at all, though an occasional tourist bus does make the short trip from the harbour up to the old town along wide tracks.

Without a doubt, the best way to see any of these islands is on foot. Detailed walkers' maps are available from most of the islands' small shops and many generations of visitors before now have left countless hundreds of footpaths covering the length and breadth of all four major islands.

TOURIST INFORMATION

Although there is no N.T.O.G. head office as such anywhere on the island group, there are innumerable small travel agencies which double as private tourist and accommodation offices. The best all-rounder is the Tourist Police office in Skiathos, around the far corner from where the ferry docks. Here you will find a goldmine of information (printed and verbal) about the islands' history, accommodation in every class and the impressive range of day-trip options by boat around the islands.

Each of the main Sporades has a similarly multi-function tourist office – all situated right by the harbour. One of the most useful pieces of literature you ought to get hold of is the glossy N.T.O.G. leaflet about the islands. This condenses virtually every piece of basic background about the islands into a couple of thousand words and a few photographs!

CLIMATE

The Sporades, in common with the rest of Greece, usually enjoy a summer of sun and cloudless skies. From Easter onwards, the temperatures climb from around 15°C (60°F) into a low 20°C (70°F) by late May. June, July and August (especially) are the warmest months with temperatures in the mid-30s°C (90°F) quite common. Even by September and October, the weather holds around the average April and May temperatures.

Prolonged rain is unheard of during the summer season, but a brisk breeze from the Aegean Sea is not uncommon. Particularly on the higher ground, this can be quite noticeable. There is, however, no end to the number of private and sheltered beach coves on all four main islands for visitors keen to retreat from these occasional gusts.

CULINARY SPECIALITIES

Seafood is the finest speciality these islands offer. Good local food is inexpensive and quite magnificent. Lobster, octopus and massive pink prawns (often baked with cheese and fresh tomatoes) are caught in the islands' waters and cooked to perfection at even the tiniest taverna on the island.

Fruit, too, flourishes in the islands' year-round sunshine. Melon, peaches, figs, or grapes make a fitting end to any good meal in the region. Skopelos particularly is famed for its prunes, and the Glossa region, near the smaller of the island's two ports, produces fine almonds.

Inexpensive local wines are produced all over the region. Although the vineyards of tiny Alonissos were devastated by pestilence, and earthquake two decades ago, the region's fruity white wines are again being bottled. Well worth trying.

Skiathos

Very green, heavily wooded and only eight miles long, Skiathos is the best-known and most cosmopolitan of the Sporades islands. Meaning 'shadow of Athos', Skiathos' sheltered southern shore boasts one magnificent golden sandy beach after another culminating at Koukkounaries, quite the most spectacular beach of any on these islands.

No less than thirty-eight British tour operators (including most of the larger ones like Intasun, Thomson, and Thomas Cook) visit Skiathos each summer. Virtually all operators go to Skiathos Town itself, or else to one of the numerous hotels around the stunning beach at Koukkounaries.

The only town on the island, called **SKIATHOS TOWN**, is built between two sweeping hills. A haphazard cluster of whitewashed houses, linked by narrow cobbled streets, cascade down to the picturesque harbour below. The waterfront is lined with fashionable boutiques, smart jewellery shops, gift and antique shops, and a multitude of tavernas and cafés.

Most of the island's 4000-strong population live in Skiathos Town but that number quickly doubles at the height of the summer tourist season. If you want vibrant nightlife, cosmopolitan company and impressive international hotels then this thriving resort can offer it all in abundance. To do that, much of the real Skiathos is sadly diluted, so if you want to see the island at its natural best come out of season – March or October – when the weather is still mild enough to be appreciated by British visitors.

Skiathos Town itself has few recognized places of interest other than a host of immaculate small churches. You can still see the home of the Greek writer Papadiamantis who immortalized the island in many of his short stories.

In relation to its size, Skiathos Town is one of the finest island shopping centres in the Aegean. If you tire of the sunsoaked beaches and waterfront cocktails the town has a bustling array of traditional and cosmopolitan shops alike to tempt visitors. Wander up any of the winding streets leading away from the harbour and you will be surprised at just how much the town has to offer.

One of the first shops you will encounter is the fur shop just off Nikgnos Street. Every conceivable fur item is in this Aladdin's cave for fur-lovers and a quaint stuffed wolf bearing a sign DO NOT TOUCH THE ANIMALS guards the shop door. Remember possible import restrictions – and the addition of V.A.T. – if you purchase a real skin item.

Just around the corner on Antoniou Riga Street you'll find the town's two banks. Both small in size, queues quickly form in summer with tourists keen to cash their traveller's cheques. You'd be well advised to avoid the rush by going early, or else cash enough on the mainland to tide you over if you're planning a fairly brief visit.

An excellent souvenir shop is only a couple of doors along from one of the banks. Fluent English is spoken at **Vociatzi's** and most English newspapers are on sale during the summer months. Equally helpful are the Tourist Police virtually next door on Antoniou Riga Street. Cheerful staff speak good English and it is open between 8 a.m. and 9 p.m. daily. The independent traveller should try here for accommodation on Skiathos once you arrive, or else write as far in advance as possible. Look out for their helpful free booklet 'This Summer in Skiathos'. All the island's useful addresses and phone numbers are updated annually, together with information about special events taking place on the island.

Skiathos Town has one or two really good places to eat. The larger hotels like the **Esperides** and **Alkyon** all have excellent – but pretty bland – international cuisine. The best food is to be found in just about any of the busy tavernas and cafés that circle the harbour front. Look out for **Taverna Stamatis** round the corner from the quay. Local seafood is cooked to perfection and served on massive oval dishes. Succulent shrimp kebabs, tender lobster and octopus salad are specialities well worth seeking out but, sadly, octopus still looks like octopus once it has been cooked and served!

Nightlife in Skiathos positively swings. A lively atmosphere is enhanced by a host of bright discos and clubs. **Captain Nemo's** is popular, air-conditioned, and advertised all round town. You'll pass its tidy exterior, if you arrive by air, just past the airfield. **Disco Charlie 'O** is a smart, new, high-class place offering the occasional 'music hall/Greek' nights. **Disco Petro** is central and a favourite with islanders but if you fancy a meal and a bop on Skiathos then head for **Bonaparte's** a block or so from the harbour. It boasts a good restaurant and stylish outdoor dance area. You'll find live Greek music at the **Hellas Club** in town.

Skiathos is the only one of the four main Sporades islands that has been extensively developed for package tourism. As a result, all grades of accommodation can be found but almost certainly you will need to book well in advance unless travelling out of season. Dozens of private rooms are available in addition to a host of well-kept hotels. The A-grade **Nostos** has good sports facilities (swimming, tennis, pool), and the impressive A-grade **Esperides** is fully air-conditioned and sits squarely by the town's nearest beach. Skiathos also has a large number of A-, B- and C-grade bungalows available for hire in and around the town.

Skiathos Town has a great number of local tour and travel agencies operating short overland excursions to **KASTRO** and other parts of the island. **Lakis Tours** offer a good-value trip round the island from 10 a.m. to 5 p.m. daily during the summer and this takes in about four stops including the beach at CALARIA and the ruined old town of **KASTRO**.

Skiathos Tours have British staff – so can be particularly helpful. In addition to boat trips they also offer day trips to VOLOS on the mainland and ninety-minute videos about the magnificent old monastery of Evagelistrias. Skiathos Tours run a very popular day trip to nearby **SKOPELOS** (which *must* be booked in advance) and includes a few hours' shopping in the main village of Skiathos' near island neighbour.

Regular flights to Athens and Thessaloniki can be booked through Olympic Airways' office at 12 Papadiamanti Street if you fancy a longer-haul excursion to the mainland. The flight to Athens or Thessaloniki takes less than an hour but due to flight scheduling it is not possible to complete an air excursion without an overnight stop.

At the other end of the island's one main road – and regular bus service – lies the simply breathtaking beach at **KOUKKOUNARIES**. Featured on many N.T.O.G. posters and in every single brochure for the island, Koukkounaries epitomizes everything the finest beach could be. Half a mile of silk-like golden sands gently curve round this idyllic inlet. Safe-bathing, shallow waters, plenty of watersports, tavernas and beach bars galore. Summer temperatures seldom drop below 27°C (80°F) and frequently reach the mid-30s°C (mid-90s°F).

In addition, hotel accommodation in the immediate vicinity is the finest anywhere in the Sporades. The region's only L (luxury) grade hotel – the 382-bed **Skiathos Palace** – basks only minutes away from the beach. A cluster of lower grade pensions hide amidst the pine greenery nearby, but do bear in mind if you're travelling independently these are always booked up well in advance by tour operators.

If you want an idyllic holiday in a luxury hotel then this is the place for you. Bear in mind the main beach (and the few others nearby) are always packed so you can forget privacy and any notion of either sampling the 'real' Greece or escaping from other British tourists who've flocked here for the same reasons as you. You could compromise and stay in a smaller hotel or pension in Skiathos and commute to the beach. Fabulous as it is, the Skiathos Palace and its numerous smaller satellites are isolated by at least half an hour by bus from the islanders and, indeed, the main communication links if you wanted to make a day trip away from the island.

The most extreme northerly point on the island is the crumbling ruin of **KASTRO**, Skiathos' former capital and main settlement. When murderous Turkish forces occupied the island in the 16th century, the surviving population fled to this massive northerly rock and built a totally impregnable fortress against the invaders. The Turks remained on Skiathos for three centuries, but the islanders on Kastro held out and the rock (which actually stands a short distance out into the sea) once held over three hundred homes and nearly two dozen churches.

Today, apart from a very few ruins, only two churches and poignant memories remain of this brave little community. Kastro was eventually abandoned in the last century in favour of what is now Skiathos Town – built from scratch. The town is best reached by boat excursion; at least one leaves the main harbour every morning if you enquire at any of the tour agencies in town. Alternatively you can choose to make a pleasant 2–3-hour stroll along the well-kept, insect-infested paths from Skiathos Town. It is well sign-posted and an enjoyable walk through the heart of the island's green vegetation.

Once there, you will be rewarded by stunning silence, broken only by other tourists, and great views seaward. The small **Church of the Nativity** is the finer of the two surviving churches with numerous icons scattered around its interior and an ancient carved wooden screen on display.

Skiathos has two further outstanding beaches which you ought to seek out if you're a real sun-worshipper. **MANRAKI** and **AGIA ELENI**, both near to Koukkounaries, are among the most popular on the island with locals and visitors alike.

Manraki is best reached by small boat from town, and has similar sand and sea to that found at Koukkounaries. A little more off the beaten track, it is famous for the dramatic reddish cliffs which have formed nearby. Even if you don't stop, you ought not to miss a glimpse of this naturally striking stretch of the island's coast.

Agia Eleni looks like Koukkounaries in miniature – and the summer crowds tend to be smaller as well. Officially this is one of several popular nudist beaches (the main one being Banana Beach just off Koukkounaries). But, in practice, Agia Eleni absorbs most of the inevitable overflow from its idyllic neighbour nearby. The nudists still come to Eleni, but as the popularity of the region grows, then so too does the nudists' shyness and most seem to have slipped away quietly to the haven of the aptly named Banana Beach.

Skiathos is definitely the finest island in the Sporades group for beaches and bear in mind that there are dozens of likely spots all along the coast from Skiathos Town to Koukkounaries. Watch out for good bathing at **MEGALI, AKLADIAS TROULOS**, and amidst the giant pebbles at **LALARIA** near Kastro.

Skopelos

Quieter, but no less lovely, Skopelos is only an hour's ferry journey away from her more famous neighbour Skiathos. Geographically larger than any other island in the group, Skopelos is covered with lush pine-sided mountains which sweep down to sheltered beaches and hidden coves. A couple of bustling villages belie a much more relaxed way of life than you'll find on Skiathos, but slowly the island is being discovered by the larger British tour operators.

The island's main population centre – and the only proper resort – is at **SKOPELOS TOWN** on the far side of the island. The town is a tiered maze of little white houses, all interlinked with unique herring-bone cobbles, and it becomes extremely busy during the summer months.

Skopelos boasts over 350 churches – many no more than ruins – and almost half that number were built in and around Skopelos Town by generations of pious Greeks. All are quite tiny and relatively easy to find in amongst the souvenir shops and tavernas. Within the town itself there is little else to see or do other than soak up the atmosphere and visit one or two of the appealing tavernas. The harbour-front has a string of useful little shops and cafés, as well as the town's small post office. Look out for the **Kapabia** cafeteria near here where good English is spoken and over 500 different types of food are on offer including cheese pie – an island speciality. (Beware of the filthy café next door. Serving only coffee and pizzas, this place is utterly inhospitable to the casual tourist.)

For a more substantial meal, head for the **Aktion** restaurant near the harbour for superb local fish or the **Spiros** taverna just one block further inland. Recommended by locals, the Spiros is immaculate and has a huge, characteristic, open grill gently cooking every conceivable meat to perfection. Mr Spiros himself speaks good English and his place is very popular with the locals. Nearby is the island's only OTE office on Skonfa Street, open weekdays till 10 p.m. and 3 p.m. at weekends.

Skopelos Town is well blessed with comfortable, homely pensions and a few decent hotels. Most of these fill up quickly with package tourists but casual travellers may be lucky to find a bed at the C-grade **Captain** hotel, 200 yards up from the seafront, or even the B-grade **Amalia** overlooking the town's modest beach. The Amalia is the island's largest with over 100 rooms and a good (international) restaurant. The town's best pension is the B-grade **Kyr Sotos** by the harbour, owned and run by an expatriate Englishman and his Greek wife.

Nightlife in Skopelos has yet to catch up with the thriving disco/club found on Skiathos but it is improving. Numerous discos have opened in recent years, among them **VIP's** on the outskirts of the town and **Studio 52** near the post office. The former is one of the busiest and certainly the trendiest, but easily the most popular is **Livadi** on the town's beach road. This is where the local disco set generally hang out. The **Fantasy Bar** in town offers another reasonable disco, but with a very European feel to its music.

If you fancy an excursion by boat from the town then head to **Madro Travel** (the best of several modest agencies on Skopelos). From here you can also purchase Flying Dolphin hydrofoil tickets and book daily excursions to Alonissos (from 10 a.m. to 4 p.m.). Twice-weekly boat trips run round the island and, less frequently, trips are possible to some of the smaller uninhabited islands in the region. The Cyclop's Cave on **GIOURA** is well worth an excursion although quite a lengthy trip when available.

Fifteen minutes by regular bus service takes you to the beach at AGNONTAS. This pebbled expanse of coast sits in a very charming cove but is extremely exposed to the nearby main road. Traffic is light but it wouldn't be the safest beach to bring young children unless they were constantly watched. There is no sand but the pebbles are fine and smooth, and the water usually warm because of the shelter created by the cove. An overpriced, seasonal café nearby does fantastic business in the summer, and the occasional small boat moors by the small man-made jetty that juts out into the far edge of the water.

The first settled part of Skopelos which you'll see will be the tiny port of **LOUTRAKI** in the north-eastern corner of the island. All ferries and hydrofoils from Volos and Skiathos stop here. You'll find only a handful of small cafés and one or two basic shops. Loutraki itself isn't worth stopping for unless you enjoy the comings and goings of a small harbour. It comes alive every hour or so when 'the Boat' arrives. Both the main ferry company and Flying Dolphin have offices here – seldom open but ask any of the locals drinking coffee nearby and you can be sure one will jump up with a bunch of keys and sell you a ticket!

Avoid eating in Loutraki if you can since only the small café **Maracana** tends to be packed with tourists waiting for the ferry. Pizzas here are good but their hastily prepared omelettes are great if you feel like something light before a ferry crossing. There are one or two hotels nearby but these are isolated from the rest of the island. Both the **Avra** and **Valentina** are clean and comfortable with large gardens.

The only other village of any size on the island is **GLOSSA** up the hill from Loutraki. Perched precariously at the summit of the steepest and most twisting road you're ever likely to encounter in Greece (and that's saying something), Glossa tends to be forgotten by tourists. Regular buses run to and from Skopelos Town, and on down the hill to Loutraki.

The lack of tourist interest isn't surprising once you spend an afternoon in Glossa. Other than the stunning views down to the sea, and a few small shops, there is little to merit a visit. A small disco, the

Cosmos, offers little action after the hours of darkness. Look out for an abandoned car standing nose-down in a ditch as you leave the village towards Skopelos Town. It is bright pink – and a local said it had been there since it crashed years ago. After all, as he said, where else could they put it?

The **Rania** restaurant is a culinary oasis in Glossa and even the café **Magic View,** despite its corny name, offers a modest seafood fare to weary visitors. You'll find Magic View at the top of the steep hill – the cafés views *are* quite spectacular – and a welcome sight if you've attempted the climb on foot from the harbour. If you do, keep well into the side of the road and walk in single file since traffic is so infrequent that drivers seem to assume no one else will be on the road.

Skopelos has some magnificent beaches, just a few of which have still to be discovered by British tourists. One of the finest is at STAFILOS just a couple of miles out of town on the main road. A well-used track disappears sharply to the left down to this idyllic cove. Circling round to a massive rock (which creeps into many of the island's postcards) this is one of the best family beaches. Secluded, but accessible, the sand is fine and the waters both shallow and warm. It can become quickly crowded in peak season but you shouldn't miss Stafilos if you're on the island.

Less than a hundred yards on the other side of the rock is the much less crowded, and only marginally less striking, VELONIO beach. It is a good size, clean and safe, and quickly reached from Stafilos after a brisk scramble over the rock. Velonio is officially a nudist beach, and as such the only one on the island. Large notices warning against nudity on any other beach on Skopelos are pinned all over the town. Be warned that you will be looked at oddly, and probably cause considerable embarrassment to other bathers, if you arrive at Velonio 'improperly dressed'. Strip off if you dare and you'll quickly become quite anonymous, otherwise *avoid* Velonio!

Just up the road from the wide pebble-cove beach at PANORMAS is the long, straight stretch of coast at MILIA. Not the easiest beach to find but worth the trek from the roadside if you ask (or point to a map) when you board one of the island buses. Milia has limited facilities but is large enough to absorb hundreds of summer sunseekers. A few cafés, water pedaloes and so on are based at nearby Panormos so bring a picnic if you visit here.

Accommodation outside the island's two large villages is practically nil, although a few British operators use the **Panormas Beach** hotel nearby. This large, well-equipped hotel is bland tourist accommodation at its most disappointing since residents are effectively isolated in a 'nice' plastic environment away from where the locals have chosen to settle. If you come to stay on this increasingly popular island, do yourself a real favour and stay in Skopelos Town.

Alonissos

[PRIVATE. Keep Out] Much smaller and quieter than even Skopelos is tiny Alonissos just a short ferry hop away. Alonissos is a green and fertile island with distant historic origins as an Athenian colony. The island today has a single road and under 2000 inhabitants spread across a couple of sleepy villages. The island remains largely untouched by tourism – only a few tour operators actually stop here and even then accommodation is limited to pensions and a few small hotels. The atmosphere here is tranquil and passive whatever time of year you come and local life tends to carry on regardless of visitors. It's a lovely sight to see many of the older women still wearing their traditional costumes as everyday clothing.

The old town of **ALONISSOS** is the island's most famous feature and lies a pleasant three-quarters of an hour (on foot) from the main harbour settlement at Patitri. A small bus runs daily during the summer if you don't feel up to the two-mile walk along a steep, but well-worn path that is clearly signposted from the harbour.

The old town was the island's capital until 1965 when an earthquake badly damaged much of it. A few cliff-edge houses toppled down towards the sea and many more were so dangerously cracked that the villagers fled to the harbour. The then Greek dictatorship government forced most of those who remained down to second-rate temporary concrete buildings at Patitri by use of financial pressure.

The old town is a maze of narrow cobbled streets and quaint houses – once busy and alive with people but now still. There is no electricity here but a few old homes are being gently restored to their former beauty. Two or three tavernas have even appeared amidst the ruins. The **Taverna Paraport** is a welcome sight to visitors when they reach the end of their hike – and is well signposted. The tidy, open exterior is perfect for this peaceful location where the utter silence is truly deafening. **Taverna Astro Fengia** does a magnificent chicken with herbs. Already one or two private rooms are available to let amidst the narrow, uneven streets. None are officially listed as hotels or pensions but that is sure to follow. Don't gamble, though, on finding somewhere to stay in the old town. There are now even a couple of overpriced general stores, as well, amidst the semi-renovated buildings. Both are signposted when you arrive.

For the time being, Alonissos will remain a poignant reminder of the island's all too recent tragedy. People may return to shatter the peace and tranquillity that has fallen across Alonissos like a huge blanket, but the commanding views to Skopelos and beyond will remain. The poignancy of this lovely spot will stay with you for a very long time.

The island's activities proper focus around the little harbour village of PATITRI. All along the attractive harbourside, the largest natural harbour on the island, there are small shops, tavernas and cafés. A massive pine-fringed crescent dominates the skyline of Patitri as you disembark from the regular ferry hydrofoil service. There are plans to complete the semi-built airstrip on Alonissos, but like many things in Greece, the islanders will get round to it when they're good and ready.

Patitri is not the most picturesque village on the Sporades islands, but it has an authentic charm which will strike you straight away. Alonissos has yet to be taken over by tour operators in the way Skiathos, and increasingly Skopelos, have been so you can expect little in the way of conventional tourist amenities, beyond basic needs, in Patitri.

For starters the island has no proper restaurants, only several adequate tavernas where foreign visitors are still greeted with a genuine Greek warmth – especially out of season. Even the island's best hotel, the B-grade **Alkyon**, has only a comfortable cafeteria. All the places to eat, drink and buy essentials and souvenirs are clustered along the seafront. The friendliest and busiest place to eat is the **Akpotiali** right in front of the village's small beach – not great for swimming since it is made up of round, fist-sized stones rather than sand. The Akpotiali serves most meats but during the summer local fish as well. Octopus and lobster are a speciality – a genuine treat, moderately priced, and tinged with one of the many peculiarly Greek herbs you'll either love or hate.

Towards the middle of the seafront is the **Metroikos** taverna, a slightly smarter but no more special eating place with equally good service. One or two souvlaki fast-food places have sprung up around the village, though these are all seasonal.

Nightlife on Alonissos is practically nil. Passing the evening on a romantic moonlit beach, or drinking in one of several tavernas is just about your lot although a couple of smallish discos have appeared for the benefit of the younger tourist market in recent years. **Disco for You** in the middle of the village has a tiny dance floor, overpriced drinks and very dated western music but is open every night in summer and is fully air-conditioned. On the outskirts of Patitri is **Disco Rocks,** keenly signposted and offering 'special programmes' of music (and occasional club-type nights) every evening. None of the island's few hotels offers much in the evening – the proprietors tend to disappear to one of the tavernas where groups of tourists and locals alike normally spend an evening's drinking, each enjoying the antics of the other. Look out for good bottled beer in the **Pub Esperides** (sic) but don't expect draught.

Both of the local ferry companies, and the Flying Dolphin hydrofoil service, have agencies along the seafront. The Dolphin office also doubles as (easily) the better of the island's two travel agencies. At Ikos Travel popular excursions are possible to Skopelos (daily) and the uninhabited islands less frequently according to demand. A number of tour companies arrange excursions to PERISTERA, a large uninhabited island right next to Alonissos popular for evening barbecues.

Good English is spoken at **Ikos Travel** by the ebullient Greek proprietor who is a sheer goldmine of information about the island's history. Here you will be able to pick up the only truly comprehensive map of the island detailing most of the isolated beaches and the myriad of tiny footpaths which criss-cross Alonissos. Ikos also cashes traveller's cheques, hazarding a generous guess about the number of drachmas to the pound! The ferry company office next door also doubles as a bank but offers less generous exchange rates.

Most guidebooks in Alonissos say there's an OTE office in Patitri open all week. This office has, in fact, closed down. Optimistic locals reckon temporarily, but the run-down shack that once housed the OTE looks pretty permanently out of commission. Direct-dial metered telephones are available in any of the tavernas at most hours of the day. You'll have to accept the background noise in these places as part of the way of life in rural Greece!

The village is blessed with a small post office, and a small chemist's, but one of the best all-round souvenir shops on Alonissos is the old Ikos shop along the Avenue Pelagon (just off the seafront). The one real blackspot this reclusive haven does possess, however, is an inhospitable, grubby, café-like ouzerie on the corner by the waterfront. It does overpriced breakfasts – bread, honey, fried eggs and flies if you're British; bread, honey and flies if you're not – best avoided.

Alonissos has many splendid beaches, all reachable only by chartering a small boat or trekking overland. Two of the island's best are **PALOVODIMOS** and **KALAMAKIA**, both located along the eastern side of the island. In season, both beaches have simple tavernas or snack bars; out of season they bring a new meaning to the word desolate. Palovodimos is one of the island's largest beaches and is quite a hike overland to reach. It is idyllic, though, in season – a vast stretch of sand with gentle waters and no noisy skyscraper hotels nearby.

KALAMAKIA deserves the edge as the island's finest beach. Another long, clean, simply beautiful stretch of coast with clear, shallow waters ideal for families with young children. Easy to find on foot but bring a picnic and take great care not to get lost in search of these lovely isolated beaches. Getting lost on Alonissos with little more than a towel and a smile would be no laughing matter.

EXCURSIONS

A host of smaller islands lie to the east of Alonissos and one or two of the larger ones make interesting places to visit if you're prepared to go on an organized trip or (preferably) hire your own boat for the day. Take extreme care never to get stranded on one of these uninhabited islands.

PERISTERA is a large, misshapen island off the eastern coast of Alonissos which from the air looks not unlike a slightly deformed map of Great Britain. Once inhabited, Peristera is easiest to reach and permanently visible from Alonissos. In addition to a few paths, Peristera still has the remains of a few old buildings and numerous stunning beaches. A few tour operators run evening excursions here for secluded barbecues by the sea. **Ormos Peristeri** is the island's finest beach – a huge sheltered inlet off the southern end of the island.

PELAGOS (also known by islanders as Kira Panagia) lies a good bit further north and is about half the size of Skiathos. Widely visited by fishermen, Pelagos has two safe, natural harbours and a few isolated beaches. High on the island sits an old monastery which is still occasionally visited by monks from Mount Athos.

Legend has it that **GIOURA**, still further north, was thrown in to the sparkling Aegean by the mythical one-eyed giant Cyclops. A massive cave is all that remains on Gioura as evidence of the isolated rock which the giant was said to have made his home. Gioura has also produced a unique herd of goats, a legally protected species now for many years, and the island sanctuary is occasionally visited by keepers from the mainland.

Much further east lies **PIPERI**. Tiny and almost never visited, the Greek authorities decreed this exposed lump of rock to be a protected haven for seals and seabirds. Sadly, no one told this to the seals or the seabirds and when several nature-loving Athenian bureaucrats visited there in 1985 expecting to find many thousands of rare seals they counted only seven!

Miles out on its own, halfway between Alonissos and Skyros, lies **SKANTZOURA**. In splendid isolation, Skantzoura is still tenuously owned by the Monastery of Grand Laura on Mount Athos. A few deserted houses survive – and yet more rare goats – but the only regular visitor is a lone Athos monk who occasionally tends the monastic state's distant colony. Skantzoura does boast one of the most powerful lighthouses anywhere in the Aegean so you won't have any difficulty spotting it if you pass by in the night!

Skyros

The largest, most beautiful, and the most unspoilt of the Sporades, Skyros is also the most barren and inaccessible for visitors other than those on package holidays. Skyros has a long and colourful past buried deep in legend: it was here that Achilles was said to have hidden as a child. Dressed as a girl, his mother Thetis did this to keep him out of the Trojan war. It had been foretold that his involvement would be vital to the success of the Greeks, but that he himself would be killed. Odysseus found the child by throwing jewellery and a sword amongst playing children.

In recent history, the English war poet Rupert Brooke died here of septicaemia during the First World War. He lies buried amidst the olive groves at **TRIS BOUKES** and is remembered by a large statue of Immortal Poetry erected outside Skyros Town.

Recent increases in the volume of tourist traffic do not seem to have marred the island's charm yet, at present, only two operators – **Madison Holidays** and **You Travel Company Ltd** – visit the island.

The main settlement is the small resort of **SKYROS TOWN** on the eastern coast of the island. Also called 'Horio' locally, Skyros Old Town clambers elegantly down a wide hill towards the sea, in a whitewashed semicircle not unlike an ancient Greek theatre.

Reckoned to be the most unspoiled town in the region, Skyros owes much of its preservation to the steep roads and passages that link the streets of quaint houses and shops. These remain impregnable to all but the most sturdy of cars and buses so few vehicles are prepared to risk the assault!

There is a lot to see in town. At the top of the huge hill are the remains of an ancient fortress, once one of the best strongholds in the

Aegean. You'll also see here the **Monastery of St George,** founded in AD 962 and with no connection to the dragon-slayer, and be able to enjoy the spectacular views down the eastern coast of the island. Near Rupert Brooke's statue in town is the **archaeological museum** with an impressive collection of Mycenaean and later relics found on the island. A free pamphlet, in English, guides you through the exhibits and the museum is open seven days a week 9 a.m. to 3.15 p.m.; 10 a.m. to 2.30 p.m. on Sundays.

Pay a visit also to the **Faltaits museum,** one of the best small folk art museums in Greece. The display includes a collection of local embroidery, carved wooden furniture, pottery and numerous rare books. Open daily from 10 a.m. to 1 p.m., and again between 5.30 p.m. and 8 p.m., the museum also has a gallery set up as a traditional Skyrian home and a modest craft shop.

The town's own beach lies 15–20 minutes away on foot and is one of the largest, and busiest, on the island. If you are in no rush to soak up the sunshine then you would do yourself no harm to either walk or take one of the regular 'beach special' buses to a beach on another part of the island. Skyros Town also offers all the usual amenities such as chemist's, post office, foodstore and currency exchange. You'll find both the post office and the telephone office (unusually) side by side below the square in the centre of town where the buses stop.

Eating out offers excellent possibilities in Skyros Town. Numerous good tavernas line the streets and only a few – quickly spotted by the dozens of plastic seats outside their front door – should be given a wide berth as obvious tourist traps. Grilled meat and chicken is excellent – head for the taverna with the 'Chicken Souvlaki' sign near the car repair garage.

Nightlife on Skyros generally grinds to a halt around 11 p.m. Most of the main street cafés, and two particularly smart pubs, **Sisyphus** and **Kosta's Bar**, stay open till midnight playing good modern music. Skyros boasts two discos, **On the Rocks** and **Skyroponlo,** which stay open well into the early hours of the morning. After about 1 a.m., Greek music tends to replace pop music.

The island's main port is at LINARIA, a modest village with little to offer but the option of numerous excursions by boat around the island or to isolated beaches. Numerous attractive beaches clutter the coast a mile or so in either direction from Linaria – all are fine and sandy with crystal-clear waters. Along the coast north of Linaria ORMOS PEFKOS has a restaurant. The sprawling beaches at AGIOS FOKA and ATSISTSA are both lined with trees and a popular alternative to Pefkos in the busy summer season.

MOGAZIA BEACH is one of the island's most popular, particularly for family swimming, and can be found within walking distance of the **Xenia Hotel.** Xenia is the only hotel of any size on Skyros since most package accommodation consists of self-catering apartments or modest pensions. Each summer, children will appreciate seeing the now domesticated Skyrian ponies being herded together in a field, near Mogazia, around 15th July. Village children look forward to this occasion to ride the ponies in a makeshift rodeo derby!

On Skyros, look out for other good beaches at GIRISMATA, AHILI and AHERANNES. In most of these isolated havens you will find small tavernas offering fresh fish, local wine and some of the island's better culinary delicacies. Don't stray right to the northernmost tip of the island since this is legally off-limits. It is reserved for personnel of the nearby air-force base which you won't find on any tourist map. Remember, too, that photography is strictly forbidden anywhere near here.

The Cyclades

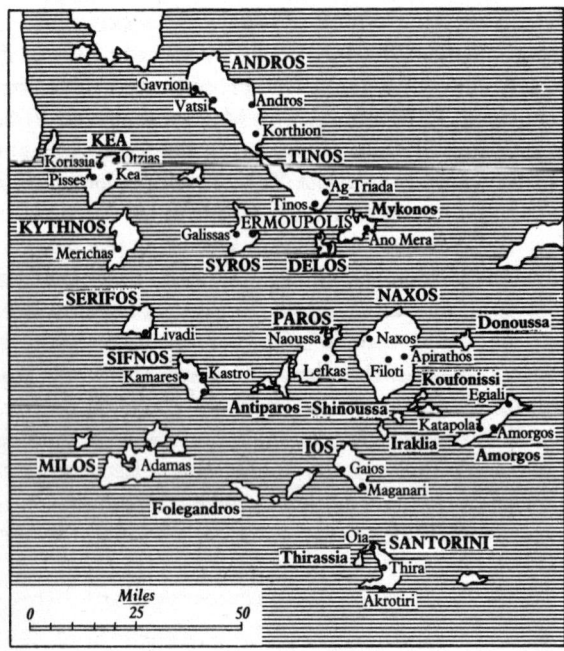

This is the largest of all the Greek island groups. It is known as the Cyclades, Greek for circle, because of the way in which the islands surround Delos, once the spiritual centre of Greece. Most of the Cyclades look as you expect Greek islands to look: very dry, with good beaches, wonderful views, white houses, windmills and churches.

The islands may have been settled in the 8th century BC, but the earliest evidence dates from the 5th century BC. By about 2000 BC the Cyclades were controlled by King Minos of Crete. He was followed by the Mycenaeans, the Dark Ages and then the Ionians, who resettled many of the islands. Some places, like Naxos, became important trading centres and founded colonies of their own. In 490 BC a huge Persian fleet took many of the islands. Athens was at war with the

Cyclades at the time and in reprisal it attacked many of the islands which had helped the Persians. This resulted in the founding of the Delian League by the Cyclades; named after the sacred island where the League's funds were kept. Like the similar League of Nations this soon came to be used for the convenience of the dominant nation rather than to benefit everyone.

In 197 BC the islands were taken by Rome, who allowed control to pass mainly to Rhodes. After the fall of the Empire the Cyclades were frequently raided by Arabs, Moors, occasionally even Vikings, and above all by pirates, so the islanders moved away from the coastal ports to fortified hill towns. After the sacking of Constantinople by the Crusaders, the Byzantine Empire was divided up amongst the victors and the Cyclades became part of Venice. During the 16th century the Turkish Empire began to grow and soon they challenged and captured most of the islands. Apart from taxing the Cyclades they left them alone, exposing them to further pirate raids. In the 1770s the Russians took many of the islands during their war against the Turks. Finally in 1821 the Greek War of Independence began in the Cyclades and the islands became part of an independent Greece.

Then, about 20 years ago, the islands were 'discovered' and turned from being quiet, idyllic settlements into major tourist centres. Most of the tour operators offer cheap and simple accommodation and the Cyclades therefore tend to attract young people rather than families. Even the undeveloped islands are no longer deserted. Every year 'the recluse' heads off to some unsophisticated island only to find it, at least during the summer months, full to overflowing with backpackers.

Most people who come to Greece simply want a lively time in the sun, and the islands that offer this type of holiday, such as Mykonos, Paros, Santorini and Ios, are the most popular. For those after quiet beach holidays such as families and sun-worshippers, Andros and Naxos are more suitable. Those who want to escape the package atmosphere should head for the still very Greek islands of Tinos and Milos. The smaller islands are all less developed, but if you take a package holiday you will probably stay at a package resort, with all that that implies.

The more developed islands like Mykonos, Paros and Santorini all have airports with direct flights from the U.K. To reach the other islands you have to travel by ferry. The Cyclades are all fairly close together and they are therefore ideal for island hopping, for you can visit several islands without having to spend all your time on the ferries. As some people find the charm of their resort begins to dim after the first week of a two-week holiday, some tour operators now offer two island holidays, which are a very popular and convenient idea.

Amorgos

[PRIVATE. Keep Out] Amorgos, the most easterly of the Cyclades, has some interesting scenery, good beaches, and outside the summer months is very quiet and ideal for the Recluse. It is still fairly undeveloped, so much so that there is nowhere to change money except the Post Office.

There are ferry connections to Kos, Tilos, Rhodes, Naxos and Paros, and on the island a bus service runs between the port and the town. You land at **KATAPOLA**, a pleasant little harbour set on a beautiful bay. Surprisingly there are some good restaurants such as the **Café Diogenis**, the **To Akroyiali** and the **Mourayou**. Half a mile south from here is the ancient site of MINO, where there are some ruins and, more interestingly, a very good view.

A 40-minute walk takes you to CHORA, a pretty little village set on cliffs high above the sea. Here you will find a telephone office and a post office. A 25-minute walk leads to the beautifully situated **Monastery of Hozoutissa**, the Presentation of the Virgin, open 8 a.m. to 2 p.m. There is a good beach 20 minutes further on at AG ANNA. At the north end of the island is EGIALI, with a good beach and several good restaurants like the **Kopali** and the **Kphitokoe**.

From Amorgos you can visit the small and uncrowded islands of **DONOUSSA**, with a good beach near the port, **KOUFONISIA**, **SHINOUSSA** and **IRAKLIA**.

Andros

Andros is one of the largest of the Cyclades, about 21 miles long and 6 miles wide, and the most northerly of the islands. Apart from some excellent beaches it also boasts beautiful scenery, which, because of the natural springs, is unusually green for a Greek island. Despite these attractions Andros is one of the few islands not swamped by tourists and backpackers. Thus for those who want a relaxing holiday, such as Families, Sun-worshippers and the Naturalist, it would be ideal, but other holiday types should be warned that there are few sights and little nightlife. The island might also appeal to the Recluse, though he may find the island too full of Greeks.

History

The island was colonized by the Ionians some time around 1000 BC and named after the General sent to govern it, Andrea. Later in the island's history, fed up with being controlled by Athens, the locals appealed to Sparta for help. As is so often the case the liberators soon became as repressive as the regime they replaced. The island was then taken by the Romans, who promptly banished the whole population for daring to resist, but soon allowed them to return. During the Middle Ages the Venetians gained control of the island before losing it to the Turks in 1566. Turkish rule was less harsh on Andros than elsewhere in Greece, but it was here that the Greek War of Independence was declared in 1821. During the Second World War the island was, like many other places in Greece, occupied by Italian troops, who later refused to surrender to the Germans and had to be bombed out.

It may seem strange that an island as attractive as this has not developed as a tourist resort. The answer lies in the fact that many of the locals are fishermen and thus do not need to turn to tourism to provide them with an income. The comparative wealth of the island becomes clear as you travel round for most of the houses are in good repair and the majority of the new buildings are not hotels, but holiday homes for people from Athens.

Practical Details

There is no airport on the island so most tour operators fly you to the island of Mykonos, or to Athens, and then put you on a ferry. For island hoppers, in addition to Mykonos, there are connections to Tinos and Syros. On the island there is a reasonable bus service and the usual selection of cars and mopeds for hire. The roads are fairly bad in many places, and if you do travel independently note that petrol is almost as hard to find as a proper signpost, so fill up whenever you have the opportunity and make sure you buy a map.

CULINARY SPECIALITIES

Andros is famous for its natural spring water, which is sold all over Greece. In addition, but less well known, there is *frontalia*, a kind of Spanish omelette which is well worth a try.

WHERE TO GO FOR WHAT

The main package holiday resort on the island is **VATSI** on the west coast, ideal for Families and Sun-worshippers. Some tour operators also offer holidays based in **GAVRION,** the port, which has a rather more Greek atmosphere.

The Island

Everyone arrives on the island at **GAVRION.** This is neither a very beautiful nor a very lively place. The brochures describe it as having a Greek atmosphere, which tends to mean that a place looks like a very dusty building site. (This is not exactly true, but Gavrion is a place to unwind rather than enjoy amazing scenery or wonderful nightlife.)

 The two best hotels are the **Galaxias,** almost opposite the ferry, and the **Gavrion Beach,** further round the harbour. In addition **Andros Camping** is a very good site and their van usually meets most of the ferries. For those staying here, or those passing through, there are some useful facilities.

The OTE office is at the bottom right of the harbour road, open 8 a.m. to 9 p.m. Just around the corner are the police (Tel: 71 220), who can provide information if you are both patient and charming enough. The Post Office is up the road to Vatsi, a few hundred yards on the right.

If you find yourself in Gavrion in the evening, there is surprisingly, one of the best tavernas in Greece just opposite the Port Police on the Harbour Road, the **O'Balmas.** Equally good is the café at the campsite. North of the town a 40-minute walk takes you to the **Tower of St Peter,** not a particularly fascinating sight, but interesting enough to make a visit worthwhile. If you are a more energetic walker, or have some form of transport, visit the beach at FELLOS on the coast, and inland, the pretty little village of AMOLOHOS.

South of Gavrion lies **BATSI,** also known as **VATSI.** With its large, sandy beach this is a very popular resort with Families and Sun-worshippers. Most of the tour operators offer pension-type accommodation, but there are some hotels, and to be recommended are the modern **Chrysi Atki** and the more simple **Krinos.**

Apart from the beach there are a few sights, but there are some useful facilities. The police are quite helpful in providing tourist information and are located at the far end of the harbour, near the small quay and up a flight of steps. The Post Office and the OTE office share the same building up another flight of steps, by the **Hotel Avra,** to the left of the bus square. The Post Office is open 8 a.m. to 3 p.m., the OTE 8 a.m. to 3 p.m., 5 p.m. to 10 p.m.

There are several good restaurants in the resort. On the harbour road try **Yiannis** for simple Greek food. In the opposite direction is the popular **Lykion** near the beach. A visit to one of the two open-air cinemas might provide a pleasant way to end an evening.

Slightly north of the resort lies the **Convent of Zoodochou,** built in the 9th century. As so often at such sites, the building itself is of little interest but the view is excellent. Heading inland is the pretty village of **KATO KATAKILOS**, and on the other coast a good, and usually fairly quiet beach at **ATENI**. A few miles down the coast is **PALIAPOLIS**, a town destroyed by an earthquake in the 4th century AD, but once the capital of the island. The earthquake left little standing, but again there are wonderful views and the water is so clear that you can see many of the buildings which slid into the sea. There is also a good beach here, but the tortuous path and the hundreds of steps make it rather difficult to reach.

The capital **ANDROS** town, is on the other side of the island. Although not a beautiful place, with its wide marble streets and large municipal buildings it does have a certain elegance that most Greek towns lack. The **statue** at the end of the promenade is dedicated to all those who lost their lives at sea and next to it is an old **Venetian castle,** destroyed mainly by German bombing in 1943. Along the main street are the **Archaeological Museum** (open 8 a.m. to 3 p.m.) and the **Modern Art Museum** (8 a.m. to 2 p.m., 4 p.m. to 6 p.m), but both should be saved for a 'rainy day' and are not worth a special trip.

Andros is not really a tourist resort and accommodation can be quite hard to find, but should you wish to stay, try the **Paradissos,** the **Xenia** or the **Aegli.** Along the main street are the Post Office and the OTE office.

North of the town is the small pebble beach of **YIALIA**. Heading south will bring you to **PALAIKOASTROU**, a pretty little village containing the ruins of a Venetian castle. This was besieged by the Turks, but fell only when a local old woman tricked her way into the castle and then threw open the gates. So contrite was she afterwards that she threw herself off what is now known as Old Woman's Leap. The road then leads down to **Korthion,** a pleasant village which makes a useful goal for an excursion.

Folegandros

This is a dry, harsh island. The guidebooks all say that it is very quiet and unsophisticated, and although the latter is very true, during the height of the summer hordes of backpackers descend on the island and crowd out the port and the town. Out of season, however, the island is very quiet and would suit the Recluse. There are ferry connections from Santorini, Sikinos, Ios, Paros, Kimolos, Naxos and Syros. The port is small but has a few pleasant tavernas. A 20-minute walk around the harbour bay brings you to a reasonable beach and a **campsite** at LIVADI. CHORA has some excellent views over the cliffs and the sea, as well as a Post Office and some small tavernas. Twenty minutes down the coast there is a good beach at AGKALI.

Ios

Ios is an island for those who are, or those who wish to be, young and single. It is something like a younger and less sophisticated version of Mykonos. Other islands may have better beaches, interesting sights, and good scenery, but nowhere has such a large amount of nightlife specifically geared to the young. This fortuitous combination of nightlife and cheap prices, and some good beaches, make it ideal for the Socialite.

History

The island's main claim to fame is that Homer may have been buried here. The argument is that he was shipwrecked on the way to Athens, but local tradition has a more enjoyable explanation. It suggests that he died of frustration when unable to answer a riddle that a fisherman asked him, 'What do we throw away when we catch, and keep when we don't catch?' (The answer is at the end of this section.) Several thousand years after Homer, the island had another famous visitor, Otto, the first King of Greece. When he arrived he bought all the islanders a drink in the local bar and promised to pay for the village to be cleaned up. Their toast of thanks in reply suggests that either they did not know who he was or were very sarcastic, 'To the Health of the King, the island's new dustman'!

To give a slightly more factual history, the island was controlled by Egypt, Rome, Naxos, Turkey and Russia, and then finally achieved independence on becoming part of Greece. In 1951 there was an earthquake which, hard though it is to believe, sucked all the water out of the bay. It rushed back in and devastated the island. Were it not for the fact that soon after the island was 'discovered' by tourists who brought money to the island, it would probably now be deserted. Ios is the oldest of the Greek resorts and has passed from being something of a large hippy commune in the 1960s to a more respectable centre with over 20 tour operators offering holidays here.

Practical Details

There is no airport on this small island and therefore no direct flights from the UK. Most companies fly you to either Athens, Paros or Santorini and you then catch a ferry from there. There are also ferries to Naxos, Folegandros, Tinos, Syros and Sikinos.

On the island itself there is only one major road and an excellent bus service runs between the port and the harbour about every 30 minutes between 8 a.m. and 11 p.m. There is no real need to hire any transport, but a moped is fun and many people get these. Unfortunately the roads are very bad and with so many young, inexperienced riders there are a large number of accidents every year. Few people have the energy or the inclination to do so, but Ios is a small island, and very suitable for hiking.

CULINARY SPECIALITIES

The only one is a hard cheese something like parmesan, called *megithra*. It is now very hard to find, since it is made by mixing the whey with perfume and leaving it to mature in a goatskin.

WHERE TO GO FOR WHAT

There are only two resorts on the island, the port and the town. They are both very similar but Gaios, the port, is slightly quieter.

The Island

The ferry comes round Ios Bay into **GAIOS**. The first sight of your holiday resort – a ramshackle port and herds of people queueing up to get on the ferries – is not too impressive. However, few people come to the island for its tremendous natural beauty.

Most people stay in rooms, but there are a number of hotels. Immediately opposite the ferry is the **Fragakis,** and slightly further round are the **Acteon** and the **Sea Breeze**. All three are, like all the hotels on the island, simple, small and fairly noisy. For those travelling independently, as you come in on the ferry you can see a **campsite,** but there is a much better one at **Milopatamos Beach.** If you are looking for a room, try the steps leading up to the town. For obvious reasons the ones at the top fill up last, so it is worth dropping your luggage and running ahead.

Your first stop may need to be the bank, conveniently situated on the main square, open Mon to Fri 8.30 a.m. to 2 p.m., but be warned that the queues can be enormous, particularly after the weekend.

Undoubtedly the best choice of nightlife is in **IOS** town, but there are a number of good cafés in the port itself. Very popular is the **New Corner,** with pleasant tables and cheap food, opposite the bus stop. Along the road to the town is **Andreas Taverna** with a limited but cheap menu. Back at the bus stop, on the opposite side of the harbour, there are two slightly more expensive and sophisticated restaurants, **Remezzos** and the **Fisherman.**

EXCURSIONS

The main places of interest on the island are the beaches. If you desire smaller crowds than are found on the town beaches, a 25-minute walk to the right from the jetty, around the church you see from the ferry, will bring you to the small, sandy beach at VALMAS. This is not deserted, but few people can be bothered to walk this far. Heading left from the jetty a path leads to KOUMBOURA, a beach just on the other side of the headland.

A 45-minute bus ride across the island takes you to AG THEODOTI, a crowded beach, but also one of the best on the island. Nearby is another good beach at PSATHIS. Heading north from here lies

Homer's Tomb. (It probably is not; there is little to see and it is very hard to find, but if you are still determined to follow scholarly pursuits, ask for directions at the police station in the town.) Near the tomb is PLAKOTOS where, although you can still see some of the ruins in the sea, only a tower remains of the ancient city that once stood here and was destroyed by earthquake.

A small boat runs to the beach at MAGANARI in the south of the island. You can also take excursions round the island, and to Sikinos and Folegandros.

About 20 minutes above the port lies the town. The bus deposits you in a rather tatty bus square to the right of this very pretty but very crowded capital. The streets are almost as full of discos and bars as they are of people, yet only a few minutes' walk outside the town you are back in rural Greece with donkeys and old women in black. There are a few hotels but most people stay in rooms. These are to be found almost everywhere, but the best place to look is behind the Town Hall on the right of the bus square.

This Town Hall also houses the Police, who can help you with information, doctors, and the Post Office, open Mon to Fri 7.30 a.m. to 3 p.m. The banks are on the street leading off the top of the Cathedral Square.

Few people come here to see the sights and indeed there are few to see. It is worth climbing to the top of the hill above the town to enjoy the view. Along the way you pass the church of **Ag Gremmictissa,** where there is little to see but an interesting history attached to the building. When Crete was being attacked by the Turks a pious man threw an icon of the Blessed Virgin Mary into the sea to prevent it falling into the hands of the infidels. It washed ashore in Ios and was placed in a local church. Every night it would 'disappear' and be found at this spot. Eventually someone took the hint and built the church. It is said that a tunnel leads from the church at the top of the hill down to Plakotos, used for hiding treasure and people in the days when the island was attacked by pirates.

During the day there are any number of cafés at which to linger. For breakfast try the **Deja Vu Café** on the bus square or the **Romantica,** a few streets up, which also serves good lunches. In the evening, for good, simple food try **Margarets** on the Cathedral Square, **Antonios,** off the top of the square near the bank, and further up the street, the **Windmills.** Recommending bars and discos is more difficult because there are so many and taste varies so much. The most popular is the **Ios Club,** situated near the top of the steps leading back down to the port. In a dramatic setting with wonderful views it is a particularly good place to listen to classical music and watch the sunset. Off the Cathedral Square the **Jazz Club** offers something of a haven from the discos. Among the best, or at least the most popular, of these are the **New Look, Mike 'n' Frankys, Jon's Electric** and the **Iliatreon.** Also worth a try are the **Why Not Pub** and the **Kalimera** near the Jazz Club; **Homer's Cave,** near the Windmills, and **Scorpions,** along the Milopatamos Beach Road. It is hard to find anywhere Greek amongst all this, but try the **Nest,** where there are usually a few locals, or for something rather more tourist-orientated, **Zorbas.**

South of the town lies the above-mentioned MILOPATAMOS BEACH, probably the best on the island, and indeed in Greece. Apart from some rooms there are also some hotels such as the **Galaxy,** the **Ios,** the **Aegean** and the **Marcos Beach.** Just behind the Ios lies the excellent **Camping Stars,** and further down the beach is the good, but slightly less well equipped, **Camping Souli.**

In the evening there are a number of bars and cafés but the best is the **Far Out,** on the left as you come into the resort. This has good food, nightly videos, and, as well might be expected, large crowds of young people. For something slightly more traditional try the tavernas to the right, the **Delfin Café,** the very pleasant **Brothers Draco** and the quite good **Up on the Rocks.**

On the east coast, along the donkey track, lies a very good beach at KALAMOS BAY.

And finally the answer to Homer's riddle? Lice.

Kea

Kea is a very popular holiday island, but mainly for Greeks rather than British tourists: it has a very Greek atmosphere and is very crowded during the summer. The island can be reached by ferry from Lavrio and Kithonos.

The main resort is **KORISSIA**. The **Karthaea** and the **Tzia Mars** are two good hotels in the town, but most of the rest of the accommodation, of which there is not very much, is organized by the Tourist Police. The two best restaurants are the **Pizzeria Dianis** and the **United Europe.** There are good beaches north of the resort at YALISKARI and OTZIAS, and at PISSES and KOUNDROS in the south. At the latter is a very good holiday development, the **Kia Beach,** with tennis courts, pools and the like. South-east of Korissia are the remains of the ancient city, the interesting monastery of **Panayia Kastriani** and the 300-ft tower of **Ag Marina.** The main excursion is to CHORA, with very dramatic views, situated on the side of a mountain. The best hotel here is the **Ioulis.** A 15-minute walk brings you to the **Lion of Kea,** a famous sculpture. In the north of the island is VOURKAI, once a fishing village but fast becoming a resort.

Kythnos

Kythnos, in the north-west of the Cyclades, is a quiet, undeveloped island suitable for the Recluse or the keen walker. It can be reached from Piraeus, Kea, Kimolos, Serifos, Milos and Santorini. Like many other of the small islands it is hard to find accommodation but there are two pleasant hotels in MERICHAS, in the port, the **Kythnos** and the **Poseidon.** Six miles away is CHORA, of little interest apart from the Post Office. At LOUTRA there is a reasonable beach and thermal springs.

Milos

Milos is a large island, about 21 miles long and 8 miles wide, in the shape of a flattened horseshoe. It has excellent sandy beaches and dramatic volcanic scenery, but the island is a major mining centre and parts of it do look like a

building site. There is very little tourist development and the island would suit those who want a quiet, Greek holiday.

History

Most of the history of the island is similar to that of the other Cyclades, for it too was ruled by Rome, Byzantium, Venice, Turkey and so on, but it was Athenian rule that had the greatest effect. In 450 BC the locals refused to help in the Persian wars and the Athenians exacted a huge penalty, killing all the men, deporting everyone else, and finally resettling the island with people from the mainland. Nothing that happened after this was, or perhaps could be, so dramatic, and Milos was of interest in modern times mainly because of its good natural harbour, and was used during the Crimean and the First World Wars. The most famous thing about the island is the statue of the Venus de Milo, found here in the 1820s and now in the Louvre in Paris. Less well known is that in the 1680s some emigrants from Milos arrived in London and the area where they settled was soon called after them, Greek Street in Soho.

Practical Details

A very small airport does exist and over the next few years it may cause the growth of mass tourism; as yet, however, most people arrive by ferry. There are links to Piraeus, Sifnos, Serifos, Kythnos, Ios, Santorini and Crete by these ferries.

The roads on the island are not very good, particularly in the west where the hire firms specifically forbid you to take any of their vehicles, but the bus service is fairly good.

The Island

The main resort is **ADAMAS,** a small town which may be one of the best harbours (in nautical terms) in the Mediterranean, but is not one of its most charming. There are some package hotels nearby at **LAGADA BEACH**, the best of which are **Venus Village** and the **Chronos Bungalows**. In the town are the well-situated **Milos,** the pleasant **Meltemi** and the slightly noisy **Georgantas.**

To the right of the ferry jetty is the OTE office, open Mon to Fri 7.30 a.m. to 9 p.m., the Post Office, and several banks. The only sights are the Catholic church, inland from here, and a monument to French sailors killed during the Crimean War.

In the evening there are some good restaurants such as the **Cavo D'Amore** and the **Ta Hana To Afroditis**, 'the arms of Aphrodite'. On the bus square is the **Milos,** hardly the place for a sophisticated evening, but with simple, cheap food. Slightly less basic is the **Aktaion** next door, and there is a good charcoal taverna nearby.

EXCURSIONS

North of the port is **PLAKA,** the capital of the island, worth a visit for its tiny, confusing streets and the wonderful view. Below the Post Office is a small **archaeological museum**, very popular on account of its excellent air-conditioning. The chapel at the top of the hill, on the site of an old Venetian castle, has a very good view. On the coast near here is Trypiti, the site of the **Catacombs,** some 2,000 years old and the oldest place of Christian worship in Greece. The tombs still contained bones when they were first opened, but these dissolved on exposure to the air. The tombs have been closed recently, so check in Plaka that they are now open. It was in this area that the statue of Venus de Milo was found by a poor peasant, of which there is now a copy in the archaeological museum.

Heading north-east from here is **PULLONIA** where there is a good sandy beach. From here an interesting day trip can be taken to the island of **KIMOLOS**, or those prepared to do without creature comforts for a few days could even stay here. This is a very quiet, barren island. You arrive at **PSATHI**, which has several pleasant tavernas. A 20-minute walk takes you up to **CHORA**, a surprisingly large village with the usual Cycladic narrow streets. Above the town, almost cut into the cliffs, is **OUPA**, with a pebble beach nearby. On the west coast there is an old castle at **PALIOKASTRO**.

Heading south-east from the port back on the main island is **Zefiria**, a pleasant village which was once the capital of the island. It was abandoned after earthquakes and disease, apparently caused by the curse of a priest who had been falsely accused by the locals of being immoral. On the coast is **PALIOCHIRI,** a large and popular beach that can be reached by bus or caique. Going through the tunnel to the right of the beach will bring you to a quieter cove, as will climbing over the rocks to the left.

South-west of the port is the excellent beach of HIVADOLIMNIS, and on the opposite coast there are two more beaches at PROVATA and AG SOSTI. From Hivadolimnis the road leads to a quiet beach at PHATOURENA and the pretty monastery of **Ag Marina**. A windy path leads to **Ag Ioannis Theologis,** a church with a very good view over the bay. This was once attacked by pirates during a mass and the congregation prayed to St Theologis. He turned the door to iron and you can still see a tiny piece of cloth, supposedly ripped off the skirt of a woman who was rushing to the church for safety. Stopped by the door the pirates tried to attack from the roof, but when one of their number fired a pistol, it blew up and his hand and gun dropped down into the church. Stirring stuff!

Mykonos

This is one of the most beautiful of the Greek islands, full of windmills, dazzlingly white, cube-shaped buildings, blue seas and golden beaches. However, all this is secondary to the main appeal of Mykonos, which is that it is probably the liveliest and most sophisticated place in all Greece, with more nightlife to the square foot than anywhere else in the world. The island is an excellent choice for the Socialite, particularly if they also happen to be a Sun-worshipper. It is one of the most famous islands, and it is also very well known as a gay holiday centre.

History

Traditionally the island is the resting place for one of the giants killed by Hercules, and a more obscure mythical character called 'Little Ajax'. The latter, shipwrecked in a storm, was rescued by the sea god, Poseidon. Later, rather than being full of humble gratitude, Little Ajax said that he was perfectly capable of saving himself. This turned out to be untrue, for his remark so annoyed Poseidon that he killed him with his trident. The factual history of the island is not quite so entertaining.

Nearby Delos was the centre of the Cyclades and for years Mykonos was simply a stepping stone on the way to this sacred island, originally for the ancients, and later for the archaeologists. After the decline of Athens the island was controlled successively by Rome, pirates, Byzantium, Venice and the Turks. In the 1960s the island became very popular with the 'jet set' and a very sophisticated nightlife grew up. As the package-tour operators moved in, the number of bars and discos grew even larger. Today you have the incongruous sight of a very traditional-looking Greek island with over 360 churches, crowded with very untraditional and un-Greek-looking people.

Practical Details

There are numerous flights to the island from Gatwick, Birmingham and Manchester, a journey taking about 3½ hours. Mykonos is also connected by air to Athens, Crete, Rhodes and Santorini.

Ferries travel to the island from Piraeus and Rafina on the mainland, and from Tinos, Syros, Andros, Ios and Santorini. On the island there is a fairly good bus service but the crowds are almost as bad as a commuter train. In addition there is the usual mixture of car and moped hire. Taxis are not cheap, but they are much more affordable than they are at home.

TOURIST INFORMATION

There is no tourist office on the island, surprisingly for such a popular resort, but the Tourist Police in the town are very helpful. You will find them on the ferry road.

WHERE TO GO FOR WHAT

Sun-worshippers should stay at the beach resorts of **PLATI YIALIS** or **SAN STEFANOS**, but Socialites should stay in the town, which is where most of the package holidays are based.

The Island

MYKONOS TOWN

The town is one of the few resorts in Greece that can be described as beautiful. From the harbour, narrow streets filled with tiny white houses lead up to a row of windmills, and another of the town's beauty spots is an elegant row of 19th-century mansions known as Little Venice. Unusually for a tourist resort the town is also largely free of cars, not because the islanders have none, but because the streets here are too narrow. Yet despite all this charm the main thing about the town is the vast amount of nightlife, and the fact that despite its popularity Mykonos is still a most attractive place to spend a couple of weeks.

ACCOMMODATION

As is the case on most of the Greek islands the tour operators tend to use small, simple hotels in the centre of town. On the waterfront is the **Delos**, small but elegant, and nearby, the **Apollo**, with good rooms. Just south of these is the town square with the old but comfortable **Delphus**. On the main street, Matoyianni, is the simple and quiet **Manto**, the **Matogianna**, with reasonable rooms overlooking a pleasant garden, and the **Cabonis**. At 32 Kalogera is the **Philipi**, a very good hotel with comfortable rooms and a pleasant garden. On the opposite side of the road is the slightly expensive **Zorzis** and the **Marios**. Just around the corner is the **Maria**, and about 15 minutes out of the town is the very popular **Mykonos**, with good views and good facilities.

Accommodation for the independent traveller is both hard to find and expensive because the island is so popular. If anyone offers you a room upon arrival you would be well advised to accept it. The Tourist Police have a very useful list of addresses. The best area to look for is Kalogera Street. For those travelling more simply, there is a campsite at **Paradise Beach,** reached by bus or one of the small boats along the harbour.

The Tourist Police are very helpful in providing information and are located by the small jetty just next to the Town Hall (Tel: 22 482). In this same building is the OTE office, open Mon to Fri 7.30 a.m. to 3 p.m. The Post Office is next to the port police and the Olympic Airlines' office on the road to the ferries, open Mon to Fri 7.30 a.m. to 4 p.m. The banks are located along the harbour road, and to avoid the queues you can also change money, at a slightly lower rate, at the travel agents. Confusingly there are two bus stations in the town. For Ano Mera, Kalafatis and San Stefanos, buses leave from the square beside the port police. For Plati Yialos, Psarou, Ornos and Ag Yannis buses leave from the other side of the town from a bus station which is, fortunately, well signposted.

SIGHTS

Few people come to Mykonos to see interesting buildings. In fact the most interesting 'sights' are probably your fellow tourists, some of whom are very flamboyant. There are, however, some more 'traditional' sights, most of which are useful for a rainy day rather than being an absolute must.

A stroll round the town will take you to the OLD TOWN and ALELKANDA, the Venetian quarter, both of which are very pretty and very crowded. Worth a look is the **Church of Paraportia,** actually four churches knocked into one. It is thought to be one of the best examples of its type in Greece and is easily recognizable from the large crowds of people standing round taking photographs of it. Next door to this is the small but interesting **Folk Museum.** Cunningly this is open from 5.30 p.m. to 8 p.m. Mon to Fri, 6.30 p.m. to 8 p.m. Sat, when people are idly strolling round the town before joining in the nightlife. A similar museum is the **People's Museum** on Enoplon Dinaemon, near the pretty **Three Wells Fountain.** Along the harbour road is the **Mykonos Library,** behind the banks, housing a collection of seals and coins which will probably only interest the expert. Towards the ferry is the **Archaeological Museum,** with the usual collection of old pottery, but one or two interesting sculptures. Open 9 a.m. to 3.30 p.m., Sun 10 a.m. to 3 p.m., closed Tues. The two most famous sights on the island, however, shown in all the brochures, are the Windmills and Petros the Pelican.

The **windmills** are at Kato Myli, above the harbour. Although only three are visible from a distance there are, in fact, five, one of which can usually be seen working in the early afternoon.

Petros, the pelican of Mykonos, is simply a tourist gimmick who has become something of an institution, at least in guidebooks. There is an interesting story attached to the original Petros, for the one you see today is a later replacement. Some years ago he left Mykonos, famed in Greece for its loose morals, and flew to nearby Tinos, well known for its sanctity. The Tinoits, always thought by everyone else to be rather 'holier than thou', were delighted at his apparent conversion. Unsurprisingly the Mykonoits were furious and accused their rivals either of bribing the bird to stay by overfeeding, or clipping his wings. The eventual return of the bird has two explanations. The first is that the Greek Prime Minister intervened and good sense prevailed, but this seems unlikely, for who ever listens to politicians? The more credible explanation is that the keeper of the bird went to Tinos and standing near Petros was 'attacked' by some friends. The bird immediately rushed to his defence and proved where his heart really lay; suggesting that like many people he preferred to live with sinners rather than saints.

NIGHTLIFE

This is really what Mykonos is all about. There are a large number of restaurants in the town, many of which are as expensive as those at home. Starting from the top of the town, among the good restaurants on the main square are **Antoni,** supposedly one of the best Greek tavernas on the island, **Klimateria** and **Androninis.** A right turn at the Matogianni Hotel brings you to the excellent **Philippi,** which must be good, for it is popular with the locals. On the same street is the **Edem,** where you probably pay more for the company of Petros the pelican than you do for the food, and the **Hibiscus Croissanterie.** Continuing down the main street, across Kalogera, is the **Lotus,** a small but very popular restaurant. The road leads on to the very pretty Enopolon Dinameon, and among the many pleasant places to eat here **El Greco's** is to be recommended. Back at the harbour, in the Venetian quarter is **Nikos,** with a high standard of Greek food. About halfway round the edge of the bay towards the windmills is the **Pelican,** one of the most popular restaurants on the island, with a good but expensive menu. Opposite is **Spiros,** not quite up to the same standard, but much cheaper.

The number of bars and discos is enormous and there is a map you can buy which shows where they all are. Starting from the Little Venice area, try the very civilized **Montparnasse** or **Kastros,** similar but slightly smaller, both of which offer good views and pleasant classical music. Near here are the **Sundown Café,** particularly good for, of course, its views of the sunset, and the **Skarpa,** one of the few places where you will see any Greeks. On K Georgiouli nearby are two good discos, the **City** and the **Rainbow**. On the pier is the **Yacht Club,** popular mainly because it does not close until 5 a.m.! At the top of the harbour road is the main square, the centre of the town's nightlife. Among the many good places here are **Apollos,** the **Mad Club,** the **Windmill,** the **Piano Bar** and the **Scandinavian Bar.** Up the main street from here lies **Pierros,** the most popular gay bar. Nearby, and with a rather different atmosphere is the **Irish Bar.** There are a few Greek nightspots in the town, such as **Thalami, Mykonos Bar** and **Babolas,** but they all tend to be very tourist-orientated and expensive. If you would like a rest from all these discos, there are also two cinemas in the town, the **Artemis,** on Ipirou, and the **Lito,** on Ag Tessarakonda.

EXCURSIONS

The best 'proper' excursion is to **DELOS** island, a very important archaeological sight and once the spiritual centre of the Cyclades (see page 301). However most people are far more interested in the beaches.

There is a sandy beach in the town, to the right of the harbour, but this gets very crowded and it is worth travelling elsewhere, either by bus or caique. South-west of the town is MEGALI AMMOS, an excellent beach backed by cliffs. The beach at KORFOS is to be avoided. ORNOS is a reasonable sandy beach and can be easily reached by bus. Continuing along the road brings you to **AG YIANNIS**, a small beach with a dramatic setting and some very good views. South-east of the town is **PSAROU**, one of the better beaches on the island with some water sports, and it must be said, considerable crowds. Similar is **PLATI YIALOS** nearby. If you have spent your life searching for paradise, a few miles round the coast, or a short boat ride from the town, and you've found it. **PARADISE BEACH** is an excellent sandy beach with a good **campsite,** but both are very popular. Another boat ride, or a stiff walk, will take you to **SUPER PARADISE**, another good beach and one very popular with gays. Continuing round the coast there are more good beaches at **AGARI** and **ELIA**, but with a steeply shelving beach, neither are very good for non-swimmers. East of the town lies **FTELIA**, with a reasonable beach and a path to a much better beach at **PANORMAS**. Inland, on the way to the pretty village of **ANO MERA**, there is a convent at Palekastrou and a monastery at Tourliani, both of which are worth a passing glance. Continuing along the road you come to more beaches at **AG ANNA** and **TARSANA**. Finally, heading north of the town there are a few sandy beaches on the way to **TOURNOS BAY**, a good beach with some water sports.

Delos

Delos is the spiritual centre of the Cyclades. As always, there is a Greek myth to explain its existence. Zeus, fearing the wrath of his wife Hera, abandoned Leto, his mistress, when he discovered she was pregnant. Everyone else refused to help her, being as afraid of Hera as her husband was. Eventually, watching her wander around without any friends, Zeus felt guilty and asked his brother, Poseidon, to help. Accordingly from the bottom of the sea he raised up on diamond pillars a haven for her, the island of Delos. Here she gave birth, hanging from a palm tree (progressive stuff), to Diana, the goddess of hunting, who a few days later assisted at the birth of her brother, Apollo, the god of music and poetry.

The factual history of the island is no less interesting. First settled around 3000 BC it became important around 1000 BC when the Ionians, who worshipped Leto, turned the island into a sacred site. The importance of Delos was further increased when an early 'League of Nations' was formed and chose to keep its funds on the island, a league which thus became known as the 'Delian League'. In 454 BC the Athenians, under the guise of protecting the money, moved it to Athens, and of course promptly spent it all on themselves. In 427 BC, after a plague, the Athenians decided that the gods must be annoyed with them and ordered a ritual purification of the island, an action which conveniently limited the powers of the locals as well as appeasing the gods. The two most natural and inevitable of actions, birth and death, were forbidden on Delos and anyone about to suffer either had to travel to the nearby island of Rheneia. Understandably the locals were a bit fed up with this and asked the Spartans for help. In retaliation, in 423 BC the Athenians deported the whole population and had their leaders killed. Later, they were losing the Peloponnesian wars and thought it prudent to follow the advice of several oracles and return the island to the locals in case the gods were angry. In about 250 BC the Romans took the island, and as a political decision to limit the growth of Rhodes, turned Delos into a free port. The religious ceremonies became something of a festival, with over 10,000 slaves being sold every day during the greatest feasts. In 88 BC the island was attacked by Rome's enemies and after this it never really recovered, so much so that in the 3rd century AD the Athenians were unable to find anyone who wanted to buy it. Since then pirates have used it as a base for their ships, locals for sheep and stone, and all the nations who have ruled the Cyclades, the Venetians, the Turks and so on, took many of the best finds home with them. Finally in 1872 a French archaeological team began to excavate the site.

Small boats run to Delos from Mykonos and there are day trips from many other nearby islands. Take a jumper to keep you warm on the crossing, and if you are determined to properly explore the site, buy the guidebook. The ferries do not allow you much time to see the site and you will have to move at a rapid pace, or decide to visit more than once.

From the harbour and heading left, the path leads to the **Agora Competialist,** built by merchants who worshipped Compita, the goddess of the crossroads, and then the **Stoa** of Philip V of Macedon, built about 210 BC. The road then leads on to the **Sanctuary of Apollo,** erected by the Athenians in the 2nd century BC and one of the most sacred places in ancient Greece. Sadly all that remains of a 30-ft statue of Apollo is the base. The path then goes past the **Great Temple,** started in 480 BC but due to political events only recommenced in the 3rd century BC, the **Athenian Temple,** and the **Bulls Shrine.** The last originally contained the ship on which Theseus returned to Athens after slaying the minotaur. Just behind this is the **Temple of Dionysus,** with the remains of huge statues of genitalia. North lies the **Sacred Lake,** where Leto gave birth, now dry and marked only by a wall. Overlooking this is the famous **Lions' Terrace,** the gifts of the Naxians in the 7th century BC. Behind this is the **House on the Hill** and the intriguingly named **House of the Comedians.**

Turning right from the harbour you come to the **theatre,** with its excellent views, and the **House of the Trident** with statues of the man who owned the house, Dioscourides, and Cleopatra. Behind this lies the **House of the Masks,** where there are excellent mosaics, the best of which is Dionysus riding a panther.

Naxos

This is the largest of the Cyclades and is also one of the most beautiful with green, mountainous scenery and some excellent beaches. Although it has begun to attract the attention of the tour operators it is not yet swamped with tourists and for Families especially, but also for Sun-worshippers, this is a good place for a holiday. The main port is the only resort on the island.

History

Traditionally, this is the island where Theseus, the man who slew the minotaur, left Ariadne, the woman who helped him by giving him a ball of string to find his way out of the maze after killing the animal.

More factually the island was settled by Crete and soon became famous for its marble, which can be seen in the sacred lions statues at Delos and in two statues of men, known as kouros, on the island itself. In the 5th century the island was seized by the tyrant Lugdamis. Not the most humble of men, he decided to build the largest buildings in Greece. Sadly, by his death all that had been erected are the columns you can see overlooking the harbour.

Little is known about what happened to the island after this until the Venetians arrived in 1207, though in the 1st century AD St John, the writer of the gospels, is thought to have brought Christianity to the island. The Venetians were followed by the Turks and the Russians, before the island finally became a part of independent Greece. Today the island is dependent upon agriculture rather than tourism, though this is beginning to change, and it is one of the major producers of Greek potatoes.

Practical Details

There is no airport on the island, though one is soon to be built, and thus from the UK you fly either to Athens or Paros and then catch a ferry. There are also ferry connections from Santorini, Folegandros, Sikinos, Mykonos and Crete.

On the island there is a fairly good bus service, which is very good for getting to the main beaches but a bit limited for those who want to explore the island. Such people should hire a car or a moped, but be warned that the roads are very bad in many places. There are plenty of taxis and for about the same price as hiring a car you could hire one for the day. The island is a good place for walking, but because of the distances involved it might be a prudent idea to take the bus on the first leg of your excursion.

The still-undeveloped nature of the island is indicated by the fact that there is no Tourist Office, and the main sources of information are the travel agents.

CULINARY SPECIALITIES

The most famous product of Naxos is a very sweet lemon liqueur called 'kitron'. You can try free samples of this in the shop on the harbour road in the town. Harder to find is a pleasant white wine called 'Promponas'.

NAXOS TOWN

This is the main resort on the island and at first sight it is a simple working port, pleasant but not over inspiring. However, up the hill above the port lie the narrow and confusing streets of the very pretty Venetian old town. The town is a very good place for a relaxed holiday, with some pleasant hotels, a surprising number of good restaurants and several good beaches nearby.

Probably the best hotel in the town is the rather unfortunately named **Grotta,** about 15 minutes' walk up from the ferry. Back in the centre is the very small, but well-kept **Anna.** In the old town is the **Panorama,** a pretty hotel with views as excellent as its name suggests, and nearby the **Apollon,** set in a pleasant little garden. Many of the tour operators use slightly bland but very central hotels like the **Oceanis,** with very good views, the **Coronis,** and the older but slightly more comfortable **Hermes.** Near the telephone office is the new and very popular **Aegon.** The area towards the beach at Ag Georgis is full of package hotels but is not one of the most scenic places on the island. On the way are the very good **Ariadne,** the **Kimata,** the **Glaros** and the **Galan.** For independent travellers there is a **Youth Hostel** in the old town, just next to the Panorama Hotel and a **campsite** at the far end of Ag Georgis beach.

Apart from the Police, located on Prantouna (Tel: 22 100), almost all the town's facilities are on the harbour road. There are several banks, open Mon to Fri 8 a.m. to 4 p.m., and nearby is **Zas Travel,** usually very helpful in providing information. Further down the road lies the OTE office, open Mon to Fri 7.30 a.m. to midnight. Follow the road to the left and just on the right is the Post Office, open Mon to Fri 7.30 a.m. to 3 p.m. In case you fall off your moped there is a small hospital on the way to Filoti (Tel: 22 346).

The main official 'sight' of the town is the gateway to the **Temple of Apollo,** overlooking the port. Close up this is really a rather scruffy area, but, if nothing else, at sunset it does provide a very good holiday snap. The more interesting sight, however, is the **Old Town,** built by the Venetians around their castle and once the central area of the capital. You will inevitably get lost as you walk round the narrow streets and may begin to wish that you had Ariadne with you to lend you a ball of string to enable you to find your way out! As you wander round note the crests of the old Venetian families that you can still see above many of the doors.

Most of the town's nightlife is relaxed rather than hectic, but there are a number of good bars. One of the best restaurants is the excellent, but slightly expensive **Faros** offering a wide choice of Greek food, situated on the corner by the bus stop. Along the harbour road there are many other places to eat. Particularly good for breakfast, or for an ice cream later in the day, are the many cafés near the jetty like the **Faros Ipidas.** Just inland from here and more suitable for an evening meal are the **Pizzeria Club,** and a little way up on the left on Nikodimou, **Stamata.** Back on the waterfront two simple Greek tavernas offering reasonable food are the **Meltemi** and **Nikos**. At the end of the harbour road is a rather expensive, tourist-type taverna, also called the **Meltemi.** Nearby is the **Karvagio,** which has a reasonable selection of non-Greek food.

EXCURSIONS

Walking straight along the harbour road will take you, via a rather dismal and dusty lorry park, to the beach at AG GEORGIS. The sand here is good, but the beach is very crowded and the bathing is not very safe because there are submerged rocks. As if all this were not enough the wind is usually very strong during the summer. Unless convenience is therefore your main priority, it is worth travelling by bus or boat to AG ANNA, a large beach with very suitable bathing for families, south of the town. There are several tavernas and an excellent view from the church up on the headland. Walking past this church is a track leading to a **campsite** and a rather crowded and tatty naturist beach.

The island does, however, have some interesting places to visit apart from the beach. Along the north coast, a scenic 2½ hour drive will take you to APOLLONAS, a small fishing village. A 20-minute walk up from the bus stop will take you to the well-signposted **Kouros,** a 30-ft figure of a man carved in about 650 BC. This was destined for the island of Delos, but somehow was never delivered. Many excursion coaches come here during the day and do make it a little touristy, but in the evening it is much quieter and has a few reasonable restaurants.

East of the town lies **SANGKI**, a maze of cobbled streets leading to a Venetian castle. Along the road is the pretty village of **CHALKI**, which has excellent views. South-east from here lies the simple village of **FILOTI**. You reach this by passing through the plain of Tragea, very green and full of olive trees. Near here is **DANAKOS**, with a few watermills and a monastery. Continuing north is the picturesque **APIRATHOS** and the road finally leads to **MOUTSOUNA**, full of the remnants of a once-profitable quarrying industry. A tricky path leads from here to a good beach at **PSILI AMMOS**. Back at the town another road heading east takes you to **FLERIO** where, in someone's garden, you can see another statue, similar to the one at Apollonas, but smaller and better carved.

Paros

Paros is, after Mykonos, the most popular of the Cyclades with British tourists. Like most of the developed islands it has a particular appeal to the Socialite with a wide variety of nightlife, but in addition there are some good beaches.

History

Paros has never enjoyed a terribly independent history. It was settled some time around 4000 BC and expanded considerably some time around 2000 BC due to trade relations with Crete. After this it was controlled by Athens and then Rome. Attacked by pirates and Arabs, the island fell into decline until it was taken over by the Venetians in the 13th-century. In 1566 the island fell, after several attacks, to the Turks. Once again the island suffered, partly because of the Turks, and partly because of the raids that the Venetians made in their attempts to recapture the island.

Paros has given two famous things to the world. The first is the Parian marble, probably the best in the world and used in the making of the Venus de Milo and the tomb of Napoleon. The other is the iambic pentameter, a verse form used by Shakespeare among others, that you may dimly remember from school. This was invented by a 7th century poet called Archliochus who came from the island and sensibly decided to become a poet when the muses turned his cows into a lyre(!).

Practical Details

There are direct flights to the island from several UK airports, and in addition Olympic Airlines fly to Athens, Rhodes and Crete.

Paros is one of the junctions for the Greek island ferries, and thus it is connected to many islands. From here you can travel to Naxos, Ios, Santorini, Sifnos, Samos, Folegandros, Sikinos, Kos, Rhodes, Irakri, Tinos and Amorgos.

A good bus service covers most areas of the island and is fine for travelling between the resorts, but it is a bit limited if you want to explore. As usual, however, there is a wide range of cars and mopeds for hire by the more independently minded.

TOURIST INFORMATION

There is a very helpful Tourist Office in the windmill immediately opposite the ferry jetty where tired, but very courteous young Greeks dispense leaflets and advice.

CULINARY SPECIALITIES

Paros produces two wines, *Lagari* and *Kavarvis* which are available in red, white and rosé form.

WHERE TO GO FOR WHAT

The most lively spot on the island is the capital, **PARIKIA,** ideal for the Socialite. Slightly less developed and with a bit more of a village atmosphere and some good beaches is **NAOUSSA** in the north of the island, probably more suitable for Sun-worshippers. On the east coast is **PISO LIVADI,** a very popular place for independent travellers.

The Island

The capital of the island is the port, **PARIKIA.** The harbour area is not very appealing, but the narrow streets of the old town are charming. In the evening the resort is very lively, very much a place to see and be seen in the most stylish clothes.

Most of the package-tour hotels are about 10 minutes round the bay at LIVADHI. They are all of the same fairly bland if reasonable standard, and some of the better ones also have a good view. Among the newer hotels is the **Polo,** and nearby the cheaper **Stella, Paros** and **Dilion.** Further up the road is the very pleasant **Asterias.** The best hotels in the centre of the resort are those in the old town, such as the clean and quiet, and usually fully booked, **Hotel Dina** on the main shopping street. In the main square up from the windmill are the stylish, but slightly old, **Kondes** and nearby, the rather more modern **Gregory.**

The island is popular with independent travellers and this makes rooms very hard to find during the height of the season. Therefore if you are offered anything, it may be wise to accept it, at least for the first night. There are several good campsites, **Paros Camping,** with good facilities at Livadhi Beach and, in the opposite direction and rather further away from the centre, **Parasporos Camping.**

The most interesting sight in the resort is the OLD TOWN with its winding streets and a wide variety of shops. The most famous sight, however, is the **Panagia Ekatontapyliani,** the large church near the ferry port. It is one of the most important churches in Greece and was supposedly built by St Helena, the mother of Constantine the Great. It is known as the 'Church of 100 Doors' but there are in fact only 99. It is said that when the 100th door is found Constantinople, now called Istanbul, will return to the control of Greece. To be honest the church itself is not that impressive and no one can ever find 50, let alone 100 doors, but it is worth a quick look round. Open 8 a.m. to midday,

4 p.m. to 8 p.m. In the centre of the old town is a **castle**, but little remains to be seen apart from the very thick walls. Nearby is an **archaeological museum,** but its appeal is fairly limited. Open 8 a.m. to 2 p.m., Mon to Sat, 8 a.m. to 1 p.m. Sun, closed Tues.

NIGHTLIFE

The best restaurants are in the old town. Along the main street, off the top of the square, left at the chemist's, and then right (it's also well signposted), is the very good but rather expensive **To Tamarisko,** serving continental food. Similar restaurants nearby are **Kriakos,** and the **Bistro Balcony.** In this same area but further down is the **May Tey,** offering of all things Vietnamese food. Round the corner is the excellent **La Creperie,** with a wide variety of those delicious French pancakes. On the square are the **Palm Tree Café** and **Rhodias.** Along the coast road from here are numerous bars and discos and **Niks,** a very good hamburger bar which also runs a book exchange service. You can tell the nature of the bars by the music you hear as you walk past. Try **Ballos, Apollos,** and the **Irish Bar** for a drink, and **Pebbles** and the **Statues** if you feel rather more elegant or want to enjoy some very good ice-creams. This same street is lined with discos. Among the most popular are **Disco 7** and **Hesperedes.**

EXCURSIONS

The most popular excursion is to the caves on **ANTIPAROS,** see page 312. Day trips can also be taken to Mykonos, Delos and Naxos, but Paros itself is worth exploring.

Neither of the town beaches are very good and they are, for obvious reasons, very crowded. The Sun-worshipper should take a caique across the bay to **KRIOS,** where beyond the main beach there are also several quieter bays. About 2 miles south of the town is PARASPOROS, one of the few official naturist beaches on the island.

Heading south of the town, many of the travel companies offer excursions to Petaloudes, or BUTTERFLY VALLEY. This is a scenic spot with a special butterfly farm, but the season is from June to August and outside this period, a visit is really a little disappointing. Try to arrive early in the morning or in the evening to see the beasties at their most active. The more adventurous may choose to reach the valley by donkey rather than coach! Off the main road along the way is an awkward path which leads to a small beach and a good view at **AG IRINI**. Back on the main road is **POUNTA**, of interest mainly because of the car ferry that runs from here to Antiparos. Further south there is a good beach at **ALYKI**.

North of the town there are several good beaches along the coast road to **NAOUSSA**, the other main resort on the island for package tours. As you drive into the village there are several good hotels such as the **Mary**, the **Atlantis**, the **Madaki** and the rather unfortunately named **Drossia**. On the main square consider the **Aliprantis**, the **Minoa** near the church or the **Cavos** if you wish to stay in the resort. For the independent traveller there is a campsite around the bay, **Camping Naoussa**, very near the sea and with reasonable facilities.

Naoussa is a rather more relaxed place than the port, but is still very crowded. There is a bank by the harbour, a Post Office at the top of the main street and the OTE office, down the road to the left from here. There are no real sights in the town and the number of visitors have turned this once very quiet place into a rather more tourist-orientated resort, but it is a pleasant and relaxing place to stay and has a surprisingly good nightlife.

Among the restaurants probably the two best are the **Christos Taverna**, situated in a garden near the church, and the **Tria Asteris**, on the road out of the town. Both offer very good non-Greek food, but both are rather expensive, at least by Greek standards. For Greek food try the **Limonaki**, a traditional taverna by the harbour with simple, but above average dishes. The main square gets very busy in the evening. A popular place with the locals for a drink is **Stratia** opposite the harbour. There are many very different and less traditional bars but if you are feeling rather more sophisticated you may enjoy the **Maimou**. Up the hill above the town, and well-signposted, lie several discos, the **Paradise**, the **Banana Moor** and the **Cave**.

This northern coast contains some of the best beaches on the island, but because of the development that is taking place in this area they are all beginning to become more crowded. About 30 minutes' walk west of the resort lies **KOLIBITHRES**, where small sandy coves, broken up by large, smooth rock offer good bathing. Near here is **MONASTIRI**, sometimes shown on the map as **AG IOANNIS**, which, set on a sheltered cove, is an official naturist beach. If you do not wish to walk, a pleasant boat trip runs from the harbour at the resort to these beaches from about 10 a.m. every day. Heading in the opposite direction, east from Naoussa, are the good but slightly crowded beaches of ANAGIRI and LAGERI, about an hour's walk away. Further east there is a very good beach at **Sancta Maria**. This is about a 20-minute drive from the resort, and because it is too far for many tourists, it is therefore usually not too full. South-east of Naoussa lies AMBELLA, once a small fishing village but now a developing resort with a reasonable beach.

On the east coast of Paros, about 13 miles from the port, is PISO LIVADI. There is a good beach here, but it is the very lively but unsophisticated nightlife that attracts large numbers of young people. There are a few hotels and a good campsite. South of the resort is the excellent and as yet undeveloped beach of LOGARES. Further south there are more good beaches at POUNDA, about 20 minutes' walk away, MEZAHDA and TZIRDAKIA, about 45 minutes away. Finally you come to the best of these beaches, CHRYSI ATKI, a long sandy bay with good swimming.

Heading north from Piso Livadi back towards the town is the small village of PRODROMOS, complete with those very Greek symbols, churches and windmills. The road continues to LEFKAS, a pretty little village with narrow cobbled streets which is well worth a visit. Once the capital of the island, it was built in a defensive pattern to protect the inhabitants from the pirates who occasionally raided the island. As you will discover, finding your way about the village is not easy, but try to walk up to the church at the top of the hill because the view is excellent. The last place of interest before the town is the marble quarry at **Marathi**.

ANTIPAROS

A 45-minute boat ride from the port takes you to the caves at Antiparos. These are not 'unmissable', but they have attracted visitors for over 2000 years and are probably the best sight around Paros. When you arrive the boat is besieged by donkey drivers offering to take you up the hills to the cave. If you are going to ride a donkey only once in your life, this is the place to do it for the hill is very steep and the ferries do not wait long.

The main point of interest about the caves, 230 ft deep, are the stalactites hanging from the ceiling, inscribed with centuries-old graffiti. Sadly the two most interesting examples were destroyed during the Second World War when resistance fighters hiding here were attacked by the Germans. Fortunately, however, a record survives of what they said. The first showed that the cave was used to hide from an enemy centuries before the 1940s, recording the names of several ancient Greeks who wrote that they were hiding here from the wrath of Alexander the Great. The second told how in 1673 the French Ambassador to Greece had an Easter mass celebrated down here. He arranged for a large charge of gunpowder to be exploded outside the cave at the most solemn moment, and even paid 500 locals to attend the mass.

Until recently you had to descend to the caves by a basket hanging from a rope, but to the relief of many there is now a set of concrete steps. The view walking back to the boat is excellent, Paros to the left and Ios and Tinos in the distance. Incidentally, as the boats do not wait very long, it is worth arriving early in the morning, and then catching a later boat back.

A few years ago all the guidebooks recommended the island of Antiparos as an ideal place for a quiet holiday and a few tour operators now include it in their brochures. Those seeking solitude have now arrived in such vast numbers that all they find is a loud and crowded tourist resort. This is particularly true during the height of the season when the place is swamped by backpackers. It is still very unsophisticated and relaxed, but it is no longer a haven for the Recluse.

Most people stay in rooms but there are a few hotels, the **Chrysi Atki,** the **Anargyros** and the **Mantalena.** For the independent traveller there is a well-signposted **campsite** about 20 minutes' walk to the east of the harbour. Almost every house is now a tiny café, and the best of these, at least for breakfast, is **Parrots.** In the evening try **Yorgos** and the nearby **Klimataria,** set among fig trees, for good, simple Greek food. To find a bar simply follow the crowds. A less active and very enjoyable way of spending an evening is the local open-air cinema, which remarkably seems to have a daily change of programme and shows major films, in English.

The caves are a 2-hour walk round the island, but there is also a minibus from the harbour for the less energetic. Somehow this manages to squeeze through the very narrow main street, but in doing so it terrifies almost every pedestrian. Apart from the town beaches, to the right and left of the harbour around the bay, there is a good beach at LIVADHI, about a 45-minute walk, and also at AG GEORGIS, a hefty 5 miles away. There are no proper roads on the island so anyone who hires a moped should be very careful.

Santorini

The capital of Santorini, Thira, set on sheer cliffs and overlooking a beautiful bay, is one of the most dramatically situated towns in the world: for once somewhere as stunning as the photos in the brochures suggest. But on its own a view, however wonderful, does not make a good holiday or explain the popularity of Santorini as a holiday resort. Naturally the island has some good beaches, unusually of black rather than yellow sand, but history has added one of the most interesting archaeological sites in Greece and tourist development has brought a considerable amount of nightlife. Over 30 holiday companies sell holidays on the island, most of which are taken up by young Socialites, but the island should also interest the Sun-worshipper. The Sightseer would also find Santorini of interest, but would probably feel happier staying on one of the quieter islands and coming here on a day trip.

History

Santorini was formed by the eruption of a volcano about 25,000 years ago, and ever since then its history has been dominated by geology. In 1600 BC there was an earthquake which devastated the island. Many people, mainly because of this destruction rather than any actual evidence, believe that Santorini is the site of the ancient sunken city of Atlantis, but the fact that the loudest exponents of this are the travel agents rather than archaeologists makes you a bit sceptical. The archaeologists do believe, however, that the earthquake set off a 700 ft tidal wave which may have destroyed Crete. Further earthquakes took place in AD 1650 and as recently as 1956.

The various names that the island has borne indicate who has controlled it. It was first known as Thira, after a Dorian general from Sparta who ruled the island. Under the Persians, the Egyptians, and later the Romans, the island became a naval base. After years of disorder and raids by the Moors, the Slovacs, and even the Vikings, control passed via Byzantium to Venice and then the Turks. For many years the island was called, appropriately, 'Kalliste', or 'most beautiful', but eventually became known as Santorini, after the patron saint of the island, St Irene. The island has now become one of the most commercialized of the Cyclades.

Practical Details

Much of the recent expansion of the island has come from the fact that it has an airport. Direct flights from the UK take about 3½ hours. There are also internal flights to Athens, Crete, Rhodes and Mykonos, but these are usually booked up months in advance.

There are ferry connections to Piraeus, Ios, Naxos, Sikinos, Folegandros, Syros, Sefinos, Mykonos, Crete, Kimolos, Milos, Siphonos and Paros. Confusingly there are three ports on the island, but most ferries dock at Athinos, and may in addition call at Thira. If you dock at Athinos and are not being met by a hotel coach, get off the ferry quickly to get a seat on the bus. Locals offering rooms meet most of the ferries in the summer, and since accommodation on the island is hard to find the independent traveller would be well advised to accept anything that they are offered for the first night. The island is also a port of call for cruise liners, which if nothing else look very pretty moored at the bottom of the cliffs at Thira.

On the island itself there is a good road network, and a good bus service. Car hire is expensive and because most people who come here are young, mopeds are more popular. For this reason there are lots of accidents, so use some common sense. In addition there are many taxis, which are cheaper than those at home and are a convenient way of returning to the hotel after the last bus.

The island is quite large and the temperatures high, so that walking does not appeal to many, but if you are determined enough there are some interesting routes.

TOURIST INFORMATION

Despite the popularity of the island as a tourist resort there is no Tourist Office; however the Police in the town, located at 25 Martiou St (Tel: 22 649), are quite helpful in providing advice. More useful are the many travel agents in the town such as **Nomikos,** next to the police, or **Domigos** on the bus square.

CULINARY SPECIALITIES

The island is well known for its strong wines. The best are two whites, *Nichteri* and *Visanto*.

WHERE TO GO FOR WHAT

THIRA has the most nightlife and would be suitable for the Socialite, but most of the tour operators use the beach resorts of KAMARI and PERISSA, ideal for Sun-worshippers. Because the bus service is quite good, the last bus being at 2 a.m., the Socialite could also stay at these resorts, which are themselves quite lively.

The Island

THIRA

The capital has a dramatic view that you will remember for the rest of your life. The centre of the town is pretty, though crowded, but the outskirts are less appealing. Almost every shop that is not an expensive jewellers is a bar or a disco and the nightlife, although unsophisticated, is considerable.

ACCOMMODATION

Only a few tour operators use the hotels in the town but there are some good places to stay. For obvious reasons the best hotels are those overlooking the bay, such as the very comfortable **Atlantis** or the slightly less lavish **Lucas**. Down the shopping street opposite are two good, simple hotels, the modern **Tataki** and the pleasant **Theoxenia**. Another good hotel is the **Asimina** near the cable car and the archaeological museum. Down past the bus square are three simple but acceptable hotels, the **Lyngos**, the **Antonia** and the **Santorini**. Taking this road out of the town it is about a 15-minute walk to another hotel area where you will find the excellent **Galina**, the comfortable **Cafiens** and the cheaper **Thira**.

For independent travellers there are rooms all round the town but finding an empty one is largely a matter of luck and patience. Straight along from the bus square towards Oia are three **Youth Hostels**, and there is another one in the town near the cable car. It is usually much easier to find accommodation in the nearby towns of **KARTERADOS** and **MERISA**, only a few miles away and well connected by bus.

Practical Details

The bus pulls up in a rather tatty square. Down to the right are the Police (Tel: 22 649), next to the Olympic Airlines' office, who are usually very helpful in providing information. The buses run from the square to the rest of the island and timetables can be found on the wall of most of the travel agents. The banks are at the bottom of the square on J Dekigala St, open Mon to Fri 8 a.m. to 2 p.m. Most travel agents will also change money and although you lose a few pence on the exchange rate you also avoid the massive queues. The Post Office lies a few hundred yards down the same street, open Mon to Fri 7.30 a.m. to 2.30 p.m. Overlooking the bay on Ag Mina Street is the OTE office, open Mon to Fri 7.30 a.m. to 10 p.m.

SIGHTS

The view over the bay is truly magnificent. Equally impressive but far less welcome are the 537 steps leading up from the harbour. One look at the sweating face of someone staggering up the steps will soon convince you of the wisdom of travelling by donkey or cable car. The donkey drivers only allowed the lift to be built on the condition that they got a percentage of each ticket sold, but this makes them no less clamouring for custom.

As you park your donkey at the top of the steps it is slightly surprising to see so many expensive jewellers. Clearly no one comes on a package holiday to buy a £2000 ring and their existence is explained by the cruise ships which stop over here. The ships look very beautiful tied up below the cliffs, but when they arrive there is a huge influx of visitors and it is a prudent idea to spend the day at the beach. Apart from this view the town has no real sights.

NIGHTLIFE

The best thing about the town is the view, and the best places from which to enjoy it are the cafés along the cliff. Try the **Scirocco** or the slightly more impressive **Francos**, near the cathedral and the telephone office. Both are very elegant and serve wonderful breakfasts and an enjoyable choice of ice creams, to the accompaniment of pleasurable classical music. Similar are the **Nea Kameni** and **Kastros**. At the end of the street, near the steps, are two tavernas serving simple Greek food at reasonable prices with a good view, **Nicholas** and **Leonidas**. Rather more sophisticated, and indeed expensive, is **Camille Stefani**. If you have had enough of the view try the **Galaxy**, a simple restaurant below the bus square on 25 Martiou Street serving good Greek dishes.

For nightlife, among the most popular places are the **Town Bar** and the **Enigma**. There are dozens of other nightspots, and if noise levels are anything to go by the better ones are **Paradise**, the **Hook Bar**, the **Banana Moon, Casablanca** and **Forum**.

EXCURSIONS

A quick look inside the travel agents will show you that there are a large number of organized excursions. The most popular is to the volcano on **NEA KAMENI,** or 'new burnt island'. The boats do not stop long here and you will need a good pair of legs and a strong pair of shoes to make the stiff 30-minute climb to the top. The volcano is not terribly exciting, though there is the odd puff of steam, but it is worth visiting for the view, not of the volcano but of Santorini. You can bathe in the hot springs here, but however therapeutic these may be they simply look like very muddy water!

On Santorini itself there are a number of interesting excursions. The nearest beach from the town is MONDITHOS. The black sand gets extremely hot during the day, as do all the other beaches, so bring a mat and a good pair of shoes. The road continues to EPISKOPI (**Misa**) **Gonias,** where a small 11th-century church is one of the very few in Greece that has been both Orthodox and Roman Catholic.

You then come to **KAMARI**. There is little to do here except flop on the beach, and perhaps for this reason it has become the island's most popular holiday resort. There are some very comfortable villas, and also some hotels. The best of the latter are the very good **Kamari**, the **Matina** and the **Sunshine**. There is a bank, open Mon, Wed and Thurs 9 a.m. to 1 p.m., and the helpful **Nomikos Travel** will also change money. The best nightlife is to be found in Thira, to which there is a good bus service running roughly on the hour 7 a.m. to 10 p.m., but one evening at least it is worth staying in the resort itself. Try **Gamos, Irinis** or **Georges,** for reasonable Greek food, or slightly further out, **Christos** and the **Cavana Roussos** by the bus stop. There are several discos in the town and among the most popular, and also the best, are the **Yellow Donkey** and the **Sail Inn**.

Just along the road from here lies ANCIENT THIRA. Although there are some ruins to see its main attraction is the excellent view. Supposedly you can see as far as Crete. Those wishing to explore fully will need good shoes and a map, but the most interesting sight is a **theatre**, dramatically set on the edge of the cliffs. The locals were so taken with this when it was rediscovered in the 1890s that the whole town band marched up here and gave a concert. On some of the buildings you will see what some of the better guidebooks politely call 'erotic graffiti'.

Back on the main road is PYRGOS, a small village with some old houses and pretty cobbled streets. From here travel to the summit of the mountain of **Profitis Ilias.** Although rather dominated by a radar station the view is very good, this time apparently stretching as far as Rhodes.

PERISSA

This resort lies on the south-east coast of the island. The large black beach is excellent, but as you will see on the long drive into the village, apart from this, and the large crowds of young people, Perissa has few attractions. Most of the people who come here are Sun-worshippers who stay at **Perissa Camping,** but the good bus service means that it is also quite popular with Socialites. Among the better hotels are the **Marianna,** the **Christina** and the **Santa Irini**. Apart from the campsite there is also a **Youth Hostel** and many rooms in the resort. Although there are a number of discos, the range of restaurants is a bit limited, and most people picnic or snack at the **Pizzeria**. The food at the **Tourist Kiosk Restaurant** is better than its drab surroundings would suggest. Few people who stay here are very interested in it, but this is the site of the largest church on the island, a remarkable 19th-century building all buttresses and supports.

In the south-west of the island nearby is AKROTIRI, an archaeological site that will interest more than the experts. Like Pompeii this is almost a whole town caught in lava, but unlike Pompeii the locals had some warning and were not caught themselves. What therefore remains to be seen are the buildings of a town which once housed 30,000 people. The site was found by a Professor Marinatos who was convinced there was a city on this part of the island and spent years searching for it. He eventually found it in 1967 and actually died here by falling off a ladder. The site is covered by a large plastic roof, so it is best to come in the early morning before it gets too hot. The guided tours are very good. Some excellent murals were found here, but sadly these are now in Athens, but the most famous, the fisherman, can be seen on most of the island's wine labels. For those with their own transport, a few miles east of here is **Exomitis,** one of the best Byzantine castles to see in Greece.

OIA

A few miles north of Thira the road leads to Oia. On the way is IMEROVIGLI, a small, not particularly interesting village, but the 2½-hour walk to it from the town is very pleasant. You finally reach Oia, a small fishing village badly damaged in the earthquake of 1956.

The Tourist Board have restored it to its original design and it is actually much prettier than Thira, and very famous for its views of the sunset. There are a number of hotels, such as the excellent but expensive **Fregada**, the pleasant **Lauda** and the cheaper **Anemones**. In addition the Tourist Board rent out a number of charming but pricey houses, but most people come here simply to see the view. The cliffs are full of small caves in which people used to live and a set of stairs leads down to a rocky beach at AMONDI where you can swim amidst pumice stone. On the return journey to Thira, those with their own transport should, during the day, take the path heading north from Oia which leads back to the town along the east coast, where there are some quiet beaches.

Most people come here, however, in the evening, in which case they would be well advised to bring a jumper for it gets surprisingly chilly. The last bus leaves at 8 p.m. so it may be worth hiring a taxi to take you back to your hotel. There are some particularly good restaurants, notably the **Kyklos** and the **Lontza**, near the castle, which both have very good views and good food. Without the view but also to be recommended are **Petros Taverna**, the **Panorama**, the **Neptune** and **Milos**.

From Oia you can reach the small island of **THIRASSIA**. To say the least this is fairly barren and deserted but it does make a good excursion. There are some good beaches on the east coast, a monastery and inland, the ruins of a castle.

Serifos

The island of Serifos is quiet and undeveloped, but the same cannot be said of the port and main resort, Livadi, suitable more for a very lazy Socialite than the Recluse. The most interesting part of the history of the island concerns Perseus. The local king wished to have an affair with Perseus' mother and therefore sent the boy himself away on a fool's errand, the task of killing Medusa, the gorgon who could turn people to stone with a look. Perseus accomplished this and returning unexpectedly early found the King in a compromising position, so promptly used the gorgon's head to turn him to stone.

The main resort is **LIVADI**, with a very scenic position and increasing crowds. The best hotels are the **Serifos Beach** and the new **Cavo d'Oro**. Slightly more basic are the **Cyclades** and the **Mai Strali**. Rooms are also available but they are not very well advertised, so ask at the bars for addresses. Two good restaurants are the **Pizza,** on the left of the main street, and the **Perseus** on the harbour road. Livadi has a surprisingly active nightlife and three good bars are the **Nyktolia, Heaven Can Wait** and **Froggies Bar.** Apart from the beach on the harbour, there is another good beach at LIVADAKI, reached by the steps next to the Scorpios Restaurant opposite the jetty. A 15-minute walk from this beach will take you to a quieter beach at KARAVI. An hour's walk, or a bus trip takes you to PSILI AMOS, the best beach on the island, and AG GIANNI, large and usually fairly deserted. Boat trips run from the town to two interesting **caves,** Cyclops and Kontaloas.

The main excursion, however, is to **CHORA,** an hour's stiff walk. This is an old town of narrow streets and excellent views. Here you will also find the Police and the Post Office. One of the best restaurants is the **Stavros,** which serves food almost as good as its view. On the north coast of the island is the very good beach of SIKAMI and the pretty monastery of **Taxiarchon,** both worth a visit.

Sifnos

Sifnos is a pretty island with lush green scenery and good beaches, more popular with Greeks than British tourists. It is also the main port linking the east and west Cyclades, with regular connections to Kimolos, Milos, Serifos, Kythnos, Paros and Syros; the combination of these factors makes the island very crowded during the summer. A daily ferry also makes the six-hour journey to

Piraeus. The main resort is **PLATI GIALOS,** ideal for Sun-worshippers.

The most interesting part of the history of the island is the explanation for the disappearance of the gold and silver mines, for which the island was once famous. Traditionally Sifnos sent a golden egg to the sacred island of Delos every year, as an offering to Apollo. One year, however, the islanders, famous for their greed, merely sent a gilded egg. Apollo was enraged and in his anger destroyed the mines.

The ferry arrives at **KAMARES,** a developed resort with a good beach and a few hotels such as the **Stavros** and the **Kamari.** From here a boat travels to VATHY, one of the best beaches on the island. A 20-minute bus ride from the capital Kamanes brings you to APOLLONIA, set on three hills. Among the best hotels are the **Sofia** and the **Anthouissa** and there are also rooms for the independent traveller. Confusingly there are two bus stops. The first is on the museum square and goes to Kamares, the second, above it, for Artemon, Kastro, Faros and Plati Yialos. There is one bank, and near the Police on the museum square there are two exchange offices. Also on this square is the Post Office, open Mon to Fri 7.30 a.m. to 2.30 p.m., and on the other square is the OTE office, open Mon to Fri 7.30 a.m. to 3 p.m. There is a small **folk museum** containing local crafts, particularly pottery, for which the island is well known, open 9.30 a.m. to 1 p.m., 5 p.m. to 7 p.m., closed Tues and Sun. It is worth walking up above the town to look down and see the views. For the evening the **Manganas** or **Alexis** are simple tavernas, slightly more sophisticated are the **Krevatina** and the **Cyprus.**

North of the town lies ARTEMONA, a village with elegant Venetian houses, and **KASTRO,** the Venetian-style former capital of the island, a charming place with narrow streets and excellent views. There are good beaches at FAROS and PLATI YIALOS.

Syros

Syros is a large island about 11 miles by 6, with some good beaches and an elegant town. There is only one major resort, **GALLISAS,** and the rest of the island is almost empty of tourists, with inhabitants considerably outnumbering tourists. For those who want a relaxing beach holiday with some nightlife the island would be a good choice.

History

The history of the island is fairly uneventful until in 1207 the Venetians took over and built the town of Ano Syros. Later the Turks captured the island but a large Catholic community survived under the protection of France. During the Greek War of Independence against the Turks the island became a refugee centre. After this Syros grew into the main port of the country, known as the Manchester of Greece. This was the heyday of the island and the merchants built large, elegant mansions, the first secondary school and the first theatre in modern Greece. However, oil replaced coal and Piraeus became the main port for Athens and Syros declined in importance.

Practical Details

There is no airport on the island so everyone arrives by ferry. For the independent traveller Syros is hard to avoid for almost every ferry stops here and the island is connected to Tinos, Mykonos, Paros, Ios, Santorini, Naxos, Ikeria, Samos, Kos, Rhodes, and many of the smaller islands.

There is a very good bus service and cars and mopeds can also be hired.

CULINARY SPECIALITIES

The island is famous for *loukomi* or Turkish Delight. You can always tell when a ferry is about to arrive because small, fat men appear with huge baskets of it to sell to the passengers. There are several shops around the town where you can see it being made and enjoy free samples.

WHERE TO GO FOR WHAT

Gallisas is the only major resort on the island and nearly everyone stays there. An alternative would be the capital, Ermoupolis, a surprisingly elegant place where although there are no beaches, there are good hotels and an active, though relaxed, nightlife.

The Island

ERMOUPOLIS

This is the largest town in the Cyclades and still very much a working port. Away from the harbour, however, it is a delightful place. A large marble square, looking more Italian than Greek and complete with a very prosperous Victorian Town Hall and even a bandstand, forms the centre of the town. Above it steps lead up to quiet streets lined with large mansions. On the hill above the town is the charming medieval town of ANO SYROS.

The best hotel is probably the **Europe** at 74 Stam Proiu. Once the town hospital it is built round a pleasant cloister, and although a bit old is a very enjoyable place to stay. Opposite the jetty is the well-appointed **Hermes**. Most of the accommodation, however, is in rooms in converted mansions. These are usually a bit tatty, but still have a certain degree of elegance. One of the better ones is the appropriately named **Central,** on the square.

On the concrete jetty by the ferry is a small but helpful Tourist Office, which can provide information and suggestions for excursions. On the corner of the main street as you enter the square is the Post Office, open Mon to Fri 7 a.m. to 4 p.m. On the corner of the square on the right is the OTE office, open 6 a.m. to midnight.

The main sight of the town is the square itself. In the afternoon this is a quiet place to linger over an ice cream, but in the evenings it takes on a very friendly atmosphere and is full of Greek families. The dilapidated building up to the right of the square is the **Apollon Theatre,** built as a replica of La Scala in Milan, but now, sadly, closed. Further up is the church of **St Nikolaos,** surrounded by large mansions with good views. Up the steps to the left of the square lies the **Archaeological Museum,** very small but pleasantly cool, open 9 a.m. to 3 p.m., closed Tues.

Two hills dominate the town. The one on the right is topped by the Orthodox church of **Anastasis,** the other by the old Venetian town of ANO SYROS, well worth a visit. From the Catholic Cathedral of **St**

George at the top of the hill there is a wonderful view. Once in Ano Syros the streets are too narrow for anything but pedestrians, but the walk up here is fairly steep, so the bus is well recommended.

The two obvious places for a meal are the harbour and the slightly more touristy main square. If you are prepared to walk a little further climb up to Anastataseos Church, below which you will find two very good and very Greek tavernas, **Tempelis,** and on Vlontado the excellent **Folia.** There are several discos back in the town, and just off the bottom left of the square, a cinema.

EXCURSIONS

There are some small beaches in the town, but you would be much better advised to catch the bus to **GALLISAS,** the main resort on the island. This is a quiet place with a good beach and excellent bathing. There are a number of hotels, including the very good **Francoise,** and several **campsites.** Good beaches can also be found at FINIKAS, a small resort to the south of the town, and KINI, to the north. Just by Finikas is Posidonia, an elegant tree-lined town with a reasonable beach nearby at ANGATHOPES. There are two other good beaches at AG DIMITROS on the east coast, where there is also a pretty church, and VARI on the south coast.

Tinos

Tinos is a pretty island with some rolling green countryside, good beaches and 1875 large dovecotes that look like castles, shown in all the brochures. The island is only beginning to be developed for tourists and away from the town it is fairly quiet. The town itself, however, is the Greek equivalent of Lourdes: it could hardly be described as a haven of tranquillity and has some surprisingly active nightlife. Tinos is basically an island for those who want a relaxing holiday in a non-package-tour resort, with a beach nearby.

History

The Venetians occupied the island in 1207 and managed to survive no less than 11 sieges by the Turks, mainly because of the very strong Exobourgo Castle. In 1714 the Turks finally took the island and the garrison commanders were executed on their return to Venice for supposedly taking bribes to make them surrender. Because of this long period of Venetian rule the island was once almost totally Catholic, and even today about a quarter of the island still is.

In 1822, an 80-year-old nun, Sister Pelagia, had a vision revealing the location of a special icon on the island. After searching for a year this was found and was almost immediately discovered to have healing properties. A new church was built and the island became one of the major pilgrimage venues in Greece. Another major event in the history of the island was in 1940 when the *Elli*, a Greek ship taking part in a special feast day, was torpedoed in the harbour. Although it was never proved everyone assumed that she was torpedoed by the Italians, and this helped to bring about Greece's entry into the Second World War on the Allied side.

Practical Details

There is no airport at Tinos and so most people fly either to Athens or Paros and then catch a ferry from there. Ferries also go to Syros, Rhodes, Kos, Ikaria, Naxos and Samos.

The bus service on the island is quite good, but hiring a car or a moped is very popular and does allow you more freedom. There is no tourist office on Tinos so you have to rely on the travel agents for information.

TINOS

The town is the main resort on the island and is a crowded, lively place based around the main street leading up to the church housing the famous icon. It soon becomes clear that this is a pilgrimage site, for the shops are full of beads and statues rather than the usual Greek equivalents of 'Kiss-me-Quick' hats. The town is also popular with weekend visitors from Athens and thus becomes very full during the summer.

Most of the hotels are small and simple but of a reasonable standard. Among the better ones are the very good **Favie Souzane,** the **Eleana,** the **Avia,** the **Tinion,** the **Aphrodite** and the **Thaleia.** Independent travellers will find accommodation hard to find, but most of the rooms are down the side streets off the main street.

There is a bank at the end of the jetty. The Post Office and the OTE office are in the same building halfway up the main street on the right.

The reason why most Greeks come here is to see the church housing the icon, **Panagia Evangelistria.** Inside you can join the queue of pilgrims and see the icon, now almost hidden behind silver and gold. Among the many votive offerings is a silver model of a ship with a fish wedged in a hole on the side, given in grateful thanks by a sea captain whose ship was saved in such a manner. Below the church is a chapel where the icon was found and there are several museums attached. Just down from here is the **Archaeological Museum**, built in the shape of a dovecote. It has a reasonably interesting collection, including a remarkable sundial from the 1st century BC. Open Mon to Sat, 9 a.m. to 2 p.m., 4 p.m. to 6 p.m., Sun, 10 a.m. to 2 p.m., closed Tues.

Tinos may be a holy island but clearly the Greeks who come here are not into penitential diets for the food is much better than in most resorts. Among the good tavernas are **Michalis,** opposite the bus stop, the **Xinari,** and down a side street on the main street, the **Good Heart.** Later in the evening try **Georges Place,** the **Seagull** and the **Vintsi.** Surprisingly there is a roller-skating rink in the town which may be of interest to some people.

EXCURSIONS

There are no spectacular sights on the island, but the scenery is interesting and there are some good beaches. An easy walk east from the town, turning right at the ferry, there is a long, narrow beach at AG FOKAS, but this gets fairly crowded. West from the ferry lies another beach at KIONIA, with a number of hotels such as the **Tinos Beach.**

South-east of the town is the old monastery of **Ag Triada** and a very good beach at AG SOSTIS. Nearby is LICHNAFTA, a very quiet village with a small beach. North-east of the town is the 12th-century **Kechrovounio,** one of the largest convents in Greece where Sister Pelagia had her visions of the icon. On the coast is KOLIBITHRA, a lovely beach with good views. North-west of the town there are more good beaches at AG NIKITAS and KAPSALIS. The road then leads to PANORMOUS, a large, pretty village, though the nearby port is less interesting. In the middle of the island is the Venetian castle which defeated the Turks so often, **Romborgo,** though the view is more interesting than what remains of the castle. For those in the second week of their holiday when the charms of the island are beginning to pale, there are excursions to **DELOS** and **MYKONOS**.

The Dodecanese Islands

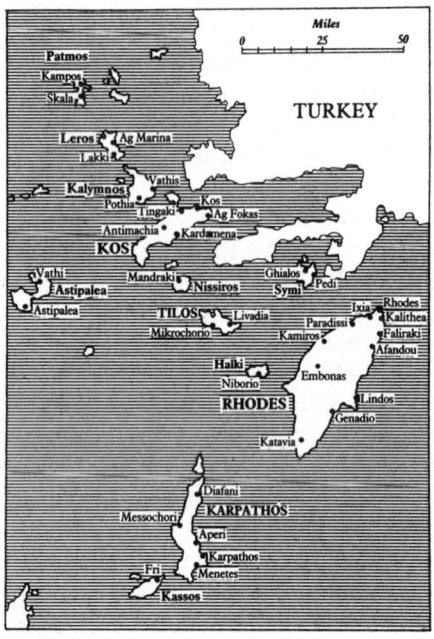

Scattered along the western coast of Turkey, from Patmos in the north to Rhodes and Karpathos in the south, are the sun-drenched Dodecanese, which means 'Twelve Islands' in Greek, though the group actually comprises fourteen main islands. While they are comparatively remote from the mainland, they nevertheless possess the qualities to keep all types of holiday maker happy: outstanding scenery, lovely old villages, fine archaeological sites, imposing medieval fortresses, and many excellent beaches which are blessed with hot sunshine nearly all year round.

The Dodecanese played an important part in the Ancient Greek Empire as can be seen from the many splendid ruins which have been recently excavated. Under the Roman Empire the islands continued to prosper, but later on their fortunes were to slowly decline under the Byzantine Empire. The Dodecanese were first distinguished as a group by the Crusader Knights of St John of Jerusalem, when they moved their operations from Cyprus to Rhodes in 1309. From this point onwards the islands were subjected to successive foreign occupations. The knights built several enormous fortresses to protect the islands from the Turks and pirates, but in 1522 they were finally ousted by Suleiman the Magnificent. The Ottomans ruled the Dodecanese for the next 400 years but the islands kept their Greek language, culture and traditions intact. In 1912 the Italians took control, building several public buildings in the major towns and conducting extensive archaeological excavations. The Italians improved the fortunes of the area but marred their reputation by their excessive cruelty towards the islanders. When the Italians surrendered during World War II in 1943, the Germans briefly took over, but it was not until 1948, three years after the Germans surrendered their control of the islands at Symi, that the Dodecanese were finally incorporated into the Greek state.

Tourist development in the region has been patchy, so that Rhodes and Kos, with their excellent communications, have become extremely commercialized in recent years, while other islands such as the ruggedly beautiful Karpathos and the smaller Tilos and Kastelorizo, remain unsullied by tourism.

In the area as a whole, however, development continues apace, and parts of Kos and Rhodes are beginning to resemble the worst excesses of the Costa Blanca. EOT (The National Tourist Organization of Greece) is fully aware of the dangers of over-exploitation, and has developed a policy of 'Social tourism' which involves consulting the inhabitants of each island to ascertain what sort of tourist development they want (if any). EOT sees the establishment of a tourist office on every island as an absolute necessity, which will be welcomed by those of us who have suffered in the past from not being able to find out practical details on many of the islands.

Practical Details
COMMUNICATIONS

Rhodes and Kos possess international airports, with several connections daily to Europe and Athens and the rest of Greece. If you are flying out to another Dodecanese island on a package trip, the chances are you will arrive at one of these airports and reach your final destination by ferry. The relatively isolated Karpathos has an airstrip, as does the smaller island of Kassos. There are plans to provide every island with its own airstrip, and should this materialize it will greatly improve communications in the area. It is worth mentioning that the ulterior motive for building these airstrips is that they would strengthen the area's defence capabilities against Turkey, Greece's traditional foe, who believes it is entitled to sovereignty over many of the Dodecanese, despite their decidedly Greek character.

There are student discounts of 25 per cent on **Olympic Airways'** flights to and from the islands with international connections, but unless you are really pushed for time it is cheaper to take the ferry.

If you are undecided whether or not to take a package holiday in this region, a good idea is to island hop. The distances involved are not great as most of the Dodecanese are arranged in a crescent shape which roughly follows the coast of Turkey, and ferry tickets are reasonably priced. The main island group, from Rhodes, through to Kos, Kalymnos, Leros and Patmos, is served daily by the main ferry lines and you can usually get a ticket – even in high season. Symi and Tilos are now easier to reach by boat than in the past, with Symi in particular receiving boats daily carrying day-trippers from Rhodes. The other islands of Kastelorizo, Halki, Nissiros, Astipalea, Kassos and Lipsi are slightly more difficult to reach, but there should be no problems getting a ferry in the high season. Buy your tickets from the ferry offices in the harbour before you embark.

A hydrofoil line, serving the main island chain, has been established recently and while journey times are considerably reduced, you will have to pay around twice the price of the average deck-class fares on conventional ferries. Also if there are not enough takers for a particular journey, the captain is likely to cancel the trip.

On the islands themselves, Rhodes and Kos have adequate bus services and all the islands on which there are roads have taxis, which are reasonably cheap. Many islands have taxi-boats for journeys along the coast, but if you are visiting one of the more out-of-the-way islands you should be prepared to do a fair bit of walking!

Warning: Given the close proximity of Turkey – only 1½ miles from Kastelorizo for example – you will find many day trips on offer, to places such as **BODRUM**. If you do decide to go on one of these trips, bear in mind that the Greek authorities may refuse to let you board your return flight home if you have a recent Turkish stamp in your passport. The Turks do not normally stamp the passports of day-trippers, but ensure that you do not stay longer than your allotted time.

CLIMATE

It is very hot and sunny nearly all year round, so Sun-worshippers need have no fear. If you travel during the peak season, do take precautions such as suncream and a hat – especially if you have a fair complexion, for the sun is really blisteringly hot during July and August.

The best times to go are from Easter to June – especially if you want to miss the hordes on Kos or Rhodes, and it is still very warm in this region up until October.

CULINARY SPECIALITIES

All the standard Greek specialities are to be found in this area, and on many islands the sea-food is particularly recommended. Individual island specialities are listed under each island heading. It is worth pointing out that all Dodecanese ports are well stocked with duty-free alcohol, and the prices are far cheaper than at the airports, or on the plane. In Kos, for example, it is possible to buy a bottle of gin for around £2.

The islands featured in this section are:
Karpathos, Halki, Kassos, Kastelorizo, Symi, Tilos, Sirna, Nissiros, Astipalea, Kos, Kalymnos, Leros, Patmos, Lipsi.

Karpathos

Rugged and splendid, Karpathos is a large mountainous island lying between Rhodes and Crete, and well off the beaten tourist track. Though it has a small airport, there are fewer ferry connections to other islands and the mainland, and correspondingly fewer tourists. If you are looking for somewhere a little bit different, where you can still experience local customs dating back thousands of years, go for enchanting mountain hikes past isolated villages, or merely relax on one of the excellent and uncrowded beaches, then Karpathos could be the place for you.

Due to its relatively remote position and the choppy seas which surround it, Karpathos was subjected to only two years of the rule of the Knights of St John, who left without building a fortress. The Venetians ruled for two hundred years and like the Ottomans who followed later, they allowed the Karpathians to preserve their own distinctive culture and traditions. At **OLYMPUS,** the most famous village on Karpathos, the villagers dress in traditional costumes and still speak a dialect which uses words and phrases dating from ancient times.

At present, relatively few companies offer package holidays to Karpathos and those that do tend to be the smaller, specialist operators. Most of the hotels are centred in or around Karpathos Town, though Amopi Beach, 5 miles to the south, has undergone recent tourist expansion. You can expect to pay less than £350 for a two-week stay (half-board) during peak season in a hotel which will be comfortable rather than luxurious.

Practical Details

There is a small domestic airport which has daily flights to Rhodes and five flights per week to Kassos and Crete. Three ferries sail weekly from Rhodes to Karpathos. The fare from Rhodes is around 1000 dr and the passage is eight hours. On the island itself Karpathos town is the administrative and transportation centre. There is a minimal bus service: four buses per day connect Aperi–Volada–Othos–Piles, and there are two to the beach at Amopi and one per day to Menetes and Arkasa (returning next morning). The road network is hardly extensive and there are no adequate roads connecting the north and south parts of Karpathos.

You can rent cars near the Karpathos Hotel on the waterfront and you can hire mopeds (from around 950 dr) near the post office. Complete bus, plane and boat information can be obtained from **Possi Travel** (Tel: 22235) on the waterfront, or **Karpathos Travel** (Tel: 22754) on Dimokratia Street.

TOURIST INFORMATION

There is no EOT office on the island yet, but the two agencies listed above will be happy to provide any information on rooms and travel arrangements. The police station is at the far end of the waterfront (to the left as you face the water) and while they are happy to be of service, their English is somewhat limited.

WHERE TO GO FOR WHAT

Most of the hotels are situated near the main town of **KARPATHOS,** which is fairly quiet with little in the way of swinging clubs for the dedicated nightlifer. You could choose to stay directly on the waterfront in the **Karpathos Hotel,** or perhaps just out of the town at a popular beach hotel such as the new **Seven Sisters,** or **Romantica** (Tel: 22460/1) hotels. Both of these have good facilities for children. It is a modern town with nothing much to interest the historian except the remains of **Agia Fotini**, a fifth-century basilica on the road north towards APERI. The town, also known as **PIGADIA** incidentally, possesses a pleasant and not-too-crowded beach, and indeed there are several excellent beaches near Karpathos town. The most popular beach resort is **AMOPI BEACH** 5 miles south of Karpathos. The beach here is clean and sandy, but relatively crowded. If you want a more secluded spot you need only walk south from here along the miles of golden beach until you arrive at a suitable spot. The best beach on the island, however, is the superb AGIA MARINA BEACH, further north at **MESSOCHORI.** You can sometimes get a bus here, but don't count on it. This bus is also supposed to call at LEFKOS, a lovely fishing hamlet which has a couple of tavernas and a splendid beach.

[PRIVATE. Keep Out] Compared with the mountainous, barren north, the southern part of Karpathos features green gently undulating scenery. There are many charming villages, isolated chapels, and fine views over the terraced hillsides to the sea. Two roads lead from Karpathos town, one south, the other to the north and west. South of Karpathos there is a fine church at MENETES, but the tiny chapel of **Agios Mammas,** a few hundred yards to the north along a dirt road, is without doubt more delightful. A miniature doorway leads to some superb 14th-century frescoes and a wonderful icon of Mary with the infant Jesus. To the west, there are some Mycenaean remains at ARKASSA, but it is to the medieval town of APERI, situated on the other road out of Karpathos town to the north-west, that the historian will be drawn. This became the medieval capital of Karpathos when Arab raiders forced the inhabitants to retreat from the coast to the hills. From Aperi, there are a number of delightful villages within walking distance, and indeed this whole area, with its lush scenery, is *the* place on the island to hike. For the less active, PILES is perhaps the prettiest town on the bus route.

The northern and southern parts of Karpathos are divided by **Mt Kalolimni,** and until recently, the only way you could reach the northern villages was by boat. This is still the best way to get to the north of the island and excursion boats will take you to **DIAFANI,** the main northern town, for around 1250 dr (return). There's nothing much of interest in Diafani, though there is an excellent beach at VANANDA, a 30-minute walk away through a pine forest. More importantly Diafani makes a good base from which to explore the village of OLYMBOS, undoubtedly Karpathos' finest attraction. This is a remarkable community, still following the traditional lifestyle, and its customs and dialect date back 3000 years. On the west side of the village two functioning windmills overlook the cliffs to the sea, and women, wearing long-sleeved white shirts and flowery aprons, still come to grind their flour here for the bread which they bake in large stone ovens set into the hillside. If you visit in August, there are two important festivals, the *Panagia* (the Virgin Mary's name-day) on the 15th and feast of *Ai-Giannis of Vourgounda* on the 29th, which are celebrated in traditional and flamboyant fashion. The latter is particularly exciting, with the women dressing up in brightly coloured clothes and festooning themselves with pounds of jewellery, while the men take up their bouzoukis and bagpipes and revel till the early hours. Below Olymbos is the oldest chapel on Karpathos, the **Agia Anna,** with frescoes dating back to the 8th century.

If you can, you should stay overnight at Olymbos, in one of the delightful pensions run by the women of the town. Here you will enjoy traditional Greek hospitality and if you stay at the **Pension Olymbos,** Nikos will even serenade you on his bouzouki as you eat in the small restaurant.

Olymbos can be reached from Diafani by minibus (around 350 dr return) or by an extremely pleasant 90-minute hike along a beautiful valley floor.

Further north is VOURGOUNDA, a good two or three hours from Diafani. Energetic historians will be intrigued at the ancient burial chambers cut into the rock overlooking the sea, and the scenery is truly dramatic. However, this trip should only be undertaken by those undaunted at the prospect of a long walk.

Halki

Despite its proximity to Rhodes, Halki remains an unspoilt, easy-going place with little or no tourist development. The island is small and hilly, and has numerous sandy beaches. Its people are said to be 'shy of strangers' and few tourists visit. It is the ideal place for those wishing to take a complete break from the pressures of city life.

Practical Details

Halki can be reached by ferries travelling between Rhodes and Karpathos three times a week. A small boat also does trips between the island and Kamiros on Rhodes for around 500 dr (one way). On Halki there are no buses or cars and if you want to go anywhere you'll have to walk, or hire a horse.

TOURIST INFORMATION

There is no EOT office, no hotels and no pensions! Some private homes have accommodation to let, which is always easy to find. **NIBORIO**, the harbour, possesses only a post office.

WHERE TO GO FOR WHAT

This is the ideal place for the Recluse. There will be no tourists annoying him and no commercialism. In **NIBORIO** there are a few tavernas and that's about it as far as entertainment goes. However, it is a lovely spot and there is a decent beach nearby at **PANDEMOS**.

Two miles further inland, **HORIO** is now a largely deserted village which thrived in the 18th and 19th centuries when islanders retreated here to avoid frequent pirate raids. There is a magnificent view of the southern coast from the medieval castle (if you're willing to climb to it). Near Horio lies the **Monastery of Stavros,** where there is a simple, yet lively folk festival on 14th September.

Kassos

This is the southernmost of the Dodecanese and the most remote and difficult island to land on. The coast is rocky, with many caves and the beaches it does possess are all very small.

Mountains rise for 2000 ft on this nearly barren island, which has a most pleasant climate. As there has been little or no tourist development, this is another ideal island for the recluse to while away a few weeks away from the pressures of the city.

Practical Details

Kassos has a small domestic airport, with connecting flights from Rhodes and Athens. Ferries sailing between Rhodes and Crete call at the island twice a week, and there are four connections to Piraeus, though if the sea is rough they won't call at the small port of **FRI**. Passengers then have to go ashore in a small caique. This trip can take up to an hour and can cause sea-sickness. There are no proper roads and no bus service, but most of the attractions can be reached by boat or on foot.

TOURIST INFORMATION

There is no EOT office on the island yet, and the Post Office is at Fri. You will stay in private accommodation.

WHERE TO GO FOR WHAT

EMBORIO, the port, and **FRI**, the principal town are both extremely picturesque, and the villages of **PANAGIA, POLI** and **AVRANITOHORIO** (literally 'Albanian village') are all delightful and worth a visit. South-west along the coast from Fri, a dirt track leads to **AGIA MARINA**, near which is situated the fascinating cave of **Selai** with its interesting stalagmites. The cave also contains the remnants of an ancient wall. There is a colourful festival at Agia Marina on 17th July (the name-day of Agia Marina) with lots of music and folk dancing.

From Emborio you can make the short boat trip to the island of **ARMATHIA,** where there is a fabulous stretch of beach. Here you will be well and truly away-from-it-all.

Kastellorizo

This is a tiny island 65 miles to the east of Rhodes, and therefore well off the tourist map. Though only 1½ miles from the Turkish coast the island has preserved its Greek character despite several foreign occupations. Megisti, the capital, is a delightfully friendly fishing village with attractive buildings and several excellent sea-food restaurants.

Practical Details

Kastellorizo is relatively isolated and there are only two ferries a week to Rhodes. The passage lasts around six hours and costs approx. 800 dr. If you go out of season the ferries only visit once a week. The main town is **MEGISTI** and as the island is only about 5 square miles in size there are no proper roads on the island. All places of interest can be reach on foot or by boat.

TOURIST INFORMATION

There is no EOT office yet, but the OTE, post office and police can be found in the same building at the north end of the harbour next to the steel tower. Hours vary but are roughly 7.30 a.m. to 2.30 p.m. Mon to Fri.

CULINARY SPECIALITIES

Kastellorizo is *the* place to eat seafood, and Megisti has several excellent, inexpensive tavernas lining the waterfront.

WHERE TO GO FOR WHAT

There really isn't that much to do on Kastellorizo: just relax, soak up the sun, and sample the excellent tavernas at night. There is little nightlife of any description: **Karpouzis,** at the south end of Megisti's harbour, is a bar-cum-discotheque during the summer, and that's about it.

You will doubtless be staying in Megisti, and while you can choose to stay in the pleasant **Hotel Megisti,** you may as well sample the local hospitality in one of the many cheap pensions in the town, such as **Estodia's Pension** or the **Pension Komninos.**

Sun-worshippers should note that there are no proper beaches on Kastellorizo. There is a decent pebbly beach at **AGIOS STEFANOS** next to the uninhabited island of **AGIOS GEORGIOS,** a mere ten minutes distance.

Megisti town itself is extremely pleasant, and possesses a modest one-room museum. Behind the town the impressive 14th-century **castle** built by the Knights of St John, has a superb view over the town and across to the Turkish coast.

A pleasant excursion can be made to the **Cave of Parasta** on the eastern coast of the island. You can hitch a lift from one of the fishermen and marvel at the superb colours inside the immense cave. If you want to purchase Turkish carpets and other artefacts, you can make the short trip to **KAS** for around 500 dr (return).

Symi

Many people arrive at the stunning port of Ghialos on a day trip from Rhodes and wonder: 'Why didn't I come here instead?' For Symi, small, picturesque and friendly, is a jewel. The landscape is virtually unspoilt and generally rocky, save for a small fertile region to the south which is covered with pines and olive and almond trees. The coastline features many delightful little coves and beaches and some of the clearest water you will find in the Mediterranean.

Well over a dozen tour operators offer packages to Symi, and while there are four or five small hotels on the island, most offer self-catering accommodation in the numerous restored villas which flank the port, thus leaving you free to sample the delights of the waterside tavernas at night.

Practical Details

COMMUNICATIONS

Symi is 25 miles north of Rhodes. Three large ferries stop here weekly. A daily boat runs to Rhodes: the trip costs 600 dr and lasts around 1 hour. There are weekly hydrofoil excursions to Kos on Sundays, provided more than twenty people sign up for the trip. The cost is a hefty 4000 dr. You can join the excursion ferries from Rhodes at Ghialos and return to Mandraki with a brief stop-over at the historic Panormitis Monastery. You can visit the numerous deserted coves of Symi in one of the caiques which depart from the harbour every morning at around ten (700–1000 dr return).

The island now has a couple of roads: one connects Ghialos with Pedi, just along the coast; the other is a dirt track, laughably described as a 'motorway' in one guide we read, from Chora, which is the upper vicinity of the main port, to Panormitis, the historic monastery on the south side of the island. There is a minibus service connecting Ghialos/Chora/Pedi every hour on the hour until ten at night, and taxis also work the same route. The bus fare to Pedi is 75 dr and taxi journeys average 100 dr per head, with a minimum charge of 200 dr. It is possible to hire scooters (from 1500 dr daily) and cars. Remember, the dirt track to Panormitis is quite dangerous and if you fall off and cut yourself there is no hospital on the island, though the chemist is perfectly willing to stitch you up, free of charge, with ouzo as your only anaesthetic!

TOURIST INFORMATION

There is a tourist office in **GHIALOS** located in the clock tower. However, there are numerous agents who can give you information about boats, services and rooms. **Surry Land**, **Symian Holidays** and **Symi Tours** on the waterfront, have information sheets and this is also the place to get your ferry/caique tickets.

The post office is situated just off the harbour road and is open Mon to Fri, 7.30 a.m. to 2.30 p.m. There are three banks in Ghialos, which are all open from 8 a.m. to 2 p.m., Mon to Fri only.

There is one chemist on the harbour road (belonging to the demon stitcher). Should you have the misfortune to fall seriously ill there are English-speaking doctors on the island: Mr Polis (Tel: 71345/71316) and Mr Christos (Tel: 71000/71290) – and there is a speedboat ambulance to take you to a hospital on Rhodes in cases of emergency.

The historical 'guides' to Symi are very expensive (at least 700 dr) and often badly written. Read up on Symi *before* you go. If you are lucky, a friendly local will show you around on the back of a Vespa at the drop of a hat.

WHERE TO GO FOR WHAT

Approaching Symi at night is a wonderful experience. The harbour twinkles magically as you approach, and when you disembark to agreeable chaos at the quayside, it seems that the entire town has come to greet you. This is the harbour town of **GHIALOS,** set into the steep hillsides surrounding the natural bay, and the postcards on sale on the waterfront fail to do justice to the town's beauty. A hundred years ago Ghialos enjoyed great prosperity under the Turkish sultans and was a main centre for sponge fishing. The population was then around 30,000 but this has since declined to around a tenth of that who now discreetly encourage tourism. The elegant, neo-classical residences built for the rich merchants around the turn of the century remain, though many are now derelict shells: a remnant of the heavy bombing the island suffered at the hands of the Germans in World War II which also destroyed the medieval castle built by the Knights of St John. In 1971 the Greek Government finally declared Ghialos a historic site and the lovely old merchants' villas are now being gradually restored. If you decide to come to Symi for a holiday, it is probably in one of these houses that you will stay, for the building of large hotels has been forbidden by a preservation order. Even the two good small hotels in Ghialos, the **Dorian** (Tel: 0241 71181) and the **Nireas,** are in the style of the merchant villas. While the facilities offered in these charming villas are often quite basic, they do provide the opportunity for holiday-makers to sample island life fully rather than being cloistered in a characterless hotel. There are now over a dozen tour operators offering villa accommodation in Symi and you should book early for the high season. **Timsway** (Tel: 0923-771266) have built up a good reputation and **Laskarina** (Tel: 6062 982-2203) always have reps on hand to sort out any problems.

There is not much of historical interest remaining in Ghialos. Apart from the attractive turn-of-the-century architecture, there is really only the medieval castle, which was razed during the blitz, but still worth a visit for the delightful views across the old town (Chora) and out to **PEDI**. In Chora you will find a tiny museum with ikons and antiques which will give you a picture of what life was like on Symi in times gone by.

The tavernas lining the waterfront are all excellent if a little samey. You should visit **Katerinettes** if only to note the plaque marking the spot where the Germans surrendered to the Allied forces on 8th May, 1945. The waterfront restaurants can get very crowded during the day as the ravenous hordes descend from Rhodes, but in the evening they regain their charm. The local speciality is Symi shrimps – and you will have to ask for these specifically as they are rarely printed on any of the menus. These menus, incidentally, provide a continual source of entertainment, offering such dubious delights as 'Fruit compost' and 'Clap sandwich' – for 'creative translation' the Greeks are unrivalled! There are also a few restaurants worth trying up in Chora, and **George's** gets quite lively when the bouzoukis are brought out after a few beers.

There's not exactly much in the way of nightlife on Symi. There are two discos down in the vicinity of the harbour: **Waves** which has the added attraction of a roof garden, and the more established **Nos,** just past the Clock Tower, which is open from July to September. During the first week of July there is a festival which livens things up featuring folk-dancing competitions at night, and swimming and boat races across the harbour during the day in which tourists may participate. Sporting-minded tourists may also like to know that the island's youth has a fanatical interest in soccer and are always more than willing to take on a tourist XI on Sunday evenings on the ramshackle football pitch up in Chora, near the school.

Once you have spent a day or so sampling the attractions of Ghialos, you will want to explore the rest of the island. One or two places are accessible on foot and you can risk hiring a moped, but the accepted tactic – especially for sun-lovers – is to pile onto one of the caiques which leave the harbour at around ten every morning, heading for a variety of destinations. These are usually deserted beaches – all offering blissful calm, with safe windsurfing and scuba-diving in crystal-clear water if you want to make the effort. The average fare on a caique is around 650 dr return – double this if you take advantage of the superb barbecues sometimes offered.

The nearest hamlet is PEDI, 1½ miles from Ghialos, and the next largest settlement on the island. It can be reached in 30 minutes on foot and many of the caïques don't bother stopping here because of the bus/taxi services connecting it with Ghialos. Pedi has a good hotel, the **Pedi Beach**, and quite a few lively tavernas such as the **Two Brothers**. Also keep an eye open for the raucous young bouzouki band which used to play at the **Villa Nithia,** which has since closed down.

Near Pedi are the beaches of ST MARINA and ST GEORGE which are easily reached in small taxi boats, and further south is the first main destination for the caiques, NANOU BAY, which has a pleasant shingle beach shaded by pine trees, with cliffs rising dramatically behind it. While this is all very well aesthetically, it also means the sun disappears from the bay at around four o'clock. You can hire a speedboat (5000 dr) in Ghialos to take you water-skiing here.

The next stop is MARATHOUNTA BAY which has the clearest water on the island, but little in the way of shade.

Arguably the best beach on Symi is not actually on the island itself, but on the little island of SESKLIA, just off the south coast. SKOMISA BAY is delightfully unspoilt and the tamarisk trees which fringe it provide the ideal location for a barbecue.

Back on Symi and in the remarkable, almost totally enclosed Panormos Bay on the fertile south coast lies the historic **Monastery of Panormitis.** Built to honour Archangel Michael the monastery dates back to Byzantine times and is Symi's chief attraction. It is fortified and contains in its centre the elegant little **Church of St Michael** whose faded walls are decorated with votive lamps and amazing icons, including the priceless icon of St Michael which dates from 1724 and dominates the whole church. The museum (entry 100 dr) is worth a visit, but the guides are overpriced. The cloisters are attractive to look at, but filled with sad old women moaning about the tourist hordes who arrive from Rhodes most days at around 3.30 p.m. In the monastery 200 rooms are available for overnight stops and you can eat in one of the quiet tavernas lining the bay.

For those who don't fancy the boat or who merely want to save 300 dr you can reach Panormos Bay by truck, and yes, it *is* as bumpy as it sounds.

There is little of interest on the west coast except for ST EMILIANOS, the sponge fishers' islet with the best snorkelling in Symi. Off the north coast is the island of NEMO which is barren and totally deserted except for one tiny chapel. The only other settlement on Symi is NIMBORIO which is a 45-minute walk westwards from Ghialos. This has a good beach and has a nice taverna and this is just one of the places which you can visit on a walking tour organized by the eccentric Hugo, who carries a mysterious green bag, the contents of which are never divulged, and who is accompanied everywhere by his faithful dogs. Other tours take in some of the eighty-odd monasteries on Symi and there is even an arduous trek to Panormitis along the island's spiral road.

Remember to pack a torch to take to Symi as only the main paths are illuminated at night – and a pair of plimsolls, as the beaches are all pebbly and some have urchins.

Tilos

Though it is conveniently situated on the main ferry routes between Rhodes and Kos, Tilos is still relatively untouched by the tourist development which has overtaken its bigger neighbours. The island is small and friendly, and there are some excellent beaches in the numerous bays which cut into the mainland. The island is very quiet, with no nightlife of any description, and with its good walking trails and the odd interesting sight, Tilos should make the ideal holiday destination for the more reclusive holidaymaker.

Practical Details

COMMUNICATIONS

Ferry connections with other islands are extensive. Both the *Nireas* and *Miaoulis* make weekly stops at Tilos on their way between Rhodes (4hrs) and Piraeus (20hrs) and the good old *Panormitis,* which spends its life chugging faithfully around the Dodecanese Islands, also stops here twice a week. You can get details of the times from the restaurant on the quay at **LIVADIA,** the port of Tilos.

On the island itself there is no public transportation so you'll either have to walk or hitch, which can be very slow at times. The best idea is to ask if anybody is leaving soon at the restaurant on the dock at Livadia or at the Tropicana at ERESTOS.

TOURIST INFORMATION

The post office and OTE are situated in the same small building in Livadia's main square. You can change money at the restaurant on the quay or at the **Hotel Livadia** in the main square but it is cheaper to ensure you have sufficient drachmas when you arrive. There's not much to spend your money on anyway.

WHERE TO GO FOR WHAT

Livadia's attractive arcaded houses are surrounded by the ruins of no less than four Genoese castles. There are plenty of places to stay at here, all concentrated around the main square. The **Hotel Livadia** has clean doubles for around 800 dr and there are also several **pensions** from which to choose. There is a white pebble beach and the locals don't mind the odd camper or two.

The main settlement is at MEGALOCHORIO, some six miles away in the north-western bay. The village is dominated by the ruins of the **Venetian Fortress** which is well worth the lengthy hike it takes to get there – if only for the superb views over the whole island. About halfway between Megalochorio and Livadia are the ruins of the deserted town of **MIKROCHORIO**, which was abandoned by its inhabitants in favour of a more convenient site after pirates ceased being a major problem.

There are several good walking trails on Tilos, especially in the fertile south, and many further north lead to attractive and deserted beaches. The best is probably at **ERESTOS BAY** to the west of the island. You can camp in peace on the red sand or stay in rooms at the **Tropicana Taverna,** a hundred yards from the beach. **PLAKA BAY**, to the north of the island, also has excellent beaches.

Nissiros

Nissiros is linked with neighbouring Kos by myth. When Poseidon, god of the sea, hurled Kos at the Titan Polybotes, Nissiros was the bit that fell off. Nowadays Nissiros is linked with Kos by ferry. Situated an hour from **KARDOMENA,** it is now a prime destination for day-trippers from Kos.

The approach to Nissiros is spectacular, with the **Polyvotis Volcana** looming enigmatically in the distance. During the day the island receives a number of visitors – all wanting to take a peek at the volcano's bubbling waters – but when the hordes depart in the late afternoon, Nissiros regains its customary charm and tranquillity.

It is certainly possible to visit the island's main attractions in a day, but it is worth taking a little more time to get the 'feel' of the island without the day-trippers. The views of the volcanic landscape are tremendous; there are some excellent beaches; and the locals are, as yet, still friendly towards tourists.

Practical details
COMMUNICATIONS

Nissiros is well connected with the rest of the Dodecanese – especially Kos, from where a number of boats offer day trips for around 500 dr.

From **KARDOMENA,** Nissiros is about an hour's journey. The *Nissiros Express* also makes several journeys to Kos each week, while other ferries connect the island with Rhodes, the Cyclades and Piraeus. The *Panormitis* calls twice a week on its regular chugs around the Dodecanese, and more information can be obtained from the port police (Tel: 31222) on the wharf in the main port of Mandraki (open Mon to Sun, 8 a.m. to 1.30 p.m.).

TOURIST INFORMATION

In the same building as the port police, situated just in front of the ferry dock houses, you will find the post office and OTE (open Mon to Fri, 7.30 a.m. to 2.30 p.m.) and the police (Tel: 31201; open Mon to Fri, 8.30 a.m. to 3 p.m.). There are no banks but you can exchange money in the hotels on the quay, and also at the grocer's in the town square.

WHERE TO GO FOR WHAT

You arrive at the main port of **MANDRAKI** which is a charming town of winding whitewashed streets and alleys, overlooked by a medieval castle which contains the **Monastery of Panagia Spiliana,** built into the crag which rears above the town. There are a couple of hotels on the left of the quay: **The Three Brothers** (Tel: 31344) with doubles for 1000 dr with bath, and the **Romantzo Hotel** (Tel: 31340) with doubles for 900 dr. The pensions on the right-hand side of the quay are cheaper though, with the **Pension Porfyris** (first on the right past public bathrooms) offering rooms right on the waterfront for 500 dr.

Just past the Three Brothers at MIRA MARE, there is a fine, sandy beach with a further good beach on the other side of the cove, about half a mile distant. Just past the promontory on which the monastery is located, at HOKLAKI, is a secluded black rock beach, which can be reached via a donkey path. You won't get lost, the donkeys have dropped plenty of hints to mark the route.

Half a mile inland from Mandraki is the **Kastro,** the ancient acropolis of Nissiros, whose long walls are magnificently carved in black trachyte. They are 12ft wide and fully 20 ft in height.

The centre of the island is occupied by the volcanic crater of **Polyvotis**, some 2 miles in diameter and it is basically this that the tourists have come to see. Buses depart for the crater from the quay at Mandraki – when they're full – and the fare is 250 dr. The buses go all the way to NIKIA, a tiny village at the edge of the great crater. From here there are superb views out to sea across the lunar landscape of the crater and its fertile volcanic valley. The outer slopes of the volcano are planted with almond trees which blossom around February, making for an exquisite sight. Some of the buses stop at EMBORIO, also near the edge of the crater, which is a picturesque if near-deserted village, containing a crumbling Byzantine fort.

Around halfway between the crater and Mandraki is the spa of LOUTRA which is open from late June until September to sufferers from a whole host of ailments.

A pleasant excursion is to PALI, a peaceful fishing village around a mile and a half from Mandraki. The beach here is excellent and the water is crystal-clear.

Astipalea

Astipalea is situated so far to the west that it is virtually part of the Cyclades. Its relative isolation from the rest of the Dodecanese means it receives few tourists. The island is barren and shaped like a bow-tie, with most of its inhabitants clustered in the central knot of Astipalea town.

Practical Details

COMMUNICATIONS

Four ferries a week stop at Astipalea on their way between Piraeus and Rhodes. The fare to Rhodes is 850 dr. In winter, it is often too windy for the ferries to stop at **ASTIPALEA TOWN,** so they dock in the more secluded port of VATHI, to the north-east.

Getting around on the island can be difficult for tourists and you will generally have to find out about the boats which connect the main settlements. The other alternative is to walk, which is no real disadvantage as most of the island's attractions – such as they are – are located on the central isthmus. A bus should still be in service, connecting Astipalea town with Analipsi and Vathi.

From Astipalea caiques run quite frequently to many points around the island, including LIVADIA, AGHIOS KONSTANTINOS and MALTEZANA (Analipsi). It is often quicker to walk to places such as Livadia, as the isthmus which connects the north-eastern and south-western parts of the island narrows to little more than 100 yards in some places.

There is an OTE office next to the **Paradissos Hotel,** which is open from 7.30 a.m. to 3.10 p.m., Mon to Fri, and a shipping agent, located just opposite, sells boat/ferry tickets. Up on the hill by the nine windmills the post office is open from 7.30 a.m. to 3 p.m. Mon to Fri.

WHERE TO GO FOR WHAT

ASTIPALEA is an attractive town in the shadow of the island's Venetian castle. There are just three hotels: the **Astynea** on the waterfront (500 dr per person); the **Paradissos** (Tel: 61224) with doubles for 900 dr; and the **Aegeon** (Tel: 61236) with doubles at 1000 dr. In the low season you may get a reduction at the last two hotels if you haggle. Apart from the castle, there is not a great deal to see.

There are pleasant beaches on both sides of the isthmus near Astipalea. A twenty-minute westward walk brings you to LIVADIA where there is a lovely beach which tends to get quite crowded in peak season. Further along the coast, to the south-west, SENAKI beach unofficially caters for nudists.

To the east of Astipalea town, MALTEZANA, also known as ANALIPSI, is a tranquil little fishing village, as is VATHI further north. From here caiques leave twice a week for AGHIOS ANDREAS, which is a fine spot for diving off rocks.

If you go at Easter or during the middle of August you will see traditional costumes worn in most villages on the island.

Kos

After Rhodes, Kos is the largest and most popular island in the Dodecanese. Tourist development has been more rapid than in any other part of Greece and, in addition to its long, sandy beaches and superb archaeological sites, Kos now possesses a glut of hotels and a highly active nightlife. Much of the recent development has been in the form of lower-category hotels, catering mainly for the huge market of Germans and Scandinavians who are apparently seeking a cut-price alternative to Rhodes. With over forty British companies offering packages to Kos, it can now be uncomfortably crowded in July and August, and independent travellers expecting any sort of accommodation *whatsoever* except the beach, can forget it during the peak period.

As with all the major Greek islands, the time to visit Kos is at Easter, when the weather is pleasantly sunny and there are no crowds to get on your nerves.

Whilst its scenery doesn't compare with that of other Greek islands, the agreeable climate and abundant fresh water in Kos ensure that it supports a remarkable variety of flora, which has led to its being nicknamed the 'floating garden'. Indeed in Kos town the exotic profusion of trees, flowers and orchards eclipses most of the buildings.

The most famous of flora is undoubtedly the Plane Tree of Hippocrates, who was born here in 460 BC. The Hippocratic Oath – now 2400 years old – is taken by doctors to this day and Kos is still generally best known as being the birthplace of the 'Father of Medicine'.

In ancient times the island prospered, becoming one of the principal maritime and trading powers of the Aegean, with its wines and fine silk fabrics being renowned throughout the classical world. With the establishment of the Asklepios and the school of medicine Kos also acquired a reputation as a centre of learning. As the Greek Empire declined, it benefited from the patronage of the Egyptian Ptolemies and the Romans, and in AD 431 became the seat of a bishop. Thereafter it shared the fortunes of the other Dodecanese islands.

Recently it has escaped the severe depopulation which has afflicted the smaller islands through its greater size.

Practical Details
COMMUNICATIONS

Kos has an international airport near Antimachia in the centre of the island, 17 miles from Kos town. There are links with most European countries (package flights only) and Olympic Airways operates internal services to Athens three times daily or more; Leros (three times per week); and Rhodes (twice daily).

Kos is also well catered for by ferries. In the summer there are daily ferries to Rhodes (4hrs) and Piraeus (14hrs) via Kalymnos, Leros and Patmos. At least three other large ferries connect Kos with Rhodes and the rest of the Dodecanese. Rhodes, Samos and Patmos are served by fast, though expensive, hydrofoils, though these are unable to operate in even slightly choppy seas.

Excursion boats make day trips to Kalymnos (approx 900 dr) Pserimos (700 dr) and Nissiros (1000 dr – or 800 dr from Kardamera on the southern part of the island). Nissiros can also be reached for free, once per week, on the *Nissiros Express*. The EOT office has a complete list of all boats, though times are subject to change at short notice. A shipping agent is next door to the EOT office on the waterfront, and others are just round the corner.

On the island itself there are plenty of taxis for hire and a reasonably efficient bus service. The last bus to many places leaves around six, so make sure you don't get stranded in some isolated spot on the island after dark. You can get complete bus schedules from the EOT office. Fares are very reasonable, and the main bus-stop is a block back from the waterfront in the main square.

As most of the northern part of the island is flat, bicycles are a good way to get around. You can hire one pretty well anywhere for around 200 dr per day. The less energetic can also readily hire mopeds, scooters and cars.

TOURIST INFORMATION

There is an EOT office on the waterfront in Kos town, which is open daily from 7.30 a.m. to 1 p.m. and from 2 p.m. to 9 p.m. (Tel: 28724).

The office has details of ferries and buses, and carries a list of hotels with prices. The staff all speak English and are helpful, if overwhelmed at times by the sheer volume of backpackers wanting to know about cheap accommodation (there isn't any) and ferries.

The Tourist Police are next door (Tel: 28227) and they have information on rooms in Kos town and around the island, but you have to make your own inquiries. Open daily 7.30 a.m. to 1 p.m. and 2 p.m. to 9 p.m.

The Port Police a few yards to the left and up the stairs carry the most complete ferry information.

There are several publications available giving information about Kos. The 'Kos' leaflet available from the EOT office is adequate and free, but look out for the more comprehensive *This Summer in Kos* magazine which is also free. It contains maps, a history of Kos, and information on accommodation, restaurants and transport.

The post office is at Venizelou Street near Meropidos Street (open Mon to Fri, 7.30 a.m. to 2 p.m.) and the OTE is on the corner of Meropidos Street and Xanthou Street (open Mon to Fri, 7.30 a.m. to midnight, Sat and Sun, 7.30 a.m. to 3.10 p.m.).

WHERE TO GO FOR WHAT

Kos certainly has a variety of tourist attractions and is one of the few Greek islands which actually caters for all our seven stereotypes. There are plenty of good, sandy beaches on the island; the scenery is varied and lush; Kos town is stuffed with sights and antiquities and has an active nightlife; and you can still escape to the mountains in the south if the crowds in the major resorts are getting to you.

SIGHTS

KOS TOWN is a historian's delight. It seems that every age has left its mark upon the city, and not only are there extensive ancient ruins, but there are also Turkish mosques, Italian mansions and a medieval fortress. The almost circular harbour is dominated by the **Castle of the Knights of St John** which was built in the 15th century to ward off attacks by the Turks. You approach the castle via a superb stone bridge which traverses the **Avenue of Palms**, and which was originally the site of the outer moat. Entry is 100 dr (50 dr students) and the castle is open Mon and Wed to Sat 9 a.m. to 3.30 p.m., Sun 10 a.m. to 3 p.m. Once inside the castle's twin walls you can admire the splendid views over the town and across to Turkey.

Behind the castle and to the left as you exit is the famous **Plane Tree of Hippocrates,** which is alleged to be the oldest tree in Europe, and under whose leafy shade the great physician is said to have written his books and taught his pupils. God knows how this rumour came about, for plane trees can only live for five or six hundred years at most, and Hippocrates was around over 2400 years ago. He didn't even live in Kos town, which didn't come into existence until 366 BC. In his days, during the 5th century BC, the capital of Kos was Astipalea, which was situated at the other end of the island, and its destruction by an earthquake is recounted by Thucydedes the historian. The Plane Tree itself is held up by numerous bits of scaffolding and now looks like a leafy children's climbing frame. In front of the tree you can take a light lunch at the **Plantanos Restaurant** which is sited in one of the many splendid Italian mansions built earlier this century. The Town Hall, which was originally the Italian Governor's Palace, is probably the best example of Italian architecture. Also near the Plane Tree is the 18th-century **Loggia Mosque,** which is perhaps the finest Turkish building on the island. Byzantine architecture is also well represented in the town and you should visit the **Cathedral of St Nikolas,** which is situated a block behind the ancient Agora on Aghios Nikolaou Street.

However, it is the ruins that you will probably be most interested in, and there are certainly enough of them. Indeed it seems that you can't walk anywhere in Kos Town without stumbling across one archaeological site or another. The largest is situated near the waterfront and is known as the **Agora**. Not much is left standing, and at first glimpse the site just looks like a couple of pillars and a lot of old stones. However, there is a small 4th-century **Roman basilica,** which is still used by practising Christians, in the corner of the site, and a few of the fine mosaic floors still remain. The 'Ancient Road' is in better condition than a lot of the modern ones on the island, and entry to the site is free. The ruins at the second major site in Kos Town, situated about half a mile from the harbour on the main Grigoriou Road, are probably more interesting: certainly the mosaics are better preserved. There is a **Temple of Dionysus** to the left of this site, and over the road, at the end of a colonnade of cypress trees is the **Odeon,** a 2nd-century theatre which has been restored and is still used for summer performances.

Near this site is the town **Museum** (open in summer Mon and Wed to Sat 9 a.m. to 3.30 p.m., Sun 10 a.m. to 3 p.m. – free) which contains a fine mosaic from a Roman house which was uncovered in 1933. In the town's main square further archaeological exhibits are to be found in the **Archaeological Museum** (open in summer, Mon and Wed to Sat 9 a.m. to 3.30 p.m., Sun 10 a.m. to 3 p.m., admission 100 dr) including some superb Hellenistic sculpture and mosaics.

Most people venture the couple of miles or so from Kos Town, past the Muslim village of PLATANI, in order to see the most photographed monument of Kos – the **Asclepion.** This was an ancient sanctuary dedicated to the God of Healing, and was for many years the workplace of Hippocrates. There were 300 or so Asclepions – the ancient equivalent of a hospital – in ancient Greece and Hippocrates' systematic research into the science of medicine during the 5th century BC led to Kos establishing its reputation as the foremost medical centre in Greece.

The ruins, most of which actually date from the 4th century BC, are built on a series of terraces on a small hill with wonderful views of Kos Town and the Aegean. The most interesting ruins are to be found on the three central terraces, known as *andirons,* which are connected by superb marble staircases. The first andiron contains what is left of the **School of Medicine,** while the second andiron contains the best-preserved remains of the Asclepion: the elegant **Temple of Apollo,** dating from the Hellenistic period. The third andiron contains the remnants of the 2nd century BC **Main Temple of Asclepius,** which was originally reputed to have been an enormous structure.

Unfortunately, and rather surprisingly, there is no bus to the Asclepion, which is open Mon to Sat 9 a.m. to 3.30 p.m., Sun 10 a.m. to 3 p.m., admission 50 dr (students 25 dr). You can walk or take a taxi, but many people choose to hire a bicycle.

If you take the main inland road you will begin to experience the real Kos. At ZIPARI, which is a modern village situated 7 miles south-east of the main port and containing the ruins of the early **Christian Basilica** of St Paul, a winding road forks off towards the Dikeos Mountains. This road leads to around half a dozen settlements, collectively known as **ASFENDIOU**, whose inhabitants still practise the traditional occupations of goat herding, farming and weaving. The most attractive village is **LAGOUDI**, but others are being affected by creeping commercialization. Reclusive nature lovers can go for long walks in the woods in this area without meeting a soul.

The road continues south from Lagoudi, degenerating into a donkey track long before you reach the ruins of **PYLI**, where there is a Byzantine castle containing a church which is decorated with well-preserved 14th century frescoes. From Pyli there is a much better road back to the island's main road which eventually brings you to **ANTIMACHIA**, near the airport. Half a mile before you reach Antimachia there is a turnoff which leads to the imposing **Castle of Antimachia,** which was built by the Knights of St John.

Continuing south, there is really not much more of interest to the sightseer. The scenery is certainly attractive but the town of **KEFALOS**, around twenty miles from Kos, is nothing to write home about.

BEACHES

If you're not too bothered about fighting to the death to preserve your precious stretch of sand, you can stay in **KOS** which is where all the after-hours 'action' is anyway. There are two beaches: the first is a rough, pebbly affair stretching south of the town, which is at least fringed with plenty of shade. The second runs north towards **LAMBI** and while it is sandy, it is totally crowded and fringed with hamburger stands and large hotels. You used to be able to avoid the crowds by cycling as far as Lambi, 2 miles from Kos, but it seems that this area too has been earmarked for heavy tourist development.

However, if you can be bothered to travel a few miles along the north coast, there is a string of very good beaches. **TINGAKI**, 6 miles west of Kos, has a good beach with plenty of fish tavernas, although again it is usually extremely crowded. Continuing west, there are good beaches at **MARMARI** and **MASTIHARI** and fewer tourists. Mastihari is an attractive fishing village with a narrow, well-shaded beach, while the windsurfing at Marmari is said to be the best on the island.

A road connects Mastihari with **KARDAMENA**, a pleasant beach resort, 7 miles away on the south coast. The beach is long and sandy and there is the additional bonus of a wide range of boat excursions to **PATMOS, KALYMNOS** and the volcanic island of **NISSIROS**.

In the extreme south-west there are more superb beaches. KAMARI BEACH is by the huge luxurious Club Mediterranean complex but further east there is a beautifully unspoilt stretch of sand, and three miles further east is the best beach on the island, the gorgeous stretch of coast that is PARADISE BEACH.

Just south of Kos town there are a couple of good resorts. AGHIOS FOKAS is 5 miles south of the main port and has a decent beach which doesn't get too crowded because it is not on the bus route from Kos. A couple of miles further along the coast THERMI has an even better beach of black sand and pebbles, backed by high cliffs. A hot sulphur spring runs into the sea here and the water is correspondingly a few degrees warmer.

ACCOMMODATION

While there are some excellent package deals on offer to Kos, the one thing you must *not* do is turn up during the peak season expecting to get cheap – or indeed any – accommodation on spec. Many of the pension owners have done deals with tourist operators and there simply isn't the room to satisfy the demand caused by the thousands of backpackers who descend on the island from around June onwards. If you are left stranded in Kos with no accommodation the alternatives are: to blow anything up to 4000 dr on a hotel room; get on the bus to somewhere like Kefalos, miles from the action; or sleep on the beach. All the tents for rent at the inconveniently situated **Kos Camping** (Tel: 23910) will have been snapped up, and you'll have to make sure you're at the EOT office on the waterfront for 7.30 sharp next morning in order to stand any chance of getting a room in town. Of course, those who have booked ahead will face none of these problems.

The best hotel on the island is probably the **Oceanis** (Tel: 23728) at PSALIDI, just south of Kos town. It is a massive structure with staggered, tiered accommodation and in the distance it looks like a white fort. The de luxe facilities are superb and if Psalidi doesn't have the best beach on the island, the three hotel pools very nearly make up for it.

Those seeking a hotel with good facilities for children should investigate the **Atlantis Hotel** (Tel: 28731) 2 miles north of town or the **Continental Palace** (Tel: 22737) a mile to the south, facing the shingle beach. The former is a busy hotel with plenty of things to do, and it operates its own shuttle bus service, connecting it with the main port; the latter is a stark but spacious hotel, with a good pool in shady gardens. Both have facilities for the disabled.

Another good choice if you've got children is the **Norida Beach Hotel** (Tel: 91220) in a somewhat isolated position near Kardamena. The hotel's grounds extend to 700 acres and a shuttle bus tours them frequently. There is a choice of two good pools – one designed especially for children – and the nearby, wide, shingle beach is safe.

Sun-worshippers who want to lie in the sun all day (and do little else) could choose worse than the **Dimitri Beach Hotel** (Tel: 28581) which is in a very isolated spot on a rocky shingle beach at Aghios Fokar. Those who want a bit more action could choose the less expensive **Valinakis Beach Hotel** (Tel: 51358), right on the beach at Kardamena. If you're keen on watersports you should check into the **Caravia Beach Hotel** (Tel: 41291) at Marmari, which despite looking like a prison, is actually very well equipped indeed, and has the best windsurfing centre on the island. There are approximately seven buses daily to Kos town, 9 miles away.

Those wanting inexpensive accommodation in the main town can choose from the **Oscar** (Tel: 28090), a lively, attractive hotel with its own restaurant, situated on a quiet city-centre street; the **Paradise** (Tel: 23916), situated minutes from every amenity and a top-of-the-range hotel of character; or the **Imperial** (Tel: 23800) and **Zikas** (Tel: 28735), two similar establishments 350 yards apart – both being clean and friendly. For budget accommodation, the **Hotel Dodecanissos** (Tel: 28460), situated not far from the waterfront, has clean doubles for around 1500 dr. You won't get cheaper.

NIGHTLIFE/RESTAURANTS

Like accommodation, food is generally more expensive here than elsewhere in Greece. The cafés along the Kos waterfront are quite expensive, with the **Limnos** or **Romantica** at the end of the waterfront being the cheapest. There are a couple of very pleasant garden restaurants in the town with the **Platon** at 3, Arseniou Street having a delightful atmosphere, as does the **Bristol** at 3–5, Vas Georgiou Street, which in addition to local specialities also serves Chinese food. A good local dish is the octopus which goes down very nicely with the local red wine.

Bars are concentrated around the harbour and along Naflklirou Street, where the **Cactus Bar** and **Blue Corner** fill up rapidly every night. The best discos are out towards Lambi with **Heaven** and the **Kailua Club** being amongst the most popular – and expensive. Try the **Aquarius II** at Lambi Beach for more traditional Greek music. All drinks cost a lot more in the clubs and discos.

Kalymnos

Kalymnos, 1½ hours north of Kos, by ferry, is famed as the island of sponge fishers, who still continue to sail for the South Mediterranean each spring to spend the whole summer diving for sponges. The Kalymnians are a friendly yet fiercely proud people who have 'always revolted against all attacks' according to a local tourist guide. In 1820 Kalymnos was the first island to revolt against Ottoman Turkey in the 1820 War of Independence and, when under Italian occupation nearly a century later, the islanders used to irritate their oppressors by painting their houses in the traditionally Greek colours of blue and white.

Kalymnos basically consists of impressively rugged mountains, with two fertile valleys across its centre. The coastline is attractive with numerous sandy beaches, though it is now not as 'unspoilt' as some tourist operators would have you believe. Kalymnos has the capacity to support increased tourist development so now would seem to be the time to go and visit the island before the large tourist operators come in and ruin it, as they have Kos.

Practical Details

COMMUNICATIONS

The nearest airport is Kos to which there are daily services with Olympic internally or with charter planes from foreign countries. There are five to seven weekly ferry connections with Piraeus and Rhodes in the summer and the fare to Athens is around 1300 dr. There are three to four daily ferries to Kos and the fare is around 600 dr. There are also good connections with the nearby islands of Leros and Patmos, and Samos further north. There are adequate connections with smaller islands such as Lipsi, Tilos and Symi but it is generally advisable to go via larger islands such as Kos.

Internally there are two bus services connecting Pothia (Kalymnos Town) with Vathis to the north-east and Massouri to the north-west. The fare is only 40 dr but the buses are hot and slow. A better option, on the face of it, is the 'taxi-bus' system operated on the island. Instead of paying the normal taxi-fare from Pothia to Massouri of 350 dr, for example, you ask for 'taxi-bus' as soon as you get in the car, thus obtaining a reduction to 80 dr per person travelling in the taxi. The only drawback with this system is that taxi-drivers tend to cram as many people as possible into their vehicles to make up the 'lost' money. The last 'taxi-bus' journey I made was with nine other people in the car! Hiring cars is possible in Pothia and Myrtics and costs from 3500 dr, but most people hire scooters. In fact there are over 6000 scooters licensed on Kalymnos and it seems that everybody rides one. They are cheap and convenient, but do make sure you have enough petrol as the distances can be quite long. From Pothia you can reach most other destinations by boat.

TOURIST INFORMATION

There is an official tourist office (Tel: 29310) in the small park after 25 Maritous in **POTHIA** harbour. The office is the kiosk at the end of the path behind the bronze statue of Poseidon. The staff are extremely friendly and will do everything they can to help you if you have a problem. They have information on rooms, buses, boats and sights (brochures only – you have to buy guidebooks at other kiosks). The office is open all day during the summer until 7 p.m.

Also helpful are **Blue Islands Travel** (Tel: 23055/23185) at the north-west corner of the harbour (first floor – mind your head as you go!). The staff are very friendly, and Themis knows just about everything there is to know about the island. You can change money here after the banks close. The hours of opening are Mon to Sat 9 a.m. to 1 p.m. and 5 p.m. to 8.30 p.m. The office is sometimes closed on Saturdays. There is no official guide to what's on, but you can find out about concerts and so on from the posters on the waterfront.

CULINARY SPECIALITIES

Kalymnos has been famed for its honey since ancient times when the Greek historian Dion Cassius (AD 155–40) recommended it in his *Geoponica* – probably one of the first-ever published cookbooks. Another repast that found favour with the ancient Kalymnians was *Lai* which consists of water, salt and olive oil mixed in a large clay bowl and served with hot brown bread on Saturdays, for some strange reason. Other bread-based dishes which have now fallen from favour are *Mirmizelli* and *Psites*.

WHERE TO GO FOR WHAT

You will doubtless arrive at **POTHIA,** which is an attractive harbour town, laid out similar to that of Symi, but without as much charm. It is everything a bustling harbour town should be and plenty of cafés, bars and restaurants line the waterfront. There was an ancient town on the other side of the island bearing the name 'Pothaea' but it was destroyed in AD 544 by the same earthquake which separated Telendos from the mainland. The town's **museum**, however, concentrates on more recent history and has a luxurious parlour, giving a good indication of how wealthy Kalymnians lived a hundred years ago (open Mon and Wed to Sat 9.30 a.m. to 2.30 p.m. and Sun 10 a.m. to 2.30 p.m. – free). The town has a **Cathedral** but the **Monastery of Agios Pantes** up on the hill overlooking the south end of town is probably more interesting. Father Savvas, a church official here, died in 1948, and when nine years later his body had still not decomposed he was canonized. Of course, as soon as Father Savvas was made a saint his body started to decompose and you can see his elaborate sarcophagus, or simply marvel at the wonderful view out to Telendos Island and beyond.

There are plenty of inexpensive pensions in Pothia and the **Hotel Alma** (Tel: 28969) is central and cheap (doubles 900 dr). A more up-market bet is the **Olympic** (Tel: 28801) but most people decide to stay in the purpose-built developments which have sprung up on the north-west coast from Kantouni to Massouri.

There are a number of decent restaurants along the waterfront but beware of expensive 'Greek nights' organized by various hotels/tour operators. You pay inflated rates for a generally tacky floor show to accompany your meal. Nightclubs are either tacky or expensive and neither **Kalymnos by Night** or the **Africaner,** which both put on Greek singing, are particularly recommended. If you want to hear good music, there are programmes of Greek music every Saturday night at the football ground in the Chora just inland from the port. The shows start at 8.30 p.m. and admittance is a very reasonable 250 dr.

There are sponges on sale everywhere and in Pothia you can see the factory belonging to Nikolas Gourlas where the sponges are cleaned and chemically treated. You should buy the brown sponges, for although they may look less attractive than the bleached ones, they will last a good deal longer. Remember also to keep them moist on your way home. The departure and return of the sponge fleet are occasions of great festivity in Pothia. The last night before the fleet leaves is known as the 'Sleep of Love' and there is much celebration when the ships return safely home in autumn.

From Pothia you can make two main excursions – not counting Kos, of course, which is only 1½ hours' distance. The first is to the rocky island of PSERIMOS which has a couple of good beaches and dozens of churches. The second is to the **Cave of Kefalas** on the south coast of Kalymnos – one of several fine caves on the island. The cave has seven sections and the largest chamber, where Zeus reputedly hid from his father before killing him, is spectacularly lit and well worth the trip. The cave is supposed to be accessible by land but there are no signposts and you will waste a day looking for it. The lack of signposts on Kalymnos is really most annoying. There's nothing worse than hiring a bike to take you to some 'spectacular grotto' or other and then not being able to find it.

The waters at the volcanic spring at the resort of **THERMA**, approximately 1 mile south of Pothia, contain numerous minerals recommended for the treatment of rheumatism and arthritis. Sufferers who have had to be carried here are said to have been dancing within a week! The baths are pretty grotty and the water doesn't smell very nice, but it doesn't matter, I suppose, if it works. There is a hotel next to the baths and a couple of small beaches which are very popular with the locals as the sea water is extra warm. The road to Therma turns into the dirt track to the settlement of **VOTHYNON** and the monasteries of **Agios Pantes** and **Agia Katherina,** from where a trail should lead to the Cave of Kefalas, but doesn't.

On the north-west road out of Pothia, the first point of interest to the historian and sightseer is one of Kalymnos' twice-ruined medieval castles, the **Kastro Chrissocherias,** which used to be the Fortress of the Knights of St John. A little further along the road and overlooking the former capital of the island Chora, 1½ miles from Pothia, is the **Pera Kastro,** also fortified by the knights with its nine tiny churches scattered throughout the ruins. Half a mile beyond the Chora is the **Church of Christ of Jerusalem,** one of Kalymnos' most important historical remains, which was built by the Emperor Arcadius in thanks to God for sparing him in a storm at sea. Also off this road – if you can find it – is the **Cave of Seven Virgins,** who came to grief in the labyrinthine cavern to escape death (and worse) at the hands of marauding pirates.

As you descend to the western coast in the haze of late afternoon, the view across to the island of Telendos is staggering. The road takes you down to the beach resort of **KANTOURI**, around 4 miles from Pothia, where there is a popular pub and the first of a string of, by Greek standards, excellent beaches. The best, if most inaccessible, is **PLATI YIALOS** just past **LINARIA**. Both **MYRTIES** and **MASSOURI** are now developing into thriving resorts and new hotels are going up rapidly, especially at Massouri, which possesses the better beach in addition to water sport facilities. The **Armeos Beach** (Tel: 47488) at Massouri has its own pool and the **Vouros Hotel** serves a mean cocktail: the Vouros Special, aka the dreaded 'sticky green'.

Down at Myrties the beach is pebbly, and near here is the popular **Delfini Hotel** (Tel: 27514) where the cocktails look prettier, but lack the punch of the Vouros Specials. You may also wish to look at the number of excellent villa holidays offered by companies such as **Timsway** and **Small World**. The villas are all well situated and represent good value for money over a hotel in many cases. From Myrties you can make excursions to 'The Holy Island' of **PATMOS** and also **LEROS**, 'The Island of Diana'. You can also sail across the 600 yards or so to the lovely island of **TELENDOS** (35 dr) which was wrenched from Kalymnos by an earthquake in AD 544. It is basically a mountain, Mt Rakhi, with a flat promontory to the south where the hamlet of Telendos is situated. Here there are some pleasant tavernas – although avoid the naff bouzouki band on Wednesday nights at **George's** on the left as you land. The main attraction, however, is the number of secluded little coves – some capable of holding a mere half dozen sun-worshippers – which line the coast facing the mainland. The island does possess a couple of proper, sandy beaches on the other side of the promontory, and even the ruins of a castle round to the north.

Back on the mainland, the taverna by the landing stage at Myrties is a good place to while away the minutes as you wait for a boat and those who enjoy nightlife can avail themselves of the rather pricey disco and cocktail bars which throng the route between Myrties and Massouri.

While there is nowhere on the island which could be said to be crowded – yet – the real recluse may wish to hire a scooter and zoom off north of Massouri and into a different world.

At ARGINONDA, 11 miles from Pothia, there is a delightful bay with a deserted sandy beach. The next village is SKALIA which has no beach but a very pleasant square. Near here is the **Cave of Skalia,** the second most important cave on Kalymnos after Kefalas. It is reputed to be a beautiful cave, but needless to say, we couldn't find it. At the end of the road, which is still being built in some places, is the tranquil hamlet of EMBORIO. Here, there is a long beach (pebbly) with plenty of shade and also a jetty, where you can land small boats.

The other road from Pothia leads to VATHIS, 3½ miles to the north-east. The scenery is dramatic here and totally unlike the rest of Kalymnos. Mountains rise steeply on both sides of the fjordal bay and the valley behind the bay is lush with a profusion of fruit trees. There is no beach here but you can take a dip off the pier and the superb scenery and dearth of other tourists more than compensates for the lack of sand. The area behind the bay is good for hiking – and it is possible to walk to Arginonda and on from there.

Leros

Leros, the island of Diana, goddess of hunting, is a quiet island possessing an understated beauty, lying between Patmos to the north and Kalymnos to the south. It generally receives far fewer visitors than its neighbours and don't come here expecting much in the way of classical antiquities or pulsating nightlife. This island's attractions are very much geared to the reclusive sun-worshipper, or sportsman who can explore the island on foot or by bicycle, indulge in water sports at Alinda, and also take advantage of the excellent diving school under whose guidance you can explore the deep, natural bays of Leros.

Practical Details

COMMUNICATIONS

There is a small airstrip around 3½ miles to the north of Platanos, the island's capital. There is a daily flight to Athens at 8 a.m. and one every Mon, Wed and Fri at 3.30 p.m. You can also fly to Kos for around 1000 dr every Mon, Wed and Fri at 2.15 p.m.

However, you will generally arrive at Leros by one of the ferries which dock at **LAKKI**. There are daily departures to Kalymnos, Kos and Rhodes. There are also weekly departures to Lipsi, Patmos, Arki, Agathonisi and Samos, every Monday and to Kalymnos, Kos, Nissiros, Tibi, Symi and Rhodes, every Thursday. A smaller boat connects Xerocampos with Myrties on Kalymnos, daily. Schedules are apt to change if the weather is bad. Tickets (in Lakki) are sold at the café across the street from the clock by a ticket agent who turns up a couple of hours before the boat is due to depart.

On Leros itself there is a bus which goes to all the major settlements from Platanos. There are six departures to Lakki and Xerocampos each day and three to Alinda and Partheni. The maximum fare is 50 dr. Taxis are reliable and cheap and can be hired from the stations in Platanos, Lakki and Aghia Marina. A good way to explore the island is by bicycle, or moped for the more lazy. These can be hired at Lakki and Alinda.

TOURIST INFORMATION

There is no official tourist office on the island but Chris Kokkonis at **DRM Travel,** just off Platanos Square (Tel: 0247 23568), is always glad to help with any problems and he supplies an information pack which tells you all you need to know about Leros.

WHERE TO GO FOR WHAT

Leros is rocky and mountainous but is greener than its near neighbour Kalymnos due to its having more water. Six deep bays eat so deeply into the island that they appear landlocked, and indeed the locals refer to Leros as an island of lakes. The water in these bays is fresh and sparkling and the bays of Vlefouti and Aghia Marina are ideal for skin-diving and fishing.

The capital of the island is **PLATANOS,** situated to the south of the medieval castle of the Knights of St John which dominates the surrounding area. Platanos is quiet and has the feel of a village rather than a town. You can stay in the pensions in this area, but most people prefer to stay nearer the beaches at **ALINDA** and **AGHIA MARINA.** Alinda is on the east coast 1½ miles from Platanos and is the island's premier resort. There is a pleasant narrow beach over half a mile in length, with plenty of shade, and there are facilities for water-skiing, windsurfing and pedaloes. Alinda has built up a reputation for having the best restaurants in Leros and most of the island's nightlife is concentrated here. The hotels are reasonably priced and you could stay at the **Maleas Beach** (Tel: 23306) or the **Alinda Hotel,** which contains the ruins of an old Christian church with fine mosaic floors in its courtyard.

There are two sandy, secluded beaches just north of Alinda. These are at PANAGIES and DIO LISKARIA, and both are ideal for sun-worshippers who wish to sport themselves in the nude. Further on there is a delightful swimming spot at KRYPHOS where there is also an interesting cave.

Just to the south of Alinda is the small port of **AGHIA MARINA**, whose neo-classical two storey villas built around the turn of the century reflect the wealth of culture of the people of that period. Aghia Marina is only around 10 minutes' walk from Platanos and contains several popular bars and souvenir shops. There are paths up to the impressive **Castle of Leros** from both Aghia Marina and Platanos. A lot of the castle has now been destroyed but various towers, walls and chapels remain and it is certainly worth the 45-minute walk (slobs can go by taxi) if only for the magnificent view of the whole island from the top of Pityki Hill.

The delightful fishing village of PANTELI lies a few hundred yards to the south-east of Platanos. The medium sized **Hotel Panteli** is located within 50 yards of the small beach, and there are plenty of pensions which offer simple yet comfortable accommodation in this area. The tiny **Hotel Rodon** has a charming garden with fruit trees and terraces and is one of several hotels available through **Lancaster** (Tel: 01 697 8181). Panteli has a disco, some bars and several excellent fish tavernas.

The distance from Panteli on the east coast, to **LAKKI** on the west is less than a mile. Lakki port is one of the Mediterranean's largest natural deep-water harbours and contains several attractive dwellings and leafy gardens. However, Lakki also used to contain prisons for political prisoners and the grimness of these surroundings seems to have rubbed off on the locals. There are hotels and pensions in Lakki but the place is deadly dull and you'd be far better off on the east coast. The one bright spot in the port of Lakki is the delightful beach at KOULOUKI, which, though pebbly, is shaded and secluded.

A short walk away through orchards and vineyards is the hamlet of XEROCAMPOS, which some feel has the best beach on the whole of Leros. However, if the locals continue to litter it with rubbish it won't retain its reputation for long. Near Xerocampos is the noted church of **St Mary** (Panagia) and the ruins of a fortress which dates back to the 3rd century BC.

Moving back up to the north, there is a fascinating spot on the west coast near GOURNA, a short walk from Alinda. On a small islet connected to the mainland by a narrow causeway is the tiny chapel of **Agios Issidoros**. There is no beach here but the scenery is wonderfully romantic.

On the north coast the bays of **VLEFOUTIS** and **PARTHENI** offer the chance for a scenic dip, and at Partheni there is the ruined temple of Artemis, said to be one of the most important Greek monuments.

 DRM Travel (Tel: 23568) offer several good tours of the island – by bus or boat – including trips to deserted coves (including fish barbecue) and the more unusual option of a diving trip, which takes place once a week.

Patmos

Patmos, the 'Holy island', was until quite recently wholly owned by the Greek church. The island is dominated by the formidable Monastery of St John the Theologian, which was actually given to Patmos late in the 11th century by Emperor Alexis I. The Monastery is dedicated to St John the Divine who wrote the Book of Revelations in a hermit's cave further down the mountain. The cave is now known as the Cave of the Apocalypse and is the most sacred place on the island.

Unlike Athos, however, Patmos never became an independent monastic republic under Greek protection. The Greek Government had other plans for the island and decided to open up Patmos to tourism, though it had long been a popular pilgrimage destination. Patmos has many attractions besides its obvious religious and historical sites. The island features strikingly beautiful scenery and possesses some excellent beaches. In addition to this, the port of Skala is lively without ever seeming crowded.

Practical Details

COMMUNICATIONS

SKALA is the port and main town of Patmos. Ferries from here travel to the Cyclades and Piraeus daily and no less than ten per week cling along the Patmos–Leros–Kalymnos–Kos–Rhodes route. Excursion boats shuttle to Samos, Iraria, Lipsi, Kalymnos and Kos and the prices on these boats are generally twice the ferry prices. The frequent hydrofoil service to Leros, Kos, Rhodes and Samos costs nearly three times the regular ferry fare and trips are liable to cancellation if the weather is rough.

On Patmos a number of small boats are available between the main beaches and buses connect all the main villages with Skala. The main bus station is on the harbour in front of the police station and the complete schedule is displayed. The most frequent bus service is between Skala and the Chora. Buses depart every hour; the fare is cheap and the distance short. There are also coaches available for tours of the main religious sites. These are more expensive but include guided tours, and (sometimes) air-conditioning. Skala has seven taxis, which will take you anywhere on the island. You can also rent mopeds on the waterfront for around 800 dr per day.

TOURIST INFORMATION

Somewhat surprisingly there is no official tourist office in Skala. The police (Tel: 31213) to the right of the main square as you disembark are quite friendly and have information on ferries (but not accommodation). There is little difficulty finding out about Patmos. Several travel agents are to be found in the harbour all of whom will be happy to help with any problems and the *Patmos Tourist Map and Town Guide* is available everywhere.

WHERE TO GO FOR WHAT

You will land at **SKALA**, the capital of Patmos, which is a pleasant harbour town with an adequate and convenient beach which usually has as many ducks as people on it. Skala possesses the usual tourist facilities, yet has managed to remain not overly commercialized. There are well over a dozen hotels in the town and over 300 rooms to let in private houses (including Netia just across the harbour). Good hotels in Skala include the **Porto Skala** (Tel: 31343), situated near the beach, and smaller and cheaper **Astoria** (Tel: 31205). The **Hotel Rodos** (Tel: 31371), one block behind the square, offers decent rooms at economy prices (doubles from 900 dr). In summer the hotels are usually full up but you can generally get a room at a pension without too much difficulty (900 dr).

There are plenty of restaurants and bars in the harbour and the local crayfish is excellent. After a dip in the sea, relax over a drink in the **Café Arion** on the waterfront.

There are two excursions you must make on Patmos. The first is to the **Cave of the Apocalypse,** the hermit's cave situated about halfway up the hill between Skala and the Chora, where St John heard the voice of God through a threefold crack in the rock. He dictated the entire Book of Revelations (the last book of the New Testament) to his disciple Prochorousim in AD 96. The present cave has been extended into the **Church of St Anne** and a further church, the **Apokalypsis Monastery,** has been dedicated to St John on this spot. Not surprisingly the cave of the Apocalypse is packed with tourists who are shunted in and out at great speed by tour guides. Remember to cover your legs before you enter (you can hire coverings from the kiosk for 60 dr) and on no account disturb any of the priests or you'll be unceremoniously booked out.

The other important excursion is to the Chora and its daunting **Monastery of St John the Theologian,** whose majestic grey walls dominate the village and indeed the whole island. The monastery was founded in 1088 by St. Christopolous who was given the island, plus financial assistance to build the monastery, by Emperor Alexis I. The monastery was fortified with formidable battlements and watch-towers to guard against the threat of Turkish pirates. As a result of these fortifications the monastery was never sacked and its 13,000 documents provide an unparalleled picture of monastic life throughout the ages. As you enter, the head of Christopolous can be viewed in the chapel to the right of the entrance. His was another of those bodies which refused to decompose after death, leading to his inevitable canonization. In the church itself the finest frescoes are the ones in the **Chapel of the Virgin.** The refectory is also interesting, and the outstanding treasury (admission 100 dr) features a superb collection of Byzantine art, with ornate liturgical garments and splendid icons. There is also a wonderful collection of manuscripts, some illustrated, including much of the original Gospel of St Mark. The monastery still has seventeen students, though there used to be ten times that amount, and if you visit out of season, one of the students may show you around some of the closed-off sections which have panoramic views over the whole island. Entry to the monastery is free (Sat to Wed 8 a.m. to midday and 2 p.m. to 6 p.m.; Thur and Fri 8 a.m. to midday) and a guided tour costs 400 dr.

The Chora itself is a fascinating hilltop town whose narrow winding lanes you can explore at your leisure. There are many attractive houses and the views across the rest of the island are superb. There are a couple of decent tavernas in the main square but little else. If you want accommodation and night life, you'll have to head back to Skala.

Elsewhere on the island there are numerous chapels – as you would expect on a 'holy' island – and several good beaches, many of which have seen recent tourist development. The best beach is at PSILI AMOS to the south, although this is comparatively remote and best reached by boat. The main beach resort on the east coast is GRIKOS where there is an attractive sandy beach. This is now a popular tourist spot and good hotels here include the **Xenia** (Tel: 31219) and the **Grikos** (Tel: 31167). Grikos is convenient for excursions to the Chora and the boat excursions to the uncrowded beaches of DIAKOFIT and Psili Amos.

Just north of Skala there is a beach at Meloi with pleasant camping nearby and further up the coast is the quiet village of KAMPOS whose beach is very popular if somewhat overrated. The best beach on the north coast is at LAMPI where there is a fine pebble beach with many attractively coloured stones.

Lipsi

Lipsi is the tiny island where Homer's Odysseus allegedly met the beautiful Calypso – and that is just about its only claim to fame. It is situated a few miles to the east of Patmos and is a rocky island with lovely scenery and just the one village.

Practical Details

COMMUNICATIONS

Most people visit Lipsi on day trips from Patmos. Boats leave **SKALA** every day at 10 a.m. and return to Patmos at around 5.30 p.m. The fare is around 750 dr and most people return the same day.

TOURIST INFORMATION

There is a post office and an OTE in the main square of the village – and that's about it.

WHERE TO GO FOR WHAT

Where to go for *anything* is the main problem on Lipsi. Its lack of tourist attractions is a standing joke on the island. However, if you want to while away a few pleasant days on a peaceful and unspoilt Greek island then Lipsi will do nicely. Accommodation is relatively cheap and there are a few pensions on the waterfront.

Lipsi has a decent town beach, but the best one on the island is **KATZADIA**, half an hour's walk south from the waterfront. Shoppers should note that there is a rug-making school on the waterfront whose products are very attractive.

Rhodes

For thousands of years now, Rhodes has been blessed with idyllic weather: the hot sun all summer, no rain, and pleasantly cool evenings. It is perhaps this, and the fact that Rhodes was placed on strategic trade routes that attracted plunderers throughout the centuries.

Today's Rhodes is one of the most tourist-orientated islands in Greece, but the plethora of beautifully preserved remains, good beaches and numerous tourist facilities make it well worth a visit. It rates among the top ten most interesting islands and is the perfect compromise for someone equally interested in getting an all-over tan and soaking up a bit of culture.

Rhodes continues to charm and plays host to half a million tourists each year. The tourist industry is now quite developed and it is an ideal place to settle down for a couple of weeks' rest and relaxation, bronzing in the sun, and dancing into the night. Likewise, the history of the island ensures that there is plenty to see. The massive walls built by the Knights of St John still control entry to the Old City and you will find yourself trying to navigate through the maze of cobbled streets, worn but little changed from the 15th century.

Rhodes is the largest of the Dodecanese islands and there is plenty to explore. Driving down the coastline will lead you to Greek villages with whitewashed houses, the ruins of ancient cities ('crumblies'), and to the dirt-tracked roads of the interior.

Rhodes is much closer to Turkey than to mainland Greece. From the north shore of the island, the Turkish coast appears to be a stone's throw away (10 miles), but the similarity ends there, or so the Rhodians would have you believe. They are one hundred per cent Greek and you will detect that they wish to have no association with the Turks, under whose yoke they lived for centuries. Consequently, the old mosques built by the Turkish conqueror, Suleiman the Magnificent, are becoming dilapidated and are no longer open to the public.

Though the Greeks have no love lost to their Eastern neighbours, they are incredibly hospitable people. The tourist industry has quickened the pace of life and has added a sense of urgency to a country that is traditionally slow, the more so, because they must earn most of their annual tourist revenues in the summer months. Take the opportunity to sit back and chat with the Greeks and you will be amply rewarded.

The island is about 40 miles long and only 25 wide. Rhodes town, the hub of island activity, lies at the top of the island. It is here that most of the package holidays come. Large hotels line the waterfront in the New Town and nothing is further than a short walk (except seclusion). A variety of restaurants, tavernas and discos make life comfortable and entertaining here, if somewhat busy. Rhodes town is especially popular with young people from Scandinavia, and a *Svensk Ordlista* (dictionary) might come in handy. Many package holidays are also available in the Old Town, which is the Greek Rhodes, as history once knew it. The Old Town is quite commercial, but the charm and the lazy mood make it ideal for just wandering about.

A chain of hills, rising to the south of the town, forms the backbone of the island, dividing the coastlines between east and west. The east side of the island is quite beautiful and it is here that the new resorts are sprouting up. Beaches abound, large and small, occasionally hidden in a cove. The golden sand here is much nicer than the pebble beach in Rhodes town. The coast is varied from the low plains around Faliraki to the lofty cliffs surrounding the beaches of Lindos, where they filmed *The Guns of Navarone* and is very popular with the British. Some of the resorts are well developed and quite busy. Others are still small and quiet, so there is quite a bit to choose from.

The west side of the island caters to package holidays and has some distinct pros and cons. A strong wind, typically 15 mph, blows in from the Aegean, making it excellent for advanced boardsailing, but not so placid for sunbathing. Furthermore, the beaches are more pebble than sand, but away from Rhodes town, the west coast is fairly quiet and can be a restful base for planning day trips. Cars, motorbikes and mopeds can be rented nearly everywhere and the package tours all offer a variety of day trips on the coach, so being isolated is not a problem.

The interior of the island is rugged. A few roads cross the island, passing through small towns. Driving up into the hills gives a good view of the island and the small towns are really worth a visit, if only because they still maintain their traditional ways and don't offer the tourist everything on a platter. Likewise the south of the island is primarily undeveloped with dirt roads and empty beaches. Exploring this area is highly recommended, but you may need to pack food and water before you leave. Motorized transport is essential.

History

Rhodes' situation at the crossroads of the Mediterranean trade routes has attracted many settlers over the years; among the earliest were the Minoans from Crete and the Achaeans from the Peloponnese. With the arrival of the Dorians in 1100 BC, the island was divided between the three cities of Ialysos, Lindos and Kamiros. These ancient cities formed half of the Hexapolis which was set up in 700 BC bringing economic and political stability to this area for four centuries. To prevent rivalry and to increase the island's standing the new city of Rhodes was created in 408 BC, which was to prosper and become a major power centre.

Throughout the 3rd century BC, Rhodes behaved like a good businessman; shifting its allegiance to whichever power best suited its commercial interest and trying for the most profitable connections. When it became apparent that Rome was going to remain in the driving seat for the foreseeable future, Rome's enemies became Rhodes' enemies, and wars were fought on their behalf. The island grew prosperous and due to the Roman connection became an influential power in the ancient world. Many considered Rhodes to be the cultural and intellectual heart of the Roman Empire, and as far back as the 2nd century BC, VIPs have been holidaying there – Brutus, Caesar and Mark Antony having a soft spot for the place in particular.

During the Civil Wars Rhodes backed the wrong horse by supporting Pompey against Caesar, and after Caesar's assassination, the islanders refused to help Brutus and Cassius in their rebellion against the Senate, an act which resulted in the sacking of their island. From the end of the Roman period to the arrival of the Knights of St John in 1306, Rhodes suffered numerous invasions including the purchase of the island by Genoese pirates, from whom the Knights took over. With the Pope's help the Knights built extensive fortifications which were to protect this Christian outpost from numerous attackers. But in 1522, Suleiman the Magnificent and 150,000 men breached the walls and took Rhodes after a six-month siege, but so impressed was he by the Knights' valiant defence, that he gave them their freedom after capturing the island. Turkish rule continued up until 1912 when the Italians helped the island gain its independence.

Practical Details

One caveat about practical information is worth mentioning. Nearly all information, be it flight arrivals, boat or bus schedules, and particularly prices, is subject to change, depending on the time of the year and the whims of the gods. Therefore, this information should serve only as a guide. For current schedules etc., stop in at the Tourist Information offices.

Rhodes is easily accessible from all directions except Turkey. Many package tours will fly you directly into the island's airport, 10 miles south-west of Rhodes town. The package operators are usually there to meet you with a coach and take you to your hotel. Alternatively, there is a public bus (120 dr) going to Rhodes town which runs all day. The airport also has an OTE office, a post office desk and facilities for car rental.

Scheduled flights with Olympic Airways run to and from Athens all week long several times a day, and from Thessaloniki twice-weekly, though the high demand may require you to book a couple of days in advance. Until recently, the price of an airfare to Athens was only marginally more expensive than the ferries. The ferries were suffering and have successfully lobbied for successive 20 per cent increases in airfares. As a result, a one-way fare from Athens to Rhodes is about 5000 dr by air and takes about an hour. The alternative is 2000 dr for the ferry (without a berth) which takes anything between 16 and 28 hours from the port of Piraeus. The boats usually visit some of the neighbouring islands in the Dodecanese en route and run daily.

COMMUNICATIONS

Island-hopping. There are flights during the summer from Rhodes to Kos, Paros, Leros, Heraklion, Karpathos, Kassos, Kastelorizo, Santorini, Mykonos and Sitia.

The ferries run daily to Kos, Kalymnos, Symi, Alimnia and Halki; three times a week to Symi, Nissiros, Kalymnos, Tilos, Karpathos, Kassos and Santorini; twice a week to Chalki, Kassos and Limnos and once a week to Kastelorizo, Haifa (Israel) and others depending on the season.

Getting Around the Island. Buses (*Ieoforio*) leaving from the **Nea**

Agora (New Market) serve the west coast of the island. Buses for the east leave from nearby **Rimini Place** by the sign for the *Sound and Light Show*. They are fairly reliable and reasonably priced; the fares vary from 100–500 dr depending on the distance of your journey. You board at the front or the back and pay the conductor. During the rush hours the buses get unbelievably busy and uncomfortably hot, so try to avoid the pre-siesta crush around 1.30 p.m. In the high season, the crowds are inevitable and you will have to push and fight to get a seat. Bus timetables which continually change are available from the Tourist Office. The major resorts are typically served every hour or two depending upon the temperament of the bus drivers, the heat etc.

Taxis are reasonable by northern European standards, despite the high cost of petrol in Greece, and if you can get four people together, a taxi can work out quite a cheap means of transport. Outside the main towns another type of taxi operates – the *agoreon*. These operate on a set-fare basis, but tend to work out quite expensive. The main town taxi rank is just off Mandraki Harbour (Tel: 27666).

Car hire is readily available although extremely expensive – you are not only charged a basic hire and petrol charge, but also a hefty kilometre rate as well. It's only really worth your while if you have a group of 4 to 6. As a jeep out on a daily rate to tour the whole island can cost as much as £40, it is often worth considering a three-day hire scheme which works out around £80.

Hiring mopeds and motorbikes is another cheaper alternative to get yourself mobile. Most of the large hotels hire them out, and there are also several obvious places in Rhodes town. The average cost is 1200 dr a day for a 50 cc machine, including insurance. No matter how young you are, it seems you are rarely asked for a licence or proof of age. Alternatively, bicycles are available for around 600 dr a day.

The Tourist Information office is on the corner of Makariou and Papagou Street. Accommodation service is offered, also maps, 'what's on', and timetables. Open Mon to Fri 8.30 a.m. to 2.30 p.m. (opens 7.30 a.m. during summer), closed Sat and Sun (Tel: 23255). There is another office on Papagou Street at Place Rimini. This too offers accommodation service, maps, 'what's on', and timetables. Open Mon to Sat 8 a.m. to 8 p.m., Sun 9 a.m. to midday. The Tourist Police are at El. Dodekanission on Lohou Street. Use them when the EOT is closed, or when serious problems arise. They speak English and are often open 7.30 a.m. to midnight (Tel: 27423). The British Consulate is at 17, 25th Martiou Street (Tel: 27306, 24963). The Post Office is on Platia Eleftherias, Mandraki Harbour. Open Mon to Sat 7.30 a.m. to 8.30 p.m. The OTE office is at 130 Amerikis St, 25 Martiou St, open 24 hrs, and the National Bank of Greece, Kyprou Sq. in the New Town is open Mon to Sat 8 a.m. to 1 p.m., 2 to 8 p.m., Sun and holidays 9 a.m. to noon, 5 to 7 p.m. In case of medical problems the Queen Olga Hospital is at Helvetsas St., Rhodes town (Tel: 25555).

CLIMATE

Rarely in Rhodes do people talk about the weather. It is what you might expect of a top holiday island, hot and sunny, day in and day out, all summer long. You can feel the heat of the sun by nine o'clock in the morning on a summer day with no respite until six in the evening. Avoid looking like a lobster; bring a hat and a long-sleeved shirt for the days when you have had a bit too much. There is always more time to lie in the sun than your body can take, so use plenty of sunscreen and take care of your skin. Surprisingly, the evenings can be cool and a warm jumper is just the thing.

The most prominent cause of illness results from dehydration from too much sun and alcohol. Make it a habit to consume water every couple of hours or pick up some fruit at the market. Bottled water is fairly inexpensive and you will want a couple of litres if you're planning a day trip to the south of the island.

The average temperature in the winter months is only in the fifties. Dress accordingly with some warm jumpers and a jacket for the evenings.

CULINARY SPECIALITIES

Finding restaurants in Rhodes is never a problem, though finding really good Greek food takes a bit of work on your part. The island is littered with tavernas and you might find that some of the smaller ones are the most traditional, operated by families and generally unpretentious. The secret of eating in Greece is not so much what you eat but how.

Why not go for a *meze*? The Greeks traditionally do not drink on empty stomachs. The custom is to have food with your drinks. This could be just about anything: *dolmades*, stuffed vine leaves, *souvlakis* or *kebabs* on a skewer or even a sweet dessert. A good *meze* can be a long affair lasting several hours. The quantity of food is not so important. It is the lazy atmosphere that counts, where you can sit back, talk and relax without hurrying or being hurried out. That is the Greek way to eat.

Rhodes is not actually known for particular specialities, but take the opportunity to learn more about Greek food in general. Begin your dinner with a starter like the Greek salad with *feta* cheese made from goat's milk, or try a *tzatziki*, a mixture of yoghurt, cucumber, and garlic which goes well with a large chunk of bread.

For the main course, experience the seafood. Freshly caught *oktapodi* hung up to dry in the sun and fried in a batter is very popular. A lot of food in the restaurants is cooked in the morning or the day before. The solution to this is to ask to see the kitchen, something quite accepted in Greece. Be inquisitive, ask when the fish was caught and they are likely to appreciate your interest as well as giving you better service.

The traditional meat dishes, *pastitsio*, *moussaka*, *souvlaki* and *keftedes* all offer some variety. Enjoy your meal with a glass of retsina with its distinctive Greek flavour. Alternatively, try one of the local wines, *Chevalier de Rhodes* or *Grand Maitre*. All Greek food has one thing in common – olive oil. A soft drink or a glass of beer often helps the food go down. For a cheap, decent meal, there are a string of tavernas on Oreos Street in the Turkish Quarter of the Old Town.

Finally vegetarians take heart. Visit Mollye at **The Vegetarian Place** on Ionos Dragoumi Street. She was the first woman to open her own restaurant in Rhodes town. The dishes are wholesome and attract the holiday hostesses who spend the whole summer on Rhodes. If your curiosity is aroused, Mollye also claims to be a psychic and consults in the mornings.

WHERE TO GO FOR WHAT

Rhodes offers a lot of variety and it's worth taking the time to think about your interests and arrange your holiday accordingly.

Socialites should head for the large, developed resorts like **IXIA, FALIRAKI, LINDOS** and particularly **RHODES TOWN** and its environs. Most hotels have discos, but you may want to walk around the town exploring. Dancing goes on late into the night at the discos, but the hot spots are not cheap. Cover charges are often as high as 700 dr and include free drinks. Others are cheaper, but they usher you directly to the bar.

Sightseers have some choice because there is much to see all over the island. No matter where you are staying, the hotels arrange tours of the island. If you are more independent, you enjoy taking your time and are willing to rent a car, you may want to pick a small resort from which to base your trips. If you are willing to rely on public transport, you ought to stay in Rhodes town (the Old Town is more picturesque) where all the buses arrive and depart. Another idea would be to stay at a pension in Lindos (there are no large hotels). The town, popular with the British, is exquisitely situated, retains its natural Greek flavour and is also on the main bus routes.

Family Holidays are quite good along the north-west coast around **KRITIKA, KREMASTI** and **PARADISSI**. Pick a large hotel with a beach, boats and entertainment, and avoid the areas like Faliraki and Rhodes town if the children are small and you don't want to be constantly worrying about them.

The Recluse and the Nature Lover will find Rhodes to be good exploring ground in the winter. Come the summer months, the Recluse should have a good think before coming to Rhodes. It is quite possible to sign up for a package holiday, take the charter flight and then explore the island on your own for the duration of your holiday. The south and the interior of the island are very undeveloped and quiet. The areas south of GENADIO and along the tip at **PRASSONISSI** will give you all the peace and quiet you want and the buses run down to **KATAVIA** once a day. However, you need to be pretty self-sufficient because there is little catering in these areas. If this suits you, fine. Otherwise, you might want to consider a smaller island with a quiet town where the ferries pass only once a week.

Healthy Holiday types will probably enjoy the east coast, but it rather depends on what you want. Boating and beaches are everywhere, but the east coast has less wind, calmer water and better sand. If you push weights and want to work out during your holiday, Rhodes town has a couple of gyms open to visitors. One spot worth recommending is AFANDOU on the east coast. It's still a fairly small resort with the usual beaches and water sports. Tipping the balance is its location, parked next to an 18-hole golf course open to visitors. Fifteen miles north, towards Rhodes town, are riding stables also catering for tourists.

Sun-worshippers; the sun shines equally on all parts of the island. A strong breeze on the west coast detracts somewhat from the sunbathing, and the beaches in Rhodes town are mediocre and covered with pebbles. As a result, the east coast resorts have been developed and are very popular. **FALIRAKI** beaches are a bit like the Costa del Sol with a good base of sand covered with tourists. The beaches in and around **LINDOS** are also quite good and not quite as crowded. Perhaps the optimum beaches are those at the up-and-coming resorts with only a few package tours. Try KOLIMBIA, PEFKI or GENADIO. If you want a private beach, you'll have to venture south of Genadio and follow the path of the Recluse.

RHODES TOWN

Rhodes was one of the ancient world's most beautiful cities with its impressive planned streets and famous schools of oratory and philosophy. Medieval Rhodes was no less noteworthy: the Knights used the very best Italian craftsmen of the time to construct their fortresses and castles. Today's Rhodes is divided into the Old Town, the medieval centre within the City Walls, and the New Town.

THE OLD TOWN

From the Tourist Office walk down Alexandrou Papagou Street towards Mandraki Harbour. Climb any of the stairs leading off the street to the right and on your right-hand side is the **Great Wall and Moat** which completely surrounds the Old Town and dates back to 1309 when the Knights arrived from Cyprus. You can appreciate the impressiveness of the Old Town by walking around the walls, tours on Mon and Sat, at 2.45 p.m., starting at the Palace of the Knights (200 dr).

Knights Quarter

Entering the Old Town via Liberty Gate you will see straight in front of you on Platia Simis the ruins of the 3rd century BC **Temple of Aphrodite**, one of the few reminders of Ancient Rhodes. Directly behind these ruins is the **Inn of Auvergne**, completed in 1507. Slightly further along, overlooking the fountain, is the **Archaeological Institute** – one of the town's oldest buildings dating from the 14th century, and considered to be the possible site of the Knights' original Hospital. Alongside the Institute is the **Musuem for Traditional Decorative Arts** (open Mon, Wed, Fri 10 a.m. to 1 p.m.). Carrying straight on past Pl. Moussiou, on your right, you will come to the 15th-century **Knights' Hospital**, now housing the island's **Archaeological Museum** (open Mon to Sat 8 a.m. to 7 p.m., Sun 8 a.m. to 6 p.m. 200 dr, closed Tues). The ground floor of the Gothic courtyard was used for storing items for the infirmary above. The 'cells' which look as though they were for the private patients as opposed to the 'National Health' wards, were actually for contagious cases. The museum contains an outstanding collection of Archaic and Hellenistic artefacts: the tombstones of the Knights, some bearing the skull and crossbones of the plague, a 3rd century BC statue of Aphrodite, otherwise known as the Marine Venus, washed up at the start of this century with the clear outline of a fisherman's watch tattooed on her chest.

Across the square is the **Inn of England** which is a 1919 copy of the original 1493 structure. The best-preserved inns, however, are those which line the Avenue of the Knights – turn right on to Ippoton Street. Walking up the avenue, you pass on your right the **Inn of Italy**, followed by the Palace of Grand Master Villiers de L'Isle Adam, and the **Inn of France**, the most elaborate of the inns; predictable when you know that fourteen of the nineteen Grand Masters were French. It is now used to display exhibitions and its small gardens are pleasantly quiet. Opposite the French Inn, behind an iron gate is a peaceful but inaccessible shaded garden and a Turkish fountain. Further up the avenue, on the right, you pass the **French Chapel** and the House of the Chaplain of the Tongue of France (now the Italian vice-consulate), and finally the **Inn of Provence**. On the other side of the avenue is the **Inn of Spain**, the other house having belonged to the Knights. The **Palace of the Grand Masters** is straight ahead on Platia

Kleovoulou (open Mon to Sat 8 a.m. to 7 p.m., Sun 8 a.m. to 6 p.m. [200 dr], closed Tues).

The Palace survived the Turkish siege, only to be converted to a prison by the victorious Turks. In 1856, it was accidentally blown up when gunpowder in the cells exploded. Under Mussolini's orders the Palace was restored to serve as a summer residence for the rulers of Italy. In all, about fourteen rooms are open to the public. Aside from the usual bricks, pillars and beautiful ceilings, there are mosaic floors from the neighbouring island of Kos, wooden chests from the Turks, and some Chinese pottery thrown in for good measure.

Turkish Quarter
Entering the Old Town through the Amboise Gate you will arrive at Orfeos Street which is lined by plane trees and portrait artists, set beneath the Palace. The clock tower on the left marks the outer limit of the Knights' Quarter. Ironically a stone's throw away stands the **Mosque of Suleiman the Magnificent**, the symbol of the Muslim faith and all that the Knights were trying to defend the island from. The original 16th-century mosque was completely reconstructed in 1808 and was, until recently, the only mosque in Greece still in active use. Decay is setting in, the Greeks don't seem interested in repairing it, and it is now closed to the public.

There are various other Turkish mosques within this quarter, though most have fallen into disrepair. Two of the most interesting are the **Mosque of the Agha**, halfway down the busy Sokratous Street and the **Mosque of Ibrahim Pasha**, off Sophokles Street.

The old *Jewish quarter* centres on the Platia M. Evreon (Square of the Jewish Martyrs) with its ornate sea-horse fountain.

THE NEW TOWN

The island's west coast bus station is outside the colourful NEA AGORA – New Market, and this makes as good a starting point as any to see round the New Town. Nearly all the sights are around Mandraki Harbour. In our opinion the harbour is best seen in the early evening when everyone is out for a stroll trying to catch the last of the sun's rays and sizing up the various excursions offered by the rival shipping companies. Legend has it that the Colossus of Rhodes once stood where the bronze deer now stands; the symbol of Rhodes. Opposite the stag is the **Church of St John** built by the Italians in 1925 as a replica of the original which once stood near the Grand Palace. A little further along is the **Mosque of Murad Reis**, named after Suleiman's Admiral who was killed during the fight for the island. The Turkish cemetery adjoining the mosque seems worlds away from the crowded beaches just a few minutes away.

The pier, on the other side of the harbour, is graced by three medieval windmills, now fully restored and equipped with sails once more. The castle at the end of the pier is the 15th-century **Fort of St Nikolas**, the patron saint of sailors, now appropriately used as a lighthouse. Back at New Market, buses leave for **Monte Smith**, the other main sight of the New Town.

From the summit of Monte Smith the British Admiral Sydney Smith watched for the movements of the French fleet during the Napoleonic Wars. Originally this was the site of the main acropolis of Rhodes and today you can see a 3rd century BC Dorian Temple to Apollo, an ancient theatre and a stadium similar to those used in the early Olympic games.

ACCOMMODATION

Rhodes town has no shortage of hotels catering for the package holiday market, and most of them are large, clean, and located in the New Town. Top of the range is the town's only officially-rated deluxe hotel, the **Grand Astir Palace** (Tel: 26284). In a prime location, opposite a magnificent shingle beach, the Grand Astir has a busy, if rather impersonal, atmosphere with three swimming pools all bordered by rather overgrown gardens. All 375 bedrooms have good views and the hotel offers some fine nightlife in the form of the Isabella nightclub and garden casino (with adjoining 'English pub'!).

The **Mediterranean** (Tel: 24661) and **Siravest** (Tel: 23551) are among the town's better A-grade hotels. Both offer live entertainment occasionally, and are located just across from the beach. The A-grade **Park**, and the B-grade **Continental**, are two rather scruffy hotels in Rhodes town which don't really deserve their good ratings.

Among the town's other hotels, in lower categories, the B-graded **Spartalis** (Tel: 24371) and **Lominiz** (no telephone number listed) can be recommended for all-round value. Both offer good nightlife and are situated opposite an appealing stretch of sandy beach which, so far, hasn't seen too much hotel development.

The C-graded hotels **Amariles** (Tel: 24522), **Astoria** (Tel: 24808), **Europa** (Tel: 22711) and **Royal** (Tel: 24601) each offer a reasonable amount of nightlife with a local flavour, and are relatively central if you want to explore any of the more cosmopolitan (and expensive) nightspots. The Amariles and Europa have the added advantage of a good beach location.

Some of the best streets to investigate for accommodation are Pythagoras, Aristotelous and Aristofanous, where doubles average 2500 dr and singles 1300 dr. **Boarding House Lia** at 66 Pythagoras (Tel: 26209) is small, clean, has showers and is nicely tucked away. Aristotelous Street sports several pensions. On Ierocleous Street the **Laluna Rooms** at number 21 (Tel: 25856) are worth a shot. If all else fails, ask a hotelier for his suggestions as often there are roofs being offered for 200–300 dr.

There are several D- and E-grade hotels in the New Town which charge around 2000 dr per double, plus a 10 per cent supplement if you are staying under three nights. Orfanidi Street and Othonas-Amilias Street, parallel to the water, are worth a try. If you are considering camping take a bus as far away from the resort hotels as possible or you could find the police hassling you.

RESTAURANTS

There are dozens of restaurants in Rhodes town, mostly along the hotel-lined coast near to Rhodes. To avoid paying over 800 dr per person it's best to go for the set menus, or the restaurants that offer main courses for around 500 dr. The Italian influence can be seen in the cuisine, with pasta dishes cropping up quite regularly. Often you'll find these are the best value, averaging 400 dr. There are no supermarkets as we know them in Britain, but it is possible to pick up bread, cheese and fruit for a reasonably priced picnic in the local shops. The other alternative to eating out at a restaurant is to use the stand-up snack bars and live off toasted sandwiches etc. Surprisingly fish dishes work out very expensive, particularly in the *Plaka* restaurant upstairs in **Platia Ippokratous**, where you are lucky to escape under 1000 dr per head.

In the **NEW MARKET**, set back from Mandraki Harbour, there are several restaurants, which are a bit touristy but quite good value. However, the best places for price and atmosphere are up in the Old Town. You will find prices at their most competitive in the open-air restaurants opposite the Clock Tower, and often the management offers free glasses of ouzo to lure you in, which is a cheap way of getting drunk, if nothing else! As usual, if you are prepared to go a bit off the beaten track, you will find restaurants frequented by the locals with cheaper prices.

NIGHTLIFE

In the evening there's a fair amount happening but none of it, apart from strolling and looking at the beautiful yachts, is free. The shops stay open late, particularly those in Socrates Street, and there are Greek Folk Dances at **Rodini Theatre** through the winter and at the **Theatre of the Old Town** in the summer. Performances begin at 9.15 p.m., except on Saturday. Admission is 500 dr (Tel: 20157). For some lively bouzouki dancing, visit the **Copacabana Club**.

The *Sound and Light Show* in the **Palace of the Knights** is a real tourist trap. For 180 dr you get an account of the Turkish siege, complete with full sound effects and lighting. Entry is on Papagou Street, opposite New Market. The English language performances are given five or six times a week. Check with the tourist information office for starting times. Here you can check the calendar of other events, and see when the next performance is due at the ancient theatre at the foot of Monte Smith.

The **Casino** at the Grand Hotel is always willing to take your money, but you must be well dressed and bring your passport. As far as discos and nightclubs are concerned, head for the stretch along by the Rodos Bay Hotel, and on into Rhodes town. There are quite a few, but you can expect to pay at least 400 dr entrance and 600 dr for the flashier ones. Often if you hang around the busier beaches you will be handed leaflets and concessionary tickets for the lesser known discos. Some discos are now charging a fixed entrance of 700 dr which includes as much as you want to drink – these seem like a good idea for those with a big thirst. The dance floors are nothing too spectacular, but if you are looking for a chum, the tourists hang around them in droves. The **J.P.S.**, the **New York** and **Highway** are some of the better discos. **Tiffs**, a bit like an English pub, plays rock and roll.

EXCURSIONS

The ancient town of Ialyssos, now called FILERIMOS, is one of the best afternoon trips you can take if you are based round Rhodes town. The **Monastery** and **Church of Our Lady of Filerimos** are well worth taking in, as is the 4th-century BC **Doric Fountain**. Don't overlook the underground **Chapel of St George** while you are up there, and note its original 14th- and 15th-century frescoes. Take the walk past the stations of the Cross to find the **Byzantine towers**, which date back to the 13th century. The site at Filerimos is open weekdays and Sats 8.30 a.m. to 6 p.m., Sun 9 a.m. to 3 p.m. As there is no direct bus, your options are to walk up the steep hill to the top, take a taxi which will cost 500 dr return trip from the centre, or hire out a moped for the day and take in this along with some of the other sights nearby.

Rodini Park is a good picnic venue with lots of trees, streams and paths. Take a no. 3 bus towards the east coast and you will find the park about 1½ miles from the centre. If in doubt, ask the bus conductor who will know. Another idea, though not one we'd recommend for those seeking peace and isolation, is the VALLEY OF THE BUTTERFLIES, also known as PETALOUDES. This is about 15 miles away from Rhodes town and gets its name from the abundance of butterflies which are out in force from June to September (ironically, the same types as you see dead and sold in cases as souvenirs all over town).

Getting there is not too difficult; follow the road south to Paradissi and just beyond the village there is a turn off to the left, well signposted. Three buses a day go directly to Petaloudes from Rhodes town, all in the mornings. Public buses leave regularly from Averof Street in the New Market three times a day, 250 dr single.

The valley's butterflies are attracted to the resin of the pine tree, and for years have been coming to this particular valley every summer. The butterflies have seen some changes in the valley in recent years. No longer does the occasional entomologist come to visit these creatures in the picturesque gorge. They have been replaced by busloads of tourists and souvenir shops. As a result, the butterflies are disturbed and expend a lot of energy flying around. One of nature's secrets is that during the summer months the butterflies do not eat, their increased activity therefore shortens their life cycle, and their numbers are dwindling. Nonetheless, they are quite beautiful, and with a little restraint, it can be enjoyable.

If you have your own transport or if you are an exceptionally energetic walker with a bottle of water, you can walk 5 miles into the interior, reaching the village of PSINTHOS. It is small, whitewashed and seems oblivious to the few tourists passing through. Fortunately, it also has a couple of small tavernas with cold drinks.

The picturesque island of Symi is a 2-hour sail from Rhodes and is one of the pleasant day trips you can take from the island. There are various boats from Mandraki Harbour, leaving either at 9 a.m. or 11 a.m., and the average cost of the return trip is 2000 dr. For further details of Symi, see under its separate listing.

LINDOS

The *pièce de résistance* of Rhodes is undoubtedly Lindos. Both historically and from the tourist's point of view, it's got a lot going for it; remains dating from the 6th century BC through to the time of the Crusaders, a lovely sandy beach, a natural harbour, and lots of whitewashed winding alleys filled with tourist shops and donkeys for hire. Tours operate here in great abundance, particularly through the summer months and are especially popular with the British. Alternatively, it is easy to make a day-trip to Lindos from Rhodes town. Buses leave Rimini Square for Lindos and return to Rhodes town eight to ten times a day. The fare is 230 dr single, and the journey lasts about an hour.

The post office is on the main street, Acropolis Street, and is open Mon to Fri 8 a.m. to 1 p.m., Sat, Sun 8 a.m. to midday. The OTE office is at number 156 and is open Mon to Sun 7.30 a.m. to 3 p.m. and the Police are to be found at number 521, open Mon to Fri 8 a.m. to 3 p.m. The 24-hour emergency number is 31223. Cars and mopeds can be rented at several places. Check around the town for competitive prices. Cars usually cost from 4000 to 6000 dr per day, including insurance and 100 km free mileage; petrol is extra.

Virtually all accommodation in Lindos is devoted to package tourists, though it is often possible to find a pension with a spare room if you are an independent traveller. The best advice is to arrive early and to head for the **Tourist Information booth** in the main square or the **Pellas Travel Agency** (Tel: 31275) at number 178, open 9 a.m. to 1 p.m., 5 to 8 p.m. They are likely to know of any spare beds in the town. Some of the pensions are not always full. Try the **Pension Lindos** at number 57, **Christina House** at number 205, **Pension Anna** at number 247, **Pension Venus** at 344, and next door **Pension Astoria** at number 345, where doubles are reasonably priced at 1500 dr.

SIGHTS

The village of Lindos dates back to at least 2000 BC, when at its peak, it supported a population of 17,000. Of the three ancient cities of Rhodes, it is the only one to have survived the ages, and today, it thrives. In spite of its small size, it was once quite powerful and had established colonies overseas. In the 7th century BC, the Lindians created a code of maritime law, belying their naval power. Touring the town provides us with signs of the town's fascinating history, a product of two natural harbours and a well-fortified acropolis.

From the main square, follow the signs for the ancient acropolis. On your way you will pass the **Byzantine Church of St Mary**. It is very peaceful and if you are in no hurry, it can take you back in time. The floor is covered with a 'chochlaki' design of black and white stones, and 18th century frescoes adorn the walls with the story of the life of Christ which, though the light is bad, are well worth a look. The woodwork of the Bishop's throne is beautiful. If you can manage, you may just squeeze up the steps of the bell tower outside, which commands an interesting view. Be careful, however, because the steps are worn and the climb is difficult and slightly dangerous.

The focal point is the **acropolis** which stands 375 ft up from the town, perched on top of a sheer cliff (which is bad news for the donkeys). Take a rest halfway up the path and look out over the town and the beach. Hundreds of years ago, traders would come to these same Lindian harbours, either seeking shelter from the storms, or merely wanting a bed for the night.

The Greeks' infinite fascination with, and commitment to, politics is unrelenting and unwithered by hundreds of years of Turkish domination. Spot the house with the PASOK sign of the present ruling socialist party painted on a roof in the middle of the town.

The acropolis is a 4th century BC temple, but as you climb the steps, you witness the large medieval walls, built by the Knights of St John. The site is open Mon to Sat 8.45 a.m. to 2.45 p.m., Sun 9.30 a.m. to 2.20 p.m. Admission 200 dr. If you want to go in style, pay the Greeks to ride the donkeys, 250 dr up, 200 dr down, and consider how the lifestyle of the people has changed since the days of the Knights.

On your last assault up the steps, look out for the relief of a 2nd-century BC Greek warship, a trireme, carved into the rock. Was this a symbol of the importance of Lindian seapower? The story goes that it was carved in 170 BC in honour of Hagesandros, a great sea-captain.

Entering the acropolis through the Castle of the Knights, you will come to the ruins of the 13th-century **Byzantine Church** which is completely dwarfed by the impressive Doric portico to its left. This 3rd-century BC arcade is all that remains of its original 42 columns. Explore each of the four levels of the acropolis. You get the feeling that it was once a great place, and there are plenty of semi-destroyed ruins to testify to this, but it's rather difficult to guess what they are.

At the highest point of the acropolis, perched on the edge of the cliff, is the 4th-century BC **Temple of the Lindian Athena**. Built in the Doric style, this temple was one of the most important religious sites in the Mediterranean. The archaeology is quite interesting, but it is the view that makes the climb worthwhile. From this vantage point, you look down on St Paul's Bay where the apostle landed in AD 51 en route to Syria. What a sight it must have been for him to arrive in the bay at the foot of this magnificent temple to the pagan gods.

The acropolis is good fun to explore, but be careful with children. The walls are not all reinforced and there are no safety fences by the steep cliffs.

RESTAURANTS/NIGHTLIFE

Because Lindos is usually packed to capacity with tourists, food is expensive, and it is a good idea to wander about and check the menu prices. A cheap three-course meal will cost around 800 dr. There are a couple of good restaurants around the main square by the bus stop. Eating at the souvlaki stalls is much cheaper, or you might want to consider making your picnics from the local shops' produce. Most shops are on the two main streets. Some of the bars offer dishes at reasonable prices, but this often varies depending on who is serving. The **Flora Bar** and **Yanni's** are good and serve English breakfasts at around 300 dr.

The nightlife in Lindos centres on dancing and drinking, neither of which is cheap. Most people drift from bar to bar around 11 p.m., but if you are counting your drachmas, beware the exodus. There are several discos located just outside the town.

The East Coast

The island's best beaches are undoubtedly on the east coast – the crowning glory being the ever-busy **FALIRAKI BEACH**, 10 miles from Rhodes town. There is a string of resorts all the way along the coast, run in conjunction with fifty or sixty tour operators. As a rule of thumb, the closer to Rhodes town you go, the busier the area. Interspersed among the large resorts are smaller ones, some of which are just developing. Further down the coast towards the south of the island are the more isolated and peaceful areas.

KALITHEA
About 5 miles south of Rhodes town is Kalithea, noted for the medicinal waters of its ancient spa. Though the spa is not currently in operation, Kalithea makes for a relaxing holiday. Packages are offered by only three operators meaning that the hordes will not be on your doorstep. Its proximity to Rhodes town gives you the benefit of easy access to its shopping, sights and sounds, without having to be stuck in the middle of it. Buses run to and from Rhodes four times a day.

The hotel **Eden Roc** (Tel: 23851) is comfortable, high class, and located on a rocky stretch of beach. It offers 261 rooms in the main hotel or in small bungalows which seem more independent and might be preferable for families. The usual array of watersports is available with entertainment for children. The **Paradise Beach** (Tel: 29220) shares the same stretch of beach as the Eden Roc. It is a large, spacious, A-grade hotel with an oblong-shaped swimming pool surrounded by a tidy sun terrace. Watch out for the children's playground which has a stony base. Entertainment in both popular package hotels is limited to discos, and occasional special evenings of Greek entertainment.

Another alternative is the **Sunwing**, a large hotel of similar size to the others.

Beyond the reaches of the hotels, Kalithea is quiet and offers little in the way of nightlife. This may be a blessing in disguise for those who want to wander the beach quietly in the evening.

FALIRAKI

Faliraki is a large resort town, just a few miles to the south of Kalithea. There are some twenty to thirty operators in the area, making it worthwhile to shop around for the best deal. Faliraki's beaches are superb, probably the best going on the east coast. In the winter, it is an ideal place to stay. In the summer, it is difficult to see the beach for the people, but it has everything going for it.

The **Hotel Apollo Beach** (Tel: 85251) is an excellent A-class hotel, located right in the middle of town, with pools, bars and terraces, and ideal for families. For something of equal class, but away from the centre of town, try the **Calypso** (Tel: 85553). Most of the A-class hotels in Faliraki have extensive facilities within the confines of the hotels. People looking for good accommodation without all the frills might try the **Hotel Evi** (Tel: 85631) or the small **Faliro** (Tel: 85483). The Evi offers particularly good facilities for families with children, including babyminding and special meals.

All the watersports including jet-skiing can be found in Faliraki. If you want to see the island from a different point of view, we'd recommend one of the sailboat excursions, cheaply available along the beach. You can usually sign up the day before, and your escape on to the water takes you along the coast for the day, stopping in at some pretty coves, which are difficult to get to otherwise. Another day might well be spent shooting a round of golf in Afandou.

Fifteen buses a day can take you the short ride into Rhodes town for the sights and a rendezvous with Scandinavia (see the section on

Rhodes town for a full description of the possibilities). If you have your own transport, there are two places of interest to stop off en route. Firstly, the **British and Italian Cemetery** which dates back to the Second World War, as well as the beautiful, deserted KALITHEA SPA. The Italians built the elaborate buildings of the Spa and promoted it as a centre for the treatment of rheumatism, diabetes and liver complaints, but unfortunately it didn't work out and the Spa closed down. Today you can swim in the beautiful little coves and sunbathe in its grounds undisturbed.

From Rhodes town to Faliraki, there are buses every half hour. If you venture a little further south than Faliraki, down to Cape Ladiko and the surrounding area, you will find some very secluded little coves, ideal for a quiet camp.

The next village on the main road is AFANDOU, a large whitewashed village, quiet, pleasant and accessible. A couple of package tours are offered down by the pebble beach a mile away. This town can give you peace, relaxation and a sample of the Greek way of life, even in the high season. It is on the major bus routes and gives you access to the other beaches and tours on the island. Nightlife, in the Western sense, will be minimal. Afandou plays host to the island's only golf course, but it has a good reputation. Clubs can be hired, as can caddies, and green fees are quite reasonable at 900 dr per day or 5000 dr per week. The medium-priced hotel **Xenia Golf** is conveniently located near the golf course, has three swimming pools and full amenities. For something smaller, consider the **Despina Pension**.

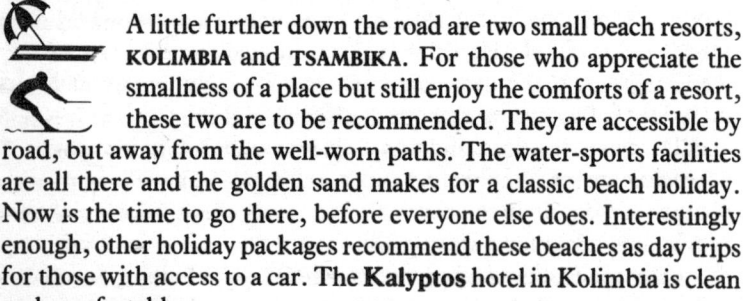

A little further down the road are two small beach resorts, KOLIMBIA and TSAMBIKA. For those who appreciate the smallness of a place but still enjoy the comforts of a resort, these two are to be recommended. They are accessible by road, but away from the well-worn paths. The water-sports facilities are all there and the golden sand makes for a classic beach holiday. Now is the time to go there, before everyone else does. Interestingly enough, other holiday packages recommend these beaches as day trips for those with access to a car. The **Kalyptos** hotel in Kolimbia is clean and comfortable.

Near Tsambika is the Byzantine cloister of **Tsampikas Monastery**, perched on top of Mount Tsampikas. The views from the top will make the climb worthwhile. **Epta Piges**, meaning 'the seven springs', flow into an aqueduct which takes the water down to Kolimbia. Following a tunnel will take you to a picturesque gorge where the springs meet.

Continuing down the road is ARCHANGELOS, Rhodes' largest village. The two churches Archangelos Gabriel and Michael are two of the most attractive on the island. The **Fivos** hotel just on the edge of Archangelos, has a large 3-acre garden and is a tranquil base from which to explore the handicrafts of the town, or just to read in peace. Closer to the centre of town is the hotel **Archangelos**. Archangelos is also on the main bus route, making it easy to get around the town.

EXCURSION TO HARAKI

Haraki lies only a couple of miles south of Archangelos. Its beautiful coves have yet to be developed. Take a day off to go to the beach here, but bring along some food and water. Standing guard atop one of the cliffs is the castle of **Feraclos**, dating from the Knights of St John, with its isolated cave and enclosed beach.

Just to the north of Lindos lies VLYHA BAY with its golden sand, protected from the main road by the large rock face. It is another strip of beach still largely undeveloped and can be the basis of a quiet relaxed holiday or a day-trip away from the crowds in Lindos.

There are a couple of hotels there now, and the British package industry is just beginning to get in there. It is accessible by foot, bike, or bus. There are now pensions, water-sports facilities and an array of bars and tavernas. Motorbikes can be rented from the hotels.

On the other side of Lindos lies the resort of PEFKOS, popular with both the British and the Greeks. It is only 3 miles down the road and has a good variety of water-sports. The beaches are reasonably good and it is a lot like some of the other small beach resorts along the coast. You can walk there, take a taxi, or flag down a donkey for a small price.

Olympic Holidays offers package holidays in Pefkos, but there are five or ten smaller operators doing the same style of holiday.

Lindos is a hop, skip and a jump away and is well worth spending a couple of days exploring and enjoying. The plush village of LARDOS, five miles inland, might also be worth a visit. Should you decide to stay the night, try the inexpensive **Phaedra Hotel**. From Lindos, everything else is accessible by buses which run five or six times daily to Rhodes town. Motorbikes can be rented in Pefkos, jeeps in Lindos.

GENADIO AND THE SOUTH OF THE ISLAND

By-passing Lindos, venture further south and you will be rewarded by quieter beaches, a series of sand dunes and down between Genadio and PLIMIRI a few miles of splendid isolation. What tourists there are here tend to be Greek, and, as a result, you will find the prices in the shops and restaurants more reasonable.

Genadio is just beginning to open up as a resort for holiday-makers and for anyone seeking a combination of good beaches, boats, peace and quiet, we recommend it. The south of the island is much less developed than the north. Buses here only run once a day. Travelling south, the bus will take you to LAHANIA, HATTAVIA, and MESSANAGROS. At the southernmost tip of the island – PRASSONISI CAPE – you are in a different world from Rhodes town or Lindos. Hardly any tourists travel this far south, making it an ideal place to pitch your tent if you want to get away from it all. **Skiadi Monastery**, up a hill between Apollakia and Messanagros, will put you up for a reasonable price, but bear in mind that there are few local shops down here, so do bring your own supplies.

The West Coast

The resorts along the north-west coast seem to be a continuous extension of the hotel shoreline coming from Rhodes town. Following the main airport road, you will come to the villages of KRITIKA, IXIA, TRIANDA, KREMASTI, and THOLOS, where many of the island's large hotels are situated. The beaches are reasonably good. Many of them are artificially made with large quantities of dark sand and pebble spread along the shoreline. A strong westerly breeze blows on to the land almost every day, ideal for the sailing and windsurfing fraternity. Sun lovers can make use of the umbrellas, not for shade, but for shelter from the breeze. The hotels are generally of a high standard, many of them catering to families. The resorts closer to Rhodes town are well located for the vibrant nightlife.

You need not limit yourself to this area. All the resorts are on major bus routes, in short range of Rhodes town, where you might want to spend two or three days taking in the sights and exploring the Old Town. The holiday operators invariably have day trips set up which will guide you through the main town, the geography of the island, or to a smaller neighbouring island. The choice is all yours. If you are more independent, you might consider renting a car or a jeep to explore the more rugged interior and desolate south end of Rhodes.

KRITIKA is only a mile outside of Rhodes town, on the main road. Getting into town is a 10 minute walk and there is no shortage of buses and taxis. The beaches are quite pleasant, but not straight out of paradise. The area is dotted with tavernas, and you should try several of them, experimenting with the Greek food (see section on Culinary Specialities). The sunsets are beautiful, but they don't mark the end of the day. The area is a haven for nightlife, particularly discos, which go on late into the night. For a good night's rest, try the **Posseidon** hotel, a fairly small, medium-priced villa. The only package hotel, as such, is the attractive A-grade **Hotel Sirene Beach** (Tel: 30638) opposite a wide shingle beach.

IXIA is about 2 miles further down the road than Kritika. It is the largest and most developed resort on the west coast, and consequently, boats, windsurfers, tavernas and discos abound.

The hotels are mostly of a high standard and offer variety. Some have swimming pools for those who want a break from the sea. All have bars and most offer enough services that they are self-sufficient. Some of the better large hotels are the **Metropolitan Capsis** (Tel: 25015) which caters for families, the **Oceanis** (Tel: 24881) and the deluxe **Rodos Palace** (Tel: 25222). For something a little less expensive, consider the **Vellois** (Tel: 24615) or the **Lito** (Tel: 23511) built on the water's edge and very private.

TRIANDA (*Ialissos*) is a large village, some 5 miles away from Rhodes town, and like Ixia, will give you a day on the beach with drinks and relaxation, the emphasis being on decadence. The tavernas warmly await you and the nightclubs rock. For villa-size accommodation, try the **Green View**. If you are looking for one of the larger, self-contained luxury hotels, you might be better staying in Ixia.

Continuing a few miles south along the main road, you will arrive at the village of **KREMASTI**, which owes much of its attractive appearance to the generosity of its inhabitants who departed to 'make good' in North America. Keep an eye out for the annual festival of the Dormition of the Virgin, held in the middle of August. Kremasti offers the same facilities as the other resorts mentioned above, and in spite of being close to the airport, it somehow seems to retain the Greek atmosphere a little better, possibly because there are fewer nightclubs.

If you fancy staying in a large luxurious hotel, try the **Blue Bay** or the **Electra Palace**, or if you feel that something less grand would suit you, the **Filerimos** apartments will be just as comfortable.

From Kremasti, you have the same opportunities to see the rest of the island, by either renting a car or joining organized tours. If you decide to go independently by bus, you should expect a 15-minute ride into Rhodes town.

If you continue driving along the main road south, you will arrive at **PARADISSI**. Once a farming village, it has changed considerably with the advent of the Rhodes airport nearby, and is a village to pass through. Five miles further takes you into **THOLOS**, a collection of road-side tavernas, one large hotel and a few others that are smaller. The **Doreta Beach** (Tel: 41441) is a large A-class hotel, worthy of the rating. Clean and comfortable, it caters for the family as well as couples. It is, however, isolated and you can occasionally hear noise from the airport 3 miles away. A hotel bus will take you the half-hour journey into Rhodes town and back in the evening. It is a popular hotel and the tour operators offer the full range of day-trips around the island. If you are on a low budget, the **Sunset** hotel across the road is spartan, but clean.

EXCURSIONS ALONG THE WEST COAST

If you are staying in any of the west coast resorts described above, you may want to look around the island, and there are some good excursions close at hand. At Trianda, take the marked turning on the left for the steep ascent to Filerimos, or Ancient Ialyssos. A little further down the coastal road on the left-hand side past Paradissi is the turnoff for Petaloudes, the Valley of the Butterflies. Ancient Kamiros is reached by taking the well-marked turning to the left. The city of Kamiros was flourishing 2500 years ago, and it remained inhabited until the time of Christ. The archaeological site here is one of the country's best and you should make a point of seeing it. If you are really interested in the archaeology, or if you are roaming the island for a day, make your own way down the coastline to Monolithos, a huge rock which commands a fantastic view.

ANCIENT IALYSSOS

Ialyssos was one of the three ancient cities of Rhodes, along with Lindos and Kamiros. It has throughout history been favoured by military commanders for its position, perched high in the sky, which you will appreciate when you make the drive there. When the three ancient cities decided to pool their glory and build Rhodes town in 408 BC, many of the inhabitants of Ialyssos migrated up to the new city. This was the beginning of the decline that led to Ialyssos being abandoned by the time of Christ.

Standing high above a forest of pines is the acropolis, with Mt Filerimos standing on top. In the Middle Ages, it was occupied by the Byzantines. When the Knights of the Order of St John took over the island, this acropolis was the first fortress to be strengthened. Eventually, the Knights, representing the tongues of Europe (see section on Rhodes – Old Town), consolidated over the whole island, but the importance of Ialyssos was not lost because in 1522, Suleiman the Magnificent used the acropolis to direct his assault against the Knights in Rhodes town.

On your way up to the acropolis, you will be able to see the remains of the **Temple of Zeus and Athena** and the early **Christian Church** from the early centuries AD. These require a bit of imagination, but the **Monastery of our Lady of Filerimos** stands today for all to see. The invaders of centuries gone by have been replaced by monks who now live quietly in the monastery.

Going back in history 500 years is the **Chapel Shrine of St George** with frescoes depicting the life of Christ, and a **fountain**, which was built 2500 years ago and has since dried up. Take heart, and realize that in spite of the ages, you have the same view of the sea and the forests as did the conquerors who stood in the same place.

ANCIENT KAMIROS

Ancient Kamiros makes for a good day-trip from any of the resorts. Buses leave from Rhodes town and stop at all the main resorts along the way, five times daily. Tours arranged through the tour operators usually go to Kamiros as part of an island tour, giving you about 1½ hours to look over the ruins. It is efficient and interesting. If you have any interest in archaeology, you will want to do this one alone; buy a pamphlet interpreting the site, and walk through the ancient ruins at your own pace, recreating the ancient town as you go.

The history of Kamiros dates back to the Mycenaean period, but much of the ruins you see are from the Doric period of the three cities of Rhodes. Kamiros, unlike Ialyssos and Lindos, was never a fortified town. Likewise, it was not a naval power, but depended instead upon its agriculture for survival. Its limited strategic value may in part explain the relatively good condition of the ruins when unearthed by the Italian archaeologists in 1929. In the 5th century BC, the town people, perhaps fed up by persistent pirate raids, abandoned the town. What remains today are the pillars and walls of the town's houses, public buildings and temples. Keep an eye out for the two columns of the **Doric Temple** and the **Agora**, which looks like an acropolis, but was in fact the marketplace where the farmers came to do much of their trading.

Even if ruins bring to your head visions of clambering up endless steps with perspiration dripping down your neck, you should still visit Kamiros. In particular, keep an eye out for the ancient water system with its drainage pipes. The remains of the city's reservoir cisterns give you an idea of these people's advanced level of civilization. Look at the pipes and see how well they are made, some 25 centuries ago.

Viewed from above, you can pick out the residential area to the right of the main street, and the resurrected pillars mark the site of a Hellenistic house. The site at Kamiros is open Mon to Sat 8 a.m. to 7 p.m., and Sun 9 a.m. to 7 p.m. Admission 200 dr.

Ten miles further south is the village of KAMIROS SKALA where boats for the tiny island of Halki leave at 5 p.m. daily and return at 9 a.m. Another castle dating from the Crusades is **Kamiros Castle**, just off the main road, though without your own transport, it is virtually inaccessible. The village of **EMBONAS**, reached by the turning at Kritini, is best known for its shows of traditional folk dancing. Ask around in the cafés for details as there are different shows every night in summer.

Proceeding south, one mile from **MONOLITHOS** village is the **Castle of Monolithos**. The Greeks proclaim this to be the 'most beautifully situated castle in the world'. This is a bit excessive, but it is nonetheless very dramatically perched atop a rock 500 ft above the sea. Not much of the castle remains today, but if you happen to catch it before the crowds, it still has a very special atmosphere.

The area further south from Monolithos is farming country, and is really of little interest to the tourist. The beaches are quieter than those further north but they are not as sheltered as those on the east coast. If you venture that way, bring your own supplies. It is difficult to find tavernas, shops or even a place to stay.

OTHER EXCURSIONS

If you are situated on the west coast, all of the excursions to the east coast are possible, and can be arranged through your tour operator. Visiting the neighbouring islands of Kos and Symi is also something to think about. Kos can be reached by a not-so-cheap ride on the hydrofoil and Symi, much closer by, can be reached by ferry. If you are going to visit Kos in a day, you probably want to arrange it through a tour company. Symi is especially nice, a small town, with a pretty harbour. For more details on either of these islands, they are listed in this book under their own headings.

Crete

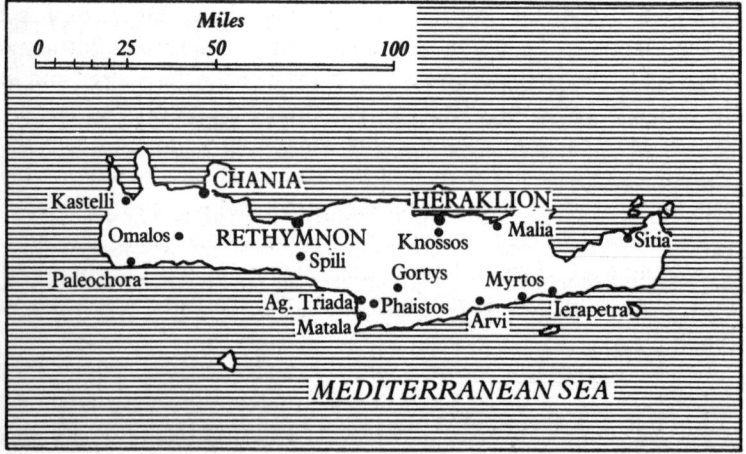

There is a perfect holiday on Crete for everyone for the simple reason that this vast island has so much to offer that whether you're a beach bum, culture vulture or recluse you'll find all the ingredients for your holiday here. The island is huge – 3,189 square miles to be exact, yet with only a population the size of Edinburgh. Away from the developed centres of Heraklion, Chania, Rethymnon, Herssonisos, Aghios Nikolaos and Elounda there are still completely unspoilt villages and quiet little coves where you can camp and run around nude for weeks on end, if that's what takes your fancy. Whatever you want in a holiday you can find it on Crete, which, as many people say, is more like a separate country than a Greek island.

The area between Malia and Heraklion, and the section around Aghios Nikolaos on the north-east coast is the most developed, while on the north-west Chania and Rethymnon are also commercialized. This leaves virtually all of the south coast, the east and west of the island untouched by the developer's concrete mixer, and it gives you the active choice to go for a back-to-nature holiday or to choose the tourist facilities.

The north coast is flat with good sandy beaches and deep bays, which is why this was the main area chosen by the holiday industry to develop. The south coast has dramatic scenery with sheer mountains plunging into the sea, but the beaches are of coarse grey sand and the rugged terrain makes access difficult. Away from the coastal plains in the south-east and the north, the land is mountainous. At the west end of the island are the White Mountains – one of the many limestone ranges of Crete; in the centre is Ida, with the Kamares Caves; and in the east, Dikti with the Dictaean Cave. Crete has a network of literally thousands of caves and gorges. The longest gorge in Europe – the Samaria Gorge – is in the west of the island and this should provide even the most active of holidaymakers with a challenging 5-hour trek.

The island is divided into four main regions or *nomoi*: running west to east there are Chania, Rethymnon, Heraklion and Lasithi. Until 1971 Chania was the administrative centre, thereafter it moved to Heraklion.

If you're going to Greece for the archaeological remains or sightseeing you can do no better than go to Crete. Included in the long list of ancient remains which are scattered all over the island are four Minoan palaces, including the famous Knossos, and of later eras there are also interesting sights such as the Venetian towns of Rethymnon and Chania and many beautiful monasteries of the Byzantine era (5 – 6th centuries).

With over eighty British tour operators running to Crete there's no shortage of holidays to choose from. Most, however, go to the big resorts and offer only basic beach holidays, so shop around if you want something different or organize it yourself – it is quite easy on Crete and there are always rooms to be found, even if you go at the last minute.

History

The strategic position of Crete, at the very crossroads of Europe, Asia and Africa has resulted in its having a turbulent past. The Minoan civilization developed and flowered here for over a thousand years until its demise around 1450 BC, and it is this culture which is most closely associated with Crete and which left some of the island's most remarkable sights.

At the height of their power the Minoans lived in considerable numbers on the island, and the town of Knossos alone had a population of over 100,000. There people originally came from Asia Minor, Egypt and Libya and were known as Minoans after their king, Minos. Their civilization lasted from 3000 BC to 1400 BC, and their sophisticated lifestyle contrasted sharply to that in the rest of Europe.

Halfway through their era an earthquake destroyed most of the structures on the island. The remains you see today, therefore, are of the rebuilt buildings. It is believed that the Minoan civilization disappeared around 1400 BC as a result of an earthquake on Santorini to the north of Crete.

The Dorians from the Balkans were the next people to occupy Crete, followed from 67 BC to AD 395 by the Romans. St Paul brought Christianity to the island in AD 59, and when the Roman Empire split between Rome and Constantinople in AD 395, Crete came under the rule of Byzantium.

In the 9th century Saracen Arabs conquered Crete and made it one of the largest and most important slave markets in the Mediterranean. The Byzantines liberated the island in AD 961, and from this period many beautiful monasteries and highly decorated, ornate churches can still be found.

When in the Fourth Crusade Byzantium fell, Venice bought Crete and 465 years of Venetian rule followed (1204–1669). Although the Cretans were subjugated to a foreign power the Venetians brought a positive force to the island. Beautiful buildings were erected (see Rethymnon and Chania) and a mini-Renaissance occurred on Crete with a school of painting and literature flourishing under the inspiration of the Venetian masters. In 1669, however, after several invasion attempts and a 21-year long siege in which 118,000 Turks and 30,000 Venetians were killed, the Turks finally conquered Crete. Their rule was to last from 1669 to 1898 and be the most repressive regime that Crete had ever had to endure. There was little advancement in any field under the Turks, who treated the people harshly and took all the island had to offer without putting anything back. No fine buildings emerged from this period and an air of deterioration hung over Crete.

In 1897, the four great European powers – Great Britain, France,

Russia and Italy intervened again in Turkish affairs. Crete was given autonomous status within the Ottoman Empire and the Greek King's second son, Prince George, took over governorship. In 1923 the last Turks left Crete.

Destruction was again brought to the island in the Second World War. The Cretans fought hard to resist the Germans, but despite their valiant resistance alongside the British, Australians and New Zealanders, in 1941 it was captured and Crete was again subjugated. When the War was over there was much damage in evidence but the last four decades have seen the re-emergence of Crete as the 'Great Island' as it was once known, and the older Cretans still give a specially warm smile and good service to the British in remembrance of their efforts to save their independence.

Practical Details

The international airport is in the capital, Heraklion. It has connecting flights to several European capitals as well as internal Olympic Airline flights to Mykonos, Paros and Santorini. Flights to Athens from Crete fly from Heraklion and Chania airport. There are four flights daily. Sitia on the north coast of Crete has a connecting flight to Rhodes and Karpathos. There are flights into Heraklion from Athens, Rhodes, Thessaloniki, and in summer from Mykonos and Santorini.

Internal flights within Greece are very reasonably priced. There are daily ferries from Piraeus to Heraklion and Chania, and the journey takes about 11 hours. There is also a catamaran service from Piraeus to Rethymnon taking 5 hours.

From Heraklion there is a ferry to Santorini daily, and from Santorini you can sail to virtually any of the Cyclades islands. There are also ferries from Gythion on the Peloponnese to Kastelli, on the north coast of western Crete; from Rhodes there is a service to Sitia and Aghios Nikolaos (weekly) which stops off in Kasos, Karpathos and Halki. There is another weekly ferry from Piraeus to Aghios Nikolaos via Milos, Folegandros, Santorini and Anafi. All these work in reverse too, making the list of places you can visit on a day-trip surprisingly large, considering Crete's relative distance from the other islands.

In addition to these trips it is possible to make boat connections to and from Yugoslavia, Italy, Egypt, Israel and Cyprus.

On Crete itself transport is limited to car hire (which is expensive but definitely the best way to see the island in comfort), or to the bus service. The buses are very cheap and good for visiting the large centres, but a bit erratic and slow in getting to the hidden corners without feeling the strain. Between all the major north coast cities there are up to 10 buses a day, costing an average of 250 dr for a 1-hour trip between two of the centres. The buses to avoid are those of the early morning rush hour. These are packed with farmers' wives bringing produce to market and office workers clamouring for seats.

The roads along the north and south coasts are good, but those linking the two, i.e. the north–south roads, are not so good. For details on car hire see the relevant section in the introduction to this book.

TOURIST INFORMATION

The two Tourist Information offices on Crete are in Chania at Akti Tombazi 6, Old Port (the converted mosque at the east end of the harbour) (Tel: 26426, open Mon to Fri 8.30 a.m. to 3 p.m., closed weekends), and in Heraklion at 1 Xanthoudidou Street (opposite the Archaeological Museum) (Tel: 222487, open Mon to Sat 7.30 a.m. to 8 p.m.).

CLIMATE

Crete enjoys a superb climate and is sufficiently warm in winter to be increasingly promoted as a winter resort. Having said this, with the meltemi wind in July and August, it is always possible to hit an 'off' period and experience the odd wet and cool day. Generally though, if you travel between April and October you will experience hot sunny weather, with the temperatures in July and August averaging 80°F.

CULINARY SPECIALITIES

Apart from the traditional Greek dishes you will find the following delicacies on Crete: in central Crete *stiffado* is likely to be on the menu. This is a rich beef casserole, braised with onions, herbs and spices. *Dolmades* is another favourite on Crete, and those served here are often of a higher quality than you will find elsewhere in Greece. Cheese-filled pastries called *bougatsa* are a speciality in Heraklion. These are sold in kiosks and in cafés and eaten as a mid-morning snack with a coffee. In Rethymnon cheese is the speciality. *Anthotyrr* is a soft, bland, fat cheese; more suited to the British palate perhaps is *graviera*, with a harder, more distinct flavour.

Feta is served with olive-oil, black pepper and oregano on Crete. Fruit is good all over the island. In the Chania region oranges and tangerines are grown, and in the rural areas all over Crete you will find the freshly made yoghurt for which Greece is now famous. The east of Crete specializes in fish dishes. Although one would expect all of Crete, indeed all of Greece, to have an abundance of fresh fish and seafood this is no longer the case and, although fish is always available, it is not cheap. Grilling the fish is the traditional method of cooking, and seafood is served without many trimmings so the true taste of the fish can be sampled. In the small town of Neapolis, between Heraklion and Aghios Nikolaos, *soumada* is made. This is a sweet, rich drink made from the extracts of pressed almonds.

Eating out on Crete can range from a meal of grilled sardines, Greek salad, bread and a carafe of the local wine, costing you around £2, to a 5-star £20-a-head seafood meal; there is scope for every taste and pocket.

WHERE TO GO FOR WHAT

As we have already said, Crete is an island of great diversity with the potential for many different types of holidays depending on your location.

Socialites and those looking for an active social life should head for the busy, large, developed resorts such as Aghios Nikolaos, Elounda, Malia, Rethymnon, Aghia Galini, Matala and Chania.

Of these the towns of Chania and Rethymnon are the most authentically Greek, for the activity here is as much for the locals as for the tourists; the other resorts are just that, holiday resorts, and what you will find in the way of discos, bars, parties and dances is laid on for the tourists.

Two up-and-coming resorts where 'one should be seen' are Matala and Aghia Galini, on the south coast of Crete. Sufficiently few operators go to these resorts as yet, and they still largely attract the yachting/villa party crowd.

Sightseers will best enjoy Rethymnon with its Venetian architecture, or Heraklion, but not if they are looking to combine sightseeing with lazy days on the beach. The Samaria Gorge is a must while on Crete, but there's no need to position yourself close to it as there are many excursions to this area, and it's possible to make it into a day-trip from most resorts. The same applies to the Palace of Knossos, which is only 3 miles from Heraklion.

Family holidays can be recommended at Aghia Marina, just west of Chania, and at Elounda and Hersonisos.

The Recluse will find many havens in the east, south and west of the island. By taking a charter flight to Heraklion and heading off by bus or thumb, away from the resorts, it is possible to have an independent holiday with no commercial trappings and no crowds. In the south head for places like the Kotsifou Gorge and Hora Sfakion, from where you can take the boat to Loutro, a delightful coastal village in the west. However, inland areas will be most attractive to the recluse. Away from the coast Crete, like most Greek islands, is still unspoilt and undeveloped. Spili, south of Rethymnon, is just one such place, and in the east of Crete places like the village of Kritsa and the plateau of Lasithi, with its thousands of windmills and dramatic mountain scenery are the perfect places for quiet, unwinding times.

Healthy Holiday types and Nature lovers will enjoy the walks in the National Park where the Samaria Gorge lies, in the west of Crete, as well as climbing Mount Ida, the highest point in Crete (8,058 ft), some 20 miles from Heraklion. The many caves on Crete, and especially the Idaian Cave, are of great interest to those keen on geological features.

Finally Sun Worshippers should head for Malia, Sitia, the area west of Rethymnon, the beach 3 miles west of Chania (Oasis Beach) and Aghia Marina. These are about the best beaches on the island, though if you're prepared to settle for a pebbly or coarse-sanded cove, you should be happy in most locations.

HERAKLION

The capital of Crete and the gateway to the island, Heraklion is the most likely point of arrival from the UK, and at some point you will probably take a day-trip to the city. Whether or not you base your holiday here depends on the type of holiday you're after. Heraklion is really not the resort to come to if you want a beach holiday. There are no beaches in the city; the nearest are about 7 miles away, and the resorts on the outskirts of the town, **AMMOUDARA** and **LINOPERAMATA**, would not live up to a real sun-worshipper's expectations. If, however, you are interested in sightseeing and an authentic Greek feel to your resort, Heraklion could be for you. There is certainly plenty going on, and it's within reach of many of the island's major tourist attractions (Knossos, Gortyna, Phaistos) making it a good base for those keen to get round the archaeological sites of Crete. (The Archaeological Museum of Heraklion is filled with the very best of the finds made on Crete, making this another reason to base yourself here if your holiday is primarily to see the remains first hand.)

Over forty tour operators base holidays from the UK in Heraklion, and a choice of hotels and self-catering accommodation is available.

Beware of Kokkini Hani and Amnisos if you're a light sleeper as they're directly on the flight path.

Practical Details

The EOT office is at 1 Xanthoudidou Street, opposite the Archaeological Museum in Eleftherias Square. They will help out with accommodation in all categories, as well as hand out maps and bus and boat timetables. The office is open Mon to Sat 7.30 a.m. to 8 p.m. The Tourist Police are at Dikeosinis Avenue (Tel: 283190) and are open 7 a.m. to 11 p.m. American Express do not cash traveller's cheques, but the banks do. The bank on 25th August Avenue is open for exchange 8 a.m. to 2 p.m., Mon to Fri. The souvenir shops on Venizelou Square also exchange currency after hours but at lower rates. The Post Office is off Gianari Street, open Mon to Fri 7.30 a.m. to 8.30 p.m. The OTE office is at El Greco Park, off Venizelou Square and is open daily 7 a.m. to 11 p.m.

Bus Station: **Terminal A** is between the old city walls and the harbour. (Buses 2, 3 or 5 from Eleftherias Square.) This handles buses to the area east of Heraklion. **Terminal B** is outside the Hania Gate of the old city walls and services areas south of the city. **Terminal C:** walking down Evans Street until you reach the city walls, turn right onto Platia Kyprou and the terminal is the first on the right. This services the south-east of Heraklion. There are no Sunday buses. For Chania and Rethymnon walk down 25th August Avenue to the water, turn left and look out for the Xenia Hotel. The terminal is on your left after a few blocks. Ferry information can be found at the boat offices at 25th August Avenue.

ACCOMMODATION

Accommodation on package tours tends to be outside the town in large new, custom-built hotels. Among the best are the **Astoria Capsis** (Tel: 229002), **Akti Zeus** (Tel: 821503), and **Atlantis** (Tel: 288241); and in the inexpensive category **Daedalos** (Tel: 22439). It is possible to find your own accommodation in Heraklion quite easily as, even in high season, most visitors get in and out of the city quickly, or make it a day-trip. Very cheap beds can be found at the **Youth Hostel** on 24 Handakos Street (Tel: 286281), or in the area around Handakos Street (e.g. **Rent Rooms Mary**, at number 48, where you can pick up a double for around 1000 dr). Another location for cheap rooms is around the Market, on Evans Street and 1866 Street. There's a very good **campsite** 3 miles west of town on bus route 6 from Eleftherias Square.

SIGHTSEEING

The monuments built during the Venetian occupation of the city are the most interesting in Heraklion. These include the **Morosini Fountain** in Venizelou Square, the **Venetian Loggia** at the same location, the 13th-century **Basilica of St Mark** on 25th August Avenue, now used as an exhibition hall with a permanent display of replicas of the frescoes of remote Cretan churches; the **Venetian Arsenal**, near the waterfront, and **Koules Fortress** which protects the old harbour. The **Venetian walls** enclose the old city and can be walked upon for good views of the layout of Heraklion.

There are three churches of particular note: the **Cathedral of Aghios Minas** on Agia Ekaterinis Square, with particularly beautiful icons; **St Catherine's Church**, in the same street. This church was used as the first Greek University, back in the 15th century, and today houses an icon exhibition (closed Sun), and **St Titus Church**, next to the 25th August Avenue. This was originally a Turkish mosque, but like many such buildings, after the Turks left it was converted into a Christian church.

For an overall impression and quick history lesson on Crete take a trip to the **Historical Museum** off Grevenon Street, near the waterfront. There is everything here, from early Christian and Byzantine treasures to photographs documenting the invasion of the Germans in World War II. (Closed Sun.)

The sight of Crete, however, is the **Archaeological Museum** which, second to the National Museum in Athens, is the finest in Greece. It houses the largest and finest collection of Minoan art in the world: vases and frescoes from Knossos, Phaistos, and Amnissos, and a superb sarcophagus from Agia Triada, dating from 1400 BC. There are also remains and reconstructions of how Crete looked up until Roman times, plus a rich collection of archaeological treasure gathered from all the sites on Crete.

This museum really deserves more than one visit, and should be of interest even to those not particularly keen on archaeology. Having visited the sites at Knossos and Phaistos, seeing the museum puts it all into perspective and gives even the uninitiated a good idea of how the early civilizations lived on Crete.

On a different note, but equally much a 'sight' of Heraklion is the open-air **Market** on 1866 Street, off Venizelou Square. This is the best place to pick up picnic supplies; fruit, cheese, meat, bread and fresh yoghurt (the shop at number 53 sells the real thing such as can only be found in Greece).

RESTAURANTS/NIGHTLIFE

Nightlife in Heraklion starts with the *volta* (evening promenade) on Plateia Venizelou and Plateia Eleftherias, then there are discos to progress to later on in the evening at Dimokratias Street; one of the best in the city is **The Piper**, below and behind the Astoria Hotel on Eleftherias Street.

Eating out is as much of an entertainment as a necessity in Theodosaki Street, where some of the most colourful and 'ethnic' restaurants are to be found. In the pedestrian zone is Platia Venizelou and Daedalou, both with open-air restaurants. (In Greece, however, the sign of a good restaurant is that it's indoors only; outdoor eating is for the peasants and the tourists!)

The **Caprice Restaurant**, close to the Morosini Fountain, is reasonable, as is **Ta Psaria**, a fish restaurant at the end of 25th August Avenue. For a great (and cheap) pizza try **Pizzeria Napoli** in Eleftherias Square. (Often pizzas and ice creams are better in Greece than in their native neighbouring home!)

EXCURSIONS

From Heraklion all of central Crete is at your feet for exploration. Most of the major archaeological sites are within an hour of the city, and also within a few miles are the beaches of Amnissos and Lindo. The nearest beach to the town, and consequently the busiest, is FLORIDA BEACH, run by EOT (or NTOG as it is referred to elsewhere in this book). Buses connect from the town but if this is too crowded head for the beaches all along the coastline, east of Heraklion.

KNOSSOS

If you're based in Heraklion you've only a few miles to travel to see the remarkable site of Knossos, a reconstructed Minoan palace which though 'restored' by the British archaeologist Arthur Evans, dates back to around 1400 BC and is one of the most impressive sights of the ancient world. Even those staying on the other side of Crete should make the journey to this unique place: unique in the sense that it is the only archaeological site to have been bought privately and restored. There exists among purists and academics a great deal of controversy as to whether Evans had the right to tamper with history and leave for posterity his personal interpretations of how the Minoan palace of Knossos would have looked in the second millennium before Christ. Whatever, the result is fascinating, and evidence does now support the view that Evans knew more than he was given credit for and that what stands here is indeed a true reconstruction of the palace which was at the centre of the first great European civilization.

The story behind the palace explains why its approximate 1200 rooms are in labyrinthical form and why you are likely to get lost on several occasions trying to find the treasures of the Throne Room and Royal Chambers. Knossos was built by King Minos, the son of Zeus, to hide the minotaur – an enormous monster; half bull, half man, conceived by his wife, Pasiphae. Here he locked the beast away from the world, sacrificing to it fourteen young Athenian youths annually until the day the Athenian prince, Theseus, volunteered to be one of the youths. The prince killed the minotaur and escaped from Knossos thanks to a coil of golden thread given to him by Minos' daughter Ariadne, whom he promised to rescue from her father's despotic rule. They escaped, and as punishment Minos imprisoned in the labyrinth Daedalus, the builder of the palace, and his son Icarus. Daedalus, a man of obvious inventiveness, designed a great pair of wings made from feather and wax so that they could both escape, but Icarus, ignoring his father's warnings, flew too close to the sun and the wings melted, plunging him down into the sea which today carries his name.

Legend and Greek myth apart, what we know about Knossos for certain is that following on from the German archaeologist Schliemann's abortive attempts to excavate Knossos, Arthur Evans bought the site in 1894 and began the excavations and renovation work to which he dedicated the rest of his life.

Knossos takes less imagination than most archaeological sites, which makes it particularly interesting for those who normally perceive ancient remains as 'a pile of old stones'; frescoes have been copied and re-painted, pillars re-erected and such sophisticated pieces of equipment as the Queen's toilet and bathtub have been excavated for the public's gaze.

The drainage system at Knossos is something to be marvelled at. Around 1650 BC, when the rest of Europe was still totally barbaric, they had their own water supplies and sanitation system here, along with a highly stratified society.

There is no set route to follow in Knossos, and unfortunately in high season, no way to escape the crowds other than to go early or late (the site opens Mon to Sat 8 a.m. to 7 p.m., Sun and holidays 8 a.m. to

6 p.m.). The palace was built around a central court, and surrounding this are the rooms: the state rooms, the bedrooms, servants' quarters, and the granaries and working quarters. Most impressive are the *Throne Room* and the *King's and Queen's Rooms*. The Throne Room is off the central court and has in it a small throne made of gypsum and frescoes of griffins. Descending the grand staircase on the left of the courtyard you come to the Royal Chambers (at least this is what Evans decided they were; others who believe the palace to have been a mausoleum say these were the embalming rooms). Note the shafts of light which penetrate these rooms, despite their being so low lying. This is achieved by opening air shafts which carried light down to the lower floors – again, remarkably sophisticated engineering. The King's and men's quarters are in the Upper Hall of Double Axes, which has been reconstructed very well, and the Queen's and women's rooms are those decorated with frescoes of blue dolphins and dancing girls. This is the location of the famous flush toilet.

Several guides to Knossos exist and if you are keen on exploring in more depth consider buying one. Travelling to Knossos independently you take bus number 2 from the 25th August Avenue or Eleftherias Square in Heraklion. There are buses every 20 minutes.

GORTYS, PHAISTOS AND AGIA TRIADA

Another excursion from Heraklion, or worthy of an excursion from any part of the island if archaeology interests you, is to the Roman ruins of Gortys and the two Minoan sites of Phaistos and Agia Triada. They are geographically located so that it is possible to combine all three in the one day-trip. Organized excursions are available, or to travel independently head for Terminal B for the bus to Phaistos. There are 7 buses daily.

At Gortys are the remains of the Greco-Roman capital whose heyday was around 500 BC. The main reason to visit this site is to see the **Law Code of Gortys**, etched on stone by the Dorians. It reads left to right one line, right to left the next, in boustrophedon manner. From the etchings we have learned much about their sophisticated liberal society where slaves could sue free men in breach of the law. Civil and criminal laws and the laws regarding adultery and marriage are laid out.

The church building is the shell of the Basilica of St Titus, which dates back to the 7th century, and the statue lying in the grass is that of Apollo.

Ten miles further on, in a wonderful setting on a plateau overlooking the mountains of Dikti and Ida and the Messara Plain, are the remains of the **Minoan Palace of Phaistos**. This palace was built, occupied and mysteriously abandoned at the same time as the palace of Knossos (around 1450 BC). It bears the same structure, centred on a courtyard surrounded by rooms and apartments. The site was excavated at the turn of the century by the Italian Halbherr but virtually all the 'finds' are now in the Archaeological Museum in Heraklion: vases, jewellery, altars, and the Phaistos disk, with its still-undeciphered symbols. Unlike Knossos, nothing here has been renovated or re-constructed; in fact it gives you a good idea how Knossos looked before any work was done on it. The royal family who lived here in the second millennium BC would have been of a similar standing to that living at Knossos. One cannot appreciate the true size of this palace and adjoining site as it now looks as though there is much still unexcavated and the palace covered far more ground than we can see today.

The site is open in summer Mon to Sat 8 a.m. to 7 p.m., Sun 9 a.m. to 6 p.m. A mile or so from Phaistos is the ROYAL VILLA OF AGIA TRIADA, which despite its small size and simple appearance has been the source of many of the most outstanding treasures now housed in the Archaeological Museum: frescoes, the painted sarcophagus and many everyday items used by the Minoans. This is thought to have been the retreat for the Royal Family at Phaistos, or a hideaway for the priest-kings. The name Agia Triada comes from the small Byzantine church on the site. To get here from Phaistos take the road to Matala (a lovely place for a swim in the Libyan Sea, see under section headed 'South Crete'), and take the right turn up the hill beyond the car park. You will come to the site a mile or so along the road. It is open Mon to Sat 9.30 a.m. to 3.30 p.m., Sun 10 a.m. to 3 p.m.

The North-east Coast

This section covers the resorts from Amnissos right along to Kato Zakros, including, along the way, the large holiday resorts of Kokkini

Hani, Herssonissos, Malia, Elounda and Aghios Nikolaos. Amnissos, Kokkini Hani and Gournes have more or less merged into one sprawling tourist development. On the plus side there are plenty of sandy beaches, but on the minus is the fact that this area is on the direct flight path, and it's not the most scenically spectacular area of Crete. Having said that, if it's a flop-on-the-beach holiday you're looking for with a bit of nightlife thrown in, any of these resorts will suit you. The **Hotel America** in GOURNES is good for this type of holiday, while more de luxe establishments are, in KOKKINI HANI, the **Arina Sands** (Tel: 761293), **Themis Beach** (Tel: 761374) and **Knossos Beach**, all with swimming pools (a big plus considering how crowded the beaches get), discos and sports facilities.

HERSSONISSOS has turned from being a sleepy fishing village into one of Greece's most bustling but attractive resorts. Its picturesque waterfront, old narrow streets and plethora of tavernas, cafés, discos and souvenir shops make this a lively resort, ideal for those who always want to have something to do. Malia, Heraklion and Aghios Nikolaos are all accessible from Herssonissos, connected by local buses, and as a base for excursions it measures up quite well. There are no actual sights in the town itself, and in character this is very much a created holiday resort.

Among the many hotels used by the package companies (over 40 run here so gather in all the brochures to ensure you're not paying over the odds for the same holiday), the hotels **Creta Maris** (Tel: 22115), **Nora** (Tel: 22575), **Lyttos Beach** (Tel: 21271) are three of the best. Nightlife is lively and the area down by the attractive waterfront is where the evening volta takes place. Excursions run to all the major tourist sights from the hotels. The beach is narrow but sandy. It is obviously very busy in high season, so head west of the headland for the beach there which is quieter and larger.

STALIS is a small resort half way between Herssonissos and Malia. It has not very much to recommend it other than its beach which is clean and sandy – good for children. Parents, however, will have to look to the neighbouring resorts for their nightlife.

MALIA is a busy resort with its attractions stemming from its excellent beaches, the remains of its Minoan palace and its highly developed tourist facilities. Behind its main street of souvenir shops and cafés lies the old town with its winding alleys and narrow lanes of old Venetian-style houses – much more interesting. The beach gets busy but is sufficiently good to compensate, and it's a particularly good place for family holidays.

The remains of the third largest **Minoan Palace**, excavated in 1921, is one of the main attractions for many visitors. This dates from the same era as Knossos and Phaistos and has as its main sights the ceremonial staircase and the nearby *chrysolakkos* or 'pit of gold' which was a royal burial chamber where the honeybee pendant now in the Heraklion Archaeological Museum was originally unearthed. The plan of this 1600 – 1450 BC building, on the site of an earlier 2000 – 1650 BC palace, is: the main entrance is on the north side, and this leads to the principal entrance hall of the palace. On the right you enter the courtyard, dating from the Mycenaean period. Right of the entrance is the Archive Room. The *kernos* in the central courtyard is an altar for offerings of fruit and seeds to ensure fertility, and this still stands in its original place. North of this is the staircase, and upstairs the throne room.

This site, unlike Knossos, requires a good deal of imagination and background knowledge in order to imagine its former splendour, as the excavations carried out by the French in the 1920s were not particularly thorough.

Even if you're not really interested in archaeological sites, the beach near here is worth the journey and is reputed to be one of the finest stretches of sand on Crete.

Hotels in Malia range from de luxe to cheap tavernas offering independent travellers a room for the night. There's even a youth hostel. Three of the best hotels are the **Ikaros Village** (Tel: 31267) – a noisy 'Greek village' within Malia designed by Germans to look like the sort of Greek village everyone dreams of but rarely finds (probably close to how Malia looked before the tourists moved in and spoiled it!); the excellent **Kernos Beach** (Tel: 31421), with its relaxing interior, landscaped gardens and shingle beach, and the slightly noisier **Sirens Beach** (Tel: 31321). Some of the better package companies use those hotels, and with all the facilities on offer they represent excellent value for the price. (To stay independently at these hotels is *not* cheap.)

Nightlife is centred on the street which runs down to the beach, but many of the best restaurants are nowhere near this commercialized centre. For authentic Greek food try somewhere like **Restaurant Ilotis**. This is on the street two blocks inland from the road to Aghios Nikolaos. **Discos Scorpio** is reputed to have the best music and attracts a young crowd.

The developing villages of SISSI and MILATOS are still attractive and have to their credit quiet pebbly coves which get better as you go east. A couple of tour operators base holidays here, and if you're looking to avoid the crowds these are two good suggestions.

ELOUNDA is the nearest resort of any size. Despite its increased popularity after the television series 'Who Pays the Ferryman' and all its new developments, it is still a beautiful resort with a wonderfully relaxing atmosphere. Forty operators base holidays here, so it's not difficult to compare prices and deals before booking.

There is superb scenery all around Elounda, with local places of interest to visit, and easy access to the towns of Heraklion (42 miles east) and the resort of Aghios Nikolaos. This does not, however, make it an ideal touring base, as it's a long drive to get to places like Chania, and Rethymnon.

Bathing is not the strong point of this resort. Keen swimmers should head for SPINALONGA ISLAND. The Venetian fortress here protected a leper colony until as recently as 1958, and sun-worshippers are best advised to head for the road north towards Plaka, where there are two coarse-sand beaches.

There are two deluxe hotels in Elounda, which offer excellent facilities in beautiful settings. If you can get into either of them at package prices, consider yourself very lucky. (Generally early booking is required.) The **Astir Palace** (Tel: 41580) in Elounda Bay has both bungalows and rooms. It is situated right on the beach, and it has everything in the way of sports facilities, nightlife, and exclusive air-conditioned luxury. The Greek President has been a guest here. The disco attracts many young northern Europeans, and this hotel is particularly suitable for the childless, young set. The **Elounda Beach** (Tel: 41412) is a slightly older version of the same. It too has a sea-front setting, sports and nightlife facilities, and attracts a wealthy, older clientele. Security is tight to ensure its facilities remain exclusive.

The **Hotel Marmin** (Tel: 41513) is another favourite for tour operators, and though not in the luxury bracket it is a most comfortable hotel offering an ideal base for those who spend less time in their hotel and more exploring the island.

The places to sit, see and be seen in Elounda are in the town square and down by the harbour. There is a path and causeway, below the much-photographed three windmills, which run along the shore and make a wonderful sunset walk. The disco set will be more at home in Aghios Nikolaos than Elounda, which still attracts an older, more monied market, making it an ideal Socialite resort.

There are numerous interesting walks up into the hill villages from Elounda, and nearby 'Ag Nik' provides all that one could want in the way of bustling nightlife and shops.

AGHIOS NIKOLAOS is a cheerful, attractive resort and the island's largest tourist resort. Despite the high degree of commercialism which has inevitably crept in, this is still a very Greek and scenically beautiful place to spend a couple of weeks in the sun. Over sixty British operators run here, and there are hundreds of hotels and rooms on offer, so, given the wide choice, the task in hand is to select the best for the best price.

Accommodation ranges from everything from a youth hostel to deluxe hotels, for this is a sizeable town, not just a holiday resort.

At the luxury end of the market is the **Minos Beach** (Tel: 22345), the **Minos Palace** (Tel: 22313) and the **Mirabello Village** (Tel: 28400). The Minos Beach is on the sea front, close to the city centre and has all the sporting facilities one could want: golf, tennis, swimming, water sports, billiards etc. It is an exceptionally attractive hotel and deserves its luxury rating. Packages to this hotel don't come cheap, but in comparison to staying there independently, it's still a bargain. Because the accommodation here is in separate air-conditioned bungalows it is a good venue for young children, and for those who like to feel they have their independence. Babysitting is available and everything from high chairs to children's portions has been taken care of.

The general consensus on the Minos Beach is that it is well worth the extra cost, and very few British holidaymakers have any complaints about this hotel.

The Minos Palace is a luxury hotel on the headland facing the town, again with excellent facilities, although not quite as luxurious as the

Minos Beach. In this same location is the Mirabello Village. This is a location for those looking to escape the crowds. Its secluded gardens and Cretan-style village accommodation is most attractive and popular with the Germans and Scandinavians.

Other hotels worth checking out are the **El Greco** (Tel: 28894) near the seafront (popular with the young crowd and close to the resort's nightlife), the **Ariadni Beach** (Tel: 22741) with its bungalow accommodation, the **Rea** (Tel: 28321) – another one for the nightlife enthusiast because of its swinging rooftop disco, and in the cheaper price categories, the **Apollon** (Tel: 23023) and the **Pension Argiro** at 1 Solonos Street.

The town of Aghios Nikolaos is actually a peninsula with beaches on three sides, and most of the buildings in the middle. The Tourist Police are at the southern corner of the lake (Tel: 22321). They will supply you with maps, accommodation suggestions and ferry and bus timetables, as well as helping out on any problems; open daily 7.30 a.m. to 2 p.m., 6 to 9 p.m.

The Post Office is at no. 9, 28th October Street; open Mon to Fri 7.30 a.m. to 4.30 p.m.

The Bus Station is at Atlandithos Square. There are car and motorbike rental companies all over the town, but you're best to stick to reliable, international names.

In the town itself the picturesque harbour is linked to an artificial lake, and round here are the restaurants and shops. The three beaches are all within easy walking distance. At the beach by the Sgouros Hotel in the east of the town are many reasonably priced tavernas. It has to be said though that this is not the best resort for beaches, and if you're really dedicated to the tan you'd be better taking a bus to IERAPETRA or better still SITIA. ALMIROS BEACH, a mile out of town, is on this road and is your best bet.

In Aghios Nikolaos itself about the only real 'sight' is the **Archaeological Musuem** with its collection of artefacts from the surrounding area, dating back to the Minoan era, (closed Tues).

Many of the restaurants in Iosif Koundourou Street are worth trying, particularly the **Vassilis** at no. 16, but all over Aghios Nikolaos are tourist menus and reasonably priced tavernas, catering for their main industry.

It's worth paying for the harbour view and the restaurants know this, but along here are some of the best (and most expensive) places to have a leisurely dinner.

Bars and discos and nightclubs (some resembling Soho) are all over the centre. Akti Koundourou and 25 Martiou Street are two of the main nightlife locations. Prices are hugely inflated by Greek standards, but more or less what you'd pay at home.

The trip to Spinalonga can be made by organized excursion from the town. Buy your tickets for this guided tour, which also takes in a stop at MAKRIKI ISLAND, home of the wild mountain goat, from K Tours next to the Hermes Hotel. This way you'll avoid the extra 10 per cent travel agent's commission.

Elounda is a possible daytrip, as is Gournia, the ancient Minoan town described on page 418.

KALO HORIO, where a couple of package holidays are based, is south of the town, and has pebbly, sandy bays, few facilities, but plenty of charm. This is where the rich are now building their villas; close enough to the town for the occasional jaunt in for nightlife, but far enough away to escape the 'great unwashed'.

KRITSA, 8 or so miles from Aghios Nikolaos, perched on a hill, is a popular daytrip from the town to see the panoramic view over the Bay of Mirabello and to shop for the local handicrafts of this town – handwoven rugs, bags etc.

This town, though only a few miles from its touristy neighbour, is a world apart in atmosphere. Organized excursions run from Aghios Nikolaos, but it's possible to make the trip yourself using one of the 13 daily buses from the town.

The sight of this village is the most impressive Byzantine building on Crete – the **Panagia Kera** – a 13th-century church with what are generally considered to be the most beautiful icons on Crete. The tiny white church is about half a mile outside the village.

A further 15 minutes' drive will take you to LATO, the archaeological site in the town of Goulas. The scenery here, however, is more spectacular than the remains.

SITIA is reached by a beautiful mountain drive from Aghios Nikolaos. This isolated port town on the north-east coast has only recently been discovered by tourism and with only half a dozen operators going there it is still a refreshingly unspoilt and attractive place. The town centre, with its Venetian buildings and the classic white cubic houses on the hillside which overlook the busy harbour and esplanade, give character to the place, and its proximity to Kato Zakros with its Minoan ruins and the beach at Vai makes it a good touring base to see eastern Crete.

The Tourist Office at 22 Sifis Street, open Mon to Fri 7.30 a.m. to 10 p.m., will help with accommodation, which ranges from a **Youth Hostel** – at 4 Therissou Street (Tel: 22693) to smart hotels, such as the deluxe **Kappa Hotel** or **Marasol Bungalows**. It is a popular base for independent travellers but because of its role as stop-off port for the Rhodes and Santorini boats cheap rooms are snapped up quickly.

Life centres on the waterfront where the restaurants are based (seafood is the speciality), and among those worth trying are **Zorba's** and **Yura's** on Dimokritou Street.

From the **Fortress** at the top of the hill there is a fine view over the Bay of Sitia. The beach is a long thin sandy strip running east of the town.

Every August the town has a festival celebrating its most famous export – raisins. This is a good excuse for drinking as much of the local vino as possible and a good time seems to be had by all. There is a fair amount of nightlife around the town square – Platia Iroon Polytechniou – everything from sleazy bars to family-filled tavernas.

The **Monastery of Toplou** dates back to the 10th century, though what you see today dates from the 15th century when it was rebuilt after the Turks razed the original to the ground. To get to this impressive site take the bus to Vai and get off at the Moni Toplou turn off, and walk from there (about a mile). For drivers it's the coast road east of Sitia and turn left at this junction. VAI is the location of Europe's only natural palm forest and many young backpackers come here to really 'get away from it all'. Because they do, you don't. The days when Vai was a peaceful unspoilt haven have passed, but just a few minutes' walk down the main stretch of beach and you do still find vast expanses of 'desert-island'-type scenery, and only the romping-nude, predominantly German tourists remind you that you're still in Europe.

KATO ZAKROS is at the very eastern end of the island. This is the site of the fourth most important Minoan palace on Crete (after Knossos, Phaistos and Malia) and like these it has the same structure, with rooms radiating off the central courtyard. The finds from it are in the

Heraklion Archaeological Museum and it would appear that it too was destroyed in the mysterious 1450 BC earthquake which wiped out the Minoan civilization.

Short of hitching or taking a taxi you must have a car to get from the village to the site, which is about 5 miles away. The route via Palekastro is fastest.

The beach at KATO is wonderful – ideal for families and camping out on.

The North-west Coast

This section covers the area from Aghia Pelagia to Falasarna, taking in Bali, the popular resort town of Rethymnon, Georgioupolis, the town of Chania, Aghia Marina, Platanias, Maleme and Rodopou. Many consider Crete's main attractions to be on this stretch of coastline; Rethymnon and Chania certainly are the most attractive of Cretan towns, and many beaches along the way are flat and sandy. The national highway runs the length of the coast, from Heraklion to Rethymnon and Chania, but far more interesting is to branch off it into the interior of the island. Excursions into the hill towns are described en route.

In a bay west of the capital Heraklion lies the village of AGHIA PELAGIA. The road to the shingle beach twists down from the highway, and the restaurants, shops and tavernas line the seafront, but there isn't much here in the way of tourist facilities, so unless you want a quiet time, you're better in nearby Heraklion. At the north end of the bay stands the **Capsis Beach Hotel** – a large, deluxe establishment offering hotel and bungalow accommodation, and around which all the nightlife and tourism flourishes.

The highway rejoins the sea, after Aghia Pelagia, at FODELE, home of the artist El Greco ('The Greek'), but there is nothing to see here to establish this fact.

The hamlet of BALI lies about halfway between Aghia Pelagia and Rethymnon. A few tour operators are now featuring this resort, and though it is attractive and an ideal place for a relaxing time, without a car there is little to do after day three of the holiday.

RETHYMNON

The third largest town on Crete is also one of the most dramatic and colourful places on the island. The Turkish and Venetian influence is strongly felt: narrow arched lanes, Arabic inscriptions and towering minarets pierce the skyline, and it wouldn't be difficult to think yourself in one of Crete's north African neighbours.

A Venetian fortress looms over the west end of the harbour, while the town itself curves around a bay of blue sea and golden sand. The harbour scene is true picture-postcard stuff – in the enclosed Venetian surroundings people sit out till the small hours dining at outdoor restaurants and enjoying watching the world go by. A few miles east the tourist industry has its headquarters. Hotel after hotel; taverna after taverna; shops, cafés, discos – all the usual trappings, and, most importantly, the beach. The beach here is one of the island's best, ideal for families and sun-worshippers: sandy, long, clean and large enough to take the crowds.

Practical Details

TOURIST INFORMATION

The Tourist Office is at 100 Kountouriotou Street (Tel: 29148). They supply maps, bus and ferry schedules, advice on accommodation, nightlife, day trips, and organize car hire. The office is open daily 8.30 a.m. to 1.30 p.m., 5 p.m. to 7.30 p.m.

The Tourist Police are on Iroon Polytechniou (Tel: 28156), open Mon to Fri 7 a.m. to 9 p.m., weekends 8 a.m. to 1 p.m. The Post Office is on 104 Kountouriotou Street, open 6 a.m. to midnight. The Bus Stations are on Dimokratias and Moatsou Streets. Buses go to Heraklion, Chania, Aghia Galini, Spili and Plakias.

ACCOMMODATION

Independent travellers have a wide choice of pensions, cheap hotels and hostels. Many of these are in the old town centre, so for atmosphere and character they leave the modern hotel complexes behind. Comfort and hygiene, however, leave a lot to be desired.

The **Youth Hostel** is at 7 Pavlou Vlastou Street (Tel: 22848). A relaxed establishment (no card even asked for) which offers basic beds for around £1.50 a night.

In the pension line Arkadiou Street is the mecca for cheap rooms. **Hotel Ahillio** at number 151 (Tel: 22581) is pleasant, as is **Barbara's** at 7a Plastira (Tel: 22319). Camping is possible a mile west of the town at **campsite Elizabeth** (Tel: 28694).

For those of you packaging to Rethymnon, the choice of hotels is impressive. With over thirty tour operators offering Rethymnon, again, do your homework to make sure you pay the going rate and no more for the accommodation offered.

The best hotel is the A-grade **El Greco** (Tel: 71281), on the beach, east of the town. It offers rooms and bungalows, sports facilities and nightlife. The luxury **Rithymna Beach** (Tel: 29491) is basically a larger version of the El Greco and its large sea-water pool should be a magnet to those who like to spend much of the holiday dipping in or sitting by the pool, as it is one of the most attractively laid out you'll find. All facilities are to be found in these two hotels: everything from shops and hairdressers to indoor pools and floodlit tennis courts.

Other hotels worth considering are the **Cretan Star** which, for a lower cost hotel, is good value because of that precious commodity – air-conditioning; **Hotel Xenia**, which is the only one actually on the town beach, and the **Ideon** (Tel: 28667).

SIGHTS

The 16th-century Venetian Loggia at the corner of Arkadiou and Paleologou Streets was the Governor's Palace, but today it houses the **Archaeological Museum**. Unless you know something about Greek archaeological remains, it's a bit of a useless expedition, as trying to interpret what all the headless statues and assorted Roman and Minoan artefacts signify is a difficult task made no easier by the lack of labelling or guides. West of the museum is the **Arimondi Fountain**, dating from 1623. The **Venetian Fortress** is the most impressive of the sights. It dates back to 1580 and though nothing much remains of its interior due to Turkish and later Nazi destruction, its solid form is still a sight worth seeing; open Tues to Fri 8 a.m. to 7 p.m., Sat to Mon 9 a.m. to 4 p.m.

The most interesting place to visit is the **Mosque of Neranzies** on Antistasseos Street. The view over the city from the balcony where the Moslem faithful were called to prayer is a favourite photograph; open daily 11 a.m. to 7.30 p.m.

Other mosques exist, and there are many more buildings of historical interest, but perhaps the best advice is just to wander round the narrow streets, soaking up the general atmosphere as Rethymnon is not so much a town of specific sights as a place to stroll in.

The nightlife scene in the tourist area of the town is what you'd expect: dances, discos and cabaret are laid on in season, and tavernas and restaurants put on the occasional Greek music performance while you eat. In the town eating out is the main form of entertainment. Along the seafront there are numerous restaurants, many specializing in seafood, and here it is both good and reasonably priced by Greek standards. Pizza is particularly good here, and for snacks there are plenty of souvlaki stalls in town. **Zizi's Tavern**, a couple of miles east of Rethymnon on the old road to Heraklion is a wonderfully authentic restaurant. Apart from the occasional young American (an American guidebook apparently also recommends this place!) you should find it filled with Greeks, eating their specialities at reasonable prices. (Closed Wed, and you do need a car to get here.)

The Wine Festival from 15 July – 2 Aug is a bit of a brash affair, but good fun if you like a knees-up. The traditional Cretan folk music and dancing is worth seeing.

EXCURSIONS

The **Arkadi Monastery**, 14 miles south-east of the town, is a monument which means more to the Greeks than to foreigners, but it is significant because of the important part it played in Greek history and merits a visit whatever your nationality.

On 8th November 1866 the monastery was the scene of great personal sacrifice by many hundreds of Cretans in the cause of Greek independence. Gunpowder had been stored in the monastery and around a thousand Cretans took shelter from the invading Turks there. When the Turks reached Arkadi and defeat looked certain the abbot decided that rather than having the building captured, and, more importantly, to bring international attention to the Greek struggle against the Turks, the gunpowder should be ignited and the whole lot go up. Each year from 7th to 9th November this enormous human sacrifice to national freedom is remembered in services at Arkadi and Rethymnon. The Monastery is open daily from 7 a.m. to 8 p.m. There is still a large section of the monastery buildings left to view as only the gunpowder room was blown up. The Sanctuary of the Heroes and the Historical Museum are worth seeing to fill you in on the story, and as a gory reminder there are thirteen skulls of Cretans who were killed in the explosion.

Organized tours from Rethymnon (and all the hotels) are offered, but it is easy to make this excursion yourself by taking one of the three daily buses from Iroon Square, Rethymnon to Arkadi.

A worthwhile beach excursion is to the **Gulf of Georgioupolis**, 7 or so miles west of the city. This vast expanse of sand can really only be reached by car, but the rewards are great.

Another alternative excursion is to take the road from Rethymnon which runs south via Spili to **Aghia Galini** (see page 432) on the south coast of Crete. This is approximately a 40-mile journey.

The village of GEORGIOUPOLIS now hosts a couple of British package holidays. The beach here is wonderful – ideal for both the dedicated beach bum and the family holiday. The village is a tranquil haven: eucalyptus trees shade the dozing old worthies who sip ouzos in the cafés, and everything looks more or less how you expect a sleepy Greek village to look. If you want a relaxing time, mainly on the beach, this is an excellent choice. For those looking for the odd bit of nightlife a hired car will quickly take you into Rethymnon, so the best of both worlds can be achieved.

CHANIA

Chania is Crete's second town and still very much a thriving commercial centre for Cretans, not tourists. Despite its popularity with the tour operators this is still a place for the proud Haniots. It is a town of character, with a busy colourful market place; a frenetic harbour of seafood restaurants, cafés, tavernas and cheap hotels, and in stark contrast an inner harbour at the centre of an old Venetian quarter, where the quiet lanes and alleys are reminiscent of Venice, and the atmosphere is one of tranquillity and peace.

The beaches are not the best, and in fact there is no town beach as such. What is referred to in the brochures as the beach is the Municipal Beach which lies just west of the town. Many hotels, however, are based 3 miles away, at the OASIS BEACH, where the sand is clean and flat, and the tour operators moved in to develop. Resorts classified as Rethymnon can stretch as far out as Aghia Marina Platanias and Maleme. Here the beaches are better, but for atmosphere you're still a bus ride away.

Practical Details

The Tourist Information Office is at the east end of the harbour (in a converted mosque). They supply maps, bus timetables and so on; open Mon to Fri 8 a.m. to 3 p.m., closed Sat and Sun. The Tourist Police are at 44 Karaiskaki Street; open daily 7 a.m. to 9 p.m. (Tel: 24477). The Post Office is at 3 Tzanakaki Street; open Mon to Fri 7.30 a.m. to 8 p.m. The Bus Station is on the corner of Kelaidi Street and Kidonias Street.

ACCOMMODATION

The **Kydon** is the deluxe choice in Chania. This large hotel offers all first-class facilities and has its own disco. In the medium price range the **Port Veneziano** is a hotel of great character (it's a converted old Venetian mansion house), as is the **Xenia**, close to the beach and the **Panorama** (Tel: 54200). There's a **youth hostel** at 33 Drakonianou Street (Tel: 53565) for budget travellers, and around the harbour is the place to hunt for cheap rooms (which are easier to find here than just about anywhere else on Crete).

Out at Maleme the **Chandris** (Tel: 91221) is a deluxe all-facility hotel, rather isolated but offered for a reasonable price by **Grecian Holidays,** and at Aghia Marina the **Santa Marina** is a medium-grade hotel on the beach.

Eating out mainly takes place on the waterfront. Standards are comparable in just about all the restaurants, and you do pay for the view. Try walking east to **Akti Enoseos** where the prices are lower and the food better. The 17th-century soap factory turned into a taverna

Aposperida, is a novelty, and for Cretan music try **Zamania's** on Apokoronou Street.

SIGHTS

The Venetian quarter lies at the west end of the harbour, and unquestionably this is the most attractive part of the town. In a restored church here is the **Archaeological Museum** which is remarkably small for the town which was until 1971 the capital of Crete, but it is an interesting and attractive collection, and worth a visit to see the remains of artefacts from the area, gathered from Neolithic times. (Closed Tues.)

Another museum where you can escape the heat of the midday sun is the **Naval Museum**. As you would imagine it houses all sorts of nautical objects and a collection of shells. (Closed Mon.) Located at the west end of the harbour.

In the shops which lie on Chalidon you will find souvenirs, while nightlife and evening strolls are best around the harbour. At one end of the harbour is the **Mosque of the Janissaries** dating from the 17th century. This is the Tourist Office. Parts of the old Venetian arsenal are still intact, and to the west of the main harbour lies the original Venetian one.

Behind the harbour is the Kastelli area. Archaeological digs here have uncovered the ancient town of KYDONIA, one of the island's major cities in the post-Minoan era.

The covered **market** on Gianari Street is worth strolling through, and if you hit a bad spell of weather and can't think what to do with the children, try the **zoo** at the end of Tzanakaki Street (it's not exactly Windsor, so don't expect too much!).

EXCURSIONS

The most obvious excursion – the Samaria Gorge – is dealt with on page 434. The following are some of the other excursions from Chania.

The beach resorts of AGHIA MARINA, PLATANIAS and MALEME hardly count as excursions as in most cases these resorts are sold as being 'Chania', but for a day's sunbathing they make good sense. The vast stretches of sand here are attracting development and the resort of

Chania is fast moving west. The beach at Aghia Marina is ideally suited to young children, and all in all this is a most attractive resort. There is little in Maleme besides the large luxurious hotel and the beach of shingle and sand. This was the site of the Battle of Crete in May 1941.

[PRIVATE. Keep Out] Carrying right on to the westernmost tip of northern Crete you reach FALASAENA – a recluse's paradise and with excellent sandy beaches. All around the west of Crete are small monasteries, Byzantine churches, and dramatic views making touring interesting.

North-east of Chania, the **Monastery of Agia Triada** is a 17th century working monastery with icons and religious relics of note, and a couple of miles further north is the **Church of Agios Ioannis**, where the monks will show your their 15th century art treasures and allow you to wander round their church.

The **Hill of the Prophet Elijah** at Akrotiri is of more significance to the Greeks than tourists for here is buried the Cretan freedom fighter Eleftherios Venizelos, Premier of Greece for many years before his death in 1936, and a son of Crete. He is buried on a hill which in 1897 was the scene of a significant act of defiance by the Cretans when they raised the Greek flag in sight of the occupying Turks until it was shot away. Around Chania are several interesting little villages with no specific sights to see, but plenty of character. The surrounding countryside is rich in flora and is a great fruit-growing area.

KASTELLI

This is the main town of western Crete – Kastelli Kissamou. The sandy beaches here are among the best on the island, and it's possible if you're sailing into Crete that this will be your docking port. There is little in the town to keep you, but the archaeological site of **Polyrrinia**, 5 miles away, is worth a visit. Not for its 8th century BC remains, for there is little to see, but for the spectacular view.

[PRIVATE. Keep Out] Buses leave hourly from Chania to Kastelli, and if you're looking for somewhere to escape the crowds, go nude, swim and sunbathe, head for Kastelli, then out to the beaches. The area east of the town is good recluse country. The beach at FALASARNA is a real Robinson Crusoe experience, but even if this isn't isolated enough for you, try 10 miles further south, in SFINARI.

GAVDOS, the tiny island off the south coast, however, is still the ultimate for those determined to see nobody and suffer for the cause of solitary sunning. A boat will take you out twice-weekly from Paleochora to this barren rock which is the most southerly point in Europe.

The South Coast

The south of Crete is untamed and wild. It offers wonderful beaches, spectacular scenery and a more relaxed pace of life. Mass tourism has only hit a few places, mainly because of the inaccessibility of the south-west, making much of the south perfect for the recluse and those who enjoy a 'get-back-to-nature' holiday.

KOLIMBOS is one of the resorts in the east not yet taken over by any tour operator, but then there is nothing much to keep you in this part of the coast. The villages round here tend to be dusty two-shop, one-bar affairs; it is the natural features of southern Crete that make it the place where increasingly the young trendies come. The beach at Kolimbos (just west of it) is most attractive, with greyish sand and a surface suitable for children.

Lusher and better placed is FERMA. Again the beaches here are good. It tends to be the two extremes of holidaymakers in this area: the very wealthy in their villas and the backpacking students camping on the secluded beaches. **Timsway Holidays** run a tour here.

IERAPETRA is the only town on the south coast. It is not an attractive town and its only saving grace is the dark sandy beaches which attract the tour operators. Lining the waterfront are shops and tavernas, and the Tourist Information office is on 25 Koraka Street, open Mon to Fri 7 a.m. to 10 p.m. The luxury hotels used by the tour operators are the (very isolated) **Ferma Beach** (Tel: 61341), with bungalows and rooms of a high standard; and the **Petra Mare** (Tel: 23341) which has its own section of private beach and a good nightclub. For an independent traveller the **Cretan Villa** on Lakerda Street is a good option.

On an adjoining promontory to the town is a Venetian castle, and in town is a museum.

As a base for exploring the south-east or a sunbathing holiday

Ierapetra, or better the villages around it, are ideal. **MYRTOS**, **ARVI** and **KERATOKAMBOS** are the best choices. The black beach at Myrtos is wonderful; the monastery and beach at the attractive (but busy) village of Arvi, enchanting; and Keratokambos really is one of the most beautiful and charming villages on Crete.

MATALA in the centre of the south coast is all set for mass commercialism to take over, but if you get in quick you can still enjoy a truly beautiful village, surrounded by sheer cliffs, and boasting mellow old buildings and nearby fine sandy beaches. It's not totally unspoilt, and among the young German and Scandinavian student set, it's already very popular, but as only a couple of organized holidays are based there it is still possible to hit it at a time when the locals still outnumber the tourists, and are keen to welcome you.

It's a good base for hiking and of interest are the caves which were originally carved out of the cliffs as tombs. Unfortunately in the 1970s the hippies moved in to these caves and lived in them and now many of them have been boarded up.

Matala is only about 8 miles from the archaeological site of Phaistos, so an excursion here is more or less obligatory. There are several pensions and campsites in the town, and sleeping on the beach is not allowed – the police will move you on as part of the keep-the-hippies-out campaign. Just outside the town's main square, on the road to Phaistos, is the **Bamboo Sands Hotel** (Tel: 42370) which has cheap and reasonable rooms. The campsite is just right of the hotel, heading inland.

Nude bathing is the norm at the **RED BEACH**, 15 minutes' walk south of the town over the hill. The town beach gets busy but is equally good. All around are quiet coves if you're prepared to walk a mile or two. One particularly good beach (with a resident young camping set) is at the ancient Minoan site of **KOMO**, 3 miles or so from the town.

Back in Matala a couple of discos and restaurants line the waterfront. The predominantly young crowd have an active nightlife, and it's not a resort recommended for the older market who are easily shocked at the beach wear (or lack of it) and frolics of the exuberant young!

From Matala there is a snaking road down to the popular resort of **AGHIA GALINI** – another informal young resort but without the charm of Matala and with more crowds and less sand. Hordes of

Germans and Scandinavians descend on this little fishing village annually, and it can become uncomfortably crowded as a result. As a base for touring, however, it has its advantages – inland SPILI on the main road to Rethymnon is one such attraction, but better still, go and stay there!

Tourist Information in Aghia Galini is just off the main square (between the road leading out of the town and Vassili Ionnis – the street where there are many outdoor restaurants). It is open Mon to Fri 8 a.m. to 3 p.m.

The beach is pebbly. Reach it by taking the road running east along the waterfront.

The **Astoria Hotel** is perhaps the best as it is close to the beach and has its own restaurant. There are many cheap rooms in the town, and just east of the town is the campsite.

This is a good base for some excursions in the area. The **Monastery of Preveli** commands a magnificent position overlooking the sea. This building hid many Allied soldiers during the last war while they were waiting to be shipped out in submarines, but is has since fallen on hard times and only a few monks remain to show you round the monastery; open 8 a.m. to 1 p.m., 5 to 8 p.m. Only those with private transport can get out to Preveli, unless you fancy a long walk uphill.

PLAKIAS is an alternative trip. This expanding resort with its beautiful beach and relaxed atmosphere is one of the most attractive places in southern Crete. Even better are the coves to the east of the village – Damnoni is particularly worth finding for a quiet day's sunbathing.

SPILI is one of the highlights of Crete, as far as I'm concerned. This oasis serves as a base for outdoor types, keen to climb the mountains in this area. The **Green Hotel** here is worth travelling to Greece for (Tel: 22225), and if you're travelling independently and are looking for a base which will allow you to sample both the lush alpine mountains and sunsoaked beaches of Crete, this should be your destination.

Still in this vein is the village of ZAROS, a good inland drive away from Aghia Galini, but well worth the effort. Set in the foothills of the Idha Mountains this alpine village is something special and offers facilities for walkers.

THE SAMARIA GORGE

  Omalos is the normal point of entry to this most famous and spectacular of trips on Crete.

The Samaria Gorge, the longest in Europe, is a 5 hour walk through a pass worn away through the White Mountains of southern Crete. It is the most popular trip on the island and in high season it is not uncommon to find two thousand people hiking through this National Park in a day. Despite this it remains an area of outstanding beauty: wild flowers, sheer cliffs and spectacular scenery. At its narrowest point the gorge measures only a few yards wide, yet the walls each side are over 1000 feet. Proper shoes and a packed lunch is recommended, and depending on your level of fitness the walk can take between four and seven hours.

Between 1st May and 31st Oct the park is open 6 a.m. to sunset. (Outside these times it is closed, but from 3 p.m. till sunset you can visit any part of the trail which is a mile from an entrance.) Organized tours operate, and regular public buses leave from Chania to get you to the plain of Omalos, where the walk commences.

As you walk through the gorge, where the sun only reaches at midday, you will see the incredible rock formations – time has worn the stones into the most unusual shapes. After a few hours you reach the 'Iron Gates', the narrowest point, and following this you come out to the village of **AGHIA ROUMELI**, a tourist trap in the middle of all this natural splendour. From here a boat sails to **HORA SFAKION**, where you can catch a bus back to Chania. (The alternative is to walk all the way back!)

If you don't fancy the whole walk start at the dramatic end section from Aghia Roumeli, and go as far as the narrowest point and back.

(See also page 39 in 'The Nature Lover' section for a description of the gorge's natural features.)

PALEOCHORA and **HORA SFAKION** are actually package holiday bases for a couple of companies. If you fancy the idea of someone taking the hassle out of organizing a trip with a difference like this, check them out.

Paleochora has to its credit a magnificent sandy beach, a wonderful pine grove and the basics in the way of tavernas, bars and rooms to let. Camping here is popular with the young, and the general atmosphere is one of a relaxed, carefree resort; ideal for the under 40s. Tourist Information is on Venizelou Street; open Mon to Fri 7.30 a.m. to 3 p.m., as are most of the tourist facilities. Tavernas, as usual, are concentrated on the waterfront, and at night, for atmosphere and enjoyment, this is the area to head for.

Independent travellers might like to consider the **Paleochora Hotel** which has rooms for only a few pounds. **Hora Sfakion** has little to keep you in it, but plenty around it to make it a good base for exploring this region. Boats connect to LOUTRO – a beautiful fishing village with a ruined castle – and the coastline between here and Aghia Roumeli is the best on Crete, so an ideal place for camping and sunbathing.

Hora Sfakion's beach is small but attractive, but the crowds of people drawn to the town because of its strategic position to the Samaria Gorge do spoil the place somewhat. Tourist Information is on the street behind the waterfront, and on the waterfront is the place to look for cheap rooms.

Saronic Gulf Islands

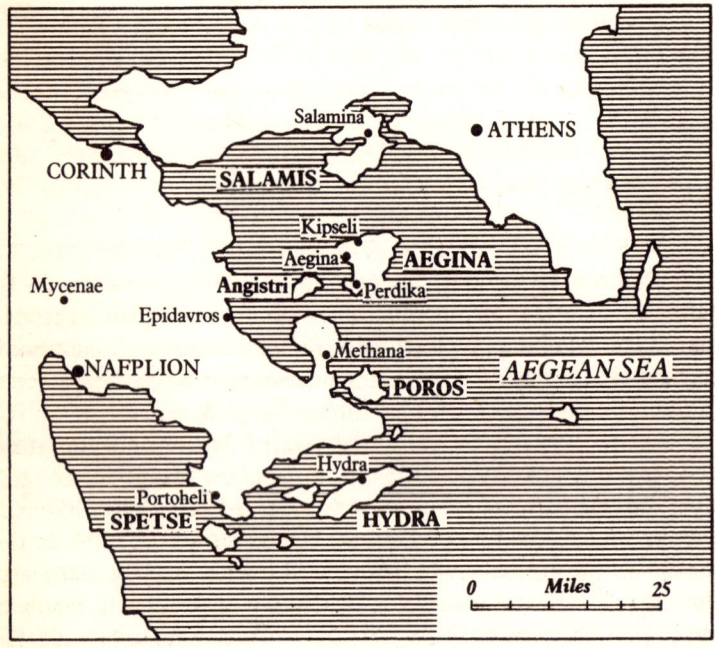

Lying to the east of the Corinth Canal, the Saronic Gulf separates south-east Attica and Athens from the Peloponnese. It is named after Saron, a King of Troizen about whom virtually nothing is known other than the fact that he was drowned in the gulf.

The Saronic Islands are the closest to mainland Greece, and although they can easily be reached by boat or hydrofoil, their very proximity to Athens has ensured that prices are high and that they are all uncomfortably crowded during the summer months, particularly at weekends, when the large influx of week-ending Athenians makes an already congested situation worse.

Many companies, such as **Grecian**, now offer two-centre holidays in the Saronic Islands with the second week of the holiday being spent on a different island. This is a good way of seeing two islands for the price of one, for although they are situated close to each other they each possess strikingly different characteristics.

Island hopping is easy and recommended, so long as you avoid July and August when accommodation is hard to find.

Aegina

Aegina is an attractive mountainous island with good beaches, situated only 1½ hours by ferry from Piraeus. Its close proximity to Athens makes it a popular island for Athenians as well as foreigners, and the main resorts are crowded during the peak season.

In ancient times Aegina was a great rival of Athens until the latter razed its walls and subjected it to the Athenian league in 459 BC. Before this the Aeginetan navy – widely regarded as the best in Greece – had performed admirably against the Persians in 480 BC at the Battle of Salamis – the greatest of all Greek naval battles. Around 200 years before this, the island earned the distinction of producing the first coins in Europe, minting the silver 'turtles' which were to provide the island with great financial power; instilling in all Greeks a respect for money which is still evident today.

In 431 BC the Athenians went so far as to expel the entire population of Aegina, replacing it with Athenian colonists. Sparta restored it in 405 BC after it had won the Peloponnesian War, and thereafter Aegina's history is quite uneventful until the 1820s, when it briefly became the capital of the new Greek state.

Today, the major sources of income for the island are tourism, shipping and pistachio nuts. Aegina is the world's third largest producer of pistachios and with typical Greek braggadocio they claim theirs are bigger and tastier than those from anywhere else in the world. Apart from the four or five main resorts on the islands there are also a number of ancient sites, the most renowned of which is the superb **Temple of Aphaia**. Try to visit in low season when the crowds are less of a nuisance.

Practical Details

COMMUNICATIONS

Ferry connections with Piraeus (from where the metro or green number 040 bus will take you to Athens) are excellent and at least five ferries depart for Aegina each day. The fare is 350 dr. The main passenger service is provided by the **Argosaronikos Line** (Tel: 4511311). In calm weather there are hydrofoil connections with Piraeus (from Zea Marina, around the corner from the main harbour) nearly every hour. The journey is twice as quick but costs nearly twice as much. Details of the hydrofoil can be obtained from the **Flying Dolphins Line** (Tel: 4531716/7) for Aegina, Tel: 452107 for other Saronics.

Passenger ferries leave twice daily for other Saronic Gulf destinations, with another three daily ferries departing from Methana and Poros alone. At weekends, especially during the summer, the frequency of the ferry service increases, and there should be at least three or four boats to all Saronic destinations. There are also two hydrofoils connecting Aegina with the rest of the Saronic islands and **PORTO HELI**, **ERMIONI** and **NAFPLIO** on the Peloponnese. These depart around 9.45 a.m. and 5 p.m. (Mon to Sat) and at 9.45 a.m. *only* on Sundays. Students should note that in the peak season discounts are very difficult to obtain on either ferries or hydrofoils. Schedules are not very consistent, so it pays to keep an eye on the posted time-tables. The port police manage a helpful booth at the ferry landing.

On the island itself there is a cheap and efficient bus service. The terminal is situated to the left of the ferry landing and buses leave hourly for Souvala, Perdika and Aghia Marina. The first bus leaves at 5 a.m. and the last bus at 10 p.m. Whenever you travel, it is usually crowded.

Bikes and mopeds can be rented easily on the island, with the nearest operator being just to the right of the ferry landing stage. Bicycles cost up to 500 dr per 'day' (i.e. 8 a.m. to 5.30 p.m.) and mopeds start at around 1000 dr with step-throughs at 1200 dr.

TOURIST INFORMATION

The tourist office in Aegina town is on Leonardo Lada Street (Tel: 22334), to the right of the ferry landing, on the other side of the road. The office is open daily from 8.30 a.m. to 9.30 p.m. and maps of Aegina can be bought here for 50 dr. You will pay more elsewhere. The Tourist Police are situated a little further up Leonardo Lada Street (Tel: 22391) and there is usually an officer on duty round the clock though the hours are officially 8 a.m. to 2 p.m. and 4.30 p.m. to 8 p.m. To the left of the ferry landing, behind the bus stop, is the post office which is open Mon to Fri 7.30 a.m. to 4 p.m. The OTE office is at Aikou Street to the right of the ferry landing, and is open Mon to Fri 7.30 a.m. to 10 p.m. You can't miss the building, which is situated towards the end of Aikou; it has a huge radar dish on its roof.

WHERE TO GO FOR WHAT

If you are after a lively holiday, with plenty of opportunities for trips to Athens and the other Saronic Islands then Aegina should satisfy you. There are two main resorts: **AEGINA TOWN**, which has all the advantages of a bustling island port, and **AGHIA MARINA** on the other side of the island, which possesses the best beach.

Accommodation is plentiful around Aegina and Aghia Marina, and it needs to be for there are plenty of tourists. In Aegina, the **Danae** (Tel: 22424) is peacefully situated 10 minutes from the town centre, with steps down through pine-woods to a small rock beach. Good quality bungalow-type accommodation is offered at the **Nafsika** (Tel: 22333) which is set in colourful gardens, opposite a shingle beach.

At Aghia Marina there are a few rather scrappy looking hotels going up and the best two are probably the **Apollo** (Tel: 32271) which is directly on a rocky beach 10 minutes' walk by cliff path from the town, and pleasantly surrounded by pinewoods, or the **Argo** (Tel: 32266) which has its own tiny sandy beach 5 minutes' walk from Aghia Marina, with extensive water sports facilities.

Five miles south of Aegina at **PERDIKA**, the **Aegina Maris** (Tel: 25130) is a stark building in an isolated spot but not far from a good sandy beach. The **Moondy Bay** (Tel: 25146) offers bungalow accommodation on a pretty coastline built on a hillside leading down to a pebble beach.

Those on a tight budget can try the **Hotel Artemis** (Tel: 25195) behind the bus station in Aegina or the cheaper **Hotel Atheia** located 5 minutes past the large domed church to the right of the waterfront.

Aegina itself has a bustling, lively atmosphere yet has managed to retain its Greek character. The waterfront is colourful, with fruit-selling boats, pony-traps and displays of local pottery. Along here there are several tavernas and the most well-known nightspots are situated at the end of the pier. A fence near the museum carries posters detailing forthcoming events.

Historians can visit the **Archaeological Museum** (open Mon, Wed to Sat 9 a.m. to 3 p.m., Sun 9.30 a.m. to 2.30 p.m.) which is located in the grounds of the **Temple of Apollo**, of which, unfortunately, only half a column remains. The admission price of 100 dr (50 dr students) covers both the temple and the sparsely filled museum but you're really better off getting on the bus to see the Temple of Aphaia.

Aegina's third main road cuts inland on its way to Aghia Marina on the east coast. Towards the middle of the island is the village of PALEOHORA where the inhabitants used to take refuge from the attacks of pirates. At one time there were 365 chapels in Paleohora but only 27 remain, crumbling and clinging to the cliff. Below, a massive modern church has been built, which contains the embalmed body of St Nektarios, the latest Greek saint, who died in 1920. The scenery becomes more and more attractive the closer you get to the east coast, and helps to contribute to the magnificence of Aegina's chief attraction – the great Doric **Temple of Aphaia**, which dominates the east coast from a beautiful mountain site, surrounded by pine woods. The temple, built with the spoils from Salamis, is one of the best-preserved temples in Greece, although it has lost its sculptures to a museum in Munich. The temple is on the Aghia Marina bus route from Aegina and is well worth the 100 dr admission fee (students 50 dr).

Aegina's two beaches, one sandy one shingly, are nothing special but other beaches are within easy travelling distance. Even Aghia Marina which possesses the best beach is only 45 minutes by bus.

There are a couple of resorts along Aegina's north coast, but before you arrive at Souvala and Vaia, there is a lovely little church at KIPSELI, 2½ miles from Aegina. Built in 1282 the basilica of **Aghios Theodorous** has beautiful frescoes adorning its interior. SOUVALA is an unremarkable fishing village with an attractive waterfront and a small, rough beach.

The west and east coasts have several beauty spots and good beaches. The west coast bus takes you to the pretty fishing village of **PERDIKA**, 5 miles south of Aegina, via Marathonas, where there is also a good beach. Perdika has some good swimming spots and there is always fresh fish in the tavernas on the waterfront. From Perdika you can catch boats to the pleasure isles of **MONI** and **ANGISTRI**. Thermi is the only Saronic island where you can legally camp, and is thus rapidly gaining in popularity with the backpackers, while Angistri is a peaceful up-and-coming resort with good beaches.

Finally, the road descends down to **AGHIA MARINA**, which has a lovely broad sandy beach with rocks at one end for diving into the crystal-clear water. However, the beach is just about the only reason for visiting Aghia Marina as the town is a horrible, prefabricated, commercialized mess. Developers of the better hotels have realized this and have located their hotels well away from the centre.

Angistri

Angistri is a tiny pleasure isle about half an hour's ferry journey from the east coast of Aegina. It has good beaches and a pleasantly wooded interior.

Three boats per day in the summer leave Aegina for Angistri. There are no connections to the mainland.

There are less than a dozen places to stay on the island and all offer basic, inexpensive accommodation. You could try the **Mylos** (Tel: 23892) or the **Anagennissis** (no phone) which is situated right on the beach, or perhaps the **Actaeon** (Tel: 23821) which possibly offers the cheapest accommodation on the island.

Package holidays here cater exclusively for people who want to laze on a decent beach all day long and then just sit in tiny, village tavernas all night; only a couple of tour operators feature Angistri.

 **SKALA** has the best beach and the villages of **MILO** and **LIMENARIA** are both worth exploring.

Methana

The peninsula of Methana juts out into the Saronic Gulf, claiming honorary island status, although in fact it is joined to the Peloponnese by a narrow isthmus at Taktikoupoli. It is served by the boats which ply between the Saronic Islands and, for this reason, it has been included in this section.

Methana was known from ancient times because of the eruptions of the volcano to the north-east of the centre of the peninsula. It is now a summer resort and spa and its modernized hydrotherapy installations, run by EOT, attract large numbers of visitors each year.

Methana is on the main ferry route between Poros and Aegina and Piraeus and there are five connections daily. A new marina just south of the harbour caters for yachts. From Methana, excursion buses lead to TRIZINA, EPIDAVROS and NAFPLION and the rest of the Argolid.

Unless you need to spend some time at the hydrotherapy installation at VROMOLIMNI (literally 'stinking lake' and so called because of the sulphur springs) there isn't any need to stay in Methana for very long. You can trek up to see the crater of the now extinct volcano near KAIMENI HORA, and the ancient citadel and sections of the walls dating from the Peloponnesian War can still be seen at VATHI, where ancient Methana was located, a couple of miles to the east.

There are no packages that we know of to this area.

Spetse

Spetse is a round, lush island at the southern end of the Saronic Gulf, offering little in the way of sights, but possessing the best beaches of any of the Saronic islands. It is very popular as a family holiday destination and you will be either delighted or depressed at the staggering amount of fellow Britons who pack the place out during the peak season. If you're after beaches and nightlife, then this is your place, but as there is little public transport on the island, most people tend to stay in Spetse town and consequently reclusive walkers will have the attractive, forested interior of the island to themselves.

There is little of any archaeological interest on the island though the discovery of pottery near Aghia Marina has led experts to believe that there were settlers on the island as long as 4000 years ago. Little is generally known about Spetse's pre-modern history and its main claim to fame is that it was the first island to revolt against the Turks in 1821.

Well over three dozen companies offer packages to Spetse and most of them are aimed at the younger end of the market. Spetse is lively and has a good nightlife, so if you're the quieter, more retiring sort you may like to consider a different destination for your holiday.

Practical Details

COMMUNICATIONS

From Spetse there is only one ferry to Piraeus daily from Sat to Tue and it usually leaves around 8 a.m. From Wed to Fri, however, there is an extra ferry in the afternoon at around 2 p.m. The fare is around 800 dr and tickets are sold in the **Pine Island Tourist office**. There are also ferry connections to Ermione, Hydra, Poros, Methana and Aegina. You can get to Spetse most cheaply from Kosta on the mainland, from where numerous small ferries will take you to Spetse town for only 50 dr. Kosta itself has a good beach and there is a bus to Porto Heli, and from there to the rest of the Peloponnese. You can take the swifter hydrofoil (less than 300 dr from Porto Heli) if you choose, and these will take you just about anywhere in the Saronic Gulf. At weekends there are anything up to thirteen crossings to Piraeus daily and the fare is around 1500 dr, tickets are sold in the **Flying Dolphin** office located up from the waterfront in Daphia Square, next to Pine Island Tours.

There is little public transport on the island. You can take a trip in a pony-trap but the bus service is negligible: just two buses to Anargyri and back daily. There are mopeds for hire (a good way of getting around the beaches without having to rely on the boats) but not cars. The few taxis in the town are relatively expensive for Greece. During the day flotillas of caiques ferry eager sun-seeking tourists out to various beaches round the island. Unless a beach party has been organized, everyone returns to the main port for the evenings and the night life.

TOURIST INFORMATION

On the wharf to the right you will find the OTE office (open Mon to Fri 7.30 a.m. to 10 p.m.) and the bank next door is also conveniently open until ten in the evenings in the summer (Mon to Fri). Up from the waterfront at Botassi Street, you will find the post office, open Mon to Fri 7.30 a.m. to 2.30 p.m., and the Tourist Police, who have good information on accommodation. Most of the accommodation on Spetse is controlled by the **Takis Travel Office**, which is on the left of the waterfront as you disembark, open 9 a.m. to 10 a.m. daily.

You probably don't need to read much about Spetse but if you feel the urge you can buy a map for 100 dr or the more costly *This Is* guide to the island.

WHERE TO GO FOR WHAT

Spetse is a pretty, gleaming town but lacks Hydra's picturesque charm and architectural distinction. There are one or two sights: the interesting **naval museum**, situated above the town and open daily 9 a.m. to 2.30 p.m. (free); the **House of Bouboulina**, who was the most renowned of Spetse's war heroines and whose courage put many men to shame during the rebellion against the Turks, is just off historic Daphia Square; and a pleasant excursion can also be made to the **Convent of Aghia Pantes**, which has a splendid view out to SPETSOPOULA, the pleasure isle of Stavros Niarchos, one of the world's richest men. However, most people are content to laze on the beach during the day, and party the whole night long.

Spetse town lacks a good beach. The town beach is called AGHIOS MEAMOS, but it is small and uninspiring. There is a larger beach 20 minutes' walk away, near a pine forest. Most people board one of the numerous caiques which leave the port, bound for various beaches around the island. The best one is probably at AGHIA PARASKEVI though ANARGYRI has a fine beach too. It is also quite near to the **Berkis Cave**, which is well worth exploring. Of the other main beaches, AGHIA MARINA gets rather crowded, and ZOGHERIA, though beautiful, is rather rocky and infested with sea urchins. Remember there are fine beaches at KOSTA and PORTO HELI on the mainland, and these places are within easy reach of Spetse town.

Hotel accommodation on the island is good, as are the pensions. The **Roumani** (Tel: 72244) is a good 'B' class hotel overlooking the harbour and the **Possidonion** (Tel: 72208) is a comfortable period hotel with a pleasant front terrace overlooking the sea on the edge of the harbour. A superior quality of accommodation is offered by the **Kasteli** (Tel: 72311) which faces a rock and shingle beach some 20 minutes' walk from the main harbour.

The cheapest hotels are the **Saronikos** (Tel: 72646) and the **Acropole** (Tel: 72219), both in the main town and liable to be booked solid in peak season. The pensions on Spetse are a good alternative to cheap hotel accommodation. Most of the rooms are controlled by the **Takis Travel Office** (Tel: 72215) and these are usually in good locations and cleaned regularly.

RESTAURANTS/NIGHTLIFE

Situated in the old harbour, the **Trechantiri** is on a rooftop, overlooking the water and the cuisine lives up to the superb setting. **Stelios** along the waterfront past Takis Travel is cheaper, but the food is still excellent, and the **Taverna Amoni** is romantically situated on a wooden jetty near the old harbour. There are plenty more restaurants and tavernas squeezed in between the hotel blocks and you can generally eat quite well in the town.

The trendy bars are situated in PALIO LIMARI at the edge of town. The roof garden at the **Hotel Myrtoon** seems popular with British holiday-makers, and you can get cheap cocktails at the **Anchor**, not far from Daphia Square. There are plenty of clubs and discos to choose from, and most are sweatily packed to the hilt until the early hours of the morning. You may not get lasers and dry ice at these clubs but they do have the latest chart sounds. **Figerio** in the old harbour is one of the best clubs, though it is far from cheap. **Fever** does its best to live up to its name, while the **Delfinia** is a popular disco near the equally popular **Rendezvous Bar**, situated on the left-hand side of the waterfront. Next door to **Fever** you can even try your hand at the syrtaki in **George's Bouzoukia**.

Salamis

Salamis (Salamina) is the closest island to Attica and Athens and there are so many ferry connections to Perama on the mainland that it seems virtually an extension of Attica. It's not really a holiday destination and when you look at it from the main road between Megara and Dafni you can see why. The north coast is barren and unattractive and you have to travel right down to the south coast before you come across any decent beaches.

The stretch of water separating Salamis and the industrial shoreline of Elefsina was the site of the Greek equivalent of the Battle of Trafalgar, the Battle of Salamis, which took place in 480 BC. The Persians were the foe, and their commander, Xirxes, had his marble throne placed on a hillside overlooking the strait in anticipation of an easy victory, for the Greek fleet was hopelessly outnumbered by the larger Persian vessels. However, the Greeks, relying on their superior seamanship and the speed of their smaller boats won a glorious victory, and Xirxes retreated hastily.

Today Salamis has little tourism and most of the Greeks who visit the island do so for business reasons. There are no packages to Salamis and we recommend a day trip only.

Practical Details

COMMUNICATIONS

There are up to 70 ferries a day between Salamina (Salamis town) and Perama, which is about 20 minutes by road from the centre of Athens.

On the island itself there is a good road network and the principal settlements are served by a network of buses and taxis.

WHERE TO GO FOR WHAT

Situated on the west coast, **SALAMINA** is the main town. Its main attractions are the **Church of Panayia tou Katharou** and the **Archaeological Museum** which exhibits noteworthy local pottery and jewellery. Four miles to the west is the imposing looking **Faneromeri Monastery** which was founded in 1661 on the site of an ancient sanctuary, though the lavish frescoes date from 1735. Four miles south of Salamina you can see ruins of the ancient city of Telamon at **Eandio**. Near here there is a good beach at MOULKI and other good beaches in southern Salamina include KAKA VIGLA, KANAKIA and PERISTERIA. Visitors should note that while there are plenty of country tavernas scattered amongst the pine-woods there are no decent hotels.

Hydra

Picturesque, fashionable and expensive, Hydra must be the choice for any socialite too old or laid-back to make it to Mykonos: the atmosphere is cosmopolitan, the food is good, and the nightlife is sophisticated. The delightful harbour is the finest in Greece, and is crammed with yachts rather than fishing boats, for this is where the well-heeled Athenian jet set come to carouse – and you can almost smell the aroma of money in the air.

The natural, crescent-shaped harbour is surrounded by tall, elegant houses in hues of white and orange. These were built around the turn of the 19th century by adventurous merchants, who had made large fortunes by supporting the British blockade during the Napoleonic Wars. Many of these merchants were originally mountain dwellers in Epirus until they were forced to flee their homes to avoid repression at the hands of the Turks. They settled in Hydra, where they had to turn to the sea to make a living as the island was barren and could not support crops. The maritime prowess developed by the Hydriots proved decisive in the 1821 revolution against the Turks, and the heroes from this struggle are remembered through statues, memorials and street names in the town. The long seafaring tradition is still maintained through the presence of the Merchant Seamen's Training College on the island.

Hydra is totally unspoilt, and does not permit new buildings or tolerate cars on the island. Its exquisite beauty has attracted countless writers and painters, and the latter are now able to seek inspiration in the lovely old mansion of the Tombazi family, which is now run as a branch of the Athens School of Art.

Not surprisingly the Greeks have been careful to keep the charms of Hydra to themselves, and as a result only a handful of rather select travel companies offer packages there. You can, however, book accommodation in advance through the Greek Tourist Agency (Tel: 01-580 3152). Do make the effort to try to visit Hydra if you're travelling in the Saronic Gulf area – it could well be the highlight of your trip.

Practical Details

COMMUNICATIONS

Four daily ferries connect Hydra with Poros, Methana, Aegina and Piraeus to the north, and Ermione and Spetse to the south. The 1990 fare to Piraeus will be in excess of 800 dr. Tickets for the ferry are sold in a booth on the wharf by the embarkation point.

Most day trippers, however, use the comprehensive hydrofoil service which gives you more time on the island. There are two hydrofoils daily from Piraeus in the summer and there are connections with thirteen destinations in the Saronic Gulf and on the Peloponnese. Hydrofoil tickets are sold by **Flying Dolphins**, situated in the right corner of the harbour as you face the water on Em. Tombaz Street (up the stairs at the side).

There are no roads on the island as no cars are permitted. You can travel round the island by caique (1000 dr) or hire donkeys for excursions from the wharf.

TOURIST INFORMATION

The post office is in an alley to the right of Ikoronou Street (open Mon to Fri 7.30 a.m. to 2.30 p.m.) and the OTE office is reached by walking along the wharf and turning left at the church. The Tourist Police (Tel: 52205) are situated opposite the OTE and are open round the clock, arranging accommodation and providing information, but you are better off going to the new tourist office (open 8 a.m. to 9 p.m.) which is in the front room of the building used by Flying Dolphins. John speaks good English and will get you a room or deal with your problem efficiently and courteously. The bank, situated in the middle of the waterfront, is open from midday to 9 p.m. to save you getting ripped off at the hands of the exchange sharks.

You can get maps and brochures from the tourist office but the best publication is called *This Is Hydra* (the series features other Saronic Islands), which contains maps, photographs, history, information on accommodation/restaurants/nightlife, and also useful snippets such as how to remove sea urchin spikes and which 'mosquito destroyer' to purchase. The book costs 250 dr and is on sale all along the waterfront.

WHERE TO GO FOR WHAT

On Hydra it can be difficult – sometimes impossible – to secure accommodation without booking in advance. Remember that it is one of the most expensive places in Greece and that accommodation is priced accordingly: the closer your room is to the harbour the more expensive it will be. Pension accommodation is invariably charming but expect to pay around 2000 dr for a double room. There are plenty situated near the harbour but if you can face the steps up the hill **George Efstathiou's** (Tel: 52392) offers peace and quiet, and **Zoe Gardelinou's** (Tel: 52114) round at Kamini, a 10-minute walk from the waterfront, is near a good beach and several excellent tavernas.

The cheapest hotel on the island is the **Sophia** (Tel: 52313) right in the centre of the wharf. Also popular but slightly more expensive is the **Leto** (Tel: 52280). This hotel is almost invariably full during the high season, so book in advance.

For those who don't have to worry about money the best two hotels are probably the **Miranda** (Tel: 52230) up A. Miaouli Street, or the **Miramare** (Tel: 52300/1) which is by the beach at Mandraki, half an hour's walk along the coast from the waterfront, or 15 minutes by boat (50 dr).

SIGHTS

At present Hydra's **museum** is being rebuilt and its exhibits are housed in the town's administrative offices. Those of a nautical bent may care to visit the **Merchant Seamen's Training School** which has various paintings, photos and models; open 8 a.m. to 10 p.m. (free).

Historians may be interested in visiting one of Hydra's 'mansions' which were great, self-contained residences, built to be siege-proof with their own bakeries, store rooms and giant cisterns. One of the most elegant is the **House of Koundouriotis**, set in a dominating position on the western side of the harbour. Koundouriotis was a distinguished Hydriot leader during the War of Independence, and a visit to his house and others belonging to famous Hydriots of his period such as **Votsis** and **Economou**, will give you a new understanding of Hydra's history. The House of Koundouriotis is still maintained by his family, and it is best to check at the Town Hall to see whether it is open. Another mansion, the former **Tombazi** residence, houses a branch of the Athens School of Fine Arts.

Bona fide artists can apply to the polytechnic (Tel: 6192119) for permission to stay at the house for a period of up to three weeks 'in order to study'.

Other sights worth visiting in Hydra town include the **Ecclesiastical Church** whose clock tower dominates the wharf, and the **Church of St John** in the Place Kamina, which possesses several attractive and historic frescoes.

If you want to see the other sights of the island you will either have to walk, or charter a donkey. There are three main trails out of Hydra town of interest to the fit sightseer, and all lead to churches or monasteries. An hour's walk south of the town are two attractive monasteries. The first is the **Monastery of the Prophet Elias** and it is located high on the hills surrounding the town. The monks are very hospitable and will be delighted to show you round. The second is the less attractive **Convent of Aghia Efpraxa**, where you can buy woven fabrics made by the nuns on their antique looms.

Well over an hour to the west from here is the deserted monastery of **Episkopi**, which is set in beautiful unspoilt countryside.

The third main trail takes you east to the **Convent of the Holy Trinity**, perhaps the most picturesque of all of Hydra's many churches and monasteries, and, situated on the east coast a good 3 hours (55 minutes by boat) hike from the main town and across difficult terrain, is the **Convent of Zourvas**. As long as you're female you can spend the night here before attempting the long walk back.

There are no real beaches as such on the island, but there are plenty of delightful little coves and the water is the clearest in the Saronic Gulf. Hydra town has a couple of concrete platforms set into the rocks for the benefit of swimmers and sun-bathers, but most people walk the 25 minute journey to MANDRAKI BAY to the east of the port, which contains the largest beach on the island. It's not an especially wonderful one and gets clogged up with the watersports facilities of the Miramare Hotel. You are better advised heading west from Hydra where the first beach will be KAMINI. Here there is a small, red pebbly beach, and a few good tavernas are within easy walking distance. The beach is at its best in late afternoon as the sun begins to sink towards the horizon. Continuing westward you soon come to the small bay and beach of CASTELLO, but it is worth continuing for a quarter of an hour or so to reach VLICHOS, where the water is quite astonishingly clear. There are two tavernas where you can eat fresh fish in this tiny village.

The other beaches are not really within walking distance, and you'll have to take one of the horrendously expensive water-taxis to discover the delights of PALAMIDA and AGHIOS NIKOLAOS BAY on the west coast, and also CAPE BISTI and MOLOS where the fishing is excellent. If you think 1½ hours is 'within walking distance' for a swim then you can also try LIMNIONIZA on the south east coast.

RESTAURANTS/NIGHTLIFE

Hydra has several excellent, if pricey, restaurants. The **Douskos Tavern** is one of the most established and has tables set out under the trees in an attractive square off D. Rafaelias Street. Also excellent are the select and somewhat pretentious **La Grenouille**, a French restaurant with tables set out in a charming courtyard; the delightful **Garden Restaurant**, up Ekononou Street; and the **Pirofani** near Kamini which caters to an arty, yuppy clientele. Grills are specialities here and the king prawns are delicious. Also at Kamini is **George and Anna's** which has cheap prices for Hydra and is always packed out: always a good sign. Back in the main town Stelios will entertain you on the bouzouki while you eat at his restaurant (**Stelios**) in Votsi Square and **The Three Brothers** restaurant, just behind the clock tower, serves just about the cheapest food in town. If you're trekking out to Vlichos you can phone up the **Iliovassilema Restaurant** who will have your fish waiting for you when you arrive.

There are quite a few discos, most situated on the right-hand side of the harbour, and up the hill. The disco **Lagoudera** is located in the stone fortress on the right corner of the harbour and offers drinks at half price for students (they're still expensive even then). Further up the stone path is the **Cavos** with great views out to the Peloponnese, and the extremely expensive **Disco Heaven** is perched up on the peak of the hill.

Poros

The channel of water separating Poros town from Galatas on the mainland is so narrow that it seems more like a river than a stretch of sea. Yet this strip of water, barely 400 yards across, is significant enough to have given the island its name, for Poros means 'passage' in Greek.

Poros is actually two islands: the attractively forested **KALAVRIA** and tiny **SPHERIA**, jutting out towards the mainland, and the site of the main town. In ancient times Kalavria formed an alliance with six other Greek cities and the 6th century BC Temple of Poseidon was the nerve centre of the alliance. In 80 BC the temple was destroyed by pirates, along with many settlements in the Saronic Gulf, thus explaining why there are so few traces left of the classical civilization in the area. In more recent times the island, with its sheltered harbour, played its part in the fight against the Turks and afterwards was for many years the main naval base in Greece.

Nowadays the island is an extremely popular tourist spot, but development has been sensible and the town has preserved its bubbly charm. No one we met seemed to have a bad word to say about the place; even though it possesses neither good beaches nor interesting sights. However, many British holiday-makers have found Poros an agreeable destination, no doubt drawn by the island's beautiful scenery and soothing shades of green which imbue the sea with a lovely turquoise hue and inspire relaxation. There is also plenty of nightlife for those who want it, and the island makes a good base from which to explore historic mainland sites such as Trizina, Epidavros and Nafplion, and, of course, the other Saronic Islands.

Practical Details

COMMUNICATIONS

There are up to three daily ferries between Poros and Piraeus, as well as the *Saronic Star* which connects the island with Hydra and Spetse daily. Ferry tickets are sold in a booth across the street from the embarkation point. In addition to the ferries there is an extensive hydrofoil service connecting Poros with various destinations in the Saronic Gulf and at weekends there are ten journeys to Athens. Hydrofoil tickets are usually sold on the landing itself.

You can also get to Poros by car or bus. From Athens you can get a bus to Galatas just across the water from Piraeus, from where small ferries plough back and forth at regular and frequent intervals.

On Poros itself, the main road circles the town before breaking into three at the point where Kalavria joins Spheria. One road heads north-west to the deserted Russian Bay, another skirts Askeli Bay before terminating at the monastery, while the final road heads north up into the hills and passes by the Temple of Poseidon before circling back round to Askeli Bay. There is just one bus service: between the harbour and the monastery. The first bus leaves the town at 7 a.m. and then departs every 45 minutes until 10 p.m. The fare is 40 dr and the journey takes around 15 minutes. A number of taxis can be hired from the rank in the harbour front (Tel: 23003) and one of these should take you to the monastery for around 250 dr.

Alternatively you can hire a bike or moped from Kostas or Stelios to the left of the pier. Bikes are 300 dr and mopeds 900 dr – but get there early as the supply runs out quickly.

Small motor boats depart from Megalo Neorian Bay every 10 minutes and for Monastery Bay every 20 minutes. There are also regular journeys to Plaka Beach on the mainland, near the famous lemon groves of Lemonodassos.

TOURIST INFORMATION

There is no official tourist office but there are half a dozen agencies which are generally quite helpful. To the left of the ferry landing **Family Tours** (Tel: 22549) will book accommodation and sell you a guide to Poros for 50 dr, open Mon to Sat 8.30 a.m. to 10 p.m., Sun 8.30 a.m. to 8 p.m., while the **Takis Travel Bureau** (Tel: 22048) is up the stairway to the right of Family Tours and along the alley to the right, open Mon to Sat 8 a.m. to 9 p.m.

The post office is in the first square to the right of the ferry landing, open Mon to Fri 7.30 a.m. to 4 p.m., and also to the right and set back from the waterfront on Aghios Mikolaos are the Tourist Police (Tel: 22462). They are open from 8 a.m. to 2.30 p.m., Mon to Fri during the summer season, and there is usually an officer present round the clock to deal with emergencies. The OTE office is in the centre of the wharf and is open Mon to Fri 7.30 a.m. to 10 p.m.

There are maps of Poros on sale all along the waterfront and at tourist agencies (50 dr) but a better guide is the *This Is* guide to Poros which will set you back 250 dr.

WHERE TO GO FOR WHAT

The good thing about Poros is that it caters for both those who want a quiet holiday *and* those who are looking for a more lively time. The town has a cheerful, bustling waterfront lined with numerous tavernas, while Kalavria offers the opportunity for several delightful hikes across beautiful, wooded terrain. Most of the beaches are on the south coast and there are plenty of opportunities for water sports and sailing.

There are two very good and well-equipped hotels: the **Sirene** (Tel: 22741) on Monastery Bay and the **Poros** (Xenia) (Tel: 22216) on one of the promontories of Neorian Bay to the west of Poros town. Both are beautifully located and offer extensive facilities including watersports, discos and bars. There is a good pebble beach below the Sirene and while there is no beach at the Poros there are two lovely coves within easy reach and numerous opportunities for swimming from the rocks.

In the town, most of the hotels are quite expensive and there is nothing below 'C' class. The **Seven Brothers** (Tel: 22412), on the waterfront, has a good restaurant. Luckily for travellers on a budget there is plenty of pension accommodation. When you get off the ferry you will be met by a host of pension owners – or more likely by their children, who invariably speak better English – and with a bit of haggling you should be able to secure yourself a decent room. There are a couple of pensions up by the clock tower with superb views and the establishments of **Nikos Douras** (Tel: 22633) and **George Douras** (Tel: 22532) are recommended. **Dimitras Alexopoulou's** pension (Tel: 22697) is excellent but a little more expensive.

There is little of interest to sightseers in Poros town. The small **museum**, open Mon, Wed to Sat 8.30 a.m. to 12.30 p.m. and 4 p.m. to 6 p.m., Sun 9 a.m. to 3 p.m., is situated just before the church along the waterfront, and has various exhibits from the archaeological site of TRIZINA nearby in the Peloponnese. Navy buffs can visit the battleship *Averof* which is permanently anchored in the harbour off the Naval School. It is one of Greece's most famous modern ships and cost one million pounds in 1911! It served in both World Wars, and at one time had a crew of nearly 700 men.

Elsewhere on the island there are just two places of interest. The **Sanctuary of Poseidon**, in a commanding position a good 3 miles from the town, has been sadly nearly totally destroyed by pirates and many of its ancient marble blocks have been plundered for building purposes. It is most famous for being the site of the great orator Demosthenes' death. He had fled from the Macedonians who were ruling Athens at the time, and though the temple was supposed to be an inviolable sanctuary for all fugitives, it soon became clear to Demosthenes that he could expect no mercy at the hands of his enemies who were waiting outside the temple. He therefore cheated his future captors of their prize; committing suicide by pretending to write a letter and chewing on the poisoned end of his quill. Today only the foundations bear witness to the size and position of the great temple, but it's still worth making the journey for the fabulous view.

The other attraction is the **Monastery of Zoodochos Pigis**, which is located in a sublime spot a mile and a half north-east of the town. Try to visit it in the early evening, just before the Monastery closes at dusk, when the wooded glade that provides the location for the monastery takes on a magical quality. The monastery itself is attractively white and green, and inhabited only by a purposeful Greek Orthodox priest. It is open from 6 a.m. to 1 p.m. and 3 p.m. to sunset and there are regular bus connections until 10 p.m. Dress modestly.

You should bear in mind that though there isn't that much to see on Poros itself, it is handily placed for excursions to interesting sites on the mainland such as TRIZINA, NAFPLION and EPIDAVROS. One excursion you shouldn't miss is the short trip to the huge lemon grove of LEMONODASSOS. This is a well-watered 187-acre site, a 10-minute walk from PLAKA BEACH on the mainland (boats 40 dr), whose 25,000 trees bear fruit three times a year. In the midst of the scented groves there is a café where you can sample a lemonade made with freshly squeezed lemons and admire the view.

Whilst on the mainland you can swim at Plaka Beach or the more attractive ALIKI BEACH nearer to GALATAS. Back on Poros there are three main beaches, all on the south coast of Kalavria, and numerous small boats ferry people to them from beachless Poros town throughout the day. The main beach is probably the rather course one at ASKELI BAY, though you would do better to stay on the boat until it reaches the pebbly but scenic beach at MONASTERY BAY. On the other side of Spheria NEORIAN BAY has a small beach which is pleasantly fringed with pines. The next cove along is the less attractive RUSSIAN BAY, but it will generally be deserted. On the other side of the island is VAGIONIA BAY, which is more difficult to get to but free from crowds.

There are good water sports facilities available from the main hotels and you can also make use of the **water sports'**

centre at Villa Galini, Lambrenki Avenue (Tel: 23635). Sailing facilities are also excellent since the bays are sheltered from the strong winds which can affect the region. For further information about sailing contact the Poros **Yachting Club** (Tel: 22774).

A good time to visit Poros is June when there are a couple of interesting festivals. During the first week there is the Flower Festival of Anthestira, held in Galatas, which is festooned with flowers and plants of all kinds grown by local gardeners. In the last week of June, the Naval School holds various sporting competitions. There are colourful parades through the attractively decorated streets and a large firework display on the last night.

RESTAURANTS/NIGHTLIFE

The waterfront is crammed with numerous tavernas although there is very little variation in the fare they offer. The **Caravella** and **Lagoudera** have tables right by the sea and offer good, inexpensive grills, while both the **Seven Brothers** and **Three Brothers** offer lively atmosphere and good-sized portions. Out of town, **Zorbas** is a large popular taverna just over the bridge between Spheria and Kalavria. The tables are arranged around a dance floor and twice a week there is an organized display of Greek dancing. On other nights tourists provide a pale substitute. For a more intimate spot try **Ta Nisia** which is situated by Monastery Beach down some steps about 200 yards after the Sirene Hotel. The seafood is delicious and you can relax over a bottle of retsina, away from the bustle of the port.

After your meal you can hit the lively **Takis Pub** on the waterfront, or maybe sink a few beers at either the **Ship** or **Nektars**, just outside the harbour. These are all open until the early hours of the morning and you'll be well tanked up by the time you want to move on to the discos which are generally situated at the extreme right of the harbour front. **Kavos** is popular and features Greek dancing at around 2 a.m., while **Corali** next door attracts the younger crowd. Round the corner from these two, the open-air **Sciroco**, with its spectacular views of the Gulf, is also beginning to pack them in. If all this sounds a bit hectic, you can spend a quieter evening at the **Diana Cinema** round the left-hand side of the port, which shows many English-language films.

Corfu

Corfu is justly famed as an ideal place for cheap and cheerful holidays in the sun. More people come here than to all the other Greek islands put together, over 500,000, two-thirds of whom are British, making it the most popular holiday destination in the world for British tourists. Yet, whatever your preconceived ideas of Corfu may be, it is one of the most beautiful islands in Greece, something that Homer, Shakespeare, Edward Lear, the Durrell family and numerous European royals have all agreed upon. It is understandable that we all treat brochure descriptions with a wry smile, but for once Corfu *is* a place that does look like the photographs, with blue skies and crystal-clear seas. The greatest attraction of the island is not its beaches, though these are very good, but its scenery.

As it rains during the winter on Corfu it is far less barren and much greener than the rest of Greece. This beauty, combined with many interesting sights and probably the best tourist facilities of anywhere in Greece, means that Corfu is not simply an island for the young and single, but one of those rare places where every type can find a holiday to suit them, even, hard to believe as it is, the Recluse.

Around the island each coast has a different attraction. The east coast is the most developed and ideal for night owls and families. The north caters mainly for quieter family holidays and the north-west provides slightly more exclusive and very comfortable hotels in excellent scenery. The west coast is much less developed than the east, but ironically has the best beaches, and finally the south coast, although no longer the haven it once was, can still offer some solitude to the recluse. Corfu also makes a good choice for those who want sun and sea but get bored lying on the beach all day, for though there are no great archaeological sites there is a lot to see and good communications to get you there.

From this you can begin to see that Corfu is not simply a place for young singles holidays, it can offer something for everyone and with over 80 companies selling holidays there your main problem will be choosing the right resort.

History

Corfu is the most northerly of the Greek islands; the nearest part of Greece to Italy and only 2 miles from Albania.

In geological terms it is something like an iceberg, for the island is the exposed tip of a mountain range which broke off from the mainland millions of years ago and is now under water. The island is usually described as sickle-shaped, though it looks like some great sea-horse some 40 miles long and between 2½ and 18 miles wide. It was originally called *skeria*, the Greek for sickle, but became known as *Stous Korfus*, literally translated as 'with the peaks', after the two hills which overlook its port. These are now the site of the Old Fort in Corfu town.

In 734 BC the island was first settled as a trading colony by Corinth. Its convenient location on the trade routes between Italy and Greece soon enabled it to enjoy a rapid economic growth and it in turn began to found its own colonies. In 634 BC Corfu was strong enough to win independence from Corinth in the first sea-battle in Greek history. After this, however, the island's power diminished and it was important solely as a colony for others rather than in its own right. However, by appealing to Athens for help against Corinth over a disputed colony, Corfu caused the epic Peloponnesian War in 427 BC, a civil war which lasted 27 bitter years. Invaded by Spartans and pirates, the island was so often defeated in war that a proverbial Roman joke grew up, 'Corfu is free, dung where you will' i.e. do what you want in Corfu, no one can stop you.

In 200 BC the Roman Empire proceeded to dung where they wished and in their first conquest across the Adriatic Sea established the island as a Roman protectorate. In theory it remained one for the next 500 years, but in reality the island was controlled successively by Macedonia, Epirus and Illyria. During this time a large number of famous Romans came to Corfu: some came as tourists, like Nero who visited simply to dance at a temple at Kassiopi, but most, such as Tiberius, Cato, Octavius, Antony and Cleopatra, and Caesar, simply stopping on the way to somewhere else.

After the collapse of the Roman Empire, the Byzantines took control of Corfu. They did not prove to be very diligent rulers and the island was sacked by Vandals, Ostrogoths, Goths and Slavs. Eventually someone took the hint and after the last attack began to build defences on the eastern seaward approach to the island, the site now occupied by the Old Fort. This did not mark the end of invasions, however, for several times between 1081 and 1185 the Normans attacked Corfu from Sicily. Understandably perturbed, the locals asked the Venetians, then among the most powerful people in Europe, for help. The Venetians won the island from the Normans, but since they were fully committed elsewhere they left others to govern it for some 200 years. In the first half of the 13th century Corfu was controlled from the mainland by the despots of Epirus, who built the castle at Paleokastritsa on the west coast. The island was then given as the marriage dowry of the daughter of one of the despots to the King of Sicily. Eight years later he died and the island passed to the rule of Charles d'Anjou and his family. During this period Richard the Lionheart stopped at Corfu on his way to the crusades. After about 100 years the Angevins died out and the nobles of the island, seeking protection from pirate raids, again asked Venice for aid. On 3 June 1386 the Venetians arrived, and this time they stayed for 411 years.

The Venetians were originally only interested in using Corfu as a naval and trading base for their ships, not in developing it as a colony. Thus Italian became the official language, the Orthodox church was suppressed, and all the important administrative posts were held by Venetians. However, once they began to realize the importance of the island they began to encourage its growth. The production of olives and currants to provide exports was particularly promoted. The olives provided olive-oil, and the currants flavouring in a time of bland, heavily salted food. The locals were unable to understand the foreigners' huge demand for currants and for some reason decided that they must be used as a dye! Although undoubtedly exploited by the Venetians, the island's development far exceeded that of the mainland at the same time. The most lasting thing they gave the island was the Old Town, but whilst the Venetians were building Corfu the Turks were destroying Europe.

In 1463 they declared war on Venice and slowly captured some of the Ionian islands and then turned to Corfu. The clash finally came in 1537 when Turkish ships were sighted heading for the island. The Corfiotes had a few days' warning and literally tore down the walls of their houses to have enough stone to rebuild the now collapsing fort walls. Whilst sailing through the narrow Corfu channel the Turkish ships rammed the Venetian galleys 'accidentally' placed there, and despite a secret treaty with Venice promising not to take such an action, the Turks besieged the town with some 30,000 men under the command of Suleiman the Magnificent. The siege failed but the island was plundered and 15,000 were taken prisoner and sold into slavery or killed. One local woman had better fortune, however. She became the wife of the Turkish Sultan! Since the attack came from the north, and the fort was on the east, the 'New' Fort was built to prevent another attack succeeding. The Turks were undaunted, however, and a mere 21 years later, in 1558, they attacked again. Once more they were defeated and the Venetians now built a new set of walls regarded as the greatest fortifications of their day.

The Turks continued to attack Europe and in 1571, 1,700 men from Corfu crewed the Venetian ships at the battle of Lepanto where, in the last major battle of oared ships, the Turkish fleet was defeated. In 1716 the Turks once again attacked Corfu in what was to be the last Turkish siege of Europe. Again the islanders had some warning and this time they hired a troop of German mercenaries to defend them. After a very tough 6-week siege it appeared that the Turks had won. Then suddenly they left, despatched by a fortuitous storm which threatened their fleet (the locals are convinced this was the work of the patron saint of the island, St Spiridon). Despite all the Turkish sieges, Corfu never fell, and was the only part of all Greece not to be controlled by the Turks.

After briefly being declared a republic between 1800–07, the first modern Greek state with self-government, the island was taken over by the French. Napoleon regarded Corfu as the 'key to the Adriatic' and with 50,000 men and 500 cannon, turned it into the most heavily defended place in the Mediterranean. This was the time of Trafalgar and Waterloo, but the British were unable to attack such a well-fortified position and could only mount a very ineffective blockade with a mere two ships. Under French rule the elegant row of houses in the town known as the Liston was built and the cultivating of tomatoes and potatoes introduced. Many of the locals were very suspicious of the humble spud and thought it to be the original fruit of the Tree of Knowledge from the Garden of Eden, and had to be forced to plant it.

In 1813 Napoleon was defeated elsewhere and the seven Ionian islands became an independent state under the care of the British. Colonial rule has always had its critics, but under it the island developed far more than the mainland with excellent roads, hospitals, water supplies and even a university. However, although a kind of Parliament did exist, all effective power was in the hands of the Lord High Commissioner of the island, who was of course British. Demands for freedom became increasingly loud and in 1854 Gladstone, the Victorian Prime Minister, was sent on a fact-finding mission to Corfu. When presented to the Orthodox Archbishop he very unexpectedly, since he was an Anglican, kneeled to receive his blessing. The Archbishop was so surprised that he hesitated for a moment and Gladstone, thinking that he was not going to give it, stood up and in the process head-butted the Archbishop. (Not vital to Corfu's history, but interesting nonetheless.)

In 1863 Prince William of Denmark became King George I of Greece and since he was pro-British, the British agreed to leave the island, an act many contemporaries regarded as an unprecedented and highly dangerous withdrawal from an overseas colony. For the first time Corfu was now part of Greece. As all the brochures tell you, the British left behind cricket and ginger beer.

During World War I the island was used as an Allied naval base. In 1916 the King of Serbia and 150,000 of his army fled here after defeat by the German army. From here in 1917 he declared the modern state of Yugoslavia, but half of his troops died of plague and are buried on Volos island just opposite the New Fort. In 1923 the Italian fleet bombed the town in reprisal for the supposed assassination of an Italian general. They occupied Corfu until forced to withdraw by diplomatic pressure, mainly from Britain. They occupied the island again during the Second World War and their actions of renaming the streets and issuing a new currency suggest that they intended to stay. But in 1943 Italy surrendered and the Germans arrived to take over. The Italian troops refused to hand over the island and only gave in after ten days of heavy bombing, in which about a quarter of the town was destroyed. Finally in 1944 the Germans were driven out by the Allies and today, after centuries of being attacked, Corfu is now besieged not by troops but by tourists, mainly British.

Practical Details

The easiest and most popular way to arrive in Corfu is by plane. There are direct flights during the summer from Heathrow, Gatwick, Stansted, Birmingham, Manchester and Glasgow, all averaging about 3½ hours' flying time. The airport is very conveniently located about 1½ miles from Corfu town and transfer time, even to the most distant resorts, should be under 1½ hours. For air travel within Greece, Olympic Airways offer flights to the mainland and to many of the other islands, with student discounts of 30 per cent on night flights to/from Corfu. Be warned if you are arriving on a charter flight that there are no buses to the town, so if you are travelling independently you will either have to take a taxi, at a vastly inflated rate of course (insist on using the meter) or walk, and although the route is actually quite pleasant, no one would wish to do it with a suitcase. As you get off the plane note the huge piles of luggage on the side of the runway and hope that yours does not end up amongst it. If you get frustrated in the small terminal building count yourself lucky for only a few years ago it was still a tin shed!

If you do not fly the alternative is a ferry. The main route is from Italy and from either Ancona or Brindisi the trip takes about 9 hours. These ferries actually go to Patras on the Greek mainland, but you can stop off at Corfu at no extra cost, *provided* that you get it written on your ticket. Be warned: if you do not have it written on your ticket you will not be allowed to get off. There are also ferries from Venice, Bari and some ports in Yugoslavia. All these international ferries usually arrive at the new Port at the west end of the harbour beyond the New Fort. Ferries leave to Igoumenitsa, roughly hourly from 6 a.m. to 9.30 p.m. taking about 2 hours, or from Patras, at least once a day taking about 10 hours. All these local ferries arrive at the east end of the harbour, near the New Fort. There are also ferries to the other Ionian islands, most frequently to Cephalonia (6½ hours) and Paxi (1½ hours), details of which can be obtained from the many travel agents. Remember that each will only tell you about the ferries it is an agent for, so to ensure that there is not in fact a more convenient ferry, enquire at more than one office.

The easiest way of travelling round the island is by car. Although very convenient, car hire can be expensive, though it is slightly cheaper when organized by your holiday company from home. Despite the cost, if you are a family or a group, car hire for at least a few days would be a good idea, particularly at the more isolated resorts when the thrill of lying on the beach has begun to diminish, but drive carefully since even the tiniest scratch can prove very expensive. If there are four of you car hire will be cheaper than taking organized excursions. Petrol is fairly freely available in Corfu town, but inland petrol stations are not so common, so when in doubt fill up. Hiring a moped is much easier than a car, and more fun on short journeys, but the accident rate every year is frighteningly high. Just because you see some idiots riding them in swim suits and flip-flops doesn't mean that this is a safe practice! Bikes can also be hired and are suitable for exploring the east coast which is relatively flat.

Most people choose to travel round the island by bus. Although crowded, they are very cheap and some even seem to have multi-lingual conductors. Be warned, however, that away from the major resorts on the east coast the service is not as frequent as the tourist might wish and the last bus is never very late, and as one brochure has marvellously understated the case, 'a modicum of patience will sometimes be needed'. Hitching is possible, and usually fairly successful, but do not expect to get direct lifts. Taxis are another option, but agree a fare first if it is a long journey. If you are driving, be careful. The main roads are quite good but the minor ones are positively dangerous and they are full of unexpected hazards round the corners. Your comments about the local drivers will rapidly become very explicit, but be warned, your fellow holiday-makers are even worse! In addition in Corfu town you can hire horse-drawn carriages. These are as much fun as they look, but they are there only for the tourists so agree a price before you decide to take a trip, or your wallet will be severely shocked.

TOURIST INFORMATION

The Greek Government have one of the best tourist organizations in the world, and the Tourist Office in Corfu town, situated on the ground floor of the large modern building in Dessila Street, is probably one of the best in Greece. The very helpful staff speak excellent English and can provide very useful maps, guides and advice for the whole island, but do be prepared to queue. The office is open Mon to Fri 7 a.m. to 3 p.m., 6 p.m. to 8 p.m.; Sat 9 a.m. to 11 p.m. during the season and Mon to Fri 7.30 a.m. to 3 p.m. outside the summer. Tel: 30520, 30730 and 30360. You should be able to find copies of the English language *Corfu News*, in Corfu town. Apart from containing some interesting articles this paper has a very useful information section on the back pages with bus times, museum opening hours and the like.

CLIMATE

The weather is best on Corfu in July and August, the air temperature is about 90°F (32°C), the sea temperature about 75°F (24°C) and there is about 12 hours of sunshine. Before such wonderful figures blind you, remember that this is of course when the island is most crowded. The most pleasant time to visit Corfu is thus either May to mid-June, or September to mid-October. A slight drawback about doing this is that the sea temperature may be a bit low. Also, winters in Corfu tend to close in much earlier than in the rest of Greece, although the rain on the island is only heavy from November to March, but if you're going anytime except in mid summer, an umbrella would be useful, though you can of course buy these on the island.

CULINARY SPECIALITIES

The choice of food on Corfu is enormous because there are a large number of 'foreign' restaurants. Whilst it's still hard to get a curry (though no doubt this won't be for long) the island is full of Italian and Chinese restaurants, as well as burger bars and even fish and chip shops. Greek food does, however, still exist and among the local dishes to try are *sofritio* (veal in garlic sauce) and *bourdetto* (a kind of fish stew in hot oil with lots of pepper). The most famous local dish, however, and certainly the most expensive, is *astakos* (lobster without the claws, officially known as salt water crayfish). More familiar foods for which the island is well known are prawns, strawberries, oranges and crystallized fruit. Also very popular is honey which, poured over yoghurt, can make a delicious replacement for cornflakes at breakfast. Another popular sweet dish is mandolato nougat, though be careful of your teeth.

There are several Corfu wines, but these are hard to find and at most restaurants they will not be on the menu. However, the best of the whites is *paloumbi*, a dry wine from the west. *Bianco*, from the south, is cheaper and *Corfio*, both red and white, is very basic. The local red wines tend to vary dramatically from season to season. *Theotoki* was once one of the greatest wines of Greece, but has now lost its flavour and simply tends to be rather expensive. Rosé wines such as *roditis* and *kokkineli* should be available should you so wish. Retsina, if you can stomach it, is by far the cheapest.

Corfu has two very famous drinks. *Kum Kwat* is a sticky, sweet, orange liqueur made from the small Japanese oranges which grow on the island and *tzinerbira*, a legacy of British rule, is a drink that you have probably had at home and one which you know better as ginger beer.

The soft drinks on the island are still rather than fizzy, but the *limonada* is very refreshing. The water is safe to drink, but most people prefer bottled spring water. The tea will probably not be up to your expectations, but console yourself that on this once-British island they probably make it more correctly than they do in other parts of Greece! On Corfu you will not invariably be served with Turkish-style coffee unless you ask for it. Instant coffee and milky coffee are widely available.

WHERE TO GO FOR WHAT

Socialites: Corfu is famous for cheap and lively holidays in the sun and the simple rule is, the nearer to Corfu town the more active the resort. The most action-packed is Benitses on the south-east coast, Kassiopi and Dassia on the north-east coast followed by Ipsos, and Moraitika, Messonghi and Perama in the south-east and Aghios Georgis in the west are also lively.

Most people who come to Corfu are families. The best resorts for them are Dassia and Gouvia on the north-east coast, Roda and Sidari on the north coast, Aghios Geordis on the west coast and Perama on the south. The beaches here are far safer and the children's facilities more extensive.

Sun-worshippers will find the best beaches, and on Corfu that is saying a lot, on the west coast at beaches like Aghios Geordis and

Barbri, Glyfada, Arillas, Aghios Stefanos, Myrtiotissa and Aghios Georgiou. Also worth checking out are Nisaki and Barbati on the north-east coast, Acharavi and Sidari on the north and Kavos in the south.

Sightseers will find plenty of interest on the island, but there is no single great 'sight'; all the places of interest are quite scattered so don't expect to be able to 'do' the island in one day. The best place to stay for a holiday of this type is Corfu town, partly because of its own charming surroundings, but mainly because of its excellent communications; but do remember it does not have a good beach. If this would bother you, choose any other resort on the main bus route. If you want somewhere more isolated you'll have to hire a car.

The Recluse will have to search out the quieter spots and may find them increasingly full of sun-worshippers, but they do exist. On the west coast are Aghios Stefanos, Aghios Georgiou, Arillas, Ermones and Yaliscari, and on the south-east coast Bourkari and Kavos. The real recluse should simply head inland, or for the coast roads in the north and south, until you find a spot which you consider suitably quiet. Check through the brochures until you come across a resort where only one or two tour operators go, or travel independently and avoid anywhere where packages are based.

Healthy holidays: Corfu is famous as one of the best places in the world for water sports, making it ideal for sporting types. The best sporting resorts are Dassia and Ipsos with water skiing, paragliding and all kinds of sailing, but almost anywhere can offer at least windsurfers and pedaloes and usually the larger the resort the larger the queue. Corfu is one of the few places in Greece where the Greek Government, usually fearful of wrecks being plundered, allow scuba diving to take place and the **Baracudian Paleokastritsa** offers a two-week course for beginners, advanced trips for the more experienced, and single days for the novice (Tel: 41211). Remember also that a large number of the bigger hotels also have a wide range of sports available, such as tennis and mini-golf. Golf enthusiasts will find one of the most beautiful courses in the world at Ropa's Meadow, Livadi tou Ropa, near Ermones, with a meandering stream on no less than 16 of its 18 holes. *Golfing Monthly* described this as one of golf's best-kept secrets and even if you have never played before this might be the place to hire a set of clubs and start (Tel: 44220/1). If whilst on holiday you find yourself missing the Test Match or Wimbledon it is possible to play both cricket and tennis in Corfu town. For tennis contact the **Corfu Tennis Club** at 4 Romonou Street, Tel: 37021, and for cricket the Tourist Office or the **Gymnasium Association**, Tel: 38736. Fishermen will find excellent fishing all round the island and should find it quite easy to hire equipment and a boat, and will not need a licence.

The Nature Lover will find Corfu one of the most scenic islands in Greece. The best walks are to Mt Pantokrator at 2,972 ft and Ag Deka at 1,889 ft, but there are many other pleasant walks all round the island, so simply take a map and head inland.

CORFU TOWN

Corfu town, *Kerkira* in Greek, is the capital of the island. Although it is often said to be 'Venetian influenced' its more beautiful areas are perhaps more helpfully described as 'Venice without the canals'. Although certain areas are less than charming, it is without doubt one of the most elegant towns in Greece, yet since most people come to Corfu for sun and sea, few people stay here because there are no good beaches nearby. If this does not concern you Corfu town, with its pleasant surroundings, excellent hotels and very good communications, can make a very enjoyable base for a civilized holiday, with more of an atmosphere of Brighton than Blackpool.

Practical Details

ACCOMMODATION

Most of the tour operators offering holidays in Corfu town use hotels in the suburbs rather than the centre. The best of these, suitable for all holiday types, is the **Kerkira Golf** (Tel: 31785) with pleasant gardens and a good figure-of-eight-shaped pool some 2 miles north of the town. Just past this hotel, and an ideal base for families, is the **Sunset** (Tel: 31203). For a quiet holiday the **Arion** (Tel: 37950) with mini-golf and a pool, or the **Marina** (Tel: 32783), more isolated and with slightly fewer facilities, should appeal.

In the town itself the best hotel is the **Cavalieri**, overlooking the town and the sea on 4 Kapodistrou Street. Originally built in the 17th century, after heavy bomb damage in World War II only the facade remained and behind this was built the elegant hotel. Its roof garden, balconies, antiques and cool marble provide a level of luxury that manages to be comfortable without being ostentatious. In the same style, but slightly cheaper, is the **Calypso**, situated opposite the Archaeological Musuem on 4 Vralia Street. Positioned in a quiet residential area and run by an English management, it is ideal for older and retired couples. Such people should also consider the deluxe **Corfu Palace** (Tel: 39485), near the Old Fort, which has a pleasant interior and a good garden. Equally central is the **Arcadion** at 44 Kapodistrou Street which has nice rooms with good views. At 39 E Voulgareos Street just behind the town hall is the **Splendid**, which although less grand than its name would suggest, is still a very comfortable place to stay.

For independent travellers looking for somewhere cheap there is quite a wide choice. In George II Square the **New York**, immediately opposite the mainland ferry at 11 Zavitsianou Street, has clean rooms, some with balconies overlooking the square. Similar are the **Constantinopolis** next door and the **Acropolis** just opposite. In the Mandouki area of the New Port are the **Ionian**, with views over the sea at 46 Stratigou Street, and next door the **Atlantis**. In the maze of streets behind are two basic but clean hotels, the **Europa** and the **Aegli**. More expensive, but very well positioned overlooking the Esplanade are the **Suisse** and the **Arcadion**. If all these are full the tourist office should be able to offer some constructive advice, and they also have a list of rooms, most of which are located in the Old Town.

If you do not want to stay at a hotel, or cannot afford to do so, do bear in mind that Corfu is not very good for youth hostels. The main one is not in the town but 3 miles away at Kontokali. Although its situation on the beach sounds marvellous, the reality is a bit disappointing. To reach it take bus no. 7 from Theotoki Square. The other hostel is miles inland, which although very pretty is in a very isolated and thus fairly useless position at Ag Ioannis. However, do not despair, Corfu is very good for camping. Your first move should be to pick up the list of sites available at the tourist office. The nearest to the town is **International Camping**, just opposite the Youth Hostel at Kontokali. Probably a better choice is **Dionysius Camping** at Kommeno, a few minutes further on the same bus. A good bus service means that it is possible to stay anywhere along this coast and travel to beaches during the day and to the town at night. If you do stay at the Dionysius walk along to the local beach since the view of the bay through the forest is beautiful, but make sure that you get very clear directions and wear sensible shoes.

TOURIST INFORMATION

The Tourist Office is in the large modern building on Desilla Street. It is one of the best in Greece and the friendly English-speaking staff should be able to provide maps and advice for everyone. Even if you have been to the island before it is worth stopping here to find out if there is anything special going on during your stay. The office is open Mon to Fri 7 a.m. to 3 p.m., 6 p.m. to 8 p.m.; Sat 9 a.m. to midday in season and Mon to Fri 7.30 a.m. to 3 p.m. outside the summer months. Tel: 30320, 30730 and 30360. The Tourist Police, useful when the Tourist Office is closed or when emergencies occur, are at 33 Arseniou on the road overlooking the coast, open 7 a.m. to 10 p.m. every day. The Tourist Police for areas outside the town are in Theotoki Square, Tel: 30669. If the queues are just too awful the numerous tourist agencies dotted around the island will also give out basic tourist information.

The Post Office is just around the corner from the tourist office. In the same building you will find the main OTE office, with self-service international telephones, open 6 a.m. to midnight. There is also a smaller office at 78 Kapedistriou Street, the Palace end of the Esplanade, open 8 a.m. to 10 p.m.

There are four banks on G. Theotoki Street in the Old Town, open Mon to Fri 8 a.m. to 2 p.m. In Theotoki Square the Ionian and the Commercial Banks also open Mon to Fri 6 p.m. to 7.30 p.m. If you should need money in the evening the National Bank at the Customs House in the mainland ferry port is open 7 a.m. to 10 p.m. every day.

If disaster should strike the British Vice Consul is at 2 Zambeli Street, 'consulting hours' 10 a.m. to midday, Tel: 28055, and a good, English-speaking hospital is at Ioulias off Polichroniou Konstanta

Street, Tel: 30562. There is also a casualty clinic just behind the Commercial Bank on Theotoki Square. For less dire emergencies the tourist office have a list of doctors and dentists, a list that is also printed in the *Corfu News*. Chemists can be found on Ioulias Andreadi and G. Theotoki Streets.

There are two types of bus. The dark blue buses are numbered and trundle between Corfu town and the relatively near settlements, while the unnumbered pale blue ones offer more comfort, at greater expense, to more distant destinations such as Sidari and Kavos. Confusingly, the buses leave from three different places. The urban service, the no. 2 to Mon Repos and Kanoni leaves the Esplanade, while the other numbered buses leave from G. Theotoki Square, which is still labelled, even more confusingly, as San Rocco on some maps – its former name. The pale blue coaches leave from New Fortress Square to the north-east of G. Theotoki Square. Prices are very reasonable; you should pay no more than 50dr on a dark blue bus and no more than 200dr on a pale blue one.

Seemingly a small point, and one that is ignored by most guide-books, but one that can occasionally loom very large in your thoughts, is the location of the public loos. Corfu is one of the few places in Greece with public conveniences, located in Theotoki Square, the Esplanade and the Old Port. Do not despair if caught short, however, as it is much more convenient, and perfectly usual to use those in hotels and bars, even if you feel very guilty in doing so.

SIGHTSEEING

Corfu town is one of the most elegant towns in Greece thanks to its plethora of buildings from the 18th and 19th centuries. Under the Turkish rule of the mainland very little building took place and thus most Greek towns have little but modern concrete architecture. Corfu, however, was controlled by the Venetians, the French and the British in this same period, and they all undertook major building programmes. The result is a town whose main appeal is not its sights, which are interesting rather than unmissable, but its atmosphere seen most clearly in the Old Town.

This is a delightful place, more Italian than Greek, which alone makes a visit worthwhile. The buildings, the Venetian equivalent of high-rise tower blocks, are all very tall because, as the town was originally walled, space was very limited and any development had to be vertical rather than horizontal. In the middle of the Old Town, just next to the banks and the Catholic church, is an attractive building decorated with sculptures which is the **Town Hall**. Problems with builders are obviously both ancient and universal for although started in 1603 it took over 30 years to finish! Originally built as a club for merchants, a kind of 17th century Round Table, it became a theatre in 1720 and the Town Hall in 1902. One of the directors of this theatre, N. C. Mantzaros, was the composer of the Greek national anthem. The vandalized bust, on the side of the building, damaged many years ago, is of Admiral Morosini, an Italian who set out to conquer Greece from Corfu in 1687 and in the process blew up much of the Parthenon in Athens. The streets in the Old Town have no pavements and as you walk down them it is somewhat alarming to think that the Venetian nobles used to have horse races and jousting competitions here. Do not worry unduly about keeping track of where you are as you stroll round; everyone gets lost but the area is quite small and so you will eventually find out where you are.

The Old Town leads out onto the **Esplanade**, the largest square in all Greece. This was originally simply an open space in front of the fort left clear to provide a direct line of fire. Slowly, however, building developed around it. When the French controlled the island Ferdinand de Lesseps, the designer of the Suez Canal, built the row of houses facing the Esplanade (which now house the expensive cafés) as a replica of the Rue de Rivoli in Paris. Although it was of interest because it provided a covered walkway without diminishing the precious floor space of the rooms above, its main function, then as now, was as a place to see and be seen. It soon became known as the 'liston' after a list of local families deemed worthy to walk 'underneath the arches'. When the British arrived they levelled the area and used it as a parade ground, and more interestingly, a cricket pitch. It is the only pitch in Greece and it is sometimes possible for visitors to play (ask for information at the tourist office). A rough matting wicket is used and boundaries count as 3 and 5 not 4 and 6, but otherwise the game should be familiar. The greatest attraction of the Esplanade, however, is probably just as a place to sit, watch the world go by and write postcards home.

As you sit drinking your tea you look across to the **Old Fort**, which was the original site of the modern town. The Venetians built the fortress and over the course of 100 years turned it into an island by digging an enormous moat some 40 ft deep and between 80 and 120 ft wide. Most of the fortifications were blown up by the British when they left and the rest have now decayed, but you can still see the Church of St George. Built 1840 as the garrison church it is a strange Christian copy of a pagan temple that looks very out of place. Although the walls and tunnels of the fort are really only of interest to the military historian, they are still interesting to explore. The best view is from the landward hill, but you can also admire the scenery from a somewhat expensive café inside the walls. In the summer there is a sound and light show Mon to Fri at 9.45 p.m., with an English commentary which is preceded by Greek folk dancing at 9 p.m. The Old Fort is open 8 a.m. to 6 p.m., and then re-opens for the evening shows. The statue at the entrance is of Count Johann Schulenburg, an Austrian mercenary who helped defeat the Turks in the siege of 1716.

The phrase 'Old Fort' implies that there must be a 'New Fort', and this, imaginatively called the 'New Fort', is located on the north side of town, overlooking the mainland ferry port. This was built by the Venetians in 1576 to protect those citizens who lived outside the walls of the Old Fort from possible Turkish invasion. Although it is now used as a training centre by the Greek navy and is not fully open to the public, some interesting walks can be taken around parts of the walls. Probably its most interesting feature is a very good food market just on the other side which is well worth a visit, particularly early in the morning.

Back at the Esplanade, in the park alongside, is a legacy of the British colonial rule – the **Rotunda**, built as a memorial to Sir Thomas Maitland, a Scotsman who was the first Lord High Commissioner of the island. 'King Tom' as he was known after his somewhat flamboyant and dictatorial style, erected the monument as a memorial to himself! The most famous story told about him is that once, when faced with yet another person begging an official favour, his reply was to drop his trousers. Presumably he meant 'no'! It would probably amuse him to know that the bandstand nearby now seems to be used by one of the many local brass bands and the Communist party on alternate Sundays, but he would be less than happy at the statue of Count John Kapodistrias at the south end of the Esplanade. A Corfoite who was the first ruler of independent Greece, he was Maitland's greatest critic. Just opposite this statue is the shell of an 18th-century building, the **Ionian Academy**. Originally built as an army barracks, in 1824 Lord Guildford turned it into a kind of university. The noble lord was in the best tradition of English aristocrats, somewhat eccentric, and made all his students dress in togas coloured according to their subject. Contemporary opinions varied as to whether he was simply remarkable or remarkably simple, but it was Corfu and not Athens that led the revival of Greek literature in the 19th century. As you walk from here back down to the Esplanade you pass a narrow lane, Moustoxidou Street, which leads to the old Ionian Parliament building and, if you turn left, to the British Vice-Consulate. In the gardens opposite the cricket pitch, you can see a statue of Lord Guildford, suitably clad in a toga and reading an ancient text.

Dominating the Esplanade is the **Palace of St Michael and St George**, built by the British between 1818 and 1824 as the residence of the Lord High Commissioner and named after the newly founded ceremonial order which was based there. After the British left in 1864 the Palace became a holiday home for the Greek Royal Family until the outbreak of World War I. It then lay empty but after damage during World War II it was restored in 1954. The Palace was considered by some to be the finest building erected in Greece since ancient times and although the Malta limestone in which is was built has now lost its original beige colour and become a rather drab grey, it is still very imposing. Outside the palace is a statue to the second Commissioner, Sir Frederick Adams, who since he was the man responsible for bringing a fresh water supply to the town would probably be pleased to see his memorial sited in a pool. Above the main entrance you can see the sculptures representing the seven Ionian islands, but the large figure of Britannia which once dominated the building has long since been removed. The only way to visit the lavish interior of the Palace is to see the **Museum of Far Eastern Art** that it now houses. This private collection of jade, ivory, prints and porcelain may sound very dull, but it is so well labelled that even a novice should find it interesting. If nothing else the museum can provide a pleasant, cool stroll away from the sun and it is open 8.30 a.m. to 12.30 p.m., 4.30 p.m. to 6 p.m. every day, closed Tues.

To see Greek exhibits go to the **Archaeological Museum** below the Esplanade on 5 Vralia Street. For the expert this is a very good collection and for the layman it is still worth a quick visit. The most striking exhibit is the Gorgon pediment, a large 6th century BC work found near Mon Repos in 1912, which shows the mythical creature who could turn men to stone with a look. Under her wings are the children who sprang from her blood, including Pegasus, the winged horse. It is not clear whether the temple on which this was placed was dedicated to her, or whether she was simply used to scare away thieves, but whatever the explanation the carving is still quite frightening. In the room next door is a sculpture which, although on a much smaller scale, is also fairly intimidating. The Lion of Menekrates as it is known, was made in the 7th century BC and along with the pediment is the best-surviving example of work of this period. The archaeological museum is open at the same hours as the Palace museum.

Very near the Archaeological Museum is one of the best of the 39 churches in Corfu town, **St Jason and St Sosipatros**, two disciples of St Paul who brought Christianity to the island. The church is set in a very pretty small garden, but probably the most interesting thing about it is that one of the tombs, neither of which belong to the saints, is that of the wife of one of the despots who ruled the island: she tried to sell what was reputed to be the head of St Andrew.

Back in the town the main church of note is **St Spiridon**, the one with the red dome situated near the Ionian Bank in the Old Town. Although the belfry is still the tallest building on the island, the church itself is quite small, but it is the most important on Corfu because it houses the bones of St Spiridon, the patron saint of the island. St Spiridon was a 4th century AD bishop, famous for his faith, who actually came from Cyprus, and to understand why every other person on the island seems to be called after him you need to know something of his story. This simple shepherd boy who became a bishop was a remarkable man. Stopped by his enemies from getting on a ship to take him to an important meeting of the church at Nicea in AD 325, he simply ripped his cloak in two and, using one half as a raft and the other as a sail, arrived several days before his opponents!

Upon his death in AD 350 his relics were taken to Constantinople. In 1453 they were smuggled out of the city just before the Turks occupied it, hidden in a sack of straw and strapped to a mule. Thus in 1460 did his bones arrive in Corfu. He is reputed to have saved the island four times, twice from plague, once from the Turks and once from famine, and this is the reason why devotion to him is so strong. If you are politely sceptical about his exploits the locals will tell you that when the Venetians tried to place a Catholic altar in the church a large amount of gunpowder was struck by lightning in the Old Fort the night before the ceremony, and that when a bomb landed next to his tomb in World War II, it failed to explode. On the four days of the year when these miracles took place, Palm Sunday, Easter Sunday, 11 August and the first Sunday in November, his relics are paraded through the streets with great ceremony and people queue up to kiss his feet. For the rest of the year his relics are kept in a silver coffin in the small side chapel. Whilst in the church cast your eyes heavenwards and you will see a very impressive painted ceiling.

The other main church is the Orthodox **Cathedral of St Theodora**, situated near the main ferry port. She was a devout Empress of Byzantium whose relics were brought to the island from Constantinople along with St Spiridon. Even though she is not known to have occasioned such dramatic miracles she is still popular and her church makes a pleasant visit. On a narrow set of steps nearby is the **Church of St Nikolas** (just off Philharmonika Street). This was used by the Serbian army as their parish church in 1916 when they came to Corfu after their defeat by the larger German army. A large number of the troops died from plague and are buried on Volos Island, opposite the New Fort. This is very scenic and well worth a visit. Some people might also be interested in the **British Cemetery** which contains graves from the World Wars as well as the British Protectorate. Located on Kolokotroni Street, a few minutes' walk from Theotoki Square, it is very peaceful and well maintained.

Very unusually for Greece, Corfu has a large Roman Catholic population. The Venetians, being Italian, were of course Catholic, but they allowed marriages with the local Orthodox and any children, apart from the eldest son, were brought up as Orthodox. Surprisingly, therefore, the Roman Catholic population comes not from the Venetian occupation of the island but from the British, who introduced a large number of Maltese farmers to Corfu during their protectorate, and also from Italian craftsmen employed on the island in the late 19th century. A Roman Catholic Archbishop, one of only three in Greece, has his cathedral just next to the town hall, where you may walk into a wedding on a summer evening. At the west end of N. Theotoki Street is the **Church of St Francis**.

NIGHTLIFE

Corfu town is the best place on the island for dining out. It has dozens of restaurants offering foreign as well as Greek food. The most obvious place for a meal is the Esplanade, and although the cafés here are quite expensive by local standards they are still far cheaper than at home, the food is still quite good and the surroundings are very enjoyable as you can watch the world go by in the form of British, Italian, French, American and German tourists. The two best restaurants in this elegant row are the **Aegli** and the **Rex**. Opposite, adjacent to the Old Fort, is the **Acteon** with another very good location, but slightly less impressive food.

The main area for restaurants is around N. Theotoki Street near the centre of town. The **Edem** looks like a very bright burger bar, but despite this serves surprisingly good Greek food. Opposite is the **Gisdakis** with a similar standard of food in rather more traditional surroundings. At 150 N. Theotoki is the very large **To Nautikon** with quite a good choice of traditional dishes. Down Di Doni, an alley just opposite, is the **Dionysus**, with some of the best food in the area. Down another alley, Mariarita, just next door to 51 Theotoki Street, is the **Elefkimi** which, although small, with very little choice and slow service, does have good food. Just past the Hotel Criti is **Makis Grill**. At 31 Sebastian Street, just off Theotoki Street, is the **Krysi Kardia**, and on Taxiarhon is **Kostas**. Not all the good restaurants are in the Old Town area, however, and in the Old Port, overlooking the sea on 4 Alipou Street, is the **Averof**, very popular but slightly expensive. Cheaper is the nearby **Taverna Ellas**.

If either your taste buds or your stomach want a break from Greek food do not despair, there are two very good Italian restaurants in the town. On Skaramanga Square, just behind the Commercial Bank, is the **Bella Napoli** with a wide choice of good food. For a meal with a view try **Pizza Pete** on the coast road overlooking Volos Island at 19 Arseniou. There are several restaurants here, but this is probably the best. The breakfasts and the ice creams, as well as the evening menus are all very good, and though at night it is too dark to see the view, you can watch the waiters trying to dodge the traffic as they run across the road from the kitchens.

Your choice of non-Greek food is not simply confined to pizza and spaghetti. Situated on the beach at 120 Kapodistriou and well signposted on the road leading down behind the Palace, is the **Faliraki** which serves excellent Chinese food, and at the top of Philharmonika Street is the **Crepi Asterix** which has a wide choice of these delicious French pancakes. Another good, if slightly expensive restaurant, is **Xenihtis**, at 12 Potamou Street, confusingly advertised as 'a Normandy restaurant with that Scandinavian touch'.

If you want a snack take advantage of the cheap and tasty offerings in the downtown snack bars. Souvlakis in pitta or cheese and spinach pies will cost around 125 dr.

If you are prepared to travel, the **Orestes** at Mandouki in the suburbs of the town, and **Gerakos** in Kontokali are both very good fish restaurants. About 12 miles away in Kinopiastes is the **Taverna Tripa** which has excellent Greek food served complete with very Greek entertainment.

If there is a large number of restaurants in Corfu town there is an even larger number of bars. Everyone has different tastes, but among the most popular are the **Black and White** at the Palace end of the Esplanade, and the **Mermaid Tavern** on Ag Panton Street.

In respect for the quieter members of the community the town's discos are situated some 20 minutes north from the centre. The **Playboy** and **La Boom** seem to be the most lively, but this changes every year and the **Bora Bora** and the **Apocalypse** would disagree. If you would prefer bouzoukis to disco lights, continue along this same road north to Alikos where you will find **Espendes**, or carry on to the **Corfu By Night** at Gouvia. Both will encourage you to fling away your inhibitions with their plates, but remember that at the end of the night someone has to pay for them – you!

There are also several cinemas in Corfu town, of which the **Pallas** on G. Theotoki Street usually has the widest choice of imported English language films. Greek films are something of an acquired taste, but watching the latest American blockbuster in an open-air cinema is an amusing experience.

EXCURSIONS

Many excursions are possible from Corfu town because it is the centre of all the island's communications. If you want to drop a really impressive line over the hotel dinner table the air service is sufficiently good to enable you to take a day-trip to Athens or any of the major islands, details of which will be available from the local travel agents. Fortunately, however, most excursions are considerably less expensive and exhausting than this.

The most popular is to **MON REPOS**, a palace set in beautiful grounds some 2 miles from the town. This scenic spot was first discovered by a Russian general, but in 1824 the British, seeking a summer residence for the Commissioner away from the heat and noise of Corfu town, knocked down the small summer house which he had built and erected Mon Repos. Sir Frederick Adams, who was married to a Corfoite woman and who had a beard which was apparently the envy of many an army officer, was the Commissioner at the time and the Palace soon became known as 'Sir Frederick's Folly'. After the British left, the folly was taken over by the Greek Royal family, and it was here that the Duke of Edinburgh was born in 1921. Nearby is **ANALIPSI**, the site of the 8th century BC Corinthian colony which was the original settlement on the island. A small path leads to a fountain, now surmounted by a Venetian lion, which once fed a 6th century BC Greek temple. British ships used to collect fresh water from here and in 1822, whilst digging to discover why the spring had dried up, a naval captain discovered this temple of Kardaki by accident. Local tradition states that any foreigner who drinks here will never return to his native land. Mon Repos itself has a beautiful setting, but you cannot see inside for, despite the abolition of the Greek monarchy some years ago, the Palace still remains closed to the public. The most convenient beach for the town is situated here, but since it is not very good and is always very crowded, it is far wiser to travel out to one of the other resorts to bathe in the sun or the sea. The easiest to reach from the town are those along the east coast such as **GOUVIA**, or for particularly good watersports **IPSOS** and **DASSIA**. The best beaches on the island, however, are on the west coast, and for the sun-worshipper at least these are well worth the small amount of extra travelling. These resorts are **GLYFADA, AG GORDIS, ERMONES, MORITIOTISSA** and **PALEOKASTRITSA**. For those who want to stay in the town itself there are another two beaches apart from the one at Mon Repos. Just behind the Palace of St Michael and St George back on the Esplanade is a steep road called Kapodistrou Street. Just opposite the Faliraki Restaurant at 110 is a small lido. Although there is no beach, just steps leading down to the sea, it is possible to swim here safely if not in wonderful surroundings. The other beach is at **KANONI**, just below the Hilton Hotel, reached either by walking round the bay or taking the number 2 bus from the Esplanade. This is quite a good beach, but it is small and gets very crowded.

Those who get bored lying on the beach all day, or those who have done so too much and now need to shade their sunburn, should consider making a few excursions. The historian will find no great archaeological sights, but a reconstruction of an 18th-century Greek village has been built at **DANILIA** (see page 485). This might sound a bit dull, but there are lots of activities for children during the day and entertainment for parents at night. To get there take bus number 4 from Theotoki Square.

If the 'village' is typically Greek, nothing could be in greater contrast than the **Achilleon Palace**, a wedding cake-type mansion set in a very beautiful location and well worth a visit.

Corfu is famous for its scenic views and the two places most often seen on postcards home are **PALEOKASTRITSA** and **MOUSE ISLAND**. Both are, regrettably if understandably, crowded but their beauty still remains. To get to Paleokastritsa take the bus from New Fortress Square and to reach Mouse Island either walk round the bay or take bus number 2 from the Esplanade. The views of the sunset from the Greek islands are justifiably famed, and for the best view of this on Corfu, or at least the most popular, head for **PELEKAS**, bus number 11 from Theotoki Square.

You do not have to limit your excursions to the island of Corfu itself, for since all the ferries call at Corfu town you can indulge in the popular Greek pastime of island hopping. Many of the tour operators and nearly all the travel agents offer special tours to the nearby Ionian islands such as **PAXOS**, but it is also possible to reach these simply on the normal ferry. You could also go across to the mainland, only 1½ hours away, but be warned that the port you land at, Igoumenitsa, is not very interesting apart from a reasonable beach and a few restaurants. However, the roads in the area are quite good and if you hire a car you could make some day-trips which would enable you to feel that you have seen a bit more of Greece than just the discos of Corfu. As you travel east from Igoumenitsa you come to ZITSA, where they make the Greek equivalent of champagne, IOANNINA, a city set on a lake which was the capital of the country under Turkish rule, and DODONI, supposedly the oldest oracle in Greece with probably the best amphitheatre in the country. You can also travel to PARGA, a beautiful medieval town with super beaches.

If you do decide to visit the mainland and explore a little by car, the trip becomes much less worrying and far more enjoyable if you spend a few days doing it rather than trying to rush round everything in the one day.

The North-east Coast

This section covers the area north-east of Corfu town as far as Kassiopi, and includes Kontokali, Gouvia, Dassia, Ipsos and Nisaki. This is the most developed coast on the island, most suitable for Socialites, because of its nightlife, and Families because of its hotels. Sporting types can also enjoy the best watersports on the island at Dassia and Ipsos, but ironically the beaches here are nearly all small and narrow and the Sun-worshipper will be much better off on the west coast.

Some of the resorts in the area are large and crowded and can look something like a builder's yard, but this coast is probably unmatched in the whole of Greece in the tourist facilities that it offers, and the natural beauty of the island, particularly the views, still remains. Once they arrive most people are quite content to stay in their resort for their entire holiday, but a good main road and an adequate bus service (number 7, about every hour from 7 a.m. to 10 p.m.), makes it possible to travel round quite a lot should you so wish. Needless to say this is not the place for the Recluse to get away from it all, but

Families, Socialites and Healthy-holiday types should all be able to find resorts ideal for their type of holiday.

Just outside of Corfu town and more of a suburb than a resort is **ALIKES POTAMOU**. This is of interest simply because of the **Kerkira Golf Hotel**, used by several of the tour operators. For details see the section headed 'Corfu town'.

KONTOKALI

The first proper resort on this coast is Kontokali, about 15 minutes from Corfu town, where although its proximity to Gouvia and the building of a large marina nearby have made it a lively resort, its small size means that it is still possible to get some sleep at night. With all the facilities at Gouvia, Ipsos and Dassia so near, and Corfu town just around the bay, Kontokali is ideal for the quieter socialite. A tourist office has been opened here for the benefit of those who arrive by yacht, but it should be of use to everyone.

The best hotel, used by over ten holiday companies, is the **Kontokali Palace** (Tel: 38736), a large development, ideal for families, two private man-made beaches and the added bonus of a charming view. In the centre of the resort the **Telesilla** (Tel: 91275), only ten minutes from the beach, provides good, clean but rather more simple accommodation that would be ideal for young singles.

Independent travellers will find a **Youth Hostel** here, just next to the bus stop. Its beach setting sounds idyllic, but the reality is a bit drab and usually very crowded. For those equipped with something to lie on, a much better bet would be **International Camping** nearby (Tel: 91202).

Kontokali's nightlife is becoming increasingly active. Two popular restaurants are the **Fish Taverna** and the **Cozy**. Should you be missing home too much the **Intermezzo**, about 300 yards past the Kontokali Palace, serves traditional British dishes like liver and onions. The **Mandarin Palace** is a very good Chinese restaurant with a varied menu, situated on the main road just outside the village, which also serves breakfasts and is open 8.30 a.m. to 2 a.m. Back in the resort **Spiti Priftis** makes a good place for a drink. With Gouvia literally only a short walk away and Corfu town only a few minutes on the bus, those after a wider choice of nightlife should not have to exert themselves too much to find it. Corfu town (much nicer than any of the north-east coast resorts) is so near that you could well regard it as your base for excursions (see page 468 for details). A little careful checking of bus times should also enable you to explore inland and the northern coast.

GOUVIA

Gouvia, about 20 minutes north-east of Corfu town, is not one of the island's most elegant resorts, but it does have a very scenic location overlooking a beautiful bay, good beaches, and many very good hotels. It has long been a popular place for British family holidays and deservedly so. Over the past few years, however, the social life of the resort has become increasingly active, partly because tour operators have begun to offer it as a place for the young and single, and partly because a large marina has been built nearby which brings in many wealthy visitors. The appeal of Gouvia as a simple beach resort for family holidays is still strong, but it is a particularly good choice for Mums and Dads who want a good time for themselves as well as the children, or for the socialite who wants a proper beach on which to nurse his hangover rather than a narrow strip of sand. Gouvia's proximity to Corfu town and its regular bus service also make it a good base for excursions and thus a good choice for those who want a good beach but get bored lying on it all day.

Of the many good hotels in the resort the best is undoubtedly the **Corcyra Beach** (Tel: 30770), a large development with some bungalow accommodation surrounded by pleasant gardens and a large pool. This would be particularly suitable for sporting types, or for those who do not enjoy lying on the beach for long periods, since it offers not merely the usual selection of watersports, but also tennis, squash and even horse riding. Young couples and families should consider the **Angela** or the **Artemis**, two new modest-grade hotels, both only ten minutes away from the beach, which allow the children to exhaust themselves during the day and provide parents with a fairly lively time at night. Equally suitable for young families, but quieter and thus quite popular with retired couples, is the **Park** (Tel: 91310). If the idea of sharing a hotel with anyone over the age of 30 horrifies you, the **Sunflower** (Tel: 91355) or the **Galaxias** (Tel: 91220) would be better choices, the Galaxias being a particularly lively hotel, very popular with people who could never be described as retiring! If, however, you simply want a hotel to use as a base, not as the centre for all your activities, consider the **Louvre**, a good, clean hotel 5 minutes from the beach which is also pleasingly cheap.

The main sight of Gouvia is the beach, which offers a good choice of watersports. Apart from this there is little of great interest in the resort and probably the most interesting sight is the Marina, situated across the bay opposite the beach. A leisurely stroll round this provides an enjoyable opportunity to see how the other half lives and to appreciate their problems: finding a mooring for your yacht during the summer is apparently even harder than finding a parking place for the car on a Saturday afternoon! A more 'traditional' sight is the old **Venetian Arsenal**, where ships were once repaired, situated just outside the resort along a minor road at the end of the first part of the bay. Although the roof disappeared years ago and the remains are not very interesting, the view does make the hike up here worthwhile as you try to imagine the scene some 250 years ago when the French fleet hid from Nelson in this bay.

If you want a change from the food at your hotel one evening and no one has invited you to dinner on their yacht, Gouvia is well supplied with good places to eat. Presumably the locals know the best restaurant, so follow their example and eat at the **Taverna Pipilas**, well known for its fish dishes. This is one of the few places in all Greece, let alone Gouvia, where you will see Greeks as well as tourists eating. If you want your meal to be a memorable evening rather than just a dinner, the **Taverna Fillipas** serves food to the accompaniment of lively Greek music and even livelier Greek dancing.

After a meal there is no shortage of places to go. If you are too full to make witty conversation, or are too exhausted after the Greek dancing, the videos at **Rumours** and **Whispers** might offer a comfortable relaxation, though both get fairly lively during the evening so do not expect to follow the dialogue too closely. Gouvia is very much a British resort and as their names suggest **the Greedy Monkey** and the **Old Barrel** both tend to attract lots of the British contingent. Slightly more Greek is the **Abracadabra**, but if you are really missing your local, do not despair, but head for the tacky **Tudor Inn**, an English pub designed in stockbroker Tudor, incongruously set in the middle of a Greek island. Among Gouvia's discos the **Station** and the **Adonis** are probably the best. The Adonis tends to be the most lively, though presumably this has more to do with the fact that it plays good music rather than its being Corfu's only underground disco.

If you are not one of those people who spend their holiday going from beach to disco and back again, you will be glad to know that because of its good location many excursions can be made from Gouvia. As in any place, at home or abroad, having a car is very convenient, but it is very expensive in Greece and the bus service is sufficiently good to enable you to travel fairly widely using just public transport.

EXCURSIONS

Corfu town is only 5 miles away and this is a most popular excursion from any resort, as well as being a popular resort town in its own right. During the day its attraction is not so much its sights, but rather its elegant atmosphere, while at night it offers a wide choice of bars and discos that can make welcome relief from those in the resort, though be warned that a sophisticated evening on the town can be somewhat marred by the desperate squeeze onto the last bus! During the day, after a 20-minute bus ride you have the choice of all the excursions listed on page 479 as possible from Corfu town. The most obvious trip to make here is to DANILIA VILLAGE (but there is no regular bus) a reconstruction of a Greek village 200 years ago which is only a mile away. This might sound less than inspiring, but there is lots for the children to do during the day and a considerable amount for parents in the evening. It is intriguing to note that simple Greek villages contained very expensive jewellery and fur shops over 200 years ago! You may recognize the church from the Bond film, *For Your Eyes Only*, for this is where the wedding scene was filmed. Gouvia lies on the road to the picture-postcard resort of PALEOKAS-TRITSA. If you would enjoy particularly good watersports head up the coast a few miles to DASSIA, though almost the same facilities are offered at Gouvia itself and the beach is much better. On the way north you pass through KOMMENO, a quieter resort that might prove interesting for a change of scene one evening. If you begin to yearn for a bit of solitude, the east coast resorts are not the place to find it, so either head inland or for the north coast, though be careful to check the bus times for the return trip, as walking along a Greek road at 1 a.m. is no fun.

KOMMENO

Your first reaction on arriving in Kommeno will probably be 'have I arrived?' for this is one of those strange, rather bland resorts without any real centre, situated along the main road. It must be admitted that Kommeno is not one of Corfu's most enchanting or exciting resorts, but that does not mean that all is gloom and despondency for it does have three major attractions. Firstly, Kommeno Bay is a heavily wooded inlet whose forested hills provide a very good view out to sea and indeed look very beautiful from the water themselves. Secondly, the hotels in the resort are very good, and thirdly, the resort's location means that the excellent beach at Gouvia, and the watersports at Dassia and Ipsos are only 10 minutes away during the day whilst in the evening, an excellent choice of nightlife lies in Corfu town, only 20 minutes away by bus. Thus Kommeno is actually quite a pleasant, quiet resort ideal for those who want a comfortable hotel with good facilities but who do not wish either to be swamped by too many people or be too isolated.

The **Astir Palace** (Tel: 91340), a little way out of the village, is one of the best hotels on the whole island. Its excellent facilities, including that so-sensible but so rare design idea of a soundproofed disco, make it very suitable for couples and very popular with the tour operators. A better choice for families is the **Radovas** (Tel: 91218), with a large garden and a pool some 5 minutes from the beach. For the independent traveller, **Dionysius Camping**, just opposite the bus stop, is a fairly luxurious campsite with good showers, a shop and a disco.

This disco is one of several in Kommeno, but in the evenings most people travel to Gouvia, Dassia or Corfu town for their entertainment, though the **Piano Bar** and the **Mimosa Restaurant** are both worth a look. The simple Greek restaurants in the area are all very convenient and very popular for a nightcap after the last bus has taken you home, or for a pleasant breakfast in the morning.

A fairly good range of excursions can be taken from here (see 'Corfu town' for details). A reasonable range of watersports is available on the beach, but as mentioned above a better choice will be found at Gouvia and Dassia.

DASSIA

Over two dozen companies offer holidays in Dassia, some 40 minutes from Corfu town, and it is probably the most popular resort on the island for family holidays, mainly because the brochures sell it as such but also because it has excellent hotels and a safe beach. Apart from its appeal to families Dassia is also well known as an excellent watersports centre, and some, mainly the local reps, maintain that it is among the best in Europe. The sporting types and the mainly young parents who come here make a very active nightlife, meaning that Dassia is an ideal resort for sporting socialites with young families!

Practical Details

ACCOMMODATION

The best hotel of the bay, on the south coast is the **Castello**, a beautiful 19th-century copy of a 14th-century mansion which is now run as a very expensive and very exclusive hotel. If you have the money this represents a very enjoyable way to spend it. More in the realms of reality for the rest of us the **Corfu Chandris** (Tel: 338171), and the **Dassia Chandris** (Tel: 338171) are two sister hotels with excellent facilities and surroundings that are justifiably the most popular places for families to stay. The beach behind the Chandris is the best beach in Dassia. In a more elegant, but similar style, and ideal for those wanting a very comfortable hotel is the **Morgarona Palace** (Tel: 24360) situated off the main road some 10 minutes from the beach. Easily one of Corfu's finest deluxe hotels the **Elea Beach** (Tel: 93490) is a good hotel for those wanting a quieter holiday, although facilities are limited, whilst the B-grade **Amalia** (Tel: 93520) is popular with young singles.

Independent travellers will be extremely fortunate if they manage to find an empty room in any of the hotels in the season, and if they do the prices will be exorbitant. They will probably have no other choice than **Karda Camping** off the main road (Tel: 93595), but even this may be full so it would be worth phoning ahead from Corfu town to find out.

SIGHTS

Dassia's main selling point in the brochures is the beach. The brochures are accurate in describing it as long and backed by trees, *but* they fail to mention that it is very narrow and gets very crowded during the season. Thus choosing a hotel with a pool when booking, saves you having to pretend that you are a guest at one when you get fed up feeling like a sausage crammed under the grill on the beach.

If all this sounds very negative it must be said that the beach does offer very safe, warm swimming and a huge range of watersports, such as paragliding and water skiing. Hiring a motor boat is quite expensive but it is a very good way of seeing the coast, and this is also one of the few places on the island where you can hire good sailing dinghies, including very fast catamarans. Be warned that however keen you may be, the local children will always be, infuriatingly, very much better than you will ever be!

NIGHTLIFE

If you manage to avoid being run over by all the speed-boats, water-skiers and windsurfers, or you are simply exhausted by your own activities on the water during the day, there are many places where you can spend a very pleasant evening. Among the most lively bars are the **Woodpecker**, the **Drunken Duck** and the **Tartaya**. For those that have any energy left **La Mirage** and the **Attalayn** are both discos that stay open long after any sensible person has gone to bed.

EXCURSIONS

Yet more nightlife is available just around the bay at IPSOS, but the most important excursion is to Corfu town. Instead of taking the bus, however, take the boat (800 dr with an early return) and see the coast from the sea.

IPSOS

Ipsos is a very popular resort used by over 25 holiday companies and some 45 minutes from Corfu town. All the brochures emphasize two things, the watersports and the nightlife. The beach here is shingle and although very long it is, like Dassia, very narrow. Since its appeal to families is thus fairly limited a concerted effort has been made to develop it as a watersports centre, and the wide range of activities now available show how well this has succeeded. The people attracted by such facilities tend to be young singles rather than families and to give them something to do in the evening, after they have spent all day falling off windsurfers and water skis, a very lively social scene has developed. Ipsos is therefore a resort for the young and active. The nightlife is considerable, but do not look for a developed 'centre', for like many other places on the island Ipsos is simply a collection of bars, cafés and hotels stretched out alongside the beach road. Just slightly along the road is PYRGI, which is technically another resort but is so small that brochures treat it as part of Ipsos.

Among the many hotels the **Ipsos Beach** (Tel: 93232) in a quiet location about 5 minutes from the beach, is probably the most comfortable for couples. In the centre of the resort the **Platanos** is clean and offers good views at a price ideal for those on a budget. Ipsos is, however, predominantly a resort for the young and the most suitable hotels for them are **Costas** (Tel: 93205) and the very inappropriately named **Hotel Mega** (Tel: 93208). Those travelling with a rucksack on their back will find two good campsites, **Corfu Camping** (Tel: 93244), and the probably slightly better, **Camping Paradise**.

Once you have arrived in Ipsos your greatest decision during the day will probably be deciding what sport to try. Apart from the usual choice Ipsos also offers a rather exciting activity, though probably one which you may already have tried at home, water-chutes. Located next to Michael's Cocktail Bar their very name, the Megaslides, suggest the type of people who go on them! Also worth a try are the waterbikes, supposedly like riding a motorbike on a very wet road, but falling off is much more comfortable than when on dry land.

If your stomach should need settling after all this activity there are a number of unexciting restaurants in Ipsos. Among the most popular are the **Albatross, Zambella's**, the expensive but good **Parrotts**, and for somewhere slightly more Greek, the **Avenita**. There are also many bars where you can nurse, or gain, a bruised head. Apart from **Michael's Cocktail Bar** mentioned above there is the **Pig and Whistle**, the **Coach House, Russel's Butterfly Bar** and the wonderfully named **Hector's House**. Those who want to be supple for the next day's activities, or are gluttons for punishment, could then go onto the two best discos, **Moons** or the **Albatross**.

EXCURSIONS

Most people who come to Ipsos tend to stay here for most of their holiday, but should you wish for a change of scene a wide range of excursions is possible. The easiest is simply to walk around the bay to Dassia, but although this offers a wider choice of nightlife it is very similar to Ipsos itself. Probably more interesting would be a walk up the hills nearby to enjoy the view over the bay. This is a particularly good area for views, in fact. The old village of AGHIOS MARKOS is especially worth a visit for its magnificent vantage point as is SPARTILAS. If you have hired a car, or are prepared to risk life and limb on a moped, you could drive up through Strinillas to **Mt Pantokrator**, Corfu's highest mountain at 2,794 ft. Although somewhat marred by a television mast it still offers a magnificent view across to Albania, the Greek mainland, Corfu itself, and further south, the other Ionian islands. On exceptionally clear days you are even supposed to be able to see Italy.

If you seek not excellent scenery but simply a better beach to lie on, BARBATI is a good bet. This has an excellent mile long pebble beach and is itself beginning to be developed as a base for simple apartment holidays.

NISAKI

Nisaki is a small, simple resort about 16 miles from Corfu town. Its main, indeed almost its only attraction is the

Nisaki Beach hotel (Tel: 91232). This is a large development suitable for all holiday types but particularly good for families, located in a slightly isolated position with its own private beach. It provides a very comfortable base for those who want a simple sun and sea holiday on an excellent beach. But be warned that apart from the hotel there is very little to do. Car hire would be a good idea if you were staying here, and if you wanted to take a break from the beach the drive to the pretty village of KOULOURA offers some wonderful views and could take you on to exploring the north coast. Those visiting Nisaki will find two good beaches, but be warned that the path down to them is very steep, or at least seems it on the way back up.

KASSIOPI

Kassiopi, about 23 miles north of Corfu town, was, ten years ago, a simple fishing village. Its small port is still a working harbour, just, but it is now rather dominated by the number of bars, cafés and restaurants that surround it. Nearly all the accommodation the travel companies offer here is in villas rather than hotels, and the resort is therefore full of young people rather than families and has as lively a nightlife as the brochures suggest. It is not one of the most beautiful resorts and its main beach is some 15 minutes away from the centre, but if you are after a good fun time in hot weather, this is probably the resort for you.

The most important feature of Kassiopi is its nightlife. Among the many restaurants are the **Kassiopi Star** and the **Taverna Imerdia Beach**. Of the many bars the most popular are **Illusions**, **Davids**, the **Wave**, the **Pirate Bar** and **Angevines**, and the most lively discos seem to be the **Kassiopi by Night** and the **Just S**. With such a wide range of things to do in the evening it would probably amuse all those who enjoy holiday romances to know that Casanova once visited here, as did Antony and Cleopatra. A 15-minute walk back along the road to Corfu town lies the **Kan Kan Bouzaki Club**, offering what its name suggests.

Much less impressive than the resort's choice of entertainment is the choice of beaches. Although there are in fact four, they are all small and a wiser choice for those wanting a good beach would be to go to AGHIOS SPIRIDON nearby.

If the resort's beaches leave something to the imagination the same cannot be said of its history, for it is one of the few tourist centres on the island which has any, though admittedly this is very hard to tell today. Founded in 300 BC in Roman times there was a large town here, inhabited by thousands. Nero once visited, and historians disagree as to whether he came simply to dance at a local temple, or as one contemporary believed, as the start of a theatrical 'World Tour' of his empire.

Kassiopi's position on the north-east coast has meant that it has always been of strategic importance and when the Norman, Robert Guiscard, tried to invade the island in the 12th century, it was here that he attacked first. To prevent such an attack succeeding a castle had been built in the 10th century, and you can still walk up and see its ruins. It was destroyed not by gun fire or by the ravages of time, but by the Venetians in the 14th century in order to prevent further rebellion by the town after it had refused to surrender to them.

A church was built in 1537 on what may have been the site of Nero's temple. It contains a well-known icon called the *Panayi Kassiopi* which was donated by a famous painter in gratitude for his having been saved from a shipwreck. Ever since then sailors have prayed to it for a safe passage and so strong was their devotion that all ships used to fire a salute to the Blessed Virgin when passing. This custom was sufficiently strong that a Venetian captain fired a salute even when it warned a waiting Turkish fleet of his approach. Perhaps it was in return for this sign of devotion that despite the lack of surprise to his attack he still defeated the Turks. The icon is not the only interesting story about the church. In 1530 a boy was falsely accused of stealing some flour. Since Roman law was then in operation he was faced with the unpleasant choice of having his eyes gouged out or his hands cut off. He chose to lose his sight and after wandering round the island for some time, he fell asleep in the church. In the morning he awoke to find his sight restored and ever since an icon in memory of his miracle has been prayed to by all those with eye problems. Another icon was reputed to tell whether an absent friend was dead or alive. A coin was held up to the picture and if the person was alive it stuck there, if he was dead, it dropped off. Common sense suggests that a lot of people must have thought that many of their friends were dead because of this, and as many cynical contemporaries pointed out, either way the priest ended up with the money.

EXCURSIONS

Few people who come to Kassiopi ever bother leaving it before the end of their holiday. Since the buses are infrequent this is understandable, but as long as you are prepared to get up early, or of course hire a car, you can still get round quite a lot of the northern coast as well as Corfu town. A boat trip along the cliffs to NISAKI, or along the north coast to AGHIOS SPIRIDON, should be a particularly enjoyable and leisurely way of seeing the island from an unusual point of view.

Kassiopi is the nearest point to Albania on Corfu, and if you are interested in taking as close a look as possible visit the small village of AGHIOS STEFANOS, set in a beautiful bay a few miles down the coast. Albania looks quite deserted from here, but anyone who enters Albanian waters, either accidentally or out of curiosity, will be picked up by the military, an experience that does tend to mar your holiday. Just a few miles further south along the coast lie KALAMI and KOULOURA, two small villages with good beaches and pleasant little harbours. The Durrell family lived in Kouloura for some years and Lawrence wrote *Prospero's Cell* and Gerald *My Family and other Animals* here. There is a delightful little fish taverna in Kouloura overlooking the tiny harbour. It's very cheap and very good. Just along from Kouloura is the tiny village of AGNISTINI where the single beaches remain quiet even in peak season.

The North Coast

This section covers the north coast from Acharavi to Sidari and takes in Platonas and Roda along the way.

This is mainly an area for simple family holidays at unsophisticated resorts with excellent beaches, but with many deserted coves along the road from Kassiopi to Sidari it should also be considered by the Sun-worshipper and the Recluse. As with the rest of the island, building is beginning to take place, but the north coast is still as undeveloped, if not always as quiet and uncrowded, as the brochures suggest. It contains what some people consider to be the best scenery on the island, particularly inland, but to explore it you must hire a car for the bus service this far north is very limited. Apart from the car, or moped, the most important thing is a good map for the roads here are poorly signposted and without a map you will find yourself doing the classic 'British abroad' trick of shouting more and more loudly at the locals in an attempt to make them understand your request for directions.

ACHARAVI

This is a small resort halfway between Kassiopi and Roda, ideal for Sun-worshippers. Its only attraction is a huge sandy beach about 2 miles long whose shallow waters offer particularly safe bathing for children. This is not the place for the recluse for by midday it gets quite crowded with day-trippers from other resorts seeking good beaches.

The number of these people make it easy to think that Acharavi is a fairly lively place, but in the evening it becomes clear that, despite the development that is beginning to take place, this is a very small resort. It contains two reasonable hotels, the B-graded **Ionian Princess** (Tel: 31410), and the **Acharavi Beach** as well as two good bars, **Skandros** and the **Barn**, a few shops and as yet very little else.

About half a mile inland lies the small Greek village from which this 'new town' resort took its name. Just around the bay is **Aghios Spiridon**, sometimes counted as part of the resort of Acharavi in some of the brochures. The sandy beach here is very small, only about 5 minutes' walk from end to end, but as the water is only a few inches deep even several hundred yards out it offers excellent bathing for little ones. Here you can see a small church dedicated to St Spiridon, Corfu's patron saint, and explore the channel leading to ANTINIOTI LAGOON, a small lake where you can sometimes see large flocks of birds that is very popular with duck hunters during the winter. The beach is one of the few on the island used by the Corfoites, and so at weekends it can become very crowded.

Most people who come to Acharavi want to do nothing but flop on the beach for a week or two, but should you wish to explore, the almost deserted village of PERITHIA, on the northern slopes of Mt Pantokrator, makes an interesting excursion and allows you to explore the many interesting coves along the way. Heading in the opposite direction you come to the pleasant town of KAROUSSADES, and at ASTRAKERI there is a reasonable but rather crowded beach.

RODA

Roda is a small resort at the top of the island, about 1½ hours from Corfu town, ideal for families where the children want a good beach and parents want to be quiet without being totally bereft of entertainment. The popularity of Roda, for over ten travel companies offer holidays here, is explained not by its excellent beach, but by the strong family appeal of the rather scruffy **Roda Beach** hotel (Tel: 31225). Aside from this the resort has very little to offer, even the watersports are fairly limited, and there is very little nightlife, so if you do not like the idea of a large hotel filled with young British families, you would be well advised to head somewhere else. There are other hotels in the resort, however, such as the **Silver Beach** (Tel: 31388), a former Hogg Robinson 'Best Small Hotel' and an ideal base for young singles, with a pool and excellent views, and situated near the beach. Roda also has one of the best campsites on the island, **Roda Camping** (Tel: 93120), which even has a pool.

Caiques, a much more enjoyable mode of transport than the bus, can provide a good day excursion by taking you to one of the other resorts along the coast.

Just inland from Roda is PLATONAS. Here there is very little but the extremely isolated hotel, the **Platonas Beach**. Surprisingly this is a very lively and popular choice for young singles, but with only four buses a day either you spend all your time on the beach or you hire some form of transport.

SIDARI

The major resort on the northern coast is Sidari, where an excellent beach and a very lively, though unpretentious, nightlife make an ideal resort for relaxed family holidays. The main beach is huge and should appeal to the Sun-worshipper, but be warned that this is very much a resort for young British families staying in simple hotels, so do not come here expecting total solitude or great luxury. The road from here to Corfu town is new and good to drive.

Most of the accommodation is simple, clean and above all, near the beach. The **Aphrodite**, the **Astoria** (Tel: 31315) and the lively **Three Brothers** (Tel: 31242) are good for young couples, and the **Mimosa**

(Tel: 31363) would suit singles wanting a good cheap base and comes complete with a nightly disco. Probably the most comfortable hotel is the **Sidari Beach** (Tel: 95215/6) small and quiet, but isolated, some 20 minutes from Sidari itself.

The beach is enormous, and is probably as good as the brochures suggest. Even 100 yards out the sea is only waist deep and thus the bathing, warm and safe, is ideal for children, though on the beach itself you will have to walk some way to escape the crowds. Some parts of the beach are broken up into little coves by outcrops of sandstone rock, themselves quite pretty, but most popular simply as places to jump off. The most famous of these is the **Canal d'Amour**, a small channel through the rock worn by the sea about 15 minutes along the beach. Tradition states that anyone who swims through here will marry the person they are thinking of, though ironically for once it is the tourists who take this seriously and the locals who are sceptical. The more adventurous members of the family who are not spending all their time swimming through this could try some of the water sports available from the pontoons moored in the deeper water.

The resort has no real centre and most of the nightlife is scattered along the main street. The **Oasis,** and a little way of town, the **Sophocles** are popular places to eat. **Legends,** the **Three Brothers, Renezzos** and the **Canal d'Amour** are all relaxed if lively discos where you can work off all the olive oil.

EXCURSIONS

One of the most popular excursions is a boat trip to the three small islands of OTHONI, ERIKOUSSA and MATHRAKI off the north-west coast. All three are very quiet, and once you have arrived there is very little to do but swim in the port and snack in one of the tavernas, but this is a very enjoyable way of spending a holiday. Of the three Erikoussa, although still quiet, is beginning to be developed a little. Those with a fertile imagination might muse over Othoni, traditionally the place where Odysseus idled away many years with an attractive nymph called Calypso. Caiques also go to the other beaches along the coast like Acharavi, but these get fairly crowded by midday.

Inland, the two small villages of MAGOULADES and KINADADES are worth a visit. Nearer to Sidari on the north-west tip of the island is

PEROULADES, a tiny village with a good beach which is very shaded in the afternoon, but is hard to get to. The drive to Corfu town goes through some particularly beautiful scenery and is worth making *before* you catch the coach back to the airport at the end of the holiday.

The West Coast

This section covers the west coast from Aghios Stefanos to Aghios Georgios, including Arillas, Aghios Georgeous, Paleokastritsa, Ermones, Glyfada, Yaliscari and Aghios Gordis.

The west coast contains some of the best beaches on the island, notably **Aghios Georgeous**, **Mirtiotissa**, **Glyfada**, **Aghios Gordis** and **Ag Georgios** (every other resort on this coast seems to be called Aghios Georgios or something similar so look at a map to check that you are reading about the right one!). The north-west coast contains some of the most beautiful scenery in Greece, particularly inland, and its excellent hotels make it ideal for those who want a quiet, comfortable beach holiday in pleasant surroundings. The south-west coast is probably the quietest part of the whole island, and although not as deserted as it once was it would be a good choice for the recluse.

AGHIOS STEFANOS

This is a quiet, undeveloped resort in the extreme north-west of the island. Over ten tour operators now offer it as a place for quiet beach holidays so it is less deserted than it once was, but it still represents a good base for those who simply want a gentle time in the sun. Most people stay in rooms but there are two plain hotels, the **Nafsika** and the **San Stefanos**.

The main attraction of the resort is the beach, so large that some people even drive on it, which has a reasonable selection of watersports. In season it can become quite crowded with day trippers from around the island, but the further north you walk the more deserted it becomes.

The green hills above the bay look very scenic from the beach and the enjoyable walk up them is rewarded by fine views. From here you should also be able to see the other parts of the island which you might wish to visit such as the excellent beach at ARILLAS nearby. The country which lies inland from here is particularly beautiful and car hire is well worth considering.

ARILLAS

This is another small, relatively uncrowded resort, set on a large bay overlooked by green hills, that is suitable for the Recluse or quiet families. Originally a private villa development it remains slightly more exclusive and less barren than some of the other beach resorts on the island, though it is still very quiet and has very little nightlife. Most people stay in villas but there are two small hotels near the beach, the **Arilla** and the **Marina Beach**. The **Sea Grill** provides a pleasant place to linger over a meal. Intriguingly the beach here 'grows' over the course of the summer as the tides deposit more and more sand, only to shrink again during the winter.

AGHIOS GEORGEOUS

This is an unsophisticated resort, dramatically situated at the bottom of steep cliffs, with an excellent beach and very little else. There is as yet no bus service and this has meant that although it is no longer as deserted as it once was, no major development has taken place here. The brochures all tell you that the last 15 yards of the road are not tarmacked because a local man refuses to sacrifice his tomatoes and sell his land to the council. Whether the tale is true or not, it does show that this is still a fairly unexploited resort. Yet, as its simple accommodation appeals mainly to young singles, a fairly lively, if relaxed, nightlife has grown up. At the moment Aghios Georgeous should appeal to those who want a fun, but not too demanding, beach holiday.

Most of the visitors stay in rooms, but the **Costa Golden Beach** and **Hotel Nathalie** are reasonable hotels. For the independent traveller **San Georgio Camping**, situated along the beach, is quite good.

The huge bay of fine sand is one of the best beaches on the island and offers a good choice of watersports. It will never be very empty, but as on any beach, the further you walk from the centre, the quieter it becomes.

In the evening the nightlife is very simple. Of the tavernas the **Marina** and the **Nathalie** probably offer the best food, particularly their fish dishes, but the **Panorama** and the **Nafsika** are slightly more lively.

EXCURSIONS

As mentioned above, Aghios Georgeous can only be reached, or left, on foot or with your own transport, so car hire is strongly recommended. The nearest bus route is to AFIONAS, a small village worth a visit for its excellent views over the bay, which is a fairly long walk down the beach, or to MARKADES, at the other end of the bay. Equipped with a car this makes an excellent base for touring the north of the island. As you probably noticed on the way from the airport, the road from Corfu town is very scenic. You travel through TROUMBETTA, 'trumpet pass' in English, which has a fine view over the island in general and its millions of cypresses in particular, all as 'gnarled' and 'weather beaten' as the guidebooks say. The view on the return journey, to Albania to the east, and the three small Othonian Islands off the north-west coast, is equally good. A small café at the summit allows you to stop and enjoy the view.

PALEOKASTRITSA

Set on wooded mountains overlooking a beautiful bay about 40 minutes from Corfu town, this is probably the most scenically located of all Corfu's resorts and understandably also one of the most popular, particularly with families and older socialites. Apart from the view, which is as magnificent as the brochures suggest, it also has some very comfortable hotels, excellent bathing nearby and, because it tends to attract rich visitors, a fairly sophisticated nightlife. Its popularity as a holiday resort in its own right, as well as a place for excursions from the rest of the island, does mean that it becomes crowded during the high season. Nevertheless its beauty remains and its central geographical location makes it a very good base for travelling round the island.

ACCOMMODATION

There are many good hotels in this resort. The **Akrotiri Beach** (Tel: 41275) situated near the beach, has excellent views and is ideal for families although the poolside and sun terraces are very scruffy. The **Paleokastritsa** (Tel: 41207) is a good hotel with quite a lively nightlife that overlooks the resort, and the comfortable **Oceanis** (Tel: 41230) is a good choice for those who want a quiet holiday. Nearer the beach the **Odysseus** (Tel: 41209) is small, but represents very good value for those on a budget. For families, or those wanting considerable comfort, the **Elly Beach** (Tel: 22255) with good facilities and a very good beach, would be a good hotel, but its slightly isolated position at Liapades, about half an hour away, might be too far from the resort for some. For those travelling on a budget **Paleokastritsa Camping** (Tel: 41204), is quite good, but since it is miles out of the resort you may feel happier staying in one of the many rooms available in the centre.

SIGHTS

Homer wrote that this was the location of King Alcinous' Palace, where Odysseus was washed ashore on his return from the Trojan wars, and though this may not be true, the description of the place is so exact that it seems likely that Homer himself visited here. More recently it is certain that Henry Miller, who wrote about Paleokastritsa in his book *The Colossus of Maroussi*, came here.

From the bus stop a 20-minute climb leads up to **Panagia Theotokos Monastery** above the sea. This has a stunning view and a pleasant shady garden from which to enjoy it. This simple monastery, originally founded in 1208 but rebuilt in the 19th century, is still in use, so swimwear, as a sign tells you, is not a very suitable form of dress; open Mon to Sun 7 a.m. to 1 p.m., 3 p.m. to 8 p.m. Paleokastritsa, Greek for 'Old Castle', is named after **Angelo Kastro**, a 13th-century castle set above a 1000 ft drop, whose ruins lie behind the monastery. Although the walk up here is tiring it is well worth the effort for the view is magnificent. Military historians may be a bit disappointed, for what appears from a distance to be the walls of the castle are in fact just natural outcrops of rock, though you can still see a reservoir dug by the Venetians. If you do not feel so energetic simply enjoy the view from the **Bella Vista Café** on a natural rock terrace about half way up. As you look round the coaches now parked here it is amusing to think that when Kaiser Wilhelm arrived here he was the first person to do so by motor car, and since no one had seen such a frightening object before, everyone assumed that he was the Devil! Offshore you can see a large rock vaguely shaped like a ship. Local tradition, as against geological fact, provides not one, but two, explanations for this. One suggestion is that this was Odysseus' ship turned to stone by an angry Poseidon, but this is awkward for legend for this is also thought to be Mouse Island. Thus a more popular argument is that this is a pirate ship which was turned to stone when it tried to rob the monastery.

Excellent swimming is to be had below the monastery and on AG TRIADHA beach reached from the path near the Paleokastritsa car rental office. If you enjoy more exotic watersports, a diving school, the **Baracuda Club** (Tel: 41211), is located in the bay. It is one of the very few in Greece, for the government fear that many of the sunken wrecks which they cannot as yet afford to raise may be plundered.

NIGHTLIFE

There is no real centre to the resort and most of the tavernas and bars are scattered along the road from Corfu town. They are well known for their fish, particularly lobster, but the fact that it is caught locally does not seem to lower the price; if anything it tends to be more expensive!

EXCURSIONS

Paleokastritsa has a very central location, and because of this it makes a good base for exploring the island. Below lies LIAPADES BAY and the somewhat hard to reach GERIFA beach. Just beyond this are the two excellent beaches of HOMOUS and STILIARI, dominated by huge cliffs etched with patterns made by the waves, which are both relatively unspoiled because they can only be reached by boat. However, in season the caiques ferry large numbers of people out to them. Some very good day trips can be made by continuing down this southern coast. The remarkable beach at MORTIOTISSA is well worth a visit, as is the beach at PELEKAS, more famous for its sunset. As a break from lying on the beach many people would probably enjoy playing golf on the course near Ermones, regardless of whether they have ever lifted a club before, because it is particularly beautiful.

If you travel from the resort the still very rural nature of parts of the island can come as a surprise to those who thought it to be nothing but one huge disco. The scenery, particularly if you head north, is also very good. The best view of the bay of Paleokastritsa itself is from the road above it leading to Lakones and Markades, itself quite an interesting little journey.

ERMONES

This is a small resort owing its existence to the very large and very comfortable **Ermones Beach Hotel** (Tel: 94241), a bungalow development with excellent facilities that even include an Olympic-sized swimming pool and a lift to the beach. Several tour operators offer Ermones in their brochures and it would be an ideal choice for those who want a fairly luxurious beach holiday.

At Ropa's Meadow nearby is the **Corfu Golf Club** (Tel: 94220). This is reputed to be one of the best golf courses in the world with excellent greens and a devious stream that meanders across no less than 16 of the 18 holes. Even if you have never played before this could well be the place to start for the surroundings are very beautiful and clubs can be hired quite cheaply. The bay here is yet another of the places where Odysseus was washed ashore. Ironically the Princess Nausicaa who found him was playing a ball game before he drifted ashore, though presumably not golf, and even though he was naked recognized him as a god or a prince.

Twenty minutes' walk away is the small village of VATOS, where the excellent **Vatos Camping** (Tel: 94269) may interest the independent traveller.

GLYFADA

About 11 miles from Corfu town is another resort popular mainly because of an excellent hotel ideal for families, the

Grand Glyfada (Tel: 37574), used by over ten tour operators and full of young British families. The other hotel in the resort, the **Glyfada Beach** (Tel: 94257) is still very good but is slightly less lavish and tends to be more popular with Germans. For a comfortable flop-on-the-beach holiday either would be ideal. Here you will find a large range of watersports, including sailing, but the resort itself is tiny and apart from the hotels there is almost no nightlife. If you are seeking solitude the north end of the beach, away from the hotels, is not deserted but it is much quieter. The beach itself is superb, but it's quickly spoiling with fast-food stalls creeping in further each year.

EXCURSIONS

Just north of the resort is PELEKAS, which has excellent views of the bay during the day and of the sunset in the evening. Kaiser Wilhelm built a small telescope tower here to enable him to appreciate the view at the turn of the century and ever since then Pelekas has also been known as the Kaiser's Throne. Few people realize that there is also a very sandy beach here: beautiful, safe for children, and usually not very crowded. The reason why this spot remains relatively unspoilt is quite simple, to get here you have to go down a very steep path which drops about 800 ft. Walking down only takes about 15 minutes, but the return journey is exhausting. Do *not* ride a moped down, for if you do, you will have to carry it back up. Just inland from here lies AGHIOS YANNIS, where a charming 1820s mansion has been converted into a **Youth Hostel**, but sadly it is too isolated to be of much use.

A few miles above Pelekas is MYRTIOTISSA, certainly one of the best beaches on the island and praised by Lawrence Durrell as the most beautiful in the world, where steep cliffs, covered with trees and with fresh water running down them, form the backdrop to an excellent beach. Despite, or perhaps because, it is so difficult to reach the beach it has become *the* venue for the young and agile cognoscenti. One half is unofficially nudist despite the occasional grumbles from the monks at the nearby Monastery of Myrtiotissa, so called after an Icon of Our Lady found by a monk in a myrtle or *miriotissa* bush. The original church was built here by a Turk who became a Christian, and although the one now standing is modern, the view makes the short climb worthwhile. The beach 'shrinks' during the winter when the tide carries away much of the sand.

YALISCARI

A few miles south of Glyfada lies Yaliscari, about 10 minutes' drive from Sinadres. This is dominated by the **Yaliscari Palace** (Tel: 31400), a large hotel with excellent facilities, ideal for those who want a peaceful beach holiday at a good hotel. If you can drag yourself away from the beach **Aghios Deka**, Corfu's second highest mountain at 1,889 ft, offers a very good view and is very near.

AGHIOS GORDIS

Slightly further along the coast is Aghios Gordis, based around the **Aghios Gordis** (Tel: 36723), a very modern hotel of a design best described as 'striking', which is very popular with families and has a fairly lively nightlife. This is very much a place for quiet holidays and even though the watersports show that the resort is not totally undeveloped, outside of the hotels there is very little to do but lie on the beach and linger over a meal. The fact that some of the locals charge visitors for parking a car in front of their house does, however, tend to suggest that it is not quite as undeveloped as some of the brochures suggest. Another good hotel is the small family-owned **Golden Nest**.

The scenery around the resort is very good, but car hire is a must if you wish to explore it. The two villages of SINARADES and KATO GAROURA make pleasant walks with excellent views, or if you are feeling more energetic, you could climb **Ag Deka**.

AGHIOS GEORGIOS

About one hour from Corfu town lies the huge beach of Aghios Georgios, slowly developing as a resort but still very unsophisticated. The people who holiday here tend to be young singles attracted by its cheap accommodation, so a fairly active, though very relaxed nightlife, has grown up. Most resorts with beaches this good tend to be swamped by day-trippers, but because the road does not allow easy access and the sea is too shallow for caiques, Aghios Georgios is quieter than would otherwise be the case.

Although the resort is fairly isolated, there is no need to spend all your time on the beach unless you wish to do so. The large village of ARGIRADES nearby leads on to many interesting trips. If you head north you come to KORISSIA LAGOON, a huge inland lake surrounded not merely by beaches but also, and almost uniquely in Corfu, by sand dunes. As Aghios Georgios grows this in turn becomes more crowded, but it is so large that it should long remain possible to find a quiet spot of your own for a picnic.

Overlooking the lagoon is **Mt Matheos**, an enjoyable climb with an excellent view, and a large village of the same name lies nearby. On the coast opposite is another good beach at PARAMONA. If you head south from Argirades, you can visit the two tiny villages of VITALDES and KRITIKA, or carry on down the island to the more developed resort of Kavos, about 20 minutes away.

The South-east Coast

This final section covers the resorts from Kanoni to Kavos and also includes Perama, Benitses, Moraitika and Messonghi. All these resorts are very popular with the tour operators and are fairly developed. The far south of the island was once almost deserted, but now with the resort of Kavos this is no longer true. The scenery is not the most beautiful on the island and you will find better beaches elsewhere, but if you want a fun time in the sun with plenty of nightlife these places are all very suitable.

KANONI

Just 10 minutes south of Corfu town, in fact almost a suburb, is Kanoni, with a very scenic location overlooking Mouse Island and many good hotels. Unsurprisingly, however, it also has a number of drawbacks. Firstly, its great beauty and easy access mean that it becomes full of day-trippers, secondly, the only good beach is at the Hilton Hotel and this is small and crowded and thirdly, and most noticeably, the airport is very nearby. The brochures do all discreetly mention the fact that you may be disturbed by aircraft noise, but understandably they fail to explain quite what this means. The airport is immediately below the cliff on which the resort stands, only about 300 yards away from some hotels, and not only can you enjoy plane spotting, at times you will feel that you can read the pilots' name badges! Flights do stop at night, however, and most of the noise then comes from the nightlife rather than the jet engines, but be warned that the days when holidays tend to start or finish, Friday, Saturday and Monday, tend to be very noisy. All this said, do not be too alarmed if you have chosen to spend your holiday here, for the sightseer it can make an excellent base for exploration during the day and you can return in the evening to some good nightlife.

The main hotel is the **Corfu Hilton** (Tel: 36540) mentioned above, very comfortable for older couples with its typical Hilton luxury, and with a good beach for families. Its most interesting attraction is that it is the only hotel on the island, perhaps in the world, with a ten pin bowling alley! Of the other hotels the **Ariti** (Tel: 33885) and the **Divani Palace** (Tel: 38980) are both well situated, pleasant and fairly lively at night, whilst the **Salvos** (Tel: 30429) is good for cheap and lively holidays. If you can stand the noise from the airport 400 yards away!

SIGHTS

Kanoni is named after the 'one cannon' that the French placed here during the British blockade and ever since then it has been a place where visitors would come to enjoy an afternoon stroll and a beautiful view over Mouse Island. So pretty is the location that not only is it probably the most popular excursion on the island, but it also graces many a travel brochure cover as well as some of the Greek Tourist Board posters.

What all these people come to see are two tiny islands set in the middle of the bay, MOUSE ISLAND, or Pontikonisi in Greek, with only a few cypress trees, and VLAKHERENA, on which there is a small white convent. Tradition has it, as mentioned previously, that Mouse Island is the ship which brought Odysseus back from the Trojan wars which Poseidon then turned into stone in his anger at the great hero for his having blinded his son Cyclops on his travels. Whether this is true or not, musing over this with a quiet drink at a café overlooking the view is a better way of spending your time than actually visiting the islands, for though the convent can be reached via a causeway and Mouse

Island by a boat, they are both something of an anti-climax. The first is small and crowded, and the highlight of the other is a collection of marble plaques noting royal visitors who came here before you and who were presumably equally disappointed.

NIGHTLIFE

Most people socialize in the hotels in the evening, or go into Corfu town since it is so near. There are, however, quite a reasonable number of places to go in the resort itself. The **Top of the Hill Bistro** and **Mama Linas**, opposite the Divani Hotel, are good restaurants, and later in the evening **Captain's Wine Bar** and the **Oriental Disco** might be of interest.

For excursions see under 'Corfu town'.

PERAMA

This is a small resort about 20 minutes from Corfu town with a lively nightlife for the socialite and good hotels for families. It is very much a tourist centre and is not very Greek, but its convenient location makes it a very good base for exploring as well as being suitable for more lazy holidays.

This is a popular resort with British tourists and the best family hotels are the **Aelos Beach** (Tel: 33132) and the **Alexandros** (Tel: 33160), both with good beaches and quite lively at night. More suitable for couples are the **Aegli** (Tel: 39812), **Continental** and the **Oasis** (Tel: 38190). For young singles there are the **Frini**, the very lively **Pontoikonnisi** (Tel: 36871) and the cheap and simple **Argo**.

Perama is located on the other side of the bay from Kanoni, and though you may not be able to walk on water, you can walk, or even ride a moped, across the causeway to the other resort and the nightlife available there. Although this makes a pleasant evening stroll, it also reminds you that the airport is quite near, though Perama suffers much less from aircraft noise than Kanoni.

In the resort itself there are a number of good restaurants. **Yannis** is particularly well known for its sea food, the **Panorama**, as its name suggests, for the view, and **Nikos Grill** for good, cheap food. Every resort on the island has at least one bar called **Spiros** and the more developed ones also feature a disco called the **Cococabana**; Perama has both but unusually they are also quite good. Other popular bars are **Georges**, **Fernando's Hideaway** and the **Zodiac Disco**.

EXCURSIONS

The resort's convenient location means that it is relatively easy to make excursions from here. Just inland lies the **Achilleon Palace**, a large mansion which the more up-market brochures would describe as a spoilt Victorian child's idea of an Italian doll's house.

The Palace was built in the 1890s for Elizabeth, Empress of Austria, a famous society beauty, who fell in love with the spot on a visit some 30 years earlier. She dedicated the building to her hero, Achilles, and a statue, holding his heel of course, can be seen in the garden, discreetly positioned so that the Empress could look at him without embarrassment. Elizabeth's taste in architecture might be somewhat questionable and she filled the garden with rather unimpressive statues of unimportant gods, but the Palace has an undoubted style and is well worth a visit simply for the view. Note how it is built into the side of the hill so that each floor leads out onto a different part of the garden. A discreet look through the windows near the summer house will enable you to see the large frescoes on the wall, best described as 'striking' rather than brilliant.

The Empress lived in the Palace only for a very short time, however, since in 1898, soon after building was finally completed, she and her family were assassinated. The Palace then lay empty for some years until in 1905, Wilhelm II, the Kaiser of Germany, came to Corfu, and having been shown round the Palace by the King of Greece, decided to buy it, and until 1914 spent his holidays here. He left the Palace much as it was, but he did install three things: a saddle from which he dictated his letters and indeed some of his battle plans for World War I; a bell by his loo should state affairs suddenly require the presence of one of his advisors, and an even larger statue of Achilles than Elizabeth had erected, simply inscribed 'To the greatest of the Greeks from the greatest of the Germans', an inscription now understandably removed. Despite all this interesting history the Palace has probably achieved its greatest fame by being the location for the Bond film *For Your Eyes Only*.

It is now run as one of the few casinos in Greece, but during the day a small museum is open which contains an exhibition featuring the

Empress and numerous photos of the most beautiful women of her day which she ordered her ambassadors throughout the world to have taken. The gardens are probably the best part of the Palace and are open, along with the museum, 8 a.m. to 8.30 p.m. Mon to Sat, 9 a.m. to 6 p.m. Sun.

The casino is open 7 p.m. to 2 a.m. Mon to Fri, 7 p.m. to 3 a.m. Sat, and a bus runs from the Ionian hotel to take you here from 7 p.m. onwards stopping at the Old Port, the Esplanade and Theotoki Sq. The casino is open to anyone, though everyone must bring their passport and men should wear jacket and tie. You may not be James Bond but you can enjoy winning, or resign yourself to losing, at roulette, baccarat, chemin de fer, and less expensively, fruit machines. If you do not wish to gamble, a pleasant restaurant is located a few yards down the road from the Palace.

If you do travel out to the Palace, some 5 miles from the Town on bus number 10, there are a few additional sights which are worth a look. **GASTOURI** is a small Greek village which is still relatively unspoilt where you can see how ordinary people live away from the resorts. On the coast nearby is **KAISER'S BRIDGE**, a small resort which makes a pleasant place to spend an afternoon. If you are feeling more active **Ag Deka**, Corfu's second highest mountain, offers a wonderful view overlooking the Achilleon, once you have recovered from the walk up!

BENITSES

About 20 minutes from the town this is very much Corfu's most commercialized resort, aimed at the young British socialite who wants a cheap and lively time in the sun. If you enjoy going out to lots of discos at home Benitses is ideal for you, but quieter types will simply find it too loud and too crowded. The small harbour which forms the centre of the resort still has some charm, but it will hardly be this, nor the small and narrow beach that attracts you, but rather the vast number of bars and discos. Benitses is not one huge party, more like lots of small ones, but it is so British that it is almost impossible even to hear Greek music, let alone find a traditional taverna. It would be wrong to say this resort is like Blackpool in the sun, for it probably is more active in the evenings, but people who would not enjoy a weekend in Blackpool would probably not enjoy Benitses. For those who would, however, a very action-packed and tiring week or two lies ahead of you.

Many of the tour operators provide self-catering accommodation, but there are still a large number of good hotels. Immediately opposite the beach, and right in the centre of things, is the huge **Potomaki** (Tel: 30889), very busy and very popular with young British holiday-makers, and with its very popular ground floor disco, tends to be very active (or very noisy depending on your point of view!). Another equally lively hotel on the sea front is the D-grade **Eros**.

More basic, though if anything even *more* active at night, are the **Avra**, and two tavernas, and the **Riveria**. However, if you want at least some sleep at night, the charming **Evgenia**, the rather shabby **Corfu Maris** and the **Benitses Archers** are quieter, but still near the beach and the nightlife. The hotels slightly outside the resort cater more for families. The best of these, and the most popular among the British, is the **Regency** (Tel: 92305) a 30 minute walk from the village with good views directly opposite a beach. Similar, but not quite so popular with families, nor so lively at night, are the **San Stefano** (Tel: 92292) and the **Achilles** (Tel: 94225) which both offer excellent facilities.

The attraction of the Benitses during the day are fairly limited, and although a wide range of watersports are available, the beach itself is more suitable for sleeping off a hangover than building sandcastles. A walk round the narrow streets of the old town makes an enjoyable stroll one afternoon, but probably the most interesting sight is watching everyone else crawl out into the sun whilst you have a late breakfast at one of the many cafés.

Ironically for a resort famous for its discos and bars Benitses is one of the few places with any archaeological remains. Most people will probably not be too interested, but hidden away behind the main street are the ruins of a 3rd-century Roman villa, destroyed by time, and not as you might expect, by the power of speakers in the discos.

At night Benitses is so active that it would perhaps be of more help to mention places to avoid rather than make recommendations, but here is a selection. For a good, British atmosphere try **Pat's Place** which, suitably bedecked in Union Jacks, is hard to miss. For somewhere at least slightly Greek consider **Costas Bar X**, or for somewhere a bit more exotic, the supposedly Hawaiian **Spiros on the Beach**, situated where its name suggests, the **Cococabana** or **Reflections**. Among the discos **Stringfellows, Paradise, Style** and the **Blue Sea** are thought to be the best, and they are as large and as crowded as any at home. Should you really be missing home, eat away your sorrows at **Jock's Fish and Chips**!

If you have any energy left during the day Corfu town is only 8 miles away on bus number 6, about every hour 7 a.m. to 9.30 p.m. However, once they have arrived here most people tend never to leave until the end of their holiday, though whether this is because they are too lazy or still hungover is not clear! If you desire a better beach the nearest will be found at MORAITIKA or MESSONGHI, though be warned that both get very crowded during the day with people looking for a better beach than the one at *their* resort! People who really do want a good beach are probably better off heading for Corfu town early one morning and catching a bus to one of the resorts on the west coast, but it would be unlikely that the dedicated sun-worshipper would come to Benitses, and such early morning activity would seem strangely out of place. If you would like something to look at, the nearest sight is the **Achilleon Palace** a mere 2o miles away.

MORAITIKA

Moraitika is a small resort about 40 minutes from the town. Its main features are a long shingle beach and a number of good hotels, a combination which makes it very popular with families. The hotels provide the centre for nightlife as well as accommodation and apart from these there is very little entertainment. The best is the **Messonghi Beach** (Tel: 92429) which, despite its name, is actually in Moraitika. This is a huge bungalow development with excellent bathing and a lively nightlife that should suit anyone who likes large hotels, but is particularly good for families, as is the rather unfortunately named **Albatross**. For those who want a quieter holiday the **Delfinia** (Tel: 30318) and the **Miramare Beach** (Tel: 23684) would be a better choice. You singles should consider the **Three Stars** (Tel: 92457) with a very good beach, and the **Solonaki** for two lively, cheap hotels.

There is a good choice of watersports here and if you would like to explore rather than just admire the scenery the mountains surrounding the village offer some very good walks. Should you care for a change of nightlife from the hotels, Benitses lies only 5 miles away.

MESSONGHI

This is a small resort which is quiet, if not quite as 'sleepy' and deserted as some of the brochures suggest. A small river leads to a long, narrow shingle beach and although an increasing amount of development is beginning to take place there is still little to do and most of the entertainment lies in nearby Moraitika.

Apart from the **Messonghi Beach Hotel** (Tel: 92429) (see above) the accommodation tends to cater only for young singles. The best of these is the rather basic **Rossis** (Tel: 92352) with excellent bathing and a fair amount of nightlife, but also worth a look are the **Melissa** and the new B-grade **Gemini** (Tel: 92398). Nearby is **Sea Horse Camping** (Tel: 65364), which is quite good.

In the evening most people head for the hotels in Moraitika, or the bright lights of Benitses, but Messonghi can provide some entertainment itself. The **Messonghi Pub** and the **Gemini Bar** are among the better places for a drink, and should you wish to dance the night away there are three good discos, **Scorpion**, **Flamingos** and the **Limbo**.

Inland from the resort lie some good excursions. Nearby are MT MATHEOS and the KORISSA LAGOON. The mountain offers a good view and near it is the 13th-century **Gardiki Castle**, still with some of its original walls and some square towers, where there is a road leading down to a good beach at PARAMONA. The lagoon has one of the best beaches on the whole island, and delightfully is also one of the least crowded. If you explore a little you will find part of this is blocked off, not to act as a dam, but to trap the fish from which the local equivalent of caviar, known as *avgotarakho*, is made. If you travel on down the island from Messonghi visit the tiny villages of AGHIOS NIKOLAOS and ROUMANADES and the quite good beach at PETRETI and also BOUKARI. Be warned that the signposts are almost as bad as the road, so if you do explore, make sure that you have a good map.

KAVOS

Finally we come to Kavos, about 1½ hours from Corfu town and the most southerly resort on the island offering cheap apartment holidays on an excellent beach. With this type of accommodation the people who come here tend to be young singles and this, combined with the fact that the resort is fairly isolated and thus everyone *has* to stay in Kavos in the evening, has meant that a fairly lively, if not over sophisticated nightlife has grown up. The beach is excellent, but it becomes very crowded with day trippers brought in by excursion boats from the other resorts. Kavos has also only begun to be developed over the past few years and thus parts of it do tend to look rather like a building site.

Most people who come here stay in apartments, but the **Passas** and the **San Marino** are two good hotels, particularly suitable for families. In the evening, the **O Naftis**, the **Karavas** and **Krinos** are among the better restaurants, and of the bars the best appear to be **Studio 1**, the **Two Georges**, the **Ship Inn** and **42nd Street**.

During the day most people simply lie on the beach, but although the scenery in this area is not the most beautiful on the island, some interesting trips can be taken. Heading south, about an hour's walk from the path alongside the Bar Metaxa is CAPE ASPROKAVOS. Here you will find the ruined **Monastery of Arkoudillas**. Although little remains it has a very beautiful view and a dramatic location a few feet away from sheer cliffs. Boat trips can be taken to the nearby island of **PAXOS**, and the resort of PARGA on the mainland, though check and recheck the ferry times if you expect to get back the same day. Heading north from the resort you come to ALYKES, with a good but crowded beach, or drift through the small villages of BASTATIKA, KRITIKA and SPARTERO. At Potami there is a bridge over the river which a few years ago the locals blockaded in an understandable protest at the hordes of tourists descending upon them, so be grateful if you return to the resort without incident!

The Ionian Islands

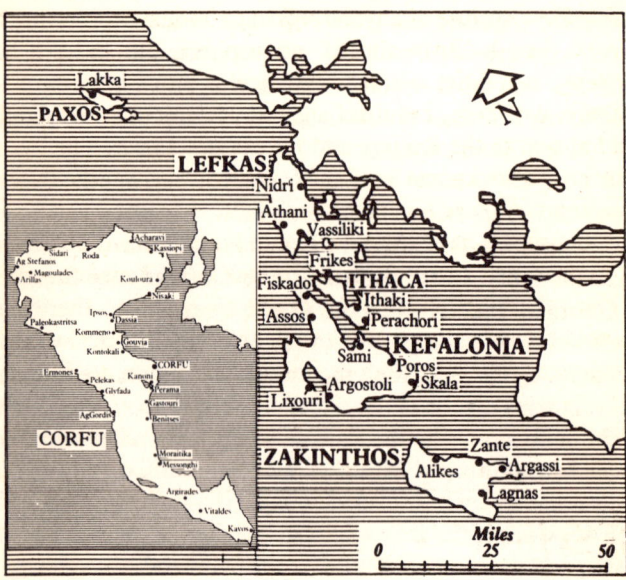

Along the west coast of Greece lie the Ionian Islands, which are named after Io, a girlfriend of Zeus who was hurriedly turned into a cow by him when he saw his wife approaching, and then, pursued by a maddening fly, dived into the sea.

The islands are most people's first sight of Greece, and yet they are also the least typically Greek of all the islands: far greener because of the winter rains, free of the strong winds that are common to a few of the other islands, and with some very elegant architecture dating from the period of Venetian control, 1388–1797, which was followed by colonial rule by France and Britain. The islands have some excellent scenery, good hotels and some of the best beaches anywhere in the world, so it is not surprising that they have become such a popular holiday centre. Even on the most popular islands like Corfu, however, it is still possible to escape the crowds.

There are six main islands. Corfu is very much a tourist resort, but it is ideal for Families, Socialites, Nature Lovers and Healthy-Holiday types. The other islands are mainly centres for villa holidays. Paxos is less crowded than Corfu and more relaxed, but is becoming increasingly fashionable. Lefkas is the least developed of the islands, suitable for a Recluse or anyone seeking a holiday with rather more of a Greek than a 'Brits abroad' atmosphere. Ithaca, the home of Odysseus, is a quiet island, of particular interest to the historian. Kefalonia is a large, beautiful and, as yet, uncrowded island which would appeal to the Recluse and the Nature Lover. Finally, there is Zakinthos, also known as Zante, another scenic island becoming increasingly popular for Family holidays.

All the islands have some very good beaches for the Sun-worshipper. There are air flights from the UK to Corfu, Kefalonia and Zante, but the others are slightly awkward to reach as there are large distances between them. This means that apart from Corfu or Paxos the independent island-hopper will not find it easy to get around.

Paxos

Paxos, also known as Paxi or Paxoi, is about 10 miles from the Greek mainland and 30 from Corfu. It is the smallest of the Ionian islands and is also one of the most beautiful, gently hilly and covered with over 300,000 olive trees. Until very recently it was completely outside the tourist circuit, indeed as late as 1968 there was no running water, but over the last few years it has begun to grow as a fairly exclusive centre for villa holidays. Almost no other accommodation is available and in the height of the season you are not allowed to land unless you have a room booked. The island is used as a base for the very popular Greek Island Club holidays, and what little accommodation is left tends to be filled by sailors. If you have chosen a holiday here, this simple and undeveloped island should provide you with a few restful weeks.

To reach Paxos from the UK you first fly to Corfu, about a 3½-hour trip, then catch a ferry to Gaios, which takes about 3 hours. If you are on a villa holiday you will then be taken to your temporary home, but everyone else will have to rush round trying to find some accommodation. Although it is more expensive for independent travellers to rent a room before embarking on the ferry (there are kiosks at Piraeus which sell rooms on various islands for a fee, for those who don't want to take the risk of arriving only to find all beds taken and a sleeping bag on the beach being the only resort), they may now begin to think that it would have been a good idea. There are some hotels, the very good **Paxos Beach**, and the **San Giorgi**, but these are *always* fully booked in season. The alternative is to find some private rooms. The police, just off the harbour road behind the post office and the telephone office (Tel: 31 222), have a helpful list, but their English is rather limited and it may be of more use to go to **Dinos Travel**. There are no banks on the island, but you can change money in a small office off the top right of the square, and in LAGGOS and LAKKA. There is no hospital and anyone who falls ill is helicoptered to Athens, although first aid can be summoned by ringing 31 466.

The small port of **Gaios** is a pleasant place centred around a marble square, though annoyingly the ferries moor a little way round the corner. The town almost looks as if it were set on the river rather than on the coast, for, like a piece from a giant jigsaw, the small island of ST NIKOLAS almost totally blocks off the sea. During the height of the season the town itself is blocked with traffic, though in the form of people rather than cars.

There are no sights in the town. The nearest is the **British Residency**, on the harbour road, which was once visited by Gladstone, but now houses the Port Police. If you ask permission from the local council official, the *kino grafio*, in the large building about 100 yards up from the square, you may be able to visit the **castle** on the island of St Nikolas, which was built in 1423 and restored in 1810. Hire a boat, take some sensible shoes, explore the castle and enjoy what is probably the best view of Gaios.

Paxos is not a place for the wild socialite and there are few discos, but because villa holidays tend to attract the better-off holiday types, the standard of food is quite high. Among the best restaurants are the **Anesis** on the square, and **Taka Taki** on the right, a little further up.

To get around the island there is the usual choice of car, taxis and mopeds; a bus also runs to Lakka several times a day. However, there is only one main road on the island and many of the minor roads are so bad that they are not suitable even for mopeds. The easiest and perhaps the most enjoyable way of getting round the island is by boat.

Staying on the land for a moment, if you head north from the town you come to MARKRATIKA, where there is a pretty little church. Continuing along this road you come to BOIKATIKI, where the simple church of **Ag Apostoli** offers a very good view. On the west coast as you drive north are the SEVEN SEAS CAVES of the island, the most famous of which is Ipparandi, which Homer said was the cave of Poseidon, covered in gold. A more recent myth has it that a Greek submarine hid here during the war and attacked German shipping, but in reality it simply sprung a leak and put in for repairs. Continuing on this road you pass near ORTHOLIHOS, best seen from the sea, where a stack of limestone rises 100 ft out of the water. As you drive, note the colour of the road, stained black by the juice of squashed olives, and the number of bridges, unusual in Greece but needed here because of the winter rains.

Turning right at Fountana you come to LOGGOS, a pretty villa resort. Continuing north you can carry straight on to Lakka, or take the scenic route along a bad road through Magazia, Manesatika and Ipanti. LAKKA itself is another villa resort with a good beach, used by the Greek Island Sailing Club. The small church here is famed, at least in the brochures, for the good quality of its Russian bells.

The most enjoyable way of seeing the island is by sea. Heading south from Gaios you come to the island of MOGONISI, now a fairly active resort, complete with water ski-ing, windsurfers and dinghies for hire. Continuing on your boat trip, about 50 minutes away, is ANTIPAXI, a quieter and more isolated resort that, but for all these boat trips, would be almost deserted. One of the best beaches in Greece is at VOUTOUMI BAY, but all round this little island you will find some excellent swimming and some very good views over the clear seas.

If you want to escape the crowds on the beaches, arrive either early or late, or more sensibly, head for the more distant parts of the island. Make sure, however, that you do not get unintentionally marooned.

If after a little while on Paxos itself you begin to feel isolated, you could catch a ferry to the mainland or Corfu and explore a little, but this would best be done on an excursion of a few days.

Lefkas

Lefkas, traditionally the home of the poet Sappho, is only separated from the mainland by a narrow canal. It is fairly rocky in the north and west, very green in the east, and in some places as pretty as Corfu. Its advantage is that it is far less crowded than Corfu because it has only just begun to feature in tour operators' brochures, mainly in the form of villa holidays. Holidays here will probably grow considerably over the next few years, but it is, as yet, the least commercialized of the Ionian islands. Quiet, with good scenery and some reasonable beaches, it would suit those wanting a relaxing, but not totally deserted holiday.

Lefka, the Greek word for 'white rock', was originally, until 540 BC, part of a mountain range on the mainland, when the Corinthians dug a canal, later kept open by the Romans, the Venetians, and now the Greek Government. The Roman Emperor Augustus built a causeway 2½ miles long, which was for centuries the only way of reaching the island, and in the 13th century the Franks built an **aqueduct** with 260 arches to take water to the castle of **Ag Mavra** which they built to defend the causeway.

The island can be reached by ferry from the mainland and occasionally from the other Ionian islands. There is no tourist office on Lefkas but the Tourist Police are usually quite helpful. Buses run to most parts of the island and there is the usual choice of car, taxi and moped hire. In addition, caiques travel to many of the resorts, of which the most important are Lefkas, Nidri, Vliho and Vassiliki.

The first thing you notice about Lefkas are the rather strange buildings, topped off with corrugated iron and scaffolding. The town was struck by heavy earthquakes in 1948 and these odd superstructures, though they may look ungainly, put the minimum stress on the foundations and prevent anyone being crushed by falling stone work. The next thing most people notice are the open gutters, but despite all this, the town does have a certain charm, particularly during August when a two-week cultural festival takes place.

The town is built along one main street, Od Zakka. The Tourist Police are situated off this street, near to the telephone office, on Mitropoleos, and the bus station and the post office are near Ag Minas Square at the bottom of the street. The best hotels are the **Lefkas**, which has good rooms and a disco, **Nicras** and the **Xenia**. All are near the beach. Cheaper accommodation can be found at the **Byzantion** and the **Averof**, the **Patrae** and the **Sant Marva** on Vlanti.

The large number of yachts that visit the town mean that the restaurants are all of quite a high standard. One of the best is **Regantos**, on Varriot Street just off the main square, and there are two good bars nearby, **Peter's Ouzerie** and the **Cafe Sunset No 2**. In the small square just inland from the ferry road is **Peter's Taverna**, whilst further south off the main street are the **Lighthouse Taverna** and the **Taverna Romantica**, all three of which serve good food in pleasant surroundings and are usually very busy.

There are a few interesting sights in the town itself, but if you want to explore the rest of the island the best way is to simply hop on to a caique. The nearest beach is the YIRO, on the sea edge of the lagoon, a visit to which you could combine with a quick exploration of the castle of **Ag Marva** across the chain ferry. For the more determined, probably the best beach on the island is a few miles further south at KALAMITISI, but the road is, to say the least, rather alarming.

Travelling clockwise round the island to the other resorts you come first to **NIDRI**, a quiet beach resort in a very good location overlooking several beautiful little islands. The best view of the bay is from NEOKHORI, a few miles inland.

A German archaeologist was convinced that Nidri was the site of Odysseus' home. Learned scholars now disagree but it makes a pleasant place to stay for a few weeks. It is mostly a villa and yacht resort, but there are a few rooms to be had, and **Camping Episcopes** (Tel: 23 043), lies about 1 mile further south. Small boats for hire from Nidri will take you round the islands, where you can admire, from a distance, SKORPIOS, owned by the Onassis family, complete with tennis courts and tomb. In the evening **Nick's** and the **Disco**

Alexander are two very different but popular nightspots as is the Nidri yacht club and the **Club de Paris**. Continuing inland a trip to the waterfall at **Dymossari Gorge** makes a pleasant excursion, as does the boat trip to the small island of **Meganisi**.

Two miles further south lies **VLIHO**, with a small secluded beach, numerous villas, and a reasonable campsite on the left before you enter the village. Continuing south there is another reasonable beach at POROS, which has a good view, some pleasant villas, and the excellent and well-designed **Poros Beach Hotel**. Further south, off the main road, lies the little village of SYVOTA, worth a look to see the bay it is situated on, and its taverna, the Delfinia run by the friendly Yannis.

The main road heads inland from here and offers wonderful views across the Bay of Vliho. Then, at the south of the island, you reach **VASSILIKI**, the other major resort on Lefkas, which has an attractive harbour with a good beach set on a huge bay. Again, most people stay in villas, but there are some hotels, the very good **Lerkatos** and also the **Paradise**. In the evening try **Pizza Pete's**, and the **Sappho** and **Yukka** discos. For some interesting excursions, it is possible to take a boat from here to Ithaca or Kefalonia, but it is very important that you check the return times.

Another caique trip, a long walk, or a very bad drive will bring you to the most famous spot on the island, NEFKADOS. Sappho, the famous Greek poetess, threw herself off here after being rejected by her boatman lover, Phaon; it is accordingly known to the locals as *Kavos tis Kyrus*, the Cliff of the Lady. When you read some of the guide books you get the impression that pagan priests, Roman criminals, and unrequited lovers have been queueing up here ever since to throw themselves off – a liturgical action for the priest, an atoning sacrifice to Apollo for the criminal and a gesture of despair by the lover. Many apparently survived the leap, which the Romans attributed to the help of the gods. Today it is simply a place with an interesting history and a 236 ft drop, which gives a very vertigo-inducing view.

If you have a car, head north and then take the minor road back down the island just before Khortata to ATHANI, where you will find some very good beaches. For the energetic, the mountain dominating the area is **Mt Stavrotas**, which also offers some very good views.

Ithaca

Ithaca is almost two small islands of equal size, both very hilly and green, joined by a narrow strip of land. It has new facilities, only average beaches, and little to do, but for those who want a quiet beach holiday, or the naturalist, it should prove ideal. Although it is, as yet, a relative tourist backwater, it is ironically one of the most famous of Greek islands, in historical terms at least, for it is thought to be the birthplace of Odysseus. In literature it has become a symbol for those who, like Odysseus, return home after a long and difficult journey. You can still see the odd scholar walking round, Homer in hand, exploring the land of their hero. Today, however, it is best known for the fact that the Prince and Princess of Wales stopped off here on their honeymoon. The lack of an airport has meant that development has been limited and although in July and August the few resorts can be crowded, the island is usually very quiet.

To reach the island from the UK you first fly to Kefalonia, about 3 hours' flying time, then catch a bus to Sami on the east coast, which is about half an hour, before finally taking a ferry to Ithaca, a 90 minute journey. There are also ferries from Lefkas, taking about 4 hours, and from Patras and Astakos on the mainland. Once on the island, buses operate from Vathi, the capital, but there is usually only one bus a day and most people get around by taxi or moped.

This is a small, undeveloped island. Most people come here for a quiet, simple holiday at either **FRIKES** or **KIONI**, both of which are ideal for families, quite good for sun-worshippers and, out of season, also suitable for the Recluse.

The most lively resort is **VATHI**, the capital, but do not expect too much sophisticated nightlife, either. Vathi is where you arrive on the ferry, a small port set on a horseshoe bay, backed by hills. You tie up so close to the houses that you almost feel that you can watch the television in the rooms opposite, but you overlook what is still quite a simple place. Accommodation is fairly limited, and thus perhaps your first action should be to turn left and head for the tourist office in the Town Hall on Odisseos Street. Of the hotels, the most convenient, situated right opposite the ferry, is the **Aktaeon**. Slightly further out, but with a good view is the **Mendor**. On practical matters, the telephone office, the OTE, is on the bottom left of the main square, open 7 a.m. to 1 p.m.; the post office is in the street behind, open Mon to Fri 7 a.m. to 3 p.m. Next door to this is the bank. Should you need them, the Tourist Police are along the road, just near the museum (Tel: 32 005), and the hospital is on Evemeou Street (Tel: 32 282).

The **museum** on An Kallinikou Street, parallel to the harbour road, contains 'one of the best collections of proto-Corinthian pottery in Greece', but, as this description indicates, its appeal is fairly specialized. In the **cathedral** on Eugeniou Street is an icon supposedly painted by El Greco. Of more interest to most people will be the **Penelope**, probably the best bar in the main square.

EXCURSIONS

You can swim off the platforms in the port, but a reasonable beach lies on the other side of the bay, around the Loutsa road to SKINOS BAY. Probably the best beach on the island is SARAKINIKO BAY, about half an hour away, reached by taking Eugeniou Karavia Street alongside the cathedral. The easiest way to get to a beach, however, is simply to take a caique from the town, although, of course, the beaches they go to tend to get rather crowded.

Ithaca is the island of Odysseus and therefore most of the sights of the island tend to be connected with him in some way. About 25 minutes south-east from Vathi is the **Fountain of Archusas**, named after a nymph who cried so much when she heard of the death of her son that she turned into a stream. Byron said a visit to this alone justified a journey to the island, but it must have changed a lot since his day, and although it is very well signposted, it is rather disappointing. Nearby are the white cliffs of **Raven's Crag**.

South-west of the town lies PERACHORI, an abandoned village, and a path from here leads to the deserted monastery of **Taxiarkhis**. Little of interest remains, but there is a very good view over the town. East of Vathi lies the **Cave of the Nymphs**, where Odysseus is supposed to have hidden some presents given to him by the Phoenicians. Continuing up the island you then come to **Mt Aetos** and **Piso Aetos**, supposedly the castle of Odysseus, but actually 700 years too late to be so, where, at the end of a tiring walk, there is a good view, but sadly a rather indifferent beach. A better beach is at AG IOANNIS, and a better view at the nearby monastery of **Kathara**.

If this list of Homeric excursions fails to excite, you could head for the fleshpots of Kefalonia or even Corfu, for a few days' break and a look at a different type of culture.

The other main resort on the island is **FRIKES** in the north; a surprisingly large port, with no shortage of rooms, and an excellent sailing centre. Nearby is thought to be the remains of the **School of Homer**, itself of little interest but lying at the end of an interesting walk, and near the **spring of Kalamos**. A few miles west from here lies KIONI, a quiet resort with a small beach which is becoming increasingly crowded as a result of villa development. South of here lies STAVROS, a simple village with a restaurant and a few rooms, and POLIS or 'city' Bay, named after the city of Ierosalem which supposedly disappeared beneath the waves in the 10th century.

Kefalonia

Kefalonia, also known by a large variety of spellings such as Cephalonia, Kefallinia and so on, has dramatic mountain scenery, some excellent beaches and should be of interest to all types of holiday-maker except the determined Socialite or the Healthy-holiday fanatic. It is slowly beginning to be developed as a holiday centre, and over twenty tour operators include the island in their brochures, though it still has no large resorts or huge crowds.

It is mainly a centre for villa holidays, but there are also a number of comfortable hotels which are very popular with British Families. The beaches are sufficiently good to be enjoyed by both the Sun-worshipper and children. Anyone but the dedicated Sightseer will probably find the beaches more interesting than the sights, but there are some Greek and Roman remains, two of the best caves in the country, a couple of good museums, and the best-preserved and probably the most attractive castle in Greece. All in all, if you are looking for a relaxing holiday with slightly more to offer than just a beach, this island would be a good choice.

Particularly of interest is the scenery. The Venetians called the island the 'Black Mountain' because of the Kefalonia silver fir trees which once darkened the island. At one time all the Greek islands were covered with forests, but as a result of the Venetians using the timber for ships, and, believe it or not, goats eating the bark of the young trees, most of the woods have now been destroyed and this is the only island with any sizeable amount of its original forests still left intact. Everyone will enjoy the scenery they provide, particularly in the north of the island, and there is enough flora and fauna to keep even the most dedicated Nature Lover happy for weeks.

HISTORY

Little is known of the ancient history of the island other than it was part of the kingdom of Odysseus and then became part of the private estate of the Roman Emperor, Augustus. In the 11th century it was taken successively by the Normans, and then, like most of the other Ionian islands, by the Turks, the Venetians, the French and the British. Byron, a man who seems to have visited more of Greece than anyone except a holiday rep, visited the island for a few months and wrote *Don Juan* here.

During the Second World War, 9,000 Italian troops occupied the island, but when the Germans arrived they refused to hand over Kefalonia and fought alongside the resistance. Later forced to surrender, most of them were then shot. In 1940 a native of the island, Gen Metaxas, was the ruler of the country and Mussolini demanded permission from him to march his troops across the north of Greece. Metaxas replied with a brevity that one could only wish all politicians spoke with, and simply said '*ochi*', which somewhat confusingly to English ears, actually means 'no'. Metaxas' defiance, symbolizing Greek independence, is celebrated with a national holiday, known as Ochi Day, on 28 October, the day he made his speech.

In 1953, the island was hit by a large earthquake and most of the buildings in ZANTE town, once considered to be more charming than Corfu, were destroyed. Faced with the desperate need to rehouse people, the council decided to develop the town in a modern style, and though this is understandable, the result is very much a modern resort. However, the village of FISKADO in the extreme north of the island survived the earthquake and offers much prettier surroundings, though for this reason it gets very crowded. Lest you become alarmed that the whole island looks like a concrete shoe box, it must be said that even in the most built-up areas of Zante town, there are some very good hotels.

Part of the reason why the island has remained much less crowded than Corfu, despite its natural beauty, is that many of the islanders are merchant seamen who earn quite a lot of money and thus do not need to depend on the tourists for their livelihoods. Many others live abroad and themselves return to Kefalonia for their holidays and are thus not too keen on vast numbers of foreigners filling their island. These two factors combine to make the island slightly more expensive than some others of the Ionian group.

PRACTICAL DETAILS

During the season there are direct flights to the island from Manchester and Gatwick which take about 3 hours. The airport is located about 20 minutes from Argostoli, and transfer time to most of the resorts should be under an hour.

A few people reach the island by ferry. Kefalonia is almost unique in that its capital is not its main port, for to get to Argostoli the ferries would have to make a long diversion round the south of the island. Most people therefore arrive by ferry at Sami on the east coast.

Once on the island, you begin to realize that this is indeed the largest of the Ionian group, particularly because the once-daily bus takes virtually the whole day to cover the island. This is much better than some places, but this is of no consolation when you wish to get around. Car hire is possible, but, as always, is very expensive and most people therefore resort to mopeds, either with too much or too little prudence, as anyone watching their erratic progress will soon conclude. You can hire bikes, but the island is very hilly and unless you are determined to get fit a taxi would be a better idea. Most people stay in the south of the island, but it is well worth making the effort to explore the beaches in the west and the scenery in the north. Some companies offer two-centre holidays, which enable you to do this without having to spend all your time driving.

TOURIST INFORMATION

There is a small but helpful office of the Greek Tourist Board in Argostoli.

CULINARY SPECIALITIES

The locals like to think that their island is famous for its wine, and indeed *Manzavino*, a white, is the only Greek wine exported to France. Also worth trying are *Rombolla*, *Monte Nero* and *Calliga*, the last being a rosé. If you simply ask for a carafe of house wine you will probably be given one of these without paying any extra.

Two local food dishes are *Bakaliaropitta*, a kind of fish pie, and *Kefalonitikipitta*, which is a mixture of goat and rice in a tomato sauce. More familiar to the British palate is the local honey, which is very good.

WHERE TO GO FOR WHAT

The most interesting sights on the island are in the south and the Sightseer will probably find ARGOSTOLI the most convenient base for excursions, though if you are prepared to hire a car, you can choose almost any resort. The Sun-worshipper will rejoice in one of the best beaches in Greece at MIRTOS on the north-west coast, and should therefore stay at nearby ASSOS, although there are good beaches close to most of the resorts. Families will be most at home in ARGOSTOLI, POROS, PLATI YALOS, LIXOURI, AG PELAGI and ASSOS.

The Island

ARGOSTOLI
The capital of Kefalonia was rebuilt after the earthquake in 1953 in a practical rather than pleasant style, but it has a number of good hotels and beaches nearby, and is a popular family resort.

ACCOMMODATION

Because of the lack of a beach in the town itself, most of the tour operators use hotels at the beaches on the outskirts. Three of these are particularly good and ideal for families. The **White Rocks** is a busy bungalow development with very good watersports, a beach and a disco at Plati Yalos. **The Mediteranne** is a good hotel dramatically set on a hill near the sea at Palioskfado beach: in addition to all the usual facilities of such places it offers a soundproofed disco (very popular with those who try to sleep at night), and even scuba-diving. At Ag Pelagi is the **Irinna**, a large, modern hotel with a pool, tennis and a very good beach. All three of these establishments provide very comfortable beach holidays but are near enough to Argostoli to enable you to make frequent trips to escape the 'not the same taverna again' feeling. On the opposite side of the bay lies LIXOURI, a developing resort which is still quite uncrowded out of season, with the good **Hotel Summery** and the pleasant **Ionios Agra** and the **Noropoula**.

In the town itself the accommodation is not that good. The **Mouikis** is a large, comfortable, though slightly expensive hotel at 3 Vironos Street. Other popular hotels are the new and fairly lavish **Regina** on 24 Georgio Vergoti; the good value **Cefalonia Star**, overlooking the harbour at 50 Metaxa; and, set on the outskirts of the town, on Platia Rizospastor, the **Xenia**, which has a pleasant garden.

The independent traveller should consider the cheaper hotels, such as the **Allegro**, at the top end of the bus station at 2A Hoida Street, the **Aenos** and the **Castello** on Valianou Square, both of which are very popular with the Greeks themselves, or the **Aegli**, at 3, 21 Maiou Street. There is also a campsite, **Camping Cephalos Beach** (Tel: 23 487), about a mile north of the town beyond the Sea Mills.

TOURIST INFORMATION

A small but helpful Tourist Office is just off Valianou Square, open 8 a.m. to 3 p.m. Mon to Fri (Tel: 22200). There is also a small information desk inside the bus station.

The Tourist Police are opposite the quay (Tel: 22200). On the other side of the road from the Tourist Office is the OTE office, with international phones, and the post office is halfway down the harbour on Lithostrato Street, off Vironos Street, open Mon to Fri 7.30 a.m. to 2 p.m.

There is a hospital at the far end of the harbour, opposite the bridge (Tel: 28332).

The buses run from the oddly-shaped building on the coast road, and just inland from here are two banks. A ferry runs from the harbour to LIXOURI, about every 90 minutes from 6 a.m. to 10 p.m., an enjoyable half-hour trip of the bay.

SIGHTSEEING

As with so many other Ionian towns, the only buildings to survive the 1953 earthquake were the bank and the main church, so sights are somewhat limited, although what remain are interesting. The town's 'must' is the **Cultural Museum** on the main square, which is open 10 a.m. to midday, 4 p.m. to 8 p.m., closed Tues. You might not usually think of visiting such a place in what is basically a beach and bar resort, but the well-displayed and labelled collection of artefacts depicting life on the island is good, and there is a particularly interesting collection of photographs of the town before the earthquake, which make everyone wish they had visited the island forty years ago. The **Archaeological Museum**, just up from the OTE, has probably the best collection of Mycenaean pottery outside of Mycenae itself. However, it is not very well displayed, and apart from a 3rd century BC bust of a man, you probably need to be very knowledgeable to enjoy it. It is open 8 a.m. to 1 p.m., 3 p.m. to 6 p.m., closed Tues. At the bottom of the harbour is the **Trapano Bridge**, leading to Sami, the original of which was built by the British in only fifteen days in 1810.

NIGHTLIFE

Kefalonia is a very popular place with Greeks and therefore there tends to be fairly lively entertainment. The most popular place for a meal is the main square. Probably the best restaurant here is **La Gondola**, where even the locals eat, which serves good Italian food at fairly expensive prices. For a more traditional meal try some of the tavernas in the square such as **Kanavia, Demosthenes** or the

Kefalos. On Georgiou B Av, just off the square, is the **Rex Cinema Café**, and a few streets inland is the **Ta Deilina**, a small restaurant with a limited choice of good food. Further south, near the Xenia Hotel on Platia Rizospastou, is **Partouras**. Along the coast road, the restaurants tend to be more tourist orientated, perhaps because this is the one road you can always find, but nevertheless there are some good restaurants, notably the **Cephalos Star**, the **Limenaki** and **Lorensatos**. Those who wish to dance the night away will have to walk to Lassi on the outskirts of the town.

EXCURSIONS

Most people's first excursion will be to the beach, but the tiny swimming area beyond the quay is not very good. The most convenient beaches are MARKIS YIALOS and PLATI YIALOS, to which a bus runs about every half an hour during the season. After a while you may want, or need, a break from the beach. If you are feeling lazy, the nearest excursion is only half a mile along the road beyond the quay.

The **Sea Mills** were built in 1835 by a Briton who accidentally discovered an underground stream and used it to drive a mill. This was converted in 1926 to an ice-producing plant. The 1953 earthquake diverted the stream and after considerable scientific investigation (i.e. they threw some dye in the water) the stream was found coming out on the other side of the island. The mills still remain, however, and are quite interesting to wander round.

Crossing the bay to LIXOURI will take you to some of the best and least-crowded beaches on the island. From here you can travel to the very scenically located **Monastery of Kipoureon**, and further north, along a very beautiful drive, the pretty little villages of AG SPIRIDON and PETARI.

A few miles south from the town itself are the 7th century BC remains of a Greek castle called **Krani**. These are not very interesting, but along the way you pass the **British Cemetery** on the right. A bit more enjoyable is the village of MOURKOUMELETA, rebuilt after the earthquake in traditional style largely through the enthusiasm, and money, of a Greek shipping tycoon. Nearby is a modest beach at AGHIOS PELAGEI.

A few miles north lies the **Castle of St George**, which is very much worth a look, especially if you remember to bring a torch. This was originally the capital of the island and had a population of over 15,000 before being destroyed in an earthquake in 1636. The capital then became Argostoli, originally the port of the island. Open 8.30 a.m. to midday Mon to Sat, 9 a.m. to 3 p.m. Sun, closed Tues.

Travelling south-west from Argostoli you come to **Mt Enos**, the highest point on the island at 5,313 ft. The view, despite a large television aerial, is stunning. If you continue along past this road you come to the caves of **Drogarati**. Almost every Greek island has caves which they claim are fascinating, but for once they are not exaggerating. Huge yellow and orange stalactites fall from the roof in a cave with such good acoustics that it was once used as a concert hall. There is a dramatic temperature drop in the cave, so take a jumper. Open 7 a.m. to 7 p.m.

Heading in an anti-clockwise direction from Argostoli, the other main resorts on the island are Skala, Poros, Assos and Fiskado.

At the end of a scenic road lies the small, quiet resort of **SKALA**, ideal for a beach holiday or as a base for exploring the south of the island. Most people stay in villas, but there are also a number of rooms and the **Skala** and the **Tara Beach** hotels. Nearby is a good beach at KATO KATELIOS, and, after a somewhat awkward drive, one of the best beaches on the island, PATZAKLI. Further up on the road to Argos lies LOUPDATA, a small villa development on a quiet sandy beach.

A few miles inland lies the village of MARKOPOULO, from which, as its name suggests, Marco Polo's ancestors are supposed to have come. Another legend which all the locals, or rather all the reps, will tell you is that on 15 August, the birthday of the Blessed Virgin, a particular type of snake, with a cross on its head and special healing powers if you touch it, suddenly appears, and is then not seen again until the same day the following year.

Round the coast from hear lies **POROS**, an attractive port slowly beginning to be developed as a resort. There is a good pebble beach and two hotels popular with families, the **Hercules** and the **Alvos Poros**. The mainland ferry to KILLINI calls here and the more adventurous can journey to the mainland for a few days and visit some of the sights.

Further up the coast lies **SAMI**, a busy and not particularly pleasant port where the ferries to Patras and the islands of Ithaca and

Corfu leave. This is not a very good place to stay and the best idea if you land here is to leap on the bus to somewhere else. If you do find yourself having to wait here, just opposite the ferry is the **Ionian Hotel**, and on the main square is the **Kyma**, near the telephone office. About half a mile west of the town lies **Caravomilos Beach Camping** (Tel: 22 480).

The north of the island is particularly beautiful. The first resort you come to is **ASSOS**, which is beginning to be developed, mainly because of the excellent MYRTOS beach nearby, again thought to be one of the best in Greece. The best hotel is the excellent **Myrto**. The resort overlooks an old Venetian fortress, once a prison island, now simply part of a lovely view. Apart from the beach at Myrtos, good swimming can also be had at AGHIOS KYRIAKI.

From Assos, you can visit the small fishing port of AGHIOS EVFIMIA, worth a trip to visit the very good **Paradise Taverna**. A few miles south from here lies the **Melissani Cave**, where you can take a boat trip across an underwater lake.

Finally we come to the other main resort on the island, **FISKADO**, supposedly named after a Norman knight called Robert Guiscard, who died trying to capture the village from the Turks. This was the only place on the island not to be destroyed by the earthquake of 1953, and though it now has an almost permanent traffic jam, it is still charming. Most people stay in rooms or in villas, and the only hotel is the **Panomos**. Sailing flotillas stop here on their travels across the Aegean and although they make the resort very crowded in season, they do mean that the nightlife is fairly sophisticated. The best restaurants are the **Nikolaos**, with a pleasant garden and good food situated near the supermarket, the **Garden Taverna** and the fairly expensive **George Thendrinos** opposite the bus stop. Among the many bars, the one most full of character and characters is the **Captain's Cabin**.

The beaches in the resort are fair, but along the very scenic road back down the island you will find some much better ones.

Ferries leave here for Lekkas and Ithaca, which would make an interesting trip for a few days.

Zakinthos

Zakinthos, or Zante, is one of the most beautiful of the Greek islands, with dramatic views, excellent scenery and very good beaches. This all sounds very similar to Corfu, and indeed many of the brochures compare the island to the Corfu of thirty years ago, before all the tourists arrived. This is true, and although the main resorts on the island could hardly be described as deserted and are very popular with Britons, the rest of the island is fairly quiet. It is not the place for the Socialite, but for Families, Sun-worshippers and the Nature Lover, it would be a good choice. Over twenty tour operators offer holidays here.

HISTORY

Traditionally the island was founded and named after Zakythos, son of the King of Troy, who built his capital on what is now the site of Zante town. With very fertile land and a good location on the trade routes from Crete to Africa, the island soon prospered and in turn founded colonies as far away as Spain. 'The neighbours' were not unaware of the commercial growth of the island, and in 214 BC the Romans invaded.

Christianity arrived sometime in the 3rd century, followed by the Vandals in AD 466. In 844 the Turks attacked, but were for once defeated by the Byzantine Empire and Zakinthos, like Corfu, was one of the few parts of Greece never to fall to the Turks. In 1182 the Normans took the island, to be replaced in 1484 by the Venetians.

Under the latter, the island became a centre for refugees from Turkish rule: with the arrival of many Cretan refugees it became a great cultural base, where the Ionian school of painting started, and a very popular type of song known as *cantades* originated here. The greatest figure of the period was a poet called Dionysius Solomos, known as the 'Byron of the East', who wrote in the ordinary Greek that most people spoke, rather than its literary form. He became particularly famous as the poet of the Wars of Independence, when a poem of his was used as the lyrics for the new Greek national anthem.

The Venetians introduced a very divisive system of government which totally ignored the poor, and at the time of the French Revolution, with the help of French troops, the islanders rebelled. The super-powers of the time felt that they could not let this happen and in 1798, after a long siege, the Russo-Turkish fleet ended the revolution. After a further rebellion in 1801 the British arrived in 1809 and stayed until 1864.

The most recurrent feature of the history of the island has been earthquakes. One in 1514 apparently destroyed the castle and Zante town, and exposed the white cliffs that now surround it. The most dramatic quake took place in 1953 and also destroyed the town. The town council, with an unusual degree of sense, decided to re-construct, rather than rebuild the town, but although compared to many Greek towns it is charming, it can no longer be considered more beautiful than Corfu town.

In holiday terms the island has long been popular with the Greeks on the mainland. Over the last few years, however, foreign tourists have begun to arrive. Although development has begun to take place, you can still see why the Venetians called the island the Flower of the Levant.

PRACTICAL DETAILS

There are direct flights to the island from several airports in the UK, which is about 3½ hours away by air. Ferries do run here from Killini on the mainland (about 75 minutes away) and from some of the other Ionian islands, but it does not lie on a major ferry route and is therefore spared the onslaught of backpackers every summer.

To get around the island you are faced with the familiar choice of car hire, taxi or bus. Car hire has the usual problem of expense, and most people turn to mopeds, though bikes make a popular, and a safer, alternative. There is a bus network covering the island, but with only one bus a day it is not very convenient. If you intend to stay on the beach all day this may not really matter and in the evening you can simply hire a taxi to take you to the town. A ride in some Greek taxis can be something of an experience, as you stop to pick up other passengers and become increasingly convinced that you are being sold into white slavery. However, they are the easiest way of getting about the island, and as long as you agree a fare before you start out you should be all right. A few horse-drawn carriages drift around the town and provide an enjoyable, if expensive, way of seeing the sights.

CULINARY SPECIALITIES

Greek food can be a bit dull and tepid, but Zakinthos is one of the places where standards are quite high. The most popular speciality of the island with the tourists is a white wine called *Kerdea*. If you are diligent you may also be able to find *Comouto*, a rosé, and a strawberry liqueur. If you fancy a nibble with your drink try *pastalis*, a small biscuit made with honey and sesame. If you are concerned for your teeth the fruit on the island is very good.

WHERE TO GO FOR WHAT

Zakinthos is really a quiet place for beach holidays, but there is some choice of resorts. The Socialite should head for ARGASSI, the Sun-worshipper for VASSILIKOS and Families for LAGNAS, TSILIVI or ALIKES.

ZANTE TOWN
Zante town was rebuilt after the earthquake of 1953, and although all the guide books will tell you that it is much less beautiful than it once was, on first impressions it is far more elegant than most holiday resorts, with a very good location and some good nightlife. In short, a lively though unpretentious resort.

ACCOMMODATION

Most people stay in the **Starda Marina Hotel**, with a rooftop swimming pool overlooking the harbour, or the **Bitzaro**, an ivy-clad hotel with a good view at 46 D Roma. Among the smaller hotels, the **Aegli** just down from the Starda Marina, the **Xenia**, just up from the Bitzaro, and the **Phoenix**, on 2 Platia D Solomau, are all quite good. The independent traveller looking for something cheaper should consider the **Ionian**, or the **Rezentsa** at numbers 18 and 36 Alex.

Roma, or the **Diana**, which has a good location overlooking Ag Markou. There are also campsites at PLANOS, TSILIVI and VASILIKOS, though the latter is rather isolated.

TOURIST INFORMATION

Conveniently, the post office and the banks are all located just inland from the pier on the left-hand side of the harbour. Here you will also find the Tourist Police on 2 Lomravdou Street (Tel: 22 550), who are very helpful in providing information. Open 8 a.m. to 2 p.m., 4.30 p.m. to 9 p.m. If you want to phone home, the OTE office is at the top left-hand corner of the main square, open 7 a.m. to midnight. If you have an accident, the hospital lies slightly inland (Tel: 22 514). The bus station is just inland from the harbour road, about halfway along between Ag Elefteriou and Filita Streets.

SIGHTSEEING

There are no great 'sights' in the town, but there are a number of places which are worth strolling round. **Plateia Solomou** is the main square of the town and is a pleasant place in which to sit. In it you will find the **NeoByzantine Museum**, next to the Town Hall. This contains a large number of icons from the period of the island's leadership of the Ionian school of painting, and though their appeal may be fairly limited, if you are interested, this is probably the best collection in the world. Open Mon to Sat 8.30 a.m. to 3 p.m., Sun 8 a.m. to 1 p.m., closed Tues.

The other main square in the town is **Ag Markou**. Here there is another good museum, the **Solomos**, which houses both an exhibition about Dionysius Solomos, the famous poet of the island, and his tomb. Even if your interest in Greek literature is not great, the museum is worth a visit to see the photographs of the town before the earthquake. Open 9 a.m. to 1.30 p.m., 6 p.m. to 8 p.m.

Only three buildings survived 1953 – the school, the bank and the **Church of Ag Dionysis, St Denis**. This huge church is on the extreme right of the harbour. Built only a few years before the earthquake, its exterior is not very impressive, although the inside is worth a look. St Denis was born in 1547 of a noble family who, until recently, still lived on the island. A bishop, he later became the abbot of a monastery, and his piety is demonstrated by the fact that he gave sanctuary to the man who killed his brother. On 24 August and 17 December his relics are taken out of their silver chest and paraded through the streets in a glass sedan chair. It is said that his slippers have to be replaced several times a year because during the night he gets up and carries out good deeds.

A few streets inland lies the **Church of Phaneroneni**, the Manifestation of the Virgin. Before 1953 this was the most impressive church on the island and although it is now much less so it makes an interesting visit. At the opposite end of the harbour is the church of **Kinas von Angelon**, Our Lady of the Angels, situated just off D Roma on Achiepiskopou Kokkini. It is not particularly stunning, but most people seem to be amused on learning that it was built by the hairdressers' guild! Incidentally, D Roma was the original coast road before the sea was pushed back by rubble from the earthquake.

NIGHTLIFE

Quite a large number of people stay in Zante town, and even more journey to it in the evening, so this makes it fairly lively. As mentioned above, the food on the island is good. Starting from the right of the harbour try the small, noisy but enjoyable **Botega Cafe**. Slightly further up the harbour road you will find the **To Stoki To Patras**. On Ag Ioannos Logothetou, leading inland, are the **Caliga Rose** and the **Hellas**, both complete with singing and dancing as well as good food, and just next to the petrol station is the very pleasant **Ship Inn**. Travelling up this same street brings you out on to Ag Pavlou, which has several small souvlaki restaurants, more popular with the locals than tourists. Carrying straight on from here you come to Alex Roma and Vass Konstantiniou, which has a few good, small restaurants on the right and left. You then come to Ag Markou Square, where there are a number of pleasant but expensive restaurants. The best is probably **Malias**, which has some very good fish dishes. Just at the bottom of the square on Vass Georgiou, is the excellent **Kallino Restaurant** and, just behind it, the **Zante Pub**.

One of the most popular places to go in the evening is the **Argassi**. It was once yet another summer residence for the commissioner from Corfu, but is now a lively disco.

EXCURSIONS

Dominating the town is the **Old Castle**, now almost covered by a forest but well worth a visit for the excellent view. To reach it, follow the signs for Vohali. On the way you will pass through BOHALI, a small village with a number of good tavernas. Another semi-military establishment is the **British Cemetery**, which contains the graves of those who died during the English occupation.

If you are staying in Zante town one of the most important excursions will be to the beach, though there is a small lido where you can bathe on D Roma. The real Sun-worshipper, however, should head for the beaches at TSILIVI in the north, VASSILIKI in the south-east and LAGNAS in the south. Those with a greater sense of adventure could explore the island, but, be warned, the maps are a little unreliable.

About 6 miles inland lies MACHAIRIDO, with the very beautiful church of Ag Mavra. Continuing on this same route will take you, via a dramatic hairpin road, to Ag Nikolaos. Along the way you catch glimpses of a large pink mansion called the **Sarakina**, which you can explore. Turning left here brings you to the pretty little village of AGALAS.

Zakinthos is famous, in the guide books at least, for its caves. The best of these is the **Blue Grotto** at Korynth on the north of the island, which for once actually deserves to be called 'blue'. You can drive up here, but it is probably more enjoyable to take a caique from the town. Boat trips can also be taken to the small islands of PELOUZO and MARATHONISISI off the south coast. If you are particularly organized, you could even consider spending a few days on the mainland.

The Rest of the Island

The main holiday resort is **ARGASSI**, about 25 minutes south of Zante town. There is no real beach, but there are a number of good hotels and, above all, a lively nightlife, which make it very popular with the British holiday-makers.

The two main hotels are the **Chryssi Atki**, overlooking the beach, and the **Mimosa Beach**, a busy bungalow development. Other fairly good hotels are **Captains**, **Levante**, **Family Inn** and **Iliessa**.

During the day the beaches at ST NIKOLAS are the main attraction, but at night Argassi comes into its own. Among the best restaurants are the **Bolero, Meno Male, Ambellos** and, just outside the village, the popular **Porto Davi**. A tour of the bars will soon show you just how popular the resort is with the British, most of whom tend to congregate in the **Magic Mushroom**, the **Three Brothers**, and **Denis' Bar**. The **Argassi** is fairly near if you want a disco, but if you are looking for something slightly more sophisticated, try the **Manhattan**.

From Argassi you can travel to VASSILIKOS, which has probably the best beach on the island, and is only about 20 minutes away by bike. This is also known as 'Golden Beach', and when you see it you can see why. It is now a nesting site for turtles, as well as a popular base for villa holidays.

In the same area good beaches can also be found at PORTO ZORRO and ST NIKOLAS, which is particularly good for children. At the bottom of the island there is a dramatically situated and very good beach at CAPE GERAKAS. The mountain nearby, **Mt Skopos** (1,640 ft), was thought by the Romans to be one of the entrances to the underworld, but most people now visit it just for the view.

Around the coast from here lies **LAGNAS**, about 20 minutes from Zante town. The brochures will tell you that this is one of the best beaches in the Mediterranean, but a much better recommendation is that many of the Greeks themselves come here for their holidays. Many tour operators now offer holidays here and the resort is becoming a bit crowded, but for a family holiday with a good beach for the children and some nightlife for Mum and Dad, Lagnas would be excellent. There are a number of watersports, and away from the centre the beach becomes less crowded. In the evening try **Tassis Taverna** and the **Sirocco**, or two discos, the **Kalamaki** and the **Cameo**.

From here you can visit the pitch springs at **Keri Bay**, but these are not really worth the trip. Travelling in the opposite direction you come to KALAMAKI, where the sea has eroded much of the shore and a bridge stands in the middle of the waves. Along the way you will probably notice the huts on stilts, originally used by peasants but now full of adventurous tourists.

The Resorts North of the Town

Nearest to the town is **TSILIVI**, which is yet another good beach set amongst olive groves, that is popular with families. Most people stay in villas, but the **Belle Helene** and the **Tsilivi Beach** are two quite good hotels.

A little further along the coast lies PLANOS, or Platanos, not so much a resort as a hotel, the **Carvelr**. This is the only 'A-class' hotel on the island and is an excellent place for a very comfortable holiday.

The other main resort on this coast is ALIKES, probably the quietest of the resorts on the island, though during the high season it does become fairly crowded, so much so that getting a table at **Kims Bar** or the **Olympian Cafe** can be quite hard. Of the hotels, the best is probably the **Astoria**, but also worth a look are the **Ionian** and the **Montreal**, or the cheaper **Alikes** and **Calmness**.

Nearby is **Kastastari**, which has a good view, also the **Blue Grotto Cave** and a ruined monastery at **Anatonitria**, which has another good view.

In the next bay from Alikes lies ALIKANAS, a villa development which is very quiet outside the main season.

Vocabulary

There's no need to try and get to grips with the Greek alphabet, as just about everywhere in the tourist areas you will find English spoken. Because of the difficulty of the different alphabet the following words and phrases are written phonetically.

English	*Greek*
Yes	Neh
No	Okhee
Please	Pahrahkalo
Thank you	Ehvkhaheesto
Good morning	Kahleemehrah
Good afternoon	Kahleespehrah
Good evening	Kahleeneektah
Goodbye	Ahneeo
Excuse me	Meh seengkhoreeteh
Where is/are	Poo eeneh
When	Poteh
What	Tee
How	Poss
Who	Peeoss
Why	Yeeahtee
I understand/don't understand	Kahtahlahvehno/dhehn kahtahlahvehno
Do you speak English?	Meelahteh ahnggleekah?
Can I have . . .?	Boro nah ehkho . . .?
I would like . . .	Thah eethehlah . . .
A single/double room	Ehnah mono dhomahteeo/ehnah dheeplo dhomahteeo
A room with a bath/shower	Ehnah dhomahteeo meh bahneeo/dooss

English	Greek pronunciation
What is the price per night/week?	Peeah eeneh ee teemee yeeah meeah neekhtah/meeah ehvdhomahdhah?
It is . . .	Eenah
It isn't	Dhehn eeneh
Is there/are there . . . ?	Eepahrkhee/eepahrkhoon . . . ?
There is/there are	Eepahrkhee/eepahrkhoon
Good/bad	Kahloss/kahkoss
Cheap/expensive	Fteenoss/ahkreevoss
Big/small	Mehgahloss/meekross
Where can I get a taxi?	Poo boro nah vro ehnah tahksee?
Take me to this address please	Peeyehnehteh meh sahftee tee dheeehftheensee pahrahkahlo
Where's the nearest bank please?	Poo eeneh ee pleesseeehstehree trahpehzah pahrahkahlo?
Where can I change some traveller's cheques please?	Poo boro nah ehksahryeerosso mehreekah trahvehlehrs tsehk?
Can you show me where I am on the map?	Booreeteh nah moo dheeksehteh sto khahrtee poo eemeh?
I'm lost	Kahtheekah
Can I have my bill please?	Boro nah ehkho ton logahreeahzmo pahrahkahlo?
Where's the ladies/gents toilet?	Poo eeneh ee tooahlehtehss/ton yeenehkonahndhron?
Can I use your telephone?	Boro nah khreesseemopeeeesso to teelehfono sahss?
Call an ambulance/police	Kahlehsteh ehnah ahsthehnoforo/ahsteenomeeah
One	Ehnah
Two	Dheeo
Three	Treeah
Four	Tehsehrah
Five	Pehndeh
Six	Ehksee
Seven	Ehptah
Eight	Okto

Nine	Ehnehah
Ten	Dhenkah
Sunday	Keereeahkee
Monday	Dhehftehrah
Tuesday	Treetee
Wednesday	Tertahrtee
Thursday	Pehmptee
Friday	Pahrahskehvee
Saturday	Shavahto
Today	Seemehrah
Tomorrow	Ahvreeo
Yesterday	Khthehss

Index

Accommodation, 82, 91–2, 97, 104–5, 106, 147–8, 155–7, 159, 161, 167–9, 170–71, 178–81, 189, 192, 194, 196–9, 206, 208–9, 210, 211, 212, 215, 217, 219, 220, 221, 222, 223, 226–7, 228, 229–30, 231, 236, 237, 238, 239, 241, 242, 243, 244–5, 250–51, 252–5, 257, 258, 265–6, 266–7, 269–70, 272, 273, 274, 279, 284–5, 290, 291, 292, 294, 297–8, 305, 311, 313, 316–17, 319–22, 325–6, 328, 335, 337–9, 343–4, 347, 348, 358–9, 364, 367–8, 370–71, 373, 381, 385–6, 390, 392–5, 397–8, 416–20, 422–5, 428, 431–3, 439–41, 445, 449–50, 455, 483–4, 486–8, 489, 491, 495–8, 500, 502–4, 506–7, 510–11, 513, 515–16, 519–23, 530–31, 534–5, 537–9
Activity Holidays, see Healthy Holidays
Aegina, 152, 437–41
  Aegina Town, 439–40
  Aghia Marina, 439, 441
  Angistri, 441
  Kipseli, 440
  Moni, 441
  Paleohora, 440
  Perdika, 439, 441
  Souvala, 440–41
  see also Saronic Gulf Islands, The
Aghios Efstratios, 42
Air travel, see Travel, Means of
Alonissos, 272–7
  Alonissos Town, 272–3
  Kalamakia, 275
  Palovodimos, 275
  Patitri, 273–5
  see also Sporades, The
Amateur Anglers and Maritime Sports Club, address, 39
Amorgos, 42, 96, 282
  Ag Anna, 282
  Chora, 282
  Egiali, 282
  Katapola, 282
  Mino, 282
  see also Cyclades, The

Anafi, 42
Andros, 281, 283–6
  Amolohos, 285
  Andros Town, 286
  Fellos, 285
  Gavrion, 284–5
  Kato Katakilos, 286
  Korthion, 286
  Palaikoastrou, 286
  Paliapolis, 286
  Vatsi (Batsi), 31, 284, 285
  Yialia, 286
  see also Cyclades, The
Angistri, 441
  Limenaria, 441
  Milo, 441
  Skala, 441
  see also Saronic Gulf Islands, The
Antikythera, 42
Antiparos, 312–14
  Ag Georgias, 314
  Livadhi, 314
  see also Cyclades, The
Apollo coast, see Attica
Astipalea, 350–51
  Aghios Andreas, 351
  Aghios Konstantinos, 351
  Analipsi, 351
  Astipalea Town, 351
  Livadia, 351
  Maltezana, 351
  Senaki, 351
  Vathi, 351
  see also Dodecanese Islands, The
Athens, 24, 141–54
Attica, 24, 154–61
  Agii Theodori, 159
  Aigosthena, 159
  Alepohori, 159
  Amfiaraion, 162
  Anavissos, 157
  Bay of Ireon, 159
  Brauron, 160
  Daphni, 152
  Dekelia, 162

546 INDEX

Elefsina, 158
Glyfada, 155–6
Kavouri, 156
Kifissia, 162
Kineta, 158
Lagonissi, 157
Lavrio, 160
Loutraki, 159
Loutsa, 160
Marathon, 161–2
Markopoulu, 160
Maroussi, 162
Mati, 161
Megara, 158
Messogia, 160
Mount Parnes, 162
Nea Makri, 161
Paleo Faliro, 155
Peania, 160
Piraeus, 39, 154–5
Porto Rafti, 160
Porto Yermeno, 159
Rafina, 160–61
Ramnous, 162
Schinias, 160, 162
Shiros, 159
Sounion, 157–8
Voula, 155–6
Vouliagmeni, 155–7

Babies, catering for, 43–4
Baedeker's Greece, 50
Baggage, *see* Luggage
Beaches, list of best, 31–2
Budgeting, 50–52
  see also Money
Bus travel, *see* Travel, Means of

Cameras, video, 35
Camping Holidays, 90–91, 105–6, 199, 212–13, 228, 234, 236, 238, 241–2, 245, 285, 287, 289, 291, 298, 301, 305, 309, 311–13, 320, 326, 358, 372, 423, 482, 486, 489, 495, 498, 500, 502, 512, 519–20, 527, 531, 535
  Hellenic Touring Club, The, 91
  N.T.O.G., 91
  tour operators, 75
  see also Independent Travel *and* Package Holidays
Car Hire, *see* Travel, Means of

Caving, 38
  see also Healthy Holidays
Central Greece, 24, 174–81
  Arachora, 179
  Arahova, 36
  Delphi, 33, 152, 174, 175–9
  Glifa, 174
  Itea, 178
  Kalambaka, 180
  Kalanera, 181
  Karena Vourla, 174
  Kira, 178
  Kissos, 181
  Lamia, 174
  Litochora, 181
  Livadia, 179
  Meteora, 33, 179–80
  Milies, 181
  Nefpaktos, 178
  Olympia, 181
  Pelion, 181
    Makrinitsa, 181
    Portaria, 181
  Rahes, 174
  Thermopylae, 174
  Tsangarada, 181
  Volos, 180–81
  Zagora, 181

Cephalonia, *see* Kefalonia
Chios, 254–6
  Anevatos, 256
  Chios Town, 255
  Emborios, 255
  Inoussa, 256
  Karfas, 255
  Komi, 255
  Limani, 255
  Litho, 255
  Mesta, 255
  Nagos, 255
  Olymbai, 255
  Pirgi, 255
  Psara, 256
  St Markella, 255
  Vallis, 255
  see also North-east Aegean Islands, The
Choice of holiday, 22–4
Climate
  Athens, 26
  Corfu, 27, 465
  Crete, 27, 406

INDEX

Dodecanese Islands, The, 333
Evia, 164–5
meltemi wind, 26
Northern Greece, 204
Peloponnese, 233
Rhodes, 379
Sporades, The, 262–3
Thessaloniki, 27
Western Greece, 184–5
winter, 28
Coach Tours
  tour operators, 78–9, 92–3, 97
  see also Package Holidays *and* Travel, Means of
Communications, 126–7
Conference arrangements, 82
Corfu, 24, 458–513
  Acharavi, 494
  Achilleon Palace, 508–9, 511
  Afionas, 499
  Ag Gordis, 480
  Aghios Georgeous, 498–9
  Aghios Georgios, 31, 504–5
  Aghios Gordis, 504
  Aghios Markos, 490
  Aghios Nikolaos, 512
  Aghios Spiridon, 491, 493, 494
  Aghios Stefanos, 493, 497
  Aghios Yannis, 503
  Agnistini, 493
  Ag Triadha, 501
  Alikes Potamou, 482
  Alykes, 513
  Antinioti Lagoon, 494
  Argirades, 505
  Arillas, 498
  Astrakeri, 494
  Barbati, 490
  Bastalika, 513
  Benitses, 509–11
  Boukari, 512
  camping, 469–70
  Cape Asprokavos, 513
  climate, 27, 465
  Corfu Town, 468–79
  Danilia, 480, 485
  Dassia, 479, 487–9
  Erikoussa, 496
  Ermones, 480, 502
  Gastouri, 509
  Gerifa, 501
  Glyfada, 31, 480, 502–3
  Gouvia, 479, 483–5
  Helios holiday village, 94, 99
  Humous, 501
  Ipsos, 479, 488, 489–90
  Kaiser's Bridge, 509
  Kalami, 493
  Kanoni, 480, 505–7
  Karoussades, 494
  Kassiopi, 491–3
  Kato Garoura, 504
  Kavos, 512–13
  Kinadades, 496
  Kommeno, 485, 486–7
  Kontokali, 482
  Korissa Lagoon, 505, 512
  Kouloura, 491, 493
  Kritika, 505, 513
  Liapades Bay, 501
  Magoulades, 496
  Markades, 499
  Mathraki, 496
  Messonghi, 31, 511–12
  Mon Repos, 479
  Moraitika, 511–12
  Moritiotissa, 480, 502
  Mt Matheos, 512
  Mouse Island, 480, 506
  Myrtiotissa, 503
  Nisaki, 490–91, 493
  Othoni, 496
  Paleokastritsa, 480, 485, 499–501
  Paramona, 505, 512
  Pelekas, 480, 502, 503
  Perama, 507–8
  Perithia, 494
  Peroulades, 497
  Petreti, 512
  Platonas, 495
  Pyrgi, 489
  Roda, 495
  Roumanades, 512
  Sidari, 495–6
  Sinarades, 504
  Spartero, 513
  Spartilas, 490
  Stiliari, 501
  Troumbetta, 499
  Vatos, 502
  Vitaldes, 505
  Vlakherena, 506
  Yaliscari, 504
  Ypsos, 31

INDEX

Corinth, Gulf of
  Antirio, 31
  Rio, 31
Credit cards, *see* Money
Crete, 24, 402–35
  Aghia Galini, 427, 432–3
  Aghia Marina, 429–30
  Aghia Roumeli, 434
  Aghios Nikolaos, 419–21
  Agia Pelagia, 423
  Agia Triada, 414–15
  Almiros Beach, 420
  Ammoudara, 409
  Arkadi Monastery, 426
  Arvi, 432
  Bali, 423
  Chania, 427–9
  Dia, 38
  Elounda, 32, 418–19
  Falasarna, 430
  Ferma, 431
  Florida Beach, 412
  Fodele, 423
  Gavdos, 431
  Georgioupolis, 427
  Gortys, 414–15
  Gournes, 32, 416
  Heraklion, 409–12
  Herssonissos, 416
  Hora Sfakion, 434, 435
  Ierapetra, 420, 431
  Kalo Horio, 421
  Kastelli, 430
  Kato, 423
  Kato Zakros, 32, 422
  Keratokambos, 432
  Kissamos, 32
  Knossos, 412–14
  Kokkini Hani, 416
  Kolimbos, 431
  Komo, 432
  Kritsa, 421
  Kydonia, 429
  Lato, 421
  Linoperamata, 409
  Loutro, 435
  Makriki Island, 421
  Maleme, 32, 429
  Malia, 416–18
  Matala, 32, 432
  meltemi wind, 25
  Milatos, 418
  Myrtos, 432
  Oasis Beach, 428
  Paleochora, 434–5
  Phaistos, 414–15
  Plakias, 433
  Platanias, 429
  Red Beach, 432
  Rethymnon, 32, 424–7
  Samaria Gorge, The, 434
  Sfinari, 430
  Sissi, 418
  Sitia, 32, 420, 421–2
  Spili, 433
  Spinalonga Island, 418, 421
  Stalis, 416
  Vai, 32, 422
  Zaros, 433
Cruises, 94–5
  companies operating, 76–7
Culinary specialities, *see* Food and Drink
Currency, *see* Money
Customs, 45
Cyclades, The, 24, 280–329
  Delos, 33
  Donoussa, 42, 282
  Iraklia, 282
  Kea, 160
  Koufonisia, 96, 282
  meltemi wind, 25
  Milos, 33
  Nea Kameni, 318
  Pserimos, 96
  Santorini, 33
  Shinoussa, 282
  Thirassia, 321
  see also Amorgos, Andros, Antiparos, Folegrandros, Ios, Kea, Kythros, Milos, Mykonos, Naxos, Paros, Santorini, Serifos, Sifnos, Syros *and* Tinos

Delos, 300–303, 329
  Ag Anna, 301
  Agari, 301
  Ag Yiannis, 301
  Ano Mera, 301
  Elia, 301
  Ftelia, 301
  Korfos, 300
  Megali Ammos, 300
  Ormos, 300
  Panormas, 301

INDEX 549

Paradise Beach, 301
Plati Yialos, 301
Psarou, 301
Super Paradise, 301
Tarsana, 301
Tournos Bay, 301
see also Cyclades, The
Dodecanese Islands, The, 24, 330–41
  Agios Georgios, 341
  Armathia, 339
  see also Astipalea, Halki, Kalymnos, Karpathos, Kassos, Kastelorizo, Kos, Leros, Lipsi, Nissiros, Patmos, Rhodes, Symi *and* Tilos

Eastern Macedonia and Thrace
  Alexandroupolis, 38, 220–21
  Audira, 219
  Batis, 220
  Kalamitsa, 220
  Kavala, 218–19
  Lagos, 31
  Nea Hili, 31
  Nea Iraklista, 220
  Nea Peramos, 220
  Philippi, 219–20
  Toska, 220
  see also Northern Greece
Eating Out, *see* Food and Drink
Educational Trips and Student Travel, 78
Emergencies, *see* Problems and Emergencies
Europe by Train, 108, 109
Evia, 24, 162–73
  Agia Ana, 171
  Agios Georgios, 171
  Aliveri, 169
  Almiropotamos, 173
  Angali, 171
  Ano Potamia, 170
  Ano Vathia, 169
  Edipsos, 171
  Eretria, 165, 168–9
  Gregolimano, 165, 168
  Halkida, 166–7
  Karistos, 31, 172
  Kehries, 171
  Kimi, 169–70
  Lepoura, 169
  Limni, 171
  Loutra Edipsou, 171
  Mantoudi, 171
  Marmari, 31, 173
  Nea Stira, 173
  Orei, 170–71
  Parolia Kimi, 170
  Pefki, 170
  Prokopi, 171
  Stira, 172

Family Holidays, 29, 43–4, 199, 205, 208, 220–21, 233, 238, 249, 251–3, 256, 264, 279, 281, 283–5, 303, 306, 354, 381, 393, 395–6, 401, 408, 423, 427, 430, 442, 466, 481–3, 486, 487, 490, 493, 495, 499, 502, 505, 507, 511, 515, 518, 526, 532, 534, 538–9
Federation of Mountaineering and Skiing, 181
Festivals, 36–7, 398, 422
Fishing, 39
  see also Healthy Holidays
Flotilla Holidays, 96
  tour operators, 77–8
  see also Package Holidays
Fly-cruising Holidays, 95
  tour operators, 75
  see also Travel, Means of
Fly-drive Holidays
  tour operators, 77
  see also Travel, Means of
Fly-yachting Holidays, 96
  tour operators, 77
  see also Travel, Means of
Folegrandros, 286–7
  Agkali, 287
  Chora, 287
  Livadi, 287
  see also Cyclades, The
Food and Drink, 120
  culinary specialities, 121–3, 165, 185, 204–5, 213, 233, 263, 284, 288, 304–5, 308, 316, 333, 340, 362, 379, 406–7, 465–6, 526, 534
  drinks, 124–5, 252, 256
  restaurants/eating out, 120–23, 152–3, 157, 167, 169, 172, 178–81, 199–200, 206–8, 210–13, 215, 218–19, 226, 235, 237–8, 239, 241–2, 255, 257–8, 265, 269, 271, 273–4, 278–9, 282, 285, 289–92, 294, 299–300, 306, 311, 313, 318, 320–22, 326, 328, 340, 344, 347, 363, 367, 371, 379–80, 386–7, 391–2, 397, 411–12, 420–21, 422, 426, 428–9,

445, 451–2, 457, 477–9, 484, 486, 490–91, 496, 498–9, 507, 513, 519–20, 531, 536, 538–9

Golf, 38, 382, 394, 502
  see also Healthy Holidays
Greek Alpine Club, 234
Greek Skiing and Alpine Federation, 37
Greek Touring Club, The, 38

Halki, 42, 337–8
  Horio, 338
  Niborio, 338
  Pandemos, 338
  see also Dodecanese Islands, The
Halkidiki, 205–18
  Afitos, 208
  Agia Triada, 31
  Agios Nikolaos, 211
  Akiti Sani, 214
  Amouliani, island of, 215
  Dafni, 216
  Dionisiou, 207
  Fourka, 213–14
  Gerakini, 31, 207
  Gomati, 215
  Haniotis, 209
  Ierissos, 215
  Kalandra, 213
  Kaldive, 207
  Kalithea, 208
  Kalomitsi, 212
  Karyes, 217
  Kassandra, 208–9, 213–14
  Kriopigi, 209
  Megaliponagia, 215
  Metamofossis, 210
  Mount Athos, 42, 216–18
  Nea Forkea, 208
  Nea Maramas, 212–13
  Nea Moudania, 207–8
  Nea Olynthos, 207
  Nea Potidea, 208
  Nea Roda, 215
  Nea Skioni, 213
  Nikiti, 210
  Ormilia, 210
  Ormos Panogias, 211
  Ouranopolis, 215–16
  Paliouri, 209–10
  Paradissos, 213
  Pefkohoro, 209
  Petralona, 206
  Poligiros, 206
  Polihrono, 209
  Porto Carras, 31, 212
  Porto Koufo, 212
  Possidi, 213
  Sani, 31, 213
  Sarti, 211
  Sikia, 211–12
  Siriri, 213
  Siviri, 214
  Stageira, 214–15
  Stratoniki, 214
  Tripiti, 215
  Torini, 212
  Vatopedi, 210
  Vourvourou, 211
  Zografou, 207
  see also Northern Greece
Health, 44, 48–9
Healthy Holidays, 29, 37–9, 156, 165, 181, 185, 205, 208, 212, 229, 238–9, 354, 381–2, 393, 394, 408, 482, 515
  caving, 38
  fishing, 39
  golf, 38, 382, 394, 502
  hunting, 38
  mountaineering, 37
  riding, 39, 382
  skiing, 37, 38
  tennis, 38
  water sports, 165, 185, 205, 208–9, 238, 253, 266, 301, 364, 367, 393–4, 397, 456–7, 467–8, 481, 489, 497, 501, 503–4, 510–11
Hellenic Alpine Club, 166
Hellenic Sailing Federation, 38
Hellenic Wind Surfing Association, 39
History of Greece, 133–7
Holiday villages, 93–4, 165, 168, 358
  see also Package Holidays
Holiday Insurance, see Insurance
Hotels, see Accommodation
Hunting, 38
  see also Healthy Holidays
Hydra, 152, 447–52
  Aghios Nikolaos Bay, 451
  Cape Bisti, 451
  Castello, 451
  Easter festivals, 36
  Kamini, 451–2
  Limnioniza, 451

INDEX 551

Mandraki Bay, 451
Molos, 451
Palamida, 451
Vlichos, 451
see also Saronic Gulf Islands

Ikaria, 259
  Ag Kirykos, 259
  Armenistis, 259
  Fourni, 259
  Nas, 259
  Rakis, 259
  Therma, 259
  Yialisea, 259
  see also North-east Aegean Islands
Independent Travel, 24, 57, 103–14
  accommodation, 91–2, 104–5, 106, 206, 209, 231, 257, 265, 297–8, 305, 309, 317, 328, 417, 422, 424, 431, 433, 435, 469, 516, 527
  air
    airlines, 106–7
    charter flights, 107–8
  bus, 93, 110, 241
    companies, 110
  camping, 90, 105–6, 199, 212–13, 234, 236, 238, 241–2, 245, 285, 287, 289, 291, 298, 301, 305, 309, 311–13, 320, 326, 358, 372, 423, 482, 486, 489, 495, 498, 500, 302, 512, 519, 520, 527, 531, 535
  car/camper, 110–12
    choice of car, 112
    petrol, 111
  coach, 110
  hitch-hiking, 112–13
  options, 103–6
  rail, 108–9
  sea, 113–14
    ferry companies, 113
  tailor-made holidays, 106
Information, see Pre-planning and Information
Inoussa, island of, 42
Insurance, 47–8
International Student Identity Card, discounts, 52
Ionian Islands, The, 24, 514–39
  see also Corfu, Ithaca, Kefalonia, Lefkas, Paxos and Zakinthos
Ios, 287–91
  Ag Theodoti, 289

Gaios, 288, 289
Gialos, 32
Ios Town, 289
Kalamos Bay, 291
Koumboura, 289
Maganari, 290–91
Milopatamos Beach, 291
Psathis, 289
Valmas, 289
see also Cyclades, The
Island-hopping Holidays
tour operators, 76
Ithaca, 515, 521–3
  Ag Ioannis, 523
  Frikes, 523
  Kioni, 523
  Perachori, 522
  Polis, 523
  Sarakiniko Bay, 522
  Skinos Bay, 522
  Stavros, 523
  Vathi, 521–2
  see also Ionian Islands, The

Kalymnos, 358, 360–65
  Arginonda, 365
  Emborio, 365
  Kantouri, 364
  Linaria, 364
  Massouri, 364, 365
  Myrties, 364, 365
  Plati Yialos, 364
  Pothia, 361, 362–3
  Pserimos, 363
  Skalia, 365
  Telendos, island of, 42, 362, 364, 365
  Therma, 364
  Vathis, 365
  Vothynon, 364
  see also Dodecanese Islands, The
Karpathos, 35, 334–7
  Amopi Beach, 335
  Aperi, 335, 336
  Arkassa, 336
  Diafani, 336
  Karpathos Town (Pigadia), 335
  Lefkos, 336
  Menetes, 336
  Messochori, 336
  Olymbos, 336–7
  Olympus, 334
  Piles, 336

Vananda, 336
Vourgounda, 337
see also Dodecanese Islands, The
Kassos, 338–9
  Agia Marina, 339
  Avranitohorio, 339
  Emborio, 339
  Fri, 339
  Panagia, 339
  Poli, 339
  see also Dodecanese Islands, The
Kastellorizo, 42, 340–41
  Agios Stefanos, 341
  Kas, 341
  Megisti, 340–41
  see also Dodecanese Islands, The
Kea, 291–2
  Chora, 292
  Korissia, 292
  Koundros, 292
  Otzias, 292
  Pisses, 292
  Vourkai, 292
  Yaliskari, 292
  see also Cyclades, The
Kefalonia, 24, 38, 515, 523–31
  Aghios Evfimia, 531
  Aghios Kyriaki, 531
  Aghios Pelagei, 529
  Ag Pelagi, 526
  Ag Spiridon, 529
  Argostoli, 526–7
  Assos, 526, 531
  Drongorati, 38
  Fiskado, 525, 531
  Kato Katelios, 530
  Lixouri, 31, 526, 529
  Loupdata, 530
  Melissani, 38
  Markis Yialos, 529
  Markopoulo, 530
  Mourkoumeleta, 529
  Myrtos, 526, 531
  Patzkali, 530
  Petari, 529
  Plati Yialos, 31, 526, 529
  Poros, 526, 530
  Sami, 31, 530–31
  Skala, 530
  see also Ionian Islands, The

Kimolos, island of, 30
Kos, 352–60
  Aghios Fokas, 358
  Antimachia, 357
  Asfendiou, 357
  Kamari Beach, 358
  Kardomena, 348, 349, 357–8
  Kefalos, 357
  Kos Town, 354–60
  Lagoudi, 357
  Lambi, 357, 360
  Marmari, 357, 359
  Mastihari, 357
  Paradise Beach, 358
  Platani, 356
  Psalidi, 358
  Pyli, 357
  Thermi, 358
  Tingaki, 357
  Zipari, 356
  see also Dodecanese Islands, The
Kythera, 42, 242
  Ag Pelagias, 242
  Chora, 242
  Kapasali, 242
  Plati Amos, 242
  see also Peloponnese
Kythnos, 42, 292
  Chora, 292
  Loutra, 292
  Merichas, 292
  see also Cyclades, The

Language, 21
Lefkas, 515, 518–20
  Athani, 520
  Kalamitisi, 519
  Lefkas Town, 31, 518–19
  Nefkados, 520
  Neokhori, 519
  Nidri, 519–20
  Poros, 520
  Skorpios, 519
  Syvota, 520
  Vassiliki, 31, 520
  Vliko, 520
  Yiro, 519
  see also Ionian Islands, The
Leros, 366–9
  Aghia Marina, 367, 368
  Alinda, 366, 367

Dio Liskaria, 367
Gourna, 368
Koulouki, 368
Kryphos, 367
Lakki, 366, 368
Panagies, 367
Panteli, 368
Partheni, 369
Platanos, 367
Vlefoutis, 369
Xerocampos, 368
see also Dodecanese Islands, The
Lesbos, 24, 252–4
  Agiassos, 254
  Eftalou, 253
  Kalloni, 252, 254
  Molyvos (Methimna), 252, 253
  Myklini, 252–3
  Petra, 253
  Plomari, 252
  Sigri, 254
  Skala Eressos, 252, 253–4
  see also North-east Aegean Islands
Let's Go: Greece and the Turkish Coast, 50
Limnos, 251–2
  Atsiki, 252
  Avlonas, 252
  Kaspakas, 252
  Kokinos, 252
  Kondaspli, 252
  Kotsimas, 252
  Myrina, 251
  Platis, 252
  Thanous, 252
  see also North-east Aegean Islands
Lipsi, 372–3
  Katzadia, 373
  see also Dodecanese Islands, The
London Student Travel, 108
Luggage, what to take, 52–4

Medical Insurance, *see* Insurance
Methana, 442
  Kaimeni Hora, 442
  Vathi, 442
  Vromolimni, 442
  see also Saronic Gulf Islands
Milos, 292–5
  Adamas, 293–4

Ag Sosti, 295
Chora, 294
Hivadolimnis, 295
Kimolos, 294
Lagada Beach, 294
Oupa, 294
Paliochiri, 295
Paliokastro, 294
Phatourena, 295
Plaka, 294
Provata, 295
Psathi, 294
Pullonia, 294
Zefiria, 294–5
see also Cyclades, The
Money, 21, 45
  banking hours, 47
  budgeting, 50–52
  credit cards, 46
  personal cheques, 46
  traveller's cheques, 46
Moni, island of, 42
Mountaineering, 37
  see also Healthy Holidays
Mountains
  Falakro, 38
  Metsovo, 38
  Parnassus, 38
  Pilio, 38
  Pindus range, 38
  Vermio, 38
Mykonos, 281, 295–301, 329
  Agios Stefanos, 31
  Megali Amos, 31
  Mykonos Town, 297–300
  Plati Yialis, 297
  San Stefano, 297
  see also Cyclades, The

National Tourist Organisation of Greece, 49
Nature Lover, The, 25, 29, 39–42, 162, 166, 167, 171–2, 185, 190, 196, 215, 250, 252, 256, 275–6, 283, 334, 354, 375, 381, 396, 434, 468, 505, 515, 521, 524
Naturist, The, 29, 30–31, 268, 271, 310, 432
Naxos, 30, 281, 303–7

Ag Anna, 306
Ag Georgis, 306
Apirathos, 307
Apollonas, 31, 306
Chalki, 307
Danakos, 307
Filoti, 307
Flerio, 307
Moutsouna, 307
Naxos Town, 305–6
Psili Ammos, 307
Sangki, 307
see also Cyclades, The
Nightlife, *see* Socialite, The
Nissiros, 348–50, 358
Emborio, 350
Haklaki, 349
Loutra, 350
Mandraki, 349
Mira Mare, 349
Niki, 350
Pali, 350
see also Dodecanese Islands, The
North-east Aegean Islands, 24
travel facilities, 249–50
see also Chios, Ikaria, Lesbos, Limnos, Samos *and* Samothraki
Northern Greece, 24, 201–30
Agia Triada, 228
Akti Thermaikou, 228
Amouliani, 42
Asvestohori, 228
Dreokastro, 229
Eyzoni, 229
Gefira, 228
Langadas, 228–9
Macedonia, 32
Mikra, 227
Nea Apolonia, 229
Nea Halkidona, 229
Nei Epirates, 228
Panorama Perea, 229–30
Pella, 33
Samothrace, 42
Stavros, 228
Thessaloniki, 223–7
Vourvourou, 42
see also Eastern Macedonia and Thrace, Halkidiki *and* Thassos

Out-of-season Holidays, 26

Package Holidays, 22, 57–103
accommodation only, 82, 97
camping, 90–91
checklist before booking, 101–3
coach tours, 78–9, 92–3, 97
conference arrangements, 82
cost-conscious holidays, 88–90
cruises, 94–6
disabled, arrangements for, 82, 97
flotilla holidays, 77–8, 96
tour operators, 77–8
holiday villages, 93–4, 165, 168, 358
private accommodation, 91–2
sailing, 96
self-catering, 79–81, 87–8, 209
special interest, 81–2, 97–100
summing up, 100–101
tailor-made, 82, 92, 97
taverna–pension–rooms, 82
two/multi centre, 83, 92
wanderer, 83, 97
Paros, 31, 34, 281, 307–14
Ag Ioannis, 311–12
Ag Irini, 311
Alyki, 311
Ambella, 312
Anagiri, 312
Antiparos, 310
Butterfly Valley (Petoulades), 310–11
Chrysiatki, 312
Kolibithres, 311
Krios, 310
Lageri, 312
Lefkas, 312
Livadhi, 309
Logares, 312
Mezahda, 312
Monastiri, 311
Naoussa, 31, 309, 311
Parakia, 308–10
Parasporos, 310
Piso Livadi, 309, 312
Pounda, 312
Pounta, 311
Prodromos, 312
Tzirdakia, 312
see also Cyclades, The
Passports
requirements, 21
visas, 44

Patmos, 358, 365, 369–72
　Diakofit, 372
　Grikos, 372
　Kampos, 372
　Lampi, 372
　Psili Amos, 372
　Skala, 369, 370–71
　see also Dodecanese Islands, The
Paxos, 480, 513, 515–18
　Antipaxi, 517
　Boikatiki, 517
　Dodoni, 481
　Gaios, 516
　Igoumenitsa, 481
　Ioannina, 481
　Laggos, 516
　Lakka, 516, 517
　Loggos, 517
　Markratika, 517
　Mogonisi, 517
　Ortholihos, 517
　Parga, 481
　Seven Seas Caves, 517
　Voutoumi Bay, 517
　Zitsa, 481
　see also Ionian Islands, The
Peloponnese, 24, 231–45
　Aighion, 99
　Aliki Beach, 456
　Ancient Olympia, 33, 243–4
　Andritsea, 243
　Areopolis, 241
　Argos, 236–7
　Assini, 238
　Bassae, 243
　Corinth, 152, 234–6
　Dyros, 31
　Egio, 245
　Epidavros, 33, 152, 238, 442, 456
　Ermioni, 239, 438
　Galati, 245, 456
　Gerolimenas, 241
　Gythion, 241
　Kaifos, 234, 243
　Kalamata, 38, 242–3
　Kastraki, 238
　Kastro, 43
　Katakolo, 244
　Kefalari, 237
　Kiparissia, 43, 243
　Koroni, 243
　Kosta, 445
　Kylini, 31
　Laganas, 31
　Lemonodassos, 456
　Loutaki Kyllinis, 244
　Loutraki, 233, 234, 236
　Loutra Kyllinis, 234
　Mani Peninsula, 33, 241–2
　Messae, 243
　Methan, 234
　Methoni, 31, 243
　Monemvassia, 242
　Mycenae, 152, 236
　Mystra, 33, 240–41
　Nafplio, 233, 237–8, 442, 456
　Nea Kios, 238
　Olympus, 243
　Palza Epidavros, 238
　Patras, 244–5
　Pelelidon, 243
　Perachora, 236
　Pilos, 243
　Plaka Beach, 456
　Porto Heli, 233, 238–9, 438, 445
　Skafidia, 43
　Sparta, 33, 239
　Tolon, 233, 238
　Trizina, 442, 456
　see also Kythera
Poros, 152, 452–7
　Askeli Bay, 456
　Kalavria, 452
　Monastery Bay, 455, 456
　Neorian Bay, 455, 456
　Poros Town, 455, 457
　Russian Bay, 456
　Spheria, 452
　Vagionia Bay, 456
　see also Saronic Gulf Islands
Post Offices, see Communications
Potted History of Greece, 133–7
Pre-planning and Information, 49–50, 114, 117–18
　electricity, 114
　free information
　　Hogg Robinson resort reports, 50
　　local libraries, 49–50
　　maps, 49
　　Thomas Cook resort reports, 50
　　tourist literature, 49
　guide books, 50
　time difference, 114
　tourist information, 117–18
　water, 114

Private Accommodation/Small Hotels, see
  Accommodation
Problems and Emergencies, 131-3
  Embassy and Consulate addresses, 132
  medical, 131
  police, 132
  women alone, 132-3
  work, 132
Psara, island of, 42
Public holidays, 21
Public Transport, see Travel, Means of

Quiet Holidays, see Recluse, The

Rail travel, see Travel, Means of
Recluse, The, 29, 42-3, 162, 172, 185,
  190-91, 205, 207, 211-12, 216-17, 220,
  223, 231, 241, 242, 250-51, 254, 259,
  272, 283, 287, 293, 334, 336, 338-9,
  346, 354, 373, 375, 381, 395, 396, 408,
  430, 467, 515, 518
Restaurants/Eating Out, see Food and
  Drink
Rhodes, 30, 32, 38, 43, 373-401
  Afandou, 382, 394
  Ancient Ialyssos, 399
  Ancient Kamiros, 400
  Archangelos, 395
  Embonas, 401
  Faliraki, 32, 381, 382, 392, 393
  Genadio, 381, 396
  Haraki, 395
  Hattavia, 396
  Ixia, 32, 381, 396-7
  Kalithea, 392-3
  Kamiros Skala, 400
  Katavia, 381
  Kolimbia, 382, 394
  Kremasti, 381, 398
  Kritika, 381, 396, 397
  Lahania, 396
  Lardos, 395
  Lindos, 32, 381, 382, 389, 390-92
  Messanagros, 396
  Monolithos, 401
  Paradissi, 381, 398
  Pefki, 382
  Pefkos, 395
  Plimiri, 396
  Prassonisi Cape, 381, 396
  Psinthos, 389
  Rhodes Town, 381, 382-8
  Tholos, 398
  Trianda, 396, 397-8
  Tsambika, 394
  Valley of Butterflies (Petaloudes), 388-9
  Vlyha Bay, 395
  see also Dodecanese Islands, The
Riding, 39, 382
  see also Healthy Holidays
Rough Guide to Greece, 50

Sailing Holidays, 38, 96
  see also Package Holidays *and* Water
    Sports
Salamis, 446-7
  Kaka Vigla, 447
  Kanakia, 447
  Moulki, 447
  Periseria, 447
  Salamina, 447
  see also Saronic Gulf Islands
Samos, 31, 256-8
  Avlakia, 258
  Gagou, 258
  Karlovassi, 257
  Kokkari, 257, 258
  Konstantinos, 258
  Le Monakia, 258
  Pirgos, 258
  Platanos, 258
  Pythagorion, 31, 257, 258
  Samos Town, 257
  Tsamadou, 258
  Votsalakia, 258
  see also North-east Aegean Islands
Samothraki, 250-51
  Ammos, 250
  Chora, 250
  Kamariotissa, 250
  Paleopolis, 250
  Therma, 251
  see also North-east Aegean Islands
Santorini, 24, 34, 281, 314-21
  Akrotiri, 320
  Amondi, 321
  Ancient Thira, 319
  Episkopi (Misa), 319
  Imerovigli, 320
  Kamari, 316, 319
  Karterados, 317
  Merisa, 317
  Mondithos, 319
  Oia, 320-21

INDEX 557

Perissa, 316, 320
Pyrgos, 319
Thira, 314, 316–18
see also Cyclades, The
Saronic Gulf Islands, 24, 436–57
see also Aegina, Angistri, Hydra,
  Methana, Poros, Salamis *and* Spetse
Schinoussa, island of, 42
Scuba Diving, 39
see also Water Sports
Self-catering Holidays, 87–8, 209, 510
see also Package Holidays
Serifos, 321–2
  Ag Gianni, 322
  Chora, 322
  Karavi, 322
  Livadaki, 322
  Livadi, 321, 322
  Psili Amos, 322
  Sikami, 322
  see also Cyclades, The
Shopping, 119–20, 222, 225–6, 264–5
Sifnos, 322–3
  Apollonia, 323
  Artemona, 323
  Faros, 323
  Kamares, 323
  Kastro, 323
  Plati Gialos, 32, 323
  Plati Yialos, 323
  Vathy, 323
  see also Cyclades, The
Sightseer, The, 24, 29, 32–3, 118–19, 146,
  148–52, 157–8, 160–62, 167, 169–70,
  175–8, 181, 185–9, 198, 205, 214, 218,
  219, 221, 224, 229–30, 231, 233, 235–7,
  239–41, 250–51, 253, 257–8, 267,
  277–8, 294, 298–9, 302–3, 305–6,
  312–14, 317–18, 328, 350, 354–6, 364,
  369, 371–2, 381, 383–5, 388, 390–91,
  399–401, 408, 410–15, 421–2, 425–6,
  429, 440, 444, 447, 450–51, 455–6, 467,
  471–7, 488, 499–501, 505, 515, 522,
  526, 528, 535–6
Skiing, 28, 37, 38
  see also Healthy Holidays
Skiathos, 31, 38, 263–8
  Agia Eleni, 267, 268
  Akladias Troulos, 268
  Calaria, 266
  Kastro, 266, 267
  Koukkounaries, 31, 266–7

Lalaria, 268
Manraki, 267–8
Megali, 268
Skiathos Town, 264–6
see also Sporades Islands
Skopelos, 268–72
  Agnontas, 270
  Glossa, 270–71
  Loutraki, 270
  Milia, 271–2
  Panormas, 271
  Skopelos Town, 31, 268–9
  Stafilos, 271
  Velonio, 271
  see also Sporades Islands
Skyros, 277–9
  Agios Foka, 279
  Aherannes, 279
  Ahili, 279
  Atsistsa, 279
  Girismata, 279
  Linaria, 278–9
  Mogazia Beach, 279
  Ormos Pefkos, 279
  Skyros Town, 277–8
  Tris Boukes, 277
  see also Sporades Islands
Small Hotels/Private Accommodation, *see*
  Accommodation
Snorkelling, 39
  see also Water Sports
Socialite, The, 29, 34–7, 125–6, 146,
  153–4, 156, 159, 178, 185, 205, 208–9,
  211–12, 222, 227, 233, 238, 252–4,
  257–8, 265, 269, 274, 278, 281, 287,
  289, 291, 297, 300, 307, 311–12, 314,
  316, 318–20, 321–2, 328, 344, 354, 360,
  363, 367, 381, 387–8, 391–2, 397,
  407–8, 416–18, 419, 422, 426, 443,
  445–6, 447, 452, 457, 466, 477–9,
  481–6, 488–91, 499, 501, 505, 507–8,
  510–11, 512–13, 515, 519–20, 528–9,
  531, 534, 536, 538
Special Interest Holidays, 97–100
  see also Package Holidays
Spetse, 442–6
  Aghia Marina, 445
  Aghia Paraskevi, 445
  Aghios Meamos, 444
  Anargyri, 445
  Spetsopoula, 444
  Zogheria, 445
  see also Saronic Gulf Islands

558 INDEX

Sporades, Islands, 24
  Gioura, 270, 276
  Pelagos, 276
  Peristera, 274, 276
  Piperi, 276
  Skantzoura, 276–7
  see also Skiathos, Skopelos *and* Skyros
Sports Holidays, 98–9
  see also Healthy Holidays
Student Travel and Educational Trips, 78
Sunworshipper, The, 29, 30–32, 146, 168, 170–71, 181, 185, 194, 205, 209, 211–12, 214, 220, 222, 233, 238, 249–54, 256, 266–7, 271, 275, 279, 281, 283–5, 293, 297, 303, 307, 309–10, 314, 316, 320, 322–3, 334, 346, 354, 357, 359, 375, 382, 389, 392–4, 401, 408, 419, 427, 429, 466–7, 481, 495, 497, 515, 523, 526, 532, 534, 537–8
Symi, 341–6
  Ghialos, 342–4
  Marathounta Bay, 345
  Nanou Bay, 345
  Nemo island, 346
  Nimborio, 346
  Panormos Bay, 345–6
  Pedi, 344, 345
  St Emilianos, 346
  St George, 345
  St Marina, 345
  Sesklia island
    Skomisa Bay, 345
  see also Dodecanese Islands, The
Syros, 323–6
  Ag Dimitros, 326
  Angathopes, 326
  Ano Syros, 325–6
  culinary specialities, 324
  Ermoupolis, 324–5
  Finikas, 326
  Gallisas, 323, 324, 326
  Kini, 326
  Vari, 326
  see also Cyclades, The

Tailor-made Holidays, 82, 92, 97, 106
  see also Package Holidays
Taverna–Pension–Rooms Holidays, 82
  see also Package Holidays
Telephones, *see* Communications
Tennis, 38
  see also Healthy Holidays

Thassos (Limenas), 221–3
  Agios Ionis, 222
  Aliki, 223
  Archangelos, 223
  Kinira, 222
  Limenaria, 221, 222
  Makriamos, 222
  Pefkaria, 223
  Potos, 223
  Skara Prinos, 221
  Thassos Town, 221–2
  see also Northern Greece
Tilos, 36, 346–8
  Erestos, 347, 348
  Livadia, 36, 347
  Megalochorio, 347
  Mikrochorio, 348
  Plaka Bay, 348
  see also Dodecanese Islands, The
Tinos, 326–9
  Ag Fokas, 328
  Ag Nikitas, 329
  Ag Sostis, 328
  Kapsalis, 329
  Kionia, 328
  Kolibithra, 329
  Lichnafta, 328–9
  Panormos, 31, 329
  Tinos Town, 327–8
  see also Cyclades, The
Tour Operators, 58–70
  resorts covered by, 71–5, 83–6
Tourist Information, *see* Pre-planning and Information
Travel, Means of, 127–31
  bus, 130–31
  car hire, 128–9, 378, 389
    companies, 128
    documentation, 128–9
  cruises, 94–6
  cycle hire, 129
  fly-cruising holidays, 95
    tour operators, 78
  fly-drive holidays, 77
    tour operators, 77
  fly-yachting holidays, 96
    tour operators, 77
  Independent, 103–6
    air, 106–8
    bus, 93, 110
    car/camper, 110–12
    coach, 110

INDEX 559

hitch-hiking, 112–13
rail, 108–9
sea, 113–14
local facilities, 143–5, 164, 174, 183–4, 202–3, 232–3, 249–51, 255–7, 261, 281–2, 284, 288, 293, 296, 304, 308, 315, 317, 324, 327, 331–2, 334, 342, 347–9, 361, 366–7, 369–70, 375, 405, 408, 410, 438, 443–4
moped hire, 129, 378
public transport, 129–31
rail, 129–30
taxis, 131, 378
Traveller's Cheques, *see* Money
Two/Multi-Centre Holidays, 92
tour operators, 83
see also Package Holidays

Video Cameras, *see* Cameras
Vocabulary, 541–3
Volus, 38

Wanderer (Voucher) Holidays, 83, 97
see also Package Holidays
Water Sports, 31, 37, 38–9, 96, 99, 165, 185, 205, 208–9, 238, 253, 254, 266, 301, 364, 367, 382, 393, 394, 397, 456–7, 481, 489, 497, 501, 503–4, 510–11, 517, 538
see also Healthy Holidays
Weather, *see* Climate
Western Greece, 24, 182–200
  Anatolika, 190
    Flambourari, 190
    Greveniti, 190
    Trisento, 190
  Arta, 193
  Ditoko, 192–3
    Mega Papingo, 192–3
    Mikro, 192–3
  Dodoni, 188–9
  Filiates, 195
  Igonmenitsa, 195
  Ioanina, 186–8
  Kanali, 194
  Kastosikia, 194
  Katsopi, 194
  Kentriko, 190–91
    Asprangeti, 191
    Dilofo, 191
    Kipi, 191
    Konkonli, 191
    Laista, 192
    Monodentri, 191
    Negades, 192
    Skemneli, 192
    Vitsa, 191
    Vrisohori, 192
  Konitsa, 189
  Matsouki, 193
  Melissopetra, 189
  Melissourgi, 193
  Messapotamos, 194
  Metsova, 189
  Mouzakei, 188
  Nikapolis, 194
  Nissi, 188
  Paramitia, 195
  Parga, 194–5, 513
  Perama, 188
  Piges Louros, 189
  Platopia, 195
  Preveza, 193–4
  Sirako-kalanites, 188
  Skoulikava, 193
  Velentziko, 193
  Zagorohoria, 190
  Zalongo, 194
  Zitsa, 189
  see also Western Macedonia
Western Macedonia, 195–200
  Alikes, 199
  Amindeon, 196
  Aridea, 196
  Dion, 199–200
  Edessa, 196
  Florina, 196
  Glanitsa, 195, 196
  Grevena, 197
  Kastoria, 197
  Katerini, 199
  Kato Vermio, 198
  Korinos, 199
  Kozani, 197
  Lefkadia, 198
  Leptokaria, 200
  Lertokana, 200
  Litohoro, 200
  Lontra Arideas, 196
  Makrigialos, 199
  Methoni, 199
  Mikra Prepsa, 196
  Naossa, 198
  Nimfeo, 196

INDEX

Ormos Methanis, 198
Paralia Skotinas, 200
Pela, 195
Perivoli, 197
Petrona, 197
Platamonas, 200
Ptolemaida, 198
Senia, 197–8
Shidra, 196
Siatista, 197
Veria, 198
Xyno Nero, 197
see also Western Greece
Windsurfing, 39
see also Water Sports
Winter sports, 198

Yacht Charterers/Brokers, 75–6, 96
Yiali, island of, 42
Young Set, The, 31

Zakinthos, 24, 30, 43, 515, 532–9
Agalas, 537
Alikanas, 539
Alikes, 534, 539
Argassi, 534, 537–8
Bohali, 537
Cape Gerakas, 538
Kalamaki, 538
Lagnas, 534, 538
Machairido, 537
Marathonisisi, island of, 537
Pelouzo, island of, 537
Planos, 535, 539
Porto Zorro, 538
St Nikolas, 538
Tsilivi, 534, 535, 537, 539
Vassilikos, 534, 535, 537, 538
Zante Town, 534–7
see also Ionian Islands, The